# THE COLLAPSE OF BRITISH POWER

*by the same author*

THE DESERT GENERALS

THE SWORDBEARERS

BRITAIN AND HER ARMY 1509–1970

9-95

CORRELLI BARNETT

# The Collapse of British Power

ALAN SUTTON

ALAN SUTTON PUBLISHING LIMITED
BRUNSWICK ROAD · GLOUCESTER


THIS EDITION PUBLISHED 1984
REPRINTED 1987

*For Calvin and Freddie*

British Library Cataloguing in Publication Data

Barnett, Correlli
The collapse of British power.
1. Great Britain—History—George V, 1910–1936 2. Great Britain—History—George VI, 1936–1952
I. Title
941.083 DA578

ISBN 0-86299-074-2

*Cover cartoon by David Low.*
*Reproduced by permission of the London Standard*

PRINTED IN GREAT BRITAIN

# *ACKNOWLEDGEMENTS*

First and foremost, I must thank my wife Ruth for deciphering and typing a convoluted manuscript, and many passages several times as they were re-written; for criticising obscurities and infelicities in the narrative; for acting in numerous ways as a highly-efficient one-woman general staff; and for supporting the author's morale in times of discouragement. My wife made it possible for me to carry this book to completion.

Secondly, I wish to express my gratitude to all those who were kind enough to read the typescript as a whole or in part: Dr Calvin Wells; Mr Paul Brown; Mr Lionel Brooks; Mr Gerald Murray; Mr Michael Preston; Dr Paul Kennedy; Mr Michael Edwardes; Miss Irene Slade; Mr C. A. Vlieland. Their kindly but acute criticisms saved me from many errors of fact and interpretation, although I fear not from those that remain.

In particular, I wish to thank my publishers Eyre Methuen, for their patience and understanding and for all their good advice, and specifically also to Miss Jane Bacon for her care and thoroughness in checking.

I am much indebted to the Rt. Hon. Julian Amery PC MP for his kindness in according me access to his father's unpublished diaries.

I wish to express my gratitude to the following for their valuable assistance in the course of my research:

Mr J. C. Dancy, the Master of Marlborough College, Mr Gerald Murray, the Librarian, and Mr Michael Preston; Dr J. C. Royds, the Headmaster of Uppingham School and Mr T. B. Belk, the Librarian; Mr Anthony Chenevix-Trench, the then Headmaster of Eton College, and Mr Patrick Strong, the Keeper of College Library and Collections; Mr J. L. Thorn, the Headmaster of Winchester College, and Mr P. J. Gwyn, the Archivist; all for information about public-school syllabuses, set-books and school life in the late nineteenth century.

Mr K. M. Reader, Commissioner and Director of Recruitment of the Civil Service Commission, for access to the *Regulations, Examination Papers and Table of Marks for Class One Clerkships* for 1885 and 1891; the *Civil Service Commission Reports* for 1895, 1896 and 1900; the *Civil Service Commission Open Competition Reports and Examination Papers* for August 1900, 1905 and 1910.

Professor Michael Balfour for allowing me to see an unpublished paper of his on the nineteenth-century public school as a source of leaders.

Mr C. A. Vlieland, late of the Malayan Civil Service, for advice and information about the colonial empire, and especially Malaya.

To Messrs Faber and Faber for access to the transcript of Victoria Sackville-West's broadcast review of Siegfried Sassoon's *Memoirs of an Infantry Officer* and for other reviews of this book; to Messrs Peter Davies for access to reviews of Frederic Manning's *Her Privates We*; to Messrs Chatto and Windus for access to reviews of Richard Aldington's *Death of a Hero* and of C. E. Montague's *Disenchantment*; to Messrs Geoffrey Bles for access to reviews of Henry Williamson's *Patriot's Progress*; to Messrs Hamish Hamilton for permission to redraw J. F. Horrabin's map (p. 314), which originally appeared in A. J. P. Taylor's *The Origins of the Second World War*; and to Messrs Victor Gollancz for permission to redraw M. Rajchman's map (endpaper), which originally appeared in Alexander Radó's *Atlas of Today and Tomorrow*.

To the Militärgeschichtliches Forschungsamt in Freiburg im Breisgau for information about the development of the Messerschmitt ME 109 and of other German aircraft.

I wish to thank particularly the staffs of the following institutions for their efficient and courteous help: The Public Record Office, London (Cabinet Records search room); the Central Library of the Ministry of Defence; the London Library; the Norwich City Library; the Library of the University of East Anglia; the Guildhall Library; the British Museum Library; the Library of the Royal United Services Institute for Defence Studies.

# *CONTENTS*

# *AUTHOR'S PREFACE*

This book does not seek to narrate the decline and fall of the British Empire, but to explain the collapse of British *power* – an entirely different and far more important question. Nor is it a work of military history in the traditional sense, for the power of a nation-state by no means consists only in its armed forces, but also in its economic and technological resources; in the dexterity, foresight and resolution with which its foreign policy is conducted; in the efficiency of its social and political organisation. It consists most of all in the nation itself, the people; their skills, energy, ambition, discipline, initiative; their beliefs, myths and illusions. And it consists, further, in the way all these factors are related to one another. Moreover, national power has to be considered not only in itself, in its absolute extent, but relative to the state's foreign or imperial obligations; it has to be considered relative to the power of other states.

It follows that a study of the decay of British power between 1918 and 1940 and of its collapse between 1940 and 1945 cannot be adequately conducted within the confines of military history, nor, for that matter, of political or economic history. This book therefore ranges from religion to technology; from education to foreign policy; from literature to grand strategy. Yet throughout the narrative the standpoint remains the single one of strategy – not, however, strategy in the limited sense, but *total* strategy: strategy, that is, conceived as encompassing all the factors relevant to preserving or extending the power of a human group in the face of rivalry from other human groups. From this standpoint, a topic like religion, for example, appears in a perhaps surprising light as a strategic factor of no less significance than first-line air strength.

The book is divided into six parts. There are no chapters, so that within each part the argument is pursued without interruption.

The first part, concerned with the summer crisis of 1940, is by way of a prologue. The second part analyses the British national character – the character of the dominant groups in British society – as it had become by the 1920s, and traces the historical influences which had served to mould it. This section is the foundation of the book, for, with a nation as with an individual, character is the key to all action, all judgement.

In the third part of the book there follows a dissection of the anatomy of British power, as it was in its world setting in 1918 at the end of the Great War. The remainder of the work – the bulk of the narrative – describes the consequent interplay between British character and British circumstance, as established in these two fundamental sections. It explores in particular how national character manifested itself in policies and decisions in every field of total strategy: imperial policy (the fourth part); and (in the fifth part and the heart of the book) foreign policy and grand strategy; defence policy, disarmament and rearmament; economic policy at home and abroad; social and industrial policy; education; propaganda and public opinion. The narrative throughout is concerned to demonstrate how tightly all these factors were linked together; how decisively, if sometimes unexpectedly, they reacted upon one another. The final part of the book briefly describes, almost as an epilogue, how the long-rotting and cumulatively over-strained structure of British power swiftly collapsed under the shock of the Second World War.

CORRELLI BARNETT
*East Carleton*
*February 1972*

# I

# I · THE AUDIT OF WAR

At 5.35 a.m. (German time) on Friday, 10 May 1940, amid fresh-smelling dawn mists that presaged another fine spring day, the German advanced guards crossed the western frontiers of the Reich, and opened the battle for the mastery of Europe. Behind the advanced guards 137 divisions were on the move, cramming the roads back to the Rhine and beyond with tanks, trucks and guns; with marching infantry; with horses and wagons.

In London the news of the German onslaught not only caught the British Government utterly by surprise,[1] but in the middle of a major political crisis. On 7 and 8 May there had taken place in the House of Commons a debate on the course of the current campaign in Norway; a debate arising from the ignominious evacuation of the Allied forces from the central part of that country. The debate had transcended the narrow topic of Allied bumbling in this secondary theatre, and had become a general inquest on Neville Chamberlain's conduct of the war. It had concluded with a decisive rejection of Chamberlain, his government and all that Chamberlain had stood for, in peace as well as in war. In the vote on an Opposition motion of censure, the Government's majority of about 240 sank to only 81; 41 Government supporters voted with Labour, and some 60 more abstained. A national coalition instead of a party administration had now become inevitable. But under whose leadership?

During the next day, 9 May, therefore, when Hitler was fixing zero hour for the attack in the west for the following dawn, a British ministerial crisis had embarked on its measured and traditional course – meetings of politicians in Downing Street, frenzied talk and rumour in the clubs and in the purlieus of the House of Commons, delicate enquiries as to who would be prepared to serve under whom. At the end of the day, however, when the German forces received a signal bearing the single code-word *Danzig* (the executive order for the offensive), Chamberlain was still the British Prime Minister. He had gone to bed awaiting the Labour leaders'

[1] Cf. the Chiefs of Staff's Appreciation of 4 May 1940, approved by the Cabinet on 9 May, which considered that a German air attack on Great Britain was more probable than a ground offensive in Western Europe.-CAB 66/7, WP(40)145. Public Record Office; Cabinet Papers. (See Bibliography for list of Cabinet Papers consulted.)

reply on the morrow, after they had conferred with their colleagues at the Labour Party's Annual Conference then taking place at Bournemouth, as to whether the Labour Party would be willing to serve under him in a national coalition.

During the morning of 10 May, while the sun climbed a blue sky and a torrent of violence by land and from the air swept into the Low Countries, the British ministerial crisis went on. At eleven o'clock Chamberlain, Lord Halifax (Foreign Secretary) and Winston Churchill (First Lord of the Admiralty) conferred in a quiet and lofty room in No. 10 Downing Street. Beyond the tall windows, towards Buckingham Palace, St James's Park was a shimmer of water and new foliage. Two hundred miles away, in Dutch cities which yesterday had been no less tranquil in the sunshine, the howl of the dive-bomber was preceding the collapse of homes into rubble and the transformation of human beings into carcasses. For Chamberlain – 'a man of peace', as he himself had once said, 'to the depths of my soul' – it had been the outbreak of war itself on 3 September 1939 which had marked the moment of personal failure, bringing down in ruins all his once-confident hopes of appeasing Europe. Now, however, he had to acknowledge to his two colleagues that his career as Prime Minister was at an end. For the Labour leaders had that morning refused to serve under him. Lord Halifax then expressed his feeling that he himself could not adequately lead a national coalition from the House of Lords. '. . . by the time he had finished', Churchill wrote in his war memoirs, 'it was clear that the duty would fall on me – had in fact fallen to me.'[1]

Churchill told Chamberlain that he would make no touch with the Opposition parties until the king had commissioned him to form a government. With that, the conversation lapsed into a brief informal chat. Then Churchill went back to his office. Chamberlain, who had been once so overweeningly self-assured, was left, a drawn and defeated old man, to tell his Cabinet of his resignation.[2]

Towards six o'clock that evening, while British people were beginning to set off on their Whitsun holiday, and the Dutch and the Belgians were fighting ever more desperately for their lives, Churchill was driven along the Mall from the Admiralty to Buckingham Palace. The interview with George VI was short and friendly, distinguished by English humour and ease rather than by a portentous awareness of a moment of destiny. Churchill returned to the Admiralty with the king's commission to form a government.

1 Winston Churchill, *The Second World War* (London, Cassell 1964), Vol. II, p. 235.
2 CAB 65/7, 116(40)1.

Between seven and eight o'clock, Clement Attlee, the Leader of the Labour Party, and his colleague Arthur Greenwood called on Churchill and accepted his invitation to join a national coalition. At about ten o'clock Churchill sent the king the names of the first five members of his war cabinet; intimation that he had in fact been successful in forming a government.

Thus, by a dramatically neat coincidence of a kind rare in history, Winston Churchill became Prime Minister of the United Kingdom on the very day when the Second World War ceased to smoulder on a slow fuse, and exploded.

Chamberlain had fallen not because of his policy, but his leadership. British grand strategy remained unchanged by Churchill's accession to power. The key to this strategy, laid down in April 1939 and confirmed by the Allied Supreme War Council in September 1939, was faith in the French army. It was assumed that the French army would hold the Western Front while Germany was enfeebled by blockade, and while Britain and her empire created their own mass army of fifty-five divisions. This process was not expected to be completed until the end of 1941.[1] If Fascist Italy entered the war during this defensive period of preparation, some cheap victories might be won over her, it was thought, by the superior Allied sea and land forces in the Mediterranean and North Africa. Finally, once the Allies had at last girded up their full economic and military strength, the offensive would be taken against Germany.[2]

If the British Cabinet and its professional advisers could rest their grand strategy so securely on the French alliance and the French army, it was not surprising that the British public, for its part, saw the war as a kind of replay of 1914–18, where in good time great British armies would take the offensive alongside the French on the Western Front and achieve final victory. Meanwhile it was expected that any German onslaught in the west would be baulked by the impregnable Maginot Line, whose wonders and strength had been assiduously peddled through the winter and spring of the 'phoney' war. After all, General Gamelin, the present French Commander-in-Chief, was the man who had been at Marshal Joffre's side in 1914, his Chief of Staff and mastermind, during the defeat of the Schlieffen Plan at the Battle of the Marne. And the French army itself, the victor of 1918, was the finest in Europe. English newspapers and

[1] CAB 65/1, 23(39)1.
[2] Stage I Report of the Anglo-French Staff Conversations, April 1939, CAB 29/159, AEC7; Meeting of the Supreme War Council, 12 September 1939, CAB 66/1, WP(39)38.

the new illustrated war magazines constantly carried features and pictures displaying the French army's tough, brilliant leaders and its splendid equipment – heavy tanks; huge railway guns; self-propelled medium artillery. As recently as 19 April 1940, in the magazine *The War*, for example, J. F. C. Fuller, the famous military critic and historian, was assuring his readers that: 'There is nothing flashy about the modern French fighting machine. It realises that war is a grim business and goes into action determined to inflict losses upon its opponent heavier than it suffers itself.'[1]

Churchill himself, in a broadcast on 30 March 1940, had both expressed and reinforced the comfortable British sense of time in hand; the total and tranquil dependence on the shelter afforded by the French army:

> We do not conceal from ourselves that trials and tribulations lie before us far beyond anything we have so far undergone, and we know that supreme exertions will be required from the British and French nations.
>
> We know all this, but we are entitled to recognise the basic facts.
>
> Our resources and our man-power, once they are fully developed, massively exceed those of the enemy.
>
> The British and French races together amount to 110 millions, against less than 70 millions of Germans ... Through our command of the sea, which is becoming continually more complete, the resources of the whole world are to a very large extent open to us and, surveying the whole scene, we may rightly feel a good and sober assurance that if we do our best we shall not fail.[2]

At the beginning of May 1940 the British Chiefs of Staff reviewed grand strategy in the light of the German invasion of Norway and Denmark. On 9 May, the eve of the German offensive in the west, their paper was discussed and approved by a Cabinet meeting attended by Churchill as First Lord of the Admiralty. While the Chiefs of Staff noted that Germany could deploy 160 field divisions in the west against 104 Allied field divisions, nevertheless – granted adequate air defence – they considered that France should be reasonably secure, even with this disparity, against land attacks by both Germany and Italy.[3]

It was therefore with confident anticipation over the Whitsun weekend of 1940 that the new British Government and the British people awaited

[1] *The War*, No. 26 (19 April 1940), p. 775.
[2] Quoted in *War Illustrated*, Vol. 2, No. 32 (12 April 1940), p. 372.
[3] CAB 66/7, WP(40)145.

the coming collision of the Allied and German armies in the Low Countries.

But instead the British were to be jerked from complacency into catastrophe with the upsetting rapidity of first-class passengers descending from the captain's dinner-table into a lifeboat, upon learning that the bottom has just been removed from the liner's hull by an unforeseen iceberg.

Up to 14 May the campaign seemed to open not unfavourably. Greeted with flowers, cheers and kisses, the French army and the British Expeditionary Force[1] advanced into Belgium. A great encounter battle opened in the Belgian plain in front of Brussels, and the Allied forces appeared successfully to be blocking what was taken to be the main German effort.

Then the scene changed with the swiftness of a revolving stage. Though unreported in the British newspapers until 15 May, German panzer forces had already smashed the French front further to the south, along the Meuse between Namur and Sedan. On 15 May, the Dutch surrendered, overwhelmed despite their inundations. That same day the French Prime Minister informed the British Prime Minister that, because of the collapse of the French front on the Meuse, the road to Paris lay open. Instead the German headed due west, and at a speed which seemed unbelievable. On 20 May the panzer spearheads reached the Channel coast, cutting off the Allied army group in Belgium from the main body of the French army. On 3 June the destruction of this army group was consummated when the last of some 330,000 survivors, with no more than their personal weapons, were evacuated from Dunkirk to England. On 5 June, 104 German divisions fell upon 49 weak French divisions and one British division holding a line from the mouth of the Somme to the Maginot Line at Malmédy. On 11 June Italy entered the war on Germany's side. On 14 June Paris fell. The exhausted and outnumbered French army finally disintegrated. On 16 June Paul Reynaud, the French Premier, resigned, to be replaced by Marshal Pétain, the aged hero of the Battle of Verdun in 1916. On 17 June Pétain's Government asked the Germans for an armistice. On 22 June the armistice was signed, and on 25 June the French forces ceased to fight. Northern France and the Atlantic coast fell into German occupation; central and southern France, under Pétain's government, into a neutrality tinged with hostility towards France's late ally, Great Britain.

In the course of just six weeks the Western Front, the French army and

[1] The British contributed 10 divisions to the battle for Europe as against the French contribution of 94 divisions from a smaller population.

the French alliance had all ceased to exist – and with them the very foundations of British grand strategy.

The consequences of the fall of France were far more immediate and dangerous than the mere conversion into waste paper of existing British plans for eventually winning the war. Britain and the British Empire now stood alone and exposed to the united aggressive force of Germany and Italy, and, all too probably, of Japan as well.

In the summer of 1940 therefore the assets and liabilities of British power were subjected to the searching audit of war. There was, in the first place, the direct threat offered by the victorious German army (some 160 divisions strong) and the Luftwaffe to the United Kingdom, which was at once the empire's industrial base, principal reservoir of 'white' population, and main source of troops. This was the danger of which the British public was most conscious at the time during that summer of pride, defiance and exaltation. Although in numbers the British land forces in the United Kingdom in June 1940 amounted to the equivalent of twenty-six British divisions and one Canadian,[1] there was only enough equipment after the *débâcle* of Dunkirk to arm the equivalent of two divisions.[2] It was therefore the Chiefs of Staff's sombre conclusion that, 'should the enemy succeed in establishing a force, with its vehicles, firmly ashore, the army in the United Kingdom, which is very short of equipment, has not got the offensive power to drive it out'.[3] Whether the navy could defeat an invasion force while at sea depended on its power to operate in the face of heavy air attacks. We could not count, wrote the Chiefs of Staff, on operating surface forces in strength in the southern part of the North Sea and the English Channel at all – the very seas that the Germans must be expected to try to cross.[4] 'The crux of the matter,' wrote the Chiefs of Staff in reply to a direct question from the Prime Minister as to whether the United Kingdom would be able to fight on, 'is air superiority.'[5]

The air defence of Great Britain had been the first care of pre-war re-armament programmes. In organisation and modern equipment (radar, excellent aircraft), Fighter Command presented a single exception to the general inadequacy and unreadiness. Even so, Fighter Command was expected to be heavily outnumbered by the Luftwaffe. It was therefore far from certain that the Royal Air Force could prevent the Germans from achieving air superiority over the Channel and southern England. And if

[1] J. R. M. Butler, *Grand Strategy* (London, HMSO 1954), Vol. II, p. 279.
[2] M. M. Postan, *British War Production* (London, HMSO 1952), p. 117.
[3] COS Appreciation of 25 May 1940, CAB 66/7, WP(40)168.
[4] Ibid. [5] CAB 66/7, WP(40)169, 26 May 1940.

Fighter Command lost the battle, the invasion and conquest of the heart of the empire would surely follow.

If the safety of the United Kingdom itself turned on a narrow enough margin, the global state of British power was even more precarious.

To secure imperial sea communications to India via the Mediterranean and the Suez Canal, and, more recently, to secure the oilfields of the Persian Gulf, a colossal but rickety structure of British involvement had been erected in the Middle East in the course of the previous century and a half – colonies, protectorates, bases, mandates, treaties – a structure militarily represented in 1940 by Middle-East Command. This Command encompassed nine countries and parts of two continents, an area some seven thousand miles by two thousand miles stretching from Cyprus to the Sudan and British Somaliland, from Iraq to the western frontier of Egypt. With the French forces in North Africa and Syria now lapsed into neutrality, the task of fighting Italy in the Mediterranean and Middle East devolved entirely on the British Empire. In the Italian colonies of Libya and East Africa there were some 18 divisions; and the Libyan force could draw on the main strength of the Italian army at home of some 60 divisions.[1] To defend the immense Middle East theatre against this formidable threat, the British could only deploy the unformed equivalent of 2 divisions, 2 brigade-groups, an armoured division well below establishment, 64 field guns and a camel corps of 500 men.

The Mediterranean sea-route, in order to secure which the British involvement in the Middle East had been incurred, had always been recognised to be vulnerable, lying as it did through the Sicilian narrows and exposed to Italian surface forces and air attack. The French Mediterranean fleet in the western basin and the British Mediterranean fleet in the eastern basin (based on Alexandria) together had just about balanced the Italian battle fleet.[2] Now, with the French neutral, the balance swung heavily against the English; and this affected not only British seapower in the Mediterranean itself, but right across the world.[3]

For it meant that a powerful squadron had to be spared from the Home fleet to replace in some measure the French in the Western Mediterranean. This dangerously reduced the strength available to protect the Atlantic convoy routes against attack by raiding German battleships. At the same time the loss of the French fleet also placed the British Empire in the Far East and Pacific in jeopardy, should Japan decide to exploit the present

[1] Butler, p. 297.
[2] S. W. Roskill, *The War at Sea* (London, HMSO 1961), Vol. I, pp. 60–1, 294.
[3] See COS Appreciation of 25 May 1940, CAB 66/7, WP(40)168.

British plight. Australia and New Zealand, nations too small in population and too extensive of coastline to defend themselves either by land or sea, utterly depended for their security on English seapower – on an English fleet being sent in good time to the naval base of Singapore. The defence of Malaya, Borneo, Burma and, in the last resort, India too, against the Japanese equally depended on there being an English fleet at Singapore strong enough to fight the Japanese battlefleet. In fact the Royal Navy had entered the war in 1939 far too small to meet all the requirements of the defence of a maritime empire. It had been therefore intended that, should Japan attack in the Far East, the British fleet in the Mediterranean would sail via the Suez Canal to Singapore, while the French navy remained to hold the Italian fleet in check. This eastwards move of the English Mediterranean fleet had now become impossible except at the cost of abandoning the Mediterranean. The English Prime Minister therefore informed the prime ministers of Australia and New Zealand on 8 August 1940 that he did not propose to make this sacrifice simply because Japan attacked in the Far East, but only if she 'set about invading Australia or New Zealand on a large scale'.[1]

The British Empire in South-East Asia, being thus deprived of all hope of its protective fleet, could now only be defended on land and by air-power. But in the summer of 1940 there were in Malaya (the hinterland of Singapore and the strategic key to the whole region) only 3 brigades instead of the 3 divisions believed to be essential; 88 obsolescent aircraft instead of the 336 modern ones considered the minimum adequate force.[2] Not a single division could be spared for Malaya either by India or by Great Britain.[3] At the same time the French collapse meant that French Indo-China was no longer a defended buffer between Malaya and the Japanese forces in China, but a potential staging post.

After the fall of France there was therefore an immense disparity between the naval, air and land forces required for the defence of the British Empire against its actual and potential enemies, and those in fact available. The disparity was compounded – especially in the Far East – by a lack of joint policy-making organs, joint command organisations, and joint headquarters, staffs and intelligence departments. The British Empire was not only ill-armed, but ill-organised.

The existence of the British Empire loaded Britain with enormous responsibilities – war with Italy in the Mediterranean and the Middle East, risk of war with Japan in the Far East – and this at a time when Britain

[1] Quoted in Butler, p. 334.
[2] S. Woodburn Kirby, *The War Against Japan* (London, HMSO 1957), Vol. I, p. 35. [3] Ibid.

herself was in peril. However, the empire's military and economic contribution to British power was by no means adequate compensation. The dominions – Australia, Canada, New Zealand and South Africa – had a combined 'white' population of over 20,000,000.[1] The population of the United Kingdom was just under 50,000,000.[2] Yet the combined navies of the dominions numbered no more than 11 cruisers and 20 destroyers or escorts, as against the 12 capital ships, 7 aircraft carriers, 50 cruisers, 94 fleet destroyers and 87 escorts in the Royal Navy[3] – hardly a proportion of 2 : 5. Nor was the dominion contribution to the imperial field army, as compared with that of United Kingdom, in the proportion of 2 : 5. Of the divisions noted as 'existing'[4] on 1 August 1940 only five were from the dominions, while thirty-four were from the United Kingdom.

India, often supposed to be a mighty buttress of imperial military strength, contributed three field divisions, a third of whose personnel was in any case British. The Indian contribution to the imperial field army merely balanced the British troops locked up in defending India and maintaining its internal security.[5]

Thus in the summer crisis of 1940 the British Empire proved strategically a net liability to Britain rather than an asset, and a heavy liability at that.

Nor did the empire's economic and industrial resources afford adequate compensation for this strategic burden. In the first place, the natural resources of the British Empire, although rich in all kinds of strategic raw material, remained in 1940 unevenly and inadequately exploited to a degree best illustrated by their later wartime development.[6] The British had preferred to obtain many commodities from Europe rather than from the empire, in order to save shipping. As a result of the loss of Scandinavia and the collapse of France, Britain now found herself cut off from European supplies, while her own imperial resources were in many cases still only potential for the future – if there was to be a future.[7]

Secondly, the dominions and India, far from adding to the industrial strength of the empire, were almost wholly dependent on British industry for the equipment of their armed forces.[8]

[1] *Statesman's Year Book 1940.* [2] Ibid. [3] Roskill, Vol. I, Appendix E, pp. 586–7.

[4] 'Existing' was a cryptic official expression which did not necessarily imply that a formation was wholly or even partially equipped, trained or organised or in any sense fit for the field.

[5] 39,100 British troops, according to the War Office Progress Report for May 1940, CAB 68/6, WP(R)(40)145.

[6] See J. Hurstfield, *The Control of Raw Materials* (London, HMSO 1953), pp. 156, 163–4, 168–9, especially Table 32, and note.

[7] Ibid. pp. 155–7.

[8] W. K. Hancock and M. M. Gowing, *British War Economy* (London, HMSO 1953), Table p. 373, figures for Sept.–Dec. 1939 and 1940. See also Postan, p. 229.

And it was here, after the fall of France, in the impact of headlong imperial re-armament and military expansion on British industrial and economic resources, that there lay a danger to British independence just as mortal as that posed by the German invasion forces across the Channel: just as mortal a danger, but certain instead of possible; as certain as the onset of an incurable disease. For while Britain had faced the peril of invasion many times before in her history, an entirely new peril presented itself in the summer of 1940, in that the mere continuance of the war for another two years would *in itself* destroy British independence; even in default of further enemy victories, even despite British victories. It was a situation that England had never before had to face since she first emerged as a great power during the wars of William III and Marlborough. For whereas the struggle against Louis XIV had been nourished out of buoyant and expanding trade, and whereas the war against Napoleon had rested solidly on British technical leadership in the Industrial Revolution and on bounding productivity, in 1940 Britain was too small, too old-fashioned an industrial base even to equip her *own* manpower, let alone equip the whole imperial military effort; let alone maintain also a sufficient volume of exports to ensure the country's solvency.[1] Unlike Nazi Germany, which could wage war out of the resources of her own industry and the skills of her own technology, or out of the extra resources of countries her armies could conquer, Britain had to turn to American industry and American technology. This dependence dated from the very beginnings of British re-armament in the mid-1930s.[2]

The dependence had become greater and greater. In peacetime Britain had relied largely on American machines to equip new British factories for producing aircraft, tanks, motor-transport, aero-engines and weapons. After the outbreak of war in September 1939, Britain, like France, had tried to repair in haste the consequences of late re-armament and industrial weakness by buying from America the aircraft, motor-transport, aero-engines and weapons themselves, as well as machine tools. At the same time, owing to the inadequacy of the British steel industry, Britain had to turn to America even for steel, the very foundation of an advanced industrial economy in peace or in war.[3]

Although up to the fall of France some attempt was made to keep British spending in the United States within bounds, to relate it to British

[1] See William Hornby, *Factories and Plant* (London, HMSO 1958), p. 34; Hancock and Gowing, pp. 107–8, 112, 114–15, 118–19.
[2] Hornby, pp. 302, 305–11, 319 and the whole of chapter XI. See also the Proceedings and Memoranda of the Defence Policy and Requirements Committee of the Cabinet, CAB 16/136–44.
[3] Hancock and Gowing, pp. 112–14.

reserves of gold and dollars and to the capability of British exports in earning dollars, England was even at that time faced with the inevitability of ultimate bankruptcy and economic collapse. In February 1940 Lord Stamp, the economic expert, in a 'Survey of the National Resources in relation to our War Effort',[1] calculated that in the first year of war Britain's adverse trade balance would be £400 million, while a Treasury estimate gave the same figure as the deficit for the sterling area as a whole. If England drew on her gold and dollar reserves to the extent of £150 million, this still left a gap of £250 million. As the Chancellor of the Exchequer explained to the Cabinet, other sources – loans from empire countries, sales of British overseas assets – were unlikely to yield more than £100 million. For although overseas investments amounted to a capital value of above £3,000 million, their nature – Argentine Railways, subsidiaries of British companies – meant that they were 'not easily realisable assets'.[2] Therefore all that could be expected from requisitioning British overseas investments and selling them for dollars was £200 million or £250 million. Since British gold reserves were only £450 million, it followed that, as the Chancellor of the Exchequer wrote in February 1940, 'the sum total of our resources is thus not more than £700,000,000 . . . It is obvious that we are in great danger of our gold reserves being exhausted at a rate that will render us incapable of waging war if it is prolonged.'[3]

And the Treasury then reckoned that, if carefully husbanded, British resources could last at the current rate of dollar expenditure no longer than two years.[4]

If this was the sombre and inescapable consequence of even the cautious policies of the 'phoney' war, when the burden of the conflict was still shared by France, what must be the effects of the headlong expansion of British imperial forces decided upon by the new British Government and its professional advisers in response to the stock-taking of imperial weaknesses in the summer of 1940?

What had been a mere general intention to create an army of fifty-five divisions by 1942, ten of them armoured, now became a firm commitment.[5] At the same time the Royal Air Force was to be vastly expanded, especially in bombers, with monthly production running at 2,782 aircraft by December 1941.[6] These programmes, competing as they did for similar productive resources and equipment, demanded immense extra

[1] CAB 65/5, 40(40)1.
[2] Ibid.
[3] Hancock and Gowing, p. 116.
[4] Ibid.
[5] Butler, p. 255; Postan, p. 128.
[6] Postan, p. 124.

quantities of American machine tools and steel.[1] Whereas, for example, it had been estimated in April 1940 that Britain would buy £12·6 million of iron and steel from the United States during the year, in July the estimated requirement had gone up to £100 million.

Yet British production itself, however increased by lavish purchases of American machines and metals, could not alone meet the speed and scale of the proposed expansion of the armed forces of the British Empire. Therefore, on top of the immensely greater dollar expenditure on American industrial equipment, the aftermath of the fall of France saw the British also turn to the United States for huge additional supplies of aircraft, aero-engines, motor-transport and war equipment of all kinds – long-term contracts as well as stop-gap aid.[2]

The loss of Europe through German conquest itself further weakened the British economy, not only cutting off one of Britain's most important markets, but also a principal source of essential raw materials – iron ore from France and Spain, steel from France and the Low Countries, Norwegian wood-pulp and pyrites, French bauxite (for aluminium), French fertilisers, Dutch and Belgian flax.[3]

These losses threw England into even greater dependence on North American supplies of raw material, which rose from 8 per cent of British imports of raw materials in 1939 to 24 per cent in 1940;[4] yet another charge on the scanty British resources of gold and dollars.

On 21 August 1940 the Chancellor of the Exchequer, in a Memorandum to the Cabinet,[5] forecast that the total cost of all British purchases in North America – munitions, raw materials, industrial equipment – over the next twelve months would be $3,200 million. Yet England's total resources in foreign exchange and American securities, now amounted to only £490 million. British holdings in American securities of some £200 million in paper value, were, the Chancellor wrote, 'virtually unsaleable at present and could only be slowly realised', while Britain's South American assets stood at 'rubbish prices'.[6] As a consequence, England, far from remaining solvent until the end of 1941 at least (as had been forecast in February 1940), would exhaust her gold and dollar reserves by December 1940. In a word, Britain would be bankrupt: incapable either of waging war or of sustaining her national life. In that summer of heroic attitudes, therefore, when the English scanned the skies for the Luftwaffe and the sea for the

[1] Hornby, pp. 329–31; Postan, pp. 156, 229–30; Hancock and Gowing, p. 206.
[2] Hancock and Growing, p. 224; Postan, pp. 230–2; H. Duncan Hall, *North American Supply* (London, HMSO 1955), chs. V and VI.
[3] Hurstfield, pp. 154–9.
[4] Ibid. pp. 159–63, especially Table 29, p. 161.
[5] CAB 66/11, WP 40(40)324.
[6] Ibid.

German army, and thrilled to Churchillian rhetoric on the wireless, England's existence as an independent, self-sustaining power was reckoned by the Government to have just four months to run.

The predicament which Churchill's Government faced after the fall of France was unique in English history: a war without an ally against two great powers, probably three; an ill-defended, ill-organised, ill-developed and immensely vulnerable empire; an inadequate industrial machine and insufficient national wealth. Yet only sixty years earlier Britain had been the richest country in the world; she had been 'the Workshop of the World'. Only twenty-two years earlier she had emerged victorious from the Great War powerful in herself, buttressed by great allies, and with her one great enemy lying smashed in defeat.

The plight of the summer of 1940 therefore marked the consummation of an astonishing decline in British fortunes. The British invested their feebleness and isolation with a romantic glamour – they saw themselves as latter-day Spartans, under their own Leonidas, holding the pass for the civilised world. In fact it was a sorry and contemptible plight for a great power, and it derived neither from bad luck, nor from the failures of others. It had been brought down upon the British by themselves.

# II

# II · ALL THAT IS NOBLE AND GOOD

Nevertheless, there was a diligent search for scapegoats during the 1940s. The prime ministers of the 1930s were personally blamed for the slide into disaster: MacDonald and Baldwin for failing to re-arm early enough and fast enough; Chamberlain for his policy of 'appeasement' of the dictators; all for failing to 'stop' Hitler in good time. When broadened to indict the Conservative Party as well as the Conservative-dominated National Government, this was a line specially favoured by writers of the Left. So well propagated was it that the national folk-memory has accepted it as the true explanation for the plight of 1940. Conservative critics, belatedly counter-attacking, have pointed out how the Labour Party in the 1930s, entranced by pacifistic illusions, doggedly opposed British re-armament until too late, and instead called inconsistently for disarmament and collective security. Apologists for Baldwin and Chamberlain – survivors of their administrations – have drawn attention to the prevailing climate of national opinion in the 1930s, deeply pacifistic and escapist as it was, which made it impossible to pursue a strong policy towards the dictators. Historians, for their part, have probed deeper, tracing the temperamental bias of English statesmen and public opinion towards policies of appeasement back as far as the Paris Peace Conference in 1919. Other critics have described the failure of British governments between the world wars to remedy British industrial backwardness, or have attacked the old-fashioned service leaders who were alleged obstinately to have obstructed the creation of modern armed forces.

All these are partial explanations; outward facets of an inner truth; but they do not explain, for example, *why* such a particular stamp of men as Baldwin and MacDonald, Chamberlain, Simon and Halifax, Henderson and Eden, held sway in British politics between the wars; *why* British public opinion was so pacifistic and internationalist; *why* 'appeasement' was so widely congenial and re-armament so repugnant; *why* British governments handled international crises in the feeble and nerveless way they did; *why* the British permitted the catastrophic decline of their industrial power; *why* the Empire was allowed to remain a source of strategic weakness and danger. The answers lie deeper, in the very springs of judgement and action: in the national character itself, as it had evolved by the early twentieth century. For it is character which, at grips with circumstance, governs the destinies of nations as it does of individual men. It is the key to all policies, all decisions.

But by what process did the British character and the British outlook on the world come to be what they were in the 1920s and 1930s?

In the eighteenth century the English ruling classes – squirearchy, merchants, aristocracy – were men hard of mind and hard of will. Aggressive and acquisitive, they saw foreign policy in terms of concrete interest: markets, natural resources, colonial real estate, naval bases, profits. At the same time they were concerned to preserve the independence and parliamentary institutions of England in the face of the hostility of European absolute monarchies. Liberty and interest alike seemed to the Georgians therefore to demand a strategic approach to international relations. They saw national power as the essential foundation of national independence; commercial wealth as a means to power; and war as among the means to all three.[1] They accepted it as natural and inevitable that nations should be engaged in a ceaseless struggle for survival, prosperity and predominance. Such public opinion as existed in the eighteenth century did not dissent from this world-view. The House of Commons itself reflected the unsentimental realism of an essentially rural society. Patriotism coupled with dislike and suspicion of foreigners were perhaps the only emotions that leavened the vigorous English pursuit of their interests; a pursuit softened but hardly impeded by the mutual conveniences and decencies of international custom and good manners.

Between 1689 and 1815, in the face of formidable rivals and despite the loss of America, England grew from a second-rank nation on the periphery of the Continent into a great power whose wealth, stability and liberty were the envy of Europe.[2]

When however Wellington waved on his red-coats after the routed French at Waterloo on 18 June 1815, it marked for the English the apparent end of centuries of struggle with European great powers. The British Empire was at last supreme and safe. And during the next thirty years of tranquil security from external menace and of bounding industrial development, the British outlook on international relations and on England's role in the world underwent profound changes. The traditional

[1] J. H. Plumb, *England in the Eighteenth Century* (Harmondsworth, Penguin Books 1959), p. 22.
[2] E. J. Hobsbawm, *Industry and Empire* (Harmondsworth, Penguin Books 1969), pp. 49–50; Plumb, pp. 109–10, 214.

strategic view became more and more discredited on two grounds: in the first place because the currently unchallenged British world supremacy in commerce and manufactures rendered protected and exclusive imperial markets and sources of raw materials unnecessary or even cramping; and secondly because it came to be more and more generally felt by public opinion that moral principle and moral purpose rather than strategy or mere interest alone should be the inspiration of English policy. For in the course of the first half of the nineteenth century a moral revolution was completed in England; a revolution which was in the long term to exercise decisive influence on the shaping and conduct of English foreign policy. It is indeed in the transformation of the British character and outlook by this moral revolution that lies the first cause, from which all else was to spring, of the British plight in 1940.

The revolution had begun to gather momentum in the late Georgian age; a peculiarly English manifestation of the romantic movement common to all Western Europe. The essence of romanticism was to value feeling above calculation or judgement. Romanticism exalted sentiment – soon crudened into sentimentality – over sense. Romantics themselves yielded willingly to their hot-flowing emotions. And, in turn, their emotions governed their thoughts and actions, inspiring visions of the noble and the ideal which freed them from the limitations of the world as it was, and human nature as it was; uplifting them from mere consideration of material interest to fidelity to high principles.

For the first time since the doctrinaire seventeenth century a concern for principle had begun to manifest itself in politics by the early part of George III's reign, when, for example, the war against the rebellious American colonies was denounced by politicians like Burke as unjust as well as unwise. Edmund Burke was himself among the most famous and eloquent of early advocates of idealistic purpose as a guide to national policy, although the Members of Parliament of his own time so little relished his high-mindedness that he was known as the dinner bell, his rising to speak being the signal for men to depart the chamber in search of mutton chops. Nevertheless abstract principle continued to wax in favour in British politics. After 1793 Charles James Fox attacked the war with revolutionary France as being an attempt to crush a noble experiment in human liberty rather than the parrying of a national danger. Radicals of the day, like Samuel Whitbread, the brewer MP, were even more passionately moralistic in denouncing English policy and excusing French actions, thereby setting a pattern of emotional response to be followed by the romantic left of politics down to the present day.

However, it was religion which was to give the romantic movement in England its singularly moralistic direction and force. The eighteenth-century founders of Methodism, the evangelists Wesley and Whitefield, although standing in an older tradition, brought to life a new religious emotionalism by loosing men's feelings in vast open-air assemblies tumultuous with mass-hysteria; the archetypes of the mass-meetings of future democracy and its political demagoguery. From the Methodists themselves, the flame of emotionalism leaped and ran through the traditional but now torpid nonconformist sects. It ignited even the Church of England, a body which in the late eighteenth century might have been regarded as wholly proof against feelings stronger and deeper than those of respect for the squire or for a well-roasted goose. The Church of England revivalists, the so-called 'evangelicals' or 'saints', such as William Wilberforce, Hannah More and their friends, carried intense religious emotion and zeal for righteousness into the upper-middle classes. By the opening years of the nineteenth century all British Churches and sects, regardless of doctrine, had been set aflame. And the evangelical attitude to religion, indeed its attitude to the whole of personal and public life, spoke to the hearts of the future rulers of England, the rising middle classes of the towns.

To evangelicals morality was no mere matter of pragmatic observance of the laws and mores of society; no unconscious affair of habit; not something to be taken for granted. On the contrary, their attitude to morality was highly self-conscious; they saw it as an intensely personal question, to be answered according to strict doctrinaire principle. For evangelicals were tormented by a sense of what they called 'sin', a term which covered most aspects of human nature, and especially its strongest and most basic impulses. 'Sin' was to be conquered by earnest prayer in the course of private struggles of conscience conducted in a state of spiritual abasement. Evangelicals therefore saw human existence in all its rich complexity in simple terms of good and evil, right and wrong. They had no doubt at all that they were, although sinful, right. Indeed, their pew-hard certainty, on which no outside evidence could make an impression, was a distinguishing characteristic.

The importance of evangelicalism in terms of future British attitudes to world affairs lay in that it did not limit itself to theology or private examination of the soul, but saw religion as a rule-book to govern every aspect of personal, social and international life. In the words of Sir Ernest Barker: 'It has indeed been a feature common to the Evangelical and Catholic sections of the English Church – and, for that matter, a feature common to both with various nonconformist societies . . . that they have all sought to make religion a general social force.'[1]

Traditional English pragmatism was therefore threatened by the onset of a rigid concern for doctrinaire principle. No less significant for the future tone of British politics and foreign policy was the emphasis of evangelical religion on humanitarian concern and pacifistic sentiment. This was the theological aspect of the new middle-class sentimentality that Dickens both tapped and stimulated, the compassion first manifested by the philanthropists of the eighteenth century. In the past religion had often served rather to justify struggle with one's fellow men. St Athanasius, for example, in the early Christian era, declared that it was lawful to kill enemies in war. There is no biblical disapproval of slavery, although the abolition of slave trade in 1807 as a result of a campaign led by William Wilberforce and of slavery itself in the British Empire in 1833 were the earliest of the great social achievements of British evangelicalism. Religious bigotry had served Cromwell and his Ironsides only to whet their resolution in battle. But while it is true that evangelical religion was to inspire some ruthless English men of action in the nineteenth century – General Gordon; the Lawrence brothers who administered the newly-won Punjab – these were nevertheless exceptions. To embrace one's fellow men in brotherly love rather than smite them with the sword of righteousness was the broad instruction of evangelicalism to the British people. As a historian of Christian pacifism observes:

> . . . our concentration on the primacy of love in the nature of God, and therefore in the Gospel . . . and therefore in the social, national and international implications of the Gospel, is a relatively modern phenomenon . . . I do not find it with any prominence earlier than about a hundred years ago.[2]

By 1870 evangelical Christianity, like a clove of spiritual garlic, had permeated British life.

> No one will ever understand Victorian England who does not appreciate that among highly civilised countries . . . it was one of the most religious that the world has ever known. Moreover its particular type of Christianity laid a peculiarly direct emphasis on conduct . . . it became after Queen Victoria's marriage practically the religion of the court, and gripped all ranks and conditions of society. After Melbourne's

[1] Sir Ernest Barker, *National Character and the Factors in Its Formation* (London, Methuen 1928), p. 201.
[2] Geoffrey Nuttall, *Christian Pacifism in History* (Oxford, Basil Blackwell 1958), p. 2.

> departure it inspired nearly every front rank public man, save Palmerston, for four decades . . . nothing is more remarkable than the way evangelicalism in the broader sense overleaped sectarian barriers and pervaded men of all creeds . . . Even Disraeli, by nature as remote from it as Palmerston, paid every deference to it in politics . . .[1]

As a consequence of this spiritual revolution English policy ceased to be founded solely on the expedient and opportunist pursuit of English interests. International relations were no longer seen as being governed primarily by strategy, but by morality. As Gladstone put it in 1870: 'The greatest triumph of our epoch will be the consecration of the idea of a public law as the fundamental principle of European politics.'[2]

Two institutions – apart from family upbringing itself – ensured that although the hot flames of evangelical moralism and romantic idealism soon burnt out, they nevertheless bequeathed, like the brandy in a *flambé* sauce, a permanent flavour to the British character and outlook. One institution was the nonconformist sect, which converted generations of the lower-middle classes and 'respectable' working classes. The other was the Church of England public school, which by 1900 had re-made the crudely *arriviste* middle classes and the old upper classes alike according to its ideal of a Christian gentleman.

The evolution of the English public school has a crucial bearing on the British plight in 1940, for most of the administrators of the British Empire, at home and overseas in the 1920s and 1930s, as well as many British business leaders and MPs, were products of the period of its ripest development between 1870 and 1900. Except for young Nazis or Communists no class of leaders in modern times has been so subjected to prolonged moulding of character, personality and outlook as British public-school boys in this era.

Over the evolution of the public school Dr Thomas Arnold, Headmaster of Rugby from 1827 until his death in 1841, exercised a decisive influence. Arnold himself expressed in his own stormy personality all the moral obsessions and emotional fervour of early Victorian evangelicalism. Arnold's Rugby was the most important and influential of the schools that served as prototypes for the numerous new public schools that opened between 1840 and 1900 to cater for the swelling middle classes. Arnold more than any other individual gave late Victorian English education

1 R.C.K. Ensor, *England 1870–1914* (Oxford, Clarendon Press 1966), p. 137.
2 Quoted in A.C.F. Beales, *The History of Peace* (London, George Bell 1931), p. 149.

both its concern with moral conduct and its distinctive mark of romanticism. Religion for Arnold, as for the rest of his generation, meant '... what the Gospel teaches us to mean by it, it is nothing less than a system directing and influencing our conduct, principles and feelings ...'[1]

It followed that the first purpose of education was to inculcate Christian morality. 'It is *not* necessary', he wrote, 'that this should be a school of three hundred, or one hundred, or fifty boys; but it *is* necessary that it should be a school of Christian gentleman.'[2]

Christian morality was thus very much more important than, for example, scientific knowledge:

> ... rather than have it [science] the principal thing in my son's mind, I would gladly have him think that the sun went round the earth, and that the stars were so many spangles set in the bright blue firmament. Surely the one thing needed for a Christian and an Englishman to study is a Christian and moral and political philosophy ...[3]

Arnold went so far as to resign from the governing body of the new London University because religion was not to be a compulsory examination subject: '... An University that conceived of education as not involving in it principles of moral truths would be an evil.'[4]

He often found it difficult to judge a work of literature merely on its creative merits or its fidelity to human nature: '... he was quite incapable of enjoying any book or poem if he disapproved of the author's principles or even if he thought that the author was half-hearted in his support of righteousness ... he was troubled by Shakespeare's apparent inability to create good men....'[5]

Arnold's own interpretation of the human past was no less immaculately ideal – a counterpart of the Middle Ages as seen in the vision of the Pre-Raphaelites. While he was writing a history of Rome, he could refer to the Romans as a people 'whose distinguishing quality was their love of institutions and order, and their reverence for law'.[6] It was an unbalanced conclusion to draw from a history replete with violence and disorder. Arnold's treatment of historical personages is less a consideration of a man's ability than a judgement of moral character. Marius was 'the lowest of democrats', Sulla 'the most sincere of aristocrats'. This is to foreshadow a common British trait in the twentieth century. It was indeed

[1] A. R. Stanley, D.D., *The Life and Correspondence of Thomas Arnold D.D.*, 2 Vols. (London, Ward Lock 1890), p. 305. [2] Ibid. p. 66.

[3] Letter of 9 May 1836, quoted in T.W. Bamford, *Thomas Arnold* (London, The Cresset Press 1960), p. 120.

[4] Stanley, p. 310. [5] Bamford, *Thomas Arnold*, p. 199. [6] Stanley, p. 116.

Arnold's purpose in writing his history of Rome to demolish Gibbon, and all the hated scepticism, cynicism and worldliness of the eighteenth century: '... my greatest desire would be, in my History, by its high moral tone and its general tone, to be of use to the cause [of religion] ...'[1]

Arnold was equally a prototype of a common later British attitude to world affairs. He strikes a very modern note over the Opium War with China in 1840 in a letter to a friend:

> ... surely you will agree with me in deprecating this war with China, which really seems to me so wicked as to be a national sin of the greatest possible magnitude, and it distresses me very deeply. Cannot anything be done by petition or otherwise to awaken men's minds to the dreadful guilt we are incurring?[2]

In yet another instance Arnold expresses a sentiment later to be widespread among the British ruling classes, a sentiment shared for example by Sir Edward Grey, Lord Curzon and Neville Chamberlain – that the British were somehow a nation with a special mission, set apart from, and above, others by virtue of their superior morals.

> ... it is very true that by our distinctness we have gained very much – more than foreigners can understand. A thorough English gentleman – Christian, manly and enlightened – is ... a finer sentiment of human nature than any other country, I believe, could furnish.[3]

From this sort of belief derived another belief later common to all British political parties and still alive after the Second World War – that Britain exercised a special and potent 'moral' influence in world affairs; a conviction that other powers would heed the pursing of British lips and the tuttings of British disapproval.

The new ideal of a Christian education went on from Rugby and other newly reformed schools to capture the universities of Oxford and Cambridge. Dr Moberly, the Headmaster of Winchester, remarked on this spiritual revolution:

> ... the tone of the young men at the University, whether they came from Winchester, Eton, Rugby, Harrow or wherever else, was [in his own day as an undergraduate] universally irreligious. A religious undergraduate was very rare, very much laughed at when he appeared; and I think I may confidently say, hardly to be found among public-school men ... A most singular and striking change has come upon our public

[1] Stanley, p. 116. [2] Ibid. p. 383. [3] Ibid. p. 498.

> schools . . . This change is undoubtedly part of a general improvement of our generation in respect of purity and reverence.[1]

Re-interpreted, watered down, sometimes debased and caricatured, this early Victorian preoccupation with morality, this romantic idealism, inspired the English public school until well into the twentieth century. As late as 1928 the Headmaster of Harrow, Dr Cyril Norwood, could write, for example:

> For what has happened in the course of the last hundred years is that the old ideals have been recaptured. The ideal of chivalry which inspired the knighthood of medieval days, the ideal of service to the community which inspired the greatest of the men who founded schools for their day and for posterity, have been combined in the tradition of English education which holds the field today. It is based upon religion; it relies largely upon games and open-air prowess, where these involve corporate effort. . . .[2]

In this book Dr Norwood allotted three chapters out of twenty to religious teaching and only ten pages to British technological backwardness and lack of trained managerial talent – without apparently noting the connection between his own weight of emphasis and the industrial backwardness he deplored. Indeed, he firmly re-stated the pristine Arnoldian doctrine: 'The first and foremost element in the life of a great school, that which is the foundation for all the rest, is religion.'[3]

He politely despised the more worldly atmosphere of the grammar school where he himself had been educated:

> I do not think that there was any clear presentation to us of the ideal of service so much as a call not to let the other schools or other people beat us. We were trained to face the full rigours of competition, and left for the most part with a real determination to get on in the world. That this was so, was due to the fact that the religious appeal was largely absent from our lives. . . .[4]

Between 1890 and 1914, however, the romanticism of Arnoldian Christianity became fused with a patriotic romanticism. The school playing-field was seen as a preparation for the battles of the ever-widening empire. To bring British rule to the coloured heathen and at the same time keep him from falling under French or German rule was seen as a

[1] Ibid. p. 104.
[2] Dr Cyril Norwood, *The English Tradition in Education* (London, John Murray 1929), p. 19.
[3] Ibid. p. 121.
[4] Ibid.

great idealistic mission: evangelism in the red coat of imperialism. As J. E. Welldon, a headmaster of Harrow, put it so movingly and characteristically in 1899:

> An English Headmaster, as he looks to the future of his pupils, will not forget that they are destined to be the citizens of the greatest empire under heaven; he will teach them patriotism not only by his words but by his example. . . .
>
> . . . He will inspire them with faith in the divinely ordered mission of their country and their race; he will impress upon their young minds the convictions that the great principles upon which the happiness of England rests – the principles of truth, liberty, equality, and religion – are the principles which they must carry into the world: he will emphasise the fact that no principles, however splendid, can greatly or permanently affect mankind, unless they are illustrated by bright personal examples of morality.[1]

Thus when the British public school did eventually take note of the real world of power, of rival great nations struggling for imperial markets and industrial success, it was in terms every bit as idealised as Arnold's original Christian teaching. Therefore public-school *alumni* after 1900, who would have shuddered at being accused of 'moralism' of the vintage Victorian brew, especially towards world affairs, nevertheless tended to be romantic idealists without knowing it:

> Naturally we believed wholeheartedly in the greatness of Britain and the permanence of the Empire. I think we believed in our hearts (though we should have shrunk from any such ethical and altruistic motives) that the creation of the British Empire was the best thing that ever happened to mankind. . . .[2]

The powerful romantic bias in the education of British ruling classes was not only religious; it was, as Arnold had again foreshadowed, intellectual as well. It meant that any subject too closely connected with the contemporary world or with the business of making one's way – or one's country's way – in the world was shunned as insufficiently noble or uplifting.

> . . . this necessity of first getting bread and then getting house-room, and then getting this, and then getting that, however far the catalogue

[1] Rupert Wilkinson, *The Prefects, British Leadership and the Public School Tradition* (London, Oxford University Press 1964), pp. 101–2.

[2] C. A. Vlieland, late of the Malayan Civil Service, in a communication to the author.

> may be taken of things which have to be taught and done before the higher education begins, does not alter the fact, that the highest education must work in the region of the highest life. Now literature is the highest thought of the highest men in the most perfect shape. It is the life of the highest men transmitted.[1]

This lofty sentiment, expressed in characteristically high-flying prose, was uttered by Edward Thring, Headmaster of Uppingham from 1883 until 1888, in a book on the *Theory and Practice of Teaching* that ran through sixteen editions between 1883 and 1910. Thring was another of the great reforming headmasters of the nineteenth century, another towering individualist of immense personal force. His book was no analysis of the problems and techniques of education; it was a vision. Although Thring wrote his book at a time when Britain was already under heavy foreign challenge, both politically and industrially, he took no note of this. On the contrary –

> ... what is a nation doing which calmly stands up and says, 'We will only regard in our schools the breeding of the strong head; and we will give all power and honour to the wielders of strength'? This is but the Vandal all over again ... glory to the strong on the reverse side of the shield is oppression to the weak.... Alas for the many, alas for the pith, and working fibre of the nation; alas for all the gentler, and finer qualities by which society lives.... All tender influences, all prevailing, patient, unpretending good may pack and be gone. There is no room for them in the heart of the modern world ... the pride of intellect is to be unchained, and with the break-up of humility, reverence, holiness and genius the child of love, the Dark Age will set in....[2]

Thring's sentiments were neither unique nor novel. John Ruskin, for example, thought that the purpose of a liberal education was to train young men to 'the perfect exercise and knightly continence of their bodies and souls'.[3]

Or as Cardinal Newman had put it: 'That perfection of the Intellect which is the result of education ... is the clear, calm, accurate vision and comprehension of all things, as far as the finite mind can embrace them, each in its place....'[4]

[1] Rev. Edward Thring, *Theory and Practice of Teaching* (Cambridge University Press 1910), p. 36.
[2] Ibid. pp. 80–2.
[3] Quoted in G. A. N. Lowndes, *The Silent Social Revolution* (London, Oxford University Press 1937), p. 108.
[4] J. H. Newman, *The Idea of a University* (New York, Longmans Green 1852), pp. 137–9.

Arnold himself had the feeling that in the ancient authors 'with a perfect abstraction from these particular names and associations, which are ever biasing our judgement in modern and domestic instances, the great principles of all political questions . . . are perfectly discussed. . . .'[1]

There was therefore a certain incompatibility between the stained-glass and white marble ideals of English education and the iron-foundries, cotton-mills and gas-works of the English industrial success that paid for it all. The incompatibility – and its dangers – was pointed out as early as 1861 by Herbert Spencer, a writer who himself looked more to Darwin than to Christ or Socrates.

> That which our school-courses leave almost entirely out, we thus find to be that which most nearly concerns the business of life. Our industries would cease, were it not for the information which men begin to acquire, as best they may, after their education is said to be finished.[2]

Spencer averred in his low, prosaic way that

> . . . it is one thing to approve of aesthetic culture as largely conducive to human happiness; and another to admit that it is a fundamental requisite to human happiness. However important it may be, it must yield precedence to those kinds of culture which bear directly upon daily duties.[3]

Spencer indeed thrust his argument into the heart of the question.

> And here we see most distinctly the vice of our educational system. . . . It neglects the plant for the sake of the flower. In anxiety for elegance, it forgets substance. While it gives no knowledge conducive to self-preservation – while of knowledge that facilitates gaining a livelihood it gives but the rudiments, and leaves the greater part to be picked up anyhow in after life . . . it is diligent in teaching whatever adds to refinement, polish, éclat.[4]

Spencer himself pleaded for science as the foundation of education – the real world systematically investigated. Here is a clue to the kind of English education, growing out of life instead of denying it, that might have been born from the eighteenth-century tradition of practical education and early nineteenth-century scientific enquiry, had it not been for the tide

[1] Stanley, p. 77.
[2] Herbert Spencer, *Education: Intellectual, Moral, and Physical* (London, Williams and Norgate 1861), p. 25.
[3] Ibid. p. 38.
[4] Ibid. p. 39.

of evangelical religion and for the decisive influence of individuals like Arnold who had lit the icy flame of idealism.

The syllabuses and set-books of the Victorian public school between 1870 and 1900 reflect a remote academicism that was slow to wane.[1] Although because of the intense individuality of the schools and their headmasters, wide variations existed between one syllabus and another, there were nevertheless common broad tendencies. In the 1860s the absolute monopoly of the classics (Greek and Latin, Greek and Roman literature, history and philosophy) had been broken. Science and other 'modern' subjects (German and French language, history and literature) were reluctantly admitted as an alternative – often in the first place partly as extras outside school hours. By the 1880s all schools had their 'modern' sides, and during that decade the courses took greater note of boys' future careers – but only in the sense that they prepared them for the qualifying examinations for various professions, such as the Army, the Indian Civil Service, medicine. And these examinations themselves were highly academic.

Thus the syllabuses and set-books, even for 'modern' subjects, remained literary, linguistic, remote from real life. 'History', for example, took no note of economic or social history; it was a matter of kings and queens and cabinets – political, constitutional, legal, even ecclesiastical – and it came to a halt in 1815, well before the late Victorian boy's own lifetime, and before the major onset of the Industrial Revolution. Even on the 'modern' sides, there was no study of the contemporary institutions, economic systems or national resources of Germany or France. Science too, when admitted with suspicion and reluctance, tended to be a low-grade study of disconnected detail – instead of the great alternative to classics in the training of the intellect that scientists like T. H. Huxley had hoped for.

Curiously enough, it was the army classes, with their emphasis on science, geography and modern history, that were least remote from the contemporary world. Did the later gulf in outlook between the civilian and military components of the British imperial ruling class first open at school – between the army class and its unacademic boys, and the academically brilliant classicists?

If the 'modern' boys never reached very close to the modern world the classical élite remained almost totally insulated from it. Edward Bowen,

[1] Cf. those at Marlborough, Winchester and Uppingham. See also Wilkinson, ch. 6; Edward C. Mack, *Public Schools and British Opinion Since 1860* (New York, Columbia University Press 1941), chs. I and II; T.W. Bamford, *Rise of the Public Schools* (London, Thomas Nelson 1967), ch. 5; David Newsome, *Godliness and Good Learning* (London, John Murray 1961), pp. 61–8.

a distinguished Assistant Master at Harrow, wrote that 'most Classical boys leave school knowing little or nothing of . . . the two chief modern languages, and the rudiments of history and English literature'.[1]

In 1887 a reader wrote to *The Marlburian*:

> The small attention paid to geography is surely an anomaly in our course of education that needs reform. I believe it is a fact that in the Upper School the only form of geography ever taught is that which is demanded for a proper understanding of the Divinity and Classical lessons of the form . . . The pressing need for change in this direction will be seen when I assure you that not one of ten boys to whom I was talking the other day could tell me in what county Birmingham is.[2]

Nevertheless there was to be no geography department at Marlborough until 1919: and Marlborough was in the vanguard in this field rather than otherwise.

Lord Vansittart, Permanent Under-Secretary of State at the Foreign Office during the 1930s recalled of his own education that 'Geography was virtually untaught at either private or public school; I only took up the subject seriously for the entrance examination of the Diplomatic Service.'[3]

This neglect of the contemporary world was the more dangerous because despite the broadening of the syllabuses between 1870 and 1890, the classics retained their overwhelming prestige. The 'modern' side was seen as a refuge for the second-rate. Most masters and all the cleverest boys were classicists. The consequences of this are shown in the *Civil Service Commissioners' Reports on the Class I Civil Service examinations*, where, to the end of the century and after, most of the candidates continued to offer classics as preferred subjects.

The late nineteenth century was a time of intense scientific progress and intellectual speculation – a time of colossal industrial developments and social change. All of this bore crucially on the future of Britain and the British Empire. Awareness of little or none of it penetrated into the public schools. The growing threat of other great nations to British predominance, for example, did not lead to a comparative examination for the benefit of pupils of the strategic and industrial foundations of British power and the power of her rivals. It merely led – in some schools – to an uncritical patriotism, in which other great powers were looked upon rather as rival schools, to be humbled by 'pluck' and team spirit.[4]

[1] W. E. Bowen, *Edward Bowen: A Memoir* (London, Longmans 1902), p. 110.

[2] *The Marlburian*, No. 360, Vol. XXII (12 November), pp. 170–1.

[3] Lord Vansittart, *The Mist Procession* (London, Hutchinson 1958), p. 20.

[4] See above pp. 27–8.

If the classics did succeed in their vaunted object of training the mind in judicious weighing of evidence and in logical thought, it was only in respect of a very few boys at the top of the school. For in judging late Victorian public-school education as a preparation for life, the methods of teaching and the size of class are as important as the content of the syllabus. Except in the sixth form, classes usually numbered over twenty boys, and the method of teaching was stereotyped – great slabs of set-books or grammar to be learned by heart and recited, repetition work, all within a fixed programme. There was little scope for personal initiative and curiosity, private research – the exploratory and experimental kind of learning. Even allowing for the out-of-class activities – music, the arts – that more enlightened schools encouraged, this was a deadening and cramping way of educating future leaders. For many it permanently divorced intellectual study from the practical activities of life.

However it was not in the classroom but in the year-in, year-out communal life itself of the school that the mould of conformity and orthodoxy was really pressed down on the raw and varied material of English boyhood – more by their fellows than by the masters. From the age of eight to sixteen or eighteen – the most formative years – an English upper-class boy lived in the closed communities of his preparatory school and his public school. This world of school did not – could not – reflect the real world outside in which the boy would eventually have to make his way.[1]

The public school was physically as well as spiritually withdrawn from the world behind its high gates and walls, looking inward to its own sweeps of lawn and its haphazard and yet harmonious architecture, Gothic and Georgian and neo-Gothic. Arnold and his fellow clerical headmasters had established the chapel as the heart of this closed community. Here in sombre religious shade, the future rulers of England heard their headmaster preaching about honour and service and sin. It was curious how many of the leaders of British life in the 1920s and 1930s seemed to reflect something of the voice and mannerisms of the parson or the headmaster – for example, Neville Chamberlain, Sir Samuel Hoare, Sir John Simon, Lord Halifax, Clement Attlee or Lord Runciman. And yet the headmasters of the late Victorian era, towering figures and strong influences though they were in their schools or even in education at large, were too often men of an extraordinary simplicity, not to say naïveté.[2]

[1] See especially Cyril Connolly, *Enemies of Promise* (London, Routledge and Kegan Paul 1938).
[2] Cf. Edward Bowen of Harrow, although not a headmaster; Almond of Loretto, Thring of Uppingham, Warre of Eton, Benson of Wellington, even Sanderson of Oundle.

Outside the walls of their schools, in the hurly-burly of a pushing, scrambling world, they might well have been lost. They could do little therefore to reflect the real world to their pupils. Nor could their staffs, for most schoolmasters had left the sheltered cloisters of their own school only to proceed to the equally sheltered cloisters of Oxford and Cambridge, and thence straight back to school again.

Arnold had recognised this artificial nature of school life and its pressures towards conformity right at the beginning of the growth of the public-school system:

> Nowhere in the world is there so keen an appreciation of those who adapt themselves to local tone, temper and custom. But nowhere is departure, however slight, from the recognised standard of propriety, visited with consequences so unfailing. The society of a public school is a world in itself, self-centred, self-satisfied. It takes but slight account of the principles and practices which obtain in the world of men. . . .[1]

In Arnold's own day however, in the 1830s and 1840s, school life had been very little organised outside the classroom and the chapel; it had been a tough and turbulent anarchy – not perhaps so totally unreal a preparation for life after all. Games like cricket and football had been scratch affairs on any old rough stretch of ground, played in any old clothes – like games in a town recreation ground today. Players were free to innovate, to invent their own rules. And poaching and other forms of delinquency had also absorbed the energies of the young in ways well-adapted to stimulate individual initiative and cunning.

By the 1880s this variety and freedom in school life had vanished.[2] The boys' time was completely filled up by organised activities. Each school had elaborated a hierarchy of petty ritual privileges – such as the seniority that entitled a boy to put his hands in his pockets or leave undone a button on his jacket. It symbolised a hierarchy of submission, obedience and authority; school life was now minutely ordered by codes of rules, manners and customs, of which the prefects were the authoritarian administrators. Though very far from being self-consciously Christian and moral, nevertheless this regimentation was strongly ethical, inculcating a way of judging and a code of behaviour.

Most important of all aspects of this regimentation was the team game. By the 1880s the playing-field had become what the parade ground is to

[1] Sir Joshua Fitch, *Thomas and Matthew Arnold and Their Influence on English Education* (London, Heinemann 1897), p. 78.

[2] Newsome, Part IV; Bamford, *Rise of the Public Schools*, pp. 76–85; Mack, pp. 123–4; Wilkinson, chs. 3 and 4.

an army – a powerful instrument for inculcating common responses, common values and outlook. Games were now formal and compulsory rituals, governed by fixed and complicated rules, dignified by special uniforms, and with their prestige enhanced by the reward of colours and tasselled caps. Sporting rivalry between the 'houses' into which schools were divided was an obsession. In the issues of *The Marlburian* for 1887, for example, letters about games are about equal in number to those about all other aspects of school life and organisation,[1] and more than twice as many as those on general current affairs or cultural or intellectual topics.

The purpose of this ritual elaboration of collective ball games was a debased version of Arnold's ideal of Christian moral education – it was to develop 'character'. This was why the emphasis on the games reports in school magazines or in school novels was not on skill, intelligence and initiative, but on 'pluck' – or 'playing up': '. . . and may the same rare combination of *vigour* and *fiery dash* with *good temper* and *perseverence* be handed down as one of the TRADITIONS [of the House].'[2]

Personal ambition was discouraged; subordination to the 'team spirit' was the ideal. Thus in 1880 the captain of a winning XV at Marlborough concluded his review of the victory by praising '. . . the unsparing devotion of individuals for the honour of the house; the mutual reliance of the whole team on one another'.[3] Success, though desirable, was not the main point. A lost game could be almost as satisfactory as a victory: '. . . though we got the worst of it, yet the spirit displayed by the losers was a most encouraging sight. . . .'[4]

If the muddy grapplings and collisions of Rugby football taught a rather mindless courage and doggedness, cricket tended to impress the importance of 'good form' and 'fair play' – of conforming to the 'laws' and the accepted code of behaviour, the accepted notions of how things should be done. A 'wrong' stroke that struck an off ball to the leg boundary was in its way less admirable than an elegant late-cut which failed to connect. Cricket's influence on the upper-middle-class British mind, with its sense of orthodoxy and respect for the rules and laws and the impartial authority of umpires, can hardly be exaggerated. As Dr Norwood, of Harrow, expressed it in 1928, cricket 'has added a new conception of fairness and chivalry to the common stock of our national

[1] 48% letters about games.
[2] Marlborough College House Reports, 13 November 1883. The special interest of these house reports lies in that they were written by boys for boys, and were never seen, let alone influenced, by a master.
[3] Marlborough College House Reports.
[4] Ibid.

ideas, since everybody English knows at once what is meant by such statements as "this is cricket" and "that is not cricket" '.[1]

Despite a minority of intractable individualists who hated life at their public schools (like Winston Churchill), the evidence of novels and memoirs is overwhelming that for most boys school was a memorably happy experience.[2] L. S. Amery, for example, a distinguished Conservative politician of the 1920s and 1930s, wrote that for him 'the Harrow School Songs were not the least important, or least abiding, part of our upbringing. They are, indeed, an all-round education in themselves, the embodiment of a manly conception of personal life, of public duty and public policy.'[3] Lord Simon, a no less distinguished Liberal Cabinet minister in the 1930s, wrote of his time at Fettes:

> I think poorly of a public schoolboy who does not feel warmly for his school, for this system of communal life in youth, with loyalties to a fine institution to which all alike belong and with the making of many close companionships, some of which last through life, seems to me to have many virtues. It teaches a small boy . . . that he must denounce injustice wherever he sees it inflicted on others and stand for fair play all round. A British schoolboy's sense of honour and of justice is a very fine quality. . . .[4]

School thus marked their generation deeply. How deeply is shown by the renegade public-school men who, violently attacking the public school, themselves argued from a romantically ideal and moral standpoint.[5]

And the generation of boys who were to reach leading places in British life in the 1920s and 1930s were the products of the public school at this period of greatest regimentation, stuffiest self-satisfaction and conformity, and most torpid intellectual life – midway between the Arnoldian era of experiment and growth, and the reforms of the mid-twentieth century.

These boys were in fact the *first* future ruling class in British history to be subjected to a powerful and uniform moulding process at all. This in itself was of the utmost significance, dooming the variety, spontaneity and open-mindedness that had hitherto been the saving-graces of the British

[1] Norwood, p. 103. See P. C. McIntosh, *Physical Education in England Since 1800* (London, George Bell 1968) for an exhaustive treatment of the subject.

[2] See Mack, ch. V, especially pp. 134–5, 143–8, 199–206.

[3] L. S. Amery, *My Political Life*, 3 Vols. (London, Hutchinson 1953), Vol. I, p. 38.

[4] Viscount Simon, *Retrospect* (London, Hutchinson 1952), p. 26.

[5] Cf. T. C. Worsley, *Barbarians and Philistines* (London, Robert Hale 1940); Alexander Waugh, *Loom of Youth* (London, Grant Richards 1917).

upper classes, while the pattern on which these boys were moulded compounded the harmful consequences of uniform moulding in itself.

Although their ignorance and lack of understanding of their own epoch might be repaired, in an intellectual sense, in later life, true sympathy with it seldom grew. For every aspect of public-school life had set the boy apart, confining him in the social isolation of an upper class. In a world spawning with conflicting ideas and ideologies, school had accustomed him to a single, common and unquestioned outlook. In an era of tremendous change, it had accustomed him to a static society, its development apparently complete. In an epoch that required in men the itch to develop, create and exploit, school had fostered (especially in its prefects) a habit of routine administration – cautious 'responsibility' rather than the taking of risk. Where continued British success and survival depended on innovation and open-mindedness, school admired conservatism and conformism – loyalty to what existed. And in a world of struggle, of infinite variation of human behaviour and morality, school inculcated expectation of common standards of gentlemanly decency and respect for the rules.

In all this the late Victorian public school, however much it coarsened the romantic Arnoldian ideal of a Christian gentleman, none the less, remained essentially true to the ideal. It did not see education as a preparation for the world, but as an inoculation against it. It was gripped by the Victorian obsession with childish or youthful innocence. It wished to preserve this innocence not only until a boy left school, but if possible all his life.

> For you will be men, [a retiring Victorian headmaster of Wellington told his boys in his farewell sermon]. You will seek purity, that the souls and bodies you offer to those you love and to all-seeing God may be white and unspotted: truth, that your speech may be sound and that the brotherhood of men may be to you no shadow.[1]

This speech, with its naïve reference to white and unspotted bodies, unconsciously touched on another aspect of Victorian public-school life which powerfully contributed to the romantically idealised outlook of its *alumni* – homosexuality, spiritual if no more. The memoirs and novels are rich in accounts of the pure, innocent but consuming love entertained by elder boys for some sweet youngster with tender face and curly locks, or by some fag for a house captain, so graceful and athletic, with the noble profile of a Greek god, in the style of Rupert Brooke. The essence of such loves lay in the distance that separated the lover from the adored one; the

[1] In 1873 – Quoted in Newsome, p. 198.

impossibility of fulfilment; the divorce from the real and the physical. As a result, in the words of Robert Graves, the 'atmosphere was always heavy with romance of conventional early-Victorian kind . . .'[1] It was an atmosphere to which the grammar schools (increasingly imitation public-schools) too were not immune; an atmosphere which was lastingly and insidiously to influence the middle- and upper-class British mind. In Ernest Raymond's novel *Tell England* and R. C. Sherriff's play *Journey's End*, for example, the heroes are indistinguishable except in name from girls, and are treated as such by the other characters.

How successful Victorian education proved to be in producing a race of innocents dedicated to romantic ideals is shown by Lord Vansittart's account of the impact on him and his fellows of the Dreyfus case, with all its revelations of human moral depravity. 'How was all this to be reconciled with the narrow standards impressed upon us at school? We were apprised of many unattainables, heard that truth was absolute, that principles must be unconnected with personal advantage, were swayed by the waning credit of Holy Writ.'[2] And Vansittart summed up the effects of their upbringing on his generation thus: 'We were easily moved and easily shocked.'[3]

Nor were the universities well adapted to bringing a more realistic influence to bear. In 1887 an Oxford man informed prospective undergraduates and their parents that to the best young men, 'Oxford will teach the graces which lend richness and interest to life, acquaintance with the great principles of literature and morality, respect of self and others, widened sympathies and admiration of human greatness.' For the average man Oxford would prove 'a means of employing pleasantly and not unprofitably, the years between boyhood and manhood, an opportunity of gaining a tone in the society of well-bred and cultivated men'. For Oxford's function was 'humanising the man rather than turning out the professional expert'.[4] Like the public schools, the universities were monasteries, more lax in rule, more convivial, although scarcely less celibate. The universities lay remote from the clank and smoke and squalor on which the ease and assurance of British upper-class life depended: they were serene, spiteful little worlds of college and university politics. The undergraduate exchanged the lawns of his own home and of his school for lawns of a finer green. Here for three years he was exposed to the silent propaganda of noble architecture deployed by the skill of centuries

[1] Robert Graves, *Goodbye To All That* (Harmondsworth, Penguin Books 1961), p. 39.
[2] Vansittart, p. 27. [3] Ibid. p. 27.
[4] See A. M. M. Stedman, *Oxford: Its Life and Schools* (London, George Bell 1887), pp. 84–5, but see the whole of ch. IV.

against trees and flowing water. He was initiated into a closed society with its own manners and humour, ceremonial and custom. Here was all the beauty and artificiality of a *fête champêtre* by Watteau. Its debilitating charm has been portrayed in the memoirs of many, including men as diverse as Harold Macmillan, Hugh Dalton and John Betjeman. It is the Oxford of Pater and Max Beerbohm, the Cambridge of Rupert Brooke and E. M. Forster.

Neither the dons nor the courses of study were likely to bring the nineteenth or the early twentieth centuries to the close attention of undergraduates. The late Victorian don was not generally a well-informed man of the world. Dr Benjamin Jowett, Master of Balliol, for example, was a personage of imposing intellectual reputation who tried to exercise as great an influence as he could on those of his pupils brilliant or well-connected enough to be likely to follow distinguished careers in politics or government. Yet Jowett's knowledge and understanding of his own country in his own time and of the Europe in which his country had to make headway were appropriate to a maiden-aunt of secluded life. On the appalling social problems left behind by the chaotic growth of Victorian industrialism, for example, Jowett could manage little more penetrating or helpful a thought than this: 'For myself,' he wrote in January 1861, 'I do little or nothing for the poor, but I have always a very strong feeling that they are not as they ought to be in the richest country the world has ever known. In theory I have a great love for them . . .'[1] Although Jowett later did become personally concerned for the poor, his naïveté about the world beyond Oxford did not lessen. In 1877 he expressed his opinion of the condition of the new German Empire, which was by then already the strongest state in Europe, in the throes of an immense industrial expansion, and beginning to pose a threat to British commercial supremacy. Jowett considered that Germany was '. . . poor, military, divided by caste, impoverished and oppressed by the conscription'.[2] And Jowett's biographers themselves, writing in the 1890s, gave vast space to his views on university and religious controversies, but found room only for a brief abridgement of his thoughts on European affairs, the future of Europe and the rivalry of great powers.

Jowett indeed, like the great headmasters, was a characteristic Victorian Englishman – characteristic in his concern for morals and ideals, his romantic love of the classical world and in his distaste for the jarring note

[1] Evelyn Abbot and Lewis Campbell, *The Life and Letters of Benjamin Jowett M.A.*, 2 Vols. (London, John Murray, 1897), Vol. I, p. 344.
[2] Ibid. Vol. II, p. 118.

of realism struck by science or other modern studies. 'I think', he wrote, 'that "the human race is inspired". But how short the moments of inspiration have been – a little stream in Greece and Judea . . . all other progress, or nearly all, is but the dilution of this water of life.'[1] Jowett believed with most of his colleagues of the epoch that science menaced 'the higher conception of knowledge and the mind'; that it was antagonistic to 'morals and religion and philosophy and history and language'.[2]

It was as a result of this entrenched attitude that the classics long retained their pre-eminence at Oxford and Cambridge as the elect field of study; the natural avenue for the brilliant man.[3] An historian of British education in the nineteenth century notes the consequences:

> Up to the close of the third quarter of the nineteenth century British universities lagged far behind those of the Continent in the matter of research; but by the beginning of the new century the relation of the universities to two at least of the important school subjects, natural science and history had been revolutionised. . . .[4]

The classics, as taught in late Victorian Oxford and Cambridge, and studied by the brilliant undergraduates who were to make many of the senior civil servants, politicians and intellectuals of the period between the world wars, followed the same idealised vision as the public schools. The Greece and Rome of this vision were as unreal and immaculate as the physiologically unfunctioning goddesses, vestals and Roman matrons painted by Victorian Royal Academicians; all was law, order, constitutions, political and moral philosophy, noble oratory.[5] A similar emphasis on law and on political and constitutional development rather than on social, economic or military history, was evident in modern historical studies. As an Oxford man expressed it, 'English Constitutional History is the backbone of the School [of Modern History].'[6] Economic history and economics were very much on the fringes of interest: 'What, therefore, is desired in the History School is probably this, that men should gain *some sort of acquaintance* [author's italics] with the chief features of the development of English Industry, Agriculture and Commerce, and with the ideas influencing and underlying it.'[7]

1 Evelyn Abbot and Lewis Campbell, Vol. I, p. 411.

2 Quoted in R. L. Archer, *Secondary Education in the Nineteenth Century* (London, Frank Cass 1966) (first edition 1921), p. 42.

3 Stedman, chs. IX and X; W. R. Ward, *Victorian Oxford* (London, Frank Cass 1965), pp. 276–90; D. A. Winstanley, *Later Victorian Cambridge* (Cambridge University Press 1947), ch. V.

4 Archer, p. 331.

5 See Stedman, ch. X and XI for details of Oxford syllabuses in Classical Honour Moderations and Literae Humaniores in 1887.

6 Ibid. p. 300.

7 Ibid. p. 303.

The Class One examinations for the civil, foreign, Indian civil and colonial services provided a documentary record of the biases and myths of the late Victorian academic mind.[1] In 1870 possible marks for Greek or Roman studies were twice the totals for French or German studies or political economy – and taken together, a third more than allotted to the entire field of science. There was no paper on current affairs. A quarter of a century later the domination of the classics had only been slightly eroded, and the relative importance of science and modern studies only slightly enhanced. It was not until 1906 – too late for the generation of senior administrators of British power in the 1920s and 1930s – that political science, psychology and economic history were included. Understanding of the contemporary world was even now seen as a matter outside formal education, as the Civil Service Commissioners acknowledged in 1917 when taking the revolutionary step of introducing a current affairs paper:

> ... candidates who, while devoting themselves to their individual studies, have nevertheless retained an alert and inquisitive mind and have kept their eyes open to the most important facts in the world about them, should have seized and retained a certain amount of knowledge – scientific, economic, and political.[2]

The content of the examination papers – the bias of the questions – is no less revealing. In 1885, for example, out of twenty questions on English history, six were on legal or constitutional topics, only four on social or economic matters and four on war or foreign relations. In the French history paper there was not a single question on France in the nineteenth century. However there was in the German paper one question devoted to the German victory in the Franco-Prussian war – the war which had made the German Empire the most powerful state of Europe and destroyed the whole traditional balance of power. The question read: 'Discuss the historical justification of the annexation of Alsace and Lorraine by Prussia after the Franco-German war.' It was not perhaps a question well-adapted to testing whether future administrators of British power had pondered the national-strategic implications of the advent of a united Germany.[3]

In 1891 all the questions in Roman history were political and constitutional, although the history of the Roman Empire is so strong in military and strategic interest. The French history paper contained no question

[1] For general surveys of Civil Service examinations in the late nineteenth century, see Cd. 7338, Cd. 7339 and Cd. 8657.
[2] Cd. 8657, p. 14.
[3] *Civil Service Commission Regulations, Examination Papers and Table of Marks* (London, HMSO 1885).

later than the reign of Napoleon I; there was no question at all in the German paper on the modern Germany created by Bismarck.[1] In 1895 ten out of eighteen questions in the English history examination were constitutional, only five on war or foreign relations, and none at all on economic or social topics.[2] In 1900 the political science paper included nothing on Marx or other socialists of the nineteenth century; nothing on the practical aspects of political science; it was all highly academic and abstract, and based on Hobbes, Locke and Rousseau. The general modern history paper concentrated on pure politics and neglected social, economic and strategic factors. In political economy there was no question dealing with the world economic system of 1900 as it existed, or with British competitive power relative to her rivals; here too the emphasis was academic, abstract – finance, economic laws, theory.

Only by 1905 was there a marked change of emphasis towards questions of national rivalry and power. There were three questions in the political science paper on the balance of power, on national decay and its causes, and on socialism. The general history paper gave greater weight to conflict, less to politics and constitutions; more importance to the relationship between war and national policy and national history. In 1906 the Greek and Roman history papers also veered towards war, foreign policy and social questions.

These changes also came too late, however, to benefit the generation that was to manage the British Empire in the 1920s and 1930s.

Because the Civil Service examinations were framed in collaboration with the universities, they fairly reflect what the best products of late Victorian English education were expected to know. Harold Macmillan, for example, wrote when he first stood for election at Stockton in 1923:

> I had no practical knowledge of the world in which I was to move. I had never been to Tees-side or even Tyneside. Apart from Glasgow, where my printer cousins lived, I had scarcely been to an industrial town. I had never seen the great ironworks, steelworks, engineering works, shipyards, which had been built up on the banks of the rivers of the North of England and of Scotland. Nor, except for the war, had I any actual experience of living among an industrial population.[3]

British governing-class education was really appropriate to a moment in history that had already vanished – that of mid-Victorian prosperity and security. As the memoirs of statesmen and civil servants make plain, they

[1] *Civil Service Commission Regulations* (London, HMSO 1891).
[2] *Civil Service Commission Report* (London, HMSO 1895).
[3] Harold Macmillan, *Winds of Change* (London, Macmillan 1966), p. 41.

left their universities unaware that that unique moment had passed away, or why. They took it for granted that the British Empire was the greatest and richest power in the world, indeed in history.[1] It had not yet occurred to them that the foundations of British power might be rotting, or that the splendid structure might seriously be threatened by other powers, such as imperial Germany. They assumed – for scepticism about fundamentals had hardly been encouraged – that the empire would just go on and on much as it was. They saw the empire romantically as a great instrument of civilisation and enlightenment, a successor to Greece and Rome; and their own role in the empire in idealistic terms of service in its civilising mission. They had been educated in fact to think of themselves as super-prefects, administering the empire justly and efficiently in the interests of the governed. They hardly thought at all of British power in terms of industrial competitiveness, science, technology or strategy.

The qualities imparted to this future ruling class by their education – probity, orthodoxy, romantic idealism, a strong sense of public responsibility – admirably fitted them for running the British Empire as they saw it: an unchanging institution of charitable purpose and assured income. Such qualities were however ill-suited to leading the empire, a great business and strategic enterprise, through drastic internal re-organisations and against ferocious and unscrupulous competition. Indeed other characteristics fostered by Victorian education – conservatism, doctrinaire orthodoxy, rigidity, inertia and unbounded complacency – are the classic attributes of an army about to suffer a catastrophic defeat.

Meanwhile, the lower-middle and 'respectable' working classes were also being moralised; by the Churches, above all by the nonconformist sects – Congregationalists, Unitarians, Methodists, Baptists and Quakers. Although the great work of conversion was complete by 1870, the chapel continued to serve these social classes as the public school served their betters, as an institution which clapped succeeding generations into a spiritual corset, the whalebone of idealism at odds with the flesh of real life. For, like the public schools, the chapels, as the historian G. M. Trevelyan put it, 'regarded life (including politics and foreign policy) as a branch of personal religion'.[2]

It was the Reform Act of 1867 which turned the nonconformist conscience into a dominant political force by enfranchising the urban lower-middle and 'respectable' working classes. The businesslike horsetrading of

[1] Cf. Viscount Maugham, *At the End of the Day* (London, Heinemann 1954), p. 99.
[2] G. M. Trevelyan, *English Social History* (London, Longmans Green 1944), p. 509.

eighteenth-century foreign policy, of which Palmerston was the last and one of the most cheerfully profane and successful exponents until his death in 1865, became increasingly difficult to carry out, even for statesmen who themselves had escaped the moralising influence of evangelical religion.

In 1876, for example, Gladstone, in Opposition, devastatingly conjured up the moral indignation of the middle classes in Beaconsfield's face over a crisis in the Balkans. It was Wesley and Whitefield in political garb – the best-selling tract or pamphlet, the evangelical crusade, the fervent preaching. Here was a prototype of a widespread response to foreign affairs in the twentieth century. To Lord Beaconsfield, the Conservative Prime Minister, the current Balkan situation appeared as a matter of British imperial and strategic interests. These seemed to require supporting Turkey against Russian pressure. To Gladstone and the audiences whose hot emotions were stirred up by his preaching, the question was a moral one, turning on the massacre of 12,000 Bulgarian Christians by the Turks. As J. R. Green, the historian, put it, Gladstone's audiences were moved by 'his warm ardour for all that is noble and good'.[1]

Although formal religious belief and attendance at church and chapel gradually ebbed after 1870 to low water in the 1920s, emotional ardour for all that was noble and good became a stronger, not weaker influence on British policy. For the evangelical spirit found new and secular outlets.

> Humanism and Humanitarianism, Liberalism and Internationalism, [wrote Sir Herbert Butterfield] . . . emerge as a result of a tendency to translate into secular terms certain movements and aspirations which had characterised a Christian civilisation ... humanitarianism, for example, is an anaemic substitute for the doctrine of New Testament love.[2]

The Liberal Party of the late nineteenth and early twentieth centuries owed much to nonconformist personnel. In 1906 there were 127 nonconformists out of 377 Liberal MPs. Nonconformists also came to dominate the trade union movement, the socialist movement and the Labour Party itself.[3] In 1918 there were 82 Methodist candidates at the

[1] Quoted in Ensor, p. 45.

[2] Sir Herbert Butterfield, *Christianity in European History* (London, Oxford University Press 1951), pp. 40–1.

[3] H. F. Wearmouth, *The Social and Political Influence of Methodism in the Twentieth Century* (London, Epworth Press 1957), especially chs. I, II, VI–IX and XII; Maldwyn Edwards, *Methodism and England* (London, Epworth Press 1943), chs. X and XI; Roland H. Bainton, *Christian Attitudes to War and Peace* (London, Hodder and Stoughton 1961); David A. Martin, *Pacifism: An Historical and Sociological Study* (London, Routledge and Kegan Paul 1965), pp. 85–90; Fenner Brockway, *Inside the Left*

General Election, of which 49 were Liberal and 26 Labour.[1] In 1925, 45 out of 192 Labour MPs were lay preachers, and 28 were active pacifists.[2] For nonconformists were natural leaders, self-educated men of serious purpose, apt for the drudgery of organisation, happy at proselytising.

Indeed the Labour Party in its whole personality was less a body for the seizing and wielding of political power than a pseudo-religion.[3] Its early days particularly illustrate its spiritual borrowings from real, evangelical religion. A socialist could write of the Labour Party work in the early 1900s in such terms as these: 'A veritable crusade was led throughout Scotland in those years with all the fervour and fanaticism of a new holy religion. . . .'[4]

There was for example the Socialist Sunday School movement of the 1890s, with its fervent socialist songs in place of hymns, and a declaration of socialist precepts, based on 'Justice and Love' and modelled on the Ten Commandments:

> We desire [proclaimed one of these precepts], to be just and loving to all fellow men and women, to work together as brothers and sisters, to be kind to every living creature and so help to form a New Society with Justice as its foundation and Love as its law.[5]

Sentiments such as these determined the attitude of the nascent Labour Party towards foreign affairs, and inspired equally party factions who might otherwise disagree over specific issues.[6] It was a picture of the world with all the charming innocence of Kate Greenaway's art, almost evoking to the mind Kaisers and Admiral Tirpitzes in muslin smocks melted into love by British kindness.

The innocence and unreality were not limited to free-trade liberals or the Labour movement. In the late nineteenth century there was a great deal of hybridising between the three original species of Victorian romanticism – rational abstraction, evangelical religion and simple sentimentalism. In terms of international relations, the result was a romantic idealism which believed that the whole world was well on the way to becoming one highly moral society – like Britain itself. Mankind

(London, Allen and Unwin 1942), chs. 1 and 3; Kenneth E. Miller, *Socialism and Foreign Policy: Theory and Practice in Britain to 1931* (The Hague, Martinus Nijhoff 1967), chs. I and II; R. Tudor Jones, *Congregationalism in England 1662–1962* (London, Independent Press 1962), pp. 341–7.

[1] Maldwyn Edwards, p. 204.

[2] J. M. Gaus, *Great Britain: a Study in Civic Loyalty* (Chicago, Chicago University Press 1929), p. 108.

[3] See Richard W. Lyman, *The First Labour Government 1924* (London, Chapman and Hall 1957), p. 12.

[4] T. Bell, quoted in Brian Simon, *Education and the Labour Movement 1870–1920* (London, Lawrence and Wishart 1965), p. 249.

[5] Ibid. p. 50.

[6] See Miller, chs. I, II and III.

was taken to be essentially good and kind and rational. His natural condition was believed to be peaceful harmony because the interests of all nations were naturally harmonious. That mankind's history to that date had been mostly concerned with struggle, ambition, greed and violence was attributed to evil governments and social systems. Once these were removed, harmony and love would prevail. The fundamental relationship between human groups was not competitive and strategic, but moral. International relations were therefore not governed by power but by moral law. Moral law was believed to be inherently capable of restraining the wrongdoer.

*Imperialism: A Study* by J. A. Hobson[1] perhaps best assembles in one bouquet the assorted beauties of late Victorian and Edwardian romantic internationalism. Hobson was a Gladstonian liberal who became a socialist after the Great War – a characteristic mutation. His book was first published in 1902, and was republished in 1938. It exercised an immense influence. By a hotly emotional tone Hobson expresses the characteristic moral indignation of the middle classes and the righteousness and biblical certainty derived from evangelical religion. By constantly appealing to reason and reasonableness, he also stands in the line of rational abstraction that runs from the classical economists to twentieth-century philosopher-commentators like C. E. M. Joad and Bertrand Russell.

Hobson set out to prove, with much useful statistical information, that imperialism was primarily economic exploitation of primitive regions, leading to a struggle between the great powers and the danger of war. Imperialism was not, he thought, an evangelical or civilising mission. He argued that imperialism was not only bad economics, but hypocritical and immoral. Indeed Hobson supported the idea of moral law against the post-Darwinian (or Hobbesian, or Clausewitzian or Marxian) view that struggle was natural and inevitable and that different human groups would always go on expanding and contracting in power or territory.

> If imperial expansion, [he writes], were really nothing other than a phase of the natural history of a nation it would be as idle to protest against it as to argue with an earthquake. But the policy of civilised States differs from that of uncivilised States in resting more largely upon deliberate conscious choice, particularly definitely of the character of conduct.[2]

Thus for Hobson it was 'collective reason' that determined national policies and could therefore resist the impulse to aggressive expansion.

[1] J. A. Hobson, *Imperialism: A Study* (London, Allen and Unwin 1902). [2] Ibid. p. 182.

In any event, the need for struggle between nations was diminishing:

> . . . the tendency of growing civilisations on the national scale has been more and more to divert the struggle for life with other nations to a struggle with environment, and so to utilise the fruits of reason as to divert a larger and larger proportion of energy to struggles for, intellectual, moral and aesthetic goods . . .[1]

Whatever the merits of this as a vision of the long-term future of mankind it hardly squared with the political facts of Hobson's own era.

Hobson ridiculed the arguments of those who believed that the nation-state was, as an observable fact, the highest effective political unit which so far existed and that consequently there was no law or sanction to govern relations between nations but the shifting equilibrium of power.

> It may here suffice to say [wrote Hobson with boundless assurance] that the maintenance under ordinary conditions of treaty relations, international credit and exchange, a common postal, and within narrow limits, a common railway system, not to mention the actual machinery of conventions and conferences for concerted national action, and the whole unwritten law of war and international courtesies, embassies, consulates and the like – all these things rest upon a basis of recognition of certain reciprocal duties, the neglect or violation of which would be punished by forfeiture of most favoured nation treatment in the future, by reprobation and possibly the combined intervention of other states.[2]

Hobson, like many others who saw international relations in idealistic terms, looked forward to the growth of world courts and congresses which would settle disputes between nations in a peaceful manner. Hobson thus spans the mid-Victorian vision of a world pacified by free trade and the post-Great-War faith in the League of Nations. He is a classic example of the romantic approach to foreign affairs, in that his argument is founded less on deduction from the evidence of real life than on an apparent refusal to accept it; an argument founded instead on optimistic assumptions. The faith in the inherent power of treaties and agreements and in the restraining effect of world reprobation is also typical. Yet Hobson wrote his book at a time when a century of wars between civilised European states had just closed, and only forty years after the American Civil War – a prolonged struggle between members of the same civil community.

Nevertheless, in place of 'the existing false antagonisms of nations'[3]

[1] Ibid. p. 183. [2] Ibid. p. 167. [3] Ibid. p. 363.

Hobson looked forward confidently if prematurely to 'both economic and intellectual community of needs and interests', once the great powers gave up policies of expansionist self-seeking based on alliances and armed force. The spread of democracy would hasten this process, for 'intelligent democracies would perceive their identity of interest and would ensure it by their amicable policy'.[1] Unfortunately for Hobson's argument, the longest and bloodiest war between 1815 and 1902 had been fought out inside a democracy. Hobson was here again typical in being unable to accept that human disputes could be irreconcilable, and therefore only to be resolved in violent conflict.

Later prophets of a world society between 1900 and 1914 tended even more than Hobson to emphasise economic and scientific arguments rather than nonconformist moralising alone. Sir Norman Angell, for example, in a high influential book *The Great Illusion*,[2] proved that the modern world was already essentially united by industry, trade, finance and communications. It followed that nationalism and ruthless pursuit of national interest were absurd anachronisms. War between great modern states in particular could profit no one, but only result in universal destruction and dislocation. The good sense of these conclusions was unchallengeable. However, in terms of the Europe of 1910, their weakness lay in their very reliance on good sense. Angell's book illustrates a general proneness within the intellectual, or rational, strain of internationalist idealism to feel that once something has been demonstrated to be absurd or self-destructive it is as good as written off. However, while you may rightly tell a drunkard that drink will kill him if he does not give it up, how do you stop him drinking?

The post-evangelical hopes of a peaceful world society founded on love or the moral law or economics took no positive account of existing human aggressiveness and irrationality, but dismissed them as morally reprehensible or rationally absurd habits that mankind ought to decide to give up. Yet even Hobson, for example, could make an admission that wrecked the whole argument of his book without noticing that it did so.

> The passion ... the instinct for control of land [he writes], derives back to the earliest times, when a wide range of land was necessary for a food supply for men or cattle, and is linked to the 'trek' habit, which survives more powerfully than is commonly supposed in civilised peoples ... The animal lust of struggle, once a necessity, survives in the blood. . . .[3]

* * *

[1] Hobson, p. 363.
[2] Norman Angell, *The Great Illusion* (London, Heinemann 1910).
[3] Hobson, p. 213.

For half a century after Waterloo the English could afford to ignore 'the animal lust for struggle', at least as between great powers. A moral conscience was the ultimate luxury afforded the middle classes by commercial success and national security. Thanks to the war-making and aggrandisement of the past they were able now to disdain and condemn unscrupulous self-seeking in other powers, just as the rich are able to rise above envy. The beneficiaries of the broadsides of Trafalgar and the volleys of Waterloo could safely indulge their humanitarian and peaceable sentiments. It was possible to look forward along an endless railway line of progress, as the moral law and free trade drew all mankind into one society, and national governments diminished into a kind of borough council. Richard Cobden and John Bright epitomised this blend of liberal doctrine and evangelical faith. As Cobden himself expressed it in a speech in 1843:

> If I were not convinced that the question [of Free Trade] comprises a great moral principle and involves the greatest moral world's revolution that was ever accomplished for mankind, I should not take the part I do in this agitation. Free Trade! What is it? Why, breaking down the barriers that separate nations; those barriers behind which nestle the feelings of pride, revenge, hatred and jealousy, which every now and then burst their bounds and deluge whole countries with blood. . . .[1]

It was a noble aspiration. But was it also a practical one? For unfortunately what men like Cobden took to be the dawning of a new age for all mankind was in fact a brief moment of security and prosperity for Britain herself between the defeat of France as a super-power and the rise of united Germany. The Liberal optimists were mistaking a local heat-wave for a general change of climate.

For after 1870 Britain was back where she had been in the centuries before Waterloo – struggling against powerful rivals, struggling economically, strategically, diplomatically.

The Crimean War, by displaying the actual state of British military power, had laid Wellington's ghost. In 1864 when Palmerston attempted to intervene in a dispute between Prussia and Denmark in the style that had been so successful in the 1830s and 1840s, his bluff was brusquely called by Bismarck. British diplomacy could no longer dine out on Waterloo; it needed fresh power and prestige if it were to carry weight. British industry too could no longer float its products without hindrance or effective competition into world markets on a tide of free trade. Britain had able

[1] Speech at a Covent Garden demonstration on 28 September 1843.

competitors now, for other nations were industrialising themselves, and enjoying all the advantages of the latest equipment and methods. The United States after 1865 and united Germany after 1871 in particular rapidly developed an immense competitive power. Worse, Britain's foreign rivals began to protect their industries and markets by tariff barriers. Free trade became free in only one direction.

For other great powers did not see the world as one great human society, but – just as the British had done up to the nineteenth century – as an arena where, subject to the mutual convenience of diplomatic custom, nation-states – the highest effective form of human society – competed for advantage. They did not believe in a natural harmony among mankind, but in national interests that might sometimes coincide with the interests of others, sometimes conflict. It followed that they considered that relations between states were governed not by law, nor even by moral principle, but by power and ambition restrained only by prudent calculation and a sense of moderation. War therefore, in their view was not a lamentable breakdown of a natural harmony called peace, but an episode of violence in a perpetual struggle. European powers looked on armed forces not as wicked, but as among the instruments of diplomacy. Indeed, whereas in Britain romantic emotion expressed itself in visions of a world society, in Europe it had given rise to a fervent nationalism. In the late nineteenth century the world was becoming not less dangerous and anarchical, but more so.

Moralising internationalism, born out of liberalism by evangelical faith, was therefore an unsuitable guide to British policy. There were those in Britain who perceived this. They argued that the continuance of British prosperity and security required more than blind faith in a free market and the moral law. They called into question the whole liberal interpretation of British history, according to which British greatness was said to derive from peaceful economic and constitutional progress. Whereas liberal thought had looked on the expansionist wars of the eighteenth century as immoral, costly and useless interruptions of progress, it was now argued that strategy and successful war had been keys to the growth of British power and influence. It was argued indeed that the British Empire ought to be revived as a collective organism for strategic purposes.

The novel case was brilliantly put by Sir J. R. Seeley, professor of modern history at Cambridge, in a series of twelve lectures, published in book-form in July 1883 under the title *The Expansion of England*[1] and

[1] J. R. Seeley, *The Expansion of England* (London, Macmillan 1883).

reprinted ten times between then and 1899. The theme of the relative power of nations inspired his whole thesis.

Seeley believed that the foundation of British greatness lay in the victories of Marlborough's army and the Royal Navy over Louis XIV, of which the Treaty of Utrecht was the consequence. 'It has been universally allowed ever since that no state is more powerful than England. But especially it has been admitted that in wealth and commerce and in maritime power, no state is equal to her.'[1]

However he warned against the smugness of 1883; 'We are not then to think, as most historians seem to do, that all development has ceased in English history, and we have arrived at a permanent condition of security and prosperity.'[2]

And '. . . as now [England] herself looks upon the business-system and banking of countries like Germany and even France as old-fashioned compared to her own, so in the Middle Ages the Italians must have looked on England.'[3]

And Seeley feared that the 'white' colonies – Australia, New Zealand, Cape Colony, Natal and Canada – might fall away in independence.

> Such a separation would leave England on the same level as the states nearest to us on the Continent, populous, but less so than Germany and scarcely equal to France. But two states, Russia and the United States, would be on an altogether different scale of magnitude, Russia having at once, and the United States perhaps before very long, twice our population. Our trade too would be exposed to wholly new risks.[4]

In Seeley's view the only alternative was

> . . . that England may prove able to do what the United States does so easily, that is, hold together in federal union countries very remote from each other. In that case England will take first place with Russia and the United States in the first rank of state, measured by population and area, and in a higher rank than the states of the Continent.[5]

From the 1880s onwards a 'hard-minded' school of imperial power and strategy challenged the believers in international moral law, the 'tender-minded' legatees of evangelical Christianity. Yet such was the romantic climate of mind in late Victorian Britain that even the businesslike pursuit of British power had to be justified by an ideal and glorified by a myth. The imperialist ideal took the form of a world civilised by Anglo-Saxons. The myth was of a British master race carrying a heavy burden of

[1] Ibid. p. 154. [2] Ibid. p. 196. [3] Ibid. p. 101. [4] Ibid. pp. 18–19. [5] Ibid.

responsibility for lesser breeds. The white man was thus not conquering or ruling unnumbered coloured men and vast territories simply in order to augment his power and wealth, but also to bring the benefits of Western administration to the benighted. The imperial myth was movingly and imaginatively expounded, above all by Rudyard Kipling; it was the myth that J. A. Hobson had wished to torpedo in *Imperialism: A Study*.

Yet another distinction between eighteenth-century empire-building and nineteenth-century imperialism lay in the latter-day need for a broad political foundation in popular sentimentality. The countervailing emotion to moral fervour was found in the crude nationalism and hatred of foreigners among the urban masses. These had largely escaped evangelical conversion, for nonconformism was weakest in the big industrial towns and in the 'unrespectable' classes.[1] The urban masses found in the navy, the army and the empire compensation for the aggression, glamour and success denied to them in their own drab and servile lives.[2] The music-hall and the pub were to imperialism what the chapel was to moralising internationalism, and beery choruses were its psalms. It was the music-hall hit of 1878, 'We don't want to fight, but by Jingo, if we do . . .' that gave the popular imperialist and nationalist state of mind its nickname of Jingoism.

By the 1890s the jingo tide was flowing strongly – so strongly that in 1899 the Liberal Party itself, in Opposition, was split between those who supported the war with the Boers and those Gladstonians who looked on the war as a moral crime against a small independent nation. In the following year, it was jingoist emotion over the war that swung the General Election in the Conservative Government's favour. However when six years later the next General Election was won in a landslide by the Liberals, a moral issue – that of the importation of Chinese coolie labour into South Africa under conditions allegedly of virtual slavery – was among the factors of their success. It was a sign that jingoism-imperialism was a superficial mood rather than a spiritual counter-revolution capable of wholly ousting the effects of evangelicalism from the British character.

During the period of armed alliances and rising European tension that preceded the Great War the opposing romantic currents of jingoism and internationalism were in constant collision in England. The jingo press had no hesitation in naming Germany as the coming enemy, and demand-

[1] See E. J. Hobsbawm, *Labouring Men: Studies in the History of Labour* (London, Weidenfeld and Nicolson 1964), ch. 3.

[2] As late as 1956 it was the middle classes, not the working class, who opposed the Anglo-French invasion of Egypt.

ing that Britain should overwhelmingly outbuild the German battlefleet. They looked forward to burning off both forks of Admiral Tirpitz's beard. There was a great deal of glorification of war as the detergent of a corrupt civilisation, a kind of romantic idealism that was to find its finest and silliest expression in Rupert Brooke. Jingo hysteria served a purpose, however, in making possible a 'hard-minded' policy of effective British preparation for war.

The 'tender-minded' still sought escape from the fact of a Europe armed to the teeth and tense with hatred and rivalry; they found it in their vision of an international society ruled by moral law. The two international conferences at The Hague, in 1899 and 1907, on the maintenance of peace, the 'law' of war and the limitation of armaments evoked preaching missions by bodies ranging from outright pacifists to internationalists of one persuasion or another. The Peace Society, the International Arbitration League, the Trade Union Congress and the Arbitration Alliance of the Churches all fervently contributed. In fact the Hague conferences demonstrated how slender was the possibility either of creating international authorities or of such authorities possessing the power to prevent war. The participating governments regarded the conferences as a pious waste of time, and although an international court was set up, recourse to it was optional, and it had no means of enforcing its judgements.[1]

The only other contribution of the idealists of the Liberal and Labour parties to the solution of the British dilemma in the face of European tension and German challenge was simply to oppose both the expansion of the British fleet and any kind of alliance. The Utopian fantasies of the 'tender-minded' were thus further removed from the realities and possibilities of Europe before 1914 than even the most bellicose fantasies of the jingoes. There was a curious – and ever-present – paradox in the temperament of romantic internationalists; while emotionally they were in the thick of the fight against evil, intellectually they might have been surveying the European scene from the basket of a balloon. Neither those who preached the moral law nor those who reasoned from economics and science displayed real understanding of what it was like to carry responsibility for foreign policy amid all the pressures and complications and limitations of the actual European situation. They seemed to think that Britain had complete liberty to choose and implement either ideal international solutions, as if other powers were naughty children who would pay instant heed to what Nanny said; or unilateral solutions, as if Britain were not only detached fom Europe but almost from the planet.

[1] Beales, chs. IX and X.

Between 1890 and 1914 moralising internationalism was on the ebb in Parliament and Whitehall as well as in the country. Not only was the Conservative Party imperialist in sentiment, but so was one wing of the Liberal Party. And yet in governing circles as well as in public opinion imperialism was more of a mood, a turn of emphasis, than a re-conversion back to the outlook of the eighteenth century. It was only after 1900 that British policy began once more to accord high importance to strategy and power, and even then it was less out of temperamental inclination and intellectual conviction than because of outside pressures. For the German naval challenge followed hard on the Boer War and its revelations of British isolation and weakness. And although Britain adhered to the Triple Entente (France, Russia, Britain) against the Triple Alliance (Germany, Austria, Italy) throughout the tensions and crises of 1905–14, Sir Edward Grey, the Liberal Foreign Secretary (as high-minded an apostle of the moral law as ever was), continued to search for a European consensus; and continued to count on the fact that the Entente was not an alliance, and therefore Britain was not automatically obliged to succour France. Nor were the nature and aims of foreign policy and national strategy a subject of grand political debate between 1900 and 1914. Except for the naval scare of 1909, when it was believed that the Germans were winning the shipbuilding race, it was domestic problems such as Ireland, social reform and unrest, and the constitutional quarrel over the powers of the House of Lords that dominated politics.

Thus although questions of strategy and national power were being more systematically studied between 1900 and 1914 than at any time since 1815, the study was largely confined to the service departments and ministers. British statesmen as a whole were far from returning to the outlook of Elizabeth I and her council or of the elder Pitt. In fact, imperialists were themselves often idealists of the true moralising and romantic Victorian model. Milner for example said of the British purpose in Egypt:

> British influence is not exercised to impose an uncongenial foreign system upon a reluctant people. It is a force making for the triumph of the simplest ideas of honesty, humanity, and justice, to the value of which Egyptians are just as much alive as anybody else. . . . If Egyptian prosperity is a British interest so is Egyptian independence. . . .[1]

With the outbreak of war in 1914 the internationalists in the Liberal and Labour parties, already losing credit, seemed to go into intellectual bank-

1 Quoted in John Evelyn Wrench, *Alfred Lord Milner* (London, Eyre and Spottiswoode 1958), p. 100.

ruptcy. The moral law was demonstrated to carry less weight than a military railway timetable. A solemn treaty was shown to have the protective power of a magic charm. The natural harmony of human interests was disproved by the spectacle of great nations at each other's throats. The pacifying and unifying effects of modern science and communications were ridiculed by the convenience with which railways launched into battle millions of men equipped with artillery and machine-guns. The liberal-evangelical faith in love, reason and the brotherhood of man was cruelly mocked by the ferocious hatreds bayed by the mobs in the great cities of Europe.

It was a sign of the internationalists' failure to study and evaluate unpalatable facts that they awoke very late to awareness that Britain was likely to be caught up in a general European war. It was not until four days after the Austrian ultimatum to Serbia that the Liberal daily, *The Manchester Guardian*, adverted to the danger of a general conflict. By contrast the Conservative press had already warned its readers that if the great powers mobilised, Britain would have to mobilise as well. *The Times* indeed first alerted its readers about the danger of war in Europe five days before *The Guardian*.[1]

The response of the post-evangelicals of the Liberal and Labour parties to the looming danger illustrates how remote they were from the European reality. *The Manchester Guardian* hastened to propagate two characteristic illusions: firstly, that Britain, having 'no direct interest in the quarrel between Austria and Serbia . . . is in no danger of being dragged into the conflict by treaties of alliance';[2] and secondly, that Britain's aloofness made her a natural and respected arbitrator. 'Can England use this favoured position to save Europe from disaster?'[3] During the final week of peace the Liberal press and peace-lovers of every shade argued more and more frenziedly that Britain should – and, more unreal, *could* – remain neutral. After all, as *The Guardian* argued, neutrality '. . . is the chief source of our moral authority in Europe'.[4] Nevertheless, with the great powers mobilising one by one, the romantic internationalists of Britain were like a man in a barrel going over Niagara Falls gabbling that he is free to navigate in any direction. There was indeed a special agony for liberals, in that it was a Liberal Government that was failing to declare Britain's neutrality, and on the contrary taking precautionary measures in regard to the fleet and the army. The heirs of Cobden and Gladstone in the Cabinet had been

[1] Irene Cooper Willis, *How We Went Into the War* (Manchester, National Labour Press 1918), ch. II.
[2] Ibid. p. 42.
[3] Ibid. pp. 42–3. [4] Ibid. p. 45.

swamped by a combination of inescapable events and pressures and their own liberal-imperialist colleagues.

On Sunday, 2 August, with Austria, Serbia, France, Germany and Russia at war, the Labour Party held an anti-war rally in Trafalgar Square. On Monday, 3 August, with German forces across the Belgian and Luxembourg frontiers, *The Guardian* still believed that it would be right and possible for Britain to stay neutral. And since it was the German violation of Belgian neutrality that was the factor most likely to impel England into war, *The Guardian*, in the tradition founded by the radicals during the Napoleonic wars, went out of its way to sympathise with and explain away the action of the German Government: '*We deeply regret it but we understand.*'[1] As to its own government's actions, *The Guardian*, again true to radical tradition, did not understand at all, although it also deeply regretted. Nor did all those others who hastened fervently and indignantly to form 'neutrality' committees of protest. Nor did the Liberal and Labour MPs who spoke and cheered against the Foreign Secretary's speech in the Commons on 3 August, when he announced mobilisation, and asserted that Britain could not watch with folded arms while Germany struck Belgium and France down.

On 4 August, despite all the frenzy of righteous indignation and passionate rejection of the inevitable, the men of peace and international understanding were swept in their barrel over the falls of war, denouncing, as they went, the danger and the violence of the waters in the hope of thereby producing a calm.

Thus in 1914 the believers in a world governed by the moral law failed to carry either national or parliamentary opinion with them. The long reaction of imperialism and jingoism since 1880 and the sharpening rivalry between England and Germany since 1900 had reduced them to a large die-hard minority. Bellicose emotion eclipsed moral indignation in British opinion. During the crisis itself, indeed, the German invasion of Belgium suggested to many Britons that the moral thing to do was to go to Belgium's aid.

Yet this defeat of the romantic internationalists was to prove only temporary. For the effects of Victorian evangelicalism on the British character were far more profound than the warlike mood of 4 August 1914; more lasting than the moment. The romantic internationalists now proceeded to turn their defeat into a victory; and the manner in which they did so demonstrates how completely their world outlook was determined by emotion. For within a matter of weeks – days even – they

[1] Irene Cooper Willis, *How We Went Into the War*, p. 57.

had psychologically taken over the war they had previously condemned, moralised it, turned it into a crusade, and given it a characteristically romantic set of characteristically impractical but inspiringly idealistic aims.

The keynote was struck in the Liberal *Daily Chronicle*, only three days after Britain entered the war, by a scientific rather than a moral Utopian, H. G. Wells. 'Every sword drawn against Germany is a sword drawn for peace. . . . The defeat of Germany may open the way to disarmament and peace throughout the earth. . . .'[1]

The Liberal *Daily News* on the following day voiced a long-lived and potent fancy:

> . . . this is not a war of peoples, but a war of despots and diplomatists. It is, we may hope, the last supreme struggle of the old dispensation and the new. . . . We have no quarrel with the German people . . . no, it is not the people with whom we are at war, it is the tyranny which has held them in its vice.[2]

The shameful war out of which Britain must at all costs keep had thus swiftly changed its nature to a war of Good against Evil. Spiritual exaltation was now manifested at a temperature not seen since the religious transports of the original evangelical movement of the early nineteenth century. As a writer in the *Daily News* put it in September 1914, 'Humanity is going to pay a great price, but not in vain . . . the reward is its liberty and a larger, nobler life.'[3]

So thus it was that the internationalists who had so passionately opposed war, instead of becoming a despised and unregarded minority, became the pacemakers of national opinion. For they called up all the latent moralism from the depths of the post-evangelical English soul, and gave it ideological expression. Even the Conservative press borrowed their ideas and their tone of righteousness; and imperialism and jingoism were swallowed up in a larger, nobler emotion.

This religious note of crusading idealism, this romantic vision of a new world, was peculiar to the British. On the whole, other European belligerents were content with patriotism, old-fashioned hatred of the enemy, and purely national war aims – survival and independence first, future security and territorial aggrandisement second.

[1] Ibid. p. 88.
[2] Ibid. p. 88.
[3] I. C. Willis, *How We Got On With the War* (Manchester, National Labour Press 1920), p. 4.

So successfully did the moralists and internationalists set the tone of British war-making and myth-making that a project for a League of Nations, originally put forward by Liberals and Socialists in 1914–15 (indeed it had figured in internationalist thought long before the war) had become an official allied war aim by 1918.[1] The project for a League of Nations combined the mid-Victorian liberal-evangelical belief in the moral law and in the essential harmony of human interests (both of course then subject to an unfortunate breakdown) with the pacifist vision of an international society without arms.

Younger imperialists too exchanged their own romantic dreams about the British Empire for an even more resplendent vision of a world order differing little from that of the internationalist moralisers. Philip Kerr (later Lord Lothian), for example, one of Lord Milner's 'Kindergarten' in South Africa, was looking as early as December 1914 for 'the voluntary federation of the free civilised nations which will eventually exorcise the spectre of competitive armaments and give lasting peace to mankind'.[2] In September 1915 Kerr was writing of the British Empire as 'the perfect example of the eventual world Commonwealth'.[3]

The project for a League of Nations was powerfully taken up by the American President, Woodrow Wilson, after the United States entered the war in 1917. The course of the war itself thus favoured the idealists, for the advent of President Wilson was decisive for their hopes, Wilson himself being a passionate moral idealist, in the American stream of descent from the common evangelical spring in the late eighteenth century. In all the agonised and sordid dealings of the Paris Peace Conference in 1919, the League of Nations was the one subject on which Wilson was inflexible. He believed that his success in getting the League of Nations 'Covenant' written into the peace treaties outweighed all their shortcomings.

Thus so far as the British and Americans were concerned, the whole atmosphere of 1918–19 was refulgent with liberal-evangelical aspirations of peace, democracy, justice and community between peoples. Even the intention of trying and hanging the Kaiser and squeezing Germany till the pips squeaked was dear to many moralising internationalists as well as jingoes, because it was clearly right to punish evil.[4]

[1] See Arthur Marwick, *The Deluge* (London, Bodley Head 1965), pp. 214–16; Willis, *How We Went Into the War*, pp. 127–8; Martin, pp. 97–9.
[2] J. R. M. Butler, *Lord Lothian (Philip Kerr) 1882–1940* (London, Macmillan 1960), p. 56.
[3] Ibid. p. 57.
[4] See R. B. McCallum, *Public Opinion and the Last Peace* (London, Oxford University Press 1944), ch. 1.

The moralising internationalists' success in setting this romantic mood of national expectation in 1918–19 marked astounding paradoxes. Before the war they had wished to confide British security to a faith in the moral or public 'law' of Europe and in neutrality. Both 'law' and neutrality had been shown in the event to be mere words. On the other hand, they, the moralising internationalists had opposed 'balance-of-power' diplomacy, alliances and the expansion of the British armed forces. Yet in the event British independence had been preserved by just those things.

Against all logic, therefore, moralising internationalism emerged into the post-war era more influential, more certain in its righteousness, than at any time. Its emotional antidotes for some forty years, imperialism and jingoism, did not survive the Great War. There was – for the moment – no longer a great enemy for jingoes to fear and hate, while the romantic element in imperialism had finally triumphed over the strategic, when the younger generation of imperialists succumbed to faith in the League of Nations. As Lord Milner's widow wrote in 1946, 'The younger men he had worked with, Curtis, Lothian, Brand, all became internationalists and supported the League of Nations. My husband greatly regretted this. He thought they dropped the substance for the shadow.'[1]

Internationalists on their part found immense encouragement and inspiration in the existence of the League of Nations at Geneva, a real, functioning authority – the heavenly vision of half a century wonderfully made flesh. The League of Nations Union, a government-blessed organisation for evangelising eternal peace and international friendship to the British public, offered a new outlet for the fervour and zeal of idealists. It became, like the Liberal and Labour parties, a pseudo-religion; and like them, alive with nonconformists.[2] Indeed its meetings were opened and concluded with hymns and prayers.

The two main streams of early Victorian idealism – the public school and nonconformism – had by now thoroughly intermingled in the middle and upper classes. In politics, liberalism – though not the Liberal Party – was triumphant. For on its protracted death-bed the Liberal Party bequeathed not only its attitudes and principles but also some of its distinguished figures to both the Labour Party and the Conservatives. As early as 1886 the bulk of the Liberal peers and the group of Liberal-Unionist MPs led by Joseph Chamberlain had joined the Conservatives because of Gladstone's home-rule policy for Ireland. Thus Austen Chamberlain, Conservative Foreign Secretary from 1924 to 1929, and Neville

[1] Vladimir Halpérin, *Lord Milner and the British Empire* (London, Odhams 1952), p. 201.
[2] See Martin, p. 168, and also Edwards, *passim*.

Chamberlain, Conservative Prime Minister from 1937 to 1940, were products of a liberal family tradition. Since they also combined public-school education with nonconformist background they were perfect exemplars of the interwoven strands in British life. After the Great War the Liberals shed more of their notable men, this time to the Labour Party; Lord Haldane, C. P. Trevelyan and Arthur Ponsonby. Finally, in the crisis of 1931, the Liberal Party bequeathed to the National Government (after 1935 essentially a Conservative Government) such leading statesmen as Lord Runciman (a nonconformist) and Sir John Simon, the Foreign Secretary from 1931 to 1935, and the son of a Congregationalist minister. In Chamberlain's Cabinet in 1938 four out of twenty-one members were 'National' Liberals – twice the number justified by their parliamentary strength. As a Cabinet Office civil servant who served Bonar Law, Baldwin, MacDonald and Neville Chamberlain put it '... we were all infected with Liberalism'.[1]

Liberal principles equally dominated public opinion at large. The rising Labour Party and the declining Liberal Party between them polled a majority of votes at every General Election from 1922 to 1929, although the anomalies of the electoral system denied them office in 1922 and from 1924 to 1929. A common Gladstonian faith in the moral nature of world affairs therefore prevailed in Parliament. It was hard to tell the Common's front benches from King Arthur's Round Table in Tennyson's *The Idylls of the King*, so knightly and Victorian was the tone. Even so sophisticated and world-jaded a statesman as Arthur Balfour could tell a meeting organised by the League of Nations Union that he was 'not prepared to discuss with any man what the future of international relations should be unless he is prepared either to accept the League of Nations in some form, or tell me what substitute he proposes for it'.[2] Indeed, as Gilbert Murray crowed in 1928; 'It is hard on many people, on naval and military circles, on Philistine newspapers, on smart society in London, just as it is hard on similar circles in Berlin, to have to give up their favourite dreams and admit themselves defeated, defeated even in the Tory Cabinet, by dull middle-class pacifism.'[3] For it was true, as Murray said on the same occasion, that 'all parties are pledged to the League . . . all Prime Ministers and ex-Prime Ministers support it . . . no candidate for Parliament dares to oppose it openly'.[4]

[1] Thomas Jones, *A Diary with Letters 1931–1950* (London, Geoffrey Cumberlege, Oxford University Press 1954), p. xxiii.

[2] Kenneth Young, *Arthur James Balfour* (London, George Bell 1963), p. 418.

[3] Gilbert Murray, *The Ordeal of this Generation: The War, the League and the Future*, being the Halley Stewart lectures for 1928 (London, Allen and Unwin 1929), p. 101.

[4] Ibid. p. 102.

In the 1920s, therefore, moralising internationalism preached a great evangelical mission to willing converts. Professor Murray expressed the common theme in a series of lectures in 1928.

> In sum it seems to me [he said], that the Covenant [of the League of Nations] is on the whole a wonderfully successful instrument, flexible, comprehensive, and exactly directed to the main evil which it was intended to cure. It does aim straight at the heart of international anarchy. . . . Its normal sanction is public opinion, its most effective weapon publicity . . . you can exert a very severe pressure on even the strongest power to mend its ways by simply putting a question to its representative at the Assembly, or at one of the permanent Commissions, and publishing its reply.[1]

Murray's lectures were delivered under the auspices of a trust founded in 1924 to help apply Christian principles to social and international problems. Yet in fact the moralising-internationalist heirs of evangelical religion were really propagating a heresy, for, in their trust in human goodwill and good nature, they had entirely left out the essential Christian doctrine of original sin. It was a crucial omission.

Nevertheless the romantic flight from the ugly truths of human behaviour into moral idealism was well-nigh universal among the British governing classes.

Thus a senior civil servant could write that what mattered to our children 'and our children's children' was that 'our nation, our people, should be great, strong, healthy, peaceful, noble and just'.[2] Another senior civil servant in a book on the nature of history could ignore Karl Marx, but acknowledge a debt to medieval lawyers for 'our belief in the theoretical supremacy of right, legal and moral'.[3] A distinguished member of the diplomatic service, Sir Victor Wellesley, referred with distaste to the methods of eighteenth-century diplomacy – 'mendacity, espionage and bribery' – while quoting Cobden with approval.[4] Sir Ralph Furse, in charge of recruitment to the Colonial Service in the 1920s, saw the public school as 'the spiritual child of chivalry', and colonial administration as 'really a crusading service'.[5] These views fairly express attitudes common to the British public servant at home and in the empire.

[1] Ibid. p. 131.

[2] Sir Stanley Leathes, *The People of England*, 3 Vols. (London, Heinemann 1920–3), Vol. II, p. 2; see also his *What Is Education?* (London, George Bell 1913).

[3] Sir Henry Lambert, *The Nature of History* (London, Humphrey Milford, Oxford University Press 1933), p. 5.

[4] Sir Victor Wellesley, *Diplomacy in Fetters* (London, Hutchinson 1944), pp. 15, 40.

[5] Robert Heussler, *Yesterday's Rulers* (New York, Syracuse University Press 1963), pp. 82–3.

The intelligentsia were hardly less romantically idealistic. They were, after all, products of the same moulding processes as civil servants or politicians: either of Victorian public schools and universities, like E. M. Forster, Bertrand Russell or Gilbert Murray; or of nonconformism, like Kingsley Martin; or of both, like Maynard Keynes. The intelligentsia were linked with the other governing spheres of British life not only by such shared backgrounds, but also by friendship, marriage, kinship and by common enjoyment of certain lawns and drawing rooms, such as those of the Astors at Cliveden.[1] Nor were the intellectuals of the 1920s a vanguard of a new outlook, as they themselves supposed, but the exhausted rearguard of Victorian romanticism. They sought refuge from an industrialised and ugly world. Some, like Virginia Woolf, found it in polishing up an exquisite sensibility. Others, like her husband Leonard Woolf and of course Gilbert Murray, found escape in designing an ideal society. This was especially the comfort of those marinated in classical humanism, like League-of-Nations men such as Lowes Dickinson, or pacifists such as Middleton Murry or Bertrand Russell.

It was a sheltered world, this of the intelligentsia of the 1920s, its inhabitants mostly shielded by private means from crude personal reminders of the outside struggle for survival. They circulated at leisure from country house to country cottage – the Bells at Charleston in Sussex, the Woolfs at Asham and Rodmell – back again to Bloomsbury or one of the ancient universities; convinced that they carried in their luggage the soul of civilisation. The memoirs of the epoch are fragrant with cultured weekends – witty chat on the lawn and brilliant profundity at the dining table. It was a circle of flimsy and precious people, of whom Lady Ottoline Morrell was perhaps the manliest. And so, while not all intellectuals were active pacifists or internationalists, they were generally more concerned with classical French and Greek culture – 'the good life' – than with 'Philistine' matters like industrial and strategic power.[2]

The change in the British since the eighteenth century went far deeper than conscious belief. Evangelical religion had modified the national character itself. The violence and quarrelsomeness that had once been noted as English characteristics had vanished, except in working-class districts; replaced by gentleness and readiness to see good in others. Kindness and gentleness indeed were now seen as prime virtues. The hardness, insolence and even arrogance with which Englishmen used to

[1] See Macmillan, ch. 7, p. 180.

[2] Cf. Martin, ch. 7; Michael Holroyd, *Lytton Strachey: A Critical Biography*, 2 Vols. (London, Heinemann 1967 and 1968); J. K. Johnstone, *The Bloomsbury Group* (London, Secker and Warburg 1954); Quentin Bell, *Bloomsbury* (London, Weidenfeld and Nicolson 1968).

deal with foreigners had given way to an unlimited willingness to see and understand the other man's point of view, even that of an opponent; indeed a willingness to assume, out of a profound though absurd sense of guilt, that his case was morally better founded than their own. Thanks also to Victorian religion – and perhaps to Dickens – the English now evinced a compassion for the underdog and a sympathy for failure, and a corresponding suspicion of ability and success, that were unparalleled in other countries. Thus it followed that the English now preferred the soft handshake of goodwill and reconciliation (in which they placed unbounded trust) to the firm grip of decision and action. Appeasement indeed had become a conditioned reflex of the British middle and upper classes. Few would now say with Palmerston that the practical and sagacious thing to do in life was to carry a point by boldness: knock an opponent down at once, and apologise afterwards if necessary to pacify him.[1]

In terms of British society at home, this transformation of national character was wholly beneficent. It was a great achievement of Victorian moralism to have softened British life and manners; to have created British civic virtue and self-discipline, and brought about standards of personal and public honesty unequalled in the world; to have rendered the law virtually self-enforcing; to have given the British their special sense of the dignity and liberty of the individual, and, as a corollary, their sense of the individual's personal responsiblity. Yet it was exactly because British life itself was now so orderly, gentle, docile, safe and law-abiding, so decent, so founded on mutual trust that the British were less fitted to survive as a nation than their ancestors, whose characters had been formed in a coarse, tough and brutal society. For the British made the fundamental mistake, catastrophic in all its consequences, of exporting their romantic idealism and their evangelical morality into international relations. They forgot that no other nation – except perhaps for America – had shared their own transforming religious experience; and that therefore no other nation now shared their world outlook. And so, in applying the qualities of gentleness, trustfulness, altruism and a strict regard for moral conduct to a sphere of human activity where cunning, cynicism, opportunism, trickery and force, all in the service of national self-interest, still held sway, the twentieth-century British stood disarmed and blinded by their own virtues.

In such a climate of opinion as now prevailed in Britain, a characteristic kind of person came to the forefront of the national life. Men of hard mind and powerful will were not in tune with the prevailing taste, and, as the inter-war period went on, their prospects in various walks of life suffered

[1] Jasper Ridley, *Lord Palmerston* (London, Constable 1970), p. 315.

accordingly. Even the newspaper cartoonists had replaced John Bull as the national symbol with meek suburban office-clerk figures like Strube's 'Little Man', and Poy's 'John Citizen'.

The home Civil Service, for example, encouraged the steady, safe, orthodox man of academic approach, rather than the man of, in the words of one senior civil servant, 'intense energy, great driving force and devouring zeal', a type of which he had known only four examples in his career in the service.[1] In the Colonial Service too 'duty and chivalry are of more account than ambition and self-seeking'.[2]

It was in that *demi-monde* where political ideas are formulated and preached where flourished the men who above all reflected in themselves the character of the age. There was Lowes Dickinson, for example, a prominent supporter of the ideals of the League of Nations, described by a recent critic as 'politically naïve . . . socially kind, and even, in a cautious docile manner, rather romantic'. His personal qualities were, in the words of the same critic, 'gentleness, generosity and pathos . . . mellowed sentimentalism'.[3] Lionel Curtis, once an imperialist, now an influential propagandist of world order and closer union of the English-speaking peoples, was nicknamed 'the Prophet'. 'It was not a bad appellation,' wrote Vincent Massey. 'He was moved always by a vision of what he thought could and should be done. No man could conceivably have been more sincere. . . .' The high-minded Curtis 'was obsessed with what he conceived to be his mission'.[4] Philip Kerr, Lord Lothian, was described by a friend and associate, Lord Brand, as being 'very absorbed . . . in trying to live the life of a Christian saint amid an otherwise very busy and active life'.[5] Yet another saint *manqué* who commanded admiration and attention in the period was the consumptive fanatic of pacifism, Clifford Allen; a man, as the *Manchester Guardian* put it, 'frail and Shelley-like'.[6]

And the very statesmen themselves who conducted England's foreign and imperial policies between the world wars were, if not saints *manqués*, then at least clergymen *manqués*. Ramsay MacDonald, for example, leader of the Labour Party, Prime Minister in 1924, and from 1929 to 1935

> really was persuaded that 'our true nationality is mankind' . . . he really did believe that men were naturally good, that they could be brought

[1] H. E. Dale, *The Higher Civil Service of Great Britain* (London, Oxford University Press 1941), p. 96–7.

[2] The Colonial Office's confidential *Appointments Handbook*, quoted in Heussler, p. 76.

[3] Holroyd, Vol. I, p. 173.

[4] Vincent Massey, *What's Past Is Prologue* (London, Macmillan 1963), p. 37.

[5] Butler, *Lord Lothian*, p. 95

[6] *Manchester Guardian*, 2 January 1932.

into line though they looked like horses at a starting gate for ever facing opposite ways and savaging each other. . . . In short and his own words [*sic*] he held that we were eternally moving in a great surge towards righteousness.[1]

And Arthur Henderson, Foreign Secretary in the second Labour Government of 1929–31, 'had the faith of a child in noble dreams, and an unshakeable confidence in the ultimate goodness of a world that might look evil, but yet had something in it of the divine'.[2]

Sir John Simon, National Liberal Foreign Secretary from 1931 to 1935, 'spent a successful life on earth without learning its ways, for he was unworldly though the reverse of other-worldly. . . .'[3] Lord Halifax, Foreign Secretary from 1937 to 1940, possessed a 'sweet and Christian nature'.[4] Even Neville Chamberlain, himself perhaps the toughest and most matter-of-fact British politician to hold high office between the world wars, could argue:

> Do not forget that we are all members of the human race. There must be something in common if only we can find it. An ancient historian once wrote of the Greeks that they made gentle the life of the world. I can imagine no nobler ambition for an English statesman than to win the same tribute for his own country.[5]

However, it was Stanley Baldwin, Prime Minister during half the period between 1922 and 1937 and also the real leader of the National Government in 1931–5 during MacDonald's senescence, who personified the spirit of the age to a greater degree than any other man. So well indeed did he focus the aspirations of his countrymen and reflect them back that the epoch seemed to take its character from him, as the Victorian age had from Queen Victoria.

Nor could Baldwin's background and upbringing have been a more perfect illustration of all the strands that went to the making of the England and the English of the inter-war period. He was born in 1867, thus passing his childhood and early manhood before the death of Queen Victoria. His father was deeply religious, firstly a Methodist and later a High Churchman. His mother, Louisa MacDonald, a woman of mixed Welsh and Highland Scots blood, also came of Methodist family. The MacDonalds, a highly talented family, were friends of the great figures of

[1] Vansittart, pp. 373–4.
[2] Mary Agnes Hamilton, *Arthur Henderson* (London, Heinemann 1938), p. 446.
[3] Vansittart, p. 427.
[4] Macmillan, p. 531.
[5] Keith Feiling, *A Life of Neville Chamberlain* (London, Macmillan 1970), p. 321.

high Victorian artistic and literary romanticism, among them William Morris. One of Louisa MacDonald's sisters married Sir Edward Burne-Jones, another Sir Edward Poynter, and a third Lockwood Kipling; their son, Rudyard, an outstanding romantic of the next generation, was thus Baldwin's first cousin. Baldwin's father, in contrast, was an ironmaster at Wilden, in Worcestershire; his firm typical of the Victorian family enterprise.[1]

In 1881, Baldwin went to Harrow: good at games, and a prizewinner in history and mathematics as well as classics. Unfortunately his headmaster, Dr Montagu Butler, made a grotesque but characteristically Victorian fuss over some piece of schoolboy smut written by Baldwin; a persecution which destroyed his interest in his school work. He left Harrow a year early, in 1885. It was Baldwin's ill-luck that a year after he went up to Trinity, Cambridge, where he got a Third in history, the ineffable Butler followed him as Master.

Thus far Baldwin had thought either of becoming an artist like his famous uncles, or, while at Trinity, of going into the Church. However, he became a director of the family firm after studying metallurgy at Owens College, Birmingham.

Baldwin met his future wife, Lucy Ridsdale, at the Burne-Jones's house at Rottingdean. He wrote to his parents that 'the first things that attracted me to Cissy were her absolute innocence and unworldliness . . .'[2] Together they enjoyed the easy, spacious life of a young married couple of the governing class, holidaying at Rottingdean or with the Kiplings at Batemans, touring Europe in the last days of the happy era when an Englishman needed no passport but gold sovereigns: the Italian lakes, the cathedrals of France, the great art collections; Vienna, Dresden and Berlin. It was not a memory of Europe which was to serve him well as a guide to the European politics of the 1920s and 1930s. In 1902 Baldwin and his wife moved to Astley Hall, near Birmingham, a small estate where Baldwin was to play, sincerely enough, his favourite role of the countryman; for a Wordsworthian love of the English countryside was one expression of his strongly romantic nature.

As a man and as a prime minister, Baldwin was patient, slow-moving, whimsical, blessed of a fine sense of humour; ruminative; shrewd and wise within his limits. He never drove his colleagues; a kindly man, he was, as he himself admitted, a bad butcher: '. . . It is not in my nature. An F. E.

[1] Keith Middlemass and John Barnes, *Baldwin: A Biography* (London, Weidenfeld and Nicolson 1969), pp. 9, 23–4.
[2] Quoted in Middlemass and Barnes, p. 28.

[Smith: Lord Birkenhead] or a Winston Churchill would not hesitate; to them public service comes before sentiment . . . I could not do that. To me it is all wrong.'[1] His kindliness and gentleness also made it impossible for him ruthlessly to attack his political opponents. On one occasion when Lloyd George mounted a tremendous assault on him in the Commons, Baldwin refused to fight back:

> I cannot rival Lloyd George at that sort of speech, full of clever thrusts, innuendoes, malicious half-truths. To Lloyd George and Winston it is all part of a game; as for me, I cannot make speeches which are sheer and mere dialectic. . . . If I had made the sort of speech about Lloyd George that I could have done, it would be a cruel attack on an old man and it would have done no good.[2]

Baldwin, believing as he did that considerateness was 'the central English virtue',[3] hated strife, shrank from conflict, constantly sought to heal division and bitterness, whether in his own cabinets, the country or the world. In this too he personified the deepest feelings of his countrymen. His speeches seldom manifested combative argument; instead they evoked moods; he was a Delius or a Debussy among political speakers. And the favourite mood was one of a sunset calm and nostalgia, in which the British nation, like an old couple in retirement enjoying the peaceful ending of the day, contemplated some sweep of English landscape and hearkened to the distant church bells. Nothing could have been more congenial to the contemporary British temperament than this tranquillity, in which desperate problems or dangers could be put out of mind, and energetic, possibly painful, action shirked or put off; nothing could have been more welcome to his hearers than this evocation of all things kindly, gentle and decent.

And Baldwin, stocky of figure, rubicund and jowly of face between his bowler hat and his wing collars, with a slightly bulbous nose which was such a gift to cartoonists, *looked* the epitome of the simple, old-fashioned virtues. It was little wonder that his countrymen saw in him all that they thought an Englishman and an English statesman ought to be. As one of his own colleagues noted in 1923 after Baldwin's first four months as Prime Minister:

> The new PM caught the public imagination . . . almost as soon as he took office. His placidity, his common sense, his moderation, his modesty and his obvious sincerity caused people to say: 'This is the

[1] Ibid. p. 807. [2] Ibid. p. 940. [3] Ibid. p. 504.

man, a typical Englishman, for whom we have been looking for so long. We are sick of Welshmen and lawyers, the best brains and supermen. We want the old type of English statesman, who is fair-minded, judicious and responsible, rather than the man who is so clever that he thinks ahead of everyone else . . .'[1]

Two years later the Lobby correspondent of *The Times* commented on the extent to which Baldwin had already begun to place his mark on the age:

> Mr Baldwin is doing remarkable work. He is restoring the whole tone and quality of British politics. He has brought into public life a pleasant savour, freshness and health. It is the fragrance of the fields, the flavour of the apple and the hazel nut, all the unpretentious, simple, wholesome, homely but essential qualities. . . . Like Lincoln, he has that rarest and finest quality of a leader, the power of liberating and calling in aid the deeper, moral motives in the hearts of men. . . .[2]

Here indeed was the fundamental clue both to Baldwin's character and career and to the esteem in which his fellow countrymen held him. Baldwin, Victorian that he was, saw politics – even international politics – as he saw the whole of human life, in terms of religion; of, in his own words, 'doing secular acts from a spiritual motive'.[3] He believed that it 'is precisely these values of right and wrong, of good and evil, of honesty and courage, which matter supremely for religion and national life . . . moral values, eternal in their quality, transient in their form and application, are the foundation of a country's greatness. . . .'[4]

Baldwin and his wife, now low church in their faith, were deeply pious, as Baron Palmstierna, the Swedish Ambassador, learned at Lord Curzon's funeral in 1925:

> 'You are a believer, Mrs Baldwin,' I whispered to her. 'I am indeed,' she replied, 'and I must tell you that every morning when we rise we kneel together before God and commend our day to Him, praying that some good work may be done in it by us. It is not for ourselves that we are working, but for the country and for God's sake. How else could we live?' She looked at me sincerely and I realised the simple earnestness of their conception of life.[5]

Such were the rulers and such was the nation to which befell after the Great War the task of preserving the power of England.

[1] Quoted in Middlemass and Barnes, p. 211. [2] Ibid. p. 506.
[3] Ibid. p. 609. [4] Ibid. p. 611. [5] Ibid. p. 168.

# III

# III · THE GREATEST POWER IN THE WORLD

In 1921 General Smuts, the Prime Minister of the Union of South Africa, told his fellow prime ministers of the British Empire that the empire 'emerged from the War quite the greatest power in the world, and it is only unwisdom or unsound policy that could rob her of that great position'.[1]

If a statesman as well-informed as Smuts could pitch his estimate of British power so high (albeit in the fervent atmosphere of imperial conference speech-making), it was not surprising that popular myth and educated opinion of almost every colour alike in Britain shared his sentiments. The message of the Great War and of the British contribution to the victory seemed clear beyond doubt – the British Empire was indeed a mighty union; mighty in military and industrial power, mighty in resources of raw materials, mighty in population, and mighty in unity itself. In 1919 the Victory Parade had impressed imperial military power on the British man-in-the-street and his family. The crowds had watched for hours while with measured stamp and ring of boots the parade had passed under the flags and the bunting: blue-jackets from the greatest navy in the world; contingents from the largest British army ever raised; slouch-hatted Australians and New Zealanders; Canadians and Newfoundlanders; Indians dark under their turbans; contingents to represent all the parts of the empire that had rallied to Britain's side in her time of peril. There were the guns that had deluged the enemy with millions of shells produced by Britain's colossal munitions industry; and, with a grinding rumble of tracks, the tanks too passed by, those wonderful new weapons of war invented by British genius and developed by British engineering resources.

And behind the armed power of the empire lay its economic and industrial resources. In 1923 the British Empire Exhibition and all its attendant publicity conveyed to the British citizen as heart-warming a picture as the Victory Parade. In the Exhibition's numerous and fanciful pavilions the empire which the British had known only from schoolroom propaganda, adventure stories and newspapers came to life. There was

[1] Cmd. 1474.

the Great Outdoors and the sun-tanned colonial cousins who inhabited it – Australians and the outback; South Africans and the veldt; Canadians and the Wild West or the lumber camps. There was Africa, so recently Dark or Darkest. There were the far-away South Sea Islands. Most imperially inspiring of all, however, was the Gorgeous, not to say Mysterious, East – Malaya, Borneo and the vast Indian Empire; rajahs and temples and elephants. All this diversity of race, religion and climate belonged to them, the British; justly governed by British proconsuls, enlightened from heathendom by British missionaries, and developed by the genius of British engineers.

Then there were the British exhibits at Wembley, proof that Britain was the greatest industrial power in the world, marvels of engineering prowess, like an express steam locomotive.

And all of it lay under the rule of George V, the King-Emperor.

Thus, it seemed to the uncritical and patriotic citizen, was British power – the Workshop of the World lying at the centre of the Empire on Which the Sun Never Set, and both protected by British Command of the Sea. And the facts and figures of the British Empire and of its effort in the Great War, when presented in a broad, bludgeoning way, seemed fully to bear out the popular myth.

The British Empire possessed the largest population of any state in the world, with 490,000,000 people (in 1931) as against 161,000,000 (estimated) for the Soviet Union and 137,000,000 for the United States. The empire's 'white' population, at 71,500,000, was greater than Germany's, one and three-quarters the size of France's, and by no means incomparable with the 'white' population of the United States, which in 1931 stood at 109,000,000.[1]

The empire produced 23 per cent of the world's wheat and 50 per cent of the rice; it owned 40 per cent of the world's cattle and 36 per cent of the sheep, and it produced 45 per cent of the wool. The empire was also the source of nearly 60 per cent of the world's rubber, over 50 per cent of the world's chrome, 46 per cent of the tin and 70 per cent of the gold.[2] In 1914 the British Empire owned 45 per cent of the world's shipping.[3] In 1913 the United Kingdom, which was the empire's industrial base, held 17 per cent of the world's trade.[4]

In the Great War the empire had raised armed forces to the astounding

[1] See D. H. Cole, *Imperial Military Geography* (London, Sifton Praed 1935), pp 42–6.
[2] Ibid. pp. 51–8.
[3] Ibid. p. 69.
[4] See S. B. Clough and C. W. Cole, *Economic History of Europe* (Boston, D. C. Heath 1952), p. 605.

total of 8,586,000 men.[1] Of these the British Isles had found 5,704,416 men; India 1,440,437; Canada 628,964; Australia 412,953; South Africa 136,070; New Zealand 128,525; and other colonies 134,202. In 1918 the Royal Air Force, with 22,000 aircraft, was the largest in the world; and the Royal Navy, with 61 battleships and 9 battlecruisers to the United States' 39 battleships, was by far the largest navy.[2] And in 1918 British industry was not only supplying without stint all the forces of the empire with weapons, ammunition and equipment, but also helping to supply the armed forces of Britain's allies, France, Italy and the United States.

The unity of the empire – common purposes and common organisation – seemed no more in doubt than its strength. Expeditionary forces from India and the 'white colonies' (or dominions) and from the United Kingdom had fought meshed together into single armies under single, and British, commands. Australian and New Zealand ships had fought as integral parts of the Royal Navy. And since 1917 high political representatives of the 'white' dominions and India (including at times prime ministers like J. M. Hughes of Australia and Sir Robert Borden of Canada) had joined with the British Government in formulating the empire's policy and grand strategy. An 'Imperial War Cabinet' came into being in London; a cabinet of governments. This collective responsibility was carried through into peacetime, when the Imperial War Cabinet took a fresh name and found another purpose in the British Empire Delegation to the Paris Peace Conference in 1918–19.

Moreover, in its power relative to the rest of the world the British Empire seemed to emerge from the Great War as strong as in the happy days of the mid-Victorian era. The empire's boundaries were set wider yet – Tanganyika, Palestine and Iraq were now under the Union flag, if in the latter two cases only in the guise of League of Nations mandates. Germany lay smashed and defeated, her navy at the bottom of Scapa Flow. Of the other great powers of 1919, France, Italy and Japan were allies of Britain, and the United States was a friend, if a tepid one.

The experiences of the Great War seemed therefore to demonstrate that British strength consisted in both Britain herself and the empire, each complementary to the other. It seemed to demonstrate also that the British Empire was as strong as any state in the world.

Yet in fact the Great War returned a far more ambiguous and gloomy verdict on the nature and the extent of British power than that suggested

[1] *Statistics of the Military Effort of the British Empire During the Great War* (London, HMSO 1922), p. 756.
[2] S. W. Roskill, *Naval Policy Between the Wars* (London, Collins 1968), Vol. I, p. 71.

by the contemplation of victory and a few blanket imperial facts and figures.

It is a commonplace that the British Empire in 1914 was no well-designed product of a grand strategy of expansion; but the random débris of successive historical episodes. The eighteenth-century maritime wars for sugar islands bequeathed the now poverty-stricken and worthless Caribbean and Central and South African possessions. The elder Pitt's struggle with the French for North America, and the American War of Independence, left Canada as a residue. A Jacobean hunt for spices eventually resulted in the Indian Empire, after eighteenth-century wars with France and hapless expansion in the nineteenth century into the vacuum created by the collapse of Moghul power. Nineteenth-century Far-Eastern trade and the demands of Indian security bequeathed Burma, Malaya, Borneo and Hong Kong. The need to protect the Atlantic route to India against Napoleon resulted, eventually, in the Union of South Africa, and British expansion into central Africa (the Rhodesias) and East Africa. The further need to protect the Suez route to India (before as well as after the Suez Canal was opened in 1869) landed Britain with Malta, Cyprus, Aden and British Somaliland, and protectorates over Egypt, the Sudan, the Persian Gulf states, and southern Persia. Long-forgotten strategic needs of the age of sail and modern requirements for coaling stations added islands in almost every sea and ocean. An idealistic early-Victorian programme to establish British communities in the Antipodes, together with a distinctly non-idealistic eighteenth-century programme of convict settlements, bequeathed the new English-speaking nations of Australia and New Zealand. And finally there was the one-third of the territory and a quarter of the population of the empire that had been acquired since 1870, mostly in the scramble for Africa.

It was a polyglot empire; a rummage-bag of an empire, united by neither common purpose in its creation, nor by language, race, religion, nor by strategic and economic design. In 1914–18 the grand audit of war showed (to those who cared to examine the evidence) what the various parts of it were worth to Britain – if worth anything; if, indeed, not a debit.

Broadly the empire fell into two distinct parts. There was the 'white' empire composed of Britain herself and the colonies (dominions) of Canada, Australia, South Africa and New Zealand – all self-governing, socially advanced Western countries. On the other hand there was the 'coloured' empire – Africa, India, the West Indies, the Far East – governed automatically from London, and mostly inhabited by people of the utmost primitiveness and poverty. And of the empire's impressive grand total (in 1914) of 425,400,000 inhabitants, no fewer than 366,000,000 were of such backward peoples.

This 'coloured' empire was itself broadly divided between the empire of India (then including Burma), which accounted for 316,000,000 people out of the 366,000,000; and the colonial empire. How valuable an asset then, in the first place, was the colonial empire?

The colonial empire was in itself a rummage-bag, scattered from Central America to the Chinese mainland, and from the Mediterranean to the South Seas, and inhabited by Greeks, Arabs, Turks, Amerindians, Negroes, Polynesians, Malayans and Chinese, and others. As the Secretary of State for the Colonies, L. S. Amery, told the first Colonial Office Conference in 1927:

> . . . there is little of what I might call structural or administrative unity. Strictly speaking, there is, of course, no Colonial Empire and no such thing as the Colonial Service. I deal in this office with thirty-six different Governments, each entirely separate from the rest. . . . The whole system with its haphazard complexity, and lack of co-ordination on any structural basis, would, I fancy, not be tolerated for one moment by our more logical neighbours across the Channel.[1]

Except for copper and tungsten in the Rhodesias, oil in Trinidad, and tin in Malaya, the colonial empire's potential mineral riches lay mostly undiscovered for want of large-scale exploratory survey-work.[2] Even in 1925–9 the colonial empire supplied Britain with only 8 per cent of her raw materials.[3] Its under-populated regions, inhabited for the most part by peoples only just emerging from the Stone Age, and even by some tribes hardly yet in it, provided in 1901 only 4 per cent of Britain's export market.[4] Nevertheless it took less than half its imports from Britain, and sent her only 42 per cent of its exports.[5]

Malaya (Straits Settlements and Federated Malay States) was the only wealthy portion of the colonial empire and the only one whose resources and potentialities had been energetically exploited. It produced 53 per cent of the world's rubber and 55·6 per cent of the world's tin.[6] Yet Britain as

[1] Cmd. 2884, p. 5.
[2] Study Group of Members of the Royal Institute of International Affairs (RIIA), *The Colonial Problem* (London, Oxford University Press 1937), pp. 317, 324; Cd. 8462 especially pp. 70, 75 and 82.
[3] RIIA, *Colonial Problem*, p. 292.
[4] J. A. Hobson, *Imperialism: A Study* (London, Allen and Unwin 1902), p. 35.
[5] 1913 figures: Hobson, Appendix VII, p. 371.
[6] 1920 and 1904 figures: Sir Richard O. Winstedt, *Malaya and Its History* (London, Hutchinson's University Library 1948), pp. 116, 118.

late as 1938 drew a fifth of her supplies of rubber from outside her empire, while in the same year Malaya sent only 10 per cent of her exports of tin to Britain.[1] And, although there was oil in Trinidad, Britain took only 36 per cent of Trinidad's exports.[2]

Thus while the colonial empire added mightily to the pink on the map of the world, it added little in the way of economic strength to Britain, although the British people perhaps found Gold Coast cocoa comforting at bedtime.

In the Great War the colonial empire raised forces of only 134,000 men out of a population of some 50,000,000 – 0·2 per cent of the population, as against 12·4 per cent in the United Kingdom and 11·6 per cent in New Zealand.[3] This scanty contribution was in any case for local defence, and added nothing to the imperial field army in Europe. Malaya paid for the battleship *Malaya*. And that was all, economically and strategically, in return for the immense British involvement in the maintenance of internal law and order, and in defence of colonial territories by sea and land in Central and South America, the Caribbean, Africa, the Mediterranean and the Middle East, South-East Asia, China and the South Seas.

However it was India that seemed to the British governing classes the real prize of the 'coloured' empire: indeed the very foundation of British world power. '. . . as long as we rule India', wrote Lord Curzon, Viceroy of India from 1899 to 1905, 'we are the greatest power in the world. If we lose it, we shall drop straight away to a third-rate power.'[4] And indeed India had exercised a colossal influence, perhaps the greatest single influence, on British policy since the beginning of the nineteenth century. It had changed England from a maritime power into a great continental power, with a frontier of thousands of miles to defend, of which 450 miles was a military frontier in a state of perpetual readiness. In the nineteenth century possession of India had made England, an island off the north-western coast of Europe, the greatest power in the East – greater than the moribund Chinese Empire, and only challenged, in the 1900s, by the rise of Japan. Because of India, British foreign policy had to concern itself with Tibet, Siam, Afghanistan and Persia as well as the Low Countries. It was because of India that England and Russia became direct antagonists in the late nineteenth century, as Russian expansion and colonisation reached south-east towards Afghanistan and Kashmir.

Yet England, unlike Germany for example, existed as a great land power

[1] RIIA, *Colonial Problem*, p. 317. [2] 1938 figure. [3] Cole, p. 43.
[4] Nicholas Mansergh, *The Commonwealth Experience* (London, Weidenfeld and Nicolson 1969), p. 256.

half the world away from the homeland. Therefore a vast fabric of secondary involvements had grown up to secure the routes to India. The British Empire in southern, central and eastern Africa had evolved out of the original seizure of Cape Colony from the Dutch during the Napoleonic Wars in order to safeguard the Atlantic passage and the continuing need to preserve this British control of the Cape.

The need to safeguard the short route to India via Suez had made England by 1914 into a major Mediterranean and Middle-Eastern as well as an Asiatic power; and, after the destruction of the Turkish Empire in the Great War, into the greatest Middle-Eastern power of all. Here were yet more fields for imperial service; governments to be manned or advised; armies and police forces to be reorganised and officered; public finances to be sorted out; justice to be administered; dams and bridges and roads and railways to be built. Like India itself, the Middle-Eastern Empire seemed to offer imposing evidence of British greatness. Yet – like India – it all meant immense political and strategic commitments. British policy had to concern itself in events in the Balkans, Turkey, the Levant and throughout Arabia, although until the coming of the age of petroleum and the discovery of oil in the Persian Gulf there was no direct British interest in the region whatsoever that would have justified so deep and vast an entanglement. British sea-borne trade via Suez, for example, accounted for only between 9 per cent and 10 per cent of British imports.[1]

The English looked upon India as the keystone of the imperial arch, but did the arch only exist to support the keystone? What in terms of economic and strategic advantage did England get in return for this immense imperial structure spread-eagled from the Mediterranean to the Bay of Bengal? Wherein lay that value of India which alone could justify – and more than justify, if India were to be profitable – the burdens and risks that England had assumed in the Middle East and Asia?

In the first place, India added nothing to the industrial capacity of the empire. Out of every hundred Indians, seventy-one worked on the land and only twelve in any kind of industry.[2] In British (as distinct from princely) India, only 6 per cent of the population were capable of writing and reading a letter in their own script.[3] And only sixteen in every thousand males and two in every thousand females were literate in English, the language of industry, administration and commerce.[4]

[1] 1937 figures: Study Group of the RIIA, *Political and Strategic Interests of the United Kingdom* (London, Oxford University Press 1939), p. 129.

[2] Census of 1921, quoted in Cmd. 3568, p. 12.

[3] Cd. 9109, p. 111.

[4] Cmd. 3568, p. 12.

Except for chromium, manganese and jute, India was also devoid of discovered or exploited sources of strategic raw materials.[1]

As a market for British products, India in 1913 was nearly equalled in value by France and Germany together (£70,273,221 as against £69,610,451),[2] and outweighed by the 'white' dominions.[3] As a source of imports into Britain, India was worth less than half the 'white' dominions.[4] As a field for British investment, India rated as not much more important than Argentina,[5] and half as important as the United States.[6]

Thus, when India's importance to England as a source of economic advantage or strategic raw materials is compared to other countries both inside and outside the empire, there was nothing remotely to justify the unique and immense diplomatic and strategic responsibilities that India entailed. Industrially indeed, India was totally dependent on British products, a circumstance the dangers of which were sharply pointed out by the U-boat during the War. The 1918 *Report on Indian Constitutional Reforms* therefore strikes a rueful note over her economic contribution to British victory:

> . . . the war has thrown a strong light on the military importance of economic development. . . . Nowadays the products of an industrially developed community coincide so nearly in kind though not in quantity with the catalogue of munitions of war that the development of India's national resources becomes a matter of almost military necessity.[7]

For the British, having given themselves such vast trouble to conquer and to hold India, had neglected adequately to exploit it; and therefore imperial interests demanded, wrote the authors of the Report, that Indian resources 'should henceforth be better utilised. We cannot measure the accession of strength which an industrialised India will bring to the power of the Empire . . .'[8]

The public schools and Oxford and Cambridge had hardly accustomed the British governing classes to think of empire in terms of raw materials and industrial capacity; rather, so far as it had induced them to think of strategy at all, in old-fashioned terms of ships and soldiers. India had no ships. The defence of India's sea-borne trade and of her 7,000 miles of coastline fell on the Royal Navy. But soldiers had loomed large in the British myth of India – from Clive and his British troops and sepoys at

[1] Cole, pp. 50–8.
[2] Cmd. 2009, p. 63.
[3] Hobson, Appendix VIII, p. 372.
[4] Ibid. Appendix VIII, p. 373.
[5] 1914 figures: India and Ceylon £378,776,000; Argentina £319,565,000. W. K. Hancock, *Survey of British Commonwealth Affairs* (London, Oxford University Press 1942), Vol. II, Pt. I, p. 27, n. 1.
[6] British investment in 1914 in the USA £754,617,000, loc. cit.
[7] Cmd. 9109, p. 268.
[8] Ibid. p. 267.

Plassey in 1757, and the young Wellesley's triumph at Assaye to those stirring and colourful battles of the Victorian age that had completed the conquest of India, all advancing lines of red-coats and charging hussars and dragoons. The Indian army seemed a splendid asset: hearts warmed at the sight of those dusky lancers, gaudy as jungle birds, who trotted beside the viceregal carriage, and at the thought of British and Indian brothers-in-arms with mule and mountain-gun carrying peace up the valleys of the North-West Frontier. The squeal of the bugle, the crunch of ironshod ammunition boots on the dusty road, red-coats and khaki, turban and topee, tents under a sky of brass – it was in these terms, touching the heart rather than the critical intelligence, that the British tended to see the power which they believed India gave them.

In the Great War India raised 1,440,437 soldiers, all volunteers.[1] It was apparently a magnificent achievement. Lloyd George expressed the gratitude of his countrymen when he said in 1921: 'No Britisher can ever forget the gallantry and promptitude with which India sprang forward to the King Emperor's service when war was declared.... The causes of the War were unknown to India; its theatre in Europe remote. Yet India stood by her allegiance heart and soul, from the first call to arms.'[2] However, despite India's unquestioned loyalty and enthusiasm, her military contribution to British power is, upon examination, not so wonderful as the British supposed.

The total number of men raised in India was no more than 0·3 per cent of her population, compared to 12·4 per cent in the British Isles, 11·6 per cent in New Zealand and about 8 per cent in Canada and Australia.[3] Of the Indian total, only 877,068 were combatants, while India sent overseas no more than 621,224 officers and men;[4] Canada, on the other hand, from a population of only 7,600,000 sent abroad 422,405 men.[5] In fact, about half of the Indian troops were recruited in the last year of the war and few of them ever reached a theatre of war.[6]

Of the troops India did send overseas, only 89,335 went to swell British strength on the decisive front in France and in the battles with England's principal enemy, Germany. Against these 89,335 troops sent to France must, however, be set the 15,000 British troops retained in India to secure internal order. The remainder of India's expeditionary forces were employed in the Middle East, a region whose importance to England derived

1 *Statistics of the Military Effort of the British Empire*, p. 756.
2 Cmd. 1474, p. 13.
3 Cole, p. 43.
4 *Statistics of the Military Effort of the British Empire*, p. 777.
5 Ibid. p. 758.
6 Sir Michael O'Dwyer, *India As I Knew It 1885–1925* (London, Constable 1925), p. 226.

almost wholly from her possession of India. And the total deaths suffered by India, with some 316 million of population, were only slightly higher than those of Australia, whose population was no more than 4,700,000. Thus India's military contribution to the British struggle with Germany in the Great War was in fact both relatively and absolutely negligible.

When therefore a final balance is struck of the value of India to Britain in the Great War, value both economically and militarily, there is only the item of a net gain of 74,000 soldiers to set against the colossal, expensive and vulnerable British involvement in territories stretching from Malta to Rangoon, from the Himalayas to East Africa. The whole British position in the Middle East and Southern Asia was in fact a classic, and gigantic, example of strategic over-extension. Far from being a source of strength to England, India served only immensely to weaken and distract her.

The 'coloured' portion of the British Empire and the 'white' were remarkably ill-assorted. Whereas in the 'coloured' empire there were technically backward races whose political and social traditions were autocratic and tribal – or caste – bound, in the 'white' empire there were free British institutions and advanced Western societies. While the 'coloured' empire was ruled by a hierarchy of upper-class British governors, the 'white' empire was peculiarly egalitarian, its British stock being mostly working class or lower-middle class. As a consequence, while it was the British governing classes who were intimately connected with the 'coloured' empire, it was the lower classes rather who had the friends and relatives overseas in the 'white' empire.

There were 25,000,000 inhabitants in the 'white' empire – more than half the United Kingdom's total of 46,000,000.[1] All but the 900,000 Boers of South Africa and the 3,000,000 French Canadians of Quebec shared common ancestry and history with the British, common political ideals, common forms of government and law. In the Great War they raised forces of 1,304,512 men; sent overseas to fight in Britain's struggle with Germany 857,450 of them; and lost 141,005 in killed.[2] This was an immense accession to British military strength.

Yet with the 'white' empire too, the balance was not as favourable to British power as the British supposed. The population, impressive in numbers when taken as a whole, was fragmented into small nations separated by thousands of miles of sea, and each dwelling in vast underdeveloped territories: Canada stretching across the whole width of North

[1] 1914 figure: Cole, p. 43.

[2] *Statistics of the Military Effort of the British Empire*, Table 1(a), p. 237; and pp. 756, 758, 762, 771, 772.

America with only 7,600,000 people; South Africa on the other side of the Atlantic in another continent, with no more than 1,200,000; Australia, a continent in itself 12,000 miles from Britain in the Pacific Ocean, with a population of 4,700,000 clustered mostly in a few cities along its coast; New Zealand, further still from the Motherland in the South Pacific, with only 1,100,000 inhabitants. Only seapower linked this scattered empire together, and it was Britain which overwhelmingly contributed the ships and the men, and paid for them. This disproportion had provided a recurrent topic of argument at pre-war colonial or imperial conferences. Nevertheless in 1914 South Africa and Canada had no ships, although Canada had paid for two cruisers in the British fleet, while the Royal Australian Navy, founded in 1911, amounted to only the battle-cruiser *Australia*, four light cruisers and three destroyers. New Zealand had paid for the British battle-cruiser *New Zealand*, and herself operated three old light cruisers.[1]

The dominion expeditionary forces that were to figure so largely and so splendidly in the folk-memories of the Great War were themselves wartime improvisations. In peacetime the role of dominion armies was local defence of their own territories, and they made no contribution to any kind of central imperial reserve, which, except for a small portion of the British regular army, did not exist. In any case the territories of the dominions were so vast in proportion to population that even the hugely expanded dominion forces of wartime would not have been enough to fend off serious attack at home. Thus the truth about the military and naval strength of the dominions was as bluntly told to the 1921 Imperial Conference by W. M. Hughes, the Australian Prime Minister: 'The Dominions could not exist if it were not for the British Navy.'[2]

This truth was obscured by the particular shape of the Great War. It was a European war; England, and not the dominions, lay under threat. The dominions were therefore free to send their forces overseas to England's succour. This fortunate situation might never recur. For example, the Japanese fleet which, under the alliance of 1902, had escorted Anzac troops to the Mediterranean might in another war threaten Australia and New Zealand with invasion. And if, through some such shift in the delicate balance of world strategy, the lucky pattern cf the Great War was not repeated, the dominions would then represent not a limited source of strength, but an immense source of weakness.

To England therefore, the 'white' dominions as well as the 'coloured'

[1] Sir Julian Corbett, *History of the Great War: Naval Operations* (London, Longmans Green 1920), Vol. I, pp. 14, 140. [2] Cmd. 1474, p. 22.

empire constituted on balance a strategic debit to Britain. In the words of another Australian Prime Minister, S. M. Bruce, at the 1923 Imperial Conference: 'The Empire is primarily the responsibility of Britain; and, while each of the Dominions is very concerned about its own particular safety, the major responsibility for the Empire is Britain's . . . it is proper that Britain has a greater share.'[1]

And the economic importance to England of the 'white' empire, like that of the 'coloured' empire, did not justify the strategic obligations. In terms of markets, raw materials and investment, countries under the Union flag meant no more to England than those under foreign, or even potentially enemy, flags. In 1913 British exports to Australia were worth less than her exports to Germany: her exports to Canada less than to France.[2] British investment in the United States was £200 million greater than in Canada. In Argentina alone Britain had sunk only £12 million less capital than in Australia and New Zealand together. And although Canada and to a lesser extent South Africa and Australia were rich in strategic raw materials – bauxite for aluminium, non-ferrous metals – Britain had almost totally failed to exploit them. For example, while between 78 per cent and 80 per cent of the world's nickel ore was being mined in Canada, all of it was refined in the United States.[3]

It was the Great War indeed that brought home to the British Government with surprise and dismay how far the raw materials with which the whole empire – 'white' and 'coloured' – was endowed had either been neglected or let fall into foreign hands. Thus, in the case of non-ferrous metals and other commodities, 'though the source of the material lay within the British Empire, some of the processes essential for their utilisation had before the war been carried out wholly or mainly in Germany. . . .'[4] Even more improvident was British dependence on foreign sources and companies for petroleum products, although the rise of the motor-vehicle, the aircraft and the oil-fired ship made these essential to national life in peacetime and survival in war. In 1918 the British Empire supplied only 2 per cent of the world's production. England was dependent on the United States for 80 per cent of her supplies.[5] *The History of the Ministry of Munitions* noted that

> even the development of her own limited resources in Egypt, Sarawak and Trinidad, were dependent, to some extent on foreign, or quasi-

[1] CAB 32/9, E-8, p. 10.
[2] £34,491,269 to £40,677,379; £23,794,955 to £28,933,072. Cmd. 2009, p. 63.
[3] Sir Robert Borden, *His Memoirs* (Toronto, Macmillan 1938), Vol. II, p. 628.
[4] *History of Ministry of Munitions* (London, HMSO 1922), Vol. VII, Pt. I, p. 3.
[5] CAB 32/1/2, p. 149.

> foreign concerns. Some supplies were also available from oilfields in Burmah, but the distance of these oilfields from Britain made import difficult, and this was also true in the case of Persian oilfields, over which Britain possessed influence. . . .
>
> [And] at the outbreak of war the petroleum trade in the United Kingdom was practically monopolised by two firms under foreign control – the [*sic*] Shell and Standard.[1]

Germany on the other hand 'through the Deutsche Bank, had obtained the monopoly of practically all the oil in Hungary, and controlled large monopolies in Roumania'.[2]

The need in the future to repair this failure and systematically to develop and exploit the resources of the empire provided the running theme of the *Final Report of the Dominions Royal Commission* of 1917[3] and of the Imperial War Conference of 1917[4] and 1918.[5] And every hope and recommendation for the future was an indictment of British improvidence in the past: the lack of organisation, worse, the lack of any desire and will, to make the empire much more than a pageant apt for a patriotic thrill. 'It is impossible to overstate the importance', the Dominions Royal Commission Final Report asserted, 'of securing to all parts of Your Majesty's Empire adequate facilities for scientific research in connection with the development of their natural resources. . . .'[6] The Report further asserted, and repeated the assertion in its final conclusions: 'It is vital that the Empire should, as far as possible, be placed in a position which would enable it to resist any pressure which a foreign Power or group of Powers could exercise in time of peace or war in virtue of a control of raw materials and commodities essential to its well-being.'[7]

There was yet another aspect of the empire's weakness as revealed by the war which troubled the imperial statesmen – the total dependence of the 'white' and 'coloured' empires alike on England for all kinds of war supplies.[8] For, despite some industrialisation in Canada, England was the empire's sole industrial base. British technology was the king post on which the whole rickety structure of the empire leaned. Yet the first two years of the Great War showed England to be incapable of fighting a major war from her own industrial resources.

This was an astonishing predicament for a country which generally still prided itself on being 'the Workshop of the World'. Far from this being

[1] *Hist. Min. Mun.*, Vol. VII, Pt. II, p. 134.
[2] Ibid.
[3] Cd. 8462.
[4] Cd. 8566, see especially, p. 6.
[5] Cd. 9177.
[6] Cd. 8462, p. 282.
[7] Ibid. paragraph 328, p. 65, repeated p. 163.
[8] See Cd. 8566, p. 6.

the case, however, England by 1914 was well on the way to becoming a technological colony of the United States and Germany. The degree of British backwardness and dependence on other nations was brought home to the Government, if not to public opinion, after August 1914 when the attempt was made to convert the British industrial machine to munitions production. For munitions production for modern war is not primarily a question of specialised armaments industries, as some suppose, but of all those varied industrial and scientific resources that in peacetime make for a successful and expanding export trade.

Iron and steel production is in the twentieth century a fundamental measure of national power. In 1910 Britain produced 7,613,000 metric tons of steel[1] – barely half the German total. The inadequacy in quantity was made the more dangerous by technical backwardness. What should have been the province of scientific research, measurement and control was left to the eye and hand of the craftsman, and there was particularly a famine after 1914 of those specialised steels of high and consistent quality now required for sophisticated industrial purposes, and formerly imported from Germany. Thus, for example, it was slow production of track-links owing to 33 per cent to 40 per cent wastage in the castings that was, with the shortage of engines, the principal reason for the delay of three years in developing the tank from a prototype to a mass weapon in the field.[2] Aircraft production too was hampered by poor quality alloy steel.[3]

The evidence given before the Iron and Steel Industries Committee in 1917 portrayed a generation of industrialists in whom ignorance vied with complacency. These were men for whom their own old curiosity shops of foundries represented the summit to which progress might aspire, and for whom the sophisticated metallurgical science of foreign competitors was not a matter worthy of the attention of a British iron- or steel-master. In Britain, steelworks equipped with modern plant laid out on scientific and economic principles were exceptional. In the words of the official *History of the Ministry of Munitions*:

> British manufacturers were behind other countries in research, plant and method. Many of the iron and steel firms were working on a small scale, old systems and uneconomical plant, their cost of production being so high that competition with the steel works of the United States and Germany was becoming impossible.[4]

[1] J. H. Clapham, *Economic Development of France and Germany 1815–1914* (Cambridge, Cambridge University Press 1923), p. 285.
[2] See *Hist. Min. Mun.*, Vol. XII, Pt. III, pp. 42–9.
[3] Ibid. Pt. I, p. 122.
[4] Ibid. Vol. VII, Pt. II, pp. 1–2.

Twenty-nine out of the fifty-nine steel firms produced only 1,000–2,500 tons of steel per week between them. Iron production was similarly in the hands of little Dickensian family firms, some of whom 'were operating furnaces seventy years old and many quite out-of-date plants'.[1] In the pig-iron industry the annual output of each man was only 380 tons compared with 599 tons in the United States.[2]

The shortcomings of the British iron and steel industry alone were proof enough that the Motherland, no less than the empire, was not the great independent power it seemed, for as *The History of the Ministry of Munitions* states: 'It was only the ability of the Allies to import shell and shell steel from neutral America . . . that averted the decisive victory of the enemy.'[3]

Yet if Britain were now backward in the great heavy industries she had once pioneered she lacked almost entirely the new industries of the second phase of the industrial revolution after 1870 – a lack that was also rammed home by the munitions crisis of 1914–16.

There were but few light engineering factories with lines of semi-automatic lathes and other machines to be converted to finishing shell-cases; few precision industries like mechanical toy and clock-making to switch to the mass manufacture of finely accurate shell fuses. Before the war Britain had imported German toys and clocks. Thus in 1915 and 1916 Britain was forced to create a light engineering industry. This attempt immediately uncovered another deficiency – there was no modern machine-tool industry capable of producing the sophisticated machines for the new production lines. 'The British machine-tool maker', wrote *The History of the Ministry of Munitions*, 'was conservative both as regards novelty in design and quantity of output.' Modern machine tools had been imported from Germany and the United States before the war. This deficiency was particularly appalling because a machine-tool industry was the key to every kind of modern large-scale production, in war as well as peace – shells, fuses, aircraft, vehicles and all sorts of equipment and instrumentation. It was the purchase of American, Swedish and Swiss machine tools that prevented a total breakdown of the British effort to create new industries between 1914 and 1916. Nevertheless shortage of machine tools exercised a pervasive throttling effect, not only on shell production, but also for example, on engines and aircraft.[4]

A no less crippling and amazing lack was that of ball-bearing manufacture. The twentieth century runs on ball-bearings. Nevertheless, except

[1] Ibid. p. 2. [2] Ibid. p. 2, n. 1. [3] Ibid. Vol. II, p. 58.
[4] Ibid. Vol. XII, Pt. I, p. 110.

for a single factory, Britain had relied for ball-bearings on Germany. In 1914 she was forced to turn to Sweden and Switzerland while she expanded her own industry; and even in 1917 Swedish supplies were equal to 55 per cent of home production. The chronic shortage of ball-bearings was a major cause of tardiness even as late as 1918 in producing internal-combustion engines of all kinds, as well as tanks and aircraft.[1]

Yet another almost unbelievable British lack was that of a magneto industry. This, together with the shortage of ball-bearings, choked back production of every kind of motorised equipment – tanks, trucks, cars, motor-cycles, aircraft. Once again Britain had become dependent on Germany: 'Only one [British] firm was producing magnetos and its output for 1913–14 was 1,140 magnetos of a simple type. In the summer of 1916 the magneto shortage became acute, as the stock of German built instruments, which had hitherto formed the staple source of supply for the Royal Flying Corps, was rapidly diminishing . . . repeated failure had attended British magneto production for the first twelve months.'[2]

As it happened, British resources and skill in making internal-combustion engines were themselves small. Tank and aircraft production were both further greatly limited and delayed by lack of enough, and good enough, engines.

In the case of aircraft engines, of which none of British design existed in 1914, it was the French who saved the British. 'On the outbreak of war it was immediately realised that a large number of French engines would be required to cover the period during which the foundations of the British industry were being laid.'[3] As it was, '. . . high-powered engines of British design did not actually become available until the middle of 1916'.[4] And even by 1918 the programme to create a strategic bomber force was curtailed by a 'serious shortage in the supply of engines . . .'[5]

For that matter, there was virtually no British aircraft industry in 1914 either. 'Both aircraft and aero-engine manufacture were infant industries in England in 1914. Most of the aircraft firms of 1917 were of quite recent growth, their financial position precarious, their works organisation underdeveloped and their equipment small.'[6]

Machine tools, ball-bearings, magnetos, internal-combustion engines – it would be hard to name a basic necessity of advanced industrial technology in which the British were self-sufficient in 1914. Thus, fine measuring equipment and instrumentation required for various exact kinds of

[1] See *Hist. Min. Mun.*, Vol. VII, Pt. I, p. 108.
[2] Ibid. p. 103.
[3] Ibid. pp. 41–2.
[4] Ibid. p. 54.
[5] Ibid. p. 14.
[6] Ibid. p. 61.

manufacture or for equipping aircraft, ships and the artillery, had also to be obtained from abroad. Lack of industrial gauges became another throttle on the creation of new shell and other factories. Aircraft production particularly suffered through shortage of instruments.

> The supply of pressure gauges . . . presented perhaps more difficulty than any other instrument. English gauge-makers had never been organised for large production, and, moreover, they relied largely on France and Germany for the component parts. . . . The difficulties were almost entirely overcome by placing orders in Switzerland for small mechanisms.[1]

Nor in 1914 did Britain make her own optical and scientific instruments. 'The manufacture of small precision measuring appliances, e.g. vernier callipers, micrometers etc. was before the war a monopoly of the United States . . .'[2] while 'ninety per cent of the optical glass used in the manufacture of instruments in this country was imported from Germany . . .'[3] For glass bulbs and tubing for electric lamps Britain was also 75 per cent dependent on Germany and Austria.[4]

Even British laboratories were German technological provinces, and it was German equipment that kept them going until 1916, when 'stocks of German chemical apparatus, upon which chemists in this country practically depended before the war, were nearly exhausted.'[5]

Perhaps the most enormous single lack that forced its attention on the British Government after August 1914 was that of a great chemical industry making drugs and dyestuffs from coal-tar, such as had contributed greatly to Germany's pre-war success in exports. For it was the same plant and raw materials that were needed to make the high explosives to fill and propel shells. 'In August 1914, therefore, the Germans were in the fortunate position of being able to turn with ease the vast resources of a flourishing coal-tar industry to the production of high-explosives.'[6]

Britain on the other hand, which had utterly depended in peacetime on Germany for dyes and drugs such as aspirin, was forced to create a chemical industry almost from scratch. Shortage of chemicals for high explosives and for other purposes such as 'doping' aircraft canvas or photography formed yet another bottleneck in munitions production, while Britain had no alternative but to continue importing German drugs via neutral countries.[7]

[1] Ibid. pp. 114–15.
[2] Ibid. Vol. XI, Pt. III, pp. 9–10.
[3] Ibid. p. 10.
[4] Ibid. p. 18.
[5] Ibid. Vol. XII, Pt. I, p. 122.
[6] Ibid. Vol. VII, Pt. IV, p. 11.
[7] Ibid. Pt. I, p. 34.

It was the German science-based chemical industry that enabled Germany so swiftly to produce in quantity suitable gases for use in war; and the British and French lack of such an industry that prevented the Allies from, for example, employing mustard gas until over a year after Germany had done so. 'In this country, when a new gas had to be made, plant had in nearly every case to be specially erected for the purpose. . . .'[1]

Thus British industry in 1914, because both of the nature of what it possessed and also because of what it lacked, was in many ways a working museum of industrial archaeology. Here clanked on tirelessly not only the actual machines but, not so tirelessly, the techniques and outlook of 1815–1850 – marvels of inventiveness and progress in their epoch, but transformed by the passage of time into quaint memorials of the original Industrial Revolution. British industry itself had, in general, failed to notice that time had moved on. For the most part, British capitalists, managers and workpeople alike still saw their methods and plant as the summit of technical achievement. They were unaware that British industries were often now on a mere cottage scale compared with the highly organised, science-based, mammoth installations of Germany and the United States. Indeed, management and men often passionately resisted the efforts of the Ministry of Munitions to jerk them out of 1845.

In the glass industry for example:

> At the outset the industry showed a singular lack of comprehension of what could be done by automatic and semi-automatic machinery, and by female and unskilled labour . . . Inspection of such machinery as existed showed it to be antiquated, and the prejudice of makers and workmen alike was in favour of maintaining a skilled man to do by hand a job a girl could do with an automatic machine. . . .[2]

This devotion to craftsmanship and fabrication in small quantities by hand was general. It was as severe a brake on British munitions production after 1914 as the lack of necessary industries. The Ministry of Munitions wished to introduce American organisation and methods along with American machines – 'dilution' of the work force by unskilled labour.

> . . . dilution meant the entire re-organisation of the workshop with a view to obtaining an output limited only by the number of skilled men available for skilled work and supervision, and by the quantity of the newest machinery obtainable at home or abroad.

[1] See *Hist. Min. Mun.* Vol. XI, Pt. II, p. 32.
[2] Ibid. Pt. III, p. 18.

> The fundamental obstacle to dilution was the opposition of the craft unions.... To avoid [unemployment and a fall in their own standard of living] they had built up a system of rules and customs, written and unwritten, which hampered production.
>
> [Such as] the limitation of the number of apprentices, the insistence that skilled men only should work certain machines, the restriction of output, the regulation of overtime, the exclusion of women and men who had not been initiated into the mysteries of the craft, the sharp demarcation between the operations proper to the various trades . . .[1]

In fact, by 1914 the British industrial system had been finely parcelled out like peasant allotments between a myriad vested interests, trade union and capitalist. It presented a positively medieval picture of complicated private and corporate customs and privileges hardened by time into absolute right legalistically defended. And as with the medieval guild and manorial systems, all these rights and privileges rigidly preserved more and more outdated and inefficient methods. It was impossible to make changes without infringing somebody's 'property right' in an existing industrial operation. Indeed the very idea of functional efficiency as the sole basis of industrial activity had given way in boardroom and on shop-floor to this conception of traditional right, status and custom. Thus by 1914 there was an overwhelming material and psychological vested interest in resisting change.

The contrast with the situation and state of mind of British industry a hundred years earlier, during the Napoleonic Wars, was sombre and striking.

Then it was other countries who were held back by rigid and outmoded internal demarcations, divisions and privileges in trade and industry – and British entrepreneurs and engineers who were untrammelled, free to carry forward the industrial revolution how they liked. Then it was the businessmen of other countries who were already committed (both materially and mentally) to an existing industrial system, and unable or unwilling to exploit new opportunities; and the British who had the open minds, the free hand. Then it was Britain's enemy, France, who depended on British products even in wartime; now it was Britain who was dependent on others.

In a hundred years British industry had thus changed its character from an army of conquest, mobile, flexible and bold, into a defensive army pegged out in fixed positions, passively trying to defend what it had won

[1] Ibid. Vol. IV, Pt. I, p. 30.

in the past. The fire of creative purpose flickered low in the blackened grate of the British industrial regions.[1]

Nor was British agriculture less decrepit. It was the German submarine which reminded the British Government after 1914 that the price of cheap food from overseas under the policy of Free Trade had been the ruin of British farms and the terrifying vulnerability of the British population to starvation by blockade. In the twenty years 1892–1912 alone British wheat production had fallen by 6 per cent; Britain was dependent on imports for four-fifths of her wheat supplies. In those twenty years 9 per cent of British arable land, once the envy of Europe for the excellence of its husbandry, had lapsed into rough grass, docks and thistles. The crumbling cottages and ill-kept farms of the English countryside marked the victory of the prairie farmers of North America. Yet in Germany, behind high protective tariffs, the area of cultivated land had increased by 8 per cent between 1892 and 1912, and while the yields of all the major crops (wheat, barley, potatoes, oats) had fallen in Britain in that period, they had risen very greatly in Germany.[2] Although there had been a slight increase in meat-raising in Britain since 1900, in 1914 40 per cent of the meat on British tables came from overseas. As an historian of the social effects of the Great War writes, 'The slight [agricultural] revival of the Edwardian era could not stand comparison with the conscious German policy of creating farm out of forest, marsh and sand dune.'[3]

Thus by 1914, behind the imposing appearance of world power which deluded Briton and foreigner alike, Britain and her empire constituted no well-articulated and muscular body, lusty in heart, tough of sinew, and trained to the highest efficiency, but a shambling giant too big for its strength.

The war crisis of 1914–15 in fact found British power essentially to consist of three elements. The first was what still remained, despite its weaknesses, a huge industrial machine capable of being mobilised and modernised. The second was vast inherited wealth invested abroad with which to buy the American technology necessary to carry out this modernisation, and the American war supplies necessary to carry on the war in the meantime. And the third element was a navy just large enough, but only just, to retain command of the sea, and thus ensure that the American

[1] For an account of the state of British industry in 1914, see *The History of the Ministry of Munitions*, vols. cited; also Cd. 9032 and Cd. 9035, especially ch. II.

[2] Wheat by 8%, barley by 44%, oats by 80%, potatoes by 79%. See R.C.K. Ensor, *England 1870–1914* (Oxford, The Clarendon Press 1966), p. 511.

[3] Arthur Marwick, *The Deluge: British Society and the First World War* (London, Bodley Head 1965), p. 18.

supplies crossed the Atlantic to Britain. However, in this buying of American technology with inherited wealth Britain was like a rich old man who hires people to do what he has become incapable of doing himself.

This swift decline in British vigour at home and the failure to exploit the empire were not owing to some inevitable senescent process of history. They shared a specific cause. That cause was a political doctrine; a doctrine blindly believed in long after it had ceased to correspond with reality.

The doctrine was liberalism, which criticised and finally demolished the traditional conception of the nation-state as a collective organism, a community; and asserted instead the primacy of the individual. According to liberal thinking a nation was no more than so many human atoms who happened to live under the same set of laws. From such a belief it followed that the State, instead of being the embodiment of a national community as it had been under the Tudors and the Commonwealth, was required to dwindle into a kind of policeman, standing apart from the national life, and with the merely negative task of keeping the free-for-all of individual competition within the bounds of decorum.

Liberalism, like evangelical religion, flowed from a late eighteenth-century intellectual spring. Like evangelical religion again, it was a manifestation of the middle-class mind, and arose with the middle classes before 1850 and with them prevailed. Indeed liberalism and evangelical Christianity were head and tail of the same idealism, often espoused by the same persons, as in the case of Richard Cobden, and fuelled from a common reservoir of moral passion.

Central to liberalism was the belief that human progress and human happiness alike were best assured by leaving individuals to compete freely with each other: *laissez-faire*; let them get on with it. What was socially necessary could be safely entrusted to spontaneous creation by private initiative. As Adam Smith, the founder of liberal economics, put it in 1776: 'By pursuing his own interest [an individual] frequently promotes that of society the more effectually than when he really intends to promote it.'[1] It was Adam Smith who formulated the doctrine of Free Trade, keystone of liberalism, which was to exercise as long-lived and as baneful effect on British power as Wesley and Whitefield's preaching. Adam Smith attacked the traditional 'mercantilist' belief that a nation should be generally self-supporting: 'If a foreign country can supply us with a commodity cheaper than we ourselves can make it, better buy it of

[1] Adam Smith, *The Wealth of Nations* (London, Dent 1929), p. 400.

them with some part of the produce of our own industry employed in a way in which we have some advantage.'[1]

Therefore the State should not protect home markets or industries from competition:

> To give the monopoly of the home market to the produce of domestic industry, in any particular art or manufacture, is in some measure to direct private people in what manner they ought to employ their capitals, and must, in almost all cases, be either a useless or hurtful regulation.[2]

Adam Smith thus looked forward to a division of labour between different countries, whereby each specialised in certain trades and industries, and therefore became dependent one on another. Nevertheless he agreed that the State should continue to regulate shipping so that the nation might always be sure of a supply of seamen, ships and naval stores, because '... defence, however, is of much greater importance than opulence'.[3] This vital distinction was totally forgotten by nineteenth-century apostles of Free Trade. Indeed Richard Cobden so lost sight of national security that he believed that Free Trade was 'the international law of the Almighty', and that 'the honest and just interests of this country, and of her inhabitants, are the just and honest interests of the whole world'.[4]

In any event, Adam Smith erected a 'scientific' theory out of the passing circumstances of his own era. He could not foresee that national defence would come to depend not just on seamen and naval stores, but on total industrial and economic capability. He could not foresee the effects of the most revolutionary technological developments in the history of mankind, just beginning when he was writing. Thus, to give one small example, he believed that Free Trade could not ruin British cattle-raising because it was impossible to transport enough meat on the hoof into the country. Yet a hundred years after this confident judgement refrigerated steamships began to bring in meat in immense quantities from all over the world.

Nevertheless Adam Smith's doctrine of Free Trade was to win unqualified acceptance by 1850, and British economic policy – or, rather, non-policy – was henceforth to be based on it, without giving the least priority to defence over opulence. It was part of the general triumph of liberalism, which confidently left all social and industrial questions to

1 Smith, p. 401. 2 Ibid. p. 401. 3 Ibid. p. 408.
4 Kenneth E. Miller, *Socialism and Foreign Policy: Theory and Practice in Britain to 1931* (The Hague, Martinus Nijhoff 1967), p. 7.

solution by private individual initiative – the layout of towns, the future of industry and agriculture, the housing, health and education of the people.

The doctrines of liberal individualism were congenial to the English temperament. Since the early seventeenth century the English had nourished a deep suspicion of the state that had hardly diminished with the waning of monarchical power. As foreigners noted, the English were anarchical and quarrelsome, renowned for their love of liberty. 'Liberty', put another way, meant dislike of being organised; a dislike vividly manifested by the extraordinary illogic and localism of English institutions in the eighteenth century. Liberal doctrine provided a new and 'scientific' justification for this English dislike. The English therefore entered the industrial era – the era of organisation – with a deep-seated horror of organisation, and the larger the organisation the greater the horror.

In fact it proved impossible to carry out liberal doctrines in unsmirched purity; awkward realities would keep breaking in. For example Acts of Parliament were passed controlling the hours and conditions of work of female and infant labour in factories, to be enforced by government inspectors. Local government was reformed. Public sanitation was undertaken. Yet such matters as these were only incidental details, and under the young Victoria the British State abandoned any pretence of generally guiding the national destiny or expressing a collective national will. As Matthew Arnold, intellectual, poet and Her Majesty's Inspector of Schools, expressed it in 1869:

> . . . we are left with nothing but our system of checks, and our notion is of its being the right and happiness of an Englishman to do as far as possible what he likes, we are in danger of drifting towards anarchy. We have not the notion, so familiar on the Continent and to antiquity, *of the State*, – the nation in its collective and corporate character, entrusted with stringent powers for the general advantage, and controlling individual wills in the name of an interest wider than that of individuals.[1]

Thus religious moralism and political liberalism advanced together; and in foreign and home affairs alike the conception of the nation and the national interest was lost to sight. Worse, liberal doctrine, which had begun as speculative theory, ended as a national faith with a truly religious force. Yet liberal doctrine did not accord with fact. What liberal theorists saw as the beneficent working of a free market was in reality (as is now

[1] Matthew Arnold, *Culture and Anarchy* (New York, Macmillan 1894, first edition 1869), pp. 43–4.

well known) appalling industrial anarchy – wasteful, redundant, scrambling effort, often small in scale and local of vision.

During the same period as liberal economic and social doctrine came to prevail, a national myth was being woven according to which British leadership in the Industrial Revolution was owing to the British being innately better engineers and businessmen than foreigners. This too was nonsense, glorifying a generation of resourceful, ingenious but often ill-educated men – jumped-up craftsmen, greedy entrepreneurs of narrow mind. For the spirit of the amateur inspired the character of British industrialism from the very beginning. Both the machinery and the business methods of which the British were so proud were crude and primitive, put together by rule-of-thumb and trial-and-error – hardly surprising since this was only the first stage of the industrial era. It was not superior native genius that put the British in the lead after 1760 but a happy set of historical and geographical coincidences – the combination of abundant investment capital, absence of internal trade barriers, abundant water power, coal and iron conveniently adjacent to each other and plenty of labour because of the destruction of the peasantry by enclosure of the old common fields.

The British faith in the 'practical man' who had learned on the job was therefore, like liberal doctrine, based on a congenial but fallacious reading of events. But the faith was not the less absolute for being misplaced. By 1860 the British were committed hearts and minds to the already passing primitive phase of the industrial era – they were like cavalrymen continuing to believe devotedly in the horse despite the advent of the machine-gun and the tank.

The cult of the 'practical man' led to a positive distrust of the application of intellectual study or scientific research to industrial problems. In 1850 *The Economist* could write that 'the education which fits men to perform their duties in life is not got in public or parish schools but in the counting-house and lawyer's office, in camp or on board ship, in the shop or factory'.

It was otherwise in Europe. In following Britain into the Industrial Revolution, European nations operated on different political and economic principles. Whereas the British had solved the problem of the inefficiency of the State by abolishing the State as far as possible, European countries like Prussia instead modernised the State and made it efficient. Whereas the British dissolved the nation into individuals and left their destiny to the free market, European countries stuck to the old notion that the State should embody the collective will of the people and guide the national development. Whereas the British believed in unrestricted international trade, European countries imposed tariff regulations to protect their infant industries, home markets and agriculture. In a word, countries like Prussia still believed, like Elizabeth I and Cromwell, that a nation was a single strategic and commercial enterprise and that the national interest as a whole came before private profit.

So European industries grew up in partnership with the State. Railways for example were planned as national systems to serve national purposes, social and strategic as well as economic. European industry was conceived from the start on a much larger scale than the small, highly individualist firms of Britain. Countries like Prussia, which had always valued good large-scale organisation in the army and the State, naturally created it in industry.

The most important – indeed in the long run decisive – contribution of the European States to their countries' industrial progress lay in elaborate and coherent systems of national education – elementary, secondary, technical and university. From the beginning European (and American) industry was served by thoroughly well-trained, well-informed, high-quality personnel – from boardroom to factory floor. Its operations were based on sophisticated intellectual study, and above all on close liaison with scientific research.

British industry and its 'practical' men were no more fit to meet this formidable attack than the British militia would have been to meet the Prussian army. From the very moment when British technology ceased to have the world's markets entirely to itself and had to face competition, its defeat was under way. As early as 1835 Richard Cobden wrote after a visit to America that 'our only chance of national prosperity lies in the timely remodelling of our system, so as to put it as nearly as possible upon an equality with the improved management of the Americans'.[1] In 1853, just two years after the Great Exhibition had seemed to crown the triumph of British industry, Dr Lyon Playfair warned in a book, *Industrial Education on the Continent*, that European industry was bound to overtake Britain if she failed to alter her outlook and methods. In the 1860s the warnings grew more numerous, though equally unheeded. In 1868 a Select Committee of the House of Commons investigated the question of scientific instruction. The Committee's report showed that already professional and technical ignorance at all levels of British industry was rotting British industrial supremacy at the roots.

[1] Quoted in R. H. Heindel, *The American Impact on Great Britain 1891–1914* (New York, Octagon Books 1968), p. 153.

> . . . the foremen are almost without exception, persons who have been selected from the class of workmen by reason of their superior natural aptitude, steadiness and industry. Their education, and that of the workmen, during the school age, has been received in the elementary schools; and owing both to the defective character of the instruction in some of these schools, and to the early stage at which children go to work, it is rarely sufficient to enable them to take advantage of scientific instruction at a later period.[1]

The knowledge of the smaller manufacturers and the managers was hardly better: 'Unfortunately, this division may be disposed of in a very few words. Its members have either risen from the rank of foremen and workmen . . . or they are an offshoot from the class of smaller tradesmen, clerks etc . . .'[2]

Even – and most dangerous of all – the proprietors and managers of great industrial undertakings themselves were found to be deficient in professional education. If they had risen from the bottom '. . . Any knowledge of scientific principles which they may have acquired is generally the result of solitary reading, and of observation of the facts with which their pursuits have made them familiar.'[3] However, 'More generally . . . the training of the capitalists, and of the managers of their class, has been that of the higher secondary schools'[4] – in other words classics and Christianity.

Indeed the public-school system, as it was now developing in the image of Arnold's Rugby, was to make no helpful contribution in the next half-century to the quality of British industrial leadership. It was not only that its syllabuses and ideals were so remote. The public school was the instrument that turned the *arriviste* middle classes into 'gentlemen', in whose scale of snobbery imperial or public service or the professions were the only careers for the brilliant man. Manipulating money in the City was just about fit for a gentleman; but trade was 'low' and productive industry lower still. In any case the output of the public schools and grammar schools, and of British universities, was too small to satisfy the growing national and imperial needs for first-class talent.

The result of British faith in the 'practical man' and the inadequacy of British education was that as early as the 1860s the British were having to lean on the more advanced technology of their rivals. For example, the

1 *Report from the Select Committee on Scientific Instruction* (House of Commons, 15 July 1868), Vol. XV, p. iii.
2 Ibid. p. vi.
3 Ibid.
4 Ibid.

Commons Committee of the Council for Education in 1868 was told in a letter:

> The Monkbridge Iron Company of Leeds have turned their attention of late to the production of cast steel for the rolling stock of railways, the manufacture of which was first carried out on a large-scale in Westphalia; they are conducting this process under the superintendence of a French engineer . . . and I was assured that they sought in vain amongst Englishmen for a director of works possessing the combination of scientific and practical qualifications. . . .[1]

The decade of the 1860s marked a great watershed in the fortunes of British industry. In 1860 Italy was unified into a nation state. In 1865 the United States emerged from the Civil War and embarked on an enormous industrial expansion. In 1868 Japan began her astonishing leap from the Middle Ages to modernity. In 1870 Prussia beat France, a victory leading in 1871 to the unification of Germany under Prussia's formidable leadership. This was the most ominous development of them all. Matthew Arnold wrote of the Prussian victory over the French:

> We have been lately witnessing in the elasticity with which every branch of Prussian organisation bore the tremendous strain upon it by the war, *the fruits of the effectiveness of the German University system.* Our breakdown at the Crimea is distinctly traceable to the ineffectiveness of our superior [i.e. higher] education.[2]

All these nations were bent on becoming great industrial powers – all based their development on the thorough exploitation of science and technology and on a high degree of organisation. All possessed (or in the case of Japan was swiftly creating) first-class education systems geared to serve national progress.

According to liberal doctrine, the entrepreneur was supposed to respond to the competition of a more efficient rival by changing his methods and becoming in his turn yet more efficient still. Unfortunately British industry between 1870 and 1914 failed to react as expected. It was now led by the sons or grandsons of its ruthless founders – too often fatly complacent men, constipated with inherited wealth. Not merely in the boardroom but throughout industry the successes of the past induced a fatal smugness. Existing methods and products evoked a devoted and emotional loyalty. The British in general could not even see that their industrial techniques

[1] Command paper 4139.
[2] Quoted in W. R. Ward, *Victorian Oxford* (London, Frank Cass 1965), ch. XII, p. 406, n. 69.

were outmoded, fit for scrapping; instead they saw a way of life that was eternally valid. They inactively watched foreign invasion of the British home market itself. Indeed, British machine-tool makers, for example, were content to act as agents for advanced machines from Germany and the United States. So the response of British industry to the challenge of foreign competition and of ever more rapid technical change was too little and too late.

Since British enterprise signally failed to be enterprising, the alternative lay in some form of government action. This might have followed the German example – a broad economic strategy to encourage and guide industrial progress in the national interest by tariffs, subsidies and rebates.

But to suggest in Britain in the late nineteenth century that the government should guide the industrial and commercial life of the nation was like suggesting medical treatment to a Jehovah's Witness. When cheap wheat from the rich virgin soils of North America began to flood into Britain in the 1870s, British agriculture was ruined despite its own high standards of husbandry. Yet such was the hold of free trade doctrine that this national disaster was acquiesced in without thought of action. On the contrary, it was thought that, thanks to this beneficent operation of Free Trade, British industrial population was now provided with cheap food. And it was true that cheap food enabled British industry to compensate to some extent for its excessive operating costs by paying low wages. British industry therefore was partly shielded from the consequences of its own inefficiency by means of allowing the ruin of British agriculture.

Thus after 1870 liberal economic doctrine itself was the most catastrophically inappropriate of all the outdated components of Britain's economic equipment. Like an enchantment, liberal doctrine seemed to blind British eyes and paralyse British willpower. The most the nation could manage in the late nineteenth century was a series of immense reports by royal commissions and other bodies on various aspects of the ever more urgent need for national reorganisation. The sombre evidence of such reports and their recommendations were either ignored or acted upon after years of delay; and then often only timorously, shadows of the original proposals.

Education was a key to industrial – indeed national – progress and efficiency. In 1870 England still had no national education system. There were the 'public' schools; there was an assortment of private schools and ancient grammar schools, but there were no State secondary schools at all. Technical education took the form of a scanty patchwork of locally or privately supported technical institutes. Lastly there were the State-aided elementary schools set up in 1861 on the rock-bottom standards of the workhouse. None of these types of education stood in any organic relationship with another. Between therefore the cult of 'the practical man' on the one hand and the high-minded pursuit of knightly ideals by the public schools (and the day schools that imitated them) on the other there was virtually nothing. It was just where there was this immense void in England that in Europe there were harmonious structures of elementary, secondary, technical and commercial, and university education; the whole designed to promote national efficiency.

In 1868 a Royal Commission, the Schools Inquiry Commission, investigated all English schools bar elementary schools and the nine premier public schools. The Commission enjoyed the benefit of a report on European education by Matthew Arnold. The Commission's report expressed the opinion: 'When we view it as a whole, the Prussian system appears at once the most complete and the most perfectly adjusted to its people, of all that now exist.'[1] The Report anatomised the English lack of such an organised national system and especially the weakness in secondary education. 'There is not (with the exception of some schools for the military and naval services) a single school in England and Wales above the class of paupers over which the State actually exercises full control.'[2]

Yet, as the Schools Inquiry Commission wrote:

> . . . we are bound to add that our evidence appears to show that our industrial classes have not even that basis of sound general education on which alone technical education can rest. . . . In fact our deficiency is not merely a deficiency in technical education, but . . . in general intelligence, and unless we remedy this want we shall gradually but surely find that our undeniable superiority in wealth and perhaps in energy will not save us from decline.[3]

As prophecy this was fully and terribly to be borne out. As a warning it was ignored. No thorough-going system of State secondary education was created for another thirty years. The idea offended liberal doctrine; it involved lavish expenditure of public money (which European countries looked on as a first-class investment). Despite piecemeal improvements there were still only 128 grant-aided secondary schools by 1895, and only

[1] *Report of the Endowed Schools Commission* (House of Commons, 1867–8), Vol. XXXVIII, Pt. I, p. 72.
[2] Ibid. p. 107.
[3] Ibid. p. 80.

some 30,000 English children were then receiving a good secondary education.[1]

Sixteen barren years after the Schools Inquiry Commission, in 1884, a Royal Commission reported on the technical education available in Britain and Europe. The Commissioners visited France, Germany, Austria, Switzerland, Belgium, Holland and Italy. Their comparison between education in these countries and in Britain was bleak; bleaker still their inferences from this to Britain's commercial future. Hardly less significant were their incidental comparisons between the human quality of the British and European industrial populations. Thus in Switzerland the Commissioners on visiting an elementary school '. . . were specially struck with the clean and tidy appearance of the boys, and there was difficulty in realising that the school consisted mainly of children of the lower classes of the population'.[2]

Of Germany they noted: 'The one point in which Germany is overwhelmingly superior to England is in schools, and in the education of all classes of the people. The dense ignorance so common among workmen in England is unknown. . . .'[3]

The Commissioners approved the evening schools in Europe where workers could continue part-time scientific and technical studies:

> . . . the evening science teaching was conducted by professors of higher standing than, and of superior scientific attainments to, the ordinary science teachers who conduct courses in some of the largest and most important of the manufacturing centre [*sic*] of this country. In the case of machine construction, the models and materials for instruction were superior to those found in similar schools at home.[4]

They noted that technical higher elementary schools like those of the Continent 'are singularly wanting in our own country'.[5] They were especially struck with European advanced technical education for managerial staff – the polytechnics.

> To the multiplication of these polytechnics . . . may be ascribed the general diffusion of a high scientific knowledge in Germany, its appreciation by all classes of persons, and the adequate supply of men competent, so far as theory is concerned, to take the place of managers and superintendents of industrial works.
>
> In England, there is still a great want of this last class of persons. . . .[6]

[1] G. A. N. Lowndes, *The Silent Social Revolution* (London, Oxford University Press 1937).
[2] C. 3981, p. 20. [3] Ibid. p. 337. [4] Ibid. p. 48. [5] Ibid. p. 84.
[6] Ibid. pp. 213–14.

Even humble members of European industry were more aware of British backwardness than British politicians or public opinion. A German foreman in a chemical works told the Commissioners: 'There is a great lack of chemical knowledge even among the foremen and managers of English dyehouses, and thus, in dealing with new colours and new effects, they are compelled to rely on "rule of thumb" experience, which is often at fault.'[1]

The Commissioners' conclusions make hardly less bitter reading than the report of their investigations:

> ... it is our duty to state that, although the display of continental manufacturers at the Paris International Exhibition in 1878 had led us to expect great progress, we were not prepared for so remarkable a development of their natural resources, nor for such perfection in their industrial establishments as we actually found....
>
> In some branches of industry, more especially in those requiring an intimate acquaintance with organic chemistry, as, for instance, in the preparation of artificial colours from coal tar, Germany has unquestionably taken the lead....
>
> Your commissioners cannot repeat too often that they have been impressed with the general intelligence and technical knowledge of the masters and managers of industrial establishments on the Continent.[2]

These and other urgent and repeated warnings that Britain was being left behind might have been addressed with equal result to a feather bolster. In the next thirty years there were to be only piecemeal improvements, inadequate developments of new products and processes. Even novel industries like electricity supply were crippled by British dislike of large-scale organisation – little local ventures, with small power stations, differing voltages and few links with one another. To give a fundamental example, while British steel production just doubled between 1880 and 1914, German steel production multiplied nearly ten times.[3] British shipbuilding came to depend largely on German steel.

After 1890 and even more so after 1900 British public opinion could not remain totally unaware of foreign progress. In 1894 there was a bestseller called *British Industries and Foreign Competition*. In 1896 there was a 'Made in Germany' press panic, on publication of a book of that title. The *Daily Express* ran a series entitled 'Wake Up England!' In 1901 the *Daily Mail* followed suit with a series on 'American Invaders'. In 1900–1

[1] Ibid. p. 369.
[2] Ibid. pp. 505–8.
[3] See Clapham, p. 285.

*The Times* itself, governing-class opinion incarnate, ran a major series of articles on 'The Crisis of British Industry' and 'American Engineering Competition and Progress'. Technical journals went into details of British backwardness in particular industries. The stubborn opposition of British trade unions to new machines and new methods was fully discussed. Lord Rosebery summed it all up for his fellow countrymen in a speech on 15 October 1901, when he averred: 'In these days we need to be inoculated with some of the nervous energy of the Americans.'[1]

Yet this prolonged and dramatic exposure produced scant result. For the inchoate carcass of British industry, the mass of small, anonymous family firms, still yielded enough for the descendants of their founders to live well; there was always a home market or easy, unsophisticated colonial markets where the competition was less ferocious than in Europe or North America. The national interest was a conception beyond the businessman's local horizon. Technical improvement and expansion for its own sake was outside the range of mind of men content to live a genteel upper-middle-class life in suburban mansions where the tram tracks ended and the rhododendrons began. When one Yorkshire ironmaster received a copy of *Principles of Scientific Management* from its American author, he sent back in reply a copy of a work of his own – an edition of Horace's *Odes* in the original Latin.[2]

Thus it was that instead of heeding the warnings and recognising the truth about their industrial decadence, the British as a whole preferred to comfort themselves with fables. German products were thought to be necessarily poor in quality because they were cheap; it was believed that they were 'dumped' in the British market at prices below the cost of production (because the prices were below the *British* cost of production). The British sneered at German thoroughness and seriousness of purpose, dubbing it a want of a sense of humour. German science became in popular British imagination a comic and owlish professor in a beard. The rivalry of American large-scale industry and mass-production was exorcised by seeing in it only Yankee bragging, pushing salesmanship and mass-produced goods cheap in quality as well as price, lacking the solid worth and high finish of British craftsmanship.

The immense national wealth accumulated earlier in the century also helped to cushion the British from the realities of their industrial decline. This wealth, more of it invested abroad than at home, was multiplying

[1] Quoted in Heindel, p. 215. For a full account of the impact of foreign, especially American, technological rivalry on Britain between 1890 and 1914, see Heindel, pp. 140–3, and chs. VIII, IX, XI and XII.

[2] Heindel, p. 95.

itself. The British grew richer while their industrial capabilities grew poorer – a gruesome paradox.

No evidence of foreign success therefore shook the general British faith in British industry and its 'practical man'. No evidence of the failure of British enterprise to be enterprising could shake the hold of liberal economic doctrine.

Thus British beliefs and myths did not serve to oil the progress of the nation (as did the nationalist myths of Europe) by justifying and sanctifying what needed to be done in social and economic policy. On the contrary, progress in Britain had to take place in the teeth of British myths, against the deepest grain of British prejudices.

The prolonged struggle to evolve a coherent national system of education remained a fundamental case in point, affecting, as the Schools Inquiry Commission had reported in 1868, the nation's 'general intelligence' – in other words, Britain's basic capability in every field of endeavour into the distant future.

For during the period 1880–1900, when the future leaders of British life in 1918–39 were being conditioned in good form and fair play in the public schools, the future managers, clerks, foremen and workers were receiving either a poor or a positively harmful education.

By 1895 there were 5,235,887 pupils at elementary schools, four million of them under ten.[1] The children themselves were a testimony to the long-term effect of anarchical industrialism on the quality of the British nation. In 1908, in the early days of the school medical service, 700–970 out of every 1,000 children were 'dirty', of whom 100 were 'very dirty', and 260 'somewhat dirty'. Among 1,000 girls in a country area some 600 would have had hair infested with nits. Out of 1,000 children 700–800 would have decayed teeth, 150–180 diseases of the nose and throat, 100–130 with malnutrition, 26–80 with diseases of the heart and circulation, 10–30 with diseases of the lung.[2] These constituted the majority of British children born in the first decade of the twentieth century – this was England's future human equipment. This was the disgraceful reality with which public-school boys made contact only through their school charity missions in the slums. For it was still accepted that it was the duty of private charity here and there to alleviate poverty and ill-health; that State action could – and should – prevent the worst effects of poverty, as it did in several European countries, was repugnant to British prejudices.

British elementary education served only to turn these sickly and filthy children into robots able to read and write and count and obey.

[1] Lowndes, *The Silent Social Revolution*, p. 4.

[2] Ibid. p. 222.

> ... when severity and constraint have done their work [wrote a retired chief inspector of schools in 1911], when the spirit of the child has been broken, when his vitality has been lowered to its barest minimum, when he has been reduced to a state of mental and moral serfdom, the time has come for the system of education through mechanical obedience to be applied to him in all its rigours.[1]

The children, according to this retired chief inspector, '... had no initiative, no spontaneous activity ... they could do nothing but sit still and wait for the word of command'.[2] It was hardly the way to create a nation of alert and resourceful people. Indeed, as yet another official report noted as late as 1909, in classes of sixty pupils: 'A not unnatural desire for orderly quiet ... leads imperceptibly to a military precision and a rapid simultaneity of movement and expression which if long continued must prove fatal to the better forms of education.'[3]

The Report went on to describe with extraordinary accuracy what were to be general British characteristics in two world wars and the peace between: 'Well-disciplined children may acquire a habit of exactness and obedience. But they will not learn self-reliance; their intelligence will not be quick to meet emergencies; their individuality and powers of initiative will not be developed.'[4]

Until 1902 Britain set up no State-sponsored system of secondary education. In 1894 therefore the odds against a pupil in an elementary school going on to secondary education were 270 to 1.[5] Even in 1909 three-quarters of the adolescents between fourteen and seventeen years of age in England and Wales were under no form of education, nor of physical training.

> The Committee finds that at the most critical period of their lives [adolescence] a very large majority of the boys and girls in England and Wales are left without any sufficient guidance and care. This neglect results in great waste of early promise, in injury to character, in the lessening of industrial efficiency, and in the lowering of ideals of personal and civic liberty.[6]

The Committee found, in a phrase, that in Britain there was '... tragic waste of early promise'.[7] Yet it was from German secondary schools, supplemented by technical education, that Germany drew that large

[1] Edmond Holmes, 'What is and might be' quoted in Brian Simon, *Education and the Labour Movement 1870–1920* (London, Lawrence and Wishart 1965), p. 118.
[2] Ibid. p. 119. [3] Cd. 4757. [4] Ibid. p. 52.
[5] Lowndes, *The Silent Social Revolution*, p. 101. [6] Cd. 4757, p. 52. [7] Ibid. p. 215.

group of well-educated and enterprising men who formed the first-class non-commissioned officers of industry and army alike. In fact some British firms in the City of London in the 1900s employed German clerks because sufficiently educated Englishmen could not be found.[1]

While British people saw the Germans as rigid and regimental, lacking initiative, and themselves as enterprising, flexible and resourceful, the reverse was the case. British educational neglect in the nineteenth century artificially created (as had been predicted) a stupid, lethargic, unambitious, unenterprising people for the twentieth century. The consequences were insidiously to affect many fields of national performance.

It was only in 1902 that the piecemeal educational developments of the previous forty years were reorganised and augmented into a coherent national system: university and technical education resting on secondary and elementary schools. Despite the foundation of the City and Guilds of London Institute in 1879 to frame courses and conduct examinations in technical subjects and the cautious and inadequate Technical Institution Act in 1889, higher and technical education still amounted to little in 1902:

> . . . when the Act of 1902 was passed the country possessed the nucleus of what are now the universities, in those days amounting, with a few brilliant exceptions such as Owen's College, Manchester, to little more than congeries of technical and literary classes; a small number of polytechnics mainly in London: a rather larger number of organised science schools and evening science and art classes. . . .[2]

Manchester College of Technology, Britain's answer to Germany's great institution at Charlottenberg, in 1902 numbered 150 day-students against thousands at the German college. There were 7 universities in England for a population of 31 million; 22 German universities to a population of 50 million; and in the United States 484 men's and 162 women's colleges and 48 schools of technology to a population of 100 million.

After the 1902 Education Act there was at last a spurt in secondary education – 94,000 pupils in State-aided schools in 1905, 200,000 in 1914. Yet the figures were still miniscule in terms of a population of school age numbered in millions. And technical education continued to lag, despite the demands for radical development made in the debates on the 1902 Education Bill. Fewer than twenty first-class technical schools were built between 1902 and 1918.[3] In 1908, when Germany possessed (apart from

[1] Lowndes, *The Silent Social Revolution*, p. 89.
[2] Ibid. p. 190.
[3] Ibid.

the polytechnics) ten technical high schools of university rank with 14,143 students[1] Britain still had no technical institutions of that rank, but thirty-one reorganised technical schools with a total of 2,768 students.[2]

In any case, despite the immense strides now being made by Britain's competitors and despite the belated development of technical education in Britain, British industry itself still devotedly believed in the 'practical man'.

> The slow growth of these technical institutions is, however, in the main to be ascribed to the small demand in this country for the services of young men well-trained in the theoretical side of industrial operations and in the service underlying them.[3]

A leading theme of the parliamentary debates on the 1902 Education Bill, one common to speakers of all parties, was the example of Germany. As G. M. Trevelyan expressed it: 'This Bill . . . is demanded by the people from a sense of shame in our possessing the worst industrial peasantry in the west of Europe, a fear on the part of our industrial population that we shall not be able to meet commercial competition. . . .'[4]

Since 1880 the whole German approach to industrial and social questions had been the admiration of a growing minority in Britain, who had watched Germany's evident success not without alarm. It began to be argued – especially during the 1890s – that this German approach was more successful, better adapted to realities, than British belief in liberal individualism. It was contended that mere private profitability in a free market ought to give way to the whole collective interest of the nation – its social cohesion, its industrial and strategic strength. There was a demand for 'national efficiency', in which reform was an essential ingredient. National efficiency in regard to home policy was the equivalent of imperialism in international relations.[5] Both were in fact aspects of a single aspiration – to enhance British power *vis-à-vis* other States. Though Bismarckian Germany was the evident model, there was a great English precedent for the aims of imperialism and national efficiency in the mercantilist state of Elizabeth I and Cromwell.

In place therefore of liberalism, Social-Imperialism (to use the term that comprises both the strategic approach to international affairs and 'national efficiency' at home) wished to return to the traditional English view of the State and the nation. Social-imperialism saw the nation as 'a social

[1] *Encyclopaedia Britannica* (14th ed.).
[2] Cd. 5246; Cd. 5130, p. 247.
[3] Cd. 5130, p. 90.
[4] Lowndes, *The Silent Social Revolution*, p. 91.
[5] See Bernard Semmel's excellent analysis *Imperialism and Social Reform: English Social-Imperial Thought 1895–1914* (London, Allen and Unwin 1960).

organism' engaged in a struggle with others for survival of the fittest. As Benjamin Kidd expressed it in his influential book, *Social Evolution*, in 1894: 'It is this quality of social efficiency that nations and peoples are being continually, and for the most part unconsciously, pitted against each other in the complex rivalry of life.'[1] Karl Pearson, another influential propagandist of social-imperialist ideas, asserted in the same year that '. . . science realises that the nation is an organised whole in a continual struggle with its competitors . . . You cannot get a strong and effective nation if many of its stomachs are half-fed and many of its brains untrained.'[2] It was a government's task to 'treat class needs and group cries from the standpoint of the efficiency of the herd at large', and therefore 'to lessen, if not to suspend, the internal struggle, that the nation may be strong externally'.[3]

Such a way of looking at things constituted a frontal assault on all that Victorian England had come to live by. It brushed aside Christian ethics as unscientific, misleading – irrelevant either to the welfare of the nation or to its success in the struggle with other nations. It placed national power before private profit, the group before the individual.

Social imperialism however was not a single, tidy prospectus, but a variety of ideas and emphases. Of these ideas, one of the earliest and most central was that of the transformation of the British Empire into a federal state, with a single foreign policy backed by an imperial army and navy. It was propounded in 1884 by J. R. Seeley,[4] who believed it was the only means by which the British race could outweigh such powers as Germany and France and match what he saw as the super-powers of the future:

> Russia and the United States will surpass in power the states now called great as much as the great country-states of the sixteenth century surpassed Florence. Is not this a serious consideration, and is it not especially so for a state like England, which has at the present time the choice in its hands between two courses of action, the one of which may set it in that future age on a level with the greatest of these great states of the future, while the other will reduce it to the level of a purely European Power looking back, as Spain does now, to the great days when she pretended to be a world-state.[5]

This was accurate prophecy. What Seeley saw as the nature of this choice appears today as no less accurate a forecast:

> . . . we have here by far the largest of all political questions, for if our Empire is capable of further development, we have the problem of

[1] Quoted in Semmel, p. 35. [2] Ibid. p. 42. [3] Ibid.
[4] In his book, *The Expansion of England.* [5] Ibid. p. 350.

> discovering what direction that development should take and if it is a mischievous encumbrance, we have the still more anxious problem of getting rid of it. . . .[1]

In any event Seeley made a sharp distinction between colonies of British stock, like Australia, New Zealand, Cape Colony and Canada, and imperial possessions inhabited by coloured and backward peoples, like, above all, India. 'It may be fairly questioned whether the possession of India does or ever can increase our power or our security, while there is no doubt that it vastly increases our dangers and responsibilities.'

Therefore: 'When we enquire then into the Great Britain of the future we ought to think much more of our Colonial (i.e. colonies of British stock) than of our Indian Empire.'[2]

In Seeley's view the solution of the imperial problem was to unite Britain and the 'white' colonies into a federal union.

This was however not at all the form the immediate imperial future took, for in the twenty years after Seeley wrote his book, great tracts of Africa with populations far more primitive than that of India were added to British responsibilities.

Despite the propagation of such ideas as Seeley's by organisations like the Imperial Federation League (1884), the British Empire League (1893) and the Imperial Federation Defence Committee (1893), federal union of the 'white' empire and a single imperial navy and army proved impossible. The federal empire was a proposition simple, bold, apparently so obvious, but politically impracticable. Seeley and other imperialists under-estimated the centrifugal tendencies caused by the trans-ocean distances that separated the 'white' communities of the empire. As Lord Salisbury told the first Colonial Conference in 1887, although the British Empire 'yields to none – it is, perhaps, superior to all – in its greatness', there was a characteristic peculiar to it as an empire; 'a want of continuity; it is separated into parts by large stretches of ocean; and what we are here for today is to see how far we must acquiesce in the conditions which that separation causes; how far we can obliterate them by agreement and by organisation'.[3] But Salisbury held out no hope of emulating the German Empire's government from the centre; and he was right.

For the 'white' colonies, isolated in their own continents or islands and moulded by their own climates, environments and histories, were swiftly becoming nations in themselves, and not merely British overseas.

[1] Seeley, p. 299.
[2] Ibid. p. 13.
[3] Mansergh, p. 128.

They were more and more jealous of their independence. Incorporation into an imperial union was thus the very opposite of their political aspirations, however unanswerable the case on strategic and economic grounds. Imperial federation was never a runner. Yet even looser forms of imperial cohesion proved unattainable. Hopes of an imperial military reserve, to which all countries in the empire would contribute fixed contingents, foundered at the Colonial Conference of 1902, despite years of arguing and scheme-mongering, and although Britain pointed out that she was spending on defence per head of population 29s. 3d. per annum, as against an average of less than 3s. in the colonies; and although the Colonial Secretary, Joseph Chamberlain, reminded the colonials: 'Justification of union is that a bundle is stronger than the sticks that comprise it, but if the whole strain is to be thrown on one stick, there is very little advantage in attempting to put them into a bundle.'[1] Hopes too for an imperial navy under Admiralty control to which each colony (dominion) would contribute a fleet unit were finally dashed at the Imperial Defence Conference in 1909. The most that could therefore be achieved were loose ties of co-operation through occasional conferences, and, after 1907, the standardisation of the organisation and equipment of the various imperial armed forces on the British model.

A no more successful runner was the project for an imperial customs union, which would have turned the whole empire into a common market protected by tariffs, as the Germans, French and American markets were protected. This too foundered because again there was no unity of interest between the industrial motherland and young colonies wishing to protect their infant industries while selling their raw materials and agricultural products where they liked. Thus in politics, defence and economics alike 'Greater Britain' foundered on the reality that the empire consisted of countries that, despite common origins, possessed increasingly separate identities and interests.

There remained for social-imperialism the national efficiency of England herself, the problems of decaying industrial power, a brutalised and ignorant urban race, a ruined agriculture – the residue of liberalism.

Here social-imperialism cut clean across old party-political distinctions. The Conservatives happily embraced imperial expansion abroad and efficiency at home; after all, Disraeli had been the precursor of social-imperialism, with his combination of imperial splendour and social

[1] Ibid. p. 134. See also R. A. Preston, *Canada and Imperial Defense* (Durham, North Carolina, Duke University Press 1967), chs. 4–10; and Donald C. Gordon, *The Dominion Partnership in Imperial Defence 1870–1914* (Baltimore, Johns Hopkins Press 1965).

reform. It was the Conservatives who created a national education system by the Act of 1902, and started the desperately needed reconstruction and modernisation of the army, navy and of imperial defence at large. Yet they split deeply over the crucial question of tariff reform. This was a shrunken version of the imperial customs union. Its aim was to shield the British home market itself behind tariff barriers against the successful invasion of foreign products. For with other countries entrenched behind tariffs, it was argued, Free Trade was free only in one direction. After 1903, there was an immense propaganda campaign against Free Trade by Joseph Chamberlain and the Tariff Reform League. Chamberlain himself came of a Birmingham business family, and the League was, of all the organs of social-imperialism, most aware that it was industry which was the basis of power in the modern age, and that British industry was in dire trouble. However the Tariff Reform League also reflected the British industrialists' illusion that the trouble was caused by 'unfair' foreign competition rather than by their own obsolescence.

Yet such was now the hold of Free Trade both on the nation at large and on the Conservative Party itself that the campaign for tariff reform succeeded only in splitting the Conservatives and helping them to lose the General Election of 1906. Conservative social-imperialism thus never extended to the rehabilitation of British industry. Although after Gladstone's death in 1894 the Liberal Party split into Gladstonian and imperialist wings over foreign and social policy, it too remained unitedly faithful to Free Trade. Thus this essential part of early nineteenth-century liberal economics survived unscathed the impact of social-imperialism. British industry and agriculture remained wide open to the smashing salvoes of foreign competition. The life of the British people continued to hang precariously on overseas and foreign supplies. Unlike Germany, Britain continued to invest more abroad than in her own industries,[1] and more in foreign countries than in her own empire, and for no better reasons than that the private investor could get higher rates of interest, and that the British banking system, unlike the German, was better adapted to foreign transactions than to co-operation in home industrial development. Indeed the liberal-imperialists tended to ignore that industrial capability was the essential muscle of modern national power; rather they put their faith in Britain's vast accumulated wealth. This was like arguing that a millionaire's fortune was more important than the talent which had created it.

Nevertheless in social policy liberal-imperialism, with its demand for

[1] See E. J. Hobsbawm, *Industry and Empire* (Harmondsworth, Penguin Books 1969), p. 192.

State action in aid of 'national efficiency', won a notable if limited victory over the Gladstonians. Liberal-imperialists dominated the Liberal administration that followed the General Election of 1906, and inspired its innovations in social reform – State old-age pensions, free meals in schools, a school medical service, a development commission for natural resources, a national system of labour exchanges, a census of production. The liberal-imperialist programme leaned on Bismarck's 'state socialism' of the 1880s, and the old-age pensions scheme was closely based on German practice. Yet the imitation of Germany, despite all the calls for 'organisation' and 'efficiency', was only superficial. British commercial and industrial life went its way unaffected. British money continued to be heavily invested in such nationally irrelevant projects as Argentine tramways while British industrial equipment fifty years old went without replacement.

It was the Fabian socialists who fully embraced not only imperialist aims abroad, but the German model of the nation organised and led by the State. The Fabians, tough-minded people like the Webbs and Bernard Shaw, had little time for the sentimental socialism of the pseudo-religious. Instead of looking rapturously forward to a world of the brotherhood of man they posed a choice between Britain as a great world-empire of the future or as two islands in the North Sea.[1] In home affairs they were less concerned with a vision of social justice as such than with national efficiency. They demanded a national minimum wage not so much for the sake of the workers themselves as to stop British industry compensating for the cost of its technical inefficiency by low wages. They wanted slum clearance and health services in order to permit the 'breeding of even a moderately Imperial race', better for all purposes, including military service, than the 'stunted, anaemic, demoralised denizens . . . of our great cities'.[2] Great advances in national education were needed because 'it is in the class-rooms that the future battles of the Empire for commercial prosperity are already being lost'.[3]

This kind of concern was common to social-imperialists of all political colours. They shared a contempt for all that Gladstone's England stood for – moralism and internationalism in foreign affairs, individualism at home. Common ground was reflected by interlocking membership of various propagandist organisations.

Yet outside social-imperialist circles, and the hard electric light of their untypically brilliant minds, 'national efficiency' and 'organisation' remained catchphrases rather than a new way of life. Despite the jingo mood

[1] Semmel, p. 71. [2] Sidney Webb in 1901, quoted in Semmel, p. 73. [3] Ibid.

before 1914, and twenty years of imperialist-inspired Conservative and Liberal Government, social-imperialism utterly failed to make the kind of conversion of the British mind that liberalism had achieved before 1850. Unlike liberalism it never found expression in a single bold doctrine espoused by one powerful political group. Its impact was weakened by its division between factions within all three political parties, by the differing emphases placed on its various ideas, and by the total disagreement over tariff reform. The England of Gladstone, and for that matter of Cobden and Bright, survived, although decayed and somewhat patched and added to by piecemeal improvement; in 1914 recognisably still the same old haphazard structure of 1860.

The British continued to 'muddle through'. To be organised for the sake of national power and efficiency had always been deeply repugnant to the British character, as even Elizabeth I and Cromwell had discovered. It took the Great War itself to make the British see that 'muddling through' was, whether they liked it or not, incompatible with the role of a great industrial and imperial power in the twentieth century – or indeed with their own very survival.

Even under German gunfire the British awakening proved slow and reluctant. The ignorance of British political leaders about the nature of modern industrial operations was astounding. Lloyd George, the Liberal Chancellor of the Exchequer and future Minister of Munitions, wrote in February 1915: '*I hear* [author's italics] that it takes months to complete . . . machinery which is essential to the turning out of rifles and cannon.'[1] Bonar Law, the Conservative leader, was himself a businessman, a member of the Glasgow Iron Exchange – and yet he believed as late as March 1915 that Britain was 'the greatest manufacturing country in the world . . . where there is immense power of adapting one form of manufacture to another. . . .'[2]

It was not until June 1915, ten months after the outbreak of war, that the Government finally assumed responsibility for organising and directing the whole industrial and economic life of the country. Until then munitions' production had been put out for tender in the open market, according to the best principles of the free play of demand and supply. When British guns on the Western Front had to be rationed to four rounds each a day, it at last became clear that liberal individualism would

[1] David Lloyd George, *War Memoirs*, 2 vols. (London, Odhams Press 1938), Vol. I, p. 100.
[2] Quoted in Lloyd George, p. 107.

not suffice. As Lloyd George informed an audience at Manchester in June 1915:

> We are fighting against the best organised community in the world, the best organised either for peace or war, and we have been employing too much the haphazard, leisurely, go-as-you-please methods, which, believe me, would not have enabled us to maintain our place as a nation even in peace very much longer.[1]

The contrast between the industrial mobilisation that now followed in Britain and the previous fifty years of drift and decline was remarkable. It was as if a portly and elderly retired gentleman had suddenly leapt from his armchair and embarked on a new career. Gone was the smugness and lethargy. Struck off were the shackles and blinkers of Victorian habits and Victorian beliefs. Once more the British tackled their problems by open-minded search for the best expedients. In three years, 1915–18, the British did much to remedy the accumulated neglect of their industrial machine, and to make good the deficiencies revealed by the demands of war.[2] This was more than just economic mobilisation – this was an industrial revolution carried through at breakneck speed. However, it was only made possible because the French were carrying the main weight of the war on land, and because the British themselves at least had not failed to maintain a navy narrowly large enough to keep command of the sea.

The wartime industrial revolution was led by a partnership between the State and private enterprise. For the first time the jealously guarded independence of the small-scale British firm was broken in favour of large productive groups. For the first time government and management tackled all the problems of planning production programmes of an immense scale and complexity. Huge extensions were built to existing private plant with the aid of government money – a heresy to make Gladstone's collars quiver under his shroud. An even greater heresy was the construction of no fewer than 218 national factories, making all kinds of products – ball-bearings, aircraft, explosives, gauges and tools, chemicals, even reinforced concrete slabs. The cost of shells made in national factories was below those made by private industry. It was the national factories indeed that received the bulk of the modern machine tools bought in America, Switzerland and Sweden, and they were laid

[1] *Hist. Min. Mun.*, Vol. III, p. 8.
[2] See pp. 83–90 above for an account of these deficiencies.

out for mass production in a way novel to British engineering. As *The Times* reported in November 1915:

> One of the new factories has grown up on a spot which last November was green fields. Now there are 25 acres covered with buildings packed full of machinery. Most of the machines are of American make, and some are marvels of ingenuity. Herein the war will prove a permanent benefactor to Birmingham. For it would be flattery to pretend that the prevailing Birmingham type of workshop is anything to boast about. It is on the whole conspicuously antiquated.

The trade unions, after much argument and a few patriotic strikes, agreed to suspend their restrictive practices and demarcations for the duration of the war in order to allow these modern factories to be worked. However they insisted on government assurances that the methods of mid-Victorian technology would be restored as soon as the war was over, so that outdated craftsmen would not lose their jobs or their status, even though they were now no more useful than a horse yoked to a motor-car. And so for the duration of the war: '. . . standardised repetition work or mass production took the place of the varied and variable output, characteristic of much British manufacture before the war'.[1]

To find the money to buy the new foreign equipment the British had to sell overseas investments. At last therefore the British were forced to invest mighty sums in the modernisation of their own country instead of in the development of others.

British electrical generating capacity doubled between 1914 and 1918, and the average output of generating stations rose from 522 kilowatts in 1914 to 7,000 in 1918 – large-scale centralised power production and utilisation at last.[2] Steam power in factories, with its jungle of clacking belts, began to give way to electricity. As the *History of the Ministry of Munitions* put it in 1922: '. . . even if a national scheme of electric power supply does not become an accomplished fact, industry as a whole has been shown by Government enterprise the value of electricity in accelerating and cheapening production. . . .'[3]

To supply chemicals for explosives, the foundations of a great British chemical industry were laid. By the end of 1916 almost all coke ovens were equipped with full plants for recovering by-products. A national dyestuff company was created. German patents were seized to provide a short-cut to technical expertise.

[1] *Hist. Min. Mun.*, Vol. IV, Pt. IV, pp. 74–5.
[2] Ibid. Vol. VIII, Pt. III, p. 105.
[3] Ibid. p. 106.

The Ministry of Munitions also developed or created many other industries '. . . the chief of which were the refining of certain non-ferrous metals . . . the production of synthetic cryolite, the manufacture of optical instruments, optical and chemical glass . . . and the development, from very small beginnings, of the aircraft and aero-engine industries'.[1]

Nor was this all:

> Among other considerable industries which were developed by the Ministry of Munitions were the manufacture of ferro-chrome, tungsten powder, and ferro-tungsten, carborundum, electrodes and magnesite coils, which had either not existed at all in this country or had been of negligible importance. The manufacture of wire rods and wire was another of the industries which was greatly developed in order to make good supplies formerly obtained from Germany and Belgium. . . .[2]

British ball-bearing production doubled during the war; the output of electric bulbs quadrupled; of optical glass increased sixty times. As a result of modern equipment and methods introduced by the Ministry of Munitions, the value of the annual output of optical and scientific instruments leaped from £250,000 before the war to about £5,000,000 by the Armistice. The manufacture of mathematical and drawing instruments was similarly modernised. These innovations were the key to making a whole range of sophisticated equipment: '. . . it became possible to manufacture for the first time in England a large number of instruments, such as panoramic dial sights, periscopes, rangefinders for aeroplanes, height finders for aeroplanes, sound ranging apparatus, travel correction apparatus. . . .'[3]

A major single contribution to an advanced British technology lay in the creation of an aircraft industry and all the subsidiary types of manufacture that served it.

> Aircraft construction was in its infancy in 1914, and aero-engine building was practically non-existent. . . . At the end of the war aero-engine production was a huge industry . . . and British engines have outstripped the productions of all other countries as to quality and quantity.[4]
>
> The advances made by subsidiary industries were remarkable. The production of magnetos was multiplied a hundred-fold; the research on alloy and steel, the development of strong lightweight metal tubing,

[1] Ibid. Vol. IV, Pt. IV, p. 34.
[2] Ibid. Vol. VII, Pt. I, p. 35.
[3] Ibid. Vol. XI, Pt. III, p. 9.
[4] Ibid. Vol. XII, Pt. I, pp. 174–5.

and of petrol-resistant rubber tubing, and the improvement in the quality of oil and petrol are all of permanent value to industry.[1]

Hardly less important than the new methods, new equipment and new industries was a new approach to the working population. British industrialists on the whole had inherited from the first industrial revolution an attitude of irresponsible exploitation of their workpeople. Few British firms imitated the paternalism of European industries, which often supplied welfare, medical care and even housing to their employees. The Ministry of Munitions opened canteens, medical centres, sports clubs and even crêches in the factories. The yard stand-pipe and a bucket gave way to wash-rooms and laundries. In Lloyd George's own words in February 1916:

> It is a strange irony, but no small compensation, that the making of weapons of destruction should afford the occasion to humanise industry. Yet such is the case. Old principles have vanished, new ideas are abroad: employees and workers, the public and the State, are favourable to new methods. This opportunity must not be allowed to let slip.[2]

The resolve to carry forward what had been begun under the pressure of war was true of the entire field of British and imperial power. From 1916 onwards imperial statesmen and committees or commissions of enquiry alike struck the same note – national and imperial renewal and development on a vast scale. As Walter Long, the Colonial Secretary, told the delegates to the Imperial War Conference of 1918, '. . . this war has already produced a new birth for the British Empire . . .'[3] And he went on: '. . . our duty certainly is to see that we take full advantage of our vast [economic] opportunities, that we make for the future what I venture to describe as a better use of our Great Possessions than we have made in the past'.[4]

In Britain itself there was the question of continuing in peacetime the second industrial revolution begun since 1915. A report in 1916 on British trade after the war made recommendations for protecting the new and still fragile home industries against foreign competition. It suggested that much more public money should be devoted to scientific and technical research.[5] In 1918 the Committee on Commercial and Industrial Policy, in its interim report on certain essential industries, seemed to sweep away the taboos of Victorian *laissez-faire* liberalism for good. It

[1] *Hist. Min. Mun.*, Vol. VIII, Pt. I, p. 35.
[2] Lloyd George, p. 210.
[3] Cd. 9177, p. 11.
[4] Ibid. p. 12.
[5] Cd. 8181 and Cd. 8275.

recommended a 'Special Industries Board' to keep a watch on industrial development and itself promote the production of strategically essential goods. The Board should offer State backing to efficient firms, and 'failing efficient and adequate output, the Government should itself undertake the manufacture of such articles as may be essential for national safety'.[1]

In its final report, the Committee considered the future of British industry in terms of commercial competitiveness as well as of capacity for war. Its recommendations, echoing as they did all the other solemn warnings about British inefficiency back to the 1860s, were drafted when the fright of 1914–15 was still vivid in the memory.

> It is in our opinion a matter of vital importance that, alike in the old-established industries and in the new branches of manufacture which have arisen during the war, both employer and employed should make every effort to attain the largest possible volume of production, by the increased efficiency of industrial organisation and processes, by more intensive working, and by the adoption of the best and most economical methods of distribution.
>
> [And] it is only by the attainment of this maximum production and efficiency that we can hope to secure a speedy recovery of the industrial and financial position of the United Kingdom and assure its economic stability and progress.[2]

Overseas, the neglected resources of the empire were to be systematically exploited by new imperial organisations. This purpose found voluminous expression in the *Final Report of the Dominions Royal Commission* in 1917. First, a great survey of imperial resources was needed, especially a co-ordinated exploration of mineral riches. Then the resources should be developed and exploited under the guidance of an Imperial Development Board.[3] This Board should consist of seven members from the United Kingdom (which would also represent India and the colonial empire) and one each from the dominions.[4] 'It is impossible to overrate the importance', stated the Report, 'of securing to all parts of Your Majesty's Empire adequate facilities for scientific research in connection with the development of their natural resources. . . .'[5]

Throughout its report, the Dominions Royal Commission emphasised the need for closer cohesion between the different parts of the empire – the making good of now inadequate imperial services, such as telegraphic, cable, mail and maritime communications; harbours and waterways on

[1] Cd. 9032, pp. 11–12.
[2] Ibid. p. 23.
[3] Cd. 8462, pp. 70–5.
[4] Ibid. p. 162.
[5] Ibid. p. 82.

main imperial arteries; news distribution; marketing of imperial products; and the utilisation of capital for development.[1]

The same theme of an empire that had been shocked by the impact of war into the repair of immense neglect inspired the Imperial War Conferences of 1917 and 1918. The Conference of 1917 resolved that an Imperial Mineral Resources Bureau should be set up.[2] It took note of the dangerous dependence of the whole empire on Britain as its single industrial base:

> . . . this Conference, in view of the experience of the present War, calls attention to the importance of developing an adequate capacity of production of naval and military material, munitions and supplies in all important parts of the Empire (including the countries bordering on the Pacific and Indian Oceans) where such facilities do not presently exist. . . .[3]

The empire, the conference also agreed, should supply its own food, and possess the means of transportation to distribute it. It should control its own natural resources, especially where essential to independence in peace or war, and be able to process these resources itself.[4]

The theme of closer unity equally inspired discussions of imperial defence. The war – the German High Seas Fleet and the U-boat – had brought home how all parts of the empire depended for life on seapower. There was therefore a fresh willingness on the part of the dominions to consider ways of taking some of the cost and responsibility of seapower off Britain's shoulders. The Imperial War Conference of 1917 resolved: 'That the Admiralty be requested to work out immediately after the conclusion of the War what they consider the most effective scheme of Naval Defence for the Empire for the consideration of the several Governments summoned to this Conference. . . .'[5]

In the highest branch of strategy too – the conduct of imperial policy – the Great War stimulated close co-operation between the governments of the empire. In 1914 Britain had declared war on Germany on behalf of the whole empire, an expression of the fact that while the dominions were self-governing at home, foreign policy was in the hands of the 'Imperial' Foreign Office in Whitehall. However the contribution of powerful expeditionary forces by the dominions inevitably carried with it the desire and the right to participate in the making of strategy and high policy; and the result was the Imperial War Cabinet, the 'Cabinet of Governments' as Sir Robert Borden, Prime Minister of Canada, had dubbed it,[6] Clearly

1 Cd. 8462, p. 159.
2 Cd. 8566, p. 6.
3 Ibid.
4 Ibid.
5 Ibid. p. 4.
6 Cd. 9177, p. 158.

Britain and the dominions could not revert to the old relationship after the war. For, as W. M. ('Billy') Hughes, the Prime Minister of Australia, expressed it, the Imperial War Cabinet, where government met government face to face, was 'a growth, a development, of the Imperial relation, to which the old formulas of administration and the old methods of correspondence are no longer applicable, and that new formulas and new methods must be developed to bring the machinery of governments into harmony with the realities'.[1]

However, it had been recognised at the Imperial War Conference of 1917 that the readjustment of the relations between Britain and the dominions was too important and too delicate a question to be settled in the middle of a war, and should be left for a special imperial constitutional conference as soon as possible after victory. The delegates nevertheless placed on record their view that any further constitution of the empire 'should recognise the right of the Dominions and India to an adequate voice in foreign policy and foreign relations, and should provide effective arrangements for continuous consultation in all important matters of common Imperial concern, and for such necessary concerted action, founded on consultation, as the several Governments may determine'.[2]

Thus even the supreme aim of the old proponents of imperial federation seemed within reach – not federation itself, certainly, but a single imperial foreign policy for which Britain and the dominions would share responsibility.

With so much accomplished during the war, and with such far-reaching plans afoot, it was scarcely surprising that the prime ministers at the Imperial War Conference of 1918 all expressed in their opening speeches passionate pride in the empire, belief in its strength, and brilliant optimism about its future growth.[3]

Yet there was an ambiguity about all the wartime achievements. Underneath the very unity of the empire which so inspired the speech-makers, the pre-war currents of dominion nationalism and separatism were still running deep and strong, especially in Canada and South Africa. Thus during the discussions on imperial naval defence at the War Conference of 1917, these dominions had emphasised local interests and autonomy, and displayed a marked aversion to joining large collective schemes, whereas Australia and, even more so, New Zealand had taken a more 'imperial' view.[4] And it was at General Smuts' (South Africa)

[1] Ibid. p. 155. [2] Cd. 8566, p. 5. [3] Cd. 9177, pp. 11–20.

[4] See Minutes of Proceedings, 4th and 5th days of the 1917 Imperial War Conference, 28 and 30 March, CAB 32/1/1, pp. 53–82.

insistence, backed by Borden of Canada, that the same conference added to its resolution postponing constitutional change until after the war, a statement that emphasised not the existence of the empire as a whole, but the separate existence of its parts: 'They [the delegates] deem it their duty, however, to place on record their view that any such [constitutional] readjustment, while thoroughly preserving all existing powers of self-government and complete control of domestic affairs, should be based upon the full recognition of the Dominions as autonomous nations of an Imperial Commonwealth. . . .'[1]

There was ambiguity too in wartime economic progress. There was, so far, immensely more of good intention than of accomplishment in the common exploitation of the empire's resources. The wartime renaissance of British technology, magnificent emergency attempt to repair the effects of seventy years of neglect and complacency though it was, marked only a beginning to the colossal task of hauling the whole industrial machine out of the mid-Victorian era. The new industries that had been created since 1915 would need careful nursing and protection if foreign competition were not again to reduce Britain to a technological colony. All in all, therefore, although Britannia had been rescued from liberalism by the Great War, it was always possible that she might abandon the hard road of rehabilitation and return to her old life.

And the British and imperial effort in the Great War had not at all altered the fundamental anomalies and weaknesses in British power. The empire remained, on balance, a colossal burden: there was India and the strategic over-extension it involved; there was the colonial empire, small return for much responsibility; there were the 'white' dominions, incapable of their own defence and yet contributing per head a fraction of what the British paid out to defend everybody under the Union flag.

Finally, and despite victory, there was an uncertainty about the future of British power that had nothing to do with the state of health of that power in itself. No man could predict how long it would be before fresh dangers arose to threaten the British Empire somewhere – or even everywhere – in its vast, vulnerable sprawl across the globe.

It all came to this: British responsibilities vastly exceeded British strength. This was not power but weakness. Responsibilities and strength therefore needed urgently to be brought into a proper ratio – either by developing the empire's strength and cohesion; or by shedding such imperial responsibilities as were unprofitable or potentially dangerous.

[1] Cd. 8566, p. 5.

# IV

# IV · AN IMPERIAL COMMONWEALTH

> . . . we have here by far the largest of all political questions, for if our Empire is capable of further development, we have the problem of discovering what direction that development should take, and if it is a mischievous encumbrance, we have the still more anxious problem of getting rid of it, and in either case we deal with territories so vast and populations which grow so rapidly that their destinies are infinitely important.

This penetrating analysis of the single problem that bore most of all on the future of British power was even more apt in the 1920s than when first written by Sir John Seeley as far back as 1883.[1]

Of the alternatives Seeley bluntly stated, that of getting rid of the empire – or parts of it – was never entertained by those who played the leading roles in British life between 1919 and 1939, although in the nineteenth century liberals had wished the empire away on practical grounds. As Gladstone had told an audience in 1879:

> . . . I wish to dissipate if I can the idle dreams of those who are always telling you that the strength of England depends, sometimes they say upon its prestige, sometimes they say upon extending its Empire, or upon what it possesses beyond these shores. Rely upon it the strength of Great Britain and Ireland is within the United Kingdom.[2]

By 1919, however, the existence of the British Empire had come to be accepted even by the Liberal and Labour parties. They now saw the empire as in a vision: a happy family of free peoples, a smaller league of nations; and the 'coloured' empire as inhabited by younger brethren whose future constituted for Britain a sacred and noble trust.[3] Under this trust – and also of course under an enlightened government – elder sister Britain would lead her brothers by the hand to independence within the Commonwealth. This happy day, when it eventually dawned, would not

[1] J. R. Seeley, *The Expansion of England* (London, Macmillan 1883), p. 192.
[2] Nicholas Mansergh, *The Commonwealth Experience* (London, Weidenfeld and Nicolson 1969), p. 126.
[3] Cf. the Labour Party's 1918 programme, quoted in Egon Wertheimer, *Portrait of the Labour Party* (London, Putnam 1929), pp. 59–60.

however mean the ending of British responsibilities, because the newly independent nations would still need the British armed forces to protect them. As Edwin Montagu, the Liberal Secretary of State for India from 1917 to 1922, wrote in the *Report on Indian Constitutional Reforms* in 1918, defence 'is the last duty of all which can be committed to inexperienced and unskilled hands'.[1]

Indeed, and especially among the truly blue, it was widely seen as a moral duty *not* to abandon the countries of the 'coloured' empire to get on with it as best they might. A former Lieutenant-Governor of the Punjab wrote in 1925 in regard to India that such an abandonment would be 'the greatest betrayal in history'.[2]

The empire, all shades of opinion were agreed therefore, was a high trust, rather than a mere source of wealth and power as our ancestors had seen it. In fact the combination of a cheerfully rapacious colonial past and a post-evangelical conscience gave the British a constant twinge of guilt – not the most effective inspiration of self-confident policy. As Sir Stanley Leathes, First Commissioner of the Civil Service Commission until 1929, told readers in his book, *The People of England*, though we had behaved badly in the past, we were making amends: '. . . we have reason to hope that the British empire as a house of peace, justice, and liberty, will be worthy of all the blood and tears that it has cost'.[3]

In this kind of mood, therefore, the thought of deliberately dismantling the empire, or portions of it, entered few heads. Equally there was no systematic attempt to dissect the anatomy of British power in order to determine which parts of the empire, if any, were showing – or could be made to show – a profit. For the British governing classes, true to their upbringing, saw the empire less as a strategic and economic enterprise than as a family estate which they had inherited, and from which derived their consequence in world society. They took their possession of this imperial estate as the most natural and unquestioned of things; and accepted as their duty the preservation of it as a whole, its improvement, and the passing on of it to their sons intact. Even the hour when the native peoples would be fit for self-government lay so distant as to be as devoid of practical implication as the Second Coming.

The British governing classes saw the native races of the colonial empire, therefore, rather as old family tenants or cottagers; as a responsibility,

[1] Cd. 9109, p. 130.
[2] Sir Michael O'Dwyer, *India As I Knew It 1885–1925* (London, Constable 1925), p. 412.
[3] Sir Stanley Leathes, *The People of England* (London, Heinemann 1920–2), Vol. II, p. 220.

rather than as instruments of British power. This attitude, coupled with the universal moralism, determined British colonial policy: the colonial empire existed first and foremost in the interests of its native peoples, not of Britain.

This was a fundamental principle, which in the words of one historian 'grew out of the circumstances and ideals of an earlier and easier age', with 'double parentage in the evangelical and free-trade movements'.[1] The principle was re-stated in 1923 under a Conservative Government with regard to India and Kenya:

> Principally, Kenya is an African territory and His Majesty's Government think it necessary to record their considered opinion that the interests of the African nation must be paramount . . . in the administration of Kenya His Majesty's Government regard themselves as exercising a trust on behalf of the African population . . . the object of which may be defined as the protection and advancement of the native races.[2]

In West Africa too, in the words of Sir George Fiddes, the Permanent Under-Secretary to the Colonial Office until 1928: 'The Colonial Office recognises two sets of clients . . . the natives and the merchants. If their interests clash, those of the natives must come first. . . .'[3]

Sir George Fiddes was aware that:

> It would be easy enough, with modern resources, to hold the country down; and it would not be difficult to obliterate all traces of native civilisation, and to impose on the inhabitants a parody of Western modes of life and habits. But if our ideal is to promote the evolution of the highest civilisation of which the native mind may be capable, it is only to be done – as it is being done – by a system of indirect rule [through the tribal chiefs].[4]

British colonial policy between the wars was therefore an essay in altruism. Yet however admirable the British respect for the cultures and personalities of the peoples under their rule, however Christian the British spirit of guardianship, British colonial policy was an absurdity when considered in terms of British power. The colonies were not so much an empire as the field for an overseas Toynbee Hall mission. The contrast with the colonial policies of the French, Dutch and Belgians was striking,

[1] W. K. Hancock, *Survey of British Commonwealth Affairs* (Oxford University Press 1942), Vol. II, Pt. I, p. 306.
[2] Cmd. 1922, p. 10.
[3] Sir George Fiddes, *The Dominions and Colonial Offices* (London, Putnam 1926), p. 153.
[4] Ibid. p. 147.

for it was the curious idea of these nations that the purpose of having an empire was to make the imperial power richer and stronger. As a British colonial servant wrote in 1947:

> British policy starts from the point that the African is the end in himself. . . . We may be muddlers but we see ourselves as Trustees who are to hand over their trust at the earliest practical moment. French policy, on the other hand, is not muddled, but it starts from the point that what matters most is not the African, but France. It never rids itself of preoccupation about military manpower, war supplies, strategic bases. The end is not the African but what he can contribute to France's political-military position as a World Power.[1]

The European colonial empires were great State enterprises, organised and directed from head office in pursuit of clear and logical policies; with efficient technical and medical services, and staffed by ambitious careerists thoroughly trained beforehand in colonial staff schools, men who were determined to turn their subject races as far as possible into their own national likenesses.[2]

The British colonial empire in the 1920s, on the other hand, had no 'policy' in the French sense: 'In my day', a colonial servant of the era told an American inquirer, 'we had not all forgotten Aristotle. I was continually asking, "What is the end or object of this endeavour?" But no one could or would give me an answer.'[3]

Such policy as there was originated less in clear strategic directives from the Colonial Office in London than from empirical decisions taken locally in the colonies. This was perhaps not surprising when the Permanent Under-Secretary at the Colonial Office from 1938 onwards, Sir Cosmo Parkinson, could assert in a book about the workings of the Colonial Office: 'Colonial Policy does not come within my present scope.'[4]

It was possible that Sir Cosmo, and perhaps his colleagues and predecessors too, thought that a clear policy was inherently a bad thing, for it was his belief that 'we think too much and feel too little. More than machinery we need humanity. More than cleverness we need kindness and gentleness'.[5]

These sentiments were shared by Sir Ralph Furse, who was in charge of

[1] W. R. Crocker, *On Governing Colonies* (London, Allen and Unwin 1947), pp. 139–40.
[2] See R. Heussler, *Yesterday's Rulers: The Making of the British Colonial Service* (New York, Syracuse University Press 1963), pp. 125, 210–16.
[3] Quoted in Heussler, p. 48.
[4] Sir Cosmo Parkinson, *The Colonial Office From Within 1909–1945* (London, Faber and Faber 1947).
[5] Ibid. p. 133.

recruitment to the colonial services from 1919 to 1948, a man who himself was, in one writer's judgement, 'a very largely unreconstructed Victorian country gentleman ... essentially an optimist and a humanist' whose view of civil service recruitment 'was moral, not scientific', and who remarked that Plato had been 'one of the main influences in his "religious life"'.[1] Furse had been at Balliol with Lord Milner, and his father-in-law was the poet and historian, Sir Henry Newbolt; he was therefore steeped in the romantic, chivalric imperialism of the late Victorian age. To staff the administration of the colonies, Furse and his colleagues looked for like-minded men 'from stock that has proved its worth, generation by generation, in the professions or in public service ... reared in the faith that duty and chivalry are of more account than ambition and self-seeking'.[2] The public schools provided just what Furse wanted; it was after all their purpose. So British colonial administrators were, in the words of the Warren Fisher Report on Recruitment to the Colonial Service in 1929, men of 'vision, high ideals of service, fearless devotion to duty born of a sense of responsibility, tolerance, and above all, the team spirit....'[3] In contrast to the French, who were always looking to Paris, they were immersed in the affairs and the peoples of their own colony, even their own district. A colonial policy in any sense of a broad conception was therefore no more likely to emerge from the colonies themselves than from the Colonial Office. On the contrary, in the words of one Cyprus and Gold Coast colonial servant: 'The best administrative officers were not those who had high-falutin' ideas [about policy] but who gave their whole minds to their daily chores – restraining here, encouraging there, advancing everywhere, with never a thought of the wider implications of their efforts.'[4]

The British colonial servants saw their task as one of efficient, fair public administration, of providing justice, law and order: the Roman imperial virtues. They tended to neglect – as did the Colonial Office itself – the modern importance of science and economics, subjects they understandably found alien and somewhat uncomfortable. Thus, although the British showed a far more tender regard for native culture than other colonial nations, British colonies were often backward in research and technical services, for the staffing of which British education in any case made small provision. In 1929 the Headmaster of Harrow, in a book on education – largely devoted to the importance therein of religion – noted that 'agriculture and production in the Dominions, and particularly the

[1] Heussler, pp. 68–70.
[2] Confidential *Appointments Handbook*, quoted in Heussler, p. 76.
[3] Cmd. 3554.
[4] Heussler, p. 216.

tropical dependencies, require the services of many trained biologists, botanists and zoologists, but they are not to be had. . . .'[1]

It was an example of this blind-spot in the British approach to colonies that, although it was in 1919 that they took over the former German colony of Tanganyika, they did not reopen the German tropical agriculture research station there until after 1927. British neglect of such technical services was compounded by the fragmentation of the colonial empire. The Committee on Colonial Scientific and Research Services reported in 1927: 'Science knows no boundaries, yet, broadly speaking, scientific investigation in the Colonial Empire depends upon the individual and unrelated efforts of over thirty distinct administrations.'[2]

Lack of research and development was one shackle on the economic exploitation of the colonies; the primacy given to the interests of the native was another shackle, and in some countries perhaps a more decisive one. Native systems of land-holding and cultivation, like peasant agriculture in Europe, were a barrier to a highly capitalised, highly efficient production. Nevertheless in British West Africa colonial governments twice, in 1907 and again in 1920, refused to allow Lord Leverhulme to set up the plantation system for the production of palm oil, under which the natives became workers on huge estates. A memorandum of 1926 by Sir Hugh Clifford, Governor of Nigeria, argued that it was 'fundamental doctrine' on moral grounds that native systems of land-holding should be protected. The only justification of British rule in the tropics, in his view, was the conferring on the native peoples of 'benefits they could not confer on themselves'. Therefore 'Land policy . . . should aim, primarily, mainly, and eventually at the development of the agricultural resources of these countries through the agency of their indigenous populations.'[3]

There was yet another shackle which the British – though again not the Europeans – forged on themselves in their colonies in the 1920s: Free Trade.

The restoration of Free Trade as an economic faith was one of the most disastrous aspects of a renewed triumph of liberal principles in British politics in the 1920s. Once the guns had ceased to fire, all the brave wartime plans and resolutions for collective imperial development and the modernisation of British industry were swiftly forgotten. For after a hundred years of liberal indoctrination the British had come to believe that war was a brief and meaningless breakdown in a natural order of

[1] Cyril Norwood, *The English Tradition in Education* (London, John Murray 1929), p. 256.
[2] Quoted in Cmd. 2883, p. 24.
[3] Memorandum of 21 March 1926, quoted in W. K. Hancock, Vol. II, pp. 192–3.

peace, rather than a facet of the continual struggle between nations, sometimes fought with diplomacy, sometimes with economic penetration, and sometimes, though more rarely, with armed forces. To the British, therefore, all the social, economic and technological lessons of the war had become irrelevant now that peacetime had returned. Thus the historian of a standard work on British Commonwealth economic affairs, writing in 1937–8, could speak sneeringly of the wartime plans for developing imperial self-sufficiency in strategic products after the war as 'the economics of siege ... affirmed as permanent policy on an imperial scale'.[1] However since his book was not published until 1942, in the middle of another war, he felt obliged in his preface to acknowledge: 'War quickly changes the perspective in which we see our problems, and – to take one example – it is improbable that I could today discuss the *Economics of Siege* exactly as I discussed them in 1937–8.'[2]

The Chancellor of the Exchequer between 1924 and 1929, whose financial policies determined the scope of British colonial development, was himself a prime example of this amnesia about the lessons of war. Although as the last Minister of Munitions he had presided over British war industry, Winston Churchill had now reverted to his late-Victorian Free Trade faith, and acted the part of Gladstone with his customary dramatic gusto. There was, therefore, no question of directing British trade, investment or purchase of raw materials to British colonies.

In various ways, therefore, the British forged such heavy shackles on their colonial policy that the most ardent ministers could achieve little. In 1919 for example Lord Milner obtained from the Treasury the far from colossal sum of £20,000 for agricultural and general research; in 1921 it was cut to £2,000 under the stringent economies known as the Geddes Axe.

It was L. S. Amery, Conservative Colonial Secretary from 1924 to 1929, who gave the greatest impetus to colonial development between the world wars. Amery had been a passionate imperialist and protectionist since a boy at Harrow in the late 1880s. During the Boer War, he had been a war correspondent and later wrote the brilliantly critical *Times History of the War*. Amery became an advocate of army reform and of conscription before 1914; and in the Great War served with gallantry and distinction as a subaltern. He was a short and stocky man, terrier-like in his bristling energy and ardent temperament. Yet he came of that late-Victorian vintage of romantic Englishmen. Like Churchill he was an adventurer, his imagination kindled by far-off peoples and distant lands.

[1] W. K. Hancock, Vol. II, p. 100.
[2] Ibid. p. vii.

On an official visit to Iraq in 1925, for example, he spent much time visiting the sites of ancient Mesopotamian civilisations, yet paid only a brief visit to the great oil refinery at Abadan, just over the Persian border, and England's principal stake in the Middle East.[1] His imperialism was more ethical than strategic, more visionary than calculating. Amery perhaps best expressed his own outlook by a comment on Israel in 1953:

> Much depends on the degree in which the restless energy and aggressive self-assurance of its people is tempered by those spiritual forces which have always inspired the Zionist movement. It is upon its influence as a cultural mission, far more than upon its effectiveness as a militarist colony, that the ultimate success of Zionism will depend.[2]

In the last resort, therefore, Amery, like so many of his class and generation – though not like Churchill – lacked the kind of ruthlessness that characterises, say, the great industrialists. Nevertheless he brought to the Colonial Office what it so often wanted – vigour and vision. It was Amery who began to remedy the scantiness of expert staff at the Colonial Office, by developing the post of Commercial Adviser (itself only set up after the Great War) into an economic and financial advisership, and by creating for the first time such essential posts as advisers on medicine, education, agriculture, fisheries and veterinary science. It was Amery who set up the Colonial Medical Research Committee in 1927 to widen and co-ordinate the work on tropical and other diseases, and on hygiene.

The centrepiece of Amery's administration was the Colonial Office Conference of 1927, which surveyed and discussed the whole field of colonial development, and to which the governments of every colony were invited. His main purpose was to win acceptance for the creation of a central research organisation and staff for the whole colonial empire, in the first place in regard to agriculture.[3]

In his opening address Amery pointed out that agriculture, transport, trade and marketing as well as the various branches of science needed co-ordination on an imperial scale. Yet he shrank from a thorough-going reorganisation of the Colonial Office and all the separate colonies into one centrally directed enterprise, like a world company, or indeed the French and Dutch empires. Instead there would be the old British painless cure-all – consultation and co-operation by conference.[4] His address also showed

[1] L. S. Amery, *My Political Life* (London, Hutchinson 1953), Vol. II, p. 316.
[2] Ibid. Vol. III, p. 116.
[3] Diary for 27 May 1929, L. S. Amery Papers.
[4] Cmd. 2883, especially p. 6.

how little the wartime intentions of a great programme to exploit the colonies had been fulfilled in ten years:

> There is real consciousness of the fact that we have immense underdeveloped resources which science, and science alone, can bring to rapid development. Now it is just here where our system of watertight compartments fails most strikingly. . . . You must give the scientist a career . . . in the sense of a field of work wide enough and varied enough to call the best out of each man. Now our present system does not offer such a career.[1]

But Amery was defeated in his main objective. The colonial governments would only accept the idea of a central research organisation 'in principle'; hardly a significant advance. The colonial governments were reluctant to join the Empire Marketing Board scheme even to the extent of contributing one quarter of one per cent of their revenues in order to finance, as a first step, a higher agricultural research service. It was an incredible situation: the minister responsible for the colonial empire thwarted by his own agents, and those agents not acting like a common board of Englishmen studying how to make the most of an empire, but rather like representatives of independent nations at an international conference.[2]

The conference also displayed a characteristic public-school-educated ignorance of, and distaste for, modern mass communications, for its discussion of this topic hinged on the negative question of censorship instead of on the immense possibilities of influencing the minds of subject peoples by systematic British propaganda through the radio and film.[3]

Amery however, a man always romantically prone to look on the bright side and search diligently for the silver lining, recorded in his diary: 'Thus ended a most successful experiment. The Colonial Office Conference has come to stay and meanwhile it has already achieved, I think, the one thing I had particularly in my mind in summoning it, namely the acceptance of the principle of a joint fund and a joint service.'[4]

Despite Amery's enthusiastic idealism about the empire, he failed to set the colonial empire on a new course during his term of office. Apart from piecemeal reforms and innovations, his most notable achievement was perhaps the eventual creation in the 1930s of a single colonial service, as a result of the report by a committee (the Warren Fisher Committee) appointed by him to consider recruitment. And despite a second Colonial

[1] Ibid. p. 9. [2] See Amery, Vol. II, p. 339 et seq. [3] Cmd. 2883, pp. 164–7, 242–8.
[4] Diary for 31 May 1927, L. S. Amery Papers.

Office Conference in 1930, only more piecemeal improvements to an unreconstructed and haphazard structure marked further progress before the Second World War. Thus the Department of Animal Health in the Gold Coast, only set up in the 1930s, had a staff of just eight in 1940. In 1940 Nigeria, England's largest and most populous West African colony, possessed only a 'skeleton Department of Geological Survey'.[1]

In the twenty years which divided the world wars, the British therefore, failed to make the colonial empire much more of an asset than it had been in 1918.

In Nigeria, for example, as a result of the government's refusal to sanction the plantation system, exports of palm-oil just doubled between 1906 and 1936, while in the Belgian Congo exports rose ten times between 1909–14 and 1924–8; and again three-fold in the next eight years.[2] In any case, Britain took only 36½ per cent of Nigeria's exports of palm-oil in 1936, while Germany took 44 per cent.[3]

Malaya remained the richest British colony and therefore equipped with the most sophisticated government services. Before the great slump of 1930–1 Malaya's total trade exceeded that of all other colonies combined.[4] Even in 1938, after the American depression had hit rubber production, Malaya's trade was greater than that of New Zealand or of all the colonies in Africa put together.[5] Malayan tin and rubber were among the empire's principal earners of dollars. Yet even Malaya was a surprisingly neglected and wasted asset. In 1914 four-fifths and in 1941 still one-third of the tin mining was in Chinese hands;[6] and while Malaya produced 31 per cent of the world's supplies of tin, and smelted most of it herself, Britain took only a tenth of her exports.[7] It was the Japanese, not the British, who began mining iron ore in Malaya.[8] And although Malaya produced 56 per cent of the world's rubber, Britain drew a fifth of her supplies from foreign sources.[9]

Although the British Empire was far from self-supporting in petroleum, Britain took only 36 per cent of Trinidad's exports and a very small part of Sarawak's.[10] As a Study Group of the Royal Institute of International Affairs noted in 1937: 'The United Kingdom, which does not seek to monopolise her colonial trade (in spite of the preferences adopted in the last few years), does not purchase from her colonies all raw materials

1 W. K. Hancock, Vol. II, p. 264.
2 Ibid. p. 195.
3 Ibid. p. 337, Appendix B.
4 Sir Richard Winstedt, *Britain and Malaya* (London, Longmans Green 1964), p. 108.
5 Ibid.
6 Ibid. p. 119.
7 Royal Institute of International Affairs, *The Colonial Problem* (London, Oxford University Press 1937), p. 317.
8 Winstedt, *Britain and Malaya*, p. 120.
9 RIIA, *The Colonial Problem*, p. 317.
10 Ibid.

she needs, even where the colonies could supply her in the full.'[1] In 1925–9 the colonial empire provided Britain with 5·4 per cent of its food and tobacco and 8 per cent of its raw materials; in 1935 with 7·9 per cent and 11·1 per cent.[2]

The extent of the continued neglect by the British of their own possessions between the world wars was demonstrated during the Second World War, when belated and hasty attempts had to be made to replace lost foreign supplies from empire sources. Sierra Leone, for example, expanded her production of iron ore from 190,000 tons in 1939 to 920,000 tons in 1941, while German occupation of France and Greece in 1940–1 forced Britain to turn to the Gold Coast and British Guiana for bauxite, the raw material of aluminium.[3]

Not only had the British failed to exploit their colonies like the French, Belgians or Dutch, but in peacetime they exercised less control over their colonial resources than Germany enjoyed over the resources of the small foreign countries of the Balkans as the result of her deliberate strategy of economic penetration.[4]

And whereas in the 1930s the fifty million people of the colonial empire only furnished armed forces to a total of 13,000 men, these forces were not available in any case for general British purposes outside their own territories.

Except for the Union flag flying above the white verandas of Government House, and for the exile of some of the best of England's scarce educated talent in jungle or desert, the colonies, in terms of British power, really differed in peacetime little from foreign countries. The principal practical difference lay in that the colonies – unlike foreign countries – swallowed up more than a sixth of the British army in garrison duties: a sixth therefore of the land force available to back British foreign policy throughout the world.[5]

Sir John Seeley's statement in 1883 that the greatest question before the British people was whether the empire was capable of further development, and if so, what kind of development, or whether it was 'a mischievous encumbrance', in which case 'we have the still more anxious problem of getting rid of it', was even more true of India after the Great War than of the colonial empire. In return for all that immense and

[1] Ibid. [2] Ibid. pp. 291–2.
[3] J. Hurstfield, *The Control of Raw Materials* (London, HMSO 1953), pp. 155–6.
[4] Ibid. p. 17.
[5] D. H. Cole, *Imperial Military Geography* (London, Sifton Praed 1938), p. 30.

potentially dangerous commitment to the Middle East and southern Asia because of India, England benefited by a market for the Lancashire cotton industry, by a major source of jute and a minor source of some minerals, and, in the greatest war she had ever fought, by some 74,000 extra soldiers for her struggle in Europe.[1] And in peacetime the field army of India amounted to no more than four divisions ill-equipped for European war, while the British forces in India amounted to some 60,000 men – nearly a third of the British army.[2] Nor was India an essential British base. Lord Derby, the Secretary of State for War, told the Imperial Conference in 1923: 'I should like to emphasise here the fact that we do not look upon, and never have looked upon, India as being the base of an Expeditionary Force, and the Force that we maintain there has been for the purpose of defending India against external attack and of providing internal security.'[3]

India was like a colossal mansion standing in the middle of a vast but ill-cultivated estate; it conferred prestige, it made the owners feel grand, and, by the cost of its upkeep, threatened them with ruin. For how could a nation of only 45,000,000 people, an industrial power not only outmatched in size but in performance by great rivals, find the diplomatic and strategic strength to carry India without dangerously weakening itself? 'It may be fairly questioned', Sir John Seeley had written more than thirty years earlier, 'whether the possession of India does or ever can increase our power and our security, while there is no doubt that it vastly increases our dangers and responsibilities.'[4]

Militarily there was no more to be got out of India. The Indian army in any case drew its strength from a fraction of the population, and from certain limited areas. The Simon Commission (Indian Statutory Commission) in its report in 1930 noted: 'The Punjab supplies 54 per cent of the total combatant troops of the Indian Army and, if the 19,000 Gurkhas recruited from the independent State of Nepal are excluded, the Punjab contingent amounts to 62 per cent of the whole Indian Army.'[5] As a result of the unwitting historical process by which the British had come to unify India, they were therefore maintaining an empire of more than twenty times the area of the British Isles, with 320,000,000 inhabitants, in which the provinces of Bombay and Madras were each bigger in extent than Italy,[6] solely for the sake, in terms of apparent military advantage, of

[1] See above pp. 76–80.
[2] Cole, p. 30; Colonel G. M. Orr, 'The Military Forces in India', *Army Quarterly*, Vol. XVIII, No. 2 (July 1929), pp. 384–95.
[3] CAB 32/9, E-10, p. 11.
[4] Seeley, p. 13.
[5] Cmd. 3568, p. 96.
[6] Ibid. pp. 10–11.

one province; and equipping the Indian army remained a burden on British industry, since the wartime intentions of developing war industries in India swiftly flagged in the post-war atmosphere of eternal peace and harmony.

Even had the British governing classes thought in terms of a colossal economic transformation of India, their powers of bringing it about were limited. The Indian Mutiny had shown the dangers that a small occupying force ran in trying to interfere with deeply entrenched prejudices, customs and patterns of life. It took the power and ruthlessness of the eighteenth-century landowners in England or the Soviet régime in Russia to prise the peasant off his patch and introduce highly capitalised large-scale agriculture, while at the same time creating new industries for the dispossessed peasant to work in. 'Five Year Plans' for India were simply not in the British mind. The corset of good and honest government and the benefit of public works, particularly irrigation schemes on a large scale, were as much as the British could hope to achieve, and as much as their imagination compassed. Only the Labour Party thought of Indian problems primarily in economic terms, and then not from the point of view of British advantage.

There was small prospect, therefore, of India ever being much more valuable to England than it was in 1918. India was indeed 'a mischievous encumbrance', to be rid of with all convenient speed. Self-interest thus chimed with the long-stated hope of British policy in India, which was, as Macaulay expressed it in a famous speech in the House of Commons on 10 July 1833, 'that the public mind of India may expand under our system till it has outgrown that system; that by good government we may educate our subjects into a capacity for better government; that, having become instructed in European knowledge, they may, in some future age, demand European institutions. . . .' When that happened, it would be, in Macaulay's opinion, 'the proudest day in English History'.[1]

Yet during and after the Great War the British governing classes failed to perceive that self-interest demanded the handing over of India to some Indian régime as quickly as it could be arranged. It was a curious aspect of all the thorough official investigations of the problem of India from 1917 to 1933, and of all the prolonged political debate, that while the British amassed the evidence that India was an encumbrance, they yet failed to draw the obvious conclusion. The Montagu–Chelmsford Report of 1918 (*Report on Indian Constitutional Reforms*) referred to India's dependence 'for her internal and external security upon the army and the navy of the

[1] Hansard, *Parliamentary Debates* (House of Commons), Third Series, Vol. 19, col. 536.

United Kingdom'.[1] The Simon Commission, in its recommendations in 1930, wrote:

> The objects for which the Army in India exists are the defence of India against external aggression and the maintenance of internal order. ... We are assured that the size of the Army in India is not artificially enlarged with a view to making some portion of it available for service elsewhere....[2]

In December 1934 Sir Samuel Hoare, the then Secretary of State for India, told the House of Commons categorically that: 'As things are now, India is not in a position to defend itself. A great part of the defence of India is dependent on British troops.'[3]

What made India even more of a drain on the British military strength available to back British foreign policy was the swallowing up of British soldiers in the maintenance of internal law and order. This too was recognised:

> It is a striking fact in this connection [noted the Simon Commission], that while in the regular units of the Army in India as a whole British troops are in a minority of about 1 : 2½, in the troops allotted for internal security the preponderance is reversed, and for this purpose a majority of British troops is employed ... about eight British to seven Indian soldiers....[4]

In all the parliamentary debates on India too it was also acknowledged, even by the die-hard opponents of Indian self-government like Churchill, that India was more of a burden than an asset. Churchill, for example, told the House of Commons on 11 February 1935 during the debate on the Second Reading of the Government of India Bill that if British protection and security 'are withdrawn and this external aid withheld, India will descend, not quite into the perils of Europe, but into the squalor and anarchy of India in the sixteenth and seventeenth centuries'.[5]

The fact that India was a liability was thus perceived; why then was the apparently obvious deduction not made? Why, indeed, in the face of this fact was so much of British opinion in favour of delaying Indian independence until some cloudy future time?

The British thought perhaps even less clearly about India than about

[1] Cd. 9109, p. 139. [2] Cmd. 3569, p. 171.
[3] Hansard, *Parliamentary Debates* (House of Commons), Vol. 296, col. 52.
[4] Cmd. 3568, p. 95.
[5] Hansard, *Parliamentary Debates* (House of Commons), Third Series, Vol. 297, col. 1654.

their other problems. They found it possible at one and the same time to recognise that India was a burden and yet feel deeply that it was the key to Britain's place as a world power. Churchill himself was a fine example of this ambivalence, for on the one hand he could admit that India was so feeble as to depend entirely on British aid and protection (see above), while on the other asserting that she was 'that most truly bright and precious jewel on the crown of the King, which more than all our other Dominions and Dependencies constituted the glory and the strength of the British Empire. . . .'[1] The Simon Commission in its recommendations of 1930 could argue that '. . . the effective defence of India is a matter in which other parts of the Empire are also closely and directly interested. Imperial foreign policy, Empire communications, Empire trade, the general position of Britain in the East may be vitally affected.'[2] Here again was the imperial arch, of which India was the keystone, that existed solely in order to support the keystone.

The British could be even more illogical; they could, and did, argue that it was the fact that India was a strategic liability which constituted the clinching reason for Britain not to leave India. The Montagu–Chelmsford Report of 1918, for example, asserted: 'The defence of India is an Imperial question; and for this reason the [British] Government of India must retain both the power and the means of discharging its responsibilities for the defence of the country and to the Empire as a whole.'[3] In 1930 the Simon Commission thought similarly: 'We hold that for many years the presence of British troops, and British officers serving in Indian regiments, will be essential.'[4] And since the army in India was the only effective barrier between India and the dangers without her gates: 'We regard it as beyond question that, having regard to the Indian and Imperial interests involved, to the dangers to be faced, and to the composition of this force, Parliament cannot wash its hands of all responsibility for this Army.'[5] And that meant, of course, responsibility for the government of India as well.

Thus the British constructed their own illogical dilemma and locked themselves up in it: India was a liability; therefore we could not abandon it. Or, to put it in another way, even if *we* had no need of India, India had need of us, and we ought to fulfil that need even at our own cost.

For in the last resort the place of India in the British mind was founded not upon calculation but upon love. India, and life in India, induced the British upper-middle and upper classes to bloom. Nothing made the

[1] Speech in 1935, quoted in K. Middlemass and J. Barnes, *Baldwin: A Biography* (London, Weidenfeld and Nicolson 1969), p. 583.
[2] Cmd. 3569, p. 174. [3] Cd. 9109, p. 130. [4] Cmd. 3569, p. 21. [5] Ibid. p. 168.

British *feel* so imperial as India, especially when their romantic souls were fed on the odd durbar, an expedition to Kabul or Lhasa, and on the writings of Rudyard Kipling or even Henty.

And nothing could *be* more imperial than India: the frontiers on the snows of the Himalayas and the dun hills of Afghanistan; the teeming peoples who looked to Englishmen for protection, order and justice; the splendid ceremonial pomp of viceregal entertainment and public progress; the tributary princes, fantastic with riches and cruelties and with a pageantry at once extravagant and absurd; the roads and railways and bridges built by British engineers which, running for thousands of miles, laced together the whole diverse and mutually hostile races and cultures; the cantonments where a third of the British army was stationed at any one time; the legend of the North-West Frontier, and the continual skirmishing with the barbarous border tribes who threatened the imperial peace; the stinks and clamour and spicy smells of the bazaars; the freshness of the countryside in the early morning when the British administrator rode out to give justice to the simple people of the villages; hill stations cool and damp under the deodars trying to provide exiles with the sensation that they were for the moment back in Surrey or Scotland; and far below in the plains the summer heat lying on the sub-continent like a brand.

The vested interest of the British governing classes in India was not only a matter of myth, legend and the imagination however. There was their vested interest in their achievement, great as it was: India, once a turmoil of anarchy and war, united; India, once a stew of corruption, oppression and incompetence, under efficient, honest government; India, once dark with religious and racial hatred, at peace under the Crown. It was hard, perhaps impossible, for them to contemplate abandoning this achievement in cold blood, possibly – as they feared – to decay and collapse under an Indian régime.

And India represented above any other 'coloured' possession the obligations of imperial service and those opportunities for advancement and honour for which the late-Victorian public school was the designed preparation. The Indian army needed officers; the administration needed men with good degrees in the classics; heathendom and 'white' exiles alike needed clergymen. For all there was the chance of living like an aristocracy: grand receptions, field sports, the elegant social round, or, for those who preferred it, a lonely life in the open air. There was also the chance of becoming aristocrats in fact, when dutiful service merited the honour of knighthood in the Order of the Indian Empire, or the Order of the

Star of India. India loomed even larger in the life of the British governing classes than the number of Britons in the senior ranks of the administration[1] might indicate. There were the British staffs of business firms; tea-planters in Assam and Ceylon; there were the British officers of the Indian army, while every officer of the British army too was almost bound to spend part of his career in India. In England itself there were the colonies of retired 'Indians', with their houses full of Indian mementoes and their conversations over-full of Indian memories. Everybody in the British governing classes had a friend or a relative who had been in India, was in India, or was going to India. India then was a habit, a custom, part of the texture of their way of life. It was therefore little wonder that to the British governing classes, India, and all the responsibilities attached to India, seemed, in Curzon's words, 'the biggest thing that the British are doing anywhere'.[2]

And so they could not tear India out of themselves. For the clue to all the agonising of the British over India between the world wars was that, whatever their political differences of opinion, they were thinking primarily not of British interests, but of Indian interests, as they conceived them. That this was so is particularly shown by the parliamentary debates on India and Indian constitutional reform; for example, during the passage of the Government of India Bill in 1935. The Labour Party alone among the three main parties advocated giving India her independence as soon as possible. Attlee argued: 'India should have charge of her own foreign affairs. We should lay down a definite term for the Indianisation of the army. . . .'[3]

However, this implied no acknowledgement that British interests would best be served by shedding India, for Attlee's speech was really devoted to the question of social injustice in India, a phenomenon which in his opinion British law and order had served to preserve, and which could only be abolished by an Indian Government. The Labour Party thus advocated what was for Britain the right policy, but for irrelevant reasons.

What was more surprising than Labour's neglect of British interests is that Winston Churchill, then so far on the Right of the Conservative Party as to be considered 'a wild man', also chose as his theme the welfare of the Indian masses. He laid oddly little emphasis on British power and British strategic needs.[4] In the violent debate on the Third Reading of the Bill Churchill argued that India required efficient, honest British autocracy

[1] 3,500 according to the census of 1921, quoted in Cmd. 3568, p. 46.
[2] Mansergh, *The Commonwealth Experience*, p. 256.
[3] Hansard, *Parliamentary Debates* (House of Commons), Vol. 296, cols. 62–3.
[4] Ibid. col. 451.

more than ever.[1] And while in his peroration he hoped that, in the government cheers when the Bill received its huge majority would not 'mingle the knell of the British Empire in the East', it was still the good of India, rather than India's usefulness to Britain which remained his dominating theme.[2]

Moral idealism not only prevented the British from leaving India between the world wars, it also created the peculiarly disadvantageous circumstances in which they stayed on. For it was the moral idealism of the liberals – first of the Liberal Party proper, and later of liberals in the Labour and Conservative parties – which gratuitously helped in raising up Indian discontent and the demand for independence in Britain's face.

British higher education in India in the nineteenth century was a smudgy copy of the English public school and Oxford and Cambridge. It therefore turned out not the engineers, scientists and technicians which India needed, with its lack of industry and its desperately backward agriculture, but unemployables of 'liberal' education, good at best for low-grade clerking, but believing themselves to be a deprived élite – apt material for political dreaming and scheming. This was what Macaulay meant by expanding the Indian public mind. The form of British education in India was a fundamental mistake. As the chief executive of a great American company, long resident in India, told an American journalist in the 1920s: 'If I were running this country, I'd close every university tomorrow. It was a crime to teach them to be clerks, lawyers and politicians till they'd been taught to raise food.'[3]

Having created an intelligentsia, the British proceeded to encourage it, step by step, to entertain larger and arger political ambitions. In 1884, under a Liberal viceroy, Lord Ripon, acting as the agent of Gladstone's second administration, Indians were given some voice in local government. In the next year an Englishman, Allan Octavian Hume, a former senior official of the government of India, and two other Englishmen convened the first Indian National Congress by writing letters to all the graduates of Calcutta University asking for fifty people to join a movement for the regeneration of India. Henceforth the unemployable and politicised Indian intelligentsia had something to do. Within twenty years the Congress movement had captured the urban Indian middle classes. It could pretend to speak for India, and did so with passionate verbosity. The rise of the Congress party and with it widespread political agitation was accompanied by a wave of political murder.[4]

[1] Hansard, *Parliamentary Debates* (House of Commons), Vol. 296, col. 1921.

[2] Ibid. col. 1925.

[3] Katharine Mayo, *Mother India* (London, Jonathan Cape 1927), p. 200.

[4] Vincent A. Smith, *The Oxford History of India* (Oxford, The Clarendon Press 1958), p. 772.

The British had thus assisted in bringing about a problem for themselves with which they now had to deal. Lord Morley, a Gladstonian Liberal, and Secretary of State for India in the Liberal administration of 1906, thought that the answer was to attach Indian nationalism to the British *Raj* by giving it a greater voice in government. The reforms of 1909, which he evolved in collaboration with the then viceroy, Lord Minto, therefore provided a majority of elected Indian members on provisional councils (assemblies). Far from associating Indian politicians with British rule, however, as Morley had optimistically hoped, his reforms provided instead an official platform for systematic criticism of British policy and subversion of British authority. Yet Liberals saw their fostering of Indian nationalism as an achievement. As Edwin Montagu, then the Parliamentary Under-Secretary of State for India, told the House of Commons in July 1910: 'When we came into India we found that the characteristic of Indian thought was an excessive reverence for authority. . . .' and '. . . when we . . . deliberately embarked on a policy of educating the peoples on Western lines, we caused the unrest because we wished to colour Indian ideals with Western aspirations. . . .'[1]

In fact: 'I think we can regard political unrest in India as being the manifestation of a movement of Indian thought which has been inspired, directly and indirectly, by English ideals, to which the English and the Government of India themselves gave the first impetus.'[2]

The Indian nationalism which liberals had fostered was now beginning to gather a momentum of its own. Yet – so far – liberals had no intention of relinquishing the British hold on India. On the contrary, Morley himself told the House of Lords in 1909: 'If I were attempting to set up a Parliamentary system in India, or if it could be said that this chapter of reforms led directly or necessarily up to the establishment of a Parliamentary system in India, I, for one, would have nothing at all to do with it.'[3]

Morley, incredibly enough, intended his reforms to help preserve the British *Raj*, a hope whose naïveté drew upon him a blast of realism from the viceroy, Lord Minto:

> . . . when you say that 'if reforms do not save the *Raj* nothing else will' I am afraid I must utterly disagree. The *Raj* will not disappear in India as long as the British race remains what it is, because we shall fight for the *Raj* as hard as we have ever fought, if it comes to fighting, and we shall win as we have always won.[4]

[1] S. D. Waley, *Edwin Montagu* (London, Asia Publishing House 1964), p. 41.
[2] Ibid. p. 42.
[3] Mansergh, *The Commonwealth Experience*, p. 249.
[4] Ibid. p. 13.

By the Great War therefore the idealism of the liberals had led them into a fine dilemma; they had nourished an Indian nationalism whose aims were inevitably reaching out towards complete independence, something the liberals had never contemplated granting. Yet even now Indian nationalism was no more than a bubble that resolute government could have easily popped. As Montagu, when Secretary of State for India, acknowledged in his Report on Indian Constitutional Reform in 1918:

> There is a core of earnest men [in India] who believe sincerely and strive for political progress; around them a ring of less educated people to whom a phrase or a sentiment appeals; and an outside fringe who have been described as 'attracted by curiosity to this new thing [self-government] or who find diversion in attacking a big and very solemn government' . . . On the other hand is an enormous country population, and for the most part poor, ignorant, non-politically minded, and unused to any system of elections. We have in fact created a limited intelligentsia, who desire advance. . . .[1]

This intelligentsia which spoke so confidently for 'India', voicing 'India's' demand for freedom and 'India's' right to self-rule, numbered in truth less than one in a hundred of India's population.[2] There was no need to take them and their secondhand liberal clichés seriously at all. The British had won India by the sword, and more than that, by the moral ascendancy behind the sword. They, a small minority lost in an alien continent, had held India ever since by moral ascendancy – by force of will. India was accustomed to autocracy; the British sat comfortably enough in the throne vacated by the Moghuls, and until the liberals created an Indian intelligentsia and told it that autocracy was wrong, no Indian resented autocracy. And even by the time of the Great War it was not the people at large but only the intellectuals who resented it. The Indian army, the British sword in India, was recruited from the villages, not from the urban intelligentsia; from Punjabis, not from Bengalis, who made better politicians than soldiers; and the army was loyal to its British officers.

There was therefore no inevitable process of history to put a term to English rule in India. In 1914–18 the future of English rule in India lay still entirely in English hands. It depended on the English nerve. For if the English could not see that they would be better off without India, if they wished rather to stay, they had only to remain true to the traditions established by the men who, during the Indian Mutiny, although only

[1] Cd. 9109, p. 116.

[2] O'Dwyer, p. 12.

some 7,000 strong, had kept their grip on the fourteen million warlike people of the Punjab and at the same time recovered Delhi from the mutineers. If they wished to stay in India the English had only to recollect the words of one English administrator in the Punjab who wrote of the measures taken to break the Mutiny: 'The Punjab authorities adhered to the policy of overawing by a prompt and stern initiative . . . and would brook nothing short of absolute, active and positive loyalty. Government could not condescend to exist upon the moral sufferance of its subjects.'[1]

For if the English could not bring themselves to abandon India, then the simplest, most effective and convenient way of holding India was by resolute autocracy – as the English in India itself indeed advocated.

However this was the twentieth century: telegraphy and the fast steamship put the English in India at the mercy of a government, a Parliament and a public opinion in Britain all of which to a greater and lesser degree were coming to believe in the sovereign powers of goodwill and kindness, to say nothing of democracy. More important still, at this crucial moment when Indian nationalism was still only a wind-bag of more noise than strength, the destiny of English rule in India came to be decided by two outstanding representatives of English romantic idealism, Lionel Curtis and Edwin Montagu.

Curtis – 'the Prophet'[2] – was the young imperialist who saw the British Empire as the working model and precursor of a world state; who during the Great War became a passionate exponent of the League of Nations, and who in 1934 was to write a book about the British Empire entitled *Civitas Dei* (the City of God). In 1916 Curtis visited India, talked a lot, listened little, impressed his hosts even less, and returned with large schemes for securing India's step-by-step advance to self-government within the empire.

At home, Curtis found an eager hearer in Edwin Montagu, who, by an unlucky chance, became Secretary of State for India in 1917. A Commission of Enquiry on the campaign in Mesopotamia had made public the appalling incompetence of the Indian army authorities – one further piece of evidence that might have made the English reflect on how much extra power India really gave them. Austen Chamberlain, the Secretary of State for India, felt obliged to resign and Edwin Montagu, a Liberal, and a radical liberal at that, became responsible for the empire in India.

Although Montagu's family was not evangelical but Jewish, political

[1] Quoted in Philip Woodruff, *The Men Who Ruled India* (London, Jonathan Cape 1954), Vol. I, p. 373.

[2] See p. 64 above.

radicalism was the tradition. Montagu himself was nervous, introspective, emotional; lonely both as a child and as a young man. His letters and speeches gush with emotion like a girl's. In 1916 he had been offered the post of Chief Secretary for Ireland, a country then, as so often, in a state of rebellion. Montagu's reasons for declining the post suggested that he was hardly fitted for the even heavier responsibility of India. 'I do not see myself in the position of being responsible for administering punishment, repression, coercion, or making up my mind to avoid punishment, repression or coercion. I shrink with horror at being responsible for punishment. . . .'

And he referred to himself for the benefit of the recipient of his letter, the Prime Minister, Asquith, as 'nervous and sensitive'.[1] A friend of Montagu wrote of him in *The Times* in 1924 after his death:

> In his lovable and complicated character great subtlety of intellect was curiously mingled with great simplicity of mind. He had the trustfulness of a child. It was often betrayed and he suffered agonies of disappointment and surprise, but his confidence always returned, ready for the next encounter . . . He never got tired of being sorry for people. . . .[2]

As Secretary of State for India, Montagu was to display all these attributes to immense effect.

India, beyond any other subject, served as the sluice which turned on Montagu's emotions.

> Lastly, as I leave my work [he told the House of Commons in his resignation speech in 1922], may I say that the fascination of India's problems has obsessed me all my life – the Princes and the Native States, each with their individual characters, the people of India, awakening, striving, often with ill-defined ideals . . . the glorious conception, as I thought it was, and I think it is, of the British Commonwealth of Nations bound together by its very freedom and the mutual respect of all the partners, acknowledging no differences of race or creed. . . .[3]

Montagu's moods of romantic exaltation alternated however with bleak moments when his sharp intelligence saw things as they really were. There had been such moments during a visit to India in 1913:

> One has here [in Madras] [he wrote in his diary], as elsewhere among the educated Indians, a desire for more power. Not, I think, for democ-

[1] Waley, p. 94. [2] Ibid. p. 286. [3] Ibid. p. 280.

racy: for, horrible as it may be for an Englishman of my way of thinking to learn, the clever Indian wants executive power and executive opportunity, but he is not a democrat. He believes in caste, he believes in wealth. . . .[1]

Yet this shrewd appreciation of the one factor upon which schemes of Indian advancement were wholly dependent was totally disregarded in Montagu's Indian policy. Such was his enthusiasm for India that in 1915 Montagu wrote to Asquith to plead for the post of viceroy. At the beginning of 1917, though then not a minister, nor connected with Indian questions for three years, he conveyed his views on Indian policy to the War Cabinet: 'There is nothing that the Indian people want more than a goal at which to look. . . . Now I believe that the actual goal, however distant, however difficult of attainment, is some form of self-government with completely representative institutions. . . .'[2]

In July and August 1917, Montagu, newly become Secretary of State, strove to commit the War Cabinet to his vision of India's future. It was a critical period of the war: there had been the long drawn-out arguments as to whether to countenance Haig's plans for a great offensive in Flanders; France was wracked with subversion and defeatism; Russia lay in the throes of revolution, an ally in liquidation; and at sea the mortal struggle with the U-boat was still going on. There was also the problem of disaffection in Ireland.[3]

The view of the outgoing Secretary of State for India, Austen Chamberlain, had been of utmost caution, for he believed that so large a matter as the future of India could not adequately be discussed in the middle of a war.[4] On 14 August 1917 the Cabinet discussed Montagu's recommendation that there was an urgent need for a declaration of government policy that ought to include the words 'self-government'.[5] It was a meeting at which the War Cabinet had also to discuss air raids on Britain, the state of the Russian front, Mesopotamia and oil supplies. In India extremist politicians seemed to be gaining ground; and since the middle of May the viceroy, Lord Chelmsford, had been despatching telegrams to London on the need for some kind of sop to attract moderate Indian opinion and cut the ground from under the extremists. Chamberlain and Curzon both agreed that some statement was necessary. The question was, what should be its content and phrasing? Montagu himself suggested 'the gradual development of free institutions in India with a view to

[1] Ibid. p. 238.
[2] Ibid. pp. 118–19.
[3] See CAB 23/3, WC172.
[4] CAB 23/3, WC176.
[5] CAB 23/3, WC214.

ultimate self-government in India'. Curzon and Balfour both thought this was highly dangerous. Curzon argued: 'When the Cabinet used the expression "ultimate self-government" they probably contemplated an intervening period that might extend to 500 years; the Indian mind determined that period by a generation only.'

Balfour went further. 'To me, then, it appears that if we promise Self-Government we shall be promising something which, in the sense already defined, we neither can nor ought to give.'[1]

So Montagu's too-definite phrasing was dropped in favour of a draft by Curzon. Nevertheless a declaration as such had been successfully wrung from 'an indifferent and reluctant War Cabinet'.[2] And on 20 August 1917 it was officially announced that the new policy of His Majesty's Government towards India was '... the gradual development of self-governing institutions with a view to the progressive realisation of responsible government in India as an integral part of the British Empire'.[3]

It was, as Montagu's 1918 *Report on Indian Constitutional Reforms* stated, the 'most momentous utterance ever made in India's chequered history ...'[4] It was indeed far more momentous than the War Cabinet intended. It was a weakness of a classical education to attach great importance to shades of linguistic meaning. Curzon and Balfour were both masters of the careful phrase. It had been thought that Curzon's watered-down and ambiguous version of Montagu's original statement avoided the dangers of too firm and precise a commitment. Yet to Indians greedy for power the import of Curzon's draft was the same as that of Montagu's would have been. The English had in effect publicly committed themselves to granting India self-government – a revolutionary change in English policy. Henceforth it was only the date of the hand-over that was in question. And henceforth Indians could use the declaration of 20 August 1917 to accuse the English of bad faith if progress towards self-government was not as swift as Indian politicians would wish; a powerful goad to the guilty post-evangelical English conscience. While Montagu had felt strongly and thrillingly about the need for a fine-sounding statement, he only began to see all the practical consequences afterwards. On the very day following publication of the statement, he wrote to Lord Chelmsford, the viceroy:

> We have promised in the name of the British Government the development of self-governing institutions and a progressive realisation

[1] All CAB 23/3, WC214.
[2] Waley, p. 136.
[3] Quoted in Cd. 9109, p. 5.
[4] Ibid.

> of responsible government in India. How far can we go in this direction safely? . . . Is there any country in the world that has attempted a half-way house in this, or a quarter-way house? An autocratic and independent executive is common. Self-governing institutions are now (I don't ever quite know why) accepted as the only proper form of government. How can you unite the two? Can you have a form of government administered by an alien agency partly responsible to the people of the country itself? . . .[1]

The agonised history of British and Indian relations in the next thirty years was to answer these questions that were now so incredibly asked by the principal evangelist of Indian self-government himself. Montagu proceeded to seek enlightenment in a tour of India. On 26 November 1917 his diary records a meeting in Delhi with 'the real giants in the Indian political world' – Jinnah, Mrs Besant, Gandhi. Giants though they might be, Montagu recognised that 'the difficulty is that owing to the thinness with which we have spread education, they have run generations away from the rest of India, and, whatever might be done in theory, in practice this would only be another and indigenous autocracy'.[2]

Montagu found that British provincial governors were disquieted about the spread of political agitation and subversion to the villages, a curious anxiety in his opinion because 'disaffection was an excellent thing if it meant you were teaching a man that he must hope for better things. Our whole policy was to make India a political country. . . .'[3]

In the course of his tour Montagu evolved specific proposals for Indian constitutional reform from all the information and impressions he was cramming in, from Curtis's ideas, and from his own intelligence on the one hand and his romantic feelings on the other. Although his proposals were to be known as 'the Montagu–Chelmsford reforms', the stolid Chelmsford had little to do with them. As Montagu confided to his diary: 'It is appalling to have to create one's schemes, and, not only that, but to create one's own criticism of one's own schemes.'[4]

The *Report on Indian Constitutional Reforms* of 1918 ran to 282 pages. Its whole argument and all its complicated proposals rested on the begging of the fundamental question. For the introduction conveniently stated: 'If we speak of "Indian opinion" we should be understood as generally referring to the majority of those who have held or are capable of holding an opinion on the matter with which we are dealing. . . .'[5]

[1] Waley, pp. 137–8.
[2] Ibid. p. 145.
[3] Ibid. p. 150.
[4] Ibid. p. 152.
[5] Cd. 9109, p. 3.

In this light, the accounts of 'Indian demands' for reform, and of the Great War's effects on 'Indian opinion' later in the report lose something of their weight. But to Montagu in any case the actual numbers or proportion of the Indian population who really wanted self-government was of 'no importance whatever', for the reason for giving them self-government 'is the faith that is in us'.[1] It was his conviction that

> . . . we have a richer gift for her people than any we have yet bestowed; that nationhood within the Empire represents something better than anything India has hitherto attained; that the placid, pathetic contentment of the masses is not the soil on which such Indian nationhood will grow, and that in deliberately disturbing it, we are working for her highest good.[2]

The core of his elaborate constitutional proposals was that as the first stage of a step-by-step advance to Indian self-government, the Indian provinces should be handed over to elected Indian administrators (except for certain departments reserved to the British governors), while the central government should remain an autocracy tempered by Indian criticism in the Legislative Council. The scheme – known as Dyarchy, after the division of responsibility within provincial governments – owed much to Lionel Curtis.[3] It was an attempt to found British rule in India on the goodwill of the Indian intelligentsia instead of on its own moral and physical ascendancy. As Montagu himself commented in his Report:

> The main principle is that instead of founding the Indian government on the confidence of the people of England, we are gradually to found it on the confidence of the people of India. We are beginning in the Provinces, maintaining the government of India as now, but subjected, I am glad to think, to more criticism, and future progress will depend on the creation of an electorate.[4]

As with the declaration of 1917, so with the *Report on Indian Constitutional Reforms* it was Montagu who sought to bundle a Cabinet immersed in a war into precipitate publication. Curzon wrote to Montagu: 'Why is it necessary to proceed at breakneck speed in a case that constitutes a revolution of which not one person in a thousand in this country realises the magnitude, and which will probably lead by stages of increasing speed to the ultimate disruption of the Empire? . . . I heard Morley say all the things that you are saying now.'[5] Curzon's reference to a revolution that

[1] Cd. 9109. p. 119.
[2] Ibid. p. 120.
[3] V. A. Smith, p. 787.
[4] Waley, p. 155.
[5] Ibid. p. 173.

might lead to the disruption of the empire 'shocked' the innocent Montagu 'very much'; this possibility had apparently never occurred to him. Wounded, he replied to Curzon, 'Surely you did not mean this!'[1]

The question of the publication of Montagu's report was discussed by the War Cabinet on 24 May 1918, immediately after they had heard a sombre report by the Chief of the Imperial Staff that the current pause in the smashing blows of the German spring offensive was not likely to last long. Curzon thought that there were three alternatives: publish the report (as Montagu wished); publish it after perfunctory study by the Cabinet; or publish it after the Cabinet had considered it carefully, together with a statement of their own views and policy. It was agreed that Curzon should prepare a memorandum for the Cabinet's guidance.[2]

The Cabinet took its final decision over Montagu's proposals on 7 June 1918, when the Second Battle of the Marne was hanging in the balance. Montagu wanted early publication, including an announcement that the Government accepted the proposals 'generally and provisionally'. In a note to the Cabinet he wrote: 'I am hopeful of receiving considerable support from sober and moderate men [in India].' Walter Long, the Colonial Secretary, was against publication at that time; Curzon and Austen Chamberlain in favour, although Curzon himself expressed deep misgivings in a note to the Cabinet of 3 June 1918.

> I think that the Secretary of State has under-estimated the fundamental nature of the change which he proposes to introduce into the Government of India, proceeding as it does far beyond anything that has been previously contemplated or discussed in this country. . . .
>
> His proposals, if accepted, will create as time proceeds (probably with little delay) a complete revolution in the governing relations between India and this country – a revolution all the more incalculable in effect, because some of these plans are admittedly only a transitory expedient, bridging the gap between the old order and an unexplored future, and are certain to give rise to an early agitation for concessions much more extreme.[3]

In Cabinet Curzon recommended that there should be no government acceptance of Montagu's proposals until it was sure that they commanded general support in Britain and India. 'A revolutionary policy of this magnitude', he argued, 'required the fullest deliberation by the Cabinet.' His considered view therefore was that while the report should be

[1] Ibid. p. 174. [2] CAB 23/6, WC428.
[3] Appendix to CAB 23/6, WC428.

published, it should carry a clear disclaimer that the government was not committed by it in any way.[1]

Despite all the misgivings, the report was published before the Cabinet had carefully considered it. Once again there was too much faith in the qualifying power of words – this time of the government declaration that accompanied the report. For once published, whatever the official qualifications, the contents had their own power and momentum – as Curzon indeed had feared. Although Montagu's proposals, enacted in 1919, did not come into operation until 1921, they caused an immediate and irretrievable change in the position of the English in India, whose authority, and with it their own belief in their moral ascendancy, had been decisively undermined. For Montagu and Curtis's new constitution for India was fundamentally absurd – a foreign autocracy, the sanction for whose existence was supposed to be the goodwill of its native subjects. Despite all Montagu's doubts in his letter of 21 August 1917 to Chelmsford, he had brought to pass the very things he had feared: 'a half-way house . . . or a quarter-way house' between autocracy and self-government; a government 'administered by an alien agency partly responsible to the people of the country itself'.[2]

The immensity of the change wrought in British authority was revealed in 1918–20, when there was a wave of political violence and subversion in India, partly the local manifestation of the worldwide civil turmoil and revolution in the aftermath of the Great War, partly the result of particular Indian grievances. In the Punjab in 1919 the violence grew from rioting into insurrection. The Lieutenant-Governor of the Punjab, Sir Michael O'Dwyer, dealt with the trouble as the English had always done – with prompt and decisive severity. Michael O'Dwyer himself was by upbringing and character hardly of the increasingly fashionable style of leader in Britain:

> Michael O'Dwyer was one of the fourteen children of an Irish landowner of no great wealth, as much farmer as landlord. He was brought up in a world of hunting and snipe-shooting, of threatening letters and houghed cattle, where you were for the Government or against it, where you passed every day the results of lawlessness in the blackened walls of empty houses. It was a world very different from the mild and ordered life of southern England. . . . One gets the impression [of O'Dwyer when at Balliol] of a man who seldom opened a book without

[1] All CAB 23/6, WC428.
[2] See p. 147 above.

a purpose, whose keen hard brain acquired quickly and did not forget but had little time for subtleties.[1]

Decisive action had indeed been the special tradition in the Punjab for a hundred years:

> There were certain unwritten rules in the Punjab service [wrote Philip Woodruff, the historian of the English in India, of the Punjab in the 1840s]. There must be no hesitation. Show a bold front, take the offensive, at once, a blow in time saves nine – that was the first commandment. And the second, supplementing it, was this; because the junior must not wait for support, the senior must back him up. . . . Every officer must be sure he will be supported.[2]

For the last occasion in time of peace the English in India unsheathed the bright blade of dominating will. The Punjab insurrections were smashed in a few weeks.[3] However in the Sikh city of Amritsar, the commander of the troops called in to maintain order, Brigadier-General Dyer, made unfortunate decisions under the stress of crisis. The city, its essential installations and its 'white' population appeared to be in acute danger of falling into the hands of the rebels. Although all public gatherings had been prohibited, a great crowd gathered in an open space called the Jallianwallah Bagh. It was led by known and identified rebels. Though Dyer did not at the time know this, they could not disperse because the walled Jallianwallah Bagh had only one narrow exit. To Dyer, faced with a vast and apparently hostile mob, it seemed that the situation was passing out of his control. He ordered the troops to fire. Three hundred and seventy-nine Indians were killed.

Unfortunately Dyer's volley at the Jallianwallah Bagh and his 'crawling order', an excessive and needless humiliation by which Indians entering a street where a European woman had been attacked were to do so only on their stomachs, provided exactly the right triggers for a spasm of moral indignation and philanthropic emotion in Britain. A hot torrent of denunciation poured on the head of the authorities in India and in the Punjab in particular, and on Dyer himself.

Jallianwallah Bagh was, equally, a perfect gift to the Congress movement, which, far from being grateful for Montagu's step-by-step plan for Indian independence, was bitterly grieved that it was not to be given greater power sooner. Congress was further upset because, the whole

[1] Woodruff, Vol. II, p. 236.
[2] Ibid. Vol. I, p. 370.
[3] See O'Dwyer, pp. 267–317.

fabric of law and order seeming threatened by insurrection, the Government of India had passed emergency laws permitting imprisonment without trial. The Congress Party, led by Gandhi, therefore began an unrelenting political war on the British, for which the names of Jallianwallah Bagh, Amritsar and Dyer were heaven-sent ammunition. In 1920 Gandhi launched his strategy of non-cooperation; boycott of schools, colleges and even of Montagu's beloved new constitution, which was soon to be put into operation. Montagu's own liberal optimism, so incandescent in 1917–18, had by now blown a fuse. His biographer records that a letter to Lord Willingdon on 9 September 1920 'is perhaps the first specific confession that Montagu had come round to the view that the policy of self-government by stages laid down by the Declaration of 20 August 1917 which Montagu had so often and so eloquently defended, was a mistake'.[1] Montagu wrote:

> I personally do not believe that the Dyer incident was the cause of the great racial exacerbation which is now in existence. . . . This racial consciousness is inevitable. As soon as the Indians were told that we agreed with them and they were to become partners with us, it instilled into their minds an increased feeling of existing subordination and a realisation of everything by which this subordination was expressed. . . . I am convinced in my own mind that that has been the fatal mistake of our policy in India. We ought to have let the Indians run their own show from the beginning, with all its inefficiency and imperfections.[2]

Indeed the history of the French, Habsburg and Russian monarchies showed clearly enough that there could be no half-way or quarter-way houses between total autocracy and total abdication. If an autocracy can no longer rule by force of will and force of guns, concessions cannot preserve it, but only determine the manner of its extinction. Yet in 1919–21 the English continued to pursue the liberal fantasy of enlisting the goodwill of the Congress movement, and it was the two facets of this policy of appeasement that really brought about the revolutionary change in the position of the English in India.

On the one hand General Dyer was sacked and disgraced: an English officer who had acted swiftly on his own judgement had not been backed by his seniors, whatever his mistakes in the heat of the moment, but publicly disowned. The effect throughout the whole British structure in India was decisive.

[1] Waley, p. 235.
[2] Ibid. p. 236.

> . . . for the rulers a new dilemma was in existence. The officer confronted with the prospect of riot had been brought up to avoid loss of life at all cost. He had been used to having very little force at his disposal and he had known he must therefore use it or display it quickly. He had acted at once with complete confidence that he would receive support, because the first object of the Government was to keep order. From now on it was not the first object of the Government to keep order. . . .[1]

On the other hand the official disowning of Dyer was turned into a parade of British self-abasement in front of all India. The new viceroy, Lord Reading, made a pilgrimage to the Jallianwallah Bagh before making his first political speech in India. 'Can we not now do our utmost', he asked, 'to banish suspicion, to cease imputing evil motives, to believe again in the sympathetic justice of the Government, to concentrate in united effort to reach by peaceful means the end which is promised under your new Reforms? . . .'[2]

The climax was provided by His Royal Highness the Duke of Connaught when he opened the new Parliament of India in February 1921 as the representative of the King-Emperor: 'The shadow of Amritsar has lengthened over the fair face of India,' ran his official speech. 'I know how deep is the concern felt by His Majesty the King-Emperor at the terrible chapter of events in the Punjab. No one can deplore these events more sincerely and terribly than I do myself. . . .'[3]

Their naïve attempts at appeasing the Congress Party instantly led to a collapse of confidence among the English in India, as the Prince of Wales discovered during an official visit to India in 1921–2. He conveyed his own shrewd reading of the situation to Montagu in a letter of 1 January 1922:

> Let me tell you at once that the newspaper accounts at home of the various visits, ceremonies and receptions have almost invariably been hopefully exaggerated. . . .
>
> [People at home] think my tour is a success, and I must reluctantly tell you that it is no such thing. . . .
>
> I make it my business to talk to as many of our people out here as I can – soldiers, civil servants, and, more especially, the police, who from the nature of their work, can normally give a more accurate picture of the whole situation out here than anyone else; and as regards the present

[1] Woodruff, Vol. II, p. 243.
[2] H. Montgomery Hyde, *Lord Reading* (London, Heinemann 1967), p. 344.
[3] Quoted in Edward Thompson, *The Reconstruction of India* (London, Faber and Faber 1933), p. 127.

> conditions of life in India they one and all say the same thing – that they won't let their sons come out here to earn a living in the Indian Army, Indian Civil Service etc. etc., and that not now would they even recommend these services to any good fellow. The reason for this is, that India is no longer a place for a white man to live.[1]

At the same time the Prince well appreciated just how much Indian goodwill had been purchased by appeasement, such as when he was made 'a b.f.' (*sic*) at Benares, where a degree ceremony had been packed with highschool boys, boy scouts and Europeans, to replace the students who had boycotted the occasion.[2]

To those of the Indian masses who were conscious of what went on outside their own villages the British *Raj's* conduct was inexplicable: 'Opposition to the ruler in the traditional systems of India, whether Hindu or Moslem, is a crime and a much more serious crime than gang robbery. No one could understand why the English had suddenly become so tolerant of one form of crime, and it occurred to some people that it might be worth an experiment or two in other kinds.'[3]

The new policy of leniency made neither for civil peace nor for economy in life. Whereas the rebellion in the Punjab in 1919 had been crushed in a few weeks at a cost of under 500 lives (including those killed at Amritsar) it took more than a year to suppress the Moplah rebellion of 1920, with 2,000 Moslem casualties at the hands of the police, and thousands of Hindu casualties at the hands of the Moslems.[4] Indeed the British political concessions, by recognising the Moslem desire for separate communal identity, as well as by weakening authority, led to a general rise in communal hatred and disorder, which was soon to become endemic – and for virtually the first time since Britain had become the paramount power in India.[5]

Thus by the time of Montagu's resignation as Secretary of State for India in 1922, the British in India had been landed in the worst of all possible dilemmas. While they were still in India, and would be for decades, they no longer stood there with the assured ease of the conqueror, but stuck like a gum-boot in a bog.

The truth of the new situation was that the Indian nationalism which the English had done so much to help create was now locked in struggle with England for the possession of India.

[1] Waley, p. 262.
[2] Ibid. pp. 263–4. [3] Woodruff, Vol. II, p. 247. [4] O'Dwyer, p. 307.
[5] Nicholas Mansergh, *Survey of British Commonwealth Affairs* (London, Oxford University Press 1952), Vol. III, pp. 342–3.

British Governments and British public opinion in the 1920s refused however to recognise the existence of a conflict in India in which one side or the other must eventually acknowledge total defeat. Instead the British proceeded to attempt to solve the colossal problem they had brought on themselves in India by appealing to goodwill and the spirit of reason. It was in fact in India that the British first displayed their characteristic response between the world wars to any conflict of interests between themselves and others – a policy of appeasement.

Lord Reading, formerly Lord Chief Justice of England, in replying to Lord Chief Justice Hewart's congratulations on his appointment as Viceroy in 1921, struck the authentic note:

> To be representative of the King-Emperor in India is to be the representative of Justice. I leave this seat, the judicial bench, not forsaking or abandoning the pursuit of justice, but rather pursuing it in larger fields. . . . I trust those in India . . . who are now at the outset of great progressive reforms introduced into their country by the King's Government may recognise that in selecting the representative of Justice in this country to take the supreme place as the King's representative in India, it is the desire of His Majesty and of His Majesty's servants to make manifest in India that justice will remain the supreme guiding factor in the destinies of India.[1]

Reading, a liberal, and a man described by his biographer as 'a romantic', made a speech on landing at Bombay which could have done duty in Munich seventeen years later: '. . . all my experience of human beings and human affairs has convinced me that justice and sympathy never fail to evoke responsive chords in the hearts of men, of whatever race, creed or class'.[2]

However Reading's policy of leniency was rewarded by widespread rioting and violence, the product of Gandhi's campaign of 'non-violent' 'Civil Disobedience'. This particular wave of non-violence culminated in the burning alive of twenty-two Indian police constables in their station at Chauri Chaura in the United Provinces. Appeasement seemed for the moment untimely; and so instead Reading's Government became feebly tough, and installed Gandhi in comfort in a jail for a time, while the civil disorders smouldered on, and Montagu's and Curtis's new constitution was boycotted by the very people it was meant to please. Here was the sequence to be revolved over and over again in the 1920s and 1930s –

[1] Hyde, pp. 327–8.
[2] Ibid. p. 337.

appeasement leading to increased subversion, riot and violence; temporary British firmness followed again by fresh efforts at appeasement.

From 1924 to 1929, however, there existed a brake on appeasement in Lord Birkenhead, the Secretary of State for India, and one of the dwindling number of sceptical and tough-minded politicians on the parliamentary front benches. 'To me', he wrote to Reading, 'it is frankly inconceivable that India will ever be fit for Dominion self-government'[1] – an opinion upon which history is still in the course of delivering its verdict. Birkenhead therefore tried to warn Reading off from too complete a faith in sympathy and justice as means of holding India: 'My reading of Indian history has led me to believe that a government founded so completely as ours is upon prestige can stand about anything except the suspicion of weakness.'[2]

In 1926 Reading was replaced as Viceroy by a politician who was to play a critical role in British national policy right up to the outbreak of the Second World War. Edward Wood, Viscount Irwin (later Earl of Halifax), was a great territorial magnate with a seat at Garrowby in Yorkshire; a man positively mid-Victorian in his conception of the place in society due to hereditary rank; and an Anglo-Catholic of extreme religiosity. By temperament he was cautious, distasteful of conflict. As he himself wrote in his early biography of Keble:

> There are few things more dangerous than the constant anxiety for doing something definite. Many diseases may only be handled with gentleness and caution; violent treatment, the determination to force the issue at all costs, will result in nothing but catastrophe. . . . Nor is it always possible to do anything but defend in the face of attack. . . .[3]

In articles and speeches about British policy towards the rebellion in Ireland when a Conservative Member of Parliament after the Great War, he had first made plain his temperamental response to conflicts involving Britain and others: '. . . instead of deluding public opinion with a notion that a sufficient application of force will provide a remedy, a wiser course would be to set about taking such steps as may be the means of recovering that consent without which society in Ireland cannot exist'.

He therefore recommended that a political offer should be made to the Irish, 'conceived on the most generous lines'.[4]

[1] A letter of 24 November 1924, quoted in Hyde, p. 382.
[2] Ibid. p. 382.
[3] Quoted in Lord Birkenhead, *Halifax* (London, Hamish Hamilton 1965), pp. 79–80.
[4] Ibid. pp. 121–2.

In India he opened his viceroyalty in 1926 by appealing, like Reading, to his audience's better nature:

> In the name of Indian national life, in the name of religion, I appeal to all in each of the two countries who hold position . . . let them begin each in their own community to work untiringly towards this end: boldly to repudiate feelings of hatred and intolerance, actively to condemn and suppress acts of violence and aggression, earnestly to strive to exorcise suspicions. . . .
>
> I appeal in the name of national life because communal tension is eating into it as a canker. . . .
>
> I appeal in the name of religion because I can appeal to nothing nobler, and because religion is the language of the soul, and it is a change of soul that India needs today. . . .[1]

At the same time he added a warning that the Government had no intention of allowing violence or the threat of violence to deter it from maintaining civil peace. There followed eighteen months bloody with communal rioting: between 250 and 300 killed and over 2,000 injured.[2] Nevertheless Irwin obstinately went on seeking that elusive Indian goodwill; even inviting Gandhi, the Government's most dangerous enemy, to a personal meeting.

In 1927 Irwin and Birkenhead decided that a statutory commission drawn from both British houses of Parliament should visit India, report on the working of the Montagu–Chelmsford reforms, and suggest future developments in Indian self-government. It was thought that such a commission would secure the goodwill of 'moderate' Indian opinion.

When the Commission arrived in India in 1928, it was put under a total boycott, both by Hindus and Moslems. And the violence went on: trains wrecked, houses burned, killings in the streets. Strong action there again had to be, but now it meant not simply a British decision, but a Public Safety Bill submitted to an Indian legislature, which rejected it. Shortly afterwards bombs were thrown inside the Legislative Chamber itself. Even Irwin saw that the limits of conciliation had been reached, at least for the time being. He took the powers of the Public Safety Bill by Ordinance.[3]

At the beginning of 1929 the Conservative Cabinet was warned by a memorandum by the Secretary of State for India and by telegrams from

[1] Ibid. pp. 223–4.

[2] Lord Irwin, speech to Legislative Assembly, 29 August 1927, quoted in Edward Thompson, *The Reconstruction of India*, p. 237.

[3] Birkenhead, pp. 262–7.

Irwin that Indian opinion had swung hard to the left in the previous year – the violent agitation being probably intended to discredit the report of the Indian Statutory Commission in advance, as in the case of Montagu's proposals ten years earlier. The Cabinet therefore believed in the importance of the Government of India not being 'hustled into making concessions fundamentally unsound'.[1]

Yet Irwin was still convinced that the solution to the Indian problem lay in securing Indian goodwill by further concessions, and for this reason he welcomed Birkenhead's replacement as Secretary of State by the Socialist Wedgwood Benn when the Conservatives lost the General Election of 1929. For, in his biographer's words, he 'found the new Secretary of State as eager as himself to make some memorable gesture of friendship, to recapture the confidence by an act of faith. He could rely upon the Socialist Prime Minister, Ramsay MacDonald, who had already, when out of office, looked forward to the day when India would become a Dominion.'[2]

The warm feelings were reciprocated when Irwin, on a visit to England, attended a Cabinet meeting on 26 July 1929. The Minutes record that the Cabinet 'congratulated themselves on the fact that Lord Irwin was now Governor-General, which gave them a sense of confidence and security . . .'[3] At this Cabinet meeting Irwin won the acceptance for his proposal that at an early date there should be an exchange of letters between the Prime Minister (Ramsay MacDonald) and the Chairman of the Statutory Commission (Sir John Simon) to the effect that dominion status for India was the Government's ultimate objective, although one to be achieved by stages.

At a later Cabinet meeting it was agreed that Irwin, on his return to India, should announce 'a Free Conference' to which all sections of Indian opinion would be invited, together with a 'Declaration of Purpose' to the effect that 'in the judgement of His Majesty's Government, it is implicit in the Declaration of 1917 that the attainment of Dominion status must be regarded as the natural issue of India's constitutional progress'.[4] These announcements were made in the fresh hope of winning over 'moderate opinion' in India. This new step, in its purpose and nature as well as in the illusions that underlay it, bore a strong and dismal resemblance to Montagu's Indian policies in 1917–22.

In the view of British public opinion, however, Irwin had gone too far by committing Britain to granting India dominion status; even his Liberal

[1] CAB 23/60, C3(29)2. [2] Birkenhead, p. 269. [3] CAB 23/61, C31(29)1.
[4] CAB 23/61, C37(29)4. See above p. 146.

predecessor, Reading, attacked him. But so far as Indian politicians were concerned, Irwin's gesture of faith, while it delighted them as a victory for them and a defeat for British authority, only encouraged them instantly to raise their demands – release of political prisoners, the Round Table Conference not merely to discuss India's future but to draft a constitution for the dominion. It was hinted to Irwin that a firm promise by Ramsay MacDonald of dominion status at the Round Table Conference might be the one thing to avoid a Congress Party decision to demand complete independence and launch another insurrectionary campaign.

'Though I am, as you know, a pacifist by nature,' Irwin wrote to Benn, 'I am not disposed to go to all lengths to meet people who seem to be behaving with utter unreason.'[1] Not all lengths, but some further lengths – the Viceroy of India agreed to meet Gandhi, the principal threat to his authority, and his Congress colleagues, and also Jinnah, the leader of the Moslem League. The meeting served as an opportunity for the Indians to deliver a staggering rebuff to Irwin's attempts at appeasement. They would not take part in the Round Table Conference unless its result was to be dominion status. When Irwin inevitably refused to give this promise, the Congress leaders went away, and on 31 December 1929 publicly proclaimed not their acceptance of the dominion status for which Irwin had risked his official neck, but their demand for complete independence. The Congress called on its members in the legislatures to resign their seats. And in a final response to Irwin's obstinate efforts to please them, they launched another campaign of civil disobedience; of which the major and most successful propaganda stunt was Gandhi's walk to the sea in March and April 1930, in order ceremonially to make and eat salt in defiance of the Government's Salt Tax. More wars and violence exploded across the country. The wild men of the North-West Frontier infiltrated round Peshawar. There was a rebellion in Burma. Eventually Irwin had to take firm action again. Gandhi and his colleagues, so recently the objects of the viceroy's wooing, were once more put in jail. Troops and police fought to restore the weakening frontier as well as the crumbling pillars of civil peace and ordered government.

The publication at this time of the Report of the Simon Commission (Indian Statutory Commission) brought therefore no joy with its modest recommendation for further stages of Indian self-government and its studied omission of any reference to dominion status. The first Round Table Conference opened in London in November 1930 under total boycott by the Congress Party.

[1] Birkenhead, p. 275.

Irwin's answer to the disastrous situation was to release Gandhi. Gandhi instantly responded by trying to embarrass him with demands that there should be an enquiry into the conduct of the police during the insurrections which Congress had fomented. Nevertheless, Irwin agreed to meet him and negotiate face to face about the future in India, as one deeply religious man to another.

Even now, after four years of failure, Irwin still saw the problem not as one of defeating, discrediting and outwitting an opponent, but as 'a question of personal appeal and conviction, rather than any argument. The cards I fancy are sympathy, understanding of his hopes, suspicions and disappointments, but above all, striving to convey to him, through what one says, a real echo of the sincerity that pervaded your doings in London. . . .'[1]

The result of the negotiations between the viceroy and the principal enemy of English rule in India was an agreement by which, in return for Gandhi calling off Civil Disobedience and the boycott on British goods, and taking part in the Second Round Table Conference, Irwin withdrew the emergency ordinances against riot and disorder (except against terrorism), released those arrested during the last Civil Disobedience campaign (except for those involved directly in violence), and compromised over the Salt Tax. However the really important consequence of the meeting was to elevate Gandhi's standing with his own people. He, a rebel, had negotiated with the viceroy as an equal, as the terms of the communiqué made plain to all who could read.

The veneer of common understanding was soon stripped away. The execution of an Indian who had patriotically murdered a British police officer detonated another blast of non-cooperation and of furious communal war between Hindus and Moslems. When Irwin's viceroyalty came to an end in April 1932, the object of his last and greatest act of appeasement – to induce Gandhi and the Congress Party to take part in the Second Round Table Conference – was therefore in doubt. Irwin, however, was not in doubt.

> Every day [he wrote to the Secretary of State] makes me feel more certain that what we are trying to do is right. We have no doubt made mistakes, but I don't think that this affects the broad perspective of the policy. Whether we shall succeed or not lies in other hands than ours, but I am quite sure that the general line His Majesty's Government has

[1] Letter of 16 February 1931 to the Secretary of State, quoted in Birkenhead, p. 296.

been taking has immensely strengthened our moral position both here and abroad. . . .[1]

Despite Irwin's return and despite the Labour Government's replacement by a Conservative-dominated National Government, their Indian policy was carried on by its own momentum. Gandhi and the Congress leaders did after all attend the Second Round Table Conference, held to discuss English proposals for an Indian Federation. However, the gulf between what the English were prepared to grant and what the Congress Party now demanded, and believed they could get, was too great for minds to meet across it. Not only this but by 1932 English policy over the previous thirty years had created yet another intractable problem in Moslem–Hindu ill-feeling and communal separatism, which was to culminate in the Moslem League's demand for 'Pakistan' – self-government for the Moslem regions of India. This aspiration threatened the fundamental achievement of the English in India; that of unifying the country. As Birkenhead had correctly prophesied in 1925:

> The greater the political progress made by the Hindus, the greater, in my judgement, will be the Moslem discontent and antagonism. All the conferences in the world cannot bridge over the unbridgeable, and between those two countries lies a chasm which cannot be crossed by the resources of modern political engineering.[2]

The results of the Round Table Conference of 1932 justified Birkenhead's scepticism. The conference broke up in total disagreement, and British relations with the Congress movement again became those of open conflict: Gandhi once more in jail and his party made illegal.

Moreover British administrators displayed little taste or talent for maintaining British rule by means of fighting a political battle with Indian politicians for the support of the Indian masses. There was no attempt to exploit the opportunities offered by the splits and factions within the Congress movement, to say nothing of the gulf between Hindu and Moslem. There was no systematic propaganda of the Government case and point of view. No effort was made to present British measures against insurrection in a sympathetic light as part of a general campaign to influence opinion inside and outside India. A Liberal journalist, Edward Thompson, noted in 1932:

> There are countries with an extensive Asiatic Empire, who, faced by political activity of a kind that in India has long been accepted as mild

[1] Letter of 18 April 1932, quoted in Birkenhead, p. 307. See idem, chs. XII–XVII, for a full and resolutely sympathetic account of Irwin's viceroyalty.

[2] Hyde, p. 387.

> and entirely constitutional, promptly shoot and hang it out of existence, and inform the outside world that it was 'communism'. If you call a thing communism, you can do what you like to it, and get away with it. (American Women's Clubs, which have suffered much distress by the spectacle of England's wickedness, never vex themselves about these other Colonial Empires.) The Indian Government, faced by murderous organisations, prosecutes their members anachronistically, for such crimes as 'proposing to wage war against the King-Emperor', 'seeking to deprive the King-Emperor of his sovereignty over India'. . . It has invented a form of martyrdom which is mostly garlands for its more distinguished practitioners. . . .[1]

Sir Charles Teggart told Thompson, for example, that there was very little communism in India, and therefore '. . . I will not . . . call a thing communism when it isn't communism, just to get political advantage'.[2]

The British failure in political warfare and propaganda was the more unfortunate because British relations with India were no longer (as they had been in the nineteenth century) a semi-private affair between the British Government of the day, the viceroy and a few Indian politicians. They were conducted in an open arena surrounded by grandstands of heartfelt and highly articulate criticism. Thanks to the creation of the League of Nations, there was now a world public opinion, to which British governments were sensitive, if few others. However, it was American opinion, with its dearly-held myths about British imperialism, and the liberal idealism in Britain itself which formed the most implacable of the pressures forcing weak-nerved and tender-minded British governments to pursue policies which publicly displayed them as trying to do good.

What Montagu had eventually perceived, but which Lord Irwin never saw, was that the question for the English in India was starkly simple – stay, or get out in short order. Irwin's promise of dominion status carried no implication of speedy withdrawal. Throughout his viceroyalty it had been Irwin's illusion that by recovering the 'trust' of the Indians in British good faith over *eventual* self-government within the empire, British and Indian might co-exist and co-operate in India indefinitely; Irwin, in fact, shared Montagu's original and absurd hope of founding an alien autocracy on the goodwill of its subjects. From Morley to Irwin, Benn and MacDonald, English policy in India provides a classic case-study in romantic liberal idealism: the naïve trust in human nature that inspires it, the

[1] Edward Thompson, *A Letter From India* (London, Faber and Faber 1932), p. 62. [2] Ibid.

appeasement by which it is carried on, and the disastrous and inevitable results of its attempts to bring about the impossible.

Few people recognised even after 1930 that English interests would be best served by getting rid of the whole encumbrance of India by simply acceding to Indian demands for independence. Apart from the deeply-felt sentiments that made abrupt abandonment of India unthinkable and unthought of, there remained the crucial question of defence. For defence was the key to an independent foreign policy and hence to the complete sovereignty the Indians wanted. It was in fact the subject round which all the elaborate constitutional arguments and proposals had revolved since the Great War. Montagu, in one of the brief passages devoted to defence in his 282-page report of 1918, had stated the dilemma:

> So long as India depends for her internal and external security upon the army and the navy of the United Kingdom, the measure of self-determination which she enjoys must be inevitably limited. We cannot think that Parliament would consent to the employment of British arms in support of a policy over which it had no control or of which it might disapprove.[1]

The Simon Commission, too, saw it as the central dilemma that England could not hand over an army including a British element for use internally and externally as an Indian government responsible to an elected legislature thought fit.[2] At the same time the Commission was convinced that India would not be able to do without British troops and officers 'for many years'.[3] The Commission's conclusions were that: 'India and Britain are so related that Indian defence cannot, or in any future which is within sight, be regarded as a matter of purely Indian concern. The control and direction of such an army must rest in the hands of the Imperial Government.'[4]

Thus in the 1930s the English continued to hang on in India for the very reason which, on a clear view of their own interests, should have prompted them to get out.

The Conservative-dominated National Government that replaced the Labour Government in the financial crisis of 1931 carried on the brave search for Indian goodwill. The new Secretary of State for India was Sir Samuel Hoare, who combined education at Harrow and Oxford with a strong nonconformist, indeed Quaker, family tradition. He was supported by Stanley Baldwin who, though the Lord President of the

[1] Cd. 9109, p. 130.
[2] Cd. 3569, pp. 168–9.
[3] Ibid. p. 21.
[4] Ibid. p. 174.

Council, was in fact the real leader of the administration headed by Ramsay MacDonald.

Baldwin shared the general British assumption that the object of British policy should be to retain India in the empire. Like Morley, Montagu and Irwin, he saw political concessions as the best – the only – way of so retaining India. In December 1934, addressing a large Conservative audience at the Queen's Hall, London, he justified the Government's coming Bill to reform the Government of India:

> It is my considered judgement . . . that you have a good chance of keeping the whole sub-continent of India in the Empire for ever. You have a chance, and a good chance, but I say to you that if you refuse her this opportunity, if you refuse it to her, you will infallibly lose India, whatever you do, before two generations are passed.[1]

The Government of India Act of 1935 was yet another blend of appeasement and caution. There was no mention of dominion status; an error of public relations. In the new Indian constitution the provinces were to be almost entirely handed over to elected Indian governments, while the responsibilities for central government were divided between elected Indian representatives and the British. Burma became a separate British colony. After 1935 therefore the English remained in India under the least convenient circumstances. They shared the central government with Indian politicians whose stated objective was the obstruction and eventually the destruction of British rule. The provinces had virtually passed out of English hands. And whereas in the nineteenth century the administration of India had been centralised, now many functions had devolved to the provinces.

It was as uneasy a constitutional half-way house, and as pregnant with trouble and executive weakness, as the English constitution under the late Stuarts. Winston Churchill no more than accurately stated the nature of the English plight in India up to and during the Second World War, when he said during the debates on the Government of India Bill in 1935 that the British Government 'have reconciled themselves to a vast degeneration in the quality and character of British administration in India, but they have not attained the peace and harmony which comes from the active consent and co-operation of those for whom their gifts are designed. . . .'[2]

He predicted the consequence:

[1] Cd. 3569. p. 176.

[2] Hansard, *Parliamentary Debates* (House of Commons), Fifth Series, Vol. 302, cols. 1919 and 1921.

> In ten years' time the foundations and pivots of British authority will have simultaneously weakened in every part of India. You will have shifted the axis of India. You will have altered the forms of Indian loyalty. Everywhere the waves of so-called popular government and democratic movements will be lapping against the foundations of your power. . . .[1]

Yet Churchill's pessimism was shared by few, even in the Conservative Party, even by an imperialist like L. S. Amery.[2]

In India the British administrators hung on, doing their routine duty, caretakers without a purpose or a future, awaiting that unspecified day when the Indians would take possession. And the caution, the moral defensiveness, the pettifogging regard for legal and departmental precedent that now permeated the machinery of British administration from India Office in London to Delhi and beyond marked in themselves a senile weakening from the 'fierce nervous energy'[3] that had once created the British Empire in India. Men like those who had conquered and ruled the Punjab in the 1840s and 1850s – 'Speed and unnatural tension are the notes of all they do; there is no pause for rest, no thought of ease. . . . All is struck off at a white heat, as in the press of battle'[4] – were not exactly characteristic of the cumbersome, slow-moving and pedantic bureaucracy or of the snobbery and etiquette of the social hierarchy of British India in the 1930s.

And militarily, in the years after 1934 when the dangers posed by Nazi Germany, Fascist Italy and Japan had become manifest, India was still a liability, not an asset. The 1937 Imperial Conference was told that the Indian field army was designed primarily for the defence of the North-West Frontier.[5] India in fact still required a British garrison amounting to over a third of the British army.[6] In 1938 the best India could offer for general imperial purposes in wartime, by agreement between the Chiefs of Staff Committee and the Government of India, was one division, three out of whose ten battalions were to be British in any case.[7] In 1938 Admiral of the Fleet Lord Chatfield headed a sub-committee of the Committee of Imperial Defence charged with investigating the need for modernising India's defences. The sub-committee found that air and coastal defences were hopelessly inadequate, while the Indian army was ill-prepared for field operations outside India.[8]

[1] Ibid. col. 451.
[2] Cf. Amery, Vol. III, p. 99.
[3] Woodruff, Vol. I, p. 324.
[4] Ibid.
[5] Cmd. 5482, p. 19.
[6] Cole, p. 31.
[7] CAB 27/653, CP187(38).
[8] See CAB 27/653, CID (38) series: Cabinet Committee on the Defence of India; Chatfield Committee Report in January 1939 in CP133(39).

Nor had the hopes and intentions expressed in 1917 in the Montagu-Chelmsford Report[1] of making India more self-sufficient in war-production been fulfilled after twenty years; constitutional rather than industrial development having been more in the English mind, and perhaps more congenial to it as well. India still depended on British industry for the majority of weapons and technical equipment required by modern armed forces.[2]

Thus in 1939, as in 1914–18, England was still responsible for the defence of India; still deeply involved, and exposed, in the Mediterranean and throughout the Middle East as a consequence. Twenty years of English policy founded on false assumptions and unrealistic hopes had in no way lightened the strategic burden laid on England; on the contrary, English policy had merely served to make the burden the more difficult to carry. India was now like a child grown into adolescence: less obedient, but no less of an anxiety and an expense.

The 'white' empire emerged from the Great War in a highly ambiguous stage of transition, or evolution; really in fact newly born. It was, after all, only in 1867 that the first self-governing dominion, Canada, had been created, while Australia only became a federal Commonwealth instead of a number of separate states in 1902. The Union of South Africa dated from 1910. It was as recently as 1887 that the first attempt had been made to induce some kind of collective imperial awareness among the small and then rather unimportant 'colonies' by inviting their representatives to a Colonial Conference. The sense of belonging to a great empire only really began to awaken in official quarters in Britain and the dominions in the late 1890s. Even then there was little imperial cohesion in any practical sense of common policies or co-operation. Until the Great War came to act as a somewhat rough and clumsy midwife, the Commonwealth was really only a foetus in gestation. The question was, therefore, when the hand-slaps of war ceased, would the Commonwealth go on breathing and grow into strong maturity? Or had it been born only to expire in the crêche?

There was another question, upon a correct answer to which by imperial statesmen depended the successful rearing of the infant Commonwealth. What kind of a political creature was it? 'We are still unconscious', A. J. Balfour told his colleagues at the Imperial War Conference of 1917, 'of the extraordinary novelty, the extraordinary greatness, and

[1] See p. 78 above.

[2] S. Woodburn Kirby, *The War Against Japan* (London, HMSO 1957), Vol. I, p. 39.

the extraordinary success of this unique experiment in human co-operation.'[1]

In the heady euphoria of wartime, high-minded and even rhapsodic attempts were made to define the extraordinary nature of the novel creature. 'The British Empire', declared Smuts, 'is the only successful experiment in international government that has ever been made. . . . It is a congeries of nations . . . not merely a state but a system of states.' W. M. Hughes, the Australian Prime Minister, believed that 'we are a League of Free Nations'. Robert Borden of Canada struck the same noble chord even more resoundingly. 'We are', he proclaimed, 'an Imperial Commonwealth of United Nations.'[2]

In practical terms, however, the 'white' empire was essentially an alliance. It was an alliance not in the restricted sense of a treaty binding the signatories to come to each other's aid in certain specific contingencies, but in the sense of wartime co-operation, such as between Marlborough, the Dutch and Prince Eugene, or between Britain and France in the second half of the Great War. The 'white' empire in 1917–19 was indeed a precursor of such permanent associations of allies as the North Atlantic Treaty Organization. The problems of the evolution of the 'white' empire were the problems of an alliance, while the problems of the British themselves in regard to the 'white' empire were those of the senior partner in an alliance otherwise composed of small powers – the problems of so managing the alliance as to keep its members sweet, while at the same time maintaining its effectiveness.

Unfortunately it was an alliance that derived not from the logic of political and strategic convenience, but from kinship, from common history and culture, and from loyalty to a common Crown. It happened, for example, that the two dominions closest to Britain in race and sentiment were furthest away in distance. Australia and New Zealand had been settled in that halcyon epoch of the early nineteenth century when the Royal Navy's supremacy had turned the oceans of the world into an English pond; when Japan had been a feudal society locked up in self-imposed isolation, the United States a purely North American continental power, and the European powers almost wholly occupied with Europe itself. The haphazard operation of history had produced what was, in the twentieth century, a strategical absurdity pregnant with difficulties and dangers; and the British had no alternative but to make the best of it.

The 'best' was clearly the utmost degree of cohesion between England

[1] Cd. 8566, p. 41.
[2] Ibid. pp. 45–7; Cd. 9177, pp. 19, 146.

and the dominions that could be attained. This had been perceived by the imperialists by the 1880s; and imperial federation had been the ideal answer advocated by them until the eve of the Great War. As Lord Milner put it in 1901:

> Until we get a real Imperial Council, not merely a Consultative, but first a Constitutional, and then an Executive Council with control of all our *world business*, we shall get nothing . . . we cannot rely *permanently* upon casual inorganisation, and more or less sentimental outbursts of national sympathy as a basis of Empire. They are but raw material out of which Statesmanship can, and should, make a good fabric.[1]

Yet by the time Milner was writing this, imperial federation – together with its concomitants, an imperial army and navy – were already beginning to prove politically impossible. Except for New Zealand, the dominions wished to rise to the status of independent nations, not sink to that of oceanic Ohios.[2] But, as Asquith reminded the Imperial Conference of 1911: 'In the early Victorian era, there were two rough-and-ready solutions for what was regarded, with some impatience, by the British statesmen of the day as the "colonial problem". The one was centralisation . . . the other was disintegration.'[3]

The experiences of the Great War and the Peace Conference had however pointed towards a third solution, that of the 'white' empire's continuation as a permanently functioning alliance. This depended on whether imperial statesmen could perceive the truth – that the empire was an alliance – through the confusing fog of anachronistic constitutional form (by which the dominions were still legally colonies subordinate to Britain), of political vapouring about empires or commonwealths of free nations, and of general sentimentalising about sister states united in loyalty to the Crown. Such a continuation as an integrated alliance would not be easy to bring about, for underneath the imperial and loyal sentiments voiced by all the leaders of the 'white' empire, strong forces of geography, strategy and history were making for imperial disintegration. Unfortunately Canada and South Africa, the two dominions which, because of their geographical situation, least needed the protection of the imperial alliance, had the strongest national motives for

[1] Quoted in J. E. Wrench, *Alfred Lord Milner* (London, Eyre and Spottiswoode 1958), p. 229.
[2] See pp. 107–9 above; see also R. A. Preston, *Canada and Imperial Defense* (Durham, North Carolina, Duke University Press 1967), chs. 4–14; Donald C. Gordon, *The Dominion Partnership in Imperial Defence 1870–1914* (Baltimore, Johns Hopkins Press 1965); W. K. Hancock, Vol. I, ch. 1.
[3] Cd. 5745, p. 22.

resenting the predominant role played in it by Britain. These dominions were therefore potential disrupters.

Both countries contained large non-British populations whose presence under the Union flag was owing to conquest by British arms.

In Canada the 65,000 French settlers of 1760, the year of British conquest, had grown into a population of some 3,000,000 out of a total of 7,600,000.[1] They formed a homogeneous linguistic, cultural and religious bloc, resentful of English-speaking supremacy, devoid of feelings of loyalty towards Britain and the British Crown. Nor was this large minority of French Canadians in Quebec the only Canadian problem of unity. Settled Canada was a narrow band of country stretching 3,000 miles from the Atlantic to the Pacific. The people, the culture and the politics of the prairie provinces of the mid-west were very different from those of the Maritimes, on the other side of Quebec; and from those of Ontario again. Canadian politics were dominated by this internal problem of preserving – or even creating – national unity. Blatantly pro-British or imperial commitments were exactly the policies to raise up the French-Canadian vote in a Canadian government's face, while the prairie provinces for their part were strongly isolationist. Canadian self-government itself derived from rebellions by the colonists against British rule in 1837–8, which had conjured up fearful memories of the American Revolution. In a classic State paper in 1839 Lord Durham had recommended self-government as the only means of keeping Canada in the empire in the longterm.

Nor did Canada stand in special need of British imperial protection in the 1920s, for the Atlantic was as directly and essential a British interest (and a United States interest as well) as a Canadian, while the Pacific approaches to North America were a key strategic concern of the United States. Canada's safety was in fact guaranteed by her contiguity with the United States.

In South Africa the people conquered by British arms formed the majority of the 'white' population, for there were 900,000 Boers to 300,000 people of British stock,[2] and the conquest of the Boers, completed only in 1902, was a fresh raw wound on their independence and pride of race. Whatever its apparent causes and issues, the Boer War had really been fought to decide whether Britain and British institutions or the Boers and Afrikanerdom should prevail in South Africa. In 1906–7, however, the Liberal Government in Britain restored self-government to the former Boer republics and in 1909 passed the Act creating the Union of

[1] 1914 figure: Cole, p. 43.

[2] 1914 figures: Cole, p. 43.

South Africa, a self-governing dominion in which the Boers formed the majority of the voters. This settlement was for long afterwards seen as a master-stroke of generous policy towards a defeated enemy, reconciling old hostilities in a new spirit of friendship and co-operation; and its success seemed to be proved by the presence of former Boer soldiers in imperial conferences, and, in the case of Smuts – when as South Africa's Minister of Defence he served as an all-purpose political and strategic adviser in London during the Great War – in British uniform. This settlement with the Boers was indeed to loom mightily in British minds as a precedent to follow, whether it was a question of kissing and making up with the Irish or the Germans. The conviction of men like Milner, on the other hand, that the settlement in South Africa really meant that the verdict of the Boer War would in time be reversed, was scornfully ignored. As Margot Asquith said of Milner himself in 1906, '... there is something out of drawing with his judgement. He has got it on the brain that we shall lose South Africa.'[1]

It was Jan Christian Smuts who did so much to convince the British how generous and wise their statesmanship had been. He was a curious mixture of Afrikanerdom and a late-Victorian English upper-class chivalry which he absorbed while an undergraduate at Cambridge, when he became, and remained, a close friend of liberals, nonconformists and pacifists like the Hobhouse sisters. During and after the Great War Smuts preached the cause of the League of Nations in high places. He therefore made all the appropriate liberal noises and took all the most congenial doctrinal attitudes in Britain while in South Africa pursuing consistently illiberal policies towards the non-whites.

However Smuts and, for that matter, General Louis Botha, his friend and the first South African Prime Minister, believed, according to Smuts' latest biographer, that 'Campbell-Bannerman's act [in giving self-government back to the Boers] had redressed the balance of the Anglo-Boer War, or had, at any rate, given full power to the South Africans themselves to redress it'.[2]

If this was the diagnosis of Britain's 'liberal' Boer friends in South Africa, it was not likely that the undiluted Bible-bred Boer nationalist would look loyally on the British Empire, or wish South Africa to co-operate closely in joint imperial policies. In fact, General J. B. M. Hertzog, the true voice of Afrikanerdom, told an audience on 7 December 1912: 'I am not one of those who always talk of conciliation and loyalty; they

[1] Quoted in Wrench, p. 261.

[2] Sir K. Hancock, *Smuts* (Cambridge, Cambridge University Press 1962), Vol. I, p. 357.

are idle words which deceive no one. I have always said that I do not know what this conciliation means.'[1]

Hertzog too saw the magnanimous constitutional gift of British liberalism to South Africa as merely a means of eventually reversing the verdict of the Boer War. He regarded the new constitution of 1910, in the words of his biographer, as 'the beginning of a process of constitutional development, for self-government contains the germ of independence and the opportunity for the organic growth of freedom, given the will to be free'.[2]

Not only were there similarities between the internal problems posed in Canada and South Africa by large non-British, British-Empire-hating racial groups, but Canadian and South African statesmen themselves felt a kinship of attitude. In the 1911 Imperial Conference, Botha of South Africa and Sir Wilfred Laurier of Canada combined to destroy, finally, the hopes of Imperial Federation, as then voiced by Sir Joseph Ward of New Zealand. As Botha wrote home to Smuts: 'Yes, Jannie, Laurier and I have renewed our friendship. He and I agree about everything. . . . The conference work is going quite well. We have destroyed root and branch the proposal for an Imperial Council of State or Parliament, and we have succeeded in keeping the Conference as a round table affair.'[3]

Similarly Hertzog, as a Boer nationalist, was deeply aware of and influenced by French-Canadian history, by the example of the rebellion of 1837, which, although suppressed, had nevertheless prodded the British into granting Canadian self-government, and by the current Quebec nationalist movement headed by Henri Bourassa, with whom he corresponded during the Great War.[4]

At the Imperial War Conference of 1917, South Africa and Canada again found themselves allies, in the persons of Smuts, the South African Minister of Defence and member of the Imperial War Cabinet in London, and Sir Robert Borden, now Prime Minister of Canada. Together they let some of the wind out of the inflated hopes for imperial unity after the war. Borden in his memoirs recollected:

> From the first our acquaintance developed into an intimate friendship. Then, as afterwards, the outlook and ideals of the Boer leaders seemed very close to my own. . . . Throughout my political life I had sounded the note of Canadian nationhood and from time to time I

[1] Ibid.
[2] C. M. van den Heever, *General J. B. M. Hertzog* (Johannesburg, APB Bookstore 1946), p. 118.
[3] Sir K. Hancock, Vol. I, p. 356.
[4] van den Heever, p. 183.

> had somewhat chafed under the control and domination which Downing Street arrogated to itself in determining the scope and destiny of foreign policy, even to the direct issues of peace and war. Thus there was in my mind a fixed purpose to set forth . . . a new conception of the status of the Dominions in their relation to the governance of the Empire. Shortly after meeting Smuts, I took this up in discussion with him and we found ourselves wholeheartedly in agreement.[1]

As a result they jointly proposed to the 1917 War Conference the resolution calling for the constitutional relationships between the members of the empire to be readjusted after the war by a special constitutional conference. Borden and Smuts also won the War Conference's agreement to the statement that the delegates 'deem it their duty, however, to place on record their view that any such readjustment . . . should be based upon a full recognition of the Dominions as autonomous nations of an Imperial Commonwealth'.[2]

And Smuts justified the resolution by saying that 'too much, if I may say so, of the old ideas still clings to the new organism which is growing. I think that although in practice there is great freedom, yet in actual theory the status of the dominions is of a subject character. Whatever we may say, and whatever we may think, we are subject Provinces of Great Britain.'[3]

These moderate and statesmanlike utterances concealed the balder, simpler motive revealed in a letter to his wife: '. . . I cannot and never shall forget that we were free republics.'[4]

In 1919 at the Paris Peace Conference, Louis Botha got on with Borden just as well as had Smuts. As Borden wrote in 1923 to a South African friend: 'Before I left Paris Botha said to me, "Do you realise that on all controversial questions discussed in the British Empire Delegation, Canada and South Africa have always been on the same side?" I had not realised it but it was perfectly true.'[5]

Australia and New Zealand, on the other hand, were inhabited by homogeneous populations of almost entirely British descent and strong ties of affection linked them to 'Home' – the Mother Country. Isolated as they were in the far Pacific, they were only too well aware that their existence depended on British protection. While Australia was in favour of all possible imperial co-operation short of diminishing her own sovereign

[1] Robert Laird Borden, *His Memoirs*, 2 Vols. (London, Macmillan 1938), p. 667.
[2] Cd. 8566; for full text of statement, see above p. 120.
[3] Cd. 8566, p. 47.
[4] Sir K. Hancock, Vol. I, p. 437.
[5] Letter of 12 December 1923, quoted in Borden, Vol. I, p. 66.

independence, New Zealand, most British of all dominions, enthusiastically favoured imperial federation itself, together with an imperial navy. At the 1911 Imperial Conference Sir Joseph Ward, the New Zealand Premier, who was unfortunately wordy and pompous, made an immense speech in favour of federating the empire under an Imperial Council of State.

Yet with these dominions too there was an obstacle to achieving close cohesion with Great Britain – geography. No small nations would have *chosen* as a protector a great power 12,000 miles away; conversely no great power would have *chosen* to incur the liability of weak allies on the other side of the globe. The 'white' empire was indeed strategically absurd. Could the absurdity be overcome by statecraft?

The operation of the British Empire Delegation at the Peace Conference appeared to mark the hopeful beginnings of a collective imperial foreign policy; it reconciled the unity of the empire towards the rest of the world with the equality and independence of its component nations. On major questions regarding the peace settlement the empire was represented by the British Prime Minister who, as one of the representatives of the Big Four – France, Britain, Italy and the US – voiced a policy already agreed by free discussion between the various Commonwealth representatives. On questions involving the immediate interests of individual dominions – South Africa and the future of German South-West Africa for example, or even Australia and German New Guinea – the dominions concerned were directly represented in the negotiations. All this intimate, frank and effective collaboration was made possible by the presence in Europe of the heads of dominion governments themselves, and by the continuance of the spirit of imperial community evoked by the war.

When the Peace Conference came to an end, however, and the dominion prime ministers went home, the imperial alliance relapsed into little more than fine sentiment disguising a truth of separate nations absorbed in their separate lives. It was awareness of this relapse that led to the 1921 Imperial Conference; a conference formally styled a 'Conference of Prime Ministers'. Because of Australian and New Zealand distaste, it was not, however, the constitutional conference asked for in 1917 by Smuts and Borden.

In March 1921, in preparation for the conference, the Colonial Office submitted a paper to the Cabinet on 'A Common Imperial Policy in Foreign Affairs',[1] which dissected the problems of joint management of

[1] CAB 23/2, E-6.

the imperial alliance with commendable clarity. Before the Great War, the paper noted, imperial foreign policy had been vested both in theory and practice in the British Government. However:

> The sudden outbreak of the Great War revealed the anomaly of this state of affairs. Effective consultation during the critical days of the negotiations in which His Majesty's Government strove to avert the catastrophe was impossible and was not attempted. ... It was clearly recognised from the very outset that such a situation could not be allowed to recur.[1]

How then could truly imperial conduct of foreign policy be substituted for purely British? The Colonial Office paper saw the Paris Peace Conference and the working of the British Empire Delegation as 'a landmark of the greatest significance in the constitutional development of the British Commonwealth'. The trouble was that since that delegation had broken up, 'the control of the ever-changing field of foreign policy has almost entirely relapsed into the hands of the United Kingdom'. Although the dominions had been kept informed about foreign affairs, they really had no greater share in shaping foreign policy than before the war. In the Colonial Office's opinion the new equality of status between dominions and Britain made it the more necessary to achieve unity in policy, while at the same time it rendered it less acceptable that 'one member of the group should exercise exclusive control over a policy which may involve the most vital interests and even the existence of the others'.

Drawing lessons from the example of the British Empire Delegation, the Colonial Office therefore saw the solution in better and more continuous communication between London and the dominion capitals; perhaps in direct and permanent dominion representation in London.

This able paper laid bare the fundamental problem with which the 'white' empire was to grapple until the Second World War; it also foreshadowed the kind of solutions that were to be canvassed in the years ahead.

The British Government itself accepted in word, if not yet in spirit, that it must now share foreign policy with the dominions. As Lloyd George told the House of Commons in December 1921:

> The Dominions since the War have been given equal rights with Great Britain in the control of the foreign policy of the Empire. That was won by the aid they gave us in the Great War. ...

[1] CAB 23/2, E-6.

> [However] the machinery is the machinery of the British Government – the Foreign Office, the Ambassadors. The machinery must remain here . . . you must act through one instrument. The instrument of the foreign policy of the Empire is the British Foreign Office. . . .[1]

This then was the British answer to the growing dominion sense of equality and independence: a share in the formulation of a single imperial policy. And a single foreign policy implied co-ordinated defence – not through an imperial navy, army and air force, but, as with foreign policy, through collaboration between 'allied' imperial forces within an 'allied' organisation. In August 1920, in a paper on the 'Co-operation of the Dominions and Colonies in a System of Imperial Naval Defence',[2] the Admiralty acknowledged that its revived wartime hopes of a single imperial navy had been torpedoed again by dominion opposition (essentially by Borden of Canada), and instead accepted the idea of separate dominion navies. The Admiralty hoped, however, that high policy might be directed by an Imperial Council or Cabinet, and that imperial strategy would lie with the heads of the British armed forces, advised by attached senior dominion officers responsible to their own Chiefs of the General Staff. In the event of war all imperial naval forces in an affected sea area should pass under a single commander-in-chief, although the administrative control of dominion ships should still remain under dominion authorities. In land and air strategy as well the British similarly believed that close co-ordination of British and dominion forces, together with joint contingency plans, was essential.[3]

At the beginning of the 1920s therefore the British were clear and convinced enough in their minds about the degree of cohesion that *must* be preserved in the 'white' empire: there must be a *single* imperial foreign policy and strategy. But how far could – and would – the British go to defend the imperial alliance against relentless attack by its internal forces of disintegration?

The Imperial Conference of 1921 marked the point when the sweeping advances of imperial collaboration during the Great War and the Peace Conference were seen to have stumbled to a halt; when it was manifest that the alternative to getting the advance moving again was retreat and

[1] A. Berriedale Keith, *Speeches and Documents on the British Dominions 1918–1931* (London, Humphrey Milford, Oxford University Press 1938), pp. 85–6.
[2] CAB 21/188.
[3] See statement of Lord Derby, Secretary of State for War, to the 1923 Imperial Conference in CAB 32/9, E-10.

disintegration. W. M. ('Billy') Hughes, the Australian Prime Minister, put it in plain words:

> Much is expected from us, and I do venture earnestly to hope that this Conference will do something which will convince the people that we have found a practical and sure way of bridging the apparently impossible chasm which divides complete autonomy of the several parts of the Empire from united action upon matters affecting us all.[1]

And he went on to give a warning: 'That we must do something is essential if this Conference is not to be the last magnificent flare of a dying illumination.'[2]

In 1921 the forces of imperial disintegration were temporarily outweighted and outnumbered, for Smuts, now Prime Minister of South Africa, found that this time his Canadian colleague, Arthur Meighen, a Conservative, was a man whose imperial sentiments were as warm as those of the Australians and New Zealanders. And Billy Hughes of Australia was a doughty enemy of all attempts to win greater formal independence for the dominions at the expense of imperial solidarity. A working-class Welshman who had emigrated to Australia as a youth, and fought his way to the top of the not over-refined world of Australian politics, Billy Hughes was rather like a pre-evangelical Englishman in his cheerful love of a fight and in his plain and gamey speech.

Smuts of South Africa had hopefully prepared a paper on the future constitution of the Commonwealth: 'It will no longer be an Empire but a society of free and equal sister states.'[3] The paper was never circulated. Billy Hughes proceeded, as he put it in his own words when he got home, 'to solder up the constitutional tinkers in their own tin-can'.[4]

> It has been suggested [Hughes told his colleagues] that a Constitutional Conference should be held next year. It may be that I am very dense, but I am totally at a loss to understand what it is that this Constitutional Conference proposes to do. . . . What new right, what extension of power can it give us? What is there that we cannot do now? What could the Dominions do as independent nations that they cannot do now? . . . What can they not do, even to encompass their own destruction by sundering the bonds that bind them to the Empire? . . .[5]

So the demand for a formal constitutional statement of the dominions' existence as completely sovereign states, legally free to stay neutral in a

[1] Cmd. 1474, p. 18.
[2] Ibid.
[3] Sir K. Hancock, Vol. II, p. 46.
[4] Ibid. p. 49.
[5] Cmd. 1474, pp. 18–22.

British war, or to secede from the Commonwealth, was postponed to another day. Nevertheless, Hughes himself wanted the dominions to have an effective voice in imperial policy, and complained that, as it was, he got information about the British Government's decisions from the newspapers before the telegrams arrived from London. It was Hughes's further contention that a fair dominion share in the cost of imperial defence was 'the corollary of our admission into the councils of the Empire . . .'[1] 'The Dominions', in his opinion, 'could not exist if it were not for the British Navy. We must not forget this. We are a united Empire or we are nothing.'[2] Hughes had indeed come to the conference determined to achieve the creation of machinery, which would effectively express that unity in the conduct of foreign policy. He argued that imperial conferences were not frequent enough. On the other hand an Imperial Cabinet sitting in London was not compatible with dominion autonomy. In any case, as Hughes pointed out: 'The Imperial Conference can only formulate a general policy. Too frequently it does not even do that. . . .'[3]

Thus the difficulties of political co-ordination were due to causes beyond South Africa's or Canada's nationalism alone. Hughes himself asked how British control over the question of peace and war was compatible with dominion rights of self-government. He attacked the loose way in which people stuck the label 'Imperial' on the British organs of government. 'Where is this Imperial Government of which some speak? There is none. People speak of the Imperial Parliament, but it does not exist; and the Imperial Cabinet. Where is it? . . . We are not an Imperial Cabinet. . . .'[4]

Because of long sea voyages, personal consultation between heads of government had to be infrequent and long premeditated. Meetings at short notice to deal with crises were impossible. Air travel offered only uncertain possibilities for the distant future. Telegrams were an impersonal and unsatisfactory link. Radio-telephony was in its infancy. Once again, it was Hughes who stated the problem: 'We are faced with this position, that while we cannot come here regularly, we must have a voice in the management of the affairs of the Empire. How are we going to get it? I ask you to consider this as the great Imperial question. . . . It affects the very existence of the Empire. . . .'[5]

The practical and political problems of strengthening the imperial alliance dominated the whole conference of 1921. W. F. Massey, Prime Minister of New Zealand, went so far as to voice a fear that the empire

[1] Ibid. p. 18.
[2] Ibid. p. 22.
[3] CAB 32/2, E-16, p. 3.
[4] Ibid.
[5] Ibid. p. 4.

was drifting apart.[1] Lloyd George repeated the British conviction that '... it is of paramount importance that in foreign affairs we should maintain the unity of the Empire'.[2] He thought that the empire's achievement in the Great War and at the Peace Conference arose out of this very unity in action.[3] But he too, like Hughes, found it easier to state the problem than find a solution: '... we must have some means of connecting and co-ordinating the voices of the Empire ... but how are you going to do it?'[4]

Finally, however, Lloyd George could only return to the original British contention that the voice of the empire must be communicated to the world through the British Foreign Office: 'I do not see any other way of doing it without breaking up the Empire....'[5]

No answer that was concrete, practical or acceptable emerged. The best that Billy Hughes himself could suggest was the establishment of dominion representatives of Cabinet rank in London, together with more frequent imperial conferences and better and fuller communication between London and the dominions.[6]

The Commonwealth had therefore once more come face to face with its fundamental weakness – a geographical dispersal which the communications technology of the epoch could not overcome.

The customary kind of fudge in the published conclusions of the 1921 Imperial Conference about 'unanimous and deep conviction that the whole weight of the Empire should be concentrated behind a united understanding and common action in foreign affairs' therefore masked the total failure of the conference to solve its problems – as Hughes himself had to admit.[7] In fact the only possible practical answer was for 'imperial' foreign policy to continue to be run, as Lloyd George had said, through the British Government and Foreign Office, this British control being at best only mitigated by a greater flow of information from London to the dominions and by extending the courtesies of consultation in advance whenever possible. Yet it was this very British monopoly that all the dominions bar New Zealand – even Australia – resented. If Hughes disliked it, then South African and Canadian nationalism was bound to hate it.

The 'white' empire was being driven by its internal contradictions towards crisis, just like the Habsburg Empire in its time. The momentary good luck of the 1921 Imperial Conference, with a man as forceful as

[1] CAB 32/2, E-22, pp. 15–17.
[2] CAB 32/2, E-23, p. 2.
[3] Ibid. pp. 3–4.
[4] Ibid. p. 4.
[5] Ibid. p. 5.
[6] Ibid. pp. 12–13.
[7] Paul Hasluck, *The Government and the People 1939–1941* (Canberra, Australian War Memorial 1952), p. 11.

Hughes fighting for imperial cohesion and the Canadian Prime Minister for once a man with an imperial rather than a narrowly Canadian outlook, could only delay this crisis. And in fact it soon began, in the very year following the conference; detonated by an international crisis in which the British Empire seemed about to go to war in Asia Minor.

The Turkish nationalist army under Kemal Ataturk had thrown the Greek army (in which Lloyd George had misplaced a philhellene faith) out of Asia Minor and was advancing towards the Dardanelles, the Sea of Marmara and the Bosporus. There was a danger that the Turks might try to cross the straits and recover their territories in Europe, removed from a supine puppet government by the Allies after the Great War in the Treaty of Sêvres. More particularly, Kemal's advance threatened the Neutral Zone established on the eastern shores of the waters between Europe and Asia Minor and garrisoned by Allied troops. The French and the Italians being already engaged in making friends with Kemal, so evidently the future leader of a new Turkey, the British contingent at Chanak in the Neutral Zone stood alone in the way of Kemal's army.

On Friday, 15 September 1922 at 4 p.m., the Cabinet met to discuss the sharpening crisis. Much of the lengthy meeting was taken up with the problem of repairing British isolation and weakness, and various extraordinary hopes and schemes were put forward by which Balkan countries should be invited to spring to the aid of the British contingent in the Neutral Zone.[1] It was therefore as one aspect of a faintly desperate whip-round for aid and comfort that the Cabinet fell in with Churchill's urging, as Secretary of State for the Colonies, that the dominions too should be asked for armed assistance. Churchill coupled this with a recommendation that Britain should issue a declaration that the Neutral Zone, the Straits and the Treaty of Sêvres would be preserved, by force if necessary. The declaration was also to make public the British appeal to the dominions. Lloyd George's personal secretary took down the draft of the announcement at Churchill's dictation.[2]

The announcement was released to the Press; the telegrams were despatched to the dominions. Unfortunately Churchill and his colleagues, under the stress of the crisis and in their impetuousness, forgot that the weekend lay ahead. Dominion governments would be able to read their newspapers, but, unless they happened to remain close at hand in their capitals, not their official telegrams. Reading in newspapers that the British Government was trying to involve them in a crisis which might well lead

[1] CAB 23/31, C49/22.
[2] Lord Beaverbrook, *The Decline and Fall of Lloyd George* (London, Collins 1963), p. 160.

to war did nothing to fire the dominion governments' imperial loyalties. Churchill's blunder had compounded the general error of judgement committed by the British Cabinet under his urging, that of assuming that Britain had only to give the lead for the dominions loyally and obediently to respond.

Chanak was the catalyst of the Commonwealth's future. New Zealand, ever loyal, at once pledged her help. Australia returned a tepid assurance of support; the tepidness reflecting Hughes's anger (privately conveyed to London) at the total lack of consultation and of any resemblance of the kind of joint policy-making discussed at the 1921 Imperial Conference. For South Africa and Canada, however, Chanak was the signal and the excuse for a renewed and sustained assault on imperial unity and on the collective existence of the Commonwealth as a world power. The assault was opened by the new Liberal Prime Minister of Canada, Mackenzie King.

Mackenzie King was the descendant of four Scots grandparents. His maternal grandfather, William Lyon Mackenzie, whose memory he treasured, had taken part in the Canadian rebellion of 1837. Anti-British feeling was thus a family tradition. Mackenzie King was deeply emotional and romantic: deeply, even neurotically, religious; a man who in domestic politics shrank from strife, and pursued the politics of conciliation.[1]

As a public man, King was withdrawn and personally lonely. And King's emotions, denied broader outlets, found remarkably intense expression in an adoration and veneration of his mother that survived her death. As a politician he was secretive, suspicious, cunning in manœuvre, personally sensitive. Before becoming Prime Minister his career had been concerned with social and labour reform; and it was the problem of internal Canadian unity that was to dominate his long premiership. King was in fact a North American isolationist, and in this he only reflected the sentiments of most of his countrymen. The Great War, the first Canadian experience of overseas involvement on the grand scale, left the Canadians in retrospect only determined to stay out of European troubles and wars in the future.

King's broad objective in imperial relations did not differ from Sir Robert Borden's; both wanted Canada to be a completely independent state, especially in foreign affairs. However, whereas Borden wished to use this independent position in order to influence an imperial foreign policy that, once agreed, would be supported by Britain and all the

[1] M. MacGregor Dawson, *William Lyon Mackenzie King: A Political Biography 1874–1923* (London, Methuen 1958), Vol. I, p. 36.

dominions, King wanted the freedom in order to have a *separate* Canadian foreign policy, like any other sovereign state – even if this freedom really meant, in view of Canadian isolationism, freedom to have no foreign policy.[1] In any case anti-British bias was, in Vincent Massey's words, 'one of the most powerful factors in his make up'.[2]

Domestic and political pressures and personal prejudices alike, therefore, impelled Mackenzie King to set out to break up the 'white' empire as an effective alliance; not directly and deliberately, but as the by-product of achieving complete freedom of action for Canada. King's aims inevitably led to a political struggle with the British, a struggle from which he did not shrink; on the contrary, as the biographer of this period of King's life relates, 'Mackenzie King was the constant aggressor'.[3]

Unfortunately for Britain there stood behind King as permanent head of the Canadian Ministry of External Affairs a displaced academic, Dr O. D. Skelton, who, according to Vincent Massey, the Canadian businessman and statesman who became Canadian High Commissioner in London in the 1930s and Governor-General after the Second World War, nourished 'a strong and lasting suspicion of British policy and an unchanging coldness towards Great Britain. In other words, to put it bluntly, but I feel not unfairly, he was anti-British. No one who worked with him, or knew him well, could, I think, fail to recognise this.'[4]

In January 1922 King had heard Skelton, then the Dean of the Faculty of Arts at Queen's University, speak to the Canadian Club of Toronto on 'Canada and Foreign Policy'. The address was a merciless attack on imperial control of policy, inspiring King to note of Skelton in his diary that 'he certainly had the knowledge and the right point of view'.[5] So King invited Skelton to help prepare the Canadian case for the forthcoming Imperial Conference in 1923, and to be a member of the delegation.

The British appeal for help over Chanak, especially in the unfortunate circumstances of the appeal's arrival in the dominions, did not therefore elicit a warm response in Ottawa. King confided his suspicions to his diary:

> I confess it annoyed me. It is drafted designedly to play the imperial game, to test out centralisation versus autonomy as regards European

[1] Ibid. p. 406; H. Blair Neatby, *William Lyon Mackenzie King: 1924–1932* (London, Methuen 1963), Vol. II, p. 32.
[2] Vincent Massey, *What's Past Is Prologue* (London, Macmillan 1963), p. 242.
[3] Neatby, p. 32.
[4] Massey, p. 135.
[5] James Eayrs, *In Defence of Canada: From the Great War to the Great Depression* (Toronto, University of Toronto Press 1964), p. 175.

> wars. . . . I have thought out my plans. . . . No contingent will go without parliament being summoned in the first instance. . . . I shall not commit myself one way or another, but keep the responsibility for prlt [*sic*]. . . .[1]

That Canadian public opinion was against sending Canadian troops to Chanak seemed to be clear, although Arthur Meighen, the Conservative leader, called for loyal support of Britain. The Cabinet approved King's tactics. Three appeals in all from Lloyd George and one from Churchill were allowed to drop to extinction like stones in a well.

However, the immediate problem of evading the British appeals was far less important than the impression made by the Chanak crisis on King and Skelton in terms of the future. That King was himself intensely pacifistic and a hater of military institutions only sharpened his apprehensions that Canada might be drawn into wars because of the imperial connection. Immediately after Chanak he wrote privately to a friend in London:

> Anything like centralisation in London, to say nothing of a direct or indirect attempt on the part of those in office in Downing Street to tell the people of the Dominions what they should or should not do, and to dictate their duty in matters of foreign policy, is certain to prove just as injurious to the so-called 'imperial solidarity' as any attempt at interference in questions of purely domestic concern.[2]

He went on to express his conviction that if membership of the British Empire meant dominions being involved in any and every British war without advance agreement, he could 'see no hope for an enduring relationship'.[3]

The Australian answer to the problem of preventing repetitions of Chanak was still to press for that joint imperial control of foreign policy which Billy Hughes had failed to achieve at the 1921 Imperial Conference. As S. M. Bruce, who became Australian Prime Minister in 1923, expressed it:

> We have to try to ensure that there shall be an Empire foreign policy which, if we are to be in any way responsible for it, must be one to which we agree and have assented. . . . If we are to take any responsibility for the Empire's foreign policy, there must be a better system . . . so that we may be consulted and have a better opportunity to express

[1] Dawson, p. 409. [2] Ibid. p. 419. [3] Ibid.

the views of the people of this country. . . . We cannot blindly submit to any policy which may involve us in war. . . .[1]

Yet this kind of communal participation in foreign policy was hardly less distasteful to King and Skelton than British control of it. In a memorandum of 1923, Skelton attacked the whole notion of an imperial foreign policy. 'A common foreign policy . . . offers the maximum of responsibility and the minimum of control. It commits a Dominion in advance to an endorsement of courses of action of which it knows little and of which it may not approve, or in which it may have little direct concern.' And he went on: 'The real way in which the Dominions may extend their power is the way in which such an extension has come in the past – by reserving for their own peoples and their own parliaments the ultimate decision as to their course of action. . . .'[2]

The Peace Conference which finally resolved the Chanak crisis and which led to the Treaty of Lausanne – and a peaceful settlement with Kemal Ataturk's new nationalist Turkey – indirectly and unintentionally strengthened King's hand. Foreign powers objected to there being present dominion delegations at the conference as well as a British delegation, the Empire being then considered by foreigners to be, like other empires, diplomatically a single state. In consequence, no invitations were sent to the dominions, which therefore did not sign the Treaty of Lausanne; two circumstances which brought only gladness to Ottawa. However, the Treaty of Lausanne raised an awkward question: since Britain had signed for the British Empire, were the dominions legally, or even morally, bound by her signature?

As the Imperial Conference of 1923 drew nearer, therefore, Australia on the one hand and Canada on the other prepared their conflicting answers to the problems of imperial policy. It only remained for the British to draw up theirs. In the summer of 1923 Lord Curzon, the Foreign Secretary, alluded in a speech to the need for

> . . . a common policy in international matters so that the Foreign Minister of this country, when he speaks, may speak, not only for Great Britain alone, but for the whole British Empire. . . . Think of the addition to his power and strength that will result if, in speaking, he knows – and the world knows – that there lies behind him the sentiments and the might of the British Empire as a whole.[3]

While this British view therefore complemented the Australian, it stood

[1] Hasluck, p. 15. [2] Dawson, p. 420. [3] Ibid. p. 458.

in four-square opposition to Canadian convictions. The issue of disintegration or cohesion thus turned on the coming battle of argument and manœuvre at the Imperial Conference.

Strategy and defence too remained aspects of the problem of imperial relations hardly less important than foreign policy. The Admiralty still believed that there must be an imperial naval authority to co-ordinate the naval efforts of the individual countries of the empire and to evolve a single imperial strategy.[1] The Air Staff sent all dominions a memorandum on air policy that also struck the 'imperial' note.[2] So in these fields as well the opposing sides prepared for conflict.

At the Imperial Conference of 1923 the British were by no means as strongly posted as in 1921. Then there had still been the afterglow of wartime co-operation to warm the memories of the overseas delegates; now there was the aftermath of Chanak, as sour as a stubbed-out cigar. S. M. Bruce of Australia, though staunch, was not so heedless and violent a fighter as Billy Hughes. There was the implacable Mackenzie King in the place of the imperially compliant Arthur Meighen. And this time there was a new delegation; a delegation from another once-conquered non-British people who had every reason to resent the British Empire.

For in December 1921 the English had concluded a treaty with the Catholic Irish rebels by which the twenty-six counties of southern Ireland were granted self-government as a dominion. In itself and as a precedent this Irish treaty was of the utmost significance to the future of British power. While Ireland was politically a vast nuisance and economically of no great value to Britain, it was still, as it had been since the Middle Ages, of immense strategic importance. Ireland offered enemies of England the opportunity of outflanking her to the West and threatening English sea communications with the world. Ireland was a back-door to England through which more than one great power had endeavoured to pass. In 1600 during Tyrone's rebellion, for example, the Spaniards had landed at Kinsale, fortunately quickly to be besieged and defeated by the English viceroy in Ireland, Mountjoy. After 1689 James II and a small French army had kept William III and his Dutch and English troops busy in Ireland for three years. In 1797, at the time of Wolfe Tone's rebellion, French troops under Humbert had landed, again fortunately to be defeated without much difficulty. In the Great War the Easter Rebellion of 1916 had served as the vehicle of German intrigue. And in the crisis of the war against the submarine in the Western Approaches and the Irish Sea, the Royal Navy's

[1] See S. W. Roskill, *Naval Policy Between the Wars* (London, Collins 1968), Vol. I, pp. 402–3.
[2] CID Paper 206–6.

use of Irish bases had been of the utmost help in defeating the U-boat. The strategic unity of the British Isles had in fact come to seem to successive English governments a fundamental principle, in pursuit of which the English had fought nasty but victorious counter-insurgency wars against the Irish on repeated occasions. By 1921 the English were beginning to win, as the Irish leaders afterwards acknowledged.

However this time the English were in fact defeated – not in Ireland, but in England, for liberal consciences flinched at the violence and human misery incidental to the maintenance of imperial power, especially when so near home. The public platform rang with reproaches; the letter columns of the newspapers were filled with lamentation. Sir John Simon, later Chairman of the Indian Statutory Commission, and later still a Foreign Secretary, was horrified. So was Edward Wood, later, as Lord Irwin, Viceroy of India, later still, as Lord Halifax, another Foreign Secretary. So was Lionel Curtis, who wrote in his journal *The Round Table* in June 1921: 'If the British Commonwealth can only be preserved by such means, it would become a negation of the principle for which it has stood.'[1] Smuts, arguing from the happy precedent of the apparent reconciliation of Boer and Briton after the Boer War, urged concessions. So Lloyd George's government embarked on a peace offer just at the moment when the rebels were being bent to snapping point. Thus the British decided the question of Ireland not in the light of whether or not, on drawing a balance of political and strategic factors, Ireland was worth holding, but out of humanitarian qualms as yet rare in a barbarous world. Yet this was a demonstration that the British ruling classes and British public opinion after the Great War were ill-suited to the preservation of their imperial inheritance. Theirs was indeed something of the confused and unhappy state of mind of teetotallers who have inherited a brewery and a chain of pubs. If the British would not hold Ireland, what would they hold?

Southern Ireland having been given its independence, as the Irish Free State, in the face-saving guise of a dominion owing a quite meaningless formal allegiance to the king, the Irish leaders were now looked upon, and welcomed, as members of the imperial family. In fact, as pessimists like Churchill warned at the time, the treaty of 1921 was the beginning of a step-by-step process in which, by the 1930s, the Irish transformed a dominion under the Crown into a state hostile to Britain, and eventually into a republic.[2] The Irish settlement certainly repeated the pattern of the

[1] Lionel Curtis, *The Round Table*, Vol. XI, No. 43 (June 1921), p. 505.
[2] W. K. Hancock, Vol. I, ch. VI.

South African settlement, but in neither case was the pattern what liberal optimists expected.

So the 1923 Imperial Conference included, in South Africa and the Irish Free State, two ex-enemies bent on expunging the last traces of British suzerainty; and, in Canada, a dominion bent on preventing the evolution of the empire into an effective alliance.

The British themselves were a weaker force than in 1921. Lloyd George had gone; his political career destroyed when the wartime coalition was broken up by a revolt of the Conservative rank-and-file. This revolt had led to Bonar Law becoming, firstly, Conservative Party Leader, and then, after winning the General Election of 1922, Prime Minister of a government described by Churchill as 'the second eleven'; mostly men only junior ministers before. After Bonar Law's retirement through ill-health, Stanley Baldwin, one of the leaders of the palace revolt against Lloyd George, became Prime Minister. Baldwin himself was the last man for a scrap. It had been a factor in the revolt which had toppled Lloyd George that Lloyd George himself was seen by Baldwin and his supporters as being both 'dynamic' and immoral, while Lloyd George's principal colleagues, Churchill and Birkenhead, were regarded as worldly, adventurous and, in the case of Birkenhead, cynical. It followed that Baldwin's government was naïve, cautious, but highly-principled. This was in fact the moment when liberal moralism came finally to triumph throughout British politics.[1] It was an administration to which the instinct to appease was native and profound.

Even before the Imperial Conference opened, L. S. Amery, the First Lord of the Admiralty, though himself a passionate believer in the imperial idea, told Beatty, the First Sea Lord, not to circulate the Admiralty memorandum on imperial naval co-operation to the dominions as it stood, as he was 'afraid that most of the Dominions, and certainly Canada, will shy off the memorandum in its present form'.[2] Amery also wrote in conciliatory fashion to Mackenzie King:

> . . . you know my own views of Imperial Co-operation well enough, but you will find the whole Admiralty staff here as definite as myself in not merely accepting as second-best, but positively as the best policy, that under which [*sic*] each unit in the Empire develops its own strength directly under the control of its own Parliament and on its own lines. The conception of a centralised Navy run by the Admiralty, and subscribed to by the Dominions, is now completely extinct . . .[3]

[1] See above p. 59–60.

[2] Roskill, *Naval Policy Between the Wars*, pp. 402–3.

[3] Eayrs, p. 173.

In imperial conferences, England occupied a unique position; she was host nation, 'the Mother Country', and the creator and present prop of the empire. It was her representatives who took the chair at most meetings. However, English statesman chose to interpret their role as one of impartial referee, concerned with the welfare of the whole empire. This inhibited them from fighting for England's own interests; too often English representatives looked on while the others argued. Thus, the Cabinet agreed before the 1923 Conference that it would not be advisable for the English representatives 'to take any initiative in suggesting any alteration in the present association of the Dominions with foreign affairs', but instead to await suggestions from others.[1]

Mackenzie King launched his offensive in his very opening speech. Under cover of a fine flow of imperial and fraternal sentiments he laid heavy emphasis on the supreme role of 'our Parliaments and peoples', of which the delegates at the conference were only representatives, and back to which the delegates would carry information from the conference for them to decide and act upon.[2] King had thus straight away called in question the very nature of imperial conferences, in particular their power to decide policy. Later in the conference, he tackled the fundamental question of an imperial foreign policy, by referring to the opening remark of Curzon's statement on foreign affairs that the dominion prime ministers came to London to assist in 'the foreign policy which is not that of these islands alone, but that of the Empire'.[3] King emphatically denied that Canadian opinion had ever accepted anything like a single channel, the Foreign Office, for all the foreign relations of the empire.[4] He saw foreign policy as falling into two categories – that which was of local and particular interest to each dominion or to Great Britain, and that which related to the whole empire.[5] By his implication, therefore, Europe might be considered a purely English concern, and the South Pacific purely an Australian, New Zealand and English concern. King also pointed out the importance of the separate public opinions in each country.

King's views were not well received. S. M. Bruce of Australia, an English immigrant who was later to return to Britain as Australian High Commissioner in London, expressed an exactly contrary opinion: '... from Australia's point of view, I have to say that, unless as a result of the discussions which take place we can evolve some policy on broad lines which we can say is the policy of the Empire, the attempt to build up

[1] CAB 23/46, C48(23). [2] Cmd. 1988, p. 13. [3] CAB 32/9, E-4.
[4] Ibid. p. 12.
[5] Ibid. pp. 12–13.

consultation and the supply of information to the Dominions are of very little use . . .'[1]

Massey of New Zealand agreed:

> I sympathise with the idea put forward by the Prime Minister of Australia, that we want . . . an Empire Council or Empire Conference that can act quickly in an emergency, and I do think before this Conference comes to an end we should decide whether it is in the interests of the Empire and of our respective countries to meet at intervals of not less than two years.[2]

Such effective dominion participation in imperial policy was indeed the Australian answer to Chanak, as Bruce privately informed Curzon: 'I left no doubts that we expected to be fully informed on foreign policy, and every intention of expressing our views. We did not want a repetition of the 1922 episode, when we were nearly involved in war with Turkey at Britain's heels, without really knowing what was going on.'[3]

While Smuts contented himself with lecturing on the constitutional relations between the various parts of the empire in regard to foreign policy, Kevin O'Higgins, for the Irish Free State, disclaimed – like Mackenzie King – any share in responsibility for British foreign policy;[4] and William Robertson Warren, the Prime Minister of Newfoundland, also supported Mackenzie King's line of argument.

The empire was thus in conflict over a fundamental issue. As the conference went on, the conflict spread inevitably from foreign policy to naval and military defence. Mackenzie King, always generous with fraternal but empty phrases, began by promising that Canada's attitude would be, as it had been in the past, one 'of hearty co-operation in matters of defence', having merely regard to the fact that the decisions as to whether, how much, and how Canada would participate in a war would lie in the hands of the Canadian Parliament at the time.[5] It gradually became clear, however, that King's 'hearty co-operation' was a euphemism for persistent obstruction. S. M. Bruce of Australia developed the ideas he and Massey had already voiced on foreign policy. He suggested that there should be an Imperial Council of Defence, charged 'with laying down the whole of the plans for united action by the Empire in a period of national danger'.[6] Imperial defence was a matter for the whole empire, and the dominions must in the future contribute more to it. Massey concurred.

[1] CAB 32/9, E-4, pp. 24–5. [2] Ibid. p. 34.
[3] Cecil Edwards, *Bruce of Melbourne: Man of Two Worlds* (London, Heinemann 1966), p. 86.
[4] CAB 32/9, E-5, pp. 13–14. [5] Ibid. p. 10. [6] Ibid.

In his view all dominions had an equal interest in the naval defence of the empire and should accept a greater share of the burden.[1]

These views of course chimed with those of the British Admiralty, whose amended memorandum, *Empire Naval Policy and Co-operation*, asking for an Imperial Naval Authority, had now been circulated to the dominions. However, the Admiralty's proposals had provoked O. D. Skelton to write an acid memorandum for Mackenzie King's benefit:

> These proposals make it clear that while the Admiralty has perforce abandoned the concept of a single Empire fleet supported by Dominion contributions, it expects to attain the same end by a somewhat more circuitous route. Each Dominion is to have its own Naval Force, but the Admiralty is to be a central controlling authority, outlining policy, and fitting the various local units into a mosaic.[2]

The conference sessions on naval matters promised therefore to be animated. Amery himself, in a conciliatory speech, argued in favour of imperial co-operation through separate dominion navies. He voiced a plea that the dominions should bear a greater weight of the burden of imperial maritime strength.[3]

Mackenzie King however took this opportunity of launching yet another major attack on the collective existence of the empire. 'I do not think it would be possible for the Dominions, whether in relation to Naval, Military or Air Forces to concur in any policy in the nature of a highly centralised policy.'[4] And he went on:

> . . . we at this table cannot be too careful not to assume powers which we have not got. We have no right, as I see it, to regard ourselves as a Cabinet shaping policy for the British Empire. We are here as the representatives of Governments, deriving what power we have from that circumstance and that fact alone. . . .[5]

King constantly emphasised what he considered to be the dangers of any phraseology that might suggest the existence of a single imperial entity in foreign policy and defence:[6] 'It is not true that the Empire is indivisible; it is divisible, and very distinctly divisible. It is divisible geographically, racially, politically, and in a thousand ways. . . .'[7]

When Lord Derby, the Secretary of State for War, stated the British view of the land defence of the empire, he did so in terms plainer and less

[1] Ibid. p. 16.
[2] Eayrs, p. 176.
[3] CAB 32/9, E-9, pp. 12–15.
[4] Ibid. pp. 15–16.
[5] Ibid. p. 17.
[6] Ibid. pp. 18–19.
[7] Ibid. p. 19.

tuned to sensitive Canadian ears than his colleague, Amery, employed over the question of seapower:

> . . . what is important is, first of all, that there should be complete agreement in the military mind not only of this country, but of the great Dominions, as to what steps should be taken in the event of an attack on any one part of the British Empire; secondly, that we should know approximately, each of us, what assistance would be forthcoming at all events at the immediate outbreak of the war. . . .[1]

After discussing the importance of common forms of training and organisation, Derby returned to his main point:

> . . . there should be the closest touch, by correspondence if necessary, between the military heads of this country and the great Dominions. The defence problem is like a great puzzle composed of many different pieces, of which the Mother Country and the Dominions each hold some pieces. We want to piece these together so as to make a complete picture.[2]

It was a metaphor exactly, though unwittingly, designed to drive O. D. Skelton into a cold rage; and at the next session Mackenzie King proceeded to disembowel Derby's hopeful proposals with the delicacy of a surgeon:

> There is one point, I think, I ought perhaps to speak of with care. Lord Derby mentioned that one thing the Government here would like to be sure of was the number of men, or rather the extent of the forces, that could be counted upon. If that has any reference to what at any time the personnel may be, what the equipment and general organisation may be, of course that is always available; but if it has reference to what numbers of men or extent of forces may be available at any given moment for participation in war, I think I ought to make it clear that as to what extent Canada would participate in a war at any time must be considered a matter which her own Parliament will wish to decide.[3]

The unfortunate Derby in reply, blundered in yet deeper: 'I appeal on two assumptions which I hope are not ill-founded. First of all, that, if any part of the Empire, wherever it is, is attacked, the whole Empire will rally to the support of the part so attacked. Secondly that it will rally to the fullest extent of its powers. . . .'[4]

[1] CAB 32/9, E-10, p. 13.
[2] Ibid. p. 14.
[3] CAB 32/9, E-11, pp. 2–3.
[4] Ibid. p. 18.

Lord Derby's assumptions were in fact thoroughly ill-founded, as Mackenzie King interrupted to tell him so. King wanted a definition of what an 'attack' meant. For example, Canadian participation in a war with Turkey, arising out of the Chanak crisis, would have been in his view unlikely. All depended on the merits of the case as seen by a dominion at the time.[1]

Thus the British conception of the empire, both in strategy and in foreign policy, and the Canadian conception were totally opposite and totally irreconcilable. Although Australia, for her part, like Canada, refused to commit herself in advance exactly as to what she would do in some hypothetical crisis, Bruce's view of imperial co-operation – and Massey's – was otherwise close to Britain's; for all three wanted a collective foreign and strategic policy; all wanted joint decisions in time of crisis; all were in favour of the co-ordination of the Royal and Dominion navies on an imperial scale. Their proposals, in fact, foreshadowed the kind of allied organisation created by the North Atlantic Treaty powers after 1949. The British Empire was therefore split open from crown to roots. It was a decisive moment, for at issue was its very future as an empire in substance as well as name. As Bruce had warned an audience in Australia before coming to London: 'We have to realise that the basis of an Empire foreign policy involves the whole future of the Empire. If we can find such a basis, then I think it is possible for the Empire to grow stronger. . . . If such a basis cannot be found, I believe the failure to find it will eventually lead to the disintegration of the Empire. . . .'[2]

The issue turned on the tactical skill and timing, the character and the force of will which each side brought to the conflict. Mackenzie King, with Skelton at his elbow, was absolutely resolved to carry the Imperial Conference, even though he was in the minority. It followed that King had either to be defeated, or he had to be bought off by concessions to his wishes. But if King was allowed to carry his point, it would decisively and ineluctably change the nature of the empire from that of a close strategic alliance into that of a loose sentimental association.

Unspoken, but always at the back of the minds of British statesmen in their attitude to the dominions and to the evolution of the empire, was the example of their eighteenth-century predecessors' policy towards the American colonies. Although the circumstantial details were very different, the quarrel at that epoch too had been over imperial defence: how far the colonies ought to contribute towards its cost, and whether the colonies ought or ought not to be pieces in an imperial mosaic. It was now a

[1] Ibid. [2] Hasluck, p. 16.

general article of belief that America might never have been lost to the British Empire if the governments of George III had only granted the American colonies 'dominion status' instead of trying to impose their own conception of a centralised empire. Yet it is hard to see what material advantage this would have offered England. The English, attaching as they did such importance to legal and constitutional form,[1] failed to perceive that, had their predecessors preserved the mere formalities of common allegiance, it could not have altered the fact of American separatism; it would have been as pointless as staying married while deciding to live apart.

There was another aspect to the Canadian problem: how far was it worthwhile toadying to Canada in order to keep her – and keep her no more than formally – within the empire? What in any case was Canada's value to England? In 1923 Canada possessed few land forces, no air force, and a navy which, in the words of a Canadian official historian, was 'scarcely more than a nominal one'.[2] Even when Canada's aid during the Great War was borne in mind, a contribution of six divisions in some future war hardly offered England adequate compensation for having to abandon the development of the empire as a close alliance and, instead, allow it to straggle off down the road to disintegration. Moreover, Mackenzie King had made it plain that England could no longer count on Canadian assistance in any crisis or conflict which did not directly touch on Canada's own interests; and Europe no longer figured among these interests.

There were therefore good reasons for not appeasing Mackenzie King. There was a further reason, perhaps the best of all: King's own tactical position was not nearly as strong as his resolution. In the Imperial Conference itself he was outnumbered by Britain, Australia and New Zealand, for Newfoundland and the Irish Free State, though sympathetic to his views, were not directly interested in the issue; while Smuts, for South Africa, was more concerned with the constitutional and legal aspects of dominion autonomy. Smuts himself was by no means averse to an imperial policy, for the proffering of advice in London on strategy and foreign affairs was by way of being a hobby of his. Nor was King's position back home in Canada invulnerable to indirect attack, for, despite his election victory, there was a great fund of imperial and pro-British sentiment among English-speaking Canadians. It was by no means certain that Canadian opinion, if it knew what was going on, would support King

[1] Cf. the fantasies of A. Berriedale Keith, the constitutional lawyer.

[2] G. N. Tucker, *The Naval Service of Canada* (Ottawa, King's Printer 1952), Vol. I, p. 328.

over the plain issue of the breaking-up of the empire as a working partnership. It is noteworthy that when the British Admiralty suggested that their memorandum on imperial naval co-operation should be published, it caused Mackenzie King and O. D. Skelton instant pangs of alarm, and they refused to allow publication. Skelton saw the dangers clearly enough: '. . . To work out this [imperial naval] policy, it will be necessary to develop a common Empire public opinion, and if need be, force the hand of the Dominion Governments; hence the Memorandum, the first, doubtless, of a series in the years to come. . . .'[1]

Skelton thus crisply sketched the outline of the strategy which the English could have carried out against King with fair hope of success. A well-phrased and nicely timed speech by an English minister, for example, or a deliberate indiscretion, could have thrown the whole crisis into the arena of public debate throughout the Commonwealth. Inside the conference itself the English could have abandoned their quasi-neutral interpretation of the role of chairman and host, and instead exploited their position with all the cheerful ruthlessness of a Palmerston.

However, to assess Canada's usefulness or Mackenzie King's political vulnerability in so cold and calculating a fashion would have been distasteful to Baldwin's Cabinet, even had it occurred to them to do so. To go further, and to consider how best to isolate and embarrass King both in the conference and at home and so beat him would have been even more foreign to their way of thinking.

It is possible that they failed even to recognise the importance and danger of the challenge which Mackenzie King was making. It is possible that they thought he was simply quibbling over a form of words because of apprehensions about being criticised in his own Parliament, while his heart was really in the right imperial place all the time. It is possible that they failed to take King, a pudgy, soft, mild, unctuous little man, as seriously as they should. It is possible that, in their guilelessness, they were completely taken in by Mackenzie King. There are indications of such a fatal series of misjudgements in L. S. Amery's diary. After King had visited Amery privately to talk about Canada's contribution to imperial naval defence, Amery recorded: 'I think he really genuinely is willing to do something but he feels himself powerless at the present moment with his majority of one. . . .'[2] When King had again privately expressed his wish to help, this time at the naval review at Spithead, Amery wrote: 'I am still not without hope that he may pluck up sufficient courage to translate

[1] Eayrs, p. 176.
[2] Diary for 24 October 1923, L. S. Amery Papers.

these ideas into practice but he is by nature thoroughly timid.'[1] During the agonising arguments in the conference over the wording of the final resolutions, Amery confided to his diary that 'the timidity of even speaking of the Empire as a single unit is getting too ridiculous'.

Amery thus displays no awareness that the empire was unbridgeably split over a fundamental question; no sense that it was facing a major crisis. And the final course of the discussions inside the conference also suggests that for the British it was all merely a question of hammering out an agreed form of words, rather than of deciding the very nature of the empire as a political and strategic institution. So they compromised and conceded in the way that came naturally to them. There was argument with King, of a tactful kind, but no relentless opposition.[2]

The final British capitulation took place over the drafting of the conference resolutions on imperial defence. Any word or phrase that could suggest the corporate existence of the empire was struck out at Mackenzie King's demand. 'Air Forces of the Empire' became, for example, 'Air Forces of the several countries of the Empire'. King would not even accept a reference to the regular exchange of service personnel, although he had no objection to this as a fact.[3] So the conference resolutions merely recognised the need for adequate defence of the territories and trade of 'the several countries of the British Empire', and merely laid down 'guiding principles' instead of common policy decisions.[4] At Mackenzie King's insistence the conference resolutions further recorded that '. . . in this connection the Conference expressly recognises that it is for the Parliaments of the several parts of the Empire, upon the recommendations of their respective Governments, to decide the nature and extent of any action which should be taken by them'.[5]

The most spirited opposition to King's wrecking tactics was provided by Lord Salisbury in a limp comment on the draft resolution on defence as amended by King: 'I cannot pretend that I like it so well as the other draft, but, so far as I am concerned, as representing the British Government, I am quite prepared to accept it, although as Mr Mackenzie King knows, there are one or two words which I should much prefer to be differently expressed.'[6]

Amery's diary well describes the circumstances and conveys the mood of this final English surrender:

[1] Diary for 3 November 1923, loc. cit.
[2] See CAB 32/9, E-11.
[3] CAB 32/9, E-15.
[4] Cmd. 1987, p. 16.
[5] Ibid.
[6] CAB 32/9, E-15, p. 2.

> The language of these [the defence resolutions] and even the sentiment was very washy in defence to Mackenzie King whom even Smuts laughs at for his timidity, but I did not suggest even the simplest verbal amendment for fear of starting a landslide by a new discussion as Salisbury and Smuts and everybody else had had hours in trying to coax Mackenzie King to accept anything.[1]

At King's yet further demand the conference added a paragraph to its statement on foreign affairs:

> This conference is a conference of representatives of the several Governments of the Empire: its views and conclusions on Foreign Policy, as recorded above, are necessarily subject to the action of the Governments and Parliaments of the various portions of the Empire, and it trusts that the results of its deliberations will meet with their approval.[2]

This made plain that all projects for a common imperial policy executed through an imperial council were now dead; more than that, it also recorded King's successful demotion of the imperial conference itself, the only existing organ of imperial co-operation over high policy.

The 1923 Imperial Conference marked an English defeat, worse, a surrender, which changed the course of the history of the empire. The possibility of greater cohesion in the imperial alliance had been destroyed, perhaps for good. Such cohesion as had been left as a residue of the Great War had been loosened. The English cabinet had chosen to preserve the *façade* of an empire entire and intact, at the cost of allowing the structure behind it to fall apart. They had placed this preservation of an outward unity above the achievement of a working partnership between England, Australia and New Zealand. Characteristically, if unconsciously, the English had chosen the ideal and not the real; the myth and not the fact.

The decisive nature of the English defeat at Mackenzie King's hands was not, like the results of defeat in battle, immediately apparent. It did not occur to English statesmen that this passing bump had doomed the ship. Thus in June 1924, the first Labour Prime Minister, Ramsay MacDonald, wrote a personal letter to his dominion colleagues to ask for their suggestions as to means to bring about closer co-operation over foreign and imperial policy. His letter drew only coldly negative replies from Canada and South Africa.[3]

[1] Diary for 6 November 1923, L. S. Amery Papers.
[2] Cmd. 1978, p. 17.
[3] Cmd. 2301, p. 5.

At the end of 1924, when the short-lived first Labour Government had been replaced by a Conservative administration, Austen Chamberlain in his first speech as Foreign Secretary talked as if the imperial alliance of 1917–21 were still in being:

> The first thoughts of an Englishman on appointment to the office of Foreign Secretary must be that he speaks in the name, not of Great Britain only, but of the British Dominions beyond the seas, and that it is his imperative duty to preserve in word and act the diplomatic unity of the British Empire. Our interests are one. Our intercourse must be intimate and constant, and we must speak with one voice in the Councils of the world.[1]

Yet this diplomatic unity was already breaking up. In 1920 Canada had, with British consent, appointed her own minister in Washington. In 1923 Canada and the United States had directly negotiated a treaty on the halibut fishery, while in the same year England, but not the dominions, had signed the Treaty of Lausanne. Such actions recognised that the different states within the empire had their own separate regional interests. In any case, the time and distance that divided one dominion from another and all from England still remained formidable obstacles to a common imperial foreign policy; obstacles which Mackenzie King had made it now impossible even to try to surmount. And so, by 1925, Austen Chamberlain was negotiating and signing the Treaty of Locarno[2] on behalf of the United Kingdom alone, without making any attempt to achieve that common voice of the empire of which he had confidently spoken only a year before. As Chamberlain himself made clear in the House of Commons:

> . . . the affairs of the world do not stand still. . . . I could not go, as the representative of His Majesty's Government, to meeting after meeting of the League of Nations, to conference after conference with the representatives of foreign countries, and say, 'Great Britain is without a policy. We have not yet been able to meet all the governments of the Empire, and we can do nothing.' That might be possible for an Empire wholly removed from Europe, which existed in a different hemisphere. It was not possible for an Empire the heart of which lies in Europe.[3]

Thus the empire as an entity in foreign policy continued to be pulled apart by the forces of geography. Mackenzie King added a tug of his own

[1] Neatby, p. 40.
[2] See below pp. 330–3.
[3] Hansard, *Parliamentary Debates* (House of Commons), Fifth Series, Vol. 188, cols. 520–1.

whenever he could. For example, it was largely at Canadian insistence that England had a clause inserted in the Treaty of Locarno specifically exempting the dominions from its provisions and obligations.[1] As a member of the Canadian Government put it: 'I do not see that Canada should assume obligations including connection with the boundaries between France and Germany . . . [or] guarantee any boundaries in central Europe or elsewhere.'[2] This isolationist distaste for entanglement in European affairs was shared not only by South Africa, but also, more unexpectedly, by Australia.[3] For while in the short term the Great War had inspired the dominions with a strong spirit of solidarity behind Britain in her European predicament, in the long term it had the very opposite effect. The post-war mood of all the dominions was fairly expressed in 1925 by the Canadian delegate to the League of Nations, when he said: 'She [Canada] is realising to-day more intensely than she did at the time of the Great War, what it has cost her: she therefore naturally hesitates to undertake in advance rigid obligations which would render her liable to intervene in conflicts so far removed from her shores.'[4]

By now English statesmen were at last becoming conscious of a disagreeable loosening one from another of the various parts of the imperial machine. They sought ways of arresting further disintegration; better, some means of tightening up the bolts again. After Amery became Colonial Secretary in 1924, he divided his ministry into a Dominions Office as well as a Colonial Office, in order to lend greater importance and intimacy to relations between England and the dominions. He attempted to outflank the Canadian embargo on the creation of official machinery for imperial co-operation by inviting the dominion representatives in London to weekly informal tea-meetings. Yet even this very English attempt to run a world alliance or empire through a tea-party brought down Mackenzie King's condemnation. It was 'one of Amery's schemes to set up a round table council in London and may create embarrassments. An effort to pull us into European affairs, Egypt etc.,' he wrote in his diary.[5] At first the Canadians simply avoided committing themselves in any way in the course of the chats over the scones and cucumber sandwiches. Eventually, however, in 1927, King took official umbrage. He pointed out to Amery that either these conferences were official or they were unofficial. If unofficial, they conveyed an erroneous impression of obligation in regard to their results. If official, then it followed that, should the Canadian Government continue to countenance them, they

[1] Eayrs, p. 7.
[2] Ibid.
[3] Hasluck, p. 36.
[4] Eayrs, pp. 6–7.
[5] Neatby, p. 41.

'would be helping to build up in London, in conjunction with the Secretary of State for the Dominions, a sort of Cabinet', whose members would have no instructions from their governments; which governments would know little about the proceedings.[1] So the experiment of imperial government by tea-party had to be abandoned.

The British Government was far from liking the current trend towards imperial disintegration; on the contrary, they now proposed – within the limits of their upbringing and outlook – to make a great effort to arrest or even reverse it. This provided one major motive for inviting the dominions to another Imperial Conference in October 1926. There was another, and connected, purpose: 'that the question of Dominion adherence to the Locarno Treaty might be discussed in the present favourable atmosphere'.[2] The principal British aim was tactfully expressed by Baldwin in his opening address:

> . . . the most pressing problem [in foreign relations], it seems to me, is whether it is possible to increase the opportunities for personal discussion, which experience has shown to be at present insufficient, particularly in relation to matters of major importance in foreign affairs where expedition is so often essential and urgent decision necessary.[3]

The omens were hardly good. Mackenzie King and his suspicions again represented Canada, while this time the South African representative was General Hertzog. Hertzog had become South African Prime Minister in 1924, when his Nationalist Party beat Smuts in a general election; it was a victory which Hertzog's biographer describes as 'the victory of Afrikanerdom'.[4] Hertzog, like Smuts, had fought the British during the Boer War, but, unlike Smuts, had failed altogether to develop later an affection for Britain or the British Empire. He was a hard man; strong, rigid; seasoned in Calvinist Afrikanerdom. The objects of his political life were to recover the lost national independence of the Boers and bring about the triumph of Afrikaner culture in South Africa; objects pursued with undeviating conviction. There was nothing here of the liberal mind, the compromising temper, of modern English politics. In 1926 Hertzog came to London determined to consummate the total reversal of the verdict of the Boer War. As his biographer put it: 'Self-government to him meant the absolute right of a people to decide in their own interests, the right to remain neutral in a British war, and the right of secession [from the British Empire].'[5]

[1] Neatby, pp. 42–3.
[2] CAB 23/52, C3(26)12.
[3] Cmd. 2769, p. 13.
[4] Heever, p. 205.
[5] Ibid. p. 134.

Hertzog was no less obsessed with legal and constitutional form than the English themselves, for although the dominions were still subordinate to the United Kingdom in law, in fact they had long been fully sovereign states. To accede to Hertzog's demand that the constitution of the empire should be formally re-defined could therefore have no practical consequences. The English, characteristically, took the whole question with immense solemnity. Statesmen and civil servants theorised voluminously on the constitutional nature of that unique institution, the British Empire. It appeared that the empire was not so much a political and strategic organisation as a kind of mystical communion. Amery, the Dominions Secretary, for example, favoured his colleagues with a paper on *The Crown As An Element In The Constitutional Evolution Of The Empire*,[1] which was far above squalid considerations of the empire as a factor in English world power. Amery believed that the empire was not a 'personal union' through the monarch, Britain and the dominions happening to share the same king, but 'a single constitutional entity, the Crown'. Therefore it was important in Amery's opinion to emphasise equally with the independence and equal status of the nations of the empire that 'all these free nations are also an organic unity'. He went on to refer to 'the intangible moral bonds expressed in the traditional form of a common sovereignty'. In this kind of thinking, the fruits of a Victorian and Edwardian classical education, the empire was nearer religion or philosophy than strategy.

Hertzog, for his part, made it clear that unless he got what he wanted he would return home and 'set the veldt on fire' with an agitation for secession from the empire.[2] The Irish Free State delegation naturally took the South African side. Here was a notable achievement of past liberal English statecraft: that two former imperial enemies should be collaborating inside a British imperial conference to break up the legal unity of the British Empire. Mackenzie King took the opportunity to act as 'honest' broker.

The English themselves had no wish to embark on this constitutional re-definition; given that there was no alternative, they wanted at least to preserve the overriding 'organic unity' of the empire in the phrasing of the new definition. Unlike Hertzog, they were not prepared to fight it out to the point of a public breach, any more than they had been in 1923 in regard to Mackenzie King. Instead they twisted and turned in their efforts to satisfy Hertzog's demand for a plain statement that the dominions were

[1] CAB 32/49, E(B)22.
[2] Heever, p. 216. See also Cmd. 2769, p. 25; CAB 32/56, E-129 and the E(IR/26) series.

wholly independent sovereign states, while at the same time drawing over this naked fact some gauzy veils of 'organic unity'. As Hertzog himself wrote afterwards: 'The whole affair was now becoming a bit ludicrous. They insisted on putting in the "Empire" in one form or another as a super-state. I could not agree to an Empire possessing a "common citizenship" and including a state unity – I will not.'[1]

The utter defeat eventually sustained by the British was disguised by a draft in which Balfour, now Lord President of the Council, rose to his supreme moment as a conjuror of high-sounding ambiguities. The Inter-Imperial Relations Committee's Report (the Balfour Report), having first blandly asserted that the position and mutual relations of Great Britain and the dominions 'may be readily defined',[2] went on to provide the definition so 'readily' reached – in fact the eighth draft:[3] '*They are autonomous Countries within the British Empire, equal in status, in no way subordinate to one another in any aspect of their domestic or external affairs, though united by a common allegiance to the Crown, and freely associated as members of the British Commonwealth of Nations.*'[4]

This sophistry satisfied Hertzog, pleased the British, and was to occasion constitutional lawyers many happy years of ingenious interpretation. But the truth was that the Commonwealth (as it was now dubbed), far from being 'united', was still profoundly sundered over the practical question of how it ought to function as a political institution, if at all. Mackenzie King was quick to repeat his contention that imperial conferences were no more than discussion and exchanges of views and contacts between, as he put it, 'those directly responsible for the government of the several parts of the Commonwealth'.[5] J. G. Coates, now the New Zealand Premier, argued on the other hand that:

> It is highly desirable . . . that in every way we should strive to make these discussions of real value and to arrive at definite decisions upon questions of real importance. . . . I feel that the importance of taking wherever possible the larger Imperial view of our problems cannot be too strongly emphasised.[6]

The British delegation wholeheartedly agreed with these sentiments. However they once again played the umpire instead of using their commanding place in the conference to drive through the policies *they* wanted to see adopted. Their attitude towards disruptors like Mackenzie King and the Irish and the South Africans remained rather like that of hosts at a

[1] Heever, p. 216.
[2] Cmd. 2768, p. 14.
[3] Heever, p. 216.
[4] Cmd. 2768, p. 14.
[5] Cmd. 2769, p. 16.
[6] Ibid. pp. 22, 23.

party who deal with awkward guests not by throwing them into the street, but by jollying them along in the hope of preserving intact the happy party atmosphere.

A principal British object in holding the imperial conference was to induce the dominions to adhere to the Locarno Treaty. The British case was put by Austen Chamberlain, the Foreign Secretary. He did not impress. Vincent Massey, a Canadian who met him now for the first time, wrote:

> Austen Chamberlain did not seem to me to be a man of first-rate mind, but he obviously possessed high character and the sort of disinterested goodness and amateur methods that now and then have enabled British statesmen to play notable roles in negotiations with foreign diplomats, even when the latter have been armed with subtler minds and the traditional techniques.[1]

Chamberlain's presentation of the British case, in fact, displayed all the diffidence of an English gentleman touching a friend for a fiver. There was only one way in which he could have applied leverage to the dominions; and that was by hinting that if they refuse to commit themselves to supporting England in Europe, England would be unable to commit herself to supporting *them* in their corners of the world. Chamberlain, in his 'disinterested goodness', threw this lever away: 'It was axiomatic in Great Britain that if the safety of a Dominion was at stake the whole resources of Great Britain would be placed at its disposal.'[2]

Chamberlain then proceeded to weaken his own argument in itself by saying that 'if they [the Dominion representatives] asked whether any serious consequences would follow from the Dominions not adhering, he would say no. He thought that people at large would think it was almost certain that in a great crisis the Empire would act together.'[3]

Nevertheless and on the other hand: 'Unanimous adherence, however, would produce great effect, if it was felt that the whole weight of the British Empire was to be used to prevent aggression.'[4]

The dominions were not keen. Bruce of Australia and Coates of New Zealand were prepared to sign the treaty if, in Bruce's words, it was the general view that 'the prestige of Great Britain would be helped by the dominions coming in'.[5] Mackenzie King refused to sign, on the grounds that the Locarno Treaty involved obligations in Europe, a continent that was not a primary concern of Canada's. Hertzog made it equally plain that South Africa would not enter 'more deeply into matters concerning

[1] Massey, p. 113.
[2] CAB 32/56, E(IR-26)7, p. 32.
[3] Ibid.
[4] Ibid.
[5] Ibid. p. 52.

Europe and Great Britain, unless cause was shown'.[1] Cause satisfactory to Hertzog was not shown, hardly surprisingly. The Irish Free State reserved its attitude – a variation on the same theme of unhelpfulness.[2]

The Commonwealth had promptly split again over a major question both of foreign policy and of imperial solidarity; and split along the old line of fissure, with Canada and the ex-enemies facing England, Australia and New Zealand. And once again the English yielded. At Balfour's suggestion, the dominions merely expressed their 'satisfaction' at the treaty and 'congratulated' the British Government on having negotiated it.[3]

It was another decisive English defeat. Its consequence was to leave England absolutely on her own so far as Europe was concerned, just as if she possessed no empire. Yet at the same time she still retained an unlimited obligation outside Europe to protect the empire. It was hardly a good bargain. The failure of the dominions to join England in the Locarno Treaty marked a critical step in the dissolution of the 'white' empire as an effective alliance useful to England. It was the opinion both of Arthur Meighen, the Canadian Opposition leader, and of Sir Robert Borden, that Britain's lone signature of the treaty meant that the attempt to frame a common imperial foreign policy had finally broken down; and that henceforth each unit of the Commonwealth was on its own.[4]

The remainder of the conference's deliberations on foreign affairs amounted to no more than the familiar cant about improving liaison between England and the dominions, perhaps by 'developing a system of personal contacts, both in London and the Dominion capitals',[5] together with some chic platitudes about supporting the League of Nations and the cause of peace. There was a total failure to fulfil the hope voiced at the opening of the conference by Coates of New Zealand for 'definite decisions upon questions of real importance'. Instead the conference only managed to recognise that in foreign affairs 'the major share of responsibility rests now, and must for some time continue to rest, with His Majesty's Government in the United Kingdom'.[6]

The conference discussions on defence saw other British defeats and surrenders. Baldwin had discreetly hinted at British policy in his opening address when he said that 'there is urgent need for constant and close co-operation' over defence policy.[7] British policy was later unveiled in detail. A War Office Memorandum entitled *General Organisation for War* pointed out that to standardise equipment and military organisation

[1] CAB 32/56, E(IR-26)7, p. 32
[2] Ibid.
[3] Ibid. p. 6; Cmd. 2768, pp. 28–9.
[4] Eayrs, pp. 23–5.
[5] Cmd. 2768, p. 27.
[6] Ibid. p. 26.
[7] Cmd. 2769.

throughout the empire was not enough: 'It is of utmost importance that what may be termed the higher organisation for war should be formulated in a well co-ordinated plan in which the efforts of the parts of the Empire are adapted to the plan as a whole.'[1] It was desirable, the memorandum continued, that the dominions should have prepared plans for mobilising and despatching expeditionary forces. This had in fact been accomplished by Australia and New Zealand, but the War Office had received no information from other dominions.[2] So as far as further military expansion after the despatch of the first expeditionary forces was concerned, the War Office recommended that the dominions should frame plans and deposit them in the War Office 'in order that the potential assistance which they may be prepared to render may be included in the schemes which are being worked out to meet the various contingencies'.[3]

This was the kind of recommendation to spoil Mackenzie King's and O. D. Skelton's breakfasts; and the Admiralty's Memorandum[4] was unlikely to restore their appetites. It likewise persisted in treating the Commonwealth as if it were a close alliance, even an empire; and once more asserted its conviction that 'in war the Naval Forces of the Empire must be considered as a single collective Empire fleet'.[5] At the moment, the Admiralty had to remind the conference, only England possessed a fleet capable of the general defence of the empire. The Admiralty therefore expressed the hope that the dominion navies would develop beyond the mere defence of their own home waters, and come to contribute 'a substantial part of the general scheme of Naval Defence, and more particularly of the Main Fleet'.[6] It added a warning in plain terms against allowing the imperial alliance to disintegrate any further: 'The problem which has to be faced by each Government is how best to organise, train and prepare its Navy in peace so that in war all the various portions of the combined Empire Navy may be able to act together for the defence of the Empire with an efficiency and striking power at least equal to that of any foreign fleet.'[7]

Yet another reminder that so far little had been done to carry out the grand resolutions of 1917–18 to develop the empire's collective strategic power was voiced by the Principal Supply Officers' Committee of the Committee of Imperial Defence.[8] 'There is, as yet, no scheme for what may be termed the general industrial mobilisation of the resources . . .

[1] CAB 32/44, IC(FPD)4, p. 1.
[2] Ibid. p. 2.
[3] Ibid. p. 3.
[4] CAB 32/44, IC(FPD)6.
[5] Ibid. p. 4.
[6] Ibid. p. 5.
[7] Appendix 5 to CAB 32/44, IC(FPD)8.
[8] Memorandum on the Supply of War Material and Other Essential Requirements, CAB 32/44, IC(FPD)-8.

which are available in the various parts of the Empire.'[1] It was therefore highly desirable, the committee wrote, that the study of supply from an imperial point of view should be begun, and that tentative arrangements should be reached.[2] In this field as well, however, the committee made all too plain, the present truth was that 'the Empire' really meant just England.[3]

These memoranda from the British service departments raised hard questions about the nature, or reality, of the imperial connection; questions which were remote indeed from the lofty consideration of such things as 'intangible moral bonds' which otherwise occupied the delegates. But it was, of all things, disarmament which posed the fundamental question as to whether or not the Commonwealth still enjoyed any kind of corporate existence as a power. For instance, when it came to allotting quotas of armed forces under some future international disarmament treaty, should the British Commonwealth be treated as one state or several? The British General Staff had to point out that a single collective quota for the empire's land forces would be founded on a wrong assumption that '. . . the forces . . . were available in any contingency and for any purpose. This is not, in fact, the case. Each [dominion] portion of the quota could be employed only when and to the extent to which the Government [concerned] decided it should be available.'[4]

And the General Staff went on to draw the gloomy conclusion that 'in weighing military risks and in considering our present military commitments they feel bound to point out that this lack of absolute certainty [about dominion assistance] exists, and, in calculating the risk, they must necessarily consider the most unfortunate possibility'[5] – i.e. that the dominions might not fight alongside England.

Here was a plain acknowledgement that, only eight years after the imperial effort in the Great War, the Commonwealth had already ceased to exist as an effective and reliable military alliance. This dissolution was the more dangerous because of the empire's geographical dispersal.

Faced with this prospect of dissolution, therefore, the English, Australians and New Zealanders tried again to advance the cause of collective imperial organisation. Bruce of Australia said: 'We take the strongest view that it is the whole Empire that is concerned in this problem [of naval defence], and that we all ought to play a reasonable part according to our population and resources.'[6] He produced comparative figures of

[1] Memorandum on the Supply of War Material and Other Essential Requirements, CAB 32/44, IC(FPD)-8, p. 1.
[2] Ibid.
[3] Ibid. p. 4.
[4] CAB 32/44, IC(FPD)-7, p. 2.
[5] Ibid. p. 2.
[6] Cmd. 2769, p. 179.

Commonwealth expenditure on defence in 1925–6, which showed that the proportion of the burden of empire carried by England had been little lightened since 1902.[1] Whereas Britain was spending annually per head of population on her sea, land and air forces 51s. 1d., Canada was spending only 5s. 10d., South Africa 2s. 2d., and even Australia and New Zealand only 25s. and 12s. 11d. respectively.[2] Bruce proceeded to draw a moral from these figures: 'I suggest that an equality of status carries with it some responsibility to share the common burden of defence, as a set-off against the great advantages we have received in recent years from our connection with the Empire.'[3]

Unfortunately Canada and South Africa, unlike Australia and New Zealand, felt no need of imperial, or really British, protection. Neither Mackenzie King nor Hertzog in the least considered that equality of status carried with it equality of responsibility for imperial defence. As a consequence, none of the hopes for a renewal of imperial strategic planning and organisation stood a chance of fulfilment.

The Imperial Conference, true to the role of impotent chat imposed on it by King in 1923, therefore came to no decisions over the urgent and crucial strategic questions that were presented to it. Its published proceedings feebly refer to exchanges of visits between British and dominion service personnel, and to joint discussions and demonstrations; and added the flaccid statement that the results of these activities 'will, it is believed, prove of much practical value in aiding the several Governments of the Empire in the determination of their policies of defence, and are commended to their most careful consideration'.[4] Since not even King could detect much danger to Canadian freedom of action in standardising organisation and equipment or in interchanging officers, the conference also invited 'the Governments concerned to consider the possibility of extending these forms of co-operation and of prompting further consultation between the respective General Staffs on defence questions adjudged of common interest'.[5]

Thus it was over the entire range of foreign policy and strategy that the firm intentions to arrest the loosening of the Commonwealth came to nothing but spongy platitudes.

What had the English gained by their appeasement of Hertzog and Mackenzie King, to say nothing of the Irish? They had preserved the empire intact, so far as their own public opinion and the world at large were concerned; preserved it in the insubstantial guise of a sentimental

[1] See above p. 109.
[2] Cmd. 2769, p. 180.
[3] Ibid. p. 181.
[4] Cmd. 2768, p. 35.
[5] Ibid.

if potent myth. In the best tradition of middle-class respectability they had kept up appearances; the neighbours need never know. The price paid was however high: no less than the complete and continued stultification of the desire of England, New Zealand and Australia to develop an imperial alliance with a common foreign policy backed by collective strategic power.

The British made the best of their surrenders. Amery, for example, wrote in his diary after the last session of the conference:

> It really has been a great clearing-up of outstanding points on a basis which eliminates friction, and leaves the way open for future co-operation. It is equally true that it leaves the way equally open to dissolution. That is a risk we have got to run, and if the will to unity is there we shall overcome it.[1]

However, the full implications of what had been allowed to happen at the 1926 Imperial Conference gradually sank in. On 1 March 1927 Amery, writing to Baldwin, the Prime Minister, to explain why he was making a forthcoming imperial tour, noted that '. . . the general principles of consultation were laid down in the sketchiest way at the Conference . . .'[2] There was therefore a need to settle with each dominion prime minister what authority was to be given to his high commissioner in London. Amery's letter also acknowledged that 'the constitutional declaration of the late conference, though it satisfied us all, is susceptible to a good many shades of interpretation, some of them in directions which would undoubtedly tend to weaken the whole unity of the Empire'.[3]

In public Amery put a brave enough face on it. While in Canada in 1928 he attempted to answer Canadian critics who argued that nothing was left to hold the empire together:

> That is quite true: no bonds except the sense of responsibility itself. That *is* the bond . . . it seems to me that in this new experiment we are trying . . . we may be justified in believing that Governments, conducting their individual affairs in absolute freedom at the same moment of time, but separate in space, can yet by the same bond of responsibility be enabled to work under the Crown for great common ends . . .[4]

And Amery went on to voice the romantic optimism characteristic not only of himself, but of post-evangelical England as a whole: 'It may be a

[1] Amery, Vol. II, p. 394.
[2] L. S. Amery Papers.
[3] Ibid.
[4] Amery, Vol. II, p. 463.

great act of faith, but we have had great acts of faith in our history before. It is on acts of faith that human progress is built. . . .'[1]

It was true enough that henceforth to explain the nature of the bonds of empire took the talents of theologians discoursing on the Trinity.[2] Yet all such optimistic glosses to the effect that the Commonwealth was 'developing' rather than disintegrating were like claiming that at the very moment when the emperor in the fable removed his pants and finally stripped himself bare, he had really finished donning fresh raiment of miraculous beauty and utility. Some sceptics refused to be taken in. Old Billy Hughes in Australia, together with some Conservative sceptics in England (including *The Times*) saw the surrender to Hertzog as a vain attempt to appease the unappeasable.[3]

However, it was Hertzog himself who, on his return to South Africa, proclaimed the truth about the Balfour Report: 'The old British Empire, as it existed in the past, now exists no longer as a result of what was done at the Imperial Conference . . . all that remains is a free society.'[4]

For Afrikaners the value of that 'free society' lay in the accompanying consummation of untrammelled Boer domination of South Africa. As one Nationalist politician exulted: 'Just think, it was from a red imperialist government, from Baldwin's Conservative administration, that our General Hertzog wrung the title deeds and transfer! Hertzog! Hertzog!'[5]

And the Cape National Party sent Hertzog a rapturous address: '. . . never, never did we dare hope that you, without arousing opposition . . . with love and peace and calm, would get what we and our forefathers have striven for so many years without success'.[6]

When in 1934 the South African Parliament passed the Status Bills which implemented the Statute of Westminster, Afrikaners could claim that South Africa was now more free and more independent than even the old Boer republics before their defeat by Britain in 1899–1902.[7]

The demolition of the 'organic unity' of the British Empire had thus been completed, or recognised, in due constitutional form; the Commonwealth had now become just a sentimental association of sovereign states under one Crown, somewhat akin to the old Holy Roman Empire. The appointment in dominion capitals of British 'high commissioners', reciprocal to the earlier appointment of dominion high commissioners in London, was itself a sign of imperial disintegration. The 'high commissioners' were simply ambassadors under a fancy name. The idea was

[1] Ibid.
[2] Cf. A. Berriedale Keith, pp. xxv–xlvii; W. K. Hancock, Vol. I, pp. 300–19, 486–507, 577–99.
[3] Mansergh, *The Commonwealth Experience*, p. 238.
[4] Heever, p. 218. [5] Ibid. [6] Ibid. [7] Ibid. p. 261.

even canvassed of fostering Commonwealth co-operation in foreign affairs through the League of Nations;[1] perhaps the ultimate absurdity of the new non-empire and non-alliance.

Unfortunately the dominions only functioned as completely sovereign and independent states when it suited them; that was, whenever Britain tentatively suggested that they might still co-operate in a Commonwealth alliance, or take some of the strategic weight off British shoulders. When there was advantage to be gained from the imperial connection – economic preferences, or worldwide diplomatic and consular representation through the British foreign services – even Canada and South Africa were quite happy to be dominions of the British Commonwealth.

Thus Mackenzie King's and Hertzog's demolition job had not served to relieve Britain totally of the burden of the Commonwealth, as might have seemed logically to follow. While Canada and South Africa enjoyed the best of both worlds of independence and imperial connection, Britain for her part suffered the worst of both. The dominions were like grown-up sons who loudly demand the independence and freedom of action of adulthood whenever there is question of contributing to the collective life of the family, and yet who are far from taking their independence to the point of dispensing altogether with the comfort and security offered by the family roof.

In the years following the 1926 Imperial Conference British politicians and public servants gradually became more aware that Britain had not done very well out of the recent changes in the nature of the imperial connection. In 1930, when the second Labour Government was making preparations for another imperial conference, the Prime Minister, Ramsay MacDonald, 'drew attention to the serious difficulties arising from the present arrangements under which the Secretary of State for Foreign Affairs undertakes the whole burden and responsibility of negotiating with Foreign Powers and yet can only speak with certainty for the United Kingdom'.[2]

It was, he thought, desirable at the forthcoming conference to discuss affairs 'on the basis of emphasising unity rather than disunity'.[3] Indeed the Cabinet as a whole 'was impressed by the difficulties created by the Report of the Imperial Conference of 1926, and more particularly by the emphasis laid on equality of status between Great Britain and the Dominions and the keeping in the background of the principle of co-operation, which is a necessary supplement to the other'.[4]

[1] W. K. Hancock, Vol. I, pp. 307–8.
[2] CAB 32/77, 1EC(30), p. 4.
[3] Ibid.
[4] CAB 23/65, C51(30), p. 1.

But such an outstandingly romantic and idealistic government of innocents as this, including as it did MacDonald as Prime Minister and the nonconformist Arthur Henderson as Foreign Secretary, was unlikely to fight any more resolutely for Commonwealth co-operation than had Baldwin and his colleagues.

The conference was in any case principally occupied with economic questions and with arguing over legalistic detail in preparation for implementing the Balfour Report by Act of Parliament (the Statute of Westminster of 1931). Here the Irish and the South Africans proved staunch allies over such important questions as the King's new style and title, insisting on the removal from the drafts of even the most harmlessly formal of words or expressions that might be suggestive of English predominance.[1] Foreign affairs were not the dominating topic at the conference, which did little more than record that virtually nothing had been done to further inter-imperial consultation since 1926, and repeat the same kind of pious hopes as in 1926 about the need for closer liaison between governments.[2]

The British Chiefs of Staff however were so perturbed at the disintegration of the empire as a strategic power that before the conference opened they wrote jointly to the Prime Minister to put forward a draft resolution by which the dominions would express their desire to extend their co-operation in the common defence of the empire.[3] Here was naïveté of a kind different from that of the politicians! The British Government would as soon have laid hand-grenades on King's and Hertzog's chairs as strike such a discordant note of strategic realism. The Chiefs of Staff nevertheless had good reasons for pleading that the question of collective imperial defence ought to be plainly and courageously faced:

> In reviewing the previous Resolutions [on defence in imperial conferences] we have been forcibly struck by the fact that whilst it is clearly laid down that each part of the Empire 'is responsible for its own local defence', no express mention is made of collective responsibility for Empire defence, and the inference, undoubtedly drawn by many of the Dominions, is that the United Kingdom would automatically shoulder the bulk of responsibility for the defence of the Empire in a major war.[4]

Hence, the Chiefs of Staff went on, the dominion forces were not taken into account in British planning, but treated as possible bonuses. But it

[1] CAB 32/88.
[2] Cmd. 3717, pp. 28–9; see also CAB 32/100, E(30)34.
[3] CAB 21/336.
[4] Ibid.

was, they noted, strange strategy to prepare to send troops all the way from Britain to Singapore when Australian troops were so much nearer.

The Chiefs of Staff were wasting their time. Imperial statesmen currently saw the Commonwealth more as a constitutional puzzle, or as a bright, hazy cloud of ideals, than as a strategic alliance. Imperial defence was in fact not discussed at all in the plenary sessions of the conference, but only by a Committee of Experts of the Fighting Services, which was debarred from discussing high policy, and could only make recommendations on points of detail.[1] The New Zealand representative on this committee did his best: he said that his government saw a two-fold responsibility, both for home defence and for co-operation in general imperial defence. He therefore would welcome guidance in order to help New Zealand co-ordinate her plans and achieve the right balance between her services. The meeting, however, agreed that it could not discuss such matters, they being 'high policy'.[2]

The discussions of the Committee of Experts of the Fighting Services therefore did little more than catalogue the items in the almost complete failure to fulfil the soaring hopes of 1917–18 for strategic planning on an imperial scale and even the more cautious intentions of 1923 and 1926. The First Sea Lord (Admiral Sir Frederick Field) said that the Admiralty still hoped that the dominions would first provide the local naval defence of their own coasts, and then sea-going squadrons for general strategic purposes. He told his colleagues that '. . . he knew the First Sea Lord had desired to impress upon the Dominion representatives the heavy burden which fell upon the United Kingdom in regard to Naval Defence. . . .'[3] Here the First Sea Lord had in fact played a record whose grooves had become somewhat worn since first put on at the Colonial Conference of 1902.[4]

Equally in the Report of the Committee of Experts of the Fighting Services, it was pointed out that not all dominions had carried out the recommendations of the 1926 conference to set up Supply Officers' Committees to study problems of industrial mobilisation. Canada was the notable defaulter. Close liaison between the British Supply Officers' Committee and their opposite numbers in the empire had only been established in the cases of India and New Zealand.[5]

Once again, however, all the hopeful suggestions for the collective organisation of defence were blocked by Canada, South Africa and the Irish Free State with the simple formula that these were questions for each

[1] CAB 32/87, E(30)37.
[2] Ibid. p. 4.
[3] CAB 32/77, E(FS)30, p. 1.
[4] See p. 109 above.
[5] CAB 32/87, E(30)37.

government to decide in the light of opinion at home. The final conference resolutions on defence were the usual thin gruel: the information obtained and opinions exchanged would, it was believed, be of much practical value in aiding 'the several governments of the Empire' to determine their own policies; which governments were also invited to consider the possibility of further co-operation and consultation between general staffs over standardising organisation and equipment.[1] As Sir Maurice Hankey, Secretary to the Cabinet and to the Committee of Imperial Defence, wrote to the Chiefs of Staff, the resolution on defence was 'necessarily an anodyne, as this section is particularly difficult from the point of view of the Irish Free State Delegation'.[2]

The British Cabinet's hope and wish that the 1930 Imperial Conference would emphasise 'unity rather than disunity' had been fulfilled by nothing more substantial than the customary fraternal sentiments expressed by the delegates in their public speeches.

So, after all, the 'white' empire had been born only to expire in infancy. It had thrived as an effective alliance only from 1916–17 until after the Peace Conference of 1919. Embalmed in myth and propaganda, however, the 'white' empire deluded the faithful in the 1930s – and public opinion at large – into believing that it still lived. Members of the Royal Family toured the dominions, to be received by loyal sentiments and Union flags. The king spoke to the Commonwealth on the wireless each Christmas Day. At George V's Silver Jubilee in 1935, and again at George VI's Coronation in 1937, dominion contingents marched in procession through London, capital of the empire, just as at Queen Victoria's Diamond Jubilee in 1897 and the Coronations of Edward VII in 1902 and George V in 1911, or at the Victory Procession in 1919 – misleading demonstrations of continued unity. There was still therefore a 'white' empire on the cigarette cards and souvenir biscuit-tins, in children's scrapbooks and the minds of men. The general public in England never realised that, whatever might happen in a general war, in peacetime England was now diplomatically and strategically on her own.

Yet this was the case. No imperial conference[3] was held between 1930 and 1937 – seven years that witnessed the transformation of the post-war world by Japanese expansion in the Far East, by the aggressive policies of Fascist Italy, and by the rise of Nazi Germany. And the imperial conference, emasculated though it had been by Mackenzie King's operations, was the only organ of high policy in the Commonwealth. Its failure to meet could only confirm the break-up of the imperial alliance.

[1] Cmd. 2768, p. 35. [2] CAB 21/336. [3] Only an economic conference in 1932.

England failed even to evolve a smaller alliance with Australia and New Zealand, dominions which shared her concern for the defence of the Far East. From before the Great War until the Second World War, New Zealand constantly urged that there should be an imperial strategy carried out by an imperial organisation. Australia too, though more jealous of her freedom of action, sought similar objectives. Even after the 1926 Imperial Conference, S. M. Bruce, the then Australian Premier, still argued: 'Our first obligation is to play a part, by consultation, in the foreign policy of the British Empire. Our second obligation is to co-operate in the defence of the Empire as a whole. . . .'[1] It was Bruce who earlier had installed an Australian liaison officer, Richard Casey (now Lord Casey) in the British Cabinet Office.[2]

Yet, so far from energetically meeting this desire for close partnership, Britain neglected even to consult Australia and New Zealand in good time over specific questions affecting their interests. Thus on 10 August 1929, for example, Sir Joseph Ward, Prime Minister of New Zealand, wrote to Ramsay MacDonald to complain about such neglect in regard to naval defence, the Singapore base and various international topics.

'Our feeling is', Ward wrote 'that sufficient time has not been made available for a study of your proposals and that there is much to be gained by taking the point of view of the Dominions in ample time to allow of a reasoned expression of their opinion before a decision is reached in London. . . .'[3]

Despite this, the Labour Government took the decision in November 1929, to halt work on the Singapore naval base without any prior consultation with Australia and New Zealand. Sir Joseph Ward again wrote to complain in strong terms.[4] Yet in 1930 Ward's successor, G. W. Forbes, was being asked by Britain for comments on vital questions 'practically by return of cable'.[5] The proposal for the five-power (the British Empire, USA, Japan, France and Italy) naval conference[6] reached Wellington only a week before the invitations were sent. New Zealand received the text of an important joint statement by the British Premier and the United States President just two days before it was to be issued.[7]

And so after the 1930s, as a consequence of the lack of sustained British effort to salvage a working alliance with Australia and New Zealand out

[1] Hasluck, pp. 19–20.
[2] Cecil Edwards, p. 87.
[3] F. L. W. Wood, *The New Zealand People At War: Political and External Affairs* (Wellington, War History Branch, Department of External Affairs 1958), pp. 15–16.
[4] Letter from the First Sea Lord of the Admiralty, Lord Passfield, to the Prime Minister, 20 May 1930. No. 223 in CAB 21/188.
[5] Wood, p. 16.
[6] See below pp. 286–71.
[7] Wood, pp. 16–17.

of the wreck of the larger imperial alliance, these loyal dominions gave up hope of intimate co-operation with Britain.[1] The British had been too accommodating to the disrupters in the imperial alliance, but not accommodating enough to those loyal to it; a sad combination of weakness and lack of imagination.

There was, it was true, the geographical obstacle in the way of a close British–Australian–New Zealand alliance. As the foreign threats of the 1930s became clearer, Australia and New Zealand looked towards Japan; England towards Germany. Thus sentiment and geography were more than ever in conflict. Yet the English failed to apply the newest resources of technology to their inherited imperial problem of distance. For example, in 1930, important memoranda concerning the Imperial Conference took six weeks to reach New Zealand.[2] The Dominions Office itself was still Victorian in its pace and methods of handling communications. It was constantly surpassed in speed by the international news agencies.[3] Vincent Massey, the Canadian High Commissioner in London, went so far as to look on the Dominions Office as less of an instrument for keeping the dominions in touch with affairs as an obstacle to this process.[4]

However the most important failure, in an empire as uniquely far-flung as the British, was in the development of air transport – despite the somewhat naïve enthusiasms of Sir Samuel Hoare, Conservative Secretary of State for Air in 1922–4 and 1924–9.[5] For modern technology, through long-distance air transport of passengers and mail, now offered the opportunity of bringing Britain and the Far Eastern and Pacific parts of the empire within days of each other instead of weeks. It was an opportunity that the British failed adequately to exploit in the late 1920s and the 1930s. Although they had created an aircraft industry in 1914–18, and in 1918 possessed the largest air force in the world, they allowed their leadership in the air to slip away in peacetime, the victim of various national characteristics of the epoch, such as a lack of awareness, understanding, interest or even liking for modern technology; sloth; and a '*laissez-faire*' reluctance to organise anything on a national scale. British aircraft in the 1920s and 1930s were backward in design and construction, except for 'shop-window' record breakers like the Schneider Trophy winners; and they were built by what was hardly more than a cottage industry when com-

[1] Hasluck, pp. 40–7; Wood, ch. 4.
[2] CAB 32/77.
[3] Cf. Mackenzie King's legitimate complaints about delayed despatches from London in the months before Chanak in 1922, in Dawson, p. 409, as well as the New Zealand complaints cited above.
[4] Massey, p. 236.
[5] See Samuel Hoare, *Empire of the Air* (London, Collins 1957).

pared with the American and German aviation industries.[1] It was only in 1931 that the College of Aeronautical Engineering was opened in Britain – with thirty-five students.[2]

The British, characteristically, shone more at individual pioneering or record-breaking flights – the romantic adventure stuff – than at the business of airline development and operation. And so, despite a lot of propaganda about an empire linked by air-power, Britain and the British Empire lagged behind other major nations in air travel. In 1930 the route-mileage of the whole British Empire, at 23,005 miles, was not much longer than the 17,900 route-miles operated by Germany, a continental power with no overseas possessions. The French, with a smaller and less scattered empire than the British, operated 19,400 route-miles. Nor did the British performance in civil aviation in 1930 look any better in terms of volume of passengers, for while the United States carried 385,910 passengers and Germany 93,126, the British Empire as a whole carried only 58,261.[3] In 1930, one year after the German airship *Graf Zeppelin* had begun her years of regular luxury travel from Germany across the South Atlantic to Brazil, a British attempt to open an airship route to India with the *R101* ended in flames at Beauvais in northern France owing to faults in design and construction.

Seven years later, when aircraft had vastly advanced in range, comfort, reliability and speed, the British had still failed to exploit the potential power of air travel to draw the empire closer together. In 1937, the and British aircraft industry produced virtually no large, long-distance airliners of modern design, and so the empire had to buy from Europe or the United States.[4] A memorandum by the Air Ministry for the 1937 Imperial Conference on a 'Commonwealth Air Route Round the World'[5] gloomily summarised the achievements of the French, Dutch, Germans and Americans (especially the latter) in developing worldwide and trans-oceanic air routes, including regular commercial flights across the South Atlantic and the Pacific. There was a German service to South America, but no British. There was no British trans-Pacific route; no trans-Tasman route. Regular commercial flights from Great Britain to Australia via

[1] See M. M. Postan, D. Hay and J. D. Scott, *Design and Development of Weapons* (London, HMSO 1964), pp. 33–4; M. M. Postan, *British War Production* (London, HMSO 1952), p. 5; William Hornby *Factories and Plant* (London HMSO 1958), especially pp. 18–19, also pp. 229–31, 240.

[2] Air Ministry – Directorate of Civil Aviation, *Report on the Progress of Civil Aviation 1930* (London, HMSO 1931).

[3] Ibid. pp. 76, 100–1. See also Air Ministry Report to the 1930 Imperial Conference on Imperial Air Communications, CAB 32/76, IEC(30)100.

[4] Policy for the Production of Civil Aircraft Within the Commonwealth. CAB 32/129, E(37)16.

[5] CAB 32/127, IC(36)10.

India were not due to start until 1938. The route from Britain to South Africa was only a project. The Air Ministry therefore wrote: 'The Conference is invited to consider the importance of meeting this foreign challenge with a concerted effort made in time to prevent the reputation and rewards of initiative from passing altogether into other hands.'[1]

However, as the Air Ministry noted, the Commonwealth faced in commercial aviation, as in every other sphere, 'problems of decentralisation and co-operation which do not confront unitary states'.[2]

And so in the 1930s dominion and English statesmen and servicemen remained further apart, both in time and in mind, than need have been the case. British backwardness in the various technologies of long-distance communications compounded the British failure to make a determined effort to create a co-ordinated alliance with the dominions of the Pacific. The Australians indeed began to question the fundamental assumption on which they had always founded their national security – whether they could depend on British 'imperial' protection against Japan. In the mid-1930s there was a great deal of informed discussion in Australia on this topic. The consensus of opinion was expressed by John Curtin, the Labour Party Leader, in the debate on the 1936 Defence Estimates.

> If an Eastern first-class power sought an abrogation of a basic Australian policy, such as the White Australia Policy, it would most likely do so when Great Britain was involved or threatened to be involved in a European war. Would the British Government dare to authorise the despatch of any substantial part of the fleet to the East to help Australia? . . . The dependence of Australia upon the competence, let alone the readiness, of the British statesmen to send forces to our aid is too dangerous a hazard upon which to found Australian defence policy.[3]

This new Australian outlook, shrewd and far-sighted as it was, made nonsense of the whole traditional relationship of Australia and New Zealand with Great Britain, based on complementary interests and mutual support. Even Billy Hughes, once so fiercely strong for collective imperial defence, now believed that Australia must look to her own security.[4]

These Australian misgivings were shared in New Zealand. In 1936 the incoming Labour Government was told by New Zealand service chiefs that Australia and New Zealand were 'open to attack as never before in

[1] Ibid. pp. 2–3.
[2] Ibid. p. 4.
[3] Hasluck, p. 83 and also pp. 44–7 for the general debate; see also the article on 'Australian Defence Policy', *The Round Table*, Vol. XXVI (December 1935).
[4] Hasluck, pp. 44–5.

their histories', and in December the service chiefs reminded the Government that on any reasonable calculation, the British fleet would be tied to its home waters.[1] So even Australia and New Zealand retreated from the imperial role into local defence.

Thus the Commonwealth, as an alliance, enjoyed but the lowliest kind of life by the mid-1930s, its constituent states linked only by half-hearted liaison between their service and supply departments over matters that never extended to joint policies, strategies, plans or organisations.[2]

As an Australian officer, Major H. C. H. Robertson, wrote in the *Army Quarterly* of July 1933: 'At the moment Imperial organisation has no real machinery. It is, at best, precariously poised on two unstable props – Imperial Conferences, which meet but seldom, and the Committee of Imperial Defence, which is merely advisory. . . .'[3] Major Robertson stated other bleak truths: '. . . there is no Imperial Defence policy on which to build a sound organisation',[4] and '. . . there can be no proper organisation and no effective plans unless there is a signed and binding agreement showing what each nation is to do'.[5]

The strategic localism of every dominion after 1930 was paralleled by individualism in foreign affairs. In the face of the first three aggressions of the 1930s – Japan's in Manchuria in 1931, Italy's in Abyssinia in 1935 and Germany's in the Rhineland in 1936 – England and each dominion formed its own opinion and decided its own policy; if policy is not too strong a word for what was often only a negative attitude of isolationism and inaction. Sometimes two or more of these individual policies might by chance coincide; but never throughout the Commonwealth as a whole. Although views were informally exchanged between England and the dominions – as was equally the custom between friendly foreign states – and although the Dominion Office sent the dominions a flood of information on foreign affairs, there was no attempt in these crises to evolve a common policy. England spoke for herself alone. On the other hand, some dominion governments did not hesitate to express their views about English policy when they felt like it. In 1935 the Australian High Commissioner in London, S. M. Bruce, the former Prime Minister, recommended, in regard to the Italian invasion of Abyssinia, that England should publicly admit that the League of Nations had failed, and that she was going instead

[1] Wood, p. 66.
[2] 'Canuck', 'Canada and Imperial Defence', *Army Quarterly*, Vol. XXVI, No. 2 (July 1933), p. 234.
[3] Major H. C. H. Robertson, 'The Empire and Modern War', *Army Quarterly*, Vol. XXVI, No. 2 (July 1933), pp. 246–53, 248.
[4] Ibid. p. 251.
[5] Ibid. p. 252.

to re-arm.[1] In 1936 the South Africans took the German side over the re-militarisation of the Rhineland.[2]

In the mid-1930s England, in regard to the Commonwealth, was therefore in every way worse off than in 1914, or even 1921. She could now speak only for herself, and support her diplomacy only with her own strength. Yet morally, as the 'Mother Country', she still felt obliged to take heed of dominion opinions, especially if she hoped to see them declare war alongside her in the event of a general conflict. Furthermore, she still felt obliged to attempt to defend them, if need be.

It might well have been that, if England were directly attacked, dominion sentiment would prove as strong as – or even stronger than – signatures on a formal treaty of alliance. Nevertheless England could not *count* on this. In any case, fighting a general war was one thing: *preventing* such a war by opposing the dictatorships with firm diplomacy backed by the pressure of countervailing force was another. In the power struggle without shooting that began and developed in the 1930s, England could rely only upon advice from the dominions; not upon a soldier or a ship.[3]

In any event, the armed forces of the dominions in the mid-1930s numbered all too few men and ships. The dominions had carried disarmament proportionately even further than Great Britain. In January 1935 the New Zealand navy possessed only two cruisers,[4] while as late as April 1939 the New Zealand authorities doubted whether 500 fully equipped soldiers could be found for Singapore in an emergency.[5] The Royal Australian Navy, with an active fleet of no more than three cruisers, three destroyers, two sloops and a survey ship,[6] was the most considerable dominion seapower. In 1935 the Australian army, on mobilisation of its citizen forces, would number only 29,000 men, with 'very incomplete' equipment.[7] None of this army was designated to form an expeditionary force. In 1935 the Royal Australian Air Force consisted of seventy aircraft.[8] By 1939 it reached the total of 131 aircraft.[9] South Africa in 1935 had no ships, few aircraft, and an army of 7,300 men short of officers.[10] Canada's regular army amounted to 3,600 men, with a mobilisable citizen force for

[1] Cecil Edwards, p. 234.
[2] Heever, pp. 266–7.
[3] Eayrs, p. 90; Tucker, Vol. I, pp. 356–8; Heever, p. 271; Hasluck, p. 47; Wood, pp. 60–1, 67–71; article on 'Australian Defence Policy', *The Round Table* especially pp. 56, 64.
[4] Cole, p. 27.
[5] Wood, p. 70; see also CAB 53/49, COS Paper 910.
[6] CAB 32/128, E-1.
[7] Memorandum on 'Australian Defence Policy' by Vice-Admiral G. E. Hyde, Australian Chief of Naval Staff (3 April 1935), CAB 21/397.
[8] Ibid.; see also Hankey's 'Report on Certain Aspects of Australian Defence', CAB 21/386.
[9] CAB 53/49, COS 910.
[10] Mansergh, *Survey of British Commonwealth Affairs*, Vol. III, p. 25; Cole, pp. 27–8; Hankey's 1934 Report on South African defence, CAB 21/385.

home defence of 136,000.[1] The Royal Canadian Navy, which was intended only for coastal defence, amounted in 1935 to four destroyers, and in 1939 to six.[2] In March 1934 the Canadian Chief of Staff received a memorandum on the state of the Royal Canadian Air Force: 'There is only one Service plane in Canada. It is a Hawker Audax, the property of the Royal Air Force, on loan to the RCAF for one year. . . .'[3]

Such, then, was the combined strategic power of the dominions during the 1930s; hardly much of an asset to England, even if that power had been freely and reliably at her disposal. In any case, it was now far from probable that all the dominions would be *able* to spring to the aid of the Mother Country in a future emergency as in 1914–18, even if they proved willing. For the singularly fortunate turn of circumstance of the Great War, whereby it was only England and not the empire that had been directly threatened, did not appear likely to recur. Instead it seemed highly possible that next time England would have to spring to the aid of Australia and New Zealand against Japan, even if she herself were simultaneously under attack in Europe.

In these menacing circumstances British statesmen began to see the Commonwealth in not quite so high-mindedly theoretical fashion as in 1926 and 1930. Considerations of power began to obtrude. With Nazi Germany arming at headlong speed, with Fascist Italy on the march in Africa, and Japan slicing up the prostrate carcase of China, it was time for the members of the Commonwealth to form a front. In 1937 the Secretary of State for the Dominions, Malcolm MacDonald, warned his Cabinet colleagues in a memorandum on the forthcoming Imperial Conference that '. . . if the main emphasis continued to be placed on the individual sovereignty of each unit in the Commonwealth the result will be a tendency towards disintegration'.[4]

The cold winds of danger continued to dispense the warm optimism of 1926–30. At the first meeting of the British delegation to the conference, MacDonald repeated his warning. He pointed out that, in recent years, '. . . great emphasis had been laid on the principle of freedom or individual sovereignty of each unit in the Commonwealth; and much less had been heard of co-operation. The Secretary of State considered that our principal aim at the forthcoming Conference should be to give an impetus towards a reassertion of the balance.'[5]

His colleagues agreed. Their purpose in convening another Imperial

[1] Cole, p. 28.
[2] Ibid. p. 27; Tucker, pp. 330–1, 356–8; CAB 53/49, COS 910 (JP).
[3] Quoted in Eayrs, p. 300.
[4] CAB 32/127, E(B)(37)1, p. 1.
[5] CAB 32/127, E(B)(37)1, p. 2.

Conference was to range the dominions behind British foreign policy for the coming decisive period of world diplomacy, while at the same time to make the Commonwealth less of a mystical bond and more of a practical, and well-organised, alliance.

So, once again, though this time with a more rightful expectation of success, the British service departments hopefully prepared their memoranda on what needed to be done in order to lessen, so far as it was within human power so to do, the weakness and vulnerability of the empire. The 'Review of Imperial Defence' by the Chiefs of Staff[1] surveyed the problems of war with Germany, Italy and Japan, and suggested how the dominions might help Britain in each case by making adequate plans and preparations in peacetime. There was, however, a certain wistfulness in the Chiefs of Staff's iteration of the conditional 'could'. In the case of war with Italy, South Africa and India 'could' help to contain the Italian forces in East Africa. In the case of war with Japan, Australia and New Zealand 'could', apart from naval co-operation, maintain air and land forces at home ready to reinforce Singapore and Hongkong, or to fight in Borneo or the Dutch East Indies. 'They might provide and maintain in peace army and air force units at Singapore as part of the permanent garrison.'[2] Canada 'could' co-operate by sea and in the air in controlling the Pacific sea-routes. And in the case of Britain's own nearest and greatest peril, from Germany, the dominions 'could' send field forces to reinforce her in Europe. However, the Chiefs of Staff thought that perhaps the most useful contribution the dominions could make in preparation for a war with Germany – and they here had Canada particularly in mind – was to provide 'sanctuaries' for war production. 'This is one direction in which large-scale co-operation in time of peace could immensely strengthen the resources of the Empire in time of war.'[3]

For expert opinion now expected German bombers to flatten British industry by way of a grand opening to the next war. The dominions, especially Canada, therefore acquired a new value as territory out of range of the Luftwaffe.[4] At the same time, it remained a general weakness of the empire that, despite the sharp lessons of the Great War on the dangers of relying wholly on one industrial base in Britain, little had been done to carry out the resolutions of the Imperial War Conference of 1917 on the development of war industries in India and the dominions. It was therefore a major British purpose at the 1937 Imperial Conference to achieve imperial planning and development of economic resources for war; and

[1] CAB 32/128, E(37); also CAB 32/127, IC(36)7–1. [2] Ibid. p. 17. [3] Ibid. p. 14.
[4] H. Duncan Hall, *North American Supply* (London, HMSO 1955), pp. 3–7.

in particular, to secure close Canadian co-operation. Although some liaison had been created between British and dominion planners as a result of previous imperial conferences, this still stopped far short of joint policies; and in any case no such links existed between Britain and Canada.[1] It was indeed a comment on the neglect of the Commonwealth as a collective power in the past twenty years that the British Supply Officers Committee, in a memorandum to the conference, virtually repeated the words of the 1917 Imperial War Conference:[2] '. . . the dominions should consider the development of internal capacity for production of armaments and munitions of war, so as to diminish as far as practicable, the degree of dependence on the United Kingdom'.[3]

Australia and New Zealand, intensely aware of the Japanese fleet and Japanese envy of their unpopulated lands, wished no less than Britain to re-create the imperial alliance of 1917–19. The Prime Minister of New Zealand, M. J. Savage, called for a Commonwealth foreign policy. 'At the present time', he argued, 'a Commonwealth Foreign Policy must mean also a Commonwealth Defence Policy.'[4] In his opening speech at the conference, he warned that there was a risk in such conferences that the delegates 'may be content with an innocuous and unhelpful formula, and be reluctant to attack and solve difficult problems merely because of their difficulty'.[5]

J. A. Lyons, the Prime Minister of Australia, wanted a clear statement from the conference that the British Empire was prepared to act together in support of international law and order.[6] Lyons told his colleagues that over both foreign policy and defence, 'Australia looks to the frankest discussion . . . of the international situation;'[7] and he and his delegation came armed with a formidably documented and strongly argued brief from the Australian departments of External Affairs and Defence.[8]

The Imperial Conference thus met in a mood of anxious awareness of crowding dangers. Australia and New Zealand were resolved that this time the conference should act as a real policy-making body and hand down hard decisions for collective execution. The English too, although less crudely forthright of mind than their antipodean cousins, at least went as far as rather to *wish* for such results. Yet they shrank once more from the conflict that must ensue if the conference were to be carried against the

[1] See two memoranda to the 1937 Imperial Conference by the British Principal Supply Officers Committee of the Committee of Imperial Defence, 'The Supply of War Material in Peace and War', CAB 32/127, IC(36)7-1, and 'Dominion Assistance in the Supply of Armaments and Munitions of War', CAB 32/129, E(37)17.

[2] See above p. 118.

[3] CAB 32/129, E(37)17.

[4] CAB 32/128, E(PD)(37)-6.

[5] CAB 32/128, E-1, p. 19.

[6] Ibid. p. 15.

[7] Ibid. p. 16.

[8] Hasluck, pp. 59–65, see below p. 223.

Canadians and South Africans. Even now, at this time of peril, the English Cabinet could not summon up the boldness, the toughness of nerve, the assertion of will, which they needed if they were not again to seek ignoble refuge in evasion and hollow compromise. Their yielding temper betrayed them again. They approached the problem of Mackenzie King in 1937 just as they always had done since 1923; just as they were currently approaching the problem of Adolf Hitler: by ingratiation and propitiation, like timid wives in the face of drunken or bullying husbands.[1] The delegation's discussions turned instead on the avoidance of trouble by dodging ticklish issues, by compromise and by the general employment of the saving unction of goodwill.[2] The feeling of the delegation was that English objectives could best be achieved by not striving too hard for their attainment; as Malcolm MacDonald, the Dominions Secretary, recommended:

> Any suggestion that there should be, in any formal sense, one British Commonwealth foreign policy or one British Commonwealth defence scheme would be regarded by some delegations at least as an attempt to derogate from their constitutional positions. But if we concede the position, and then proceed to discuss the principles inspiring, for example, our several foreign policies, I believe we shall discover that in fact there is a coincidence of principles between them which will make mutual understanding and co-operation natural.[3]

In their anxiety to avert the unpleasant consequences that must arise should the conference come to face the crucial issues of the time, the English delegation, with Byzantine cunning, chose to keep many topics out of general discussion altogether, and instead make them the subjects of less strenuous unilateral talks between England and individual delegations. As a result, the Imperial Conference itself, in the words of the Australian official historian, 'never ventured beyond the edge of those vital questions of survival which were facing the British Commonwealth and each of its members'.[4] The English resorted to yet another serpentine manœuvre, as a letter from Sir Archdale Parkhill, the Australian

[1] The English state of mind is illuminated by an exchange between the Dominions Office and the Joint Planning Committe of the Committee of Imperial Defence in the course of the year before. The Dominions Office warned the Joint Planners of the 'necessity for extreme delicacy of approach to Canada on defence questions . . .' (CAB 53/28, COS 489 (JP)). The Joint Planners, in obediently drafting what they called a 'deferential memorandum', nevertheless had the hardihood to protest that 'we feel . . . that the time has come to face realities and that a memorandum in deferential terms will not fulfil the real object in view . . . .'

[2] CAB 32/127, E(B)(37).

[3] CAB 32/127, E(B)(37)1, p. 2.

[4] Hasluck, p. 56.

Minister of Defence, to Casey, the Australian High Commissioner in London, describes:

> It is known that since the Statute of Westminster the United Kingdom Government is reluctant to *originate* any proposal for Imperial consultation, and prefers the initiative to come from the Dominions. . . . It is felt that the Commonwealth [of Australia] should give a lead in this matter [of co-operation], as the part we are playing in Empire naval defence qualifies us to speak with candour.[1]

Yet the English did face a real dilemma, if only of their own past making. On the one hand the gathering dangers of a violent world made it urgently necessary for the Commonwealth to come together again as a strategic team. On the other hand, any attempt to bring this about must at once uncover the gaping fissure right through the Commonwealth which the Balfour Report of 1926 and the Statute of Westminster of 1931 had curtained over with a fabric of fine words. The harder the English strove at the coming conference to turn the Commonwealth into a real force in world affairs instead of a kind of Ancient Order of Elks, the more they were bound to find Mackenzie King and Hertzog hardening into implacable opposition; perhaps eventually even, if they strove tenaciously enough, to the departure of those gentlemen in public dudgeon. Yet so strong was the hold on public opinion of the imperial myth, the myth of a united and powerful empire (1937 was Coronation Year, and the empire was on all the biscuit-tins and tea-caddies again), that it was unthinkable to English statesmen to take the risk of shattering it. The English in the 1930s were not the first or the last people to be trapped by their own myth; unable under its spell to face and cope with the truths of real life.

In his opening speech Baldwin sounded the English theme for the conference: 'We are partners in a joint enterprise, jointly responsible for a new experiment. . . .'[2]

He proceeded to give a reminder, couched in the prevailing headmasterly style, that 'fulfilment of duty to the community' was as true of a community of nations as of individuals. And then came the nub of the whole business: strategy and defence. Baldwin touched on these bristling topics in language which all too aptly expressed the degree of vigour and tenacity which the English brought to the conference: '. . . it will be our task to consider whether, while preserving our individual rights of decision and action, we can co-ordinate our various policies in such a way as to assist one another . . .'[3]

[1] Hasluck, p. 59. [2] CAB 32/128, E-1, p. 9. [3] Ibid. p. 10.

The task of consideration at once led to the conflict which had been dreaded. As soon as Baldwin, Lyons and Savage had outlined their hopes and wishes in their opening speeches, Mackenzie King, in *his* opening speech, trod them flat, by repeating his old assertions of 1923 that it was no part of the functions of imperial conferences to formulate or decide policy.[1] The conference therefore divided into two factions: Australia and New Zealand versus Canada and South Africa. The English, wincing whenever a blow was struck, acted as referee. The contest turned, as expected, on foreign policy and defence; and most particularly on defence.

The Australian Government submitted a memorandum on 'Co-operation in Imperial Defence',[2] which referred to the, as yet, unfulfilled platitudes in the final statements of the 1923 and 1926 Conferences for closer imperial co-operation, and put forward a draft resolution in which the delegates were to call for contingency plans (both strategic and economic) to cover all possible developments in the international situation. Each dominion was to agree to contribute to the general defence of all fellow members of the Commonwealth as well as to undertake its own local defence. Disagreeable though all of this was to Mackenzie King, the Australian proposals contained yet more outrageous ideas: '. . . owing to the fact that delay in developing the necessary power through lack of organisation may be perilous, the necessary organisation would be established in peace . . .'[3]

King, on the contrary argued that, in his words, because of Canada's sense of safety and her distaste for war, no Canadian political party contemplated preparing forces for operations overseas. Canada would therefore undertake no prior commitments.[4] His Minister of National Defence elaborated Canadian dislike of British and Australian proposals by recalling at length the past demise of plans for an imperial navy and an imperial strategic reserve. He said that 'the best contribution that Canadians could make either to Canada or the Commonwealth was to keep Canada united. That was the object of their present policy [of non-cooperation and non-commitment].'[5]

In these discussions on defence, English spokesmen presented the English case with the air of a butler laying something unpleasant on a silver salver before his employer for his inspection. Sir Thomas Inskip, the Minister for the Co-ordination of Defence, who qualified for that part by being a lawyer and devout evangelical churchman who had played a major role in a recent controversy over the revised Church of England Prayer

[1] CAB 32/128, E-2, p. 7.
[2] CAB 32/129, E(37)27.
[3] Ibid.
[4] CAB 32/128, E(PD)(37)3.
[5] CAB 32/128, E(PD)(37)5, p. 16.

Book, hastened to assure his listeners that Britain had no intention of interfering with dominion independence over the question of the co-ordination of imperial defence, and went on ingratiatingly to say that he 'hoped in due course to hear in general terms from the Delegations of the Great Nations overseas what they had begun and what their intentions were'.[1]

Sir Samuel Hoare, now First Lord of the Admiralty, put on yet again the old record about the disproportionate burden of naval defence carried by the United Kingdom. However, he did manage discreetly to imply that, as things stood, the empire was a liability to England rather than an asset, and he even unveiled a modest, though oblique, little threat:

> A great proportion of the expenditure on Naval Defence is required to meet our Imperial, as distinct from our United Kingdom, obligations. The question must occur to all of us whether this little island can continue to shoulder the financial strain involved in maintaining, to so great an extent, the requisite standard of naval strength to ensure our Imperial security. It may well be that the safety of the British Commonwealth of Nations will depend on increased naval support from the Dominions.[2]

It was now thirty-five years since Joseph Chamberlain had made the same point, though much more incisively, to another group of imperial delegates.

The purposes of the conference soon ran aground on Mackenzie King's obstructionism, and, despite some noble work at the pumps, foundered. King refused to co-operate in any way either in military and naval planning and strategy, or in that imperial development of war industries and sources of raw materials, of which the English had entertained such hope.[3] The crab-wise English wooing of the Canadian Premier failed to achieve any results. At the same time, this Canadian refusal to co-operate nullified the principal motive for appeasing Canada. Nevertheless, appeasement went on. The final battle of the conference between the disappointed Australians and New Zealanders and Mackenzie King, now the master of the proceedings, took place over the draft resolutions on defence and foreign policy. For King was resolved that these resolutions should carry not the slightest hint of imperial co-ordination. He made use of the stratagem first employed over Chanak in 1922 – of justifying all his own objections by reference to the touchiness of Canadian opinion or of the Canadian Parliament. Thus he objected, by way of a start, to the resolu-

[1] Ibid. p. 7. [2] CAB 32/128, E(PD)(37)-7, p. 8. [3] Hurstfield, pp. 41–2; Hall, pp. 5–8.

tions being called 'resolutions' at all, on the grounds that Canadian opinion would be alarmed at any implication that the conference had reached collective decisions. He preferred the resolutions on defence and foreign policy to take the form of 'statements' only. In the case of foreign policy, for example, he argued that 'the draft would be liable to interpretation as constituting a single foreign policy for the Empire. This would create considerable political difficulties in Canada. . . . There was in Canada a great dread lest the country should be committed at the Imperial Conference to some obligation arising out of the European situation.'[1]

The British delegation made haste to concede that the 'resolutions' should be gelded into 'statements'. As Neville Chamberlain, who was now, as the newly appointed Prime Minister, leading the British delegation, said: 'Everyone must recognise the force of what Mr Mackenzie King had said. There was no use in making agreements here in London, if they are to cause difficulties in other parts of the Empire. He felt that the Conference must be guided by Mr Mackenzie King on the Canadian aspect.'[2]

Unfortunately the Canadian aspects were guiding the whole conference, and the alternative to making agreements in London that would cause difficulties in Canada was to make no agreements at all. Indeed, so completely did Mackenzie King now hold the whip that the final statements of the conference owed their phrasing on crucial points almost entirely to him. Yet the Australians and New Zealanders, though unsupported by England, spoke out with the traditional English bluntness now so out of fashion in the Mother Country itself. When King objected to the British draft paragraph about standardising training and equipment throughout the empire on the grounds that it 'rather gave the impression of some central committee which arranged co-ordination', Sir Archdale Parkhill of Australia retorted that 'any such impression would give great satisfaction in Australia'.[3] Later, when King took exception to a turn of phrase in the British drafts which in his view indicated that Canada was represented on the Committee of Imperial Defence, it was Savage of New Zealand who became exasperated: 'Mr Savage recalled that those present were at an "Imperial Conference" and discussing Imperial ideas. Why this objection to a Committee of Imperial Defence?'[4]

But King was not abashed. He thought, for example, that the British

[1] CAB 32/130, E(FP)(37)1, p. 2; see CAB 32/127, E(B)(37)6 for the equivalent argument on the defence resolution.

[2] CAB 32/130, E(FP)(37)1, p. 3.

[3] CAB 32/127, E(D)(37)1.

[4] CAB 32/127, E(D)(37)2, p. 5.

draft on the defence of sea communications tended 'to suggest the impression of Empire Forces'. It would be impossible to get defence appropriations through the Canadian Parliament unless it was clear that they were intended for Canada's defence only. Casey, for Australia, nevertheless, said he preferred the original draft. But Neville Chamberlain accepted an amendment by King, which avoided the appalling implication that those assembled round the table belonged, in any meaningful sense, to one empire.

And so it went on – Mackenzie King, backed by Hertzog whenever an ally was needed, tussling with the Australians and New Zealanders, while the British gave way or suggested the kind of lame compromises that only masked surrender. The final 'statement' on defence was indeed a reedy trumpet call to a troubled world. Mention of imperial co-ordination was limited, as on previous occasions, to exchanges of personnel and standardisation of training, organisation and equipment. In case even this was too strong, the statement added: 'At the same time the Conference recognised that it is the sole responsibility of the several Parliaments of the British Commonwealth to decide the scope and nature of their own defence policy.'[1]

The statement was only redeemed by paragraphs put in at the insistence of Australia and New Zealand in order to assert that they themselves attached 'the greatest importance' to close co-operation in Commonwealth defence.[2]

The drafting of the final statement on foreign policy followed a similar dismal course. King even found fault with a paragraph saying that 'they [the delegates] welcome regional agreements between individual members of the Commonwealth'. He preferred 'they have noted . . .'[3] For once his suggested amendment was mildly resisted by Chamberlain and by Lord Halifax, the Foreign Secretary. The published version therefore reads: 'They note with interest . . .'[4]

The fifth paragraph of the British draft resolution on foreign policy constituted the very core of the purpose of the conference: 'They [the delegates] agree that the Members will consult and co-operate with one another with a view to the preservation of the vital interests of the British Commonwealth.'[5]

Hertzog, for South Africa, argued that this paragraph would be fatal if the word 'agree' was interpreted in the sense of a *legal* agreement. King

[1] Cmd. 5482, p. 20.
[2] Ibid. p. 18.
[3] CAB 32/130, E(FP)(37)1, p. 3.
[4] Cmd. 5482, p. 15.
[5] CAB 32/130, E(FP)(37)1.

asked whether by committing himself to the paragraph, 'he had undertaken to participate, say, in the defence of the Suez Canal'?[1]

But Walter Nash, the New Zealand Minister of Finance, asked: 'Ought the members [of the Commonwealth] not to consult and co-operate if its life was at stake?'[2]

It was the central question the conference had to answer. Mackenzie King himself answered it in his most Uriah-Heepish manner by assuring his colleagues that he was 'anxious to help as much as possible', [but] 'this draft would be interpreted as committing Canada to take action over all the vital interests of the Commonwealth'.[3] He implied without saying so that it must be self-evidently ridiculous to expect this of a member of the Commonwealth. Another wrangle ensued, in which King again remained adamant, and the British showed themselves again eager to find a formula acceptable to all. Eventually the draft was diluted down to King's satisfaction into '. . . they declared their intention of continuing to consult and co-operate with one another . . .'[4] – but no longer however in order to preserve the Commonwealth's vital interests; only 'to enhance their individual influence for peace by common agreement'.

Finally there was the statement of aims in foreign policy. Here too all the hopes of imperial solidarity behind English leadership crumbled away into a rubble of negative platitude in King's best style: 'While no attempt was made to formulate commitments, which in any event could not be made effective until approved and confirmed by the respective Parliaments, the representatives of the Governments concerned found themselves in close agreement upon a number of general propositions. . . .'[5]

And general they were indeed: peace and the solution of international problems by negotiation, not force; support of the ideas of the League of Nations; disarmament. Propositions as broad and trite as these constituted no foreign policy. Nor did dominion approval of the British intention to seek a settlement in Europe by appeasement imply acceptance in any way of a share in the responsibility.

The conference ended; the delegates went home; and England was left as alone and unsupported as ever. Not one of the English objectives in promoting a co-ordinated imperial alliance – in strategy, military and naval organisation, industrial development or diplomatic effort – had been achieved.[6] All the carefully argued British and Australian memoranda – to be proved so right in the event – went to join all the other carefully argued memoranda of the past thirty years on imperial defence now tied

[1] Ibid. p. 7. [2] Ibid. [3] Ibid. [4] Cmd. 5482, p. 15.
[5] Ibid. p. 14. [6] For an Australian judgement, see Hasluck, pp. 70–1.

up in tape and deposited in dusty registries. The English Government had allowed all the great and crucial purposes of the conference to be aborted. They had followed that very road of evasion against which the New Zealand Premier had warned the conference at its first meeting; they had in the event proved content, in his words, 'with an innocuous and unhelpful formula'; they had indeed proved 'reluctant to attack and solve difficult problems merely because of their difficulty'.[1]

Or, as Neville Chamberlain put it more comfortingly in his closing speech to the conference:

> In estimating the results of our labours, there is no need to look for spectacular decisions or for startling changes in policy. Our Imperial Conferences differ, as it seems to me, from most International Conferences in one important respect. They are not summoned to solve any particular problem or to achieve any specific result. They rather take the form of family gatherings held at more or less regular intervals. . . .[2]

And with a sententiousness reminiscent of a new headmaster's remarks on his first Prizegiving Day and which accorded well with his pedagogic appearance and personality, Chamberlain spoke also of a 'general harmony of aims and policy' and of a 'renewed sense of comradeship'.[3]

This complacent summary of the achievements of the conference might be put down to an understandable wish to put the best public face on a disaster, were there not evidence that the English Cabinet really did still fail to distinguish between the realities of grand strategy and the romance of the mystical bond of empire. In reviewing the results of the conference in a Cabinet meeting, Malcolm MacDonald, the Dominions Secretary, recalled that the aim of the British delegation had been to emphasise co-operation within the Commonwealth. He expressed the conviction that in this they had been successful, and that the general result had been 'to re-assert somewhat the principle of co-operation'. Despite the differences of viewpoint in the conference, 'a spirit of co-operation had grown'. MacDonald thought that one of the main results of the conference was that the United Kingdom 'had won the confidence of the Dominion Ministers who had sat round the table and who had come to trust in our sincerity, decency and wisdom'.[4]

It might have been Lord Irwin reviewing the splendid successes of British policy in India.

The practical value of this trust of the dominions in British sincerity,

[1] See above p. 220. [2] Cmd. 5482, Appendix III, p. 61. [3] Ibid.
[4] CAB 23/87, 24(37)5.

decency and wisdom to the conduct of the diplomatic struggle with Nazi Germany was to be demonstrated within a year of the 1937 Imperial Conference. The crisis which arose in 1938 because of the German demands on Czechoslovakia – the Munich crisis – was decisive for the future course of European history, even of world history, as was well recognised at the time, though not entirely for the right reasons.[1]

Yet Chamberlain negotiated only on behalf of England, and only with England's own weight behind him, just as if England were a purely European power, without an empire to look to for strength and support. There were, it was true, intensive discussions during the crisis between the Dominions High Commissioners in London and the Dominions Secretary; discussions in which all the High Commissioners were free with opinions as to what England ought to do.[2] However this was far from the 'imperial council' jointly managing the foreign relations of an imperial alliance that some had hoped for in the 1920s. The dominions were now happily seated in the back seat, refusing to take responsibility for the policy they sought to influence; refusing to contribute a gramme of strategic weight to back it. Hertzog, for South Africa, was even determined to stay neutral or 'non-belligerent', should England actually be involved in war over Czechoslovakia: 'The existing relations between the Union of South Africa and the various belligerent parties shall, so far as the Union is concerned, remain unchanged and continue as if no war were being waged. . . .'[3]

Smuts agreed with him that there was no reason why South Africa should be drawn into a European conflict.[4] Canadian policy remained wholly negative and passive over Czechoslovakia, although Massey, the High Commissioner in London, took part in the discussions between the Dominions High Commissioners and the Dominions Secretary. English statesmen could not count upon a corporal's guard from Canada in peacetime for any strategic move in support of English diplomacy. As a spokesman of the Canadian General Staff had publicly stated in 1934: 'I can say definitely that no contracted military understanding exists between the Department of National Defence and the War Office, Admiralty or Air Ministry. . . .'[5]

Nor could England even count on Australian or New Zealand strategic support over Czechoslovakia; and the English knew better than to ask for it. Robert Menzies, the Australian Attorney-General, told the Australian Parliament during the subsequent debate on the Munich settlement: 'The simple fact is that at no time from the beginning to the end of those

[1] See below pp. 469–76, 505–50. [2] Massey, pp. 259–62. [3] Heever, p. 275.
[4] Mansergh, *Survey of British Commonwealth Affairs*, Vol. III, p. 255. [5] Eayrs, p. 90.

discussions [between the British Government and the Dominions High Commissioner] did the British Government ever ask us to say whether we would send troops out of Australia. At no time did it ever ask any question at all about troops. . . .'[1]

Therefore the most dangerous and most decisive crisis in European history since 1914 provided only fresh proof that the British Commonwealth did not exist as a factor in international relations in times of peace. England alone of Commonwealth countries guaranteed the territorial integrity of Czechoslovakia after the Munich Agreement. She alone gave the guarantees to Poland, Romania and Greece in 1939 against German aggression. She gave them indeed without even bothering to consult the dominions, so completely was it now implicitly accepted that the Commonwealth did not exist as a political entity. In terms of English policy in Europe, the Commonwealth remained nothing but a source of moral enfeeblement, in the form of voices calling for caution in dealing with Hitler.[2] Nor could England even now take it for granted that she would enjoy the support of the whole Commonwealth in the event of war itself. In the two years that followed the 1937 Imperial Conference – two years of accelerating rivalry in armaments, of unfolding ambitions on the part of the Berlin–Rome–Tokyo Axis, and of international tension screwed ever tauter – the Commonwealth remained a mere spectre of an alliance. In October 1938 the British General Staff acknowledged: 'Each Dominion now had the responsibility for deciding for itself the extent and nature of its defence preparations in time of peace as well as the questions whether to employ those resources in a common cause with the remainder of the Empire.'[3]

Of the dominions, only Australia and New Zealand had publicly stated that they would fight if England had to fight, and even they still refused to commit themselves as to how, where and with what forces. Thus England had to assume that even if war broke out with Germany, as seemed more and more certain, she might find herself on her own.

Yet at the same time she still lay under an unlimited liability to defend Australia and New Zealand against Japan. This obligation demanded not just the sending of help, as Australia and New Zealand themselves had rendered help to England in the Great War, but the undertaking of the principal burden of the conflict. For while in any case the Pacific dominions were too small in population to defend their vast territories themselves,

[1] Hasluck, p. 96. See also Wood, p. 71.
[2] Massey, pp. 259–62; Mansergh, *Survey of British Commonwealth Affairs*, Vol. III, pp. 168–9, 443–4.
[3] Wood, p. 57.

they had also failed to spend per head on defence anything near the sum the English spent – and despite the noble protestations of their statesmen that the dominions ought to bear their fair share of the burden. And English statesmen had flabbily acquiesced in this failure, instead of indicating that the provision of English protection was absolutely dependent on the dominions bearing their fair share, instead of merely talking about it. In 1939 therefore Australia and New Zealand still utterly relied on England for their survival.[1] According to an unofficial report for the Constitutional Association of New South Wales, Australia, for example, was defenceless against serious attack. While the Australian navy was too small to prevent an invasion, the army was too weak to prevent an enemy landing, or defeat him once ashore. Australia also lacked the seapower to cut the communications of an isolated enemy bridgehead, or to transport the troops by sea to drive him out of it. It was questionable, said the report, whether Australia could defend herself against air or sea bombardment, while it was certain that she could not break a blockade of her coasts or commerce.[2]

In April 1939 a Commonwealth Conference on Defence in the Pacific was held in Wellington at the invitation of Savage, the Labour Prime Minister of New Zealand. Its purpose was to attempt to remedy what the New Zealand official historian calls 'the intractable chaos of British Commonwealth strategy in the Pacific'.[3] The holding of such a conference at all at this time provided in itself a gloomy epitaph on the previous twenty years. The conference was attended by senior civil servants and servicemen from New Zealand, Britain and Australia. It recommended the creation of a Pacific Defence Council of nine members (three each from Britain, Australia and New Zealand) to co-ordinate policy and strategy in the region lying between Singapore and Fiji (north) and Albany, Australia, and Invercargill, New Zealand (south). The Council was to control the New Zealand and Australian navies, armies and air forces, the British China Fleet and British troops in South-Eastern Asian and Pacific colonies.[4] These proposals went the way of all the other previous proposals for turning the Commonwealth, or even part of it, into an organised and effective alliance. The result of the 1939 Wellington Conference was to promote closer co-operation between the Australian and New Zealand navies; and that was all. The British Empire in the Far East and Pacific as a whole remained without strategic plans or organisation – defensible only on the premise that England would be able as well as willing to allot her main fleet and a large portion of her air-power to fighting Japan.

[1] Ibid. pp. 101–8. [2] Hasluck, p. 108. [3] Wood, p. 72.
[4] See CAB 53/49, COS 910.

During the twenty years that had elapsed since the Great War the 'white empire had therefore been allowed to fade away into a political institution more akin to the Holy Roman Empire than to the Roman – the reverse of that intimate political and strategic association which had seemed to imperial statesmen in 1917–21 to offer the only hope of overcoming the centrifugal forces of geography and history. And yet, little value though the Commonwealth was to England as an alliance, it still entangled England in great strategic risks and obligations. In addition to the naval and military burden, there was the industrial burden, for, owing to the almost complete failure to remedy the industrial weakness of the dominions, Britain was to have to supply, in the first year of the Second World War, over 90 per cent of the entire empire's munitions.[1] Nor were the exploited sources of raw material in the dominions either large enough or vital enough to compensate for the costs and risks England incurred in defending them; costs and risks not necessarily incurred in regard to no less important foreign sources of supply.[2]

The simple truth was that in terms of England's material interests as a great power the 'white' Commonwealth, like India, was not an asset but a predicament. But, unlike India, it was a predicament from which kinship forbade even the thought of escape. The 'white' Commonwealth represented the triumph of sentiment over strategy.

Taken as a whole therefore, the British Empire, 'white' and 'coloured', constituted on balance a source of weakness and danger to England rather than of strength. The English in their romantic idealism about the empire had failed to see it and deal with it in terms of English power. They had failed to bring responsibilities and strength into due proportion. There the empire stood, proud under the Union flag, a ramshackle, anomalous but immense structure of entanglement extending from the Mediterranean to the South Pacific; resting almost wholly on the human, military and industrial resources of a nation of only forty-five million people; one of the most outstanding examples of strategic over-extension in history.

It was only, therefore, if the favourable circumstances of the Great War were repeated in the future, with solely England under attack, that the empire could once more bring its modest aid to England's succour. On the other hand, however, if the empire itself were to be attacked simultaneously, then its demands would pump away from England the military resources she needed for her own war in Europe. For England was hardly a big enough power to fight one other great nation, let alone two or three.

[1] Figure for September–December 1939 and 1940: W. K. Hancock and M. M. Gowing, *British War Economy* (London, HMSO 1949), p. 373.

[2] Hurstfield, pp. 153, 163, 167.

From this it followed that it was vital, absolutely vital, for English statesmanship to avert that contingency which the empire made so possible – embroilment with more than one first-class power in more than one region of the world at a time.

# V

# V · COVENANTS WITHOUT SWORDS

It was here, in the field of national strategy – foreign policy + grand strategy + defence policy + economic policy + propaganda – that the British character, as it had become by the 1920s, was most ill-matched to circumstance. How the dominant groups in British society saw their country, and its relation to the world, found perfect expression in the British pavilion at the 1937 Paris international exhibition:

> When you went in, the first thing you saw was a cardboard Chamberlain fishing in rubber waders and, beyond, an elegant pattern of golf balls, a frieze of tennis rackets, polo sets, riding equipment, natty dinner jackets and, by a pleasant transition, agreeable pottery and textiles, books finely printed and photographs of the English countryside. . . . Almost all the photographs were of pastoral scenes and old churches, not a single factory chimney, not a gun or battleship or aeroplane. . . .[1]

The members of the diplomatic and foreign services themselves were for the most part recruited from the gentry or aristocracy and educated at Eton or Harrow and at one of the fashionable Oxford or Cambridge colleges: they were more at home with French literature than with German technology.[2] Although they were somewhat more worldly-wise and less imbued with earnest moral purpose than the solid upper-middle-class ranks of the imperial administration and home Civil Service, their outlook nevertheless owed more to Dr Arnold than to Signor Machiavelli. They even for the most part accepted the Covenant of the League of Nations as the guiding principle of British policy. In January 1932 Sir Robert Vansittart, then Permanent Under-Secretary at the Foreign Office, referred in a memorandum to the Cabinet to our 'sympathy' and 'faith' in regard to the League, and feared a return to 'the old – and vicious – "balance of power" '.[3] The Victorian public school's teaching of duty and public responsibility was reflected by the British diplomat's concern with

[1] Kingsley Martin, inappropriately enough, in *Editor: A Second Volume of Autobiography 1931–45* (London, Hutchinson 1968), p. 209.
[2] See Gordon A. Craig and Felix Gilbert (eds.), *The Diplomats 1919–39* (Princeton N.J., Princeton University Press 1953), p. 45.
[3] CAB 27/476, CP(4)32.

the general well-being of the world as well as with the pursuit of British interests. Thus Sir Hughe Knatchbull-Hugessen, the British Ambassador to Turkey from 1939 to 1944, wrote in 1949:

> . . . it is indeed true that the object of the diplomacy of some countries has been and even still is to score points for themselves, to gain something at the expense of another country. . . . Enlightened countries have long since realised the futility of such diplomacy and much of our energy nowadays is directed to the wider and more honourable task of serving the cause of international welfare and harmony. . . .[1]

This was a representative view. Sir Sidney Barton, Ambassador to Abyssinia in 1935, thought that an Italian invasion of that country would be widely regarded as 'an international crime'.[2] Sir Robert Craigie, Ambassador to Japan from 1937 to 1942, praised a certain Japanese diplomat as 'a citizen of the world and a staunch believer in the efficacy of peaceful methods in the settlement of international disputes . . .'[3] Sir Nevile Henderson, Ambassador to Germany from 1937 to 1939, admittedly a special case, although a crucially important one, believed that his appointment to the Berlin embassy 'could only mean that I had been specially selected by Providence for the definite mission of, as I trusted, helping to preserve the peace of the world'.[4] Even Sir Robert Vansittart, who won himself a disastrous reputation as a disturber of reposeful illusions about Germany, was as emotional and romantic in his idealism as any. The rising generation in the Foreign Office in the 1930s, more middle-class in complexion than their elders, men who had joined the service during or just after the Great War, were if anything more idealistic and chivalric; League of Nations men and strong for righteousness, especially if trench veterans. As one historian put it, they shared 'a streak of genuine romanticism'.[5] Ambassadors like Sir Horace Rumbold, who, as the ambassador in Berlin from 1928 to 1933 saw clearly and reported pungently the bleak truths about Nazism and its ambitions, were not abundant in the key capitals of the world in the 1920s and 1930s. In particular the Berlin embassy was held from 1919 to 1928 and from 1937

[1] Sir Hughe Knatchbull-Hugessen, *Diplomat in Peace and War* (London, John Murray 1949), pp. 34–6.
[2] Quoted in the Earl of Avon, *The Eden Memoirs* (London, Cassell 1962), Vol. I, p. 198.
[3] Sir Robert Craigie, *Behind the Japanese Mask* (London, Hutchinson 1946), p. 11.
[4] Sir Nevile Henderson, *Failure of a Mission* (London, Hodder and Stoughton 1940), p. 13. See also Sir Victor Wellesley, *Diplomacy in Fetters* (London, Hutchinson 1945), pp. 15, 40, and also Lord D'Abernon's Sidney Ball Lecture at Oxford, 31 October 1930 quoted on p. 192; for Wellesley's belief in moral influence see p. 205.
[5] John Connell, *The Office: A Study of British Foreign Policy and its Makers 1919–1951* (London, Allan Wingate 1958), p. 218.

to 1939 by men very different in themselves but equally steeped in hopeful illusion: Lord D'Abernon and Sir Nevile Henderson. In the Foreign Office itself, the most able official between the world wars, Sir Eyre Crowe, Permanent Under-Secretary until his death in 1925, could hardly have been more untypical, born as he had been at Leipzig, educated at Düsseldorf and Berlin, with a German mother and a German wife; poor, austere and devotedly professional as a Prussian officer; 'a dowdy, meticulous, conscientious agnostic with small faith in anything but his brain and his Britain'.[1]

Upbringing told too in the whole style and pace of British diplomacy, which had something of the air of a British family motorist of the era, proceeding with cautious deliberation and much hand signalling down the middle of the road in one of the under-powered and upright saloons then produced by the British motor industry; and British diplomacy was, like the British driver, apt to be at once bewildered and indignant when cut up by faster operators. Propaganda and public relations, for example, were at once alien and distasteful, for a late-Victorian education provided little understanding of modern developments in the mass dissemination of news and opinion, and less sympathy. When a press department was set up within the Foreign Office in 1918, 'the first thing done was the abolition of the propagandist activities of the old [wartime] organisation. Neither the British Government nor the British people had ever regarded propaganda as other than a regrettable and wasteful war-time expedient. . . .'[2] Gentlemanly diffidence and good manners too often muffled the language and blunted the impact of British diplomacy. There was here neither the cunning and stealth of the Elizabethans nor the peremptory authority of the Commonwealth of England, nor the shrewdness of men of the world like Castlereagh and Wellington, but an essentially naïve public-school decency ill-adapted to the unscrupulous self-interest of contemporary foreign diplomacy.[3]

Nevertheless the diplomats were, by the nature of their profession, closer to the realities of world affairs than the politicans. Growing foreign

[1] Lord Vansittart, *The Mist Procession* (London, Hutchinson 1958), p. 45.

[2] Sir John Tilley and Stephen Gaselee, *The Foreign Office* (London, Putnam 1933), p. 285.

[3] For the professional outlook and personnel of British diplomacy between the world wars, see Vansittart; Sir Ivone Kirkpatrick, *The Inner Circle* (London, Macmillan 1959); Sir Lancelot Oliphant, *Ambassador in Bonds* (London, Putnam 1946); Sir David Kelly, *The Ruling Few* (London, Hollis and Carter 1952); Sir John Tilley, *London to Tokyo* (London, Hutchinson 1942); Wellesley; Lord Strang, *The Foreign Office* (London, Allen and Unwin 1955); Tilley and Gaselee; J. D. Gregory, *On the Edge of Diplomacy* (London, Hutchinson 1929); Viscount D'Abernon, *Ambassador of Peace*, 2 Vols. (London, Hodder and Stoughton 1929–30); Lord Hardinge of Penshurst, *The Old Diplomacy* (London, John Murray 1947); Craig and Gilbert; Connell; James Pope-Hennessy, *Lord Crewe 1858–1945: The Making of a Liberal* (London, Constable 1955).

perils were perceived and promptly and fully reported, first to London and then to ministers. Some permanent officials, such as Crowe in his time and later Vansittart, struggled hard to convince governments of the need for a strong foreign policy, and to puncture the prevailing euphoria with a bodkin of realism. They failed. They failed because there was another, competing influence on politicians, a more congenial and therefore in the end a more effective influence: a constellation of moralising internationalist cliques, each with its ideas-peddlers, its contact-men in high places, and its tame press.[1] These busy romantics – from Philip Kerr (Lord Lothian) and Lord Robert Cecil on the Right, through liberals like Smuts and Gilbert Murray in the middle to Kingsley Martin and Clifford Allen on the Left – not only believed, admirably enough, that morality rather than power *ought* to govern relations between states but acted as though it *did*. They conversed, corresponded and combined in their efforts to sway British governments, on whose members they worked by private letter, the telephone and by personal persuasion during the long English country weekend. Their task was made the easier because of the smallness and intimacy of the British governing world, with its friendships, kinships, schools and universities in common. The internationalists successfully imposed on governments their pretension to speak for the inarticulate and unsounded body of the British nation; that is, to represent public opinion at large. They also occupied the key strongholds of 'informed' public opinion, to which governments paid special deference, such as the League of Nations Union, the Institute of International Affairs (Chatham House), the *New Statesman*, *The Times*, the *Observer*, the *Manchester Guardian* and the *News Chronicle*,[2] the Common Room at All Souls, the lawns at Cliveden and the parterre at Blickling. It was their counsel, intimate, insidious, bigotedly certain, that prevailed.

British policy was therefore the child of their insemination of the politicians – politicians like Baldwin and MacDonald, the Chamberlains, Simon and Henderson, Halifax, Eden. It was as if the encumbents of quiet early-nineteenth-century rectories and nonconformist ministers' houses had been miraculously transported into the great offices of State of a hundred years later. Instead of the suspicious minds of pre-Victorian statesmen, there was trustfulness; instead of a worldly scepticism, a childlike innocence and optimism. And instead of a toughness, even a ruthlessness, in the pursuit of English interests, there was a yielding readiness to appease the

[1] See above p. 64.

[2] For a summary of the attitudes of the British press towards international affairs in the inter-war period, see Franklin Reid Gannon, *The British Press and Germany 1936–1939* (Oxford, The Clarendon Press 1971), pp. 4–8.

wrath of other nations. For the very bedrock of the national character had been crumbled since the eighteenth century. Whereas the pre-Victorian Englishman had been renowned for his quarrelsome temper and his willingness to back his argument with his fists – or his feet – now the modern British, like the elderly, shrank from conflict or unpleasantness of any kind. In Lord Vansittart's words: 'Right or Left, everybody was for a quiet life.'[1]

How did the rulers of a great but vulnerable power convince themselves that a quiet life was possible? The answer lay in the convenient, congenial but ill-founded assumptions they made about the British place in world affairs, about the nature of the post-war world and about the functioning of international relations in general.

In the first place British statesmen convinced themselves that Britain stood outside, or above, the brawls of nations. They further believed that no national interests were so opposed that they could not be reconciled by mediation and compromise. By means of these beliefs the British were able to find intellectual escape from the inevitability of struggle and absolve themselves from the painful experience of having to take sides. British statesmen enjoyed the pleasant illusion that they could be friends equally with all the parties to all the disputes of a distracted world. This assumption of benign impartiality further enabled the British to allot themselves the role of umpire, or honest broker, assiduously seeking to reconcile the irreconcilable. Such an exalted role clearly required high moral authority. The British believed that they enjoyed this moral authority, owing to the altruism of their foreign policy, concerned above all, as it was, for the public weal. As Lord Curzon put it with classical stateliness in 1923:

> We have endeavoured to exercise a steadying and moderating influence in the politics of the world, and I think and hope that we have conveyed not merely the impression, but the conviction that, whatever other countries or Governments may do, the British Government is never untrue to its word, and is never disloyal to its colleagues or its allies, never does anything underhand or mean; and if this conviction be widespread – as I believe it to be – that is the real basis of the moral authority which the British Empire has long exerted and I believe will long continue to exert in the affairs of mankind.[2]

Belief in the efficacy of Britain's moral authority is a recurrent strain in the memoirs and documents of the period. It carried with it a devout faith

[1] Vansittart, p. 474.
[2] CAB 32/2, E-4.

in the potency of moral force. However, what was meant by moral force was not that power of personality that enables one man to impose his will on another, but simply the force of world – or British – disapproval of wrong-doing. As late as 1938, for instance, after Hitler's invasion of Austria, but before he staged the Czechoslovakian crisis, it was the conviction of the British Minister for the Co-ordination of Defence, Sir Thomas Inskip, that the German dictator 'would be affected by the consequences of world public opinion which would be roused if Germany took action against Czechoslovakia similar to that which she had taken against Austria'.[1]

Moral force, or righteous indignation, was in fact the only means the British left themselves with which to influence the course of world affairs. For their parsonical belief in the powers of moral reprobation was accompanied by an equally parsonical dislike of 'immoral' forms of pressure, such as bribery, threats or force. The British ruling classes deliberately rejected from their thinking the fundamental operating factor in international relations – power. To take note that power existed, and was the prime mover, was denounced as a cynical and immoral wish to play 'power politics'. This was about as sensible as denouncing aircraft designers who took note of aerodynamics. To the post-evangelical British, however, power in the relations between States was like the sexual urge in the relations between people: elemental, frightening, and to be denied. It was an era when Bismarck and D. H. Lawrence were equally ill-thought of. The British approach to diplomacy was therefore rather like their approach to sex, romantically remote from the distressing biological crudities. They had insufficient understanding of the nature of the bargaining process; indeed they eagerly sought to open negotiations when and where their own bargaining position was feeble in the extreme. A negotiation was seen in fact not so much as an arena of pressure and manœuvre as a meeting of minds in good faith; as an interplay of reasoned persuasion.

This failure to take adequate account of the paramount role of power in international relations was equally reflected in the astonishing British faith in treaties. They really believed that seals, signatures and parchment had some inherent force that could regulate the conduct of nations. They were sincerely convinced that foreign statesmen would honour their countries' signatures even if it became highly inconvenient to do so. They were perfectly prepared to confide British interests and security to agreements that could never be enforced.

Faith in parchment, belief in moral force and a denial of the reality of

[1] CAB 27/624, FP(36)29.

power all found their ultimate expression in British membership of the League of Nations. After 1919 the balance of power as the guiding principle of English policy was formally and finally given up in favour of the Covenant of the League of Nations. This document, although written into the peace treaties at the insistence of President Wilson, was largely the fruit of the thinking and, more, the fervent evangelising, of notable British internationalists. The signatory nations pledged themselves not to resort to war as a means of settling disputes until the matter had been submitted to various League processes of peaceful settlement for at least three months. They accepted the obligation to take prompt financial and economic action against any League member who went to war in breach of the Covenant. They also undertook to preserve the political independence and territorial integrity of League members. At the same time they were to disarm to the lowest level 'consistent with national safety and the enforcement by common action of international obligations'.[1]

It was the ambitious hope and intention of the framers of this document to usher in a new era in the life of mankind. The nobility of their vision is beyond question: a world society regulated by law instead of the power struggle, often violent, that had hitherto shaped the course of history. But its nobility does not redeem its impracticability in the circumstances of the epoch. The new world order rested on nothing more solid than another signed folio of parchment. Even League-of-Nations evangelists like Gilbert Murray had to admit that in practice the League might not be able to enforce the Covenant.[2] Murray himself, for example, looked instead to 'the whole-hearted acceptance of the League spirit' for the future of the new system.[3] an expectation at once excessively optimistic and faintly desperate. Naturally enough, in the prevailing atmosphere, much weight was also laid on the moral influence of the League, speaking as the voice of the world's conscience. It appeared therefore that the success of the new system of international law and order depended on there being no lawbreakers. 'Covenants without swords are but words,' bleakly wrote Thomas Hobbes in the seventeenth century. The League of Nations possessed no sword. How could it? The League, as such, enjoyed no kind of independent existence and authority at all. The widely made assumption that it did, as when men spoke of 'support for the League' or 'loyalty to the League', was founded on mass self-deception. For the League was no more than, or other than, its member states. In the nature

[1] Article 8 of the Covenant; F. P. Walters, *A History of the League of Nations*, 2 Vols. (London, Oxford University Press 1952), Vol. I, pp. 40–64.

[2] Gilbert Murray, *The Ordeal of this Generation: The War, the League and the Future* (London, Allen and Unwin, 1929), p. 91.

[3] Ibid. p. 97.

of things the smaller nations looked to the greatest powers for leadership; to Britain and France, since America had refused to join. If the League were ever to coerce a lawbreaker, it would be not the Paraguayan army or the Liberian navy that would do the coercing; but the Royal Navy and the French army. So when British internationalists demanded that Britain should disarm and entrust her security to 'the League', they were really proposing that Britain should rest her safety on her own weakness. When they demanded that the French too should disarm they were unwittingly trying to deprive the League of the only swords ever likely to be unsheathed against breakers of the Covenant.

There was therefore a fundamental and fatal flaw in the internationalists' new world system, glossed over in their idealistic enthusiasm. Without the sanction of overwhelming force behind the new international morality, the League of Nations had no chance whatsoever of putting an end to the anarchy of the power struggle between nation-states. It was like hoping to end the Wars of the Roses by creating a League of Barons pledged to keep the peace and obey the law of the land. But even had the internationalists fully realised that the Covenant could only prevail if backed by force adequate to restrain a rogue great power, the problem remained of finding the force. Britain and France were hardly strong and rich enough to keep the peace right across the globe, even had they been willing to do so.

Yet it was in the ambiguous obligations under the Covenant to maintain the *status quo* of the entire world against forcible change that the heavy burdens and gratuitous perils to England of membership of the League of Nations were to be found. Here was an infinitely greater and more dangerous task than the traditional pursuit of purely English interests, carrying with it the risks of embroilment with powers with which England had no direct quarrel. On the other hand membership of the League of Nations conferred on England herself no greater advantage than the traditional kind of alliance – now forsworn – except the possible but unlikely, and in any case valueless, support of a rabble of small nations.

The flaws and inconsistencies in the idea of a league of nations did not go unremarked, even at the time of its conception. When, in 1916, Lord Robert Cecil formally put the idea forward to the War Cabinet in a long and emotional memorandum, his proposals were subjected to a ruthless critique by Sir Maurice Hankey in a memorandum of his own to Balfour, the Foreign Secretary, on 1 May. Hankey, a former Royal Marine officer and now Secretary both to the Cabinet and to the Committee of Imperial Defence, was uniquely qualified to consider the project of a league of nations in the stark light of strategic and political reality. His memorandum opened prophetically enough: 'Generally it appears to me that any such scheme is dangerous to us, because it will create a sense of security which is wholly fictitious.'

Hankey attacked even the pre-war faith of British governments and the Foreign Office in the sanctity of treaties, despite the then warnings of the armed forces; and he went on to analyse the folly of entrusting our future national security to yet more treaties. In Hankey's view, a league of nations, together with some universal treaty, would merely lull the British to sleep. Nor were there grounds for hope that nations would ever combine to coerce a wrongdoer such as Germany. Hankey concluded his memorandum with a measured warning, every word of which was to be borne out in the course of the 1920s and 1930s:

> It [a league of nations] will only result in failure and the longer that failure is postponed the more certain it is that this country will have been lulled to sleep. It will put a very strong lever into the hands of the well-meaning idealists who are to be found in almost every Government, who deprecate expenditure on armaments, and, in the course of time, it will almost certainly result in this country being caught at a disadvantage.[1]

Sir Eyre Crowe was no less scathing. He pointed out in a memorandum of 12 October 1916 that 'a solemn league and covenant' would be 'a treaty, like other treaties', and asked: 'What is there to ensure that it will not, like other treaties, be broken?'

Like Hankey, Crowe doubted whether 'the pledge of common action' against disturbers of the peace would be kept; he thought that the action of individual nations would be determined in the future as in the past by the balance of power and by consideration of national interest. He poured scorn on the internationalists' proposal for an economic boycott or blockade of wrongdoers. 'It is all', he wrote, 'a question of real military preponderance' – and not merely in numbers, but in cohesion, efficiency and geographical location. Crowe also dismissed the other great hope of the internationalists – universal disarmament – as a practical impossibility.[2]

Nevertheless, the idea of a league of nations gained ground inside governmental circles. In 1917 it was discussed by a special committee of the Imperial War Conference under Lord Milner; its members included Arthur Henderson (Labour, Methodist and internationalist) and H. A. L.

[1] Both Lord Robert Cecil's and Sir Maurice Hankey's Memoranda are in CAB 27/626, FP(36)2.
[2] CAB 27/626, FP(36)3.

Fisher (Liberal and internationalist). The committee reported itself impressed with the danger of the complete destruction of the civilised world if there were to be another war like the present one, and with the need to devise some means of diminishing the risk of such an occurrence. On the other hand, the committee also felt that any scheme for an international league ought not to be over-ambitious. On 26 April 1917 the Milner Committee's report came before the Imperial War Cabinet. Lloyd George, the Premier, was an ambiguous and ambivalent figure. Though now the bellicose war leader who owed his place to his public determination to award Germany what was called 'the Knock-out Blow', he was by origins a left-wing liberal of nonconformist origins. Now, in this discussion about a league of nations, he expressed himself sorry that, in his words, cold water had been thrown on the idea. On 1 May 1917 the Imperial War Cabinet came to agree with Lord Robert Cecil's suggestion that the peace terms should provide for a conference to decide international disputes, with a three-months' cooling-off period for negotiation before resort to war. There were to be economic sanctions against offending powers. The Cabinet also agreed that the question of limitation of armaments should be included in discussions to be held with President Woodrow Wilson about a 'league of peace'. Smuts of South Africa, in one of his timely and decisive interventions, urged the Imperial War Cabinet to declare itself in favour of the general principle of sanctions; the details could be worked out later. Thus, and not least because of the wish to sweeten the President of the United States, the idea of a league of nations was officially blessed.

Late in 1917 a Foreign Office committee under Lord Phillimore was set up to enquire into the means of creating some alternative to war as arbiter of international disputes. The Phillimore Committee did not invite evidence or opinion from the heads of the armed forces. On 20 March 1918, on the eve of the great German offensive in the west, the committee rendered its report, along with a draft convention for setting up a league of nations. On 23 December 1918 the Admiralty submitted the only memorandum on the proposed league and convention ever composed by a service department. The Admiralty argued that 'it is a serious matter to enter into such covenants, which will in certain contingencies result in the obligation to take joint naval and military action with certain Powers against another Power or Powers, without regard to the wisdom of the step as a purely naval and military consideration'.

The Admiralty pointed out that the aggressor was, self-evidently, likely to be better prepared than the nations which would have to move to restrain it, and – descending like Hankey and Crowe into questions of nuts and bolts – noted the operational weaknesses of hastily assembled international fleets. These were objections valid enough, but incidental; however, the Admiralty also pointed out the fundamental danger to England of membership of a league of nations: that if no complete confidence could be placed in the naval co-operation of other league members, then a covenant obliging Great Britain to take action other than for self-protection actually *increased* British strategic responsibilities, and might require a larger navy.[1]

On 24 December 1918 both the Phillimore Report and the Admiralty memorandum were discussed by the Imperial War Cabinet. By now the war was over, and President Wilson, given consequence by dollars, was in full evangelical flight, cheered on by rapturous internationalists.[2] The Cabinet's discussion turned less on the Phillimore Report, still less on the Admiralty's pessimistic analysis, than on an enthusiastic memorandum in favour of a league by General Smuts. The long Cabinet discussion did not stoop, like Hankey, Crowe and the Admiralty, to the detail of how collective security could ever work in practice. Lord Robert Cecil himself laid weight on the league of nations' role of conciliation as the means of peace, rather than sanctions; an evasion followed by other speakers. As a result the league of nations finally won acceptance as the guiding principle of English policy. Never again, not even in the proceedings of the British Empire Delegation at the Peace Conference, was there the kind of root-and-branch critical analysis carried out so unavailingly by Hankey, Crowe and the Admiralty.[3]

How was it that the arguments against a league of nations and its covenant, unanswerable as they were and are, were so lightly dismissed? They were a defiance of the spirit of the age; they appeared absurdly irrelevant and archaic at this time of Woodrow Wilson's first coming. For British governing circles, as well as internationalist opinion at large, reposed their faith in a league of nations upon another fundamental yet characteristic misapprehension about the world they lived in. They took it for granted that the overwhelming majority of the governments and peoples of mankind now shared their own hopeful idealism. They so took it because they thought that the victory of the Allies marked the final triumph of liberal principles throughout the world; and because they also believed that, as a result of the horrors and calamities of the war, mankind

[1] CAB 27/626, FP(36)2.

[2] See above p. 58.

[3] See Hankey's Memorandum for Cabinet Committee on Foreign Policy 1 May 1936, summarising the history of deliberations on the proposal for a league of nations, in CAB 27/626, FP(36)2.

had repented and begun afresh – a sort of Wesleyan mass-conversion on a global scale. Nothing of the kind had taken place; nor, except to those who wished to believe, was there much evidence to suggest that it had. But it was on this supposed change of heart that the British governing classes really founded their hopes that the Covenant of the League might prove self-enforcing.[1] There was also the British belief in the infinite healing powers of conciliation.

For all these reasons, and perhaps most of all because of the impact on their own minds of the Great War,[2] the British in general felt that a new way must be found of conducting world affairs. They therefore convinced themselves that disputes between nations would henceforth be peacefully settled by means of the League's machinery of talk, and that the unpleasant question of armed coercion of a bandit great power might never rise. Thus even those few statesmen like Austen Chamberlain whose hopes of the League were but modest nevertheless saw advantage in British membership rather than entanglement and danger. The League of Nations, whose Covenant now supplied the place of strategy as the guiding principle of English policy, was therefore the noblest and most perilous of all the romantic illusions that were to bemuse and mislead the English between the world wars. It was a Grail that enticed the well-meaning knights of liberalism into adventures where, unfortunately for them and their country, they found themselves playing Cervantes' Don Quixote rather than Lord Tennyson's Sir Galahad, as they would have wished.

When the German delegates signed the Treaty of Versailles on 28 June 1919, it consummated the defeat of the most formidable rival England had ever had to fight. Under the peace treaty Germany was forbidden ever again to become a great seapower. Her navy was in future to comprise no more than six obsolete battleships, six light cruisers, twelve destroyers and twelve torpedo boats. Submarines were forbidden. New ships built as replacements were to be no heavier than 10,000 tons. All naval installations and defences within fifty kilometres of the German coast were to be demolished; so too were the fortifications of the island of Heligoland, the outer barbican of the German North Sea bases. Germany was completely prohibited naval and military aircraft.[3] The German High Sea Fleet was already scrap metal, lying scuttled by its own crews deep in the swirling currents of the British base at Scapa Flow.

This total destruction of German seapower marked for Britain the

[1] See for example Philip Kerr (Lord Lothian) in J. R. M. Butler, *Lord Lothian* (London, Macmillan 1960), p. 191. [2] See below p. 424–35. [3] Cmd. 153, Articles 181, 185, 198–202.

supreme gain of the Great War, since the British Empire was a maritime empire and Britain herself, owing to some seventy years of Free Trade, depended on sea-borne supplies for her very existence. The year 1919 therefore appeared to witness the apogee of English supremacy at sea. Sixty-one battleships flew the White Ensign: more than the French and United States fleets together; more than twice as many as the Japanese and Italian fleets together. There were 120 cruisers and light cruisers and 466 destroyers to escort the battlefleet and protect the tens of thousands of miles of sea-routes that converged on the British Isles from all over the world. This was nearly twice as many cruisers and destroyers as the French and United States navies combined; nearly three times as many destroyers as the Japanese and Italian navies together.[1] England and the empire rested secure again behind the overwhelming gun-power of the Royal Navy.

On land, England's principal ally, France, with a great army, faced a Germany to be disarmed under the Versailles Treaty to 100,000 long-service soldiers without tanks or heavy artillery, or a general staff, that essential piece of equipment for large-scale war; a Germany forbidden to manufacture armaments or munitions.[2] Allied forces occupied the Rhineland, the assembly area for the German offensive which had opened the war in 1914, and also bridgeheads over the Rhine which put the Ruhr, Germany's principal industrial region, at the mercy of swift occupation. Under the treaty, Allied forces were to remain in the Rhineland and the Rhine bridgeheads until 1935.[3] So that the Rhineland could never again be used as a springboard for a German invasion of France and Belgium, the region was to be permanently demilitarised: no permanent camps or barracks or supply dumps; no military railways and roads; no fortifications. This demilitarised zone included a band of territory along the *eastern* bank of the Rhine fifty kilometres deep.[4] If enforced, these various provisions would make it utterly impossible for Germany ever to revive as a great military power; impossible for her ever to launch another offensive in the West. And any German violation of this demilitarised zone was to constitute 'a hostile act',[5] justifying the immediate march of Allied forces.

The destruction under the Versailles Treaty of the German power to make war now was not all. The Hohenzollern military monarchy itself had fallen, to be replaced by a flimsy republican régime of dingy, well-meaning but inexperienced working-class and middle-class politicians. This régime was gasping for survival in the face of nationalist violence

[1] S. W. Roskill, *Naval Policy Between the Wars* (London, Collins 1968), Vol. I, p. 71.
[2] Cmd. 153, Articles 159–70.
[3] Ibid. Article 428. [4] Ibid. Articles 42–3. [5] Ibid. Article 44.

and communist revolution, and in the face of all the social and economic consequences of Germany's defeat and collapse. The huge industries lay almost at a standstill which before 1914 had been steadily conquering British world markets and even transforming Britain itself into a German technological colony.

Not since 1815 therefore had England been able to survey the world with such assurance of safety and power. For the collapse of Germany was not all: imperial Russia too, England's principal anxiety throughout the nineteenth century, had disintegrated. In 1919 Russia was convulsed by civil war between the precarious 'red' bolshevik régime in Moscow and the 'white' counter-revolutionary armies which sought to overthrow it.

Yet even in this very moment of victory two new threats could be perceived, like the smudges of smoke on the horizon that betray the far-off approach of a fleet. There was the rise of Japan as a great industrial and military power in the Far East; and there was America's emergence as yet another challenge to English naval supremacy.

Japan was, as Lord Curzon, the Foreign Secretary, expressed it in 1921, a 'restless and aggressive power, full of energy, and somewhat like the Germans in mentality'.[1] The astonishing modernisation of Japan since she had abandoned her self-imposed isolation from the West in 1868 had left her traditional society and its moral code little changed. She had copied German and American industry, the German army and the English and German navies. She had not copied the liberal assumptions by which English statesmen governed their actions. The Japanese view of international relations owed nothing to Christianity, evangelical or otherwise; and the internationalist moralising and idealism then current in Britain were as foreign and incomprehensible to the Japanese as to thirteenth-century English barons. For Japanese society remained feudal, hierarchical, obedient, each man looking to his patron and so on upwards to the emperor, who was not only the ruler of the country, but divine and therefore an object of religious worship. The Japanese venerated the ideal of the warrior brave in battle, jealous of honour, loyal unto death and achieving fulfilment in dying by violence. It was not therefore the gentle dreams of League-of-Nations believers in the West, but bloodthirsty reveries of a destiny of conquest which inspired the most powerful groups in Japanese society, the leaderships of the armed forces. For although Japan enjoyed a Western-style constitution, complete with parliament (Diet), prime minister and cabinet, it was, like the Japanese army, a constitution copied from Imperial Germany. The emperor was executive

[1] CAB 32/2, Pt. I, E-8.

ruler of the State; ministers were responsible to him rather than to Parliament; Parliament could criticise and obstruct but not rule. In particular, the emperor directly commanded the armed forces, whose leaders were responsible personally to him and not to Parliament.

Japan had already grown great by war: against China in 1894, Russia in 1904. China still remained, in 1919, a first object of Japanese penetration and exploitation, especially since China was now sunk in an anarchy of warlords and revolution. For the Japanese, with a multiplying population penned in narrow islands, hungry for markets and raw materials, the temptation of what Curzon called 'the great helpless, hopeless and inert mass of China'[1] was not to be easily resisted. However it was England which of all foreign nations held the largest single existing stake in trade and investment in China, and enjoyed the greatest political influence. And to the southwards of Japan lay other, more distant temptations: the fat, sleepy European colonies of South-East Asia, rich in rubber, oil, tin and rice – Indo-China, Malaya and Borneo, the Dutch East Indies. Further off still, isolated in the blue wastes of the South Pacific, beckoned the under-populated lands of Australia and New Zealand.

The potential dangers of Japanese power and ambition to British interests and territories in the Far East were plain enough. British statesmen immediately after the Great War suffered no illusions as to Japanese morality. As Curzon said with some understatement: 'Japan is not at all an altruistic power.'[2] Lloyd George, Prime Minister until 1922, also acknowledged to his colleagues that the 'Japanese might have no conscience'.[3] However, Japan and England were joined by a formal alliance, due for renewal in 1922; an alliance to which, as Lloyd George also had to acknowledge, the Japanese had always been scrupulously loyal.

The alliance had been negotiated in 1902, when England, faced with Russian expansion in the Far East, began to emerge from her Victorian diplomatic isolation. With the emergence of Germany as a potential enemy by 1904, however, the Japanese Alliance acquired a new and unlooked-for value. It freed England from anxieties about Russia in the East – about the Far East in general – and enabled her to concentrate her fleet at home to meet German naval power in the North Sea. In its 1905 form, the Anglo-Japanese Treaty provided that either party should go to the aid of the other in the event of unprovoked aggression by third party. As time went on, China or America came more and more to seem the likely third parties with whom Japan might find herself at war, and against whom she might invoke the Anglo-Japanese alliance. Embroilment with

[1] Ibid. [2] Ibid. [3] CAB 23/25, 42/21(2).

the United States was the last thing the English then required. When therefore Sir Edward Grey renewed the alliance in 1911 for ten years, a new article[1] was included by which it was agreed that the treaty should not oblige either contracting party to go to war with a power with whom a treaty of arbitration was in force. In 1914 England formally notified Japan that a treaty for a peace commission, which had just been concluded between herself and the United States, consisted such an arbitration treaty. As a consequence, and in the words of Lord Curzon to the Imperial Conference of 1921, 'war with the United States because of the Anglo-Japanese alliance was wholly out of bounds of possibility'.[2]

In the Great War Japan had proved a useful as well as a loyal ally. As Curzon admitted: 'I suppose it is not to be denied that our alliance with her, and the assistance of her naval forces, assured the complete safety of our possessions in the Pacific.'[3] Australia and New Zealand were particularly conscious of this service, since their expeditionary forces had been escorted to the theatres of war not only by the Royal Navy, but also by the Imperial Japanese Navy. The New Zealand Prime Minister, Massey, pointed out to his colleagues at the 1921 Imperial Conference that 'supposing Japan had been on the enemy side, one result would have been quite certain, that neither Australia nor New Zealand would have been able to send troops to the front, neither could we have sent food or equipment . . .'[4] Billy Hughes, the Australian Prime Minister, was even more forcefully eloquent:

> Look at the map and ask yourselves what would have happened to that great splash of red down from India through Australia down to New Zealand, but for the Anglo-Japanese Treaty. How much of these great rich territories and portions of our Empire would have escaped had Japan been neutral? How much if she had been our enemy? It is certain the naval power of the Empire could not have saved India and Australia and still been strong enough to hold Germany bottled up in the narrow seas. . . . Had [Japan] elected to fight on the side of Germany we should most certainly have been defeated.[5]

The Japanese alliance had thus been of immense value to England in the recent past; but in the future? This was another question, and one which had to be answered by 1922, when the decision would have to be taken whether or not to renew the alliance.

The original reasons for the alliance had become void with the disap-

[1] Cmd. 153, Article 4.
[2] CAB 32/2, Pt. I, E-8.
[3] Ibid.
[4] CAB 32/2, Pt. I, E-2.
[5] CAB 32/2, Pt. I, E-10.

pearance of the threats from Germany and Russia. Nevertheless, as Curzon was to warn the 1921 Imperial Conference, both dangers could recur. There was even a further possible danger, that some combination between Russia and Germany might eventually evolve.[1] Worse: Lloyd George expressed the opinion to his Cabinet colleagues in May 1921 that if Britain snubbed Japan, there was a risk of the Japanese falling a prey to Russo-German advances.[2] There was also the spectre raised by Hughes and Massey of the British Empire's vulnerability in the face of Japanese ambition, once Japan was freed from the curb of an alliance. Holland and France, for their parts, both wanted the treaty to be renewed, since their Far Eastern empires were almost wholly defenceless.[3] Not to renew the alliance, on the other hand, carried with it the likelihood of changing Japanese forbearance towards the British Empire into hostility. The British ambassador in Tokyo warned indeed that Japan would be so mortified and humiliated by British refusal to renew the treaty as to produce an 'attitude of resentment and a policy of revenge'.[4]

There were very strong grounds, therefore, for renewing the Japanese alliance; and not the least strong was the negative advantage that while she was an ally she could not be an enemy. Unfortunately, however, renewal of the Japanese alliance carried with it the certainty of American ill-will.

Japanese and American rivalry in the Far East had been steadily sharpening since 1900, especially over the question of China. America resented and opposed the ruthless Japanese penetration of China; partly because of chivalry about China's freedom and independence, partly because Japanese penetration was mostly directed into Manchuria, the principal area of America's own investment in the country. Since 1898 American imperialism had carried the Stars and Stripes to the Philippines and transformed the United States into a great Pacific naval power. American and Japanese policies in the Pacific and Asia were thus on converging courses. It followed that even if, as Curzon was certain, England incurred no danger of war with America through the Japanese alliance, she would unquestionably forfeit American goodwill and friendship if she renewed it. In 1921 the US Secretary of State, Charles Evans Hughes, bluntly informed the British Ambassador in Washington that 'he viewed the renewal of the Anglo-Japanese Alliance in any form with disquietude', and made the ambassador's flesh creep with references to the effects such a renewal would produce on American opinion.[5]

The approaching date for renewal of the Japanese treaty therefore

[1] CAB 32/2, Pt. I, E-8.
[2] CAB 23/25, 43/21(2).
[3] Ibid.
[4] Ibid.
[5] CAB 32/2, Pt. I, E-8.

presented the British Government with that task so uncongenial to the British temperament, the taking of a decision; the making of a choice, and a choice between mutually exclusive alternatives. What made the task the more painful was that, whichever way the choice was made, it was bound to lead to ill-feeling and unpleasantness.

The choice lay between an alliance (with Japan) and kindly sentiment (from America); or, to put it the other way round, between the disadvantages either of incurring Japan's active hostility towards the vulnerable British Empire in the East, or America's unfriendliness. For the fair alternative to a Japanese alliance – an alliance with the United States – was not open to Britain. Far from concluding new alliances, the United States in 1920–1 was in full ebb from world commitments into isolationism; refusing even to join the League of Nations and to ratify the Treaty of Versailles.

Nevertheless, when stripped of qualification, the choice the English had to make was between Japan and the United States. It was one of the most crucial national-strategic decisions England had ever had to reach in her history. What guidance could the traditional wisdom of past English foreign policy offer? As super-powers had successively risen towards domination of the Western World, from Spain to Imperial Germany, England had thrown her weight into the opposite scale, along with other powers of lesser might than the super-power. At first instinctive, this policy eventually became deliberate, enshrined in the doctrine of the balance of power, and re-stated, in terms of opposition to Germany, by Sir Eyre Crowe in 1907 in a classic memorandum. To side with the weaker against the stronger was doubly wise; it prevented the strong becoming over-mighty, while it preserved England herself from the fate of those states who were misguided enough to ally themselves with powers much greater than themselves. For example, Holland's alliance with England in the wars against Louis XIV cost her her independence of action and began her decline; while Austria in the Great War ended up as the helpless satellite of her great partner, Germany.

Traditional English policy therefore might have suggested that the correct choice for England was to renew the Japanese alliance. For Japan's total national power – military, naval and industrial – made her a state of about England's own weight. The United States on the other hand, with a population of 100,000,000, with ever-bounding industrial power – steel production four times as great as Britain's – was clearly the super-power of the future, and able, and willing, to outbuild the Royal Navy. That American power was bound to eclipse that of England had been foreseen by English writers and statesmen as long ago as the 1870s. Gladstone wrote in 1879: '... it is she alone who, at the coming time, can and probably will wrest from us our commerical supremacy.... We have no more title against her than Venice or Genoa or Holland has had against us....'[1]

Since the 1890s England had felt the accumulating pressure of American power against her interests. In 1895 America intervened in a dispute between England and Venezuela in which she had no direct concern whatsoever, over the boundary between Venezuela and British Guiana. President Grover Cleveland sent a bellicose message to Congress tantamount to an ultimatum to England to submit the dispute to arbitration, or risk war with the United States. England acquiesced.[2] Between 1898 and 1902 America transformed the whole strategic balance in the Caribbean by placing the Panama Canal under her own exclusive control and fortifying the canal zone, although the original arrangement had been for an international and neutralised canal. The passage of the British battlefleet from the Atlantic to the Pacific would now be by courtesy of the United States. The consequences of this American action, unresisted by England, was, in the words of the Admiralty, that 'from a purely naval and strategical point of view ... the preponderance of advantage from the canal would be greatly on the side of the United States ...'[3]

The American victory over Spain in the war of 1898 led to a further expansion of American power, to the economic disadvantage of Great Britain. The Philippines, Cuba and Puerto Rico, now American colonies, were gradually closed to British merchants by protective tariffs, for the benefit of their American rivals.[4]

In 1898, much to Canadian disgust, Great Britain yielded to United States pressure over a dispute about the borders between Canada and Alaska, by agreeing to submit the dispute immediately to decision by an international tribunal. The resulting award, in 1903, 'was almost wholly favourable to the United States'.[5]

This persistent encroachment, little softened by tact or grace, was

[1] *Kin Beyond the Sea* quoted in H. C. Allen, *The Anglo-American Relationship Since 1783* (London, Adam and Charles Black 1959), p. 82; see also J. R. Seeley, *The Expansion of England* (London, Macmillan 1883), p. 350.

[2] See Charles S. Campbell Jr, *Anglo-American Understanding 1898–1903* (Baltimore, The Johns Hopkins Press 1957), p. 5; A. E. Campbell, *Great Britain and the United States 1895–1903* (London, Longmans 1960), Introduction.

[3] Quoted in Charles S. Campbell, Introduction; Lionel Gelber, *The Rise of Anglo-American Friendship 1898–1906* (Hampden, Connecticut, Archon Books 1966), p. 102.

[4] See Charles S. Campbell, pp. 58–62; R. H. Heindel, *The American Impact of Great Britain 1898–1914* (New York, Octagon Books 1968), p. 161.

[5] Charles S. Campbell, p. 340; see his ch. 14 for a full account of the question.

similar enough to those French encroachments of the seventeenth and eighteenth centuries which had won for the French monarchy the unyielding opposition of the then English ruling classes. They were similar enough to those encroachments, and even those threats, of Kaiser Wilhelm II and his ministers which had caused England to reverse within a decade her traditional friendships and enmities, and side with France against Germany. However, they were not all. British markets throughout the empire and the East (including China) had been more and more invaded by United States exports; even the British home market itself was falling to American competition. America was therefore no less a dangerous industrial and commercial rival than pre-war Germany.[1]

Nor had the brief association between England and America during the Great War[2] for long halted American expansion at British expense. US relief teams in Asia Minor, for example, served as a cloak for pushing American influence and trade. When the senior American naval officer in the eastern Mediterranean arrived in a Turkish port he was accompanied by representatives of Standard Oil and the National City Bank of New York.[3] In Iraq, a major battle for oil concessions was under way between American and British interests.

And lastly there was the huge and rapid expansion of the United States Navy. This was aimed specifically, like the Imperial German High Seas Fleet, against England, and not to satisfy essential national needs as represented by the size of the American overseas empire, or of her sea-borne trade or merchant marine, or the length of her sea-routes.[4] In 1919 the Admiralty warned the British Government that if Great Britain built no new ships while America completed her 1916 building programme, then by 1923 'we shall have passed to the position of being the second naval power'.[5]

This worldwide American diplomatic, naval and economic pressure over the previous twenty-five years was fed not only from interest and from the inevitable dynamic of national expansion, but also from hostility and dislike. Ill-feeling and resentment towards England was widespread among the American people, especially the 18,400,000 Americans of German extraction[6] and the Irish. The Venezuela dispute in 1895[7] and the

[1] See Heindel, ch. VIII, expecially pp. 180–4.
[2] It was *only* an association, for President Wilson refused to become an ally of France and England, insisting on the detached status of 'an associated power'.
[3] Report by British naval authorities in the Mediterranean to Lord Curzon, quoted in Roskill, *Naval Policy Between the Wars*, p. 23.
[4] See Roskill, *Naval Policy Between the Wars*, p. 20 and ch. V. [5] Ibid. p. 216.
[6] Nearly a third of the total white population of 66,990,000: 1900 figures. Allen, p. 104n.
[7] See above p. 255.

Boer War particularly inflamed American popular feeling against England.[1] In 1900 England was so much hated that it was only by a narrow majority that the annexation of Canada failed to get adopted as a Republican plank in the presidential election.[2] In the United States Navy after the Great War, as in the Imperial German Navy before 1914, anti-British feeling was particularly strong: every American admiral seemed to have been issued with a chip to carry on his epaulettes.

There was therefore every strategic, economic and psychological justification for England to see in the United States the successor to Imperial Germany, Napoleonic and Bourbon France and Philip II's Spain as an overwhelming super-power dangerous to English prosperity and independence, even if armed aggression itself was hardly to be expected.

On the other hand, Japan's ambitions had as yet impinged on British interests to nothing like the same degree, whatever might be the future danger of Japanese attack in the Far East. It was only in China that so far British and Japanese interests had run foul of each other: Britain as the great trading and political influence *in situ* and Japan as the interloper. Whereas Britain favoured the 'Open Door' policy, whereby all trading nations were equally free to exploit China as best they could, Japan hoped for an exclusive sphere of influence, like those carved out of Africa by the European powers at the end of the nineteenth century. However, Japan was mainly interested in that part of China nearest to herself, north China and in particular Manchuria. British interests lay preponderantly in central and southern China. A division of China into spheres of influence would thus entail small sacrifice on the British part while removing a principal cause of present and future Anglo-Japanese friction, and steering Japanese ambitions away from the European empires in South-East Asia into the vast mainland of China. Such a division would have been in the tradition of such pre-war deals as the Anglo-French *entente* of 1904, whereby France acknowledged Egypt and the Sudan as a British sphere of influence in return for recognition that Morocco was a French sphere.

The traditional wisdom of the doctrine of the balance of power and a weighing of the comparative dangers from Japan and the United States to British world power suggest alike that the right course for England was to cleave to the Japanese alliance. And indeed Balfour, the Lord President of the Council, speaking not for himself but as a mouthpiece of the Committee of Imperial Defence, said as much to the Imperial Conference of 1921. He pointed out that the United States was now adding to her world

[1] See Charles S. Campbell, pp. 5, 175–9, 205.
[2] Ibid. p. 205.

strength in the Pacific. Even if it were a friendly navy, and there were no possibility of war with America,

> yet if you look at the thing from a purely strategic point of view, and omit politics and sentiment and look at it with an open mind, undoubtedly it is a fact that if we had not Japan on our side we should be second or third Power in the Pacific after a considerable number of years . . . we are in a relatively unprepared condition in that part of the world. . . . Therefore, in our view, so long as our relatively unprepared condition lasts, it is, from a strategic point of view, of very great importance that the Japanese Alliance should be maintained. . . .[1]

However the British governing classes did not look at America from a purely strategic point of view, omitting politics and sentiment. On the contrary, they saw the United States as a nation with whom the British enjoyed a special, almost family, relationship. The British had accepted the American encroachments of 1895–1902 with complacency.[2] As an historian of the Anglo-American relationship at the turn of the century writes: 'There was an assumption of goodwill, and readiness to believe that there must have been some mistake, which is not to be found in British dealings with the European powers.'[3] The British governing classes went so far as to assume that a strong American world policy, far from being a menace, could only be of help and benefit to England, thus ignoring the very real collisions of interest which had already taken place since 1895, and which had led England to sign 'what *were* virtually treaties of surrender on a number of occasions. . . .'[4]

The British indeed displayed towards the United States the forgiveness, the blindness towards blemishes of character and conduct, commonly found in a man infatuated. For the British governing classes *were* infatuated with America – or, rather, with a mythical America conjured up by their own romantic vision.

The origins of the myth lay in the 1880s, before which decade the British ruling classes were not very acutely aware of America, nor much interested in it. The myth was a grander version of the imperial myth about the mission of the Anglo-Saxon race to conquer, colonise and civilise the world. The United States was regarded as an Anglo-Saxon country, although by the end of the nineteenth century the proportion of English stock in the 'white' American population had sunk to only one-

[1] CAB 32/2, Pt. I, E-8.
[2] See A. E. Campbell.
[3] Ibid. See also pp. 3, 45, 146–55, 189–90, 193; Gelber, p. 97.
[4] Ibid. p. 193.

third.[1] It was also regarded as a kind of British colony at one remove; a daughter country that, but for an unfortunate misunderstanding in the distant past, would stand in the same relationship to Britain as Australia and Canada. This assumption of identity of race was central. By the 1890s references to 'our American cousins' and 'the Transatlantic branch of our race' repeatedly decorated the speeches of British statesmen, especially among imperialists.[2] In 1898 for example Joseph Chamberlain in a famous speech celebrated the idea of the Union Jack and the Stars and Stripes waving together over an Anglo-Saxon alliance.[3] From this false assumption of identity of race, the British went on to assume identity of political and cultural traditions and national aspirations.[4] Here they relied not only on the common language and the now distant common historical origins but also on a recent study of American life and institutions by James Bryce, afterwards Lord Bryce.[5] First published in 1888, *The American Commonwealth* exercised profound influence on the British governing classes' notions about America. Bryce, although optimistic and affectionate towards the United States, fully documented all those habits of life and mind, those social and political institutions, and those new racial elements which made modern America distinctly more a foreign than a cousinly nation. It is to be supposed therefore that the British noted in Bryce's book what was congenial to their romantic feelings, and ignored the rest.

During the 1890s – at the very epoch of American encroachment on British interests – British myth-making about America began to be enthusiastically promoted by leagues, committees and associations, although the first such body, the Anglo-American Association, was founded as early as 1871.[6] In 1898 there was the short-lived Anglo-American Alliance Society, and in the same year the beginning of the Anglo-American League. In 1901 there followed the Atlantic Union, and, at the time of Edward VII's coronation, that redoubtable promoter of inspirational clichés, the Pilgrims.[7] The statement of purpose issued by the Anglo-American League at its inaugural meeting aptly expresses in its content and tone how the British governing classes had come to regard the emerging super-power across the Atlantic:

> Considering that the people of the British Empire and the United States are closely allied by blood, inherit the same literature and laws,

[1] Allen, p. 104n. For an analysis of racial links between Britain and America, see Allen, ch. 4.
[2] A. E. Campbell, pp. 45, 195–8. [3] Charles S. Campbell, p. 47. [4] Heindel, p. 126.
[5] James Bryce, *The American Commonwealth*, 2 Vols. (New York, Macmillan 1911).
[6] Heindel, p. 38. [7] Ibid. pp. 38–40.

> hold the same principles of self-government, recognise the same ideas of freedom and humanity in the guidance of their National policy and are drawn together by strong common interests in many parts of the world, this meeting is of the opinion that every effort should be made in the interests of civilisation and peace to secure the most cordial and constant co-operation on the part of the two nations.[1]

It was not only statesmen or imperialists who saw America in this glowing light, as through stained glass. Radicals and Liberals regarded the American war against the Spaniards in 1898 as a blow against a cruel colonial tyranny.[2] British churchmen and nonconformists, ignoring the Roman Catholicism of the Irish, Italians and Poles in America, the Judaism of the large Jewish minority and the Greek Orthodoxy of Ukrainian and Balkan immigrants, perceived in America a reflection of their own evangelicalism. The American evangelists, Moody and Sankey, must be considered no less than James Bryce as among the founders of the 'special relationship'. As the Bishop of London put it in 1898: 'The question of the future of the world is the existence of the Anglo-Saxon civilisation on a religious basis.'[3]

English writers too, fêted on their lucrative lecture tours of the United States, formed an impression of cultural kinship from their highly partial experience of American life, and also from that unrepresentative group, American writers visiting Europe.[4]

The British governing classes in particular, aristocratic though they were in complexion, found the life of the rich Anglo-Saxon East-Coast oligarchy, which dominated American federal politics before the Great War, completely congenial and familiar.[5] The myth of a common Anglo-Saxon destiny flowered on the lawns of the pseudo-European pseudo-manor houses of Long Island. The accord became more intimate in the warmth of London ballrooms where American heiresses were picked up by the sons of the English aristocracy. For by 1914, 130 American girls had married into the English peerage. Joseph Chamberlain (the apostle both of Imperialism and Anglo-Saxonism), Rudyard Kipling, Lord Randolph Churchill and Lord Curzon were among the influential Englishmen blessed with American wives. This connection by marriage between the

[1] Quoted in Charles S. Campbell, p. 46.
[2] Charles S. Campbell, pp. 43–5.
[3] Quoted in Heindel, pp. 129–30. See also pp. 62–3 for British evangelical sects' attitude to the Spanish-American War of 1898; and pp. 112–14, 363–71. See also Allen, p. 111; Charles S. Campbell, p. 43.
[4] Heindel, pp. 130–1, 312–17; Allen, ch. 5.
[5] See D. C. Watt, *Personalities and Policies* (London, Longmans 1965), pp. 27–8.

then ruling American oligarchy and the English governing class supplied a further powerful and understandable stimulus to the notion of 'kinship' between the nations.[1]

Yet these social and cultural exchanges between various groups within the two countries led to an essentially false impression of the degree of 'kinship' that existed between Britain and America, when considered as nation-states. Except for Bryce, those who did most to create the British myth about America really only knew highly unrepresentative segments of American life, for they naturally gravitated to what survived there of Englishry. Yet it was from these segments that they generalised their impressions of 'America'.

However, outside the ken of statesmen, peers, clerics, dons and writers, there was another and more important America – the America of soaring industrial production, of lawlessness and violence; the America of two-thirds of the population who were not of English stock, and for whom the ideas of common history and common cultural inheritance meant nothing whatsoever. This was the America that British businessmen and technologists saw; and they recognised it as the most dangerous of threats to British prosperity and independence – more dangerous than that of Imperial Germany.[2]

While the sentimentalising about 'our cousins across the Atlantic' was in full spate among the British governing classes, a very different kind of public discussion about America was therefore also taking place in Britain. Especially between 1898 and 1903, but also in the years up to 1914, the Press treated the threat of American business penetration into British markets and into the United Kingdom itself as a major topic. There was also a spate of books and lectures to add further warning.[3] The ruthlessness and alleged sharp practice of American business methods evoked a general expression of suspicion and dislike.[4] Yet, extraordinarily enough, this prolonged public analysis of the American industrial threat seems to have made no impression on the makers of the pan-Anglo-Saxon myth, if indeed they were aware of it. Two highly discordant pictures of America were thus painted simultaneously by two different groups in British society, working, as it were, in separate studios. However it was not the harshly realistic portrayal by the industrialists which won general acceptance but the vision of the statesmen and intellectuals.

That this myth of cousinhood and common interest was at least partly

[1] Ibid.; Allen, p. 111; Heindel, pp. 126 and 349.
[2] Heindel, chs. VII, VIII and IX.
[3] Ibid. pp. 139, 141, 180–4.
[4] Ibid. pp. 185–8.

false to fact and in consequence misleading to British political judgement was not the least of its dangers. For necessarily underlying British belief in the myth was an assumption that the Americans too believed in it: that *they* for *their* part saw the *British* as less 'foreign' than other nations, to be judged according to special standards of charity and understanding; that they too felt there to be a natural harmony between British and American interests and policies. The assumption was mistaken. Except again for unrepresentative circles on the East Coast, America did not reciprocate British sentiments towards her. Where not actively hostile to Britain, American opinion was indifferent.[1] The special 'relationship' was a British fantasy. It was love in the perfect romantic style, unrequited and unencouraged, yet nevertheless pursued with a grovelling ardour.[2] Although from time to time realistic observers warned the British that their feelings were not reciprocated, it was to no purpose.[3]

The passing of two decades did little to cool this British infatuation. Co-belligerency during the Great War provided the opportunity for the British Government to court President Wilson and for President Wilson to keep it at arm's length; and for Wilson to win the hearts of all British moralising internationalists. By 1920–1, owing to America's withdrawal into isolation and to a ferocious, though covert, struggle over oil concessions and over cable and radio communications, the British recognised that things were not quite as they believed they should be. Nevertheless the myth of the special family relationship had become part of the furniture of the British mind. The younger generation of imperialists, men like Lionel Curtis and Philip Kerr (Lord Lothian), were to propagate it throughout the 1920s and 1930s through journals like *The Round Table* and bodies like the Royal Institute of International Affairs (Chatham House), as one aspect of their larger idealism. For they believed that a great English-speaking association could be evolved out of the British Empire and Anglo-American cousinhood, and that this association would be a stepping-stone to a democratic world state.[4] Of Lloyd George's Cabinet in 1920–1, Churchill was half-American by blood and a life-long romantic about the destiny of the English-speaking peoples, while Arthur Balfour and Austen Chamberlain had been early believers in pan-Anglo-Saxonism. Balfour had visited America in 1917, and the warmth of his reception had melted even his frosty detachment. On his return, he made a classic statement of the pan-Anglo-Saxon myth to a Pilgrim's Dinner:

[1] Charles S. Campbell, p. 1; Allen, pp. 164, 176; A. E. Campbell, p. 198.
[2] See Allen, pp. 222–3; A. E. Campbell, pp. 198, 204–5; Heindel, pp. 125–6.
[3] Heindel, p. 126.
[4] See Butler, *Lord Lothian*, p. 115 et seq.

> We both spring from the same root. . . . Are not we bound together forever? Will not our descendants, when they come to look back upon this unique episode in the history of the world [the War], say that among the incalculable circumstances which it produced, the most beneficent and the most permanent is, perhaps, that we are brought together and united for one common purpose in one common understanding – the two great branches of the English-speaking race? . . . This is a theme which absorbs my thoughts day and night. It is a theme which moves me more, I think, than anything connected with public affairs in all my long experience.[1]

And it was Balfour who, as a former Prime Minister and Foreign Secretary, as a founder of the Committee of Imperial Defence and as the head of the British delegation to the Washington Conference in 1921, was to exercise a most powerful influence over the final settlement of British relations with Japan and the United States.

Whether or not to renew the Japanese alliance in 1922 was discussed by the Committee of Imperial Defence on 14 December 1920.[2] Lloyd George, the Prime Minister, pointed out the heavy British handicaps in a naval race: if Britain decided to build a fleet against the United States, America would immediately demand payment of their war debts. In any case Britain, unlike Japan and America, was now burdened by an immense national debt. An attempt to maintain British naval supremacy carried with it the danger of bankruptcy.

Churchill, the Secretary of State for War and Air, argued that '. . . no more fatal policy could be contemplated than that of basing our naval policy on a possible combination with Japan against America'. Lloyd George retorted by suggesting that 'there was one more fatal policy, namely, one whereby we would be at the mercy of the United States'. It was an inconclusive discussion.

On 30 May 1921 the Cabinet itself took up the problem of the Japanese alliance.[3] Curzon, the Foreign Secretary, pointed out that the alliance did provide a means of controlling the aggressive Japanese character. He also warned of the resentment the Japanese would harbour if the alliance were not renewed. Churchill described the dangers of naval rivalry with the United States. Balfour expressed himself in favour of renewing the treaty for a short period, to tide England over her current weakness in the Far

[1] Quoted in Kenneth Young, *Arthur James Balfour* (London, George Bell 1958), p. 385.
[2] CAB 2/3, 134.
[3] CAB 23/25, 43/21(2).

East. Lloyd George himself mentioned the dangers of Japan falling into a Russo-German orbit. He was against dropping her.

The Cabinet therefore came to the decision to renew the alliance, but for a shorter term than ten years. However, this decision was hedged by such qualifications as to make it virtually impossible of fulfilment. For the new treaty was to be drawn so as not to offend the susceptibilities of the League of Nations or the United States. At the same time the Cabinet agreed to push a proposal at the forthcoming Imperial Conference that the President of the United States should be asked to summon a general Pacific Conference. A general conference! – here again was a favourite British cure-all of miraculous efficacy. As Lloyd George himself put it: '. . . the work of a Conference is to reconcile the irreconcilable, and I think the same thing would happen if we had a Conference between the United States of America, Japan and ourselves.'[1]

It was at the 1921 Imperial Conference that the problem of the Japanese alliance was exhaustively debated. The debate split the empire. Billy Hughes of Australia and Massey of New Zealand were wholeheartedly in favour of renewal, although Hughes thought that a tripartite pact including America would be even better. As Hughes argued:

> should we not be in a better position to exercise greater influence over the Eastern policy [of Japan] as an Ally of that great Eastern power, than as her potential enemy? Now, if Japan is excluded from the family of great Western nations – and, mark, to turn our backs on the Treaty is certainly to exclude Japan – she will be isolated, her national pride wounded in its most tender spot.[2]

What was more, as Massey pointed out and British statesmen agreed, the course of the Great War showed clearly enough how vital was Japanese friendship; how dangerous would be her hostility.

Arthur Meighen, the Prime Minister of Canada, on the other hand, was wholly against renewing the alliance: 'If we now in this new state of affairs renew a confidential and exclusive relationship with Japan it is wholly impossible to argue convincingly, to my mind, that it is not going to affect detrimentally our relations with the United States. . . .[3]

There was therefore in his opinion a danger of drifting insensibly into opposition to the United States, but he warned that there was no hope that Canada would see a menace in her. Smuts of South Africa too argued

[1] CAB 32/2, Pt. I, E-11.

[2] CAB 32/2, Pt. I, E-2; for other arguments advanced by Hughes and Massey, see E-10, E-11, E-12, E-31 and CAB 32/2, Pt. II, E-25.

[3] CAB 32/2, Pt. I, E-9.

for the closest possible co-operation between the British Empire and the United States in foreign policy.[1]

However, it was, as Hughes remarked, easy for Canada, snug alongside the United States and far from Asia, to advocate that Japan should be discarded; less easy for Australia and New Zealand, acutely aware as they were of their vulnerability in the face of Japan's economic need to expand. Furthermore, there was another aspect to Meighen's argument, as Billy Hughes pointed out in a sharp rebuttal.

> He [Meighen] says we ought not to renew this Alliance . . . because America does not desire us to do so. . . . The policy he thinks right is one which the 'Voice of America' would acclaim. But what we have to ask ourselves is this: Is this Empire of ours to have a policy of its own, dictated by due regard to its own interests, compatible with its declared ideals . . . or is it to have a policy dictated by some other Power?[2]

Hughes wanted to know: 'What is the substantial alternative to the renewal of the Treaty? The answer is, there is none. If Australia was asked whether she would prefer America or Japan as an Ally, her choice would be America. But that choice is not offered her.'[3]

And whereas Meighen doubted whether Japan really would be estranged if the Treaty were not renewed, Hughes drew attention to the forces of enmity towards the British Empire inside America, and doubted whether America's friendship would be won by dropping Japan.[4] Nevertheless Hughes thought it vital that the treaty should be seen not to be directed against the United States.

Then there was the related and subsidiary choice between Japan and China. China was both a cause and a theatre of Japanese and American rivalry; and America was hot in defence of China's integrity, at least with words. In any case, England's freedom of manœuvre over China was now gratuitiously restricted by her own promotion of, and present adherence to, the principles of the Covenant of the League of Nations. To carve up China as Africa had been carved up barely two decades previously was no longer possible.

The speeches of the British delegation revealed for their part a state of immobility rather like that of the louse in the experiment, starving to death in a tube half-way between a bright light and its dinner, unable to forgo the attractions of either. Lloyd George in his opening speech referred to the need for good relations both with Japan, 'a loyal ally', and

[1] CAB 32/2, Pt. I, E-6. [2] CAB 32/2, Pt. I, E-9. [3] Ibid.
[4] CAB 32/2, Pt. I, E-10.

with America. It was in his view important to avoid a division of the world over race.[1] Curzon recognised how completely the security of the British Empire in the Far East had depended on the Japanese alliance during the Great War. He conveyed the opinion of Sir Charles Eliot, British Ambassador in Tokyo, that failure to renew would lead to a Japanese policy of revenge, and also Eliot's warning that if the present alliance were replaced by an Anglo-American understanding, a link-up between Japan and Germany was possible.[2] On the other hand Curzon spoke of the importance of close relations with the United States; he noted how 'both our national interests and our sense of moral responsibility' pointed towards co-operation.[3] Then again he thought it was essential to take note of China's views; China 'a great British market, a country where we should work hand in hand with America; a country we did not wish to see swallowed up'.[4] When similarly gallant sentiments about China were uttered by Arthur Meighen, Billy Hughes brutally and prophetically pointed out their fatuity; it was impossible, he said, to defend China against Japanese ambitions: 'Is the "Voice of America" going to stand against the Japanese fleets and the Japanese army? . . . or does he suggest we should organise in China an army capable of defending China?'[5]

How completely the British Government's powers of decision were paralysed by what they took to be the fine balance between the advantages (or penalties) of renewing (or not renewing) the Japanese alliance is shown by a Cabinet meeting on 30 June 1921, which discussed the opinions expressed in the Imperial Conference. Lloyd George summed up the view of the Cabinet by saying that while Britain could not quarrel with the United States, it was 'essential not to insult Japan by doing anything which would be tantamount to casting her aside . . .'; while at the same time China must be a party to any fresh agreements over the Far East.[6]

It was the resolute opposition of Meighen of Canada which finally sank the Japanese alliance. Even before the advent of Mackenzie King, Canada was thus allowed to exercise a decisive influence over British policy, shackling it to North American opinion. Canada was in fact the British Empire's hostage to American power. However, the failure to choose Japan did not mean choosing America, partly because that choice was not open, and partly because the British Government still believed that the whole complex of Pacific and naval problems could be solved without the need for choice. Balfour, for example, personally suggested turning the

[1] CAB 32/2, Pt. I, E-1.
[2] CAB 32/2, Pt. I, E-8.
[3] CAB 32/2, Pt. I, E-4.
[4] CAB 32/2, Pt. I, E-8.
[5] CAB 32/2, Pt. I, E-10.
[6] CAB 23/26, 56/21 (2).

Anglo-Japanese Treaty into a general Far Eastern and Pacific treaty under League of Nations auspices.[1] Smuts and Meighen were both in favour of a Pacific Conference. Lloyd George agreed that Japan, the United States and China should be invited to such a conference. There was, in his view, no need to choose between American or Japanese friendship and enmity.[2] There was therefore general joy when, while the conference was still in session, President Harding issued the British Empire an invitation to take part in just such a conference, to be held in Washington.[3] But Billy Hughes did not share in the joy: 'Japan is our potential enemy, though our present friend. You propose to substitute for the Anglo-Japanese alliance and the overwhelming power of the British Navy, a Washington Conference.'[4] He wanted the Anglo-Japanese Alliance renewed as a preliminary to the proposed Pacific conference. He did not prevail.

The final communiqué of the Imperial Conference revealed the continued paralysis of decision. For Japan, according to the communiqué, was 'an old and proved ally', but China, her intended victim, was a people 'whose interests we . . . desire to assist and advance'. And the United States, the inveterate opponent of our old and proved ally, was 'the people closest to our aims and ideals'. And what, according to the communiqué, had been the purpose of the discussions in the Imperial Conference? – 'to find a method combining all these three factors in a policy which would remove the danger of heavy naval expenditure in the Pacific . . .'[5] This amazing conjuring trick was now to be finally performed at the Washington Conference.

Yet although the British Government did not acknowledge it, even to themselves, they were already in the process of making their choice between Japan and America, for it was America's displeasure which they shrank from incurring. The idea of continuing an exclusively Anglo-Japanese alliance was already dead. The new conference was to be held under American auspices in Washington, a circumstance known to evoke the sharpest Japanese apprehensions.[6] And the British delegation was to be strongly pro-American in its sentiments. Arthur Balfour, Lord President of the Council, was its leader. Lord Lee of Fareham, who as First Lord of the Admiralty would play a major role in negotiations on naval disarmament, had been military attaché in Washington during the honeymoon of Anglo-Saxon cousinhood in the 1890s, a friend of Theodore Roosevelt. He was married to an American. His qualifications for his crucial post were not apparent, since his experience of naval affairs was

[1] CAB 32/2, Pt. I, E-8.
[2] CAB 32/2, Pt. I, E-12.
[3] CAB 32/2, Pt. II, E-20.
[4] CAB 32/2, Pt. II, E-27.
[5] CAB 32/2, Pt. I, Appendix.
[6] CAB 32/2, Pt. II, E-5.

limited to three years as Civil Lord under Balfour in 1902–5, and his principal interest and fund of information lay in the fine arts. Lee was in fact chosen as First Lord by Lloyd George mainly because of his friendship for – and friendships in – the United States.[1] For a principal aim of the Washington Conference from the British point of view was to restore the somewhat tarnished cousinly relationship to its supposed former intimacy.[2]

The Washington Conference of 1921–2 was really three conferences in one: a 'nine-power conference' on a general political settlement of Far Eastern problems; a 'five-power' conference on the limitation of naval armaments and a 'four-power' conference on the Pacific area.

The nine-power conference comprised Holland, Belgium, Portugal and China, as well as Japan, the British Empire, the United States and Italy. By the resulting Nine-power Treaty, the signatories agreed to respect the independence and integrity of China and maintain the principle of the Open Door – equal opportunities for all powers to trade and invest in China. The Open Door was, of course, traditional English as well as American policy, and the English could therefore congratulate themselves on its preservation in the face of those who might have preferred exclusive spheres of influence, such as the Japanese. It followed however from this that British signature of the Nine-Power Treaty marked a further drift towards opposition to Japan, although the treaty might appear to justify the British faith in the ability of general settlements to avert the distasteful need to take sides.

The Nine-Power Treaty held further dangers. It contained no provision for deciding whether or not it was being honestly carried out. It was the kind of treaty which effectively bound up governments like the British, scrupulous about obeying the parchment they had signed, yet left the less scrupulous free to follow their own interests whenever they saw fit. And, as Billy Hughes had pointed out in the 1921 Imperial Conference, neither Britain nor America could preserve China from violation by Japanese military power. Worst of all, adherence to the Nine-Power Treaty completely destroyed Britain's own freedom of political manœuvre in the Far East, making it impossible, given the British conscience, ever in the future to conclude a deal with Japan at the expense of China.

The discussions on naval disarmament and on the Pacific in Washington also turned on the relations between Japan, the United States and England, although France and Italy took part in the former; and France in the latter.

The British Empire delegation went to Washington armed with a

[1] Roskill, *Naval Policy Between the Wars*, p. 31.
[2] Watt, p. 38.

statement of aims drawn up by the Standing Sub-Committee of the Committee of Imperial Defence.[1] It was essential, according to the statement, to safeguard the interests of the British Empire; it was essential that the conference should have stable results – without, that was, America backing out later as she had done with the Versailles Treaty. Descending from the broad and banal to the merely incidental, the committee recommended that no political engagements should be accepted which would weaken the British position in Kowloon or endanger the building of a fleet base at Singapore. The delegation was in the event able to secure these two points. More important and interesting are references in the sub-committee's statement of aims which make it clear that England entered the conference with a weak enough bargaining position. For, unlike America – or even Japan – she desperately needed to avoid a naval race. As the sub-committee wrote, disarmament was important from the point of view of the Exchequer, otherwise the consequent higher taxes would lead to unfortunate political and economic consequences at home.

The problem went deeper than this. Britain's Victorian prosperity, briefly and delusively restored in a post-war boom, had now finally collapsed. Her traditional exporting industries, decrepit as they were, had succumbed to foreign competition. Her new industries, the fruits of wartime expansion and still immature, had withered in the blast of renewed Free-Trade imports from their long-established and powerful German and American competitors. In June 1921 the number of unemployed passed two million. In the coal, cotton and engineering towns – the foundations of nineteenth-century British industrial supremacy – unemployment amounted in some places to half the insured population.[2] Thus the very heart of British power, her own industrial machine, beat slow and feeble within the vast body of British world involvement. Suddenly, only two years after the triumphant celebration of victory in the Great War, the British governing classes found that they were conducting policy not from strength, but from weakness; weakness so far disguised from other nations by the outward show of imperial pomp and power. It was a weakness which the general public, but especially the moralising internationalists calling upon Britain to take the lead in settling the affairs of mankind, were never to comprehend.

Already, as the Standing Defence Sub-Committee's statement of aims for the Washington Conference pointed out, Britain had disarmed further than other powers: not a single new warship had been laid down since the

[1] CID Paper 280-B, in CAB 30/1A.
[2] A. J. P. Taylor, *English History 1914–1945* (Oxford, The Clarendon Press 1965), p. 145.

Armistice. The statement also noted the shortage of troops and the weakness of the RAF. All this owed as much to the search for economy as to the hope of a new world order; in fact, by an unhappy but understandable process, the search for economy and the hope of a new world order served to encourage one another.

Charles Evans Hughes, the American Secretary of State, opened the Washington Conference by unexpectedly presenting cut-and-dried proposals for the future limitation of the United States Navy, the Royal Navy and the Japanese navy, thus achieving all the tactical advantages that comes from surprise. He proposed, firstly, that all capital-ship building programmes, whether approved or projected, should be abandoned; secondly, that the number of capital ships should be reduced by scrapping some old ships; thirdly, that future relative national strengths in capital ships should be proportionate to their existing relative strengths.[1] When existing fleets had been reduced by scrapping, the maximum tonnage for capital ships should, according to Hughes, be maintained at 500,000 tons each for Britain and the United States and 300,000 tons for Japan. This was not all: no capital ships should be replaced for ten years, and when eventually built they should be limited to 35,000 tons displacement. Hughes also said that he had proposals ready to introduce for the limitation of other kinds of ship, such as cruisers, aircraft carriers and submarines.

The British delegation had now to decide how to meet these unexpected American proposals. Beatty, the First Sea Lord and chief professional adviser to the delegation, realistically accepted that Britain was no longer wealthy enough to remain the world's greatest seapower in the face of American competition. He therefore expressed his agreement to the 5 : 5 : 3 ratio, though preferring the ratio to be expressed in numbers of ships rather than total tonnage.[2] A ten-year naval holiday from new construction, on the other hand, would in his view lead to the decay of the specialised technology necessary to build battleships and their armour and guns. It would also, in Beatty's view, lead to feverish building once the ten years were up. He preferred a slow and steady programme of replacement. The Admiralty itself pointed out in a signal to the British delegation that Britain had already undergone a self-imposed naval holiday of five years, while the Americans had been building new ships. At the end of the ten-year holiday the Royal Navy would therefore be inferior in quality and striking power to the American fleet.[3]

[1] For a detailed analysis of the American proposals and of the course of the conference, see Roskill, *Naval Policy Between the Wars*, ch. VIII.

[2] CAB 30/1A, BED 48.

[3] Roskill, *Naval Policy Between the Wars*, p. 313.

There was also the question of limiting the number of cruisers. Here Beatty argued that the nature of the British Empire and British dependence on overseas trade meant that Britain had a special need for cruisers over and above those that formed part of the battlefleet.

What neither Beatty nor the Admiralty pointed out, however, was the essential fallaciousness of the American proposal to base the strengths of the three nations in battleships on an arbitrary ratio between them. Hughes's proportion of 5 : 5 : 3 might reflect the present proportion between the fleets; it did not reflect the ratio between each country's maritime dangers and responsibilities. Japan was solely a Pacific power; America not a European power. Only English responsibilities were worldwide; and therefore the only logical way to calculate the future size of the English fleet was in relation to those responsibilities, not in relation to the current and purely coincidental sizes of the Japanese and American fleets. The Great War would have been a better guide to the size of fleet which the English really required.

Balfour, speaking to Baron Kato, the leader of the Japanese delegation, in the presence of the American Secretary of State, himself acknowledged both the fallacy and the disadvantages of the 5 : 5 : 3 ratio. He said the British Government had accepted it not as a result of exact calculation of the needs of the three nations but rather as 'a practical principle of easy application . . . If the basis adopted had been a precise calculation, he thought he would have no difficulty in showing that of the three nations concerned in the agreement, the British Empire came out worst.'[1]

There was yet another danger in a fixed ratio: it placed future British freedom of action in a further department of national policy in a strait-jacket, making it impossible to build against new strategic threats that might have nothing to do whatsoever with the size of the American, or even the Japanese, navy. Before 1914 the English had built against Germany without reference to the size of the United States fleet; why then now so bind English naval policy?

The English acceptance of the principle of a ratio at all, let alone in the arbitrary proportion of 5 : 5 : 3, was a disastrous mistake. It was motivated, as Balfour's remarks indicate, by the desire to reach agreement; by the instinct to appease.

But while the decision to accept the 5 : 5 : 3 ratio was at least taken with the concurrence of the British naval advisers, the hardly less damaging acceptance of the American proposal for a ten-year holiday in the building of new capital ships as replacements was taken in the teeth of naval

[1] CAB 30/31, p. 46.

opposition. On repeated occasions the naval advisers pointed out that such a holiday must inevitably end with the decay or disappearance of the resources and skills needed to build modern capital ships, and with a British fleet of ageing vessels, weaker in fighting power than its numbers might indicate.[1]

Finally there was the acceptance of a limit of 35,000 tons displacement for capital ships. Since the limit was not to be – could not be – supervised, the provision was another shackle on the honest; another potential source of advantage to powers less bountifully endowed with conscience, powers who might, when convenient, build heavier ships – ships with thicker armour and more powerful guns that would make a further nonsense of the 5 : 5 : 3 ratio.

The naval terms agreed at the Washington Conference did not constitute the full sum of disaster. The Japanese, harder bargainers than the English, refused to accept their inferiority of 3 : 5 in capital ships in respect of England and the United States unless those countries would make major concessions over naval bases in the Pacific and Far East. In the new Four-power Pacific Treaty, the British therefore agreed not to construct and fortify new bases north of Singapore, while the Americans agreed not to fortify the Philippines and Guam. This was tantamount to turning the waters off the China coast into a Japanese lake; it deprived British and American concern for China's integrity of all substance; one treaty signed at Washington made nonsense of another.

The single mercy of the conference was that no agreements were reached over restrictions on the numbers of cruisers – so vital to British trade protection – or destroyers and submarines.

Nevertheless British opinion saw the Washington Conference as a splendid success, for which Balfour fully deserved his reward of the Garter. After all, all the parties had come to agreements and signed their names on them, and it was ever the fact of agreement rather than what was agreed upon which made the British people applaud the results of a conference. Furthermore the British taxpayer was relieved of the cost of an adequate and up-to-date navy, while internationalists could be pleased at the first successful international effort to control armaments.

But in fact the Washington Conference was one of the major catastrophes of English history, whose effects were to be soon felt, and which was to exercise a cumulative and decisive effect on the future of English power.

In the first place, although the British at the time congratulated themselves that the Washington Treaties had finally absolved them from the

[1] Cf. the statement by the Assistant Chief of Naval Staff, Chatfield, in CAB 30/1A, BED 129.

need to choose between Japan and America, they had in fact so chosen: they had chosen Japan, and as an enemy. For the Japanese did not regard the vague and woolly Four-Power Treaty signed at Washington by herself, England, America and France along with the naval treaty as a fair substitute for the hard, specific treaty of alliance with England which England now abrogated. It was the later judgement of Sir Robert Craigie, the British Ambassador to Tokyo from 1937 to 1942, that the effects of the British termination of the alliance on Japanese feeling were 'profound. Once more the all-important question of "face" intervened. It was felt that the procedure used in terminating the treaty had been unnecessarily formal and abrupt.' As a consequence, in Craigie's judgement, the influence of 'liberal' sympathisers with the West was to be on the wane in Japanese life.[1]

Henceforward all British discussions of Far Eastern and Pacific problems were to assume that Japan was a potential enemy against whom the British Empire ought to guard itself. Within three years of the Great War therefore, England had, quite gratuitously, raised up a new danger in her face. As Beatty told the 1926 Imperial Conference on behalf of the Chiefs of Staff, whereas before 1914 the strategic centre of gravity had been in Europe, now it had shifted to the East.[2]

On the other hand, whether or not British conciliatoriness at the Washington Conference had averted American ill-will or even evoked American goodwill, it certainly failed to win material American support, either in Europe or in the Far East. Indeed the Washington Treaty deprived England of even the possibility of such support in the Far East, for America was now prohibited under the Treaty from creating and fortifying a main fleet base west of Hawaii. As Lord Salisbury, the Lord President of the Council, explained to the 1923 Imperial Conference: 'The effect, therefore, is that, so far as the Western Pacific is concerned, the British Empire is left face to face with Japan; no one else, practically, will be there to intervene. . . .'[3]

And the view of Lord Curzon, the Foreign Secretary, in 1923 was that 'the strategic position of Japan has been greatly strengthened as a result of the Naval Treaty'.[4]

Spurred by thrift and by hope of a better world, the British at once reduced their fleet according to the treaty, in what L. S. Amery, an imperialist First Sea Lord in a Conservative government, described as an 'act of faith', an example and inducement to others, and 'a great and hopeful augury'. Amery went on to demonstrate to his listeners, the delegates

[1] Craigie, pp. 12–13. [2] CAB 32/46, E-9. [3] CAB 32/9, E-8. [4] CAB 32/9, E-3.

to the 1923 Imperial Conference, just how much the security of the empire had now come to depend on faith and hopeful auguries: 'The result of the Treaty undoubtedly is that we have substituted what the [Imperial] Conference of 1921 had laid down as the minimum standard of our Naval security – we have made it, as far as capital ships are concerned, the maximum.'[1] Nor was the expression of British faith and hope in terms of naval affairs limited to mere obedience to the treaty: 'We have gone in every way further than the actual letter of the Treaty obliges us. . . .'[2]

Amery went on to sum up the naval policy now adopted by the nation which once, under the governments of the Tudors, the Cromwellian Protectorate, and the gentlemen of Georgian England, had risen to greatness by winning and holding the command of the sea: it was 'a defence policy reduced to the lowest limits possible, even in a relatively peaceful world, for our security'.[3]

The British Government was at pains to assuage the anxieties of Australia and New Zealand. Curzon assured the 1923 Imperial Conference: 'I do not think that, although the Japanese Alliance has terminated, there is any weakening in the ties that unite us.'

To this self-evidently absurd remark the Foreign Secretary added his opinion that, although there was nothing to stop the Japanese from expanding in China, he thought they had changed their minds about an aggressive policy.[4] Lord Salisbury, the Lord President of the Council, was happy to say that 'there is not a cloud, so far as I know, between us and Japan, not a cloud in sight. But,' he went on somewhat less euphorically, 'you must not leave everything to chance; you must take care that you are fully protected . . . ,' and this was why it was essential to build a naval base at Singapore.[5]

The Pacific dominions did not share the British trust in Japan's benevolence, at least so far as the future was concerned. Massey of New Zealand warned against hasty disarmament; pointed out that re-armament took a long time, especially the building of warships; and, referring in this context to Salisbury's anodyne remarks about a cloudless horizon, reminded the conference that 'there are no clouds on the horizon to-night, but there may be plenty here to-morrow'.[6]

This lively sense of the instability of Japanese liberal attitudes was never to leave the governments of Australia and New Zealand during the remainder of the 1920s. But there was little sympathy for such alarmist sus-

[1] CAB 32/9, E-9. [2] Ibid. [3] Ibid.
[4] CAB 32/9, E-3. [5] CAB 32/9, E-8. [6] Ibid.

picions in London. As the decade wore on, British governments and public opinion took it more and more for certain that tomorrow's international horizon, like today's, would be cloudless. Danger and conflict were things of the past, belonging to that primitive era in the affairs of mankind before the League of Nations was created. Only the reactionary and obscurantist leaders of the British armed services failed to comprehend that a new era had dawned; 'We take', wrote the Imperial General Staff in 1923, 'the great War to be not exceptional, but the greatest lesson we have ever had, and that being so, foresee the possibility of our country again at some future time being drawn with all its resources into the vortex of a great struggle. . . .' [1]

The view of enlightened intellectual opinion on these topics was expressed by H. G. Wells in 1923 in an article attacking the decision to create a base at Singapore:

> On the supposition that the world is to go on divided among aggressive sovereign states, with phases of war preparation known as peace and acute phases of more and more destructive war, it is quite a good move in the game. On the supposition that the world is growing up to an age of reason, and that a world civilisation is attainable, it is a monstrous crime.[2]

Winston Churchill, Chancellor of the Exchequer in the Conservative Government of 1924–9, was of all people no less convinced that this was a world safe enough to warrant neglect of imperial defence. He ridiculed the Admiralty with all the power of his orotund eloquence for mistakenly looking on Japan as they had looked on Germany before the war, and for wishing to push on naval preparations as fast as they could. 'For what? A war with Japan! But why should there be a war with Japan? I do not believe there is the slightest chance of it in our lifetime.'[3]

Churchill's Treasury civil servants, for their part, were opposed to naval expenditure on principle as well as because of a departmental desire to save money; they shared in the prevailing internationalist and pacifistic aspirations of the country. At the beginning of 1925, for example, one such senior Treasury official wrote that a British Government decision not to build any warships at all in the current year would be taken 'as a symbol of a really pacifistic attitude by Great Britain', which would 'reassure Japan'.[4]

[1] Quoted in Young, p. 441.

[2] *Westminster Gazette*, 13 October 1923.

[3] Letter of 15 December 1924, Baldwin Papers, quoted in Keith Middlemass and John Barnes, *Baldwin: A Biography* (London, Weidenfeld and Nicolson 1969), pp. 327–8.

[4] Baldwin Papers, quoted in Middlemas and Barnes, p. 333.

In July 1926, the question of the Singapore base provoked Churchill into a fresh tirade, declaimed to the Committee of Imperial Defence: 'When he agreed in principle to the base at Singapore, he had never imagined that that decision would be used as a peg on which to hang far-reaching schemes of alarmist policy and consequential armament. He did not believe there was any danger to be apprehended from Japan. . . .' [1]

He could not imagine 'what incentive could possibly move Japan to put herself in the position to incur the lasting hostility of England and run the risk of being regarded as a pariah by the League of Nations'.[2]

He would never have agreed to the base if he had known that it was 'to be used as a gigantic excuse for pouring out money with a view to conducting war at the other end of the world. . . . Nor was he able to accept the view of the First Sea Lord that our possessions in the Far East existed on sufferance. . . .' [3]

And so the passionate periods rolled on, in a prolonged statement of the need to economise at the expense of the armed forces.[4]

Nor could the Foreign Office understand the Admiralty's concern about English impotence and defencelessness in the Far East. Like Churchill it saw no danger in Japan. On 5 January 1925, Sir Austen Chamberlain, the Foreign Secretary, gave it as his opinion that the prospect of war in the Far East was very remote. Only if there came about a new European alliance against us, and led to, for example, a German–Russian–Japanese combination, was it likely. There was, however, no sign of this at all.[5] On 2 April 1925 the Committee of Imperial Defence decided that there was no danger of war in the Far East for ten years. Nineteen months later it considered a memorandum on foreign policy towards Russia and Japan drafted by Sir William Tyrell, Permanent Under-Secretary at the Foreign Office since Crowe's death in 1925. Tyrell wrote that he 'fully' shared the Chancellor of the Exchequer's dislike of alarmism in regard to Japan, and went on: 'I have no hesitation in stating that our policy should be based upon the assumption that Russia is the enemy and not Japan. The most we have to fear from the latter is commercial rivalry.'[6] However, in an appreciation earlier that year the Foreign Office had acknowledged that, given the nature of Japanese politics and society, a change in her present 'liberal' policy could not be discounted.[7]

The year 1926 was generally an encouraging one for romantic optimists. Germany took her place in the League of Nations to a salute of sentimental

[1] CAB 2/4, 215. [2] Ibid. [3] Ibid. [4] Ibid. [5] CAB 2/4, 193.
[6] Meeting of 25 November 1926, CAB 2/4, 218.
[7] Roskill, *Naval Policy Between the Wars*, p. 464.

oratory on the part of the spokesmen of the nations she had so narrowly failed to crush in the Great War. A League of Nations Preparatory Commission began the immense technical task of preparing for a world conference on disarmament by land, air and sea. Even Austen Chamberlain shared in the general complacency about the success of the League of Nations and the happy state of the world.[1] Nothing therefore could have been more absurdly out of fashion, more apt for scorn, and generally calculated to bore than the statement made by the three British Chiefs of Staff in their annual review for 1926, and reiterated the following year: 'We wish to place on record our view that the forces available for Imperial Defence are now reduced to a minimum and are hardly capable of dealing with the problems that are liable to arise either singly or simultaneously.'[2]

However often the Chiefs of Staff cared to record such views for the benefit of the inner circle of government, they had no chance whatsoever of being taken seriously. And outside government, the public at large basked ever more relaxedly in the prevailing sunshine of international amity and goodwill. '. . . you can have no conception how profoundly pacific our people are now,' wrote Austen Chamberlain, himself no man of strife, to the British Ambassador to China.[3] The possibility of cloud tomorrow, to which the New Zealand Premier had drawn attention at the 1923 Imperial Conference, was further and further from the dreaming British mind.

Refusal to contemplate the possibility of future danger had even been erected into a formal guiding principle of British defence policy. The armed services were to plan on the assumption that there would be no major war for ten years. The 'ten-year-rule', as it came to be called, was urged on the coalition government as early as August 1919 by the then Secretary of State for War and Air, Winston Churchill. Several times extended during the early 1920s, the rule was made self-perpetuating in 1928, urged on Baldwin's Conservative Cabinet by the Chancellor of the Exchequer, Winston Churchill. Henceforward, until and unless specifically countermanded by the government, the ten-year-period without war automatically advanced every day. Like tomorrow, the possibility of war was never to come – thanks to British Government decree. The rule may be contrasted to General Hans von Seekt's first order of the day to the new Reichswehr in 1921: 'The sword must be kept sharp.'

[1] CAB 32/46, E-2. [2] COS 41 in CAB 53/12.
[3] Sir Charles Petrie, *The Life and Letters of Sir Austen Chamberlain*, 2 Vols. (London, Cassell 1939), p. 367.

The leaders of the armed forces recognised at the time, as have most historians since, that the 'ten-year-rule' was a calamitous act of policy. It took all sense of urgency and reality of purpose from strategic planning and defence policy. It provided the Treasury with a simple and effective weapon for crushing any service demand for funds for research or development. The 'ten-year-rule' was one of Churchill's least happy contributions to English history, and was to be a major cause of his own difficulties as War Premier after 1940. As Balfour vainly pointed out in the Committee of Imperial Defence meeting which adopted Churchill's recommendation: '. . . nobody could say that from any one moment war was an impossibility for the next ten years . . . we could not rest in a state of unpreparedness on such an assumption by anybody. To suggest that we could be nine and a half years away from preparedness would be a most dangerous suggestion.'[1]

It was in this entirely hostile climate of opinion inside and outside government that the leaders of the armed forces struggled during the 1920s to preserve English strategic power from wasting away altogether. The varying fortunes of the Singapore base project provide a case history in that struggle, for on its completion depended whether English policy towards Japan was to rest on anything more substantial than faith and hope.

The decision to construct a new fleet base in the Far East was taken in principle in 1921, before the end of the Japanese alliance, largely because of the change-over of the fleet from coal to oil-firing. For there were not enough oil tankers in the world to fuel the fleet on a voyage to the East and maintain it there at sea. It was essential to have a fixed base with huge oil stocks in Eastern waters.[2]

The conversion of Japan from an ally into a potential enemy in 1922 therefore rendered the building of a base an urgent matter. After exhaustive study the Committee of Imperial Defence and the Oversea Defence Sub-Committee had chosen Singapore as the best site. The anchorage itself was good; suitable in size and depth and with a secure entrance. Strategically Singapore was the best of all alternatives, as Beatty, the First Sea Lord, had explained to the 1921 Imperial Conference:

> Singapore stands at the western gateway of the Pacific. It flanks the route from Eastern Asia to Australasia and covers the main entrance to the Indian Ocean from the eastward. . . . Of the other conceivable sites for our main base in the East, one in Australia would be too remote, and

[1] CAB 2/5, 236.
[2] CAB 27/407, (30), Enclosure No. 2; CAB 2/3, 140.

> to station our fleet in those waters would be tantamount to a defensive naval strategy by which our vital interests to the north and west would be left uncovered. . . .[1]

However, in the 1923 Imperial Conference, Smuts of South Africa, always wiser as a strategist than as a liberal, doubted whether a base there was any protection to Australia and New Zealand at all unless Britain could send the fleet – and Japan was unlikely to attack unless she had support in Europe, in which case, Smuts asked, would it be feasible to divide the navy, now we no longer enjoyed the old huge superiority?[2]

Amery, the First Lord of the Admiralty, admitted in reply: 'Of course it is perfectly conceivable that, if there were a European combination against us at the same moment as war was declared against us by Japan, we should be in a position of extraordinary difficulty.'

But even so: '. . . I should think against such a combination we might find allies, and the fact that Singapore could hold out for a good many weeks, possibly for a good many months, might be a very strong inducement to a Power like the United States to come in quickly . . . before the situation in the Far East had been entirely and irretrievably altered.'[3]

Both Smuts and S. M. Bruce, now Prime Minister of Australia, wanted to know whether Singapore would in fact be able to hold out until the British battlefleet arrived.[4] Amery answered:

> No doubt if there were no navy in those waters, and no navy which could reach it for many months, you could only hold Singapore by an overwhelming land force. . . . But given the great distance of Singapore from Japan . . . given the presence of a swift if not very powerful squadron in Pacific waters, aided by long-range submarines, given the fact that the main fleet can go out normally in from four to six weeks, there is no reason to suppose that Singapore could not hold its own against a powerful naval raid, or the raid of a navy with a small landing force such is likely to be directed against it.[5]

The broad lines of British Far Eastern and Pacific strategy after the demise of the Japanese alliance were thus drawn. The strategy depended wholly on the creation of a fleet base at Singapore, complete with graving dock, repair shops, oil storage, garrison and defences. Until the base was completed England would remain helpless and impotent in the East. In 1922 Beatty, the First Sea Lord, speaking for the naval staff, wanted the base to be completed and functioning by 1925.[6]

[1] CAB 32/2, Pt. I, E-14. [2] CAB 32/9, E-8. [3] CAB 32/9, E-9.
[4] Ibid. [5] Ibid. [6] CID Meeting of 14 December 1922. CAB 2/3, 168.

That autumn the Conservative administration, which had replaced Lloyd George's coalition government, took the decision to go ahead with the base – but, because of financial stringency, to do little work on it for two years. In March 1924 however the first Labour Government, under Ramsay MacDonald, cancelled work on the base, despite vigorous protests by Australia and New Zealand (who were contributing, along with Malaya, to its cost).[1] The Labour Government explained their motives to the nation: they were convinced that if they went on with the base

> . . . our action would exercise a most detrimental effect on our general foreign policy. . . . We stand for a policy of international co-operation through a strengthened and enlarged League of Nations, the settlement of disputes by conciliation and judicial arbitration, and the creation of conditions which will make a comprehensive agreement on the limitation of armaments possible.[2]

To develop Singapore therefore would 'lay our good faith open to suspicion'.

In November 1924 Baldwin's incoming Conservative Government decided to re-commence work on the base; but only in principle, which cost nothing and really marked little material change of policy. In the meantime, as a substitute for action, it set up a Sub-Committee of the Committee of Imperial Defence under Curzon (after his death, under Baldwin himself) to investigate all the technical and strategic problems of the future base. Between February 1925 and July 1926 this Sub-Committee produced three reports.[3] The first report recommended that work on the dock area should be limited to what was necessary to allow the dock itself to be used when it eventually arrived.[4] The fleet would have to make do with existing facilities for repairs. This report was approved by the Cabinet on 2 March 1925.[5]

The second report gave estimates of the cost of building and installing the floating dock; recommended the scale and type of naval, military and anti-aircraft defences; asked that the Air Ministry be authorised to construct an airfield; and recommended that construction of the main defences should be postponed until 1926. This report was approved by the Cabinet on 11 November 1925.[6] Thus by the end of the year when Beatty had hoped to see the base completed, it had scarcely been begun.

[1] Cmd. 2083.
[2] Hansard, *Parliamentary Debates* (House of Commons), Fifth Series, Vol. 171, cols. 319–21.
[3] CID papers 243-C, 253-C, and 273-C.
[4] It was a floating dock, to be built in Britain and towed out to Singapore.
[5] CAB 27/407, CP173(30), Enclosure No. 2.
[6] Ibid.

The third report in July 1926 gave detailed recommendations about the defences on land and in the air. The future of Singapore had now become complicated by a prolonged and bitter argument between the Admiralty and the Air Ministry as to whether 15-inch guns or torpedo-bombers could best keep off a Japanese fleet. To provide both, and make sure, was apparently unthinkable. Therefore the report recommended that although the first stage of the gun defences should be completed, the rival merits of guns and aircraft should again be explored before the second stage was started. The naval base area itself should be continued on a reduced scale, at a cost of £7,700,000 instead of £11,000,000. It was at this point that the Singapore project, whose postponements and curtailments under the Conservative Government already owed most to the hostility of the Chancellor of the Exchequer, Winston Churchill, ran foul of a particularly spectacular Churchillian attack on the Admiralty's folly in preparing to meet an imaginary danger from Japan.[1] Fortunately and not for the first or the last time, Churchill undid his own case by sheer extravagance of language. Singapore survived; although only in the much truncated and slowed-down version recommended in the third report on the CID Sub-Committee. This report was approved by the Cabinet on 3 August 1926. Haltingly the work went on. The defences were the subject of endless debate and investigation. In March 1927 Lieutenant-General Sir Webb Gillman was sent to Singapore to investigate and report. In October the Admiralty decided that 1937 instead of 1935 must now be the date for completion of the base, on the understanding that the floating dock at least should be ready by 1929.[2] Early in 1928, at Baldwin's direction, the Chiefs of Staff reviewed the whole question of the likely weight and nature of a Japanese attack and of the best defence against it, in the light of Gillman's findings. The Chiefs of Staff's report recommended yet further delays in construction, both because of the shortage of money and because of present uncertainty about various tactical and strategic factors. Even the first stage of the gun defences was not now to be completed until the end of the financial year 1932–3. This report was approved by the Cabinet on 4 April 1928.[3] On 19 December 1928 the Cabinet agreed to CID recommendations that no progress should be made in 1929–30 on installing heavy coastal defence artillery at Singapore, in order to give time for fresh investigations into their effectiveness.

When the Conservative Government went out of office in June 1929 therefore, the Singapore base was still in the most rudimentary state. The

[1] See above pp. 275–6.
[2] CID paper No. 306-C.
[3] CAB 27/407, CP173(30), Enclosure No. 2.

floating dock at least was now in place. The contract for the truncated scheme for the naval repair and storage base, only placed in September 1928, would not be completed until 1935. The first stage of the defences, on which work was now going on, would not be finished until 1932–3.[1] Thus seven years after the Japanese alliance had been jettisoned, the British Empire in the East and the Pacific was still denied the possibility of the protection of the battlefleet; British policy still rested on faith and hope instead of power. Even the local attack of the ramshackle Chinese Kuomintang régime on the International Settlement at Shanghai in 1927 had stretched British capabilities in the Far East to the limit.

The Royal Navy itself had survived Churchill's five years at the Exchequer shrunken in numbers, even in categories of vessel not limited by the Washington treaty, and worn-out and obsolescent in much of its *matériel*, especially in cruisers. It was over the building of new cruisers as replacements that the battles between Beatty and Churchill had been largely fought.[2] Mercifully, another naval conference, this time at Geneva in 1927, had broken down in total failure, owing to a stubborn American refusal to agree to the British contention that the defence of the British Empire, its trade and communications required a minimum of seventy cruisers.[3] However, Lord Cecil, the Conservative Government's leading disarmer and League-of-Nations man, and a member of the British delegation to the Geneva Conference, resigned because the Cabinet allowed the negotiations to break down rather than give way over the seventy cruisers. His resignation served to blacken the Conservative reputation among internationalists, who now perceived that Baldwin and his colleagues were ferocious war-mongers.[4]

The advent of the Second Labour Government in 1929 and its tenure of office until 1931 marked the blooming high summer of moralising internationalism in Britain between the world wars. Although a minority government, as in 1924, its parliamentary strength fell only twenty-one seats short of an absolute majority, while the fifty-nine Liberals on whose support the Government depended were no less warm in their romantic idealism. Among the five major objectives listed in the Labour Party's election manifesto was that of establishing '. . . peace, freedom and justice by removing from among the nations the root causes of international disputes, by conciliation and all-in arbitration, by renouncing war as an

[1] CAB 27/407, CP173 (30), Enclosure No. 2.
[2] See Roskill, *Naval Policy Between the Wars*, ch. XII; Robert James, *Churchill: A Study in Failure 1900–1939* (London, Weidenfeld and Nicolson 1970), Pt. Four; Middlemass and Barnes, ch. 13.
[3] Roskill, *Naval Policy Between the Wars*, ch. XIV.
[4] Middlemass and Barnes, pp. 368–72.

instrument of national policy, by disarmament and by political and economic co-operation through the League of Nations'.[1]

It was an ambitious foreign policy. Yet for those who had faith – and they were by no means limited to the Labour Party – this vision of a world rid of its ancient corruptions and villainies seemed in 1929 capable of fulfilment. In 1928, at the invitation of the United States Secretary of State, Frank Kellogg, the nations signed in Paris a pact solemnly renouncing war as an instrument of policy. This new piece of parchment was also taken at its face value by internationalists. The League of Nations was now at the height of its prestige. Chancellors, premiers and foreign ministers followed each other to the rostrum of the League assembly at Geneva to uplift the multitude with sermons praising the reconciliation of ancient enemies and the growing unity of mankind. The League's believers had come more and more to take it for granted that the League really possessed the power of a world authority, and not just the trappings. The League of Nations Union busied itself in the schools, assuring the children that there could never be another war, because the League would 'stop it'. By 1929 therefore internationalists had convinced themselves, and others, that a new era in the life of mankind was well on the way to being established.

And yet the more reflective internationalists remained uneasy, their intellects at odds with their faith. Gilbert Murray, for example, delivered a series of lectures in 1928 whose general burden was to affirm a passionate belief in the League of Nations, and yet which contained penetrating, even lethal, criticisms of it. He noted the weakness of conciliation as a means of solving international disputes: '. . . the strong Power has the issue in its own hands. It can simply refuse all terms until it gets what it wants, while the weak will accept almost any compromise.'[2]

However, Murray hopefully but somewhat feebly continued: 'This state of affairs is in practice modified by conscience, by the influence of public opinion in the rest of the world, by the knowledge that flagrant and repeated acts of rapacity would probably bring, and even for the strongest Powers, unpleasant consequences. . . .'[3]

To solve this problem he proposed that all nations should agree to submit disputes to compulsory arbitration by the International Court, so that 'if things came to the worst, the last resort would be Law and not Force'.[4]

But here Murray was relying once more on belief in the power of parchment, for a determined and unscrupulous aggressor was hardly

[1] Quoted in Connell, pp. 96–7.
[2] Gilbert Murray, p. 82.
[3] Ibid. p. 82.
[4] Ibid. p. 83.

likely to honour its obligation to submit to arbitration when force offered more certain results. It was this very possibility of force that raised the fundamental problem which the League had to face: in Murray's own words, 'what should be done if, in spite of Conference and Covenant, some nation staked its fortune on War? After all,' Murray had to admit, 'the Great War had begun with a flagrant breach of treaty.'[1]

He believed that the answer was for the League to unite to coerce the war-maker. But to raise the question of coercion immediately exposed that impotence of the League which Murray, in his intellectual honesty, had to admit and explore:

> The real difficulty of the situation lies in the practical working of the coercion. Let it be laid down that the League as a whole will take the necessary action, economic or military. Well and good; but the League is not a military or economic unit and possesses no central executives. It is a society of sovereign states. . . . I doubt whether the League as a League could declare war or wage war. The force would have to be supplied by each state separately, of its own deliberate will.[2]

However, who in the event would turn out to coerce the aggressor?

> One cannot expect Canada or Siam to mobilize because one Balkan state attacks another . . . the question is whether, in a world that increasingly detests war and mistrusts force . . . the various Parliaments or Governments will in general have sufficient loyalty to the League, sufficient public spirit and sense of reality, to be ready to face the prospect of war not in defence of their own frontiers or immediate national interests, but simply to maintain the peace of the world.[3]

It was an acute analysis. Murray himself had to acknowledge that there was 'no perfect solution' to the problem. Nor, in his view, would blockade do as a substitute for armed coercion, because it was too slow and too easily evaded.[4]

On the other hand Murray ruled out the use of the most powerful and readily available armed forces at the disposal of the League:

'One of the most advanced French advocates of the League once said to me that the true guarantee of peace in Europe was a strong French army and a strong British navy. The sort of man who thinks that is the sort of man who ought never to be allowed to touch international affairs.'[5]

First disarm the French army and the Royal Navy, in order that all

[1] Gilbert Murray, p. 86. [2] Ibid. p. 91. [3] Ibid.
[4] Ibid. p. 92. [5] Ibid. p. 88.

nations should be equally weak and then, wrote Murray, sanctions become both a genuine expression of the will of the community of nations and a safe and a necessary part of the Covenant.[1] It was an argument of less than Murray's usual clarity.

But general disarmament was indeed widely seen, especially in the Labour Party, as essential if the new world order was to be made secure. Disarmament would at once remove the nations' fears of each other and make aggression or resistance to the League's authority impossible. In this view, the Covenant needed not a sword of its own in order to prevail, but the destruction of all other swords. The problem here was, however, how to induce the nations to disarm while they were afraid to do so, because, as Murray all too clearly perceived, 'war can still be made, and there is no certainty that the nation attacked will be defended by the rest of the League'.[2]

Nor were stricter and more elaborate obligations to support the League the answer, although desirable in themselves, because, Murray pointed out, the present obligations were perfectly adequate, if only – if only – the members of the League lived up to them.[3]

That a man like Gilbert Murray could see so plainly the paradox on which the League of Nations was insecurely built, and yet remain the League's wholehearted supporter and propagandist, indicates how easy it was for faith in the League to blind the faithful.

The new Labour Government was well-endowed with such faith. It was determined to entrust the safety of the British Empire jointly to the League of Nations and to disarmament. It saw international affairs as the field for a great evangelical mission. The Word would be preached, and the spirit of peace would move within the statesmen and the peoples of the world. The new Prime Minister, Ramsay MacDonald, saw Britain as uniquely qualified for this task of conversion, for he nursed the common British illusion 'that mankind everywhere looked to Britain for guidance . . . We talked much of our moral leadership'.[4]

Born a bastard in 1866 in Lossiemouth, Scotland, he was brought up in his Celtic grandmother's two-roomed cottage. The grandmother loomed over MacDonald's childhood: a great teller of folk stories and legends, a believer in the supernatural. MacDonald grew up a curious mixture of romanticism and emotion – 'fey' in the Celtic sense – and a hard, selfish ambition. 'The key to him', wrote Sir Robert Vansittart, 'was the commonest in human nature – illusion. . . .'[5] He owed his leadership of the

[1] Ibid. pp. 88–9.
[2] Ibid. p. 106.
[3] Ibid. p. 131.
[4] Vansittart, p. 385.
[5] Ibid. p. 373.

Labour Party to his romantically distinguished appearance and personality, to his record of opposition to the Great War and to his reputation as one of the intellectuals of the movement.[1] With his beautiful voice and its folksy Scottish accent, and his pseudo-Gladstonian rhetoric, as woolly as his own romantic looks, but pulsing with emotion, he exactly supplied the psychological needs of his followers. He himself unwittingly summed up in his first election address in 1903 the theme and style of his whole career: 'There is a time for details and definite proposals, and there is a time for general principles which may even be so vague as to be little more than *yearnings* and *aspirations*.'[2]

MacDonald believed in human progress because, as he told his constituents in 1918, '. . . there are men and women like yourselves thinking, working and organizing, believing fine things and dreaming noble dreams, and determined that, in so far as you can, you are going to embody them in the practical government of this country'.[3]

World peace was one of MacDonald's noble dreams; Anglo-American friendship one of the fine things he believed. In 1929 both, in MacDonald's view, could be served by a fresh attempt at an international agreement on further naval disarmament and limitation.

By 1929, however, relations between the British and the American branches of the great Anglo-Saxon family had deteriorated to the stage of Christmas cards only. In both Britain and the United States political power had passed, or was passing, out of the hands of the oligarchies which had got on so well together before the Great War.[4] Thus British appeasement at the Washington Conference was rewarded in general by America's continued retreat into isolationism, and in particular by the ruthlessly hard bargain driven by America in 1923 over the terms of repayment of British war debts. The virulently anti-British line adopted by the American delegation at the miscarried Geneva Naval Conference in 1927 further seemed to suggest to the British that their courting of America was failing to evoke a reciprocal warmth of affection. Neville Chamberlain, himself one of the new generation of British leaders and no great lover of the United States, recorded that 'S.B.[5] says he has got to loathe Americans so much that he hates meeting them'.[6] England had in fact gained small, if any, advantage *vis-à-vis* the United States in return for her sacrifice of the Japanese alliance. Even Churchill at this period was against making fresh attempts to win American goodwill.[7]

[1] L. Macneill Weir, *The Tragedy of Ramsay MacDonald* (London, Secker and Warburg 1938), pp. 104–11.
[2] Quoted in Weir, p. 38.
[3] Weir, p 91.
[4] Watt, pp. 41, 52.
[5] Stanley Baldwin.
[6] Middlemass and Barnes, p. 375.
[7] Ibid. pp. 374–5.

MacDonald on the other hand had not experienced the rebuffs endured by Baldwin's administration. He saw America in terms of Wilsonian idealism, and in this spirit set about repairing Anglo-American relations. The price he was prepared to pay for American friendship was the further weakening of the Royal Navy. He saw no danger in this, for reasons explained to the Committee of Imperial Defence during a discussion on Singapore in July 1929: 'It is our duty to take into account the possibilities of Naval agreements and the general effect of the pact of Peace [the Kellogg Pact] upon the handling of international policy, which used to depend as a last resort on available forces.'[1]

While preliminary negotiations were taking place between the British and American governments, intended to ensure the success of the naval conference when it eventually met, the Admiralty therefore had once more to defend British seapower against a British Government. It was a battle in which the Labour First Lord of the Admiralty, A. V. Alexander, staunchly fought on the navy's side against his own colleagues. On 16 September 1929, in a memorandum to the new Cabinet Fighting Services Committee,[2] he pointed out: 'War as an instrument of policy has been abolished by the [Kellogg] Pact, but the possibility of a war in self-defence still remains. . . .'[3] There were therefore strong arguments for going on with the Singapore base.

The arguments applied equally to maintaining the fighting strength of the navy. When MacDonald had returned from a successful and highly puffed trip to the United States a-courting President Hoover, and when the politicians' intentions of making major concessions in the forthcoming conference had become all too clear, Admiral of the Fleet Sir Charles Madden, the First Sea Lord, struggled to save the existing 1929–30 building programme. He pointed out in November 1929 that since 1926–7 Britain alone of major powers had cut spending on new construction: therefore our ships were ageing in comparison with those of our rivals.

> With naval commitments beyond comparison with those of European powers and on a far greater scale than those of the United States and Japan we are therefore relatively losing ground; and if there is curtailment of the construction vote in this or in future years we shall find ourselves, in effect, in a position of inferiority in Cruisers, Destroyers and Submarines.[4]

[1] CID 337-C in CAB 27/407.

[2] A committee whose activities, on the contrary, were devoted to weakening the services' fighting power.

[3] CAB 27/407, FS(29)11.

[4] CAB 27/407, FS(29)16.

The Treasury on the other hand presented a case for making immediate cuts, based on the expectation of achieving all-round reductions at the coming conference, although to anticipate future benefits in this manner hardly accorded with the principles of sound finance.[1]

The Fighting Services Committee agreed with the Treasury. The government wished to demonstrate their spirit of goodwill by a gesture; what better and warmer gesture than to make immediate cuts in the 1929–1930 naval programme? The gesture was made in the teeth of a formal objection by the navy, as a note, initialled 'J.R.M.', attached to the Committee's decision makes plain: 'It is only fair to the Sea Lords of the Admiralty that we should place on record . . . that they are not satisfied that this programme provides the minimum amount of naval construction essential for national security'.[2]

On top of the naval cuts, the Singapore base was again found by the Labour Government, as in 1924, to be handy material for a demonstration of sincerity of purpose. The Fighting Services Committee reported on 22 October 1929: '. . . we consider that to continue the entire Singapore scheme in complete disregard of the possibilities of the [Naval] Conference would be indefensible.'[3]

It therefore recommended that, pending the results of the conference and a final decision on the base's future, work already contracted for should be slowed as much as possible; that all work which could be suspended should be suspended; and that no new work should be started.[4]

This decision too was taken in defiance of a measured warning by the naval staff:

> . . . our great and growing interests and responsibilities embracing India, Burma, Malaya, Australia and New Zealand demand that there shall be a naval stronghold . . . in the absence of such a stronghold the Fleet cannot be there, the security cannot be given; our trade can only continue and our people overseas maintain their freedom on sufferance.[5]

There was in fact nothing in common whatsoever between the Labour Government's picture of the world and that of the armed forces. Instead, there were the mutually incomprehensible exchanges of the romantic and the realist. The Government for its part was, in Ramsay MacDonald's own words, 'working steadily towards international agreements to remove

[1] CAB 27/407, FS(29)20.
[2] CAB 27/407, CP2(30).
[3] CAB 27/407, CP195(29).
[4] Ibid.
[5] Memorandum of 9 July 1929, CAB 27/407, FS(29)8.

those questions which have hitherto been the cause of disputes from a settlement by force to one by conciliation or arbitration'.[1]

The naval staff on the other hand were uncharitable enough to doubt the goodness and trustworthiness of other nations, especially of Japan; a doubt which it tried diplomatically to convey to the Government: 'The growth of peaceful aspirations in Europe and America and its translation into practical politics may possibly fail to produce the anticipated reaction on the Asiatic mind at a different stage of civilisation, guided by a different code, inspired by different ideals. . . .[2]

But arguments like this were as vain and untimely as pointing out to a woman in love that the adored object is a notorious bounder. As the naval conference approached, the Labour Cabinet became more and more eager to give away British power. In this they were much encouraged by the advice and pressure of Lord Cecil of Chelwood, founding father of the League of Nations.[3] In return for new American concessions over the sizes of cruisers and their calibres of gun, it was proposed to reduce the number of cruisers in the Royal Navy to fifty; the very point over which the 1927 Geneva Naval Conference had broken down, and over which Lord Cecil had resigned from the previous Conservative Government. Yet it had always been and still remained the Admiralty's conviction that seventy was the very lowest number of cruisers consistent with the special needs of British trade and the British Empire. In 1926 the Admiralty had written and underlined: 'It is . . . the opinion of the Admiralty *that the British Empire should agree to no proposals for disarmament which do not recognise its special need for cruisers*.'[4]

Now in 1929 Madden, the First Sea Lord, told the Government that fifty cruisers was 'a starvation number'.[5] In January 1930 Admiral of the Fleet Earl Jellicoe, Commander-in-Chief of the Grand Fleet at Jutland and later First Sea Lord, and now Governor-General of New Zealand, submitted a memorandum to London on the cruiser question at the request of the New Zealand Government. 'Personally I cannot agree', he wrote, 'that a total of fifty cruisers, as set forth in the British proposals, is sufficient for the security of our sea communications.'[6] Jellicoe pointed out that while in 1914 the Royal Navy had possessed 114 cruisers, a number which in the course of the war had proved to be not large enough, today the figure was only fifty-four, with four building. 'To cut this number down

[1] CID 337-C: Prime Minister's Statement on Singapore to the CID, 25 July 1929, in CAB 27/407.
[2] Memorandum by the Navy Staff on the Singapore base, 9 July 1929, CAB 27/407, FS(29)8.
[3] See above pp. 244–7.
[4] CAB 32/44, IC(FPD)-6.
[5] CAB 29/117, LNC(29)5.
[6] CAB 29/117, LNC(29)3.

to fifty,' Jellicoe therefore concluded, 'appears to me to be a highly dangerous step which I could not recommend.'[1]

How far MacDonald was lost to such arguments is illustrated by his pained reaction to the French proposals to the naval conference. He told members of the British delegation on 16 February 1930 that when he next met the French delegates

> . . . he was inclined to point out that the French figures contained no indication of any reaction to the improved [international] situation, the League of Nations, the Kellogg Pact, and so forth. It was a military programme similar to that in which the Admiralty's original estimate of seventy cruisers had been drawn up. Owing to the political situation our estimate had been brought down to fifty. . . .'[2]

Yet the Labour Foreign Secretary, Arthur Henderson, went even further and suggested that 'we should either initiate or support a proposal to abandon the construction of capital ships, or reduce them to a size of between ten and fifteen thousand tons'.[3] The suggestion was not adopted.

The London Naval Conference of 1930 turned out a resounding success, at least so far as agreement between England, Japan and the United States were concerned; Italy and France however failed to agree on their own ratio of strength. Although under the Washington Treaty the construction of new battleships was due to re-commence in 1931[4] it was agreed instead to extend the 'naval holiday' until 1936. The British accepted virtual parity in total cruiser tonnage with America, which would yield them, as foreseen, no more than fifty cruisers. Japan however successfully stuck out for a ratio of 70 per cent of the British (and of the American) cruiser tonnage, instead of the 60 per cent ratio the British and Americans hoped they would accept. The British concessions were thus in the event even more dangerous than British naval opinion had originally thought. Destroyers and submarines were now also to be limited by the Washington Treaty proportions of 5 : 5 : 3 for England, the United States and Japan.[5]

The maiming of English seapower, begun by the Conservatives in Washington in 1922, continued by Churchill between 1924 and 1929, was thus completed by the Labour Government in London in 1930. In May

[1] CAB 29/117, LNC(29)3. [2] CAB 29/128. [3] Ibid.

[4] In Britain's case two new ships to be started in 1931, two in 1932, and then one or two in alternate years until all the ageing and obsolescent vessels had been replaced.

[5] For a full account of the London Naval Conference and the roles of MacDonald, Henderson and of their internationalist and pacifistic mentors, Lord Cecil of Chelwood and Philip Noel-Baker, see David Carlton, *MacDonald Versus Henderson* (London, Macmillan 1970), chs. 5 and 6.

of that year the Naval Staff gloomily surveyed the consequences in a Memorandum to the Fighting Services Committee: 'It should . . . be noted that the London Naval Treaty will result in an increase in the relative strengths of the USA and Japan as compared with ourselves. French and Italian programmes also foreshadow considerable increases. Great Britain is reducing her strength as compared with the others. . . .'[1]

The Government for its part believed, on the contrary, that the London Naval Treaty had enhanced the security of the British Empire, a security which in any case rested ever more reliably on the League of Nations:

> . . . the advance within the last few years in the development of international machinery for the settlement of disputes by pacific means had greatly reduced the risk of any outbreak of war. . . . Japan in particular having joined the British Commonwealth of Nations and the United States of America in signing the London Naval Treaty, . . . was unlikely to disturb the peace.[2]

It was in these terms that the Labour Government justified to the 1930 Imperial Conference its decision to stop work on the Singapore base for five years. Although Australia and New Zealand had no alternative but to agree to this decision, they did not accept the British reasoning. When Arthur Henderson, the English Foreign Secretary, pointed out that since the Singapore base project had first been mooted Japan 'had definitely pledged herself to settle her disputes by peaceful means', G. W. Forbes, the Prime Minister of New Zealand, questioned the value of pledges like the Kellogg Pact, saying that they were in the last resort 'only ink and paper'. Henderson, horrified, replied that 'in his opinion Japan could be as much relied upon to stand by her obligations under the Kellogg Pact as we ourselves'. When Forbes disputed the expressed British conviction that there would be no war for ten years, Henderson again affirmed his faith in international peace machinery and also in the forthcoming world disarmament conference. 'Surely,' he pleaded, 'these things must count for something.' But Forbes answered that he thought they counted for less than Henderson thought.[3]

'Henderson', as his biographer expressed it, 'had the faith of a child in noble dreams, and an unshakable confidence in the ultimate goodness of a world that might look evil, but yet had something in it of the divine.'[4]

Henderson was born in 1863 in Glasgow, the son of a manual worker,

[1] Memorandum on the effects of the Treaty on the Singapore base, CAB 27/407, FS(29)25.
[2] CAB 32/91, E(30)36. [3] Ibid.
[4] Mary Agnes Hamilton, *Arthur Henderson* (London, Heinemann 1938), p. 446.

and brought up in direst poverty. Reared on the Bible by his mother, he was converted to Methodism at the age of sixteen by a noted evangelist. His elder brother recorded that 'for Arthur, life began with his conversion'.[1] Broad and solid of body, ruddy-faced, blue-eyed, hair combed sideways over a broad skull, Henderson was the embodiment of the solid character and plain virtues of the late Victorian working and lower-middle classes: a local trade-union organiser who eventually became President of the Ironfounder's Union; a town and county councillor; a man whose family life achieved a particular quality of warm cosiness. He began his political career as a Radical and an admirer of Gladstone; became one of the first four Labour MPs in 1903, and Secretary of the Labour Party in 1911, a post he was to hold for twenty-three years. His interest in foreign affairs stemmed from the Great War. 'The effort to mobilise a diplomacy of democracy was his object now; it was to go on being his object, to the day of his death.'[2]

Henderson therefore brought to the corrupt, vicious and power-ridden business of foreign affairs all the decencies of English life in a red-brick Victorian suburb; the simplicity, the honesty, the guilelessness, the warmth of heart, the neighbourliness; the complete insularity. Insularity was a singular quality to find in a passionate internationalist; however it was Henderson's sentiments that were internationalist, not his knowledge that was international. 'Any language but his own he never learned. To the last, he was to shock people by his cheerful ignorance of geography.'[3]

> The general cast of his mind was simple [wrote his biographer]. Problems that tease the analytical intelligence were not there, for him. Faith was a fact, not to be affected or disturbed by scientific discovery, philosophic enquiry, or the alien attitude of others. He was not a subtle thinker, nor a wide or curious reader. . . . He knew his Bible. He read George Fox and John Wesley constantly. He read sermons, Methodist periodicals . . .[4]

A glimpse into the soul of the man who now occupied the seat of Castlereagh, Palmerston and Salisbury is offered by Henderson's habit for years of carrying about in his pocket a little set of verses addressed to 'Mothers of Little Sons'. 'Wholly innocent of literary quality, these artless rhymes said something to him. . . .'[5]

With Henderson religion became the inspiration of British policy more openly than ever before or since.

[1] Hamilton, p. 5.
[2] Ibid. p. 166.
[3] Ibid. p. 92.
[4] Ibid. p. 34.
[5] Ibid. p. 445.

> The core of Wesleyanism, and its distinctive feature, is that it is a religion of conduct and fellowship. The social fact is stressed . . . on every line, co-operation in an effort to realise the pattern of the good life here on earth is a duty. So . . . he took the spirit of his church into politics and into Unionism, and found many men there who did the same; who believed, as he did, that politics and Trade Unionism could be instruments for the realisation of religious ideals. . . .[1]

The League of Nations at Geneva provided the perfect habitat for Henderson. '. . . the moral climate at once elevated and rather dowdy was entirely congenial. Here was a place dedicated expressly to high purposes in which he believed.'[2] In turn, Henderson was exactly the kind of man to please Geneva. In 1929–31 he achieved the kind of dominance over the League that Castlereagh had enjoyed at the Congress of Vienna. Long experience of trade-union work had him skilled in negotiation and conciliation. His patent integrity and the massive strength of his personality inspired the League delegations with his own confidence in the League's future. It was a form of faith-healing. It was in doing so much to encourage the League to believe in itself that Henderson probably rendered the greatest disservice to the world on which he wished to confer the blessings of eternal peace.

Henderson himself was aware that the League had its flaws; yet he conceived of them as legal loopholes in the obligations undertaken by League members under the Covenant. Plug these holes with more agreements, supplement the Covenant with yet more obligations, he believed, and all would be well. It was beyond Henderson's comprehension that all these solemn undertakings might simply not be fulfilled; beyond his imagination that men could and would fail to keep their pledged word. For while he acknowledged that under the Covenant there was no specific obligation on League members to use force to enforce the Covenant, 'surely', he argued, 'loyal and effective co-operation in support of the Covenant is what may confidently be expected from every member of the League of Nations. Otherwise their membership is a fraud and a delusion.'[3] On behalf of Britain therefore he confidently signed in 1929 the so-called 'Optional Clause', by which nations committed themselves to submit disputes to compulsory arbitration by the International Court, if conciliation failed. In 1930 he signed the so-called 'General Act', providing for the pacific settlement of all disputes by various methods. The new obligations, together with the original Covenant of the League and the

[1] Ibid. pp. 35–6.
[2] Ibid. p. 321.
[3] 22 March 1930, CAB 29/128.

Kellogg Pact, thus abolished war as an instrument for resolving disputes between nations – abolished it, that was, to the complete satisfaction of believing internationalists. As Henderson himself put it, thus year by year, stone by stone, the members of the League were building on a firm foundation the structure of enduring peace.[1] But, in fact, it was a structure of fantasy, like an immense and gorgeous palace in an engraving by Piranesi. Just as the gigantic arches of Piranesi's imagination defy the laws of physics and geometry, so the paper edifice of the League defied the factors that really determined the course of international affairs: the still untrammelled power of sovereign states, and the inevitable collision of their interests and ambitions.

Like Gilbert Murray and most other internationalists, Henderson believed that the problem of the power of nation-states and the problem of their mutual fear could both be solved by universal disarmament. Indeed Henderson shared the widespread conviction that it was armaments that caused the fear between nations rather than the fear that led to the armaments. The Great War was now widely if simple-mindedly blamed on 'the armament race', rather than on all the profound and complex social, economic, political and psychological tensions of pre-war Europe. The forthcoming World Disarmament Conference in 1932 was regarded therefore as the final and necessary step in the construction of the new international order. It was hoped to reduce national armed forces to mere gendarmeries for internal security, incapable of foreign aggression. Disarmament was thus the core of Henderson's policy.

Moreover Henderson and some of his colleagues in the British Government were so sanguine that this conference was going to succeed that in anticipation they were ready further to dismantle the British armed forces. Philip Snowden, the Chancellor of the Exchequer and no less Gladstonian than Churchill in his pursuit of peace and retrenchment, and encouraged by his Parliamentary Under-Secretary, Hugh Dalton, and Philip Noel-Baker, his Parliamentary Private Secretary, a particularly emotional pacifist, also wanted to cut the navy's building programme to below even the London Naval Treaty standards until the results of the Disarmament Conference were known.

The Treasury had indeed displayed a vested interest in disarmament throughout the 1920s; for it was the unfortunate Treasury that had to cope with the discrepancy between the cost of the commitments of a world empire and the financial resources of an obsolete industrial power with a partly ruined export trade. Economy was not the least among the com-

[1] Walters, Vol. I, p. 456.

plicated British motives in pushing disarmament and the League of Nations.[1] And in 1930–1, as the world slump deepened, and British exports collapsed even further, the Treasury's motives were rendered the stronger and more urgent. The British were like a family which, having a large house and rich possessions but a currently reduced income, wished to save money on anti-burgler devices. What cheaper and better way than to persuade all likely burglars that larceny is immoral, and that they should give up their jemmies?

The question of anticipating the disarmament conference by further economies in the British forces was only one element in a deep division between MacDonald and Henderson, a division partly owing to long-standing personal antipathy and rivalry, partly to MacDonald's greater and growing (relative) realism over foreign affairs.[2] On 28 November 1930, during a discussion in the Committee of Imperial Defence on the Chiefs of Staff Annual Review, MacDonald said that 'one of the chief difficulties of the present situation was that a great many people in these islands . . . were now moving in an exaggerated atmosphere of peace prophecy'.[3] It was his view that while Britain ought to give a lead, she should not disarm in advance of firm agreements.[4] On 26 January 1931, MacDonald told the Fighting Services Committee that 'the [naval] construction programme was already down to the bone and could not be cut further'.[5] He argued that if Britain did not build up to the limits allowed under the London Naval Treaty, she would have no bargaining power in the disarmament conference.[6] Alexander, the First Lord of the Admiralty, supported him by pointing out that to delay new construction now would make the financial situation worse after 1933, if Britain were not to shrink to a second-rate naval power.[7]

The arguments inside the Labour Government in 1931 over further unilateral disarmament turned on differing diagnoses of the current trend of world affairs. The general prosperity of 1925–9, which had done so much to foster internationalist optimism, had deflated into a catastrophic world slump. In Japan and Germany the traditional forces of nationalism and militarism were thriving on the consequent unemployment and social distress; and parliamentary liberalism, ever a tender exotic ill-suited to the German and Japanese character and history, sickened swiftly. In Japan a

[1] See the Minutes of the Cabinet Committee on Preparations for the League of Nations Disarmament Conference, CAB 27/476, 512, 514, and the Cabinet Committee on Reductions and Limitations of Armaments Policy Committee CAB 27/361–63, 443.

[2] See Carlton, especially chs. 4 and 6.

[3] CAB 2/5, CID 251.

[4] Ibid.

[5] CAB 27/407, FS(29)4.

[6] Ibid.

[7] Ibid.

*coup d'état* organised by the army in March 1931 narrowly failed.[1] In Germany parliamentary government had come to an end in March 1930, when the new Chancellor, Heinrich Brüning, began to rule by emergency decree. In the General Election of July 1930 Adolf Hitler's National Socialist Party had leaped from 12 to 107 parliamentary seats, and become the second largest party. In both Germany and Japan physical violence was a commonplace of political life.

From these well-reported and disagreeable developments MacDonald had formed the opinion by 1931 that '... despite all the efforts of the Government, the risks of war were greater today than they had been twelve months ago, and a militarist spirit was controlling Europe more to-day than it had been for many years'.[2]

Henderson on the other hand, expressing the optimism of the pacifistic wing of the Labour Party, insisted that he 'could not support the view ... that the political situation in Europe was deteriorating'.[3]

MacDonald wished not only to preserve the armed forces from further weakening, but also to abolish the 'ten-year-rule', which now seemed to him no longer in the least justified by the current state of the world. He was bitterly opposed by Henderson and the internationalists behind him in the Government, speaking for the naïve and sentimental idealism of the Labour rank-and-file. Once more British strategic power – what was left of it – lay in jeopardy. In the end, MacDonald succeeded in saving the navy from yet further unilateral cuts, but was not strong enough to overcome the opposition of Henderson and his supporters to the revocation of the 'ten-year-rule', for to revoke it would be officially to admit what was according to their faith inadmissible – that the sun of international amity was going in; that it was a time for umbrellas, not for further disrobing in a world disarmament conference.

At least, however, British disarmament would go no further. It was small enough comfort. In April 1931, the First Sea Lord, now Admiral of the Fleet Sir Frederick Field, surveyed the cumulative effects of ten years of internationalist escapism, both Conservative and Labour, on the Royal Navy.[4] While America, Japan, France and Italy had all spent more on their navies in recent years, the British Commonwealth on the other hand 'has accepted a naval strength which, in certain circumstances, is definitely

[1] Richard Storry, *A History of Modern Japan* (Harmondsworth, Penguin Books 1960), ch. 7, especially pp. 177–81; Marmoru Shigemitsu, *Japan and Her Destiny* (London, Hutchinson 1958), Bk. I, chs. II–VII.

[2] January 1931, CAB 27/407, FS(29)15.

[3] Ibid.

[4] In a report to the Committee of Imperial Defence Sub-Committee on the League Disarmament Conference, CAB 27/476, CDC(31)2.

below that required to keep our sea communications open in the event of our being drawn into war. In defensive material, in the modernisation of ships . . . we are below the standard of the other powers. . . .'[1]

Field went on to spell out British weaknesses item by item, the worst of them being printed in his report in heavy black type: 'The number of our capital ships is now so reduced that should the protection of our interests render it necessary to move our fleet to the East, insufficient vessels of this type would be left in Home Waters to ensure the security of our trade and territory in the event of any dispute arising with a European power.'[2]

Repeating Jellicoe's reminder that in the Great War 116 cruisers had proved too small a number, he once again stated the Naval Staff's conviction that the fifty cruisers allowed under the London Navel Treaty was 'definitely insufficient'.

In destroyers too the navy was dangerously weak. In 1918 the Royal Navy had had 433 destroyers, all of which had been needed. The figure under the London Naval Treaty was some 120. By 1936, fifty-five of these would be over-age.

The Fleet Air Arm, the First Sea Lord continued, had only 159 aircraft, ship-borne and land-based, compared with America's 689 ship-borne and 311 land-based and Japan's 115 ship-borne and 296 shore-based. Under current plans the Fleet Air Arm would still only number 225 aircraft by 1937.

There were no adequately defended ports in the British Commonwealth.

Field capped his gloomy survey by making clear that the Royal Navy had not only declined in its *relative* strength, but 'owing to the operation of the "ten-year-decision" and the clamant need for economy, our *absolute strength* also has . . . been so diminished as to render the fleet incapable, in the event of war, of efficiently affording protection to our trade'.[3]

The fortunes of the British army and the Royal Air Force during the 1920s had been even worse than the navy's. A memorandum by the Army Council in November 1931, anatomising the army's strength in relation to its actual and potential commitments and describing the obsolescence of its equipment in all its details, summed up the state of British land forces by saying that they were 'barely sufficient' to perform their peacetime duties.[4]

Yet, in addition to her limitless general obligations under the Covenant

[1] CAB 27/476, CDC(31)2. [2] Ibid. [3] Ibid.
[4] Memorandum to the Cabinet Committee on Preparations for the Disarmament Conference, November 1931, CAB 27/476, CDC(31)4.

of the League of Nations, England had also committed herself, under the 1925 Treaty of Locarno, to go to the aid of either France or Germany if one were attacked by the other. But the Army Council warned that if England were called upon to take action under the Locarno Treaty, the British army, 'except for the moral effect of its presence on the Continent . . . could have little effect on the fortunes of the campaign'.[1] The plight of the British army in 1931 therefore exemplified the final results of the double policy pursued by successive British governments of adding to British commitments while at the same time dismantling the means of fulfilling them.

The subtle minds of the Foreign Office, however, were able to offer a happily ingenious answer to the apparent paradox: 'The more the nations of Europe became convinced of our readiness to fulfil our guarantee, the less the likelihood will there be that we shall be called upon to do so.'[2]

As Gilbert Murray remarked in 1928, although apparently without taking alarm at the stark implication of his own words, 'the safety of the British Empire . . . depends absolutely on the tranquillity of the world'.[3]

Thus by 1931 moralising internationalism had run its full course in disarming England materially and spiritually. It was a course which had completely borne out Sir Maurice Hankey's warning in 1916 that the creation of a League of Nations would lead to 'a sense of security which is wholly fictitious'; that it would lull the country to sleep; that it would put 'a very strong lever into the hands of the well-meaning idealists . . . who deprecate expenditure on armaments . . .'[4]

It only remained for the final part of Hankey's warning to be fulfilled: his prediction that the creation of a League of Nations would almost certainly result in this country being caught at a disadvantage.[5]

On the night of 18 September 1931, this omission was repaired. The Japanese army began to take over the Chinese province of Manchuria by force of arms. This was a patent breach of the Covenant of the League of Nations; an insolent challenge to the efficacy of the elaborate confections of paper and parchment on which the League rested. And England, according to her own obligations under the Covenant, was bound to support the League in resisting this aggression. It was a situation which therefore carried the risk of war; a situation in which a British Government that wanted fully to live up to all the brave internationalist sentiments of the 1920s might wish to *choose* war in support of the Covenant of the League

[1] Ibid.
[2] Memorandum quoted in the Chiefs of Staff Annual Review for 1930, CAB 53/21, COS 247.
[3] Gilbert Murray, p. 215. [4] See above p. 245. [5] Ibid.

of Nations. Yet according to the 'ten-year-rule', the possibility of war was not supposed to occur until 1941; according even to the Foreign Office predictions of 1926, there was to be no danger of war in the Far East until 1936.

This was the moment when the minds of moralising internationlists were jolted at last by the impact of reality. For Britain in particular, it was that inconvenient moment in life when an injudiciously given IOU is finally presented for payment – and at a time when equal injudiciousness had emptied the bank account.

In regard to British relations with Japan in particular, the fighting in Manchuria made nonsense of all the confident pronouncements of Chancellors of the Exchequer, Foreign Secretaries and the Foreign Office in the mid-1920s to the effect that Japan offered no threat to peace. It vindicated all the warnings by dominion statesmen and British service leaders about Japan's untrustworthiness and ambition; warnings so scoffed at during the heyday of internationalist intellectual arrogance.

The launching of the Japanese aggression in itself broke both the Kellogg Pact and the stipulation under the Covenant of the League of Nations that there should be no recourse to war as a means of settling a dispute until after a delay of three months for attempts at conciliation and negotiation. The subsequent course of Japanese conquest in Manchuria continued to mock the hopeful trust placed in the efficacy of League machinery for peaceful settlement of disputes. While Geneva squawked frenziedly like a fowl-run with a fox in it the Japanese completed their conquest of Manchuria with the despatch of an efficient butcher; and in February 1932, long before the League had taken any decisive action, they proclaimed the existence of a new state, Manchukuo, independent of China. At the end of January the Japanese had extended their aggression to central China by a fresh offensive at Shanghai, using the International Settlement there as a base. This attack, unlike the earlier action in Manchuria, directly threatened British interests rather than merely the authority of the League of Nations.

England was therefore presented with a double set of problems: as a professed supporter of the League of Nations, and as a nation-state threatened in its own interests. To England as a nation-state, however, the Japanese conversion of Manchuria into an exclusive sphere of interest at long last was not greatly damaging, since English commercial interests and political influence lay in central and southern China. A mutual acknowledgement of spheres of interest between Japan and England in order to avert hostility and rivalry was still possible, though now – unlike in 1921–2

– it would have to be made under the shadow of Japanese *force-majeure*. The attack at Shanghai on the other hand was another matter; a direct menace to English trade, investments and predominance. Nevertheless it was possible that the Japanese might prove willing to abandon this expansion in the south in return for English acknowledgement of their conquest of Manchuria. The alternative to a deal with the Japanese was resistance. Resistance raised two questions: what scale of resistance was warranted by the importance of English interests in China? – and secondly, of what scale of resistance in the Far East was England now capable? The English economic stake in China formed only 6 per cent of English overseas investment. British trade with China constituted no more than about 1½ per cent of Britain's total trade;[1] English interests in China were not therefore worth a war with Japan. But in any event the decisive question was whether England was *capable* of resisting Japanese expansion; it was decisive not only in terms of England's direct interests as a nation-state, but also in terms of her chosen role as a leading power in the League of Nations.

For the League of Nations itself the Japanese aggression raised as an urgent practical issue that fundamental question of power – military and naval power – which had so troubled Gilbert Murray in theory, but which had always been ignored or played down by most other moralising internationalists. Here was a bandit state engaged in open robbery; now therefore was the time for the law-abiding powers of the world to uphold the law against the wrongdoer; to act as policemen. Unfortunately the policemen had been persuaded to give up their truncheons.

Sir Frederick Field, the First Sea Lord, remarked on 29 February 1932 on 'how powerless we would be in the Far East in an emergency in the present circumstances. As things stood, the amount the Navy could do to provide protection for Singapore and Hong Kong was very small.'[2] He also referred to Singapore's 'present defenceless situation'. Without a defended naval base in the East, England was almost wholly incapable either of defending her own interests or of acting on behalf of the League of Nations. Admiral of the Fleet Sir Ernle Chatfield commented to his colleagues in the Chiefs of Staff Committee that when the British main fleet arrived at Singapore it might either find the Japanese in occupation, or the vital oil stocks destroyed by Japanese raiders. The Chiefs of Staff counted the tallies of Japanese strength by land, sea and air and of British weakness; and Chatfield voiced their general sentiment by remarking on the dangers of pin-pricking the Japanese into further action.[3]

[1] Knatchbull-Hugessen, p. 96.
[2] CAB 53/4, COS 102.
[3] CAB 53/4, COS meeting on 28 February 1932, COS 107.

Now, suddenly the politicians became more ready to hearken to their service leaders. On 23 March 1932 the Cabinet agreed to rescind the 'ten-year-rule'. Nevertheless the Chancellor of the Exchequer, Neville Chamberlain, true to the tradition of his predecessors, had at first opposed the rescindment on the grounds that the country could not afford it, not even to remedy the deficiencies in the navy. In 1933 it was decided to speed up the completion of Singapore. All this offered a painful and dangerous lesson that it took longer for England to build ships and naval bases than for a foreign country to change its government and policy.

In the meantime England remained incapable of action in the Far East. The problem of dealing with the consequences of moralising internationalist policies of the 1920s fell, justly enough, on a National Government, composed of representatives of all three political parties: Conservative, Labour and Liberal. This government had been formed under MacDonald's premiership in August 1931, when the Labour Government collapsed in the face of the economic and financial crisis caused by the world slump. Baldwin, the Lord President of the Council, shrewdly summed up the Government's dilemma in a letter of 27 February 1932:

> ... The very people like Bob Cecil who have made us disarm, and quite right too, are urging us forward to take action. But where will action lead us to? If we withdraw Ambassadors, that is the first step. What is the next? and the next? If you enforce an economic boycott you will have war declared by Japan and she will seize Singapore and Hong Kong and we cannot, as we are placed, stop her. You will get nothing out of Washington but words, big words, but only words.[1]

Words, and big words, were in fact all the Americans offered. On 7 January Stimson, the United States Secretary of State, sent a note to Japan and China declaring that America would not recognise any agreement between them which impaired American treaty rights in China, nor any situation brought about by means contrary to the Kellogg Pact. Stimson had expressed the hope to the British and French governments beforehand that they too would make similar declarations. Further American support during 1932 equally went no further than the private and public enunciation of fine sentiments that committed America to no form of action; the climax of American activity against Japanese aggression in China being provided by her public endorsement – whatever that was worth – of the settlement finally recommended by the League in February 1933, and ignored by the Japanese. The British had sacrificed their

[1] Middlemass and Barnes, p. 729.

alliance with Japan in order to obtain American goodwill; and now that they were face to face with Japan in arms, goodwill was exactly what they got from America. It did not prove much help.

At Geneva the small members of the League looked to France and England for a lead. What had the states of Scandinavia, central Europe or South America to do with China, full though they might be of the League spirit? How useful was the contribution they could or would make to the coercing of Japan? Thus at the first challenge it became apparent that, in terms of real power and not of simply the moral power of the conscience of the world, the League of Nations amounted to England and France. At the same time it was equally manifest that, when it came down from lofty generalisation to a hard case like the present, the Covenant of the League, if it meant anything more than hollow words, meant English and French willingness to risk, and perhaps to fight, a land war in China and a maritime war in the China Seas.[1] A Far Eastern *imbroglio* was the last thing the French, more and more fearful of reviving German nationalism, wished to contemplate, while the English themselves, whose own interests were more engaged in China than those of any other European power, were physically incapable of action because of disarmament and the failure to complete Singapore. Yet the English and French stood committed by their membership of the League and all their past sermons from the League pulpit to doing something.

But what?

Sir John Simon, the National Liberal Foreign Secretary in the new National Government, well expressed the Government's continuing dilemma in February 1932, in a meeting of the special Cabinet Committee set up to consider the crisis in China:

> . . . he had never for one moment favoured the adoption of the League of any kind of sanctions, not even of an economic character. For him the application of Article XVI was quite out of the picture. The point that concerned him was lest, by a declaration [against Japanese actions] we might provoke a situation that precipitated Japanese resentment.[2]

As for all the other members of the League, he 'was convinced that none of the Powers at Geneva meant business; they wanted to find a way out'.[3]

The British Government was thus trapped between the truth of British (and League) impotence, and the myth of the League of Nations as a preserver of world law and order. Yet the Government did not dare pass

[1] See Billy Hughes' prophetic comments at the 1921 Imperial Conference: above p. 266.
[2] CAB 27/482, CJC(32)2.
[3] Ibid.

on to the general public the truth as they knew it and as bleakly enunciated by Simon. They did not dare to expose the League of Nations as the sentimental myth it was, any more than they dared, at this same epoch, to acknowledge publicly a similar truth in regard to the new 'British Commonwealth of Nations'. It was an essential aspect of the British tragedy then and later that public discussion on world affairs was almost wholly conducted in terms of idealistic humbug rather than in terms of the uncomfortable and unlovely reality. And this was very largely the fault of governments, which feared to affront the dearly cherished romantic prejudices of public opinion, even when they did not share these prejudices themselves.

The Government's dilemma over Japan and China remained. The facts of relative power and of British interest called for a deal with Japan which would avert her hostility and if possible concentrate her ambitions on Manchuria rather than further afield. A realistic stroke of policy like this, however, was hardly such as would occur to politicians like MacDonald, Baldwin or Simon; it was in any case ruled out not only by the prevailing climate of public opinion, but also by British adherence to the Covenant of the League of Nations. Such adherence demanded on the contrary a display of knight-errantry. Yet at the same time it was essential, in view of British strategic weakness, that this knight-errantry should not actually go so far as an attempt at the rescue of the maiden in distress, because this might dangerously annoy the dragon.

All that was really left therefore were two old stand-bys: Britain's moral authority, and Britain's role as the umpire above the struggle. The Government adopted these roles more by instinctive response than as the result of clear-sighted analysis.

Sir John Simon, the Foreign Secretary, was a man well-adapted to the roles. He looked like a cleric, but was a lawyer. As a lawyer he saw, and could ably present, the arguments on both sides of the case. This however impeded the process of making up his own mind; it made him reluctant to take a side and fight for it, even if the side were England's.[1] Simon's grandfather was a staunch dissenter, four out of six of whose sons became Congregationalist ministers. His father, one of the ministers, and his mother had both loyally supported Gladstone. Simon, born in 1873, was educated at Fettes and Wadham, winning scholarships to both institutions. A life-long Liberal, he had been a pro-Boer during the Boer War,

[1] See Neville Chamberlain's opinion in Keith Feiling, *Life of Neville Chamberlain* (London, Macmillan 1946), p. 249; Eden's in Avon, Vol. I, pp. 219–20; Macmillan's in H. Macmillan, *The Winds of Change* (London, Macmillan 1966), p. 314.

and, in 1914, it had been only by the personal persuasion of Sir Edward Grey that Simon had not resigned from the Liberal Government over the decision to go to the war. However in 1916 Simon did resign; and in this case rather than support the introduction of conscription. Simon's was therefore an almost too-perfect exemplar of the ancestry of the post-evangelical generation of British politicians. An unfortunate habit of concealing prompt cards for a speech in his hands, and shuffling them in the course of his oration, added to the air of a hand-washing and sanctimonious cleric. At Geneva during the Manchurian crisis this habit earned him the nickname of Uriah Heep.[1]

Simon exercised Britain's moral authority over Manchuria by administering a sorrowful wigging to the Japanese for their wrong in taking the law into their own hands. At the same time he displayed Britain's lofty stand above the squabbles of nations by pointing out, justly enough, that there were many faults on the Chinese side too, for Chinese administration in Manchuria had indeed fallen into a state of chaos. Developing this evasive yet high-minded refusal to take sides, Simon persuaded the League to send a commission of enquiry to Manchuria to gather all the facts and report back. This commission, under Lord Lytton, departed for the East on 3 February 1932, and only made its report on 4 September, nearly a year after the original Japanese attack. While the need for action was thus being postponed for the highest possible motives, and while the Japanese grasp on their conquests was being tightened, Simon persuaded the League Assembly to pass a unanimous resolution pledging its members not to recognise any changes brought about by force: a resolution no less morally admirable, no less vain, and no less apt to irritate the Japanese than Stimson's similar declaration in January on behalf of the United States.

The report of the Lytton Commission, when it at last appeared, placed the British Government firmly in the quandary which it had sought so long to evade. For although elaborately impartial as between China and Japan, the Commission on balance had to acknowledge that right lay more with China than with Japan. In particular, it recommended the restoration of Chinese sovereignty over Manchuria. If Britain accepted the report and proposals of the Lytton Commission, she would therefore be forced to take sides – against Japan. Simon therefore mounted an impressive display of objectivity, deftly bringing out all China's sins, striving to avert the threatened confrontation between the League and Japan, hoping that China and Japan might come to an agreement between themselves.

[1] Sir Basil Liddell Hart, *Memoirs* (London, Cassell 1965), Vol. I, p. 205.

Unfortunately for him, and despite his fashionably moralistic canting, Simon's obvious reluctance to lead the League into taking a strong hand against Japan destroyed his credit both with the small powers at Geneva and with internationalists at home. At the same time his procrastination and evasion ended in failure. On 24 February 1933 the General Assembly of the League adopted a statement on Manchuria completely based on the Lytton Report, a statement for which the British delegation could hardly fail to vote. On 27 March Japan left the League of Nations. And that was that, so far as Japan and the new world authority and the new international order and the power of the moral conscience of the peoples of the world were concerned.

But for England the Manchurian episode was a major disaster. She had gratuitously made an enemy out of a formidable military and naval power with which she had no necessary quarrel of her own. For the fact was that, whatever Simon's equivocations, England had exercised the leading role not only in reproving Japan in public, an experience unacceptable to the Japanese sense of honour and 'face', but also in the whole business of the Lytton Commission, and in the final vote in the League Assembly on the resolution which adopted the Commission's proposals.

Henceforward even politicians and the Foreign Office had to recognise that England and Japan faced each other as hostile powers. Moreover they had to recognise that the Japanese threat was not merely sleeping, as the service chiefs had seen it in the 1920s, but awake and ever-present; a threat England was as yet incapable of parrying.[1]

It was in this year of 1933, when their romantic idealism had finally betrayed the British into raising up a formidable menace in the East and the Pacific, that the German danger began to stalk again in Europe.

From the cliffs of Dover on a clear day it is possible to see a grey rim of land shutting in the south-eastern horizon. It is not the coastline of Asia; nor of Japan; nor of Arabia, Africa or Asia Minor, but of Europe. England lies only twenty-two miles from the European shore. Simple, obvious, indeed well-known a fact as this was, the English were prone from time to time to forget all the implications which it bore for English policy and strategy.

England was at once detached from Europe and yet so near as to be inevitably caught up in European rivalries; at once a refuge behind the sea and the Royal Navy from the march of conquering armies, and a base

[1] See CAB 53/22, COS 296: Chiefs of Staff Report analysing the British inability to wage war against Japan.

from which British expeditionary forces set forth to help to decide European destinies. Just as the geographical location of England in relation to Europe was ambiguous, so, consequently, was the outlook of English statesmanship. Those twenty-two miles of dark and broken waters commanded by English ships-of-war made it too easy for English governments to succumb to the delusion that it was possible to remain safely and tranquilly insulated from the troubles of Europe. And yet, again and again, from the time when Elizabeth I was forced to fight for the Dutch to the time in 1914 when a Liberal Government was forced to fight for Belgium, England was taught by the event that she was still inescapably a European power.

The paramount political interest of England, therefore, an interest which no English Government had been able to ignore in the end, was the maintenance of an equilibrium between the great powers of Europe, so that no single state became so mighty as to dominate the Continent. In order to maintain this balance of power England had gone to war over such unlikely matters as the succession to the thrones of Spain and Austria, and the assassination of an Austrian archduke in a remote Balkan town. The occasion of war, the location of the quarrel or event which led to war, hardly mattered; it was the balance of power for which England took up arms.

From 1643, when Condé defeated the Spaniards at the Battle of Rocroi, to 1815, Europe had lain beneath the shadow of France. In population, wealth and military strength she had greatly exceeded any other state; her power was only to be balanced by coalitions often inspired and cemented by England. However, Napoleon's defeat at Waterloo marked the end of France as a super-power. The gutting of her manhood in Napoleon's battles and the vigilance of the victors prevented the recovery of her former ascendancy in the short run, while in the long run the growth of the population of other European states during the nineteenth century, so much more rapid than France's own, wiped out her old advantage of numbers. By the time of the Franco-Prussian War in 1870, the French nation numbered only 36,000,000, against the 40,000,000 of Prussia and her German allies.

With this eclipse of France after 1815 there ensued a period of forty-five years in which Europe was free of the incubus of a super-power. Instead there were five leading powers of roughly equivalent weight, a circumstance limiting to the ambitions of all. This happy but transient condition became known, especially in nostalgic retrospect, as 'the Concert of Europe', and was romantically attributed to the moderation, wisdom and public spirit of the European statesmen of the era. It encouraged the English gradually to withdraw during the latter part of the century from close embroilment in European affairs; a withdrawal which occasional English diplomatic sorties like Disraeli's presence at the Congress of Berlin in 1878 only served to emphasise. This English isolation was also fostered by England's world-wide trading interests and by the rise of imperialism. The empire distracted the gaze of Englishmen to distant coasts and frontiers, whence loomed dangers not to the English themselves, but to the possessions and responsibilities with which they had encumbered themselves.

Unfortunately the English mis-timed their spiritual withdrawal from Europe; for it was completed *after* the short halcyon era of 'the Concert of Europe' had begun to pass away, and a fresh super-power emerge to disturb the equilibrium.

In 1871 Bismarck consummated both the Prussian victory over the French and the unification of Germany under Prussian leadership by inaugurating the German Empire in the Hall of Mirrors at Versailles. It was a fateful achievement. From its moment of birth the new German Empire was of an order of magnitude greater than that of the other states of Europe; and which became greater still during the next forty years. To the modern Europe of the industrial age, Germany was what Spain and France had been in turn to pre-industrial Europe, a giant overtopping its neighbours. From 1871 onwards the salient fact of European politics was German power. By 1914 Germany's population, at 67,000,000, was more than half as much again as either that of France or Great Britain, and was exceeded only by that of Russia among European powers. Moreover, German industry and technology were immensely stronger and more vigorous that those of either her friends or rivals. Her steel production, to give a basic index, amounted to 17,320,000 tons in 1914, as against a French total of only 5,000,000 tons and a British total of 7,000,000 tons (average for 1910–14). Nor could any other European country match the thoroughness of Germany's application of scientific research to industrial development or her system of national or technical education.[1] Unfortunately Germany was not a democratic and unmilitary state like the other industrial giant of the world, the United States. She was a military monarchy, just as France had been in her own days of greatness. Like France, Germany had been united by the sword. She inherited the martial traditions and myths of Prussia, and she also possessed the most efficient,

[1] See Correlli Barnett, *The Swordbearers* (London, Eyre and Spottiswoode 1963), pp. 192–3, 228 and 237 for brief comparisons between German, British and French industrial power in this epoch.

best equipped and incomparably the most powerful army in the world. Moreover, Germany was geographically so placed as to command Europe from its heartland; able to expand diplomatically, economically and, if necessary, militarily to the east or the west. The advantage of this central position was enhanced by a superb strategic railway system planned by the Prussian general staff. And, lastly, all Germany's powers and resources were rendered the more effective by the German talent for organisation.

When in 1888 the Kaiser Wilhelm II dismissed Bismarck and removed his restraining hand, Germany, in its eager ambition, its consciousness of its swelling might, came to present the supreme problem around which European politics revolved.

It was Germany's strength and her policy of expansion which eventually compelled England, after 1902, to emerge from her isolation and resume in some measure her traditional task of redressing the balance of power. While the German violation of Belgian neutrality in 1914 provided the moral goad needed to stir the modern British into action, Great Britain really went to war for those most realistic and traditional of reasons, the balance of power and the preservation of the Low Countries. She went to war because not even a Liberal Government was able to resist the stark strategic imperatives when it came to the event. It was just not possible to stand aside and see France go down; to contemplate Germany triumphantly bestriding Europe from Poland to Flanders.

The Great War itself provided a grim demonstration of Germany's gigantic strength. Between 1914 and 1917, nourishing her war-effort entirely from her own technological resources, and assisted by only one major, though unreliable, ally in Austria-Hungary, she smashed Imperial Russia and successfully held France and Great Britain to a draw, in spite of their being able to draw on the vast resources of American industry. In 1918 Germany came within an ace of defeating the French and British armies in the field before the United States Army could decisively intervene. Indeed Germany only lost the war because of American intervention: intervention before 1917 in the form of munitions, steel and machine-tools, and after midsummer 1918 in the form of rapidly growing and completely fresh forces on the Western Front.[1]

Thus the course of the Great War proved that Germany was more than a match for France and Great Britain together. It proved indeed that no purely *European* combination was capable of defeating her. Here was a

[1] For an analysis of the decisive nature of the American contribution to the Allied victory, see Correlli Barnett, 'The New Military Balance' in *The History of the Twentieth Century*, 24 (1968).

formidable truth; here was the salient fact of which a peace settlement had to take note. For the single great problem which faced the victorious Allies in 1918, a problem beside which nothing else really mattered, was that of Germany's power.

Throughout the Paris Peace Conference of 1919 and its preliminaries this problem obsessed the French. It was, after all, on their soil that Germany had most convincingly demonstrated German power; they also stood in the nearest and greatest danger from a fresh demonstration in the future. The French therefore conceived of a peace settlement almost wholly in terms of expedients for permanently reducing Germany's overwhelming strength to a degree commensurate with that of France herself. They believed that the German problem must be solved once and for all by making use of the Allies' fleeting moment of victory and military supremacy to take away for ever from Germany her *capacity* to disturb the equilibrium of Europe. This desirable consummation might be achieved best, in the French view, by undoing Bismarck's work and again dividing Germany. The French in 1919 wished to contrive the kind of situation which came about by luck after 1945: Germany sundered, and its parts permanently placed under the surveillance of foreign armies; the largest portion of the former German state being of a weight no greater than that of France; Germany therefore enfeebled as a power, even if its parts might in sum be economically strong and prosperous. As a consequence the separatist movements which sprang up in Bavaria and elsewhere in the wake of Germany's defeat were welcomed and encouraged in Paris.

In particular, the French wished to detach the Rhineland from Germany and turn it into a separate buffer state under French protection. In January 1919 Marshal Foch argued the case in a memorandum to the allied plenipotentiaries to the Peace Conference:

> Henceforward the Rhine ought to be the Western Military Frontier of the German countries. Henceforward Germany ought to be deprived of all entrance and assembling ground, that is, of all territorial sovereignty on the left bank of the river, that is, of all facilities for invading quickly, and threatening the United Kingdom, the Rhine, Meuse, conquering the Northern Provinces and entering upon the Paris area. . . .
>
> [Therefore] . . . we demand, at least temporarily, a guarantee . . . against a Germany with twice the population of France, a Germany whose word it will not be possible to trust for a long time – we demand a physical guarantee. . . .[1]

[1] E. R. Troughton, *It's Happening Again* (London, John Gifford 1944), pp. 17–18.

Both as compensation for the wrecking of the French mining industry by the occupying German forces, and so as further to reduce the population remaining to the German state, the French also demanded the cession of the Saar coalfield area. In order to make good the appalling devastation inflicted on France by invasion and war, and at the same time to bridle Germany's economic vigour, the French demanded that Germany should pay the full cost of all damage suffered by the Allies in the course of the conflict.

The French, in their attitude to making peace, were thus preoccupied with the question of Germany's power in the future; a future which they saw as one of continued rivalry between nations.

The British and the Americans, on the other hand, had no such hard, clear-cut policy; felt no such overriding concern with German power. In the first place they shared the liberal assumption that the normal human condition was what they called 'peace'; a natural harmony in which 'war' was simply a meaningless and regrettable breakdown. They did not agree with the Clausewitzian view that 'peace' and 'war' were alternating aspects of a perpetual conflict of interest between organised human groups, a conflict which can express itself in mere economic and diplomatic rivalry; in threats of force; in covert violence or open pressure; in local use of force; in limited war; or finally, in total war. The notion that the Allied victory in the Great War was just one episode in a continuing struggle, from which the maximum advantage must be derived for the next episode, was therefore alien and repellent to them. Anglo-Saxon statesmen in Paris in 1919 hoped above all things to re-create 'peace', a static golden age. It was not only an idealist like Woodrow Wilson, or a radical like Lloyd George who failed to share the French conception of the future; it was even a Conservative statesman like Balfour:

> They [the French] draw a lurid picture of Franco-German relations. They assume that the German people will always far outnumber the French; that as soon as the first shock of defeat has passed away, Germany will organise herself for revenge; that all our attempts to limit armaments will be unsuccessful; that the League of Nations will be impotent; and, consequently, that the invasion of France, which was fully accomplished in 1870, and partially accomplished in the recent War, will be renewed with every prospect of success.[1]

Although Balfour acknowledged that he did not 'wish to deny the

[1] Memorandum of 18 March 1919, quoted in Blanche E. Dugdale, *Arthur James Balfour* (London, Hutchinson 1936), p. 204.

importance of those prophesyings', he took refuge in the belief that if Germany revived her ambitions, she would look to the East and not to the West. He went on to express the Anglo-Saxon belief that future European security lay not in calculations and adjustments of power, as the French believed, but in a change of heart, not least on the part of Germany:

> If Germany is going again to be a great armed camp, filled with a population about twice as great as that of any other state in Europe; and if she is going again to pursue a policy of world domination, it will no doubt tax all the statesmanship of the world to prevent a repetition of the calamities from which we have been suffering. But the only radical cure for this is a change in the international system of the world – a change which French statesmen are doing nothing to promote, and the very possibility of which many of them regard with ill-concealed derision.[1]

Balfour admitted that the French might indeed be right, but if they were, 'it is quite certain that no manipulation of the Rhine frontier is going to make France anything more than a second-rate power, trembling at the nod of its great neighbour in the East, and depending from day to day on the changes and chances of a shifting diplomacy and uncertain alliances'.[2]

It was a gloomy diagnosis, suggesting that, short of the vouchsafing of a miracle by way of human moral regeneration, the Allied victory, though achieved at such a cost, was worth little.

The British and American delegations therefore placed their main hope for the future in a peace of reconciliation between victors and vanquished, and in the removal of tensions between the other peoples of Europe by permitting each ethnic group to govern itself in its own national state – so-called 'self-determination'. Woodrow Wilson in particular also reposed a fanatical faith in the ability of a League of Nations to substitute reasoned and peaceful co-operation for rivalry and war. Universal disarmament was eventually to complete this notable reversal of the pattern of European history.

At the same time however the Anglo-Saxon muddied this ideal scheme with other considerations. The English, whom Germany had badly frightened during the war, especially by the near victory of the U-boat, were less gone in idealism than Woodrow Wilson. They demanded – and achieved – the destruction of German seapower and the German overseas empire. They saw that German national power needed to be reduced to some extent by cession of territory and population, although they shrank

[1] Ibid. pp. 205–6.

[2] Ibid.

from the drastic surgery desired by the French. And, by a pleasing irony, their own doctrinaire moralism itself compromised their attempt at a peace of reconciliation, by transforming a traditional war for the balance of power into a crusade against evil.[1] When Right eventually triumphed it necessarily followed that Wrong must be condemned and punished. Most moralising internationalists believed this in 1918 and 1919.[2] Thus a cool and businesslike settlement of Europe's affairs, such as was achieved at the Congress of Vienna, was rendered impossible by the heat of Anglo-Saxon moral indignation. Germany was seen not simply as a defeated country like France in 1713 or 1815, to pay the customary material penalties of being defeated; but a criminal to stand in the dock to receive the judgement of the victors. The Treaty of Versailles loaded Germany and her pre-war leaders with full responsibility – 'guilt' – for the Great War. Wilhelm II, the former German emperor, was arraigned 'for a supreme offence against international morality and the sanctity of treaties',[3] although war was in 1914 a perfectly legal resort of policy. Reparations too were made into a moral issue as well as a question of finance or relative national power, and Article 231 of the treaty stated:

> The Allied and Associated Governments affirm, and Germany accepts, the responsibility of Germany and her allies for causing all the loss and damage to which the Allied and Associated Governments and their nationals have been subjected as a consequence of the war imposed upon them by the aggression of Germany and her allies.[4]

This was what later became known as 'the war-guilt' clause, a useful tool in the skilled hands of German nationalist agitators. Yet even before the Armistice of 1918 moral indignation and doctrinaire liberalism, in the person of Woodrow Wilson, had exercised its perhaps most damaging effect on the post-war settlement. When Germany made preliminary enquiries about the terms upon which the Allies would grant an armistice, Wilson made it plain that the essential requisite was that Germany should first have jettisoned the Hohenzollern monarchy. So Wilhelm II abdicated under duress and fled to Holland; down in turn fell the other German monarchies and princes; and German life, intensely monarchical as it was by sentiment and political tradition, was left a formless, centreless void. The Allies had destroyed the institution which alone enjoyed the prestige and stability to cover and cushion the fact of

[1] See above pp. 56–8.
[2] See R. B. McCallum, *Public Opinion and the Last Peace* (London, Oxford University Press 1944), chs. I and II.
[3] Cmd. 153, Article 227.
[4] Ibid. Article 231.

Germany's defeat,[1] and instead called into being a régime repugnant to the deepest German feelings and loyalties; a régime which, further, was forced to sign its acceptance of the 'guilt' of its predecessors. To this fragile vessel, overloaded with the bitterness of defeat and the shame of 'war-guilt', the British and Americans confided their hopes of a parliamentary and democratic Germany devoted to European peace and reconciliation.

The general influence both of Anglo-Saxon doctrinaire moralism and of romantic idealism on the peace settlement was therefore immense and calamitous. Paradoxical in themselves so far as the treatment of Germany was concerned, they were married uneasily in British policy to a residual strategic realism. The British therefore acted appropriately enough as agents of compromise between the French, who thought only of Germany's potential power, and Woodrow Wilson, who thought much of righteousness and the brotherhood of man. The French, outnumbered, conscious of their dependence on British and American friendship, were forced to accede to the dilution of their original demands in the name of 'justice' towards Germany. Instead of a separate Rhineland buffer-state under permanent French military protection there was only to be a demilitarised zone,[2] to be garrisoned by Allied troops until 1935. France had to rest content instead with a guarantee by Britain and America that they would spring to her aid if Germany attacked her again. When Foch protested that the security provided by this guarantee was less reliable than that of a Rhineland buffer-state, Clemenceau told him to mind his soldier's business and leave statesmanship to statesmen. Unfortunately Foch was to be proved right: the American Senate later disavowed Woodrow Wilson's guarantee, and the British guarantee, being conditional on the American, lapsed also. France had to sustain yet a further major setback in the peace conference. Instead of the outright cession to her of the Saar, she was only to receive the coal mines themselves, while the region was to be administered by the League of Nations until 1935, when a plebiscite would be taken as to the inhabitants' wishes for their political future. Otherwise in the west, Germany gave back the Alsace-Lorraine territory to France, who had originally ceded it in 1871, after the Franco-Prussian War, and suffered only very small losses of territory and population to Belgium and Denmark.

It was in the east that her losses and resentments were greatest. The province of Posen and (after a plebiscite in 1921) part of Upper Silesia were taken from Germany and given to the new state of Poland. The

[1] In 1945 the then American President did not make the same error over Japan and the Japanese Emperor.

[2] See above p. 249.

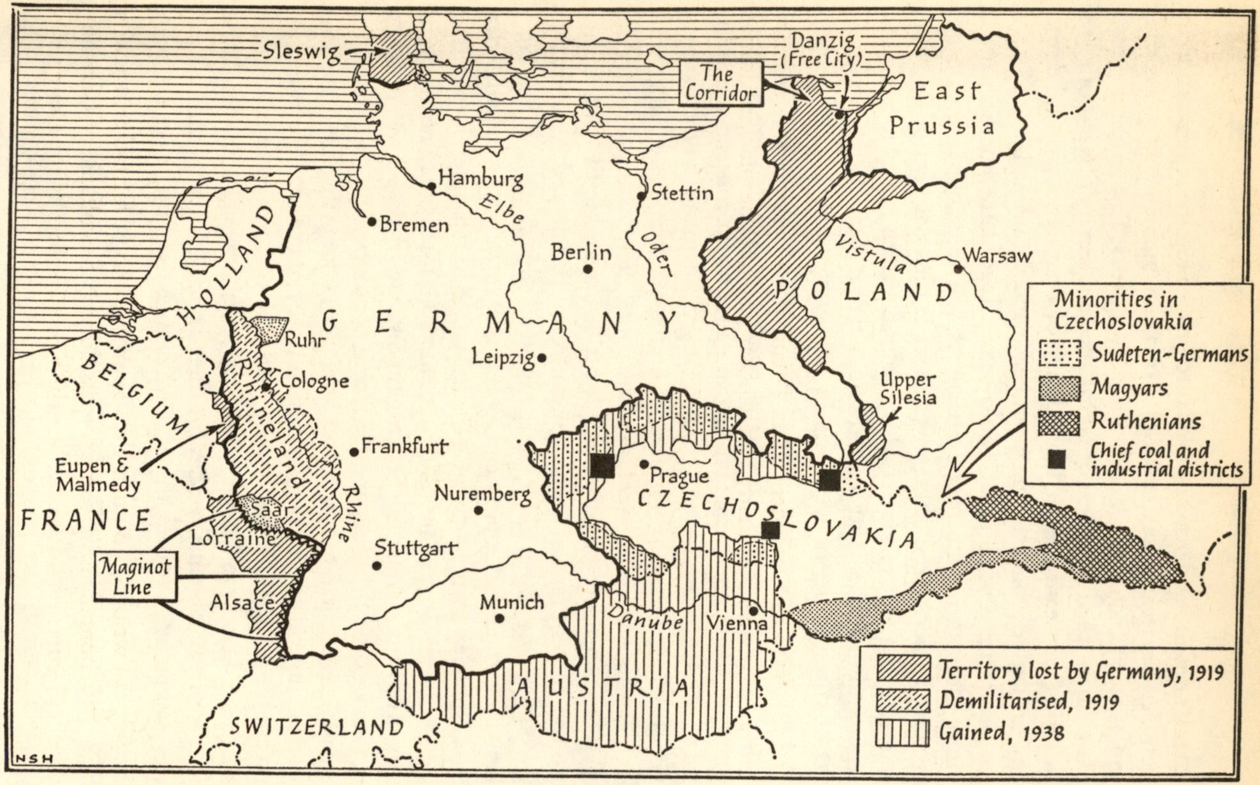


Central Europe between the World Wars.

so-called 'Polish corridor' was driven to the Baltic between East and West Prussia in order to provide the Poles with access to the sea. Memel went to another new state, Lithuania, while the great port of Danzig became a free city under League of Nations rule. This eastern settlement, not only in regard to Germany and Poland, but also Czechoslovakia (another new state) and Hungary, had caused the peace-makers much tedious and well-intentioned effort. The intermixture of different races was such as to render the task of delineating tidy nation-state frontiers, as required by the doctrine of self-determination, about as easy as Shylock's in cutting flesh while leaving the blood behind. Of the new creations, the states of Poland and Czechoslovakia offered the greatest potential dangers, as was well recognised at the time. Balfour had pointed out as early as November 1916 that an independent Poland could serve only as a theatre of intrigue between Germany and Russia, just like the old kingdom of Poland in the eighteenth century. He doubted whether Poland could be strong enough to act as an effective buffer-state; and concluded that '. . . its existence, so far from promoting the cause of European peace, would be an occasion of European strife'.[1] He had suggested at that time that Poland should receive home rule within the Russian Empire; a solution vitiated by the Russian revolution in 1917, but revived by Stalin after the Second World War. Balfour even at this early date also had his doubts about an independent Bohemia, for he wrote that whether she 'could hold her own, from a military as well as from a commercial point of view, against Teutonic domination – surrounded as she is at present by entirely German influences – I do not know . . .'[2]

Smuts, a no less influential voice within the British Empire delegation to the Paris Peace Conference, argued that 'the fact is, neither Poland nor Bohemia will be politically possible without German goodwill and assistance . . .'[3]

However, the dangers and anomalies of the post-war settlement of eastern and central Europe are not mainly to be laid at the door of Wilsonian idealism. By 1919, the Allied powers in Paris had become militarily too weak to do other than approve, except for tinkering, what had already spontaneously come to pass during the collapse of Germany, Austria and imperial Russia. Unlike their predecessors at the Congress of Vienna, the Allied governments had no power to impose a workmanlike settlement on the whole of Europe; for being, again unlike their

[1] Dugdale, p. 325.
[2] Ibid. p. 324.
[3] Sir K. Hancock, *Smuts: Biography* (Cambridge, Cambridge University Press 1962), Vol. I, p. 511.

predecessors, at the mercy of the wishes of mass electorates, they had had to demobilise their forces at utmost speed.[1]

Nevertheless this new political pattern in eastern and central Europe completed the disastrous work of Anglo-Saxon moralism and idealism at the peace conference. For the combined effect was to leave Germany even less adequately balanced by countervailing power in 1919 than before 1914. In 1914 Germany had common frontiers in the east with two great powers, Russia and Austria, both of which had acted in the past, and could always act again, in restraint of German (or Prussian) ambition.[2] Now Austria had vanished as a great power. In her place there was the middling state of Czechoslovakia, with its large Sudeten minority of former Austrian citizens of German race, and the German-speaking rump of Austria itself, forbidden by the peace treaties to unite with Germany. Russia, for her part, was currently paralysed by revolution and civil war; but, should she ever revive, Poland would now lie between her and Germany. And Poland was a new state, of only 20 millions against Germany's 60 millions, while the Poles were a nation politically incompetent by long tradition. In the east therefore Germany now faced only states very much smaller and weaker than herself; states whose German minorities and former German territories offered her the liveliest possible incentive for renewed expansion in the future.

In the west, Germany was balanced by only France and Belgium, for between 1919 and 1922 Britain and the United States ducked out of the wartime alliance, leaving the League of Nations, the Treaty of Versailles and the spirit of reconciliation to keep the peace. By the mid-1920s Germany, with 62,539,098 of population and a steel production of 12,193,454 tons, faced only one rival at all capable of making head against her – France. And France's population numbered fewer than 40,000,000 (of whom a much smaller, and continually falling, proportion was of military age), and her steel production no more than 6,900,000 tons.[3]

The less-than-halfhearted attempts under the peace treaties to weaken Germany by territorial losses had therefore wholly failed in their object of reducing Germany's national power relative to other European states; on the contrary, she emerged from the Great War with this power much enhanced. It was an astonishing and hardly looked-for result.

Yet even before the draft treaty had been presented to the Germans it

[1] Cf. Balfour's comments on the impotence of the victors to the Supreme Allied War Council in July 1919 in Dugdale, p. 198, and also p. 208.

[2] Cf. Austria in the War of the Austrian Succession and the War of 1866; Russia in 1914; both together during the Seven Year's War.

[3] *Statesmen's Yearbook 1926*, pp. 919, 929, 844, 861.

was being argued inside the British Empire delegation that its provisions were too severe. It was Smuts who, as so often in the coming decades, acted as the beguiling voice of leniency: 'I am seriously afraid that the peace to which we are working is an impossible peace, conceived on the wrong basis; that it will not be accepted by Germany, and, even if it is accepted, that it will prove utterly unstable. . . .'[1]

Smuts then went on to deploy what was to become the classic case for appeasement during the 1920s and 1930s: 'To my mind certain points seem quite clear and elementary: 1. We cannot destroy Germany without destroying Europe; 2. We cannot save Europe without the co-operation of Germany. . . .'[2] He therefore arrived at the conclusion that 'the fact is, the Germans are, and will continue to be the *dominant* factor on the Continent of Europe, and no permanent peace is possible which is not based upon that fact'.[3]

Like Balfour in 1916, Smuts was really saying that the Allies should now accept the very supremacy of German power in Europe which they had gone to war to prevent. It was tantamount to acknowledging that the war effort of the Allies had achieved nothing but a change in régime in Germany and the demolition of the German armed forces. Yet liberals saw this as achievement enough, because, in their view, England had not been fighting to redress the balance of power against Germany but to destroy 'militarism'. Now that the Hohenzollerns had departed, there was to liberal thought nothing alarming therefore in a European state nearly twice as powerful as its biggest neighbour.

Smuts, however, having been himself defeated in war and also the delegate of a defeated nation at a peace conference, was moved by a poignant fellow-feeling for the Germans. So too was Botha, the South African Prime Minister. And to the Boer leaders, British magnanimity towards them after the Boer War provided exactly the right guide as to how Germany should be now treated. Since liberals of all parties in Britain also believed that the South African peace settlement had been a master-stroke of policy, Smuts was able cunningly to exploit this curious article of faith in working on Lloyd George: 'My experience in South Africa has made me a firm believer in political magnanimity, and your and Campbell-Bannerman's great record still remains not only the noblest but also the *most successful* page in recent British statesmanship. . . .'[4]

Smuts saw no danger in a peace which failed to reduce Germany's national power, for in his opinion, 'her complete economic exhaustion

[1] Letter of 26 March 1919 to Lloyd George, quoted in Sir K. Hancock, Vol. I, pp. 510–11.
[2] Ibid. [3] Ibid. [4] Ibid. p. 512.

and disarmament would prevent her from becoming a military or naval danger in this generation, and her appeasement now may have the effect of turning her into a bulwark against the on-coming Bolshevism of Eastern Europe. . . .'[1]

These too were early expressions of British beliefs which were to enjoy a long and vigorous life.

Thus over Germany in 1919, as over Ireland in 1921, Smuts and the baneful precedent of the British settlement with the Boers operated together on British minds; and 'appeasement' began even before the Germans were presented with the draft treaty, when Lloyd George endeavoured to soften some of its terms in the unrealistic hope that Germany might then accept the treaty as equitable, and harbour no resentments in the future. It was owing to Lloyd George's efforts that Danzig became a free city and that the future nationality of Upper Silesia was to be decided by plebiscite instead of both passing forthwith under Polish rule.

The critical weakness of the Versailles Treaty consequently lay in its failure to deal with the problem of German national power. The British were instrumental in this failure. It was they who held the balance between the Americans and the French. They and the French together had the strength, in the Royal Navy and the French army, to enforce a settlement on Germany. If the British had been so minded, Germany could have been divided and permanently weakened in the very springs of power, as the French so desperately wanted. Yet instead they succumbed to the threats exerted by President Wilson; threats to outbuild the Royal Navy, to cut off American aid, and to appeal to European public opinon over the heads of governments. In any case, the British themselves had fallen into a confusion between realism (over such matters as the German fleet and colonial empire) and idealism; between weakening Germany and at the same time attempting to win her future co-operation and goodwill. It was an attitude paralleled by the final peace treaty itself, which penalised Germany materially and morally just enough to sting her into an abiding desire to demolish its provisions when time should serve, while at the same time leaving her stronger, relatively, than ever. It was an unhappy combination.

The military clauses of the treaty – the disarmament of Germany, the demilitarisation and occupation of the Rhineland – had to make do in place of the destruction of Bismarck's united Germany, and render it impossible for Germany to transform her overwhelming strength in people and industry into the equivalent in military might. These clauses suffered

[1] Letter of 26 March 1919 to Lloyd George, quoted in Sir K. Hancock, Vol. I, p. 512.

however from a serious and dangerous drawback; they would not enforce themselves. On the contrary, the ability of the treaty to restrain German power in the future depended entirely on the readiness of the victors to enforce it to the letter. Here was the difference between weakening a beast and chaining it down. And should the will-power of the victors ever falter, should their military capabilities ever weaken, the chains of Versailles would become no more than mere chains of parchment.

As a consequence the French could never relax; they must stand rigidly on every clause of the treaty. They must maintain perpetual vigilance over Germany. For their whole security depended precariously on opposing to Germany's *potential* military superiority their own superiority in forces *in being*.

By failing to solve the problem of German power, the peace settlement of 1919 hence bequeathed to Europe two tragic and inter-related consequences: an enduring French fear of Germany, and an enduring German determination to wipe away as soon as possible the effects of a defeat suffered at the hand of a purely transient combination of enemies.

For the English too this failure of the peace settlement carried heavy implications; implications which, however, they did not perceive. The equilibrium of European power had not been restored; England had failed in her main purpose in taking part in the Great War. The conclusion of the war could not therefore mark the end of the struggle with Germany, but – as in the case of the wars with France in the eighteenth century – only of a violent episode in a continuing effort, diplomatic, economic and strategic. In this effort, of which the key factor must be the enforcement to the letter of the treaty, Germany could only be balanced, as it had been in the war itself, by an alliance of England and France. Yet in fact the wartime alliance, already cracking apart at the peace conference, had wholly disintegrated by 1923, replaced by ill-concealed mutual hostility between France and England. While incidental friction over passing problems of the day and personal antipathies between particular French and British statesmen were partly responsible for this, the principal reason lay in their opposite post-war policies towards Germany; policies founded on no less opposite diagnoses.

The French, for their part, recognised that the Great War had ended in no more than a partial and precarious advantage to them. Since America and England had reneged on their military guarantees, the French felt themselves to be left almost alone as a defender of the peace settlement – and because alone, afraid. These apprehensions were well known in England. In January 1920 Austen Chamberlain noted that the French 'live in nightmare terror of Germany ...'[1] In addressing the 1921 Imperial Conference, Curzon referred to the appalling damage and loss sustained by France in the war and her fear of a German revival.[2] In 1925 Chamberlain, then Foreign Secretary, heard Edouard Herriot say: 'I tell you I look forward with terror to her [Germany] making war upon us again in ten years.'[3]

In 1932 Lloyd George had to acknowledge that France's continuing, and indeed by then sharpening, anxieties had some justification:

> Stripped of some of its richest provinces, Germany still has a population 50 per cent above that of France. The German is industrious, intelligent and resourceful, and although he is poor today such qualities soon make riches. He will therefore, so Frenchmen realise, once more become a formidable menace. The Teuton is on French nerves. This accounts for the anxiety to keep him chained by Treaties, impoverished by levies, and overawed by armaments.[4]

As a consequence, French policy towards Germany in the 1920s was squarely based on strategy. But, the English had no sympathy with such an approach, as Balfour argued to the Committee of Imperial Defence in February 1925: 'I do not think it is good policy to do what the French always do, that is, to assume that there must be a Great War, and then set to work to deal with the situation from the point of view of their General Staff. I think that it is absolute lunacy.'[5]

For after 1919 the English less and less thought of Germany in terms of suspicion and power rivalry. Instead they were enchanted with the prospect of reconciliation. As Churchill put it to the Imperial Conference of 1921, he was anxious 'to see friendship grow up and the hatred of war die between Britain and Germany'.[6] This wish for reconciliation swiftly grew as the short English memory forgot how narrow had been the margin between victory and defeat. In October 1923, in a speech of immense impact which was enthusiastically welcomed by British newspapers and by weekly and religious journals, Smuts preached in public his old sermon about the beneficent effects of British magnanimity towards the Boers:

> The Boers were not treated as moral pariahs and outcasts. Decent human relationships were re-established and a spirit of mutual under-

[1] Petrie, Vol. II, p. 155. [2] CAB 32/2, Pt. I, E-4. [3] Petrie, Vol. II, p. 263.
[4] David Lloyd George, *The Truth About Reparations and War Debts* (London, Heinemann 1932), p. 68. [5] CAB 2/4, 196. [6] CAB 32/2, Pt. I, E-4.

standing grew up. . . . South Africa today is perhaps the most outstanding witness in the realm of politics to the value of a policy of give and take, of moderation and generosity, of trust and friendship, applied to the affairs of men. . . . Human nature is the same in all continents, and what could have been done for the descendants in Africa can surely also be done for the parent peoples in Europe.[1]

It would have been impossible better to give expression to the sentiments which now prevailed in England. In five years the mood of the English had completely changed. The violent, even hysterical, hatred of Germany during the war, and the moral zeal for her punishment in 1918–19, had given way to pity for poor Germany in her plight of defeat and ruin, oppressed as she also was by the hard-hearted French. For Dickensian sentimentality towards the underdog now benefited Germany instead of France and Belgium.

There were more specific reasons for the English refusal to join with France in a perpetual anti-German combination. It was believed that the restoration of British trade, now much debilitated in the slump which had followed the post-war boom of 1918–20, depended on Germany's own recovery.[2] It was believed that British interests as a whole, political as well as economic, depended on Europe settling down with a strong Germany at its centre, as Lord Curzon explained to the 1921 Imperial Conference:

. . . our policy is frankly the re-establishment of Germany as a stable state in Europe. She is necessary with her great population, her natural resources, with her prodigious strengths of character . . .; and any idea of obliterating Germany from the comity of nations or treating her as an outcast is not only ridiculous but insane.[3]

As early therefore as this, British policy was influenced by a desire for German goodwill; for it was the risk of forfeiting this valuable asset which, in Curzon's view, stood in the way of renewing the lapsed military guarantee to France against German attack. To renew it 'might be regarded as an affront by her [Germany] at a moment when I believe that she is conscientiously and sincerely doing her best to carry out the terms of the Ultimatum [on the payment of reparations] recently agreed upon'.[4]

In paying this handsome tribute to German conscientiousness and sincerity, Curzon touched yet another divergence between the English

[1] Sir K. Hancock, Vol. II, p. 135.

[2] Cf. Curzon's speech to the 1921 Imperial Conference, CAB 32/2, Pt. I, E-4; see also Baldwin's view in 1923 in Middlemass and Barnes, p. 180.

[3] Ibid.

[4] Ibid. E-18.

and the French views of the German question; for whereas the French credited the Germans with every possible duplicity, the English reposed a gentlemanly trust in the new German régime.

The French drew no comfort from the existence of the Weimar Republic, with its beautiful constitution and its top-hatted presidents. They noted, rather, the continuing force of nationalism and militarism, the private armies that marched and fought in German streets, the assassination of democratic politicians; they noted that German industry lay still firmly in the hands of the great industrialists who had backed Germany's pre-war policies of expansion; that *Junkers* still dominated the army. The French were certain from reports by their intelligence sources that from the very moment the peace treaty was signed, its provisions for disarming Germany and forbidding her to design and manufacture tanks, heavy guns and military aircraft had been deliberately and systematically evaded; an evasion which was continued throughout the 1920s.

In Britain, however, the Weimar Republic was widely taken at its face value as a splendidly successful new achievement of liberalism. With a characteristically naïve optimism the British believed that Germans had renounced their history, and that as a consequence the new Germany merited the trust of Europe. At the same time the British governing classes convinced themselves that in any case Germany could no longer present any kind of strategic danger because of her disarmament under the Versailles Treaty.

It was unfortunate that the British Ambassador to Berlin from 1920 to 1925, far from disabusing his government at home of such innocence, fully shared in it, and devoted his official career to fostering it. In September 1921 Lord D'Abernon was writing that the success of the Allied disarmament commission meant that there would be no military danger from Germany for many years; and that it would be impossible for Germany to conceal the manufacture of heavy weapons.[1] In February 1922 he failed to see what advantage England could derive from a formal military alliance with France.

> The fundamental criticism ... is that England undertakes definite and very extensive responsibilities in order to avoid a danger which she believes to be largely imaginary. An armed attack by Germany on France within the next twenty-five years is admittedly improbable, an attack by Germany on England in the same period even more so. . . .[2]

[1] Viscount D'Abernon, *An Ambassador of Peace* (London, Hodder and Stoughton 1929), Vol. I, p. 14.
[2] Ibid. p. 259.

D'Abernon complained that 'the whole tone of the French is to assume that the real danger to the future peace of Europe is military aggression by Germany'.[1] Did this, he asked, square with the facts or make for future peace? He argued that there were two possible attitudes to Germany, and which could not be combined in one policy: either she was 'a danger [to be] held in check by military conventions and overwhelming force, or . . . an ex-enemy whom it was desirable to treat with fairness and generosity in order to strengthen the elements of peace and reconciliation within her borders. . . .'[2]

From 1923 to 1925 D'Abernon continued to assure himself and others that Germany had ceased to be a military danger.[3] Yet such belief in Germany's faithful compliance with the disarmament provisions of the Versailles Treaty, a belief upon which successive British governments rested their European policy, was the result not of mere ignorance, but of a positive effort of will. For the members of the Inter-allied Commission of Control in Germany sent back to their governments constant reports of German evasions and of Germany's concealed military strength; reports quietly muffled because of their untimely and untactful nature.[4] In 1924 Brigadier-General J. H. Morgan, then Deputy-Adjutant to the Inter-allied Commission of Control, was tasteless enough to sound the discordant note of suspicion of Germany in public; and to repeat his warning later in the same year: '. . . the least idealist nation in the world, and the most realist, watches, waits, plans, and despite all her dynastic catastrophes and changes of political form, remains after the war more identical with what she was before it than any nation in Europe'.[5]

Unfortunately for Morgan, it was the year of Ramsay MacDonald's courting of Gustav Stresemann, the new German Foreign Minister, which led to an agreement between victors and vanquished over reparations and to a vast deal of high-minded speechmaking; and British opinion was not in the listening mood for sombre warnings. Next year the Imperial General Staff itself attempted to awaken the (by now Conservative) Government to awareness that Germany was not quite as disarmed and reformed as she might seem; and drew down on themselves D'Abernon's ridicule.[6]

In 1928, two years after Germany had been welcomed into the League

[1] Ibid. p. 260. [2] Ibid.
[3] Ibid. pp. 167–8 and Vol. III, pp. 120–1, 158–9.
[4] Vansittart, pp. 276, 341.
[5] Quoted in Arthur C. Murray (Lord Murray of Elibank), *Reflections on Some Aspects of British Foreign Policy Between the World Wars* (Edinburgh, Oliver and Boyd 1946), p. 10.
[6] D'Abernon, Vol. III, pp. 120–1.

of Nations, the Committee of Imperial Defence discussed a memorandum by the Chief of the Imperial General Staff on the military situation in Germany, in which he estimated the German army's total strength, including reserves, at 2,000,000 men, instead of the 100,000 allowed under the treaty; and in which he also pointed out the large sums Germany was spending on arms and equipment.[1]

Resolved therefore to believe that Germany was now not only reformed but in any case powerless to make trouble, the British pursued their policy of reconciliation. Appeasement, set in motion even at the peace conference, continued to be the theme of English policy towards Germany; appeasement in the sense of soothing and conciliating as well as of bringing peace. By 1920, what was to be the enduring relationship between England and Germany between the world wars had been established: England, though the victor, the suitor of the vanquished; Germany, although defeated, in the dominating position of the courted. And the more touchy and standoffish Germany became, the more anxiously solicitous a wooer was England. It was an absurd reversal of what ought to have been. It yielded the initiative to Germany, enabling her to fight diplomatically from the strongest of positions, strategically offensive, tactically defensive. This initiative was ruthlessly and successfully exploited by German governments from 1920 through to 1938.

Lord D'Abernon, as ambassador to Berlin, was a particularly influential and effective proponent of this policy of courting Germany. In November 1925 he summed up what he had constantly urged during his five years in Berlin: 'One cannot repeat too often that the German view is largely what Allied action makes it; recognise goodwill, show appreciation of German action, and you have a different Germany from that produced by unjustified suspicion and unrestrained criticism.'[2]

Yet it is hard to understand how D'Abernon could come to such an opinion, for it was belied by the very judgements of the German mind and character which he himself recorded during his ambassadorship. In July 1922, for example, he wrote:

> I was impressed, as I frequently am impressed when talking to Germans, of the immense difference between our estimate of the breadth and generosity of our policy and their estimate of it . . . it always surprises me how slow they are to recognise – or to acknowledge in words – the extent of the assistance we believe we have given.[3]

[1] CAB 2/5, 239. Meeting on 13 December 1928.
[2] D'Abernon, Vol. III, p. 203.
[3] Ibid. Vol. II, p. 58.

D'Abernon indeed recognised that the German mind was generally unlike the English, lacking as it did, in his view, idealism; holding a more materialistic conception of society than either the French mind or the English; and more highly prizing success, and material success at that.[1] Nor ought he to have been under the illusion that Germans had really undergone a change of heart as a result of war and defeat, because he himself recorded his own belief that they were not in his words, 'morally disarmed': 'No one that I have met here [he wrote in May 1922] would think a successful war morally reprehensible; nor would anyone advocate a war likely to prove unsuccessful, on the ground that it was morally defensible.'[2]

D'Abernon, in a key official position, offered therefore a particularly fine specimen of the romantic British ability to hold fast to beliefs and policies that ran directly contrary to observed fact; an ability which characterised British policy towards Germany between the world wars.

While the British were resolutely viewing an ex-enemy with benevolence and charity, their attitude to their old ally and friend, France, grew colder.[3] Towards her they adopted an exactly opposite kind of irrationality; darkly suspecting her aims and actions; seeing her as an ogre of militarism and power; ignoring or dismissing in a passing phrase the gigantic human and material losses she had suffered during the war, and which left her critically weakened. The post-evangelical English mind did not always seem to remember that whereas Christianity taught us to love our enemies, it did not at the same time require us to dislike and suspect our friends.

The *Entente Cordiale* between France and England, which since 1919 had been ever less founded on cordiality and understanding, finally collapsed, as a combination against Germany, in 1923. The French, under the premiership of Raymond Poincaré (who was by no means a romantic idealist) exasperated by what they took to be Germany's deliberate attempts to evade treaty obligations to pay reparations, proposed to occupy the Ruhr industrial region by way of applying torsion to the German arm. The English denounced such action as illegal and imprudent, and unavailingly did their best to dissuade Poincaré. As a consequence only the Belgians accompanied the French in their march into the Ruhr. The British suspected that the ulterior aims of French policy went well beyond the exaction of reparations. This was true. Germany, with her

[1] See numerous references in D'Abernon, but especially Vol. III, p. 245.
[2] Ibid. Vol. I, p. 279.
[3] See McCallum, ch. V; see also Gannon, pp. 12–14, for a survey of press hostility to France, a hostility shared by newspapers of the Right as much as of the Left.

principal industrial area in French hands and her economic life hobbled, began to disintegrate; pulled apart by communist and nationalist putsches, and by renewed separatist movements in Saxony and Bavaria. The feeble parliamentary central government was dependent for survival on the sanction and bayonets of the Reichswehr. The French saw here their opportunity to achieve that division of Germany of which they had been balked by the British and Americans at the peace conference; and they encouraged a further separatist movement in the Rhineland.

Far from applauding these purposes, which might well have destroyed that German dominance of size which Bismark had bequeathed to Europe, the British Government and British opinion in general deplored them. Warren Fisher, then Head of the Civil Service, for example, believed that for the British to acquiesce in French actions would involve 'the most cynical disregard of the Treaty as interpreted by our highest legal authorities', treating it 'as a scrap of paper'.[1] There was a fear that France – France with her 1,500,000 dead and her eleven devastated departments which had been reconstructed only at colossal cost to herself – might regain the European predominance she had enjoyed in the days of Richelieu, Louis XIV and Napoleon. Germany, on the other hand, the British saw not as much in terms of power, but as a potential market for Britain's ruined export industries. It followed that their first interest was to restore German prosperity. In any case it was only from a single and prosperous German state that in their view, there was hope of getting reparations. So, as Curzon informed the 1923 Imperial Conference, 'our attitude can only be the attitude of saying that anything done to disrupt the German Reich or the German state meets with our emphatic disapproval'.[2] He drew a distinction between spontaneous separatist movements, such as had arisen in Bavaria, and the artificial régime set up in the Rhineland under French auspices;[3] but the distinction was academic for he despatched a telegram to Paris, Brussels and Rome elaborating on 'the grave consequences' that would follow the setting-up of independent sovereign states out of territories in present-day Germany. The telegram also pointed out that it would be inconsistent with obligations under the peace treaty and with the signatories' own interests to recognise such independent states; and the attempt to create them should not receive countenance.[4]

Yet while the British Government was so sedulously preserving the unity of the German state, Curzon could say to the Imperial Conference –

[1] Quoted in Middlemass and Barnes, p. 184.
[2] CAB 32/9, E-13.
[3] Ibid.
[4] CAB 32/9, E-14.

though only briefly in passing – that Germany 'is out for revenge and to rebuild herself'.[1]

France, led by the stubborn Poincaré, eventually succeeded in her purpose of taking out of the Ruhr the reparations the Germans had been unwilling to make; on the other hand, and partly owing to British diplomatic opposition, the separatist movements failed. Germany survived politically intact, her hapless parliamentary régime preserved from its communist and nationalist enemies only by the intervention of the Reichswehr under its *Junker* leadership. And the French people themselves ceased to share Poincaré's readiness to act strongly and if necessary alone. In 1924 France too, under a new left-wing government, took the road of reconciliation with Germany, her hand held by Ramsay MacDonald, now Prime Minister in the first Labour administration; and with the aid of General Dawes, an American financier, a new plan for reparations was agreed between Germany and the victors.

This *démarche* was welcomed in Great Britain as an auspicious beginning to the fulfilment of long-standing British desires and efforts. In fact the course of the Ruhr crisis marked a major shift of power from the victors towards Germany. In the first place it demonstrated to Europe, and in particular to Germany, that England was no longer at France's side; that the wartime *entente* no longer existed as a counter-balance. In the second place France had failed to make successful use of her present military superiority finally to destroy Germany's capacity to revive in the future as a super-power. The result was a decisive French moral defeat; never again was France to hold the upper hand over Germany which she had enjoyed from 1918 to 1923. As Sir Denis Brogan writes: 'Germany was still open to French invasion, but the will to invade was dead.'[2] Henceforward that military strength with which France could alone offset the potentially overwhelming superiority of German national power, relapsed into a posture of defensiveness and passivity, of which the plan, drawn up in 1928 and approved in 1930, of building an elaborate system of fortifications along the frontier with Germany was the ultimate expression.

This defensiveness was dangerously inconsistent with French grand strategy as a whole. For, deprived by circumstances of her great pre-war ally, Russia; deprived too of British and American military guarantees; deprived even of the diplomatic support of Britain, France had sought to make good her weakness by creating a new alliance in eastern Europe. The so-called *Little Entente* consisted of the middling or small states of

[1] CAB 32/9, E-13.
[2] Sir Denis Brogan, *The Development of Modern France* (London, Hamish Hamilton 1967), p. 580.

Poland, Czechoslovakia, Romania and Yugoslavia, two of which were neighbours of Germany. Although the French motive in creating the *Little Entente* was understandable enough, France had nevertheless made the same mistake over her weak new allies as Britain made over her Indian and dominion 'allies', the mistake of believing that they increased her strength, whereas in fact they weakened her by burdening her with the obligation to protect them. And the only way France could possibly protect Poland or Czechoslovakia against German aggression was by the indirect means of repeating her Ruhr invasion. This was an offensive strategy, requiring a mobile, ever-ready army. Instead the French Government and people had accepted the defensive; and the French general staff was designing a mass-army, apt for such a defensive, but unable to fight until after a long delay for general mobilisation. The French system of alliances therefore rested on strategic nonsense.[1]

The course of the Ruhr crisis and its aftermath, in which the English had so great a hand, thus marked a fateful change in the anatomy of power in Europe. It went unnoticed by English statesmen, who in 1924 were concerned with reconciling France and Germany and with perfecting the new world order at Geneva. By the proposed 'Geneva Protocol'[2] all members of the League of Nations were to agree to submit to arbitration disputes which had proved insoluble by negotiation, instead of resorting to war. At the same time they were to bind themselves to offer 'loyal and effective co-operation' in aiding the victim of an aggressor.[3] The Labour Government thought well of this document, believing that it ought to satisfy the French craving for security, although the Chiefs of Staff of the British armed forces and the Foreign Office denounced it as adding indefinitely to British dangers and responsiblities.[4] The succeeding Conservative administration refused however to go on with the Geneva Protocol, which came to nothing, much to the regret, then and later, of internationalists.

The problem of France and Germany remained to be solved. For until France ceased to keep watch on the Rhine in fear and suspicion, Europe could not achieve that state of 'peace' for which British opinion so yearned. The new English Foreign Secretary, Austen Chamberlain, at once loved France and sympathised with her, while also suspecting and disliking Germany; an attitude now out of fashion not only in England at large, but in the Cabinet, although Baldwin, the Prime Minister, was

[1] See General André Beaufre, *1940 The Fall of France* (London, Cassell 1967), pp. 39–40.
[2] 'Protocol for the Pacific Settlement of International Disputes.'
[3] Walters, Vol. I, pp. 272–4.
[4] CAB 2/4, 190, CID Meeting on 4 December 1924.

himself tepidly Francophile.[1] Chamberlain proposed that the old project should be revived of a formal Anglo-French alliance.

This did not mean that he wished to re-create the alignment of the Great War, with England and France balanced against Germany; or that he at all conceived of foreign policy in terms of equilibriums of power, and its execution in terms of winning advantages for England. Austen Chamberlain was in the judgement of his biographer, a 'practical idealist';[2] in that of Anthony Eden, 'warm-hearted, considerate and generous ... incapable of a mean action and conscientious to a fault'.[3] Chamberlain, the son of a famous father, was born in 1863 and brought up as a Unitarian. 'Scratch me', he wrote in 1927, 'and you will find the Nonconformist. . . .'[4] He was educated in classics at Rugby (entering in 1878), and at Trinity, Cambridge (going up in 1882), a product therefore of high Victorian education; and he began his political career as a Liberal. Coldly handsome, distinguished by eyeglass and orchid, he was an image of Edwardian formal elegance and courtesy. His looks did not belie his character; there was little here of shrewdness, nothing of pugnacity; none of his father's dynamism; rather, a fear of being thought pushful.[5] 'It was cruelly said of Austen Chamberlain', wrote Harold Macmillan, 'that he always played the game and always lost it. But that is really a tribute to his deep sense of honour and loyalty.'[6]

Chamberlain's European policy, like Curzon's, like MacDonald's, was to restore and perfect the supposed 'Concert of Europe' of the mid-Victorian age. It was not therefore reasons of grand strategy which impelled Chamberlain to make his proposal for a formal Anglo-French alliance, but the wish to soothe French fears of Germany so that general relaxation might then be achieved. Nevertheless the proposal stirred violent opposition from his Cabinet colleagues, for the tide of British isolationism was now running at full flood. Balfour, with all his prestige, was against a French alliance; so too were Birkenhead, Curzon and Churchill. At the end of February 1925 Churchill circulated one of his vehement papers to the Cabinet, arguing against accepting any Continental commitment over which England would have no control in the event – the old Liberal stance of 1906–14. He questioned whether England and France represented a convincing counter-balance to a re-armed Germany. In any case, it was Churchill's belief – as of many – that Germany's ambition in the future would be towards the East, which

[1] Middlemass and Barnes, p. 181.
[2] Petrie, Vol. II, p. 246.
[3] Avon, Vol. I, p. 7.
[4] Petrie, Vol. II, p. 321.
[5] See Amery's judgement in Amery, *My Political Life* (London, Hutchinson 1953), Vol. I, p. 386.
[6] Macmillan, p. 174.

apparently seemed to him quite acceptable. He questioned whether England wished to bind herself to the course of preventive war against Germany. He declined 'to accept it as an axiom that our fate was involved in that of France'. He argued on the contrary that England's role was to prevent a future war and to retain her freedom of action; not to commit herself to France, whose ambitions might then become overwhelming. Since England now lacked military power, England must stand aloof until France and Germany had settled their disputes; 'when France has made her real peace with Germany, Britain will seal the bond with all her strength'.[1]

Thus even Churchill of all people, strategist, war leader and historian, brushed aside the traditional wisdom of the balance of power, and turned his back on the course of English history, with its repetitive involvements in European conflicts; the inescapable nature of which the Great War offered a recent proof. But he was only expressing with Churchillian power convictions now common to almost all sections of British opinion; convictions again springing – though not in Churchill's own case – from that deep distaste for taking sides and choosing friends and enemies which equally inspired British policy in the Far East and towards the empire. Chamberlain's proposal therefore seemed likely to end in nothing but his own resignation.[2]

It was Stresemann, the German Foreign Secretary, who put forward an alternative which offered the English the role they so much preferred, that of being friends with both sides. Stresemann suggested that England should not only guarantee the French frontier against German aggression but also the German frontier against French aggression. D'Abernon acted as man-midwife to this German proposal, and proceeded assiduously to nurse it.

The new proposal still ran counter to the powerful current of British isolationism. In the Cabinet almost all agreed with Birkenhead when he said that while in the event England would again fight for France and Belgium, neither public opinion nor the dominions would sanction a formal commitment to do so.[3] With negotiations deadlocked, Sir Eyre Crowe warned that a complete rupture with France was possible.[4] There were fears that the French, deprived of assurance of their security, would decide to hold on to the Rhineland after the date specified by the Versailles Treaty for its evacuation by allied forces; there was talk of an ultimatum to the French to the effect that Britain would withdraw her own military contingent.[5]

[1] The Baldwin Papers, quoted in Middlemass and Barnes, p. 349.
[2] Middlemass and Barnes, pp. 349–50.
[3] Ibid. pp. 353–4. [4] Ibid. [5] Ibid. pp. 352–3.

It was Baldwin, working in his emollient way behind the scenes, who resolved the crisis. On 20 March 1925 the Cabinet, after prolonged discussions, authorised Chamberlain to state in Parliament that the German Government's proposals offered the best basis for European security; that they could not be carried out without British co-operation; and that this co-operation would be limited to the western frontiers of Germany.[1] No one, certainly not Austen Chamberlain, would consider involving England in the preservation of the unstable new frontiers between Germany and her eastern neighbours. As Chamberlain wrote to Crowe on 16 February 1925, Great Britain was not to be called upon to defend the Polish Corridor, 'for which no British Government ever will and ever can risk the bones of a British grenadier'.[2] The French, on the other hand, not least because of their alliances, believed that a new treaty ought not to ignore eastern Europe; that a conflict in the east could not fail eventually to draw in the western powers, as in 1914. But on 16 June they at last gave way and accepted the British (or German) proposals. In October the European great powers, including Italy, met in conference in Locarno, the southern Swiss lakeside resort, all pastel villas, Mediterranean flora and benign autumnal sunshine; a highly suitable venue for a collective act of escapism.

For such the group of treaties known under the generic title of the Treaty of Locarno proved to be.

As a folio of parchment the treaty was handsome enough. Germany, Belgium and France bound themselves to recognise as inviolable not only their existing mutual frontiers, but also the demilitarisation of the Rhineland. Thus Germany now voluntarily accepted in respect of the Rhineland and her western frontiers what had been imposed on her at Versailles. The three countries further pledged themselves that in no case would they attack, invade or resort to war against one another. All these obligations were guaranteed by Italy and England; in other words, the guarantors were immediately to intervene against a power which broke the treaty by violating the frontier of another. Not only this, but they were similarly to intervene if Germany violated the demilitarised zone.[3]

The treaty was rapturously applauded in England for bringing about real peace at last. This belief was shared inside the Government; inside the Foreign Office even. In 1926 a Foreign Office memorandum on the treaty noted that while Versailles had concluded the war, 'it cannot be said it

[1] Ibid. pp. 355–7.
[2] Austen Chamberlain Papers, quoted in Middlemass and Barnes, p. 356.
[3] See Walters, Vol. I, pp. 291–2.

brought peace. Its result was rather a prolonged, and sometimes even a precarious, armistice. The problem . . . has been to turn that armistice into a real peace. The significance of Locarno is that the solution of the problem was, we may hope, found there. . . .' For France had been given, in the Foreign Office view, a real sense of security.[1] The treaty also fulfilled the Chiefs of Staff's advice that English foreign policy should provide that war be kept as far as possible from the Channel, the Straits of Dover and the southern shore of the North Sea.[2] As Austen Chamberlain pointed out to the 1926 Imperial Conference: 'We have a peculiar interest because the true defence of our country, owing to scientific development, is now no longer the Channel . . . but upon the Rhine.'[3]

So far as western Europe was concerned, therefore, the Locarno Treaty fully secured English and French strategic interests; it formally obliged England to hold the European balance of power. But the treaty only did these things on paper. Unfortunately the treaty was, so far as England and her guarantee were concerned, no more than a hollow gesture to soothe the French; a bogus commitment, a fraudulent IOU that was given only because the English Government never thought for a moment that they would ever have to make it good. For as Austen Chamberlain himself remarked to colleagues in February 1928: 'The essence of the Locarno Treaty was not the provision of a guarantor but the fact that it was a pact between old enemies.'[4]

In any case the British forces were now so reduced and ill-equipped as to be wholly incapable of fulfilling the British guarantee, as the Chiefs of Staff pointed out in their annual review for 1926 and on many later occasions.[5]

In regard to Europe, therefore English policy did not merely display a characteristic escapism and self-deception but, the realities of power and strategy having been left so far behind, now veered positively into fantasy, like an unsound financier who, devoid of cash resources, deludes himself and his creditors with grandiose paper transactions.

Yet the Locarno Treaty did not protect the frontiers of Germany's *eastern* neighbours even on paper; the English had steadfastly refused to enter into even a hollow commitment towards eastern Europe, holding that developments in this region were not, and could not be, among the

[1] CAB 32/47, E-117.
[2] Austen Chamberlain's concluding statement to the 1926 Imperial Conference, CAB 32/46, E-8.
[3] Ibid.
[4] CAB 27/361, Reports and Proceedings of the Cabinet Committee on Reduction and Limitation of Armaments Vol. I, PRA(27)4.
[5] COS 41 in CAB 53/12.

interests of England. This reflected the English belief, which had been gathering strength and currency since 1919, that in future Germany would conveniently expand eastwards.[1] It was indeed well recognised that even the reformed Germany of the Weimar Republic had designs on Poland.[2] For this reason, Stresemann had refused to extend the Locarno Treaty in its western form to eastern Europe. D'Abernon's opinion therefore was that 'now Locarno has diminished danger on the German–French frontier, the Polish Corridor is the danger-spot in Europe'.[3] Marshal Foch, for his part, had stated as early as 1919 that the Polish Corridor would occasion the next war. But English statesmanship still convinced itself that the Polish Corridor and similar eastern focuses of German resentment were no direct concern of England's.

Locarno ushered in the era of the high romantic euphoria of internationalism. Stresemann and Aristide Briand, the French foreign minister, enjoyed a celebrated friendship, vying in the utterance of 'European' sentiments. Germany was invited to join the League of Nations, by way of signifying that she was no longer regarded as 'guilty'; an invitation which in fact Germany found neither flattering nor particularly welcome,[4] although she accepted it. On the far side of the world, Japan enjoyed a 'liberal' government, and would offer, in British conviction, no threat for at least ten years.[5] In 1928 the Kellogg 'Peace' Pact was signed, by which the Nations renounced war as an instrument of policy. A vast work of study and preparation was in hand for the coming world disarmament conference. Churchill in the Committee of Imperial Defence on 8 November 1928 'urged that, having regard to all the developments in the international sphere with the object of ensuring peace between nations, there was every reason to secure a reduction in the total amount of the Service Estimates'.[6]

Yet reality was otherwise. Locarno marked a further ebb of life and power from the Versailles Treaty. For, under cover of the humbug of apparent British commitment to defend the Rhineland demilitarised zone and the integrity of France and Belgium, England had really completed the liquidation of her wartime strategic involvement in Europe. All that remained was the small contingent of British troops among the occupying forces in the Rhineland; a symbol of past, not future, co-operation. France was left alone except for the Locarno guarantees and for her weak

[1] See below, p. 391, see also Balfour in March 1919, quoted in Dugdale, p. 204.
[2] Cf. D'Abernon, Vol. III, pp. 87–8, 207–8, 221.
[3] Ibid. p. 221.
[4] Ibid. especially p. 147.
[5] See above p. 276.
[6] CAB 2/5, CID 238.

allies in eastern Europe; alone, and morally and militarily on the defensive; her population static, her birthrate declining, a nation ever more enfeebled by the continuing effects of her catastrophic losses in the Great War.

And beyond the Rhine, the factory chimneys of Germany belched smoke like the guns of Hipper's relentless battle-cruisers at Jutland; the smoke of bounding economic strength. In 1929 German production *per capita* was 12 per cent higher than in 1913; German exports doubled between 1924 and 1929.[1] Germany was investing – at a time of British industrial decay – the astonishingly high average net figure of nearly 12 per cent.[2] She was in fact reorganising, reconstructing and re-equipping on the most up-to-date lines an industrial machine which had in any case been the most powerful and modern in Europe. By 1931 the Chief of the British General Staff was reporting that the 'enthusiasm for modernisation and rationalisation has caused the capacity of German industry in general to outstrip that of any other continental nation. . . .'[3] The CIGS also drew attention to the active participation of the German State in the country's industrial development, especially where this development strengthened the potential for waging war;[4] and noted that the large German parliamentary votes for war material were being invested in manufacturing capacity rather than in military equipment itself.[5]

This immense augmentation of German national power *vis-à-vis* both her European neighbours and England was paid for by American loans. The skill of German diplomacy in harping on a grievance and exploiting tender Anglo-Saxon consciences, a skill equalled perhaps only by Gandhi, succeeded in getting both the total of reparations and the pace of payment reduced in 1924 and again (under the Young Plan) in 1929. At the same time it was represented that without American loans these sums could still not be paid. The loans were forthcoming – to an amount three times greater than the total reparations paid by Germany during the 1920s.[6] The difference went largely into creating Germany's new industrial power. Thus it was becoming ever more vital for France to preserve her precarious advantage in armed forces in being; ever more vital for her to cling to those clauses of the Versailles Treaty which demilitarised the Rhineland and forbade Germany to re-arm.

But to put an end to this French military superiority and to the Allied occupation of the Rhineland now became the next objects of British

[1] Michael Balfour, *West Germany* (London, Benn 1968), pp. 85–6. [2] Ibid.

[3] Memorandum to the Cabinet Committee of Preparations for the Disarmament Conference, 31 March 1931: Appendix on foreign armies, in CAB 27/476, CDC(31)11.

[4] Ibid. [5] Ibid. [6] Balfour, p. 86.

policy. In 1929 the second Labour Government was determined to complete the appeasement of Europe by removing yet more of the disabilities under the peace treaty which so upset Germany by reminding her that she had lost the war instead of winning it. Make Germany a contented and fully equal member of the human brotherhood, the Labour Government believed, and the task of achieving lasting peace in Europe would be completed. The British delegation to the Hague Conference on reparations in 1929 (led by Snowden, the Chancellor of the Exchequer, but including Arthur Henderson, the Foreign Secretary) proposed to achieve this by bringing about a major reduction in the amount of reparations to be paid by Germany and by inducing the French to agree to an evacuation of the Rhineland forthwith, instead of in 1935. Surprisingly enough, the British, in the person of Snowden, unleashed at the conference a ruthless diplomatic offensive whose language was of a bluntness and brutality as had not been heard from the lips of English statesmen since the death of Palmerston. But this unlikely display of commanding will-power, unique in British foreign policy between the world wars, was principally directed against an old British ally; directed – if unwittingly – at enhancing the position of the nation which was already, except in the present strength of its armed forces, the paramount power in Europe.

Snowden's ruthlessness completely succeeded, although his bargaining position was by no means strong – an indication that the high hand might well have also won in other and better causes between 1918 and 1939. The British proposals in regard to reparations were carried almost entirely.[1] Over the linked question of the Allied occupation forces in the Rhineland, Henderson, placing all the weight of his formidable personality on Stresemann's side against Briand, was no less successful than his colleague Snowden over reparations. Briand, beset by misgivings, unwilling to forfeit what tenuous English goodwill remained to France, was forced into surrender. It was agreed that all the Allied occupation forces should be out of the Rhineland by June 1930.

The British 'achievement' at the Hague was acclaimed by almost all sections of British opinion.[2] When the last of the British troops returned to England from the Rhineland in time for Christmas 1929, the event was greeted with joy, not foreboding. When in June 1930 the last of the French too marched home, the British believed that a gigantic stride had been made towards lasting European peace. But Snowden and Henderson had brought about a strategic catastrophe.

The French military frontier had been brought back from the Rhine

[1] Carlton, pp. 48–9.

[2] Ibid. pp. 53–5; see ch. 2 for a full account of the conference.

and its bridgeheads to the French national frontier. There was no longer a military presence physically to prevent Germany from sending in troops to re-occupy and re-militarise what had now become a strategic No-Man's-Land. The integrity of the demilitarised zone, upon which the security of both France and the Low Countries so depended, rested now either on Germany's good faith, or, in default of that hitherto fragile safeguard, upon the readiness and willingness of the French to march forward and turn invading German forces out again – a major military operation, indeed an act of war. The evacuation of the Rhineland led therefore to a calamitous weakening of France's defensive position. But this was not all. Perhaps more serious, it removed the last positive French hold over Germany. As long as the French were on the Rhine, the Ruhr industrial area lay at their mercy. In the last resort, if Germany's internal situation had ever seemed dangerous enough to merit it, France could always have pounced from her Rhine bridgeheads and destroyed German power at the heart. Now the whole depth – and virtually the length as well – of the Rhineland, with the difficult and broken country that lies north-east of the French frontier, lay between the French army and the Ruhr.

The European balance of power, heavily tilted at Locarno, had taken a great lurch away from France and England towards Germany.[1]

Not for the first or the last time, British statesmen now discovered that their well-meaning attempts to please others had failed to elicit the looked-for gratitude and contentment. In 1930 the Germans, like good troops, pushed on vigorously towards further objectives: the Saar was mentioned; the intolerable nature of the Polish Corridor trumpeted forth. And now there was a hectoring stridency about German diplomacy which had been absent during the era which ended with the death of Stresemann in 1929. The world slump was deepening, and as the unemployed on German streets multiplied, so the nationalist parties and the communists exultantly closed in on failing German democracy from both sides. On 27 March 1930 the Socialist Chancellor resigned, an event which many historians regard as marking the end of parliamentary government in Germany.[2] The new Chancellor, Heinrich Brüning, of the Catholic Centre Party, proceeded to rule by emergency decree, as was legal under the constitu-

[1] Carlton (ibid. pp. 55–6) argues that the policy of Snowden and Henderson was reasonable enough, given the prevailing climate of opinion and the hopes, assumptions and knowledge of the time; and that they cannot be criticised for failing to know what was to happen in the future. However, the gravamen of the charge against them – as against British policy between the world wars as a whole – is not that they failed to foresee the future, but that they deliberately rejected the lessons offered by the past.

[2] Balfour, p. 90.

tion. In the General Election of September 1930 the National-Socialist German Workers' Party (or Nazis), leapt from 12 seats to become the second strongest party in the Reichstag, with 107 seats. The Nazi Party's foreign policy, as endlessly and raucously proclaimed by Adolf Hitler, the party leader, was totally to destroy the Versailles Treaty and to restore Germany to her former power and extent. In the winter of 1930–1 German unemployment reached five million.

The disquiet engendered in the British Government by this rising tide of nationalism, and a violent and neurotic nationalism at that, was deepened in 1930 by fresh evidence that Germany was systematically evading the disarmament provisions of the Versailles Treaty.[1] At the same time the British Chiefs of Staff warned in their annual review for 1930:

> . . . we have received no instructions to work out plans in fulfilment of that guarantee [to the mutual frontiers of France and Belgium with Germany, and to the demilitarised zone of the Rhineland, under the Locarno Treaty], and in fact detailed plans have not been worked out. This country is in a less favourable position to fulfil the Locarno guarantees than it was, without any written guarantee, to come to the assistance of France and Belgium in 1914.[2]

Here, in this new European situation, was a sombre reality inconsistent with the political faith of Arthur Henderson, the English Foreign Secretary. But Henderson did not adjust his faith accordingly; instead, in the face of facts placed before him about the course of affairs inside Germany, he persisted in 1930 with his policy of appeasement and reconciliation.[3] As 1931 succeeded 1930, however, and Germany sank deeper into economic and social dislocation, and the nationalists and communists bayed closer and closer to the struggling Chancellor, Brüning, the motives behind British appeasement began subtly to change. In the 1920s appeasement had sprung as a positive faith from within the post-evangelical British nature itself. Now there was another, external element – the influence of fear. For by 1931 Henderson, while refusing openly to admit even to his Cabinet colleagues that the state of Europe was worsening,[4] was beginning gradually to accept the fact of the growing menace of the German situation. He accommodated this fact to his political prejudices by coming to believe that the best way of staving off German nationalism was to save Brüning by further concessions to German demands. Henderson explained

[1] Carlton, p. 72.
[2] COS 247 in CAB 53/21.
[3] Carlton, p. 72.
[4] See above p. 296.

to Sir Horace Rumbold, the British ambassador in Berlin, in February 1931:

> The fall of the Brüning Government might easily have far-reaching detrimental effects on international relationships. If, therefore, there is real danger of its not being able to weather the storm to which it is likely to be exposed in the near future, it ought, I consider, to be the policy of His Majesty's Government to give it such support and encouragement as they properly can, in order to fortify the position.[1]

Rumbold too strongly believed in this policy.

It was in the long-pending World Disarmament Conference that Henderson placed his principal hope of finally appeasing German resentments; it would, he believed, remove that inferiority of status whereby Germany was largely disarmed while her neighbours were not. At the same time, universal and agreed reductions in armaments would exorcise the fears European nations entertained of each other. However, by the time the conference finally opened in February 1932, Henderson was no longer Foreign Secretary, being a casualty of the collapse of the second Labour Government, but instead had become chairman of the conference itself; an international tribute to his personal prestige.

The advent of Sir John Simon to the Foreign Office in the new National Government in 1931 brought less a change in policy than in style of performance. Yet this change was of the first importance, for it was a change from courage and strength of character towards ambiguity and weakness. Simon himself would have more fitly graced the judicial bench or an episcopal throne than the saddle whence the Foreign Secretary of England must ride the whirlwind and direct the storm.[2] MacDonald, the Prime Minister, was no man for lucid thought or clear-cut decision. And Baldwin, the Lord President of the Council, despite his sanity, shrewdness even, and decency, was no man for a battle, no thruster of limp colleagues.

The League of Nations World Disarmament Conference now became the principal arena of British attempts to satisfy France and Germany at the same time and thus lay the foundation of a secure peace in Europe. As Simon himself was to put it to the House of Commons in November 1933, when in fact they had already failed in this hopeful task of reconciling opposites:

> The central political issue is how to reconcile Germany's demand for equality with France's desire about security. . . . Can one say that either

[1] Quoted in Carlton, p. 70.

[2] See above pp. 303–4.

sentiment is unnatural, and that in like circumstances we should not feel it ourselves? I do not think so, and for that reason the whole of British policy had been directed, not to denying or belittling either sentiment, but in the effort to promote reconciliation between them and to meet the supreme need of the world for peace, by turning the minds of both from the past and inviting their co-operation in the future.[1]

At the conference, the British therefore adopted their favourite post of umpire: 'Britain had the difficult role', wrote Simon in his memoirs, 'of trying to be fair to each.'[2] For what was at stake, in the British view, was not a matter of grand strategy, but moral justice, as Simon informed the House of Commons in 1932. 'I aimed', he said, 'at getting rid of a series of merely legal propositions in order to insist that the principal issue is a moral and not a legal one.'[3]

Yet in the event the British interpreted their high-minded role as requiring pressure on their late French ally to give up her present military superiority in order to satisfy the German clamour for equality of status. For anxiety over Germany was becoming an ever more important element in the British pursuit of appeasement, adulterating the original motive of idealistic hope; a change which British statesmen and the public concealed from themselves.

Thus the more Germany became unstable and truculent, the more the British Government yielded up the initiative which they had originally begun to let slip on the very morrow of the Paris Peace Conference of 1919. Yet it was not as if the British had no alternative but to yield; as if German diplomacy in 1931 and 1932 was backed by superior strategic power. Although the position of the old wartime allies was now much weaker than before 1925, or before the evacuation of the Rhineland in June 1930, the German armed forces were in no way yet a match for the French army. In March 1931 the British Chief of the General Staff reported that: 'The French army is undoubtedly the most formidable military machine in the world to-day . . . France with the aid of her allies should have no difficulty in defeating Germany. . . .'[4] The response of the British Government to the rise of nationalist passions within Germany in 1931–2 was therefore dictated not by necessity, but by temperamental inclination.

The discussions during December 1931 and January 1932 of the Cabinet

[1] Viscount Simon, p. 186.
[2] Ibid. p. 185.
[3] Quoted in Study Group of the RIIA, *Political and Strategic Interests of the United Kingdom* (London, Oxford University Press 1939).
[4] CAB 27/476, CDC(31)11: Military Appreciation of the Situation in Europe.

Committee on Preparations for the Disarmament Conference display the British Government's dilemma (as they saw it) and the British state of mind at this critical juncture.

There was an all-pervading anxiety about Germany and what Germany might do. Fears were voiced that she might leave the Disarmament Conference in dudgeon – an absurd way of looking at it, since Germany, as the defeated power disarmed under present treaty arrangements, was, or ought to have been, in the position of suppliant. The character of Adolf Hitler provoked alarmed discussion; thus two years before Hitler actually came to power, he had already become a factor in British policy-making; already intimidating the British into greater alacrity in appeasement. For the National Government at the turn of 1931–2 still held fast to Henderson's conviction that the best way of fending off Hitler and other German nationalists was to bolster Brüning's position by concessions.

It was in these Cabinet Committee discussions too that the politicians first began to recognise that Britain might really be called upon to fulfil her signature of the Locarno Treaty. Simon gave vent to his worries on this score, and returned to them later. Then again he was troubled by the dilemma of being caught between France and Germany. There was the problem of whether to give France further guarantees in order, as he put it, to afford her assurance of security in compensation for her own disarmament. This, in turn, raised the awkward question of entanglement in the affairs of eastern Europe; and Simon went on to remind his colleagues what such further guarantees to France might involve: 'It might mean, for example, if we accepted that price, that British troops would be called upon to maintain the *status quo* of the Polish Corridor.' And in this connection he drew attention to British public opinion.[1]

Several speakers noted the superior strength of Germany's 'moral case' over the question of disarmament, taking this as a factor of some importance. Yet despite all the British anxieties about Germany, the British Government no more shared the wholly pessimistic French diagnosis now than they had in the early 1920s, for, in Simon's words, 'French public opinion was much more alarmed about a revived Germany than about a bankrupt Germany. This view was obviously quite wrong. . . .'[2]

The Cabinet Committee's discussions as a whole evinced perplexity and anxiety enough, but little coherent thought; no impulse to command events, but rather to submit to them. It occurred to no one that the answer to German nationalism might be to stand pat with the French on the letter of the Versailles Treaty and let the Germans do the courting.

[1] CAB 27/476, CDC(31)2.

[2] Ibid.

Nor had the experts of the Foreign Office anything much more purposeful to suggest. On 1 January 1932 Sir Robert Vansittart, Permanent Under-Secretary, and a man sometimes flattered in retrospect for strength of mind, submitted for the guidance of the Cabinet a *Memorandum on the British Position in Relation to European Policy*.[1] It was marred by a mannered style more appropriate to an undergraduate journal, and even in its more lucid passages failed to achieve the force and clarity of purpose of Crowe's memorandum of January 1907 on English policy towards Imperial Germany, to which it might be fairly compared. Vansittart noted the awkwardness which the French were displaying over the question of disarming themselves, but thought:

> In taking stock of things as they are in France, we must be careful to guard against any undue leaning towards Germany. 'The Nazis are coming.' Their violent, and often ridiculous, programme is known . . . Hitler seems to be trying to instil some, at least ostensible, moderation into his wild and dense followers. His success remains to be seen. There is lamentably little ability in the Party. The old German spirit is abroad in plenty and predominance. . . .[2]

Yet on the other hand Vansittart agreed with the British Cabinet's conclusion on 15 December 1931 that the German case on disarmament was legally and morally a very good one, and the French case a bad one. 'If, then, it comes to a show-down between the two conflicting theses, neither international policy, nor Imperial policy, nor domestic policy will permit any British Government to side with the French against the Germans.'[3]

Vansittart therefore proceeded to outline various ingenious proposals for escaping from this state of paralysis by pleasing at once both the Germans and the French. He ended his paper by pointing out the danger consequent upon failure of the Disarmament Conference, and therefore of the League itself, in view of the decay of England's own strength. If the conference came to nothing, the Government would then in his opinion have three options: a programme of re-armament such as no British Government 'could well face in the immediate future, financially or politically – and by politically I mean *internal* politics'; the acceptance of a continued French hegemony, which he thought 'unendurable'; or, finally, 'a return to the old – and vicious – "balance of power" '.[4]

[1] CAB 27/476, CP(4)32.
[2] Ibid. [3] Ibid. [4] Ibid.

So Vansittart too, like his government, thought that the only practicable course for England lay, as of old, in shirking a choice between France and Germany.

Hence followed the foredoomed British attempt during the Disarmament Conference to juggle technical formulae so that Germany might enjoy equality of status in armed strength while at the same time France did not lose her military security. In 1932 it therefore fell to the adroit and sanctimonious Simon to pursue both over disarmament and over Manchuria the familiar British object of reconciling the irreconcilable.

Yet the British Government was not only the prisoner of its own character, but, as Vansittart justly pointed out, of British public opinion, and of the expectations raised by the advent of the so-long-awaited World Disarmament.

The minds of the leaders of the armed forces, however, were fixed upon the urgent need to rebuild England's own strategic power rather than on universal disarmament. Indeed, the Chiefs of Staff's annual review for 1932 constituted a relentless analysis of the consequences of the fantasy-life lived by the British since the Great War in regard to world affairs.

The Chiefs of Staff noted the revolutionary change in the world situation since June 1931: the slump, the departure of the pound sterling from the gold standard, Manchuria, and what they called the 'general malaise in Europe', which was nevertheless 'overshadowed by this menacing situation in the Far East, which sheds a sinister light on the basis of our existing arrangements for Imperial Defence'.[1]

They proceeded unkindly to recall in some detail how earlier Foreign Office predictions of a peaceful future for the world had already collapsed; and then described the pernicious effects of the 'ten-year-rule' which had been founded on those confident predictions:

> . . . there is nothing approaching a bare margin to-day in the matter of defence against air attack [on the United Kingdom].
>
> For major military liabilities, such as might arise under the Covenant of the League of Nations or the Treaty of Locarno, we are but ill-prepared. In 1914 we intervened on the Continent with six well-equipped and well-trained divisions within the first month of war. If to-day we committed our Expeditionary Force to a Continental campaign in response to our liabilities under the Pact of Locarno, its contribution during the first month would be limited to one division, and during the first four months to three divisions, arriving piecemeal;

[1] COS 295, in CAB 53/22.

and except for the moral effect of its presence on the Continent it could have little effect on the fortunes of the campaign.[1]

The Chiefs of Staff found it extraordinary that 'we alone among the Great Powers should have neglected our defences to the point of taking serious risks. The reason is to be found in a difference in national outlooks. . . .'[2] For, the Chiefs of Staff pointed out, other countries inculcated that defence of their country was the first duty of a citizen. In Great Britain, instead, and with the encouragement of the State, intense propaganda of an opposite kind was carried out in schools, universities, churches, press and radio.[3] 'We think it right to invite the attention of the Committee [of Imperial Defence] to the fundamental weakness of Imperial Defence involved in the present state of public opinion.'[4]

And the Chiefs of Staff wound up their indictment by summarising the effects of the 'ten-year-rule': 'A terrible deficiency in essential requirements for all three Defence Services and a consequential inability to fulfil our major commitments. The decay of our armaments industry. . . . A complacent optimism in public opinion.'[5]

The Cabinet's response to this paper was to end the 'ten-year-rule', though only after much debate, and to ask the Committee of Imperial Defence to embark on a general review of the whole field of imperial defence; a painless substitute for action and decision. Nothing was actually set in motion to repair the weaknesses the Chiefs of Staff had catalogued. Instead, 1932 was the year of the Disarmament Conference; after all, if it succeeded, as the Government so much hoped, these weaknesses would no longer signify, and the need for disagreeable decisions leading to costly armament programmes would be averted altogether.

In the meantime there remained virtually no power at all behind English policy either in Europe or in the Far East. Yet the British public, who did not realise this impotence, and the Government, which did, equally took it for granted that England ought to be playing the headmaster's role in world affairs. For they still saw no necessary connection between strategic power and policy.

While the Disarmament Conference ground on its laborious way, Germany was falling step by step to the Nazi Party and other nationalists; a process that did nothing to encourage the French to yield to British suggestions that they should accept some form of eventual parity in armed forces with Germany. There were five German elections in nine

[1] Ibid. [2] Ibid. [3] Ibid.
[4] Ibid. [5] Ibid.

months – a symptom of political chaos and paralysis. In the General Election on 31 July 1932 the Nazis doubled their vote over 1930, won 230 seats in the Reichstag and became the largest single party. Yet they were still short of that absolute majority they needed for Hitler to become Chancellor. In September in a second General Election, the Nazi tide ebbed from 37 per cent of the votes to 33 per cent. There succeeded four months of intense political intrigue between the Nazis, the Nationalists and the leaders of the Reichswehr. On 30 January 1933, as a result of a final backstairs deal, Adolf Hitler became Chancellor of the German Reich. That evening, for over five hours, the Nationalist and Nazi storm troops marched through Berlin by the flaring light of torches and to the exultant crash of military bands; a barbarian army entering a conquered city.

Adolf Hitler was now master over 70,000,000 Germans and an industrial machine second in the world only to that of America. The implication of this fact became as plain as that of a clenched fist as the early months of 1933 passed by. By October the British Chiefs of Staff were writing in their annual review: '... we should like to put on record our opinion that Germany is not only starting to re-arm, but that she will continue this process until within a few years hence she will again have to be reckoned as a formidable military power'.[1]

The Chiefs of Staff believed that Germany would go on re-arming 'either openly or covertly' whatever the outcome of the Disarmament Conference.[2] In fact, only a month later, Germany walked out of the conference and announced her withdrawal from the League of Nations. By March 1934 the British Cabinet was debating the question as to whether '... we take Germany as the ultimate potential enemy against whom our "long-range" Defence policy must be directed'.[3]

So it had come to pass that within some fifteen years of the entry of British troops into Cologne on the heels of a German army utterly beaten in the field, England once again faced a great German state mighty with power and ambition, and this time bent on expunging both the ignominy and the consequences of defeat.

It was a situation which would have been far less menacing than it was if British and French troops, representing a firm alliance between their countries, had still occupied the Rhineland and those bridgeheads over the Rhine that put the heart of Germany at their mercy, as the Versailles Treaty had entitled them to do until 1935.

[1] CAB 53/23, COS 310. [2] Ibid.
[3] CAB 23/78, 10(34)3, meeting of 19 March 1934.

It was a situation which would have been rendered wholly impossible by the French proposals at the Peace Conference of 1919, for it was exactly what the French had feared and wished to prevent.

It was therefore a situation for which the British themselves bore a great, perhaps decisive, responsibility. For it was they who had gambled away all that had been achieved by the Great War; gambled it on German democracy, a runner about whose chances the greenest punter ought to have been somewhat sceptical. Even if the victors, as some have urged, had made so generous a peace as to lay no handicaps whatsoever on the 'new' Germany other than the inescapable fact of defeat itself, it is still far from certain that German democracy would have proved a winner over the distance.

The untoward and unlooked-for product of England's well-meaning kindness towards Germany, when coupled with the consequences of her no-less-public-spirited policy towards Japan, was pointed out by the British Chiefs of Staff in 1933: not only was the Far East still a danger zone, but Europe had become one as well.[1]

England now faced a strategic predicament potentially more hazardous than she had ever known in her history. This was not only because England was at present disarmed. Even at her 1918 strength, it would have been beyond her capabilities to wage successful war against two great powers at opposite ends of the earth, one of which alone enjoyed nearly twice her population and economic strength.

In February 1934 the anatomy of the problems facing England was dissected by the report of the Defence Requirements Sub-Committee of the CID (the DRC), which had been appointed in November 1933. The DRC recognised that a worldwide empire could not be secure at every point against every conceivable menace. It considered that Japan offered the more immediate threat, in view of her naval and military preparedness and 'the danger created by our total inability to defend our interests in the Far East'. Germany on the other hand was not yet fully armed: 'In her case we have time, though not much time, to make defensive preparations.' Yet, these two threats, the report pointed out, were not separate but linked one to the other. For while Japan did not appear at the moment to be planning aggression against the British Empire, she might be tempted into such action by events elsewhere, 'and elsewhere means Europe, and the danger to us in Europe will only come from Germany'. Therefore 'we take Germany as the ultimate potential enemy against whom our "long range" policy must be directed'.

[1] Annual Review for 1933, CAB 53/23, COS 310.

The DRC therefore argued that England ought to try to cultivate better relations with Japan, and avert a Japanese *rapprochement* with Germany; and in this connection acidly recorded 'that our subservience to the United States of America in past years has been one of the principal factors in the deterioration of our former good relations with Japan'.

In order to free England's hand to meet the German threat, the DRC was in fact advocating a reversal of the policy towards Japan and America which had been followed by England since the decision in 1921 not to renew the Japanese alliance.

This proposal split the Government and its advisors into embattled factions.[1] The Prime Minister, MacDonald, was himself a sentimental Americanophile whose pro-American sentiments were shared by most of his colleagues. Neville Chamberlain, the Chancellor of the Exchequer, on the other hand, was strongly in favour of a *rapprochement* with Japan because, in his often voiced conviction, 'it was impossible for this country to fight both Germany and Japan'.[2] In any case, Chamberlain deeply disliked and distrusted America.[3] Vansittart and Sir Warren Fisher, Permanent Secretary to the Treasury (and a major influence on English policy), also shared Chamberlain's convictions. This was a powerful enough lobby. Chatfield too, the First Sea Lord, favoured friendship with Japan, although he was at the same time reluctant to forfeit American co-operation over naval questions.[4] For, just as in 1920–2, English policy towards the United States and Japan was complicated by the problem of agreement on the relative strengths of the navies of the three powers, since there was to be another naval conference in 1935. Warren Fisher pointed out that '. . . in any collaboration with the United States in regard to a naval agreement the difficulty was that on the one hand Great Britain antagonised Japan while on the other she could not be absolutely certain of United States assistance'.[5]

This was indeed the core of the matter, and not only in regard to a naval agreement. The pro-Japanese lobby therefore argued that England should no longer hesitate to approach Japan. As Neville Chamberlain said in November 1934: 'We have been restrained up to date by our own desire to keep on good terms with the United States of America. . . .'[6]

But this desire was still widespread and strongly felt in British governing circles. A backstairs alliance of influential contact-men and ideas-peddlers,

[1] See Watt, Essay 4.
[2] CAB 32/125, PM(35)2.
[3] See his comments in the meetings of the Ministerial Committee on the Naval Conference 1935, CAB 29/147.
[4] CAB 29/158, LNC(35)(BC)1.
[5] Ibid.
[6] CAB 29/147, NCM(35)9.

characteristic of the period, sprang up to give it effective expression and thus to prevent the threatened reversal of English policy. Lord Lothian, idealist, Christian Scientist, internationalist, preacher of the common destiny of the English-speaking peoples, was, together with his friends of the Round Table group, prominent in this alliance. *The Times* and the *Observer* played their part. Smuts, as ever on the scene at a decisive moment to advance the liberal point of view, intervened.[1] Together all these parties successfully worked upon English susceptibilities concerning cousinhood with America, and rallied a powerful opposition inside the Government.

However, the prolonged governmental discussions over an understanding with Japan turned not so much on the question of America as of China. Here too the National Government in 1934–5 found itself traversing the old battlefield of 1920–1, albeit encountering some new entanglements which did not then exist, like the Nine-Power-Treaty of Washington of 1922, by which England and the other signatories agreed to 'respect the sovereignty, independence, and the territorial and administrative integrity of China. . . .'

For it was China that sprawled inconveniently in the way of Anglo-Japanese concord. And over China, just as over America, English prejudices remained at odds with English interests. The delicate English dilemma is well summed up by an exchange between Neville Chamberlain and Simon, the Foreign Secretary, on 16 April 1934. Chamberlain wondered whether it would be possible to come to some arrangement with Japan over China in order to avoid the risk of a collision, such as the creation of two spheres of influence and trade. But Simon replied that he thought this was not possible because of the Nine-Power-Treaty.[2] And yet, as a memorandum of 29 October 1934 on Anglo-Japanese relations by the Commercial Counsellor to the British embassy[3] and circulated to the Cabinet pointed out, 'the only condition upon which we could induce Japan voluntarily to afford us relief from her competition [author's note: economic in this case] would, in my opinion, be an undertaking from us to give political support to Japan'.[4]

The Commercial Counsellor himself did not like the prospect of such a deal 'at all'.[5] Nor did the chief of the Far Eastern Department of the Foreign Office, C. W. Orde. In a memorandum of 7 January 1935 Orde listed Japanese aggressions against China from 1915 to the 'rape' of

[1] See Watt, pp. 95–9. [2] CAB 29/147, NCM(35)1. [3] G. B. Sansom.
[4] Cabinet Committee on Political and Economic Relations with Japan, CAB 27/596, CP8(35).
[5] Ibid.

Manchuria, and argued that 'we cannot morally afford in the present-day world to put ourselves in the same camp with an exponent of such policies'.[1]

The Government shared these paralysing scruples. Even Chamberlain, the strongest voice inside the Cabinet in favour of friendship with Japan, agreed that our obligations under the Nine-Power-Treaty and the Covenant of the League of Nations ruled out any kind of arrangement to the effect 'that she will leave us alone at the price of giving her a free hand'.[2] When, during the meeting of Commonwealth prime ministers in 1935, Lyons of Australia suggested that the recognition of Manchukuo, the Japanese puppet state of Manchuria, would assuage Japanese antagonism, Simon answered that this could not be done: 'In so far as the matter was one for the League of Nations, this country would have to act as a good member of the League. . . .'[3]

We had, Simon said, to keep in line with the United States over the Far East; and to consider the strained relations with China that would ensue 'if we were to say that her dismemberment was of no account'. When change came about in China, 'let it be', Simon pleaded, 'with the goodwill of the Chinese Government and with their willing co-operation'.[4]

And so, after all the arguments and lobbyings of 1934–5, the proposal to make friends with Japan in order to free English resources to meet the German menace petered out.

It had indeed really been foredoomed from the start, for while its proponents had been shrewd enough in their object, they had been unrealistic to the point of naïveté in thinking that it might be possible to win Japan's friendship without coming to a deal over China. In any case, even if the Government itself had been willing to conclude such a deal, it would have been vetoed by public opinion. For in 1934–5 the National Government was not in the position of an eighteenth-century administration, looking to a body of opinion composed of solid country squires, with the hardness and realism born of life on the land, and a relish for a shrewd and profitable deal. Instead there was a volatile mass electorate; an urban, rootless and emotional middle class, always ready to get in the fidgets of moral indignation.

So Japan remained a potentially hostile power, a source of perpetual

[1] Memorandum by C. W. Orde, in CP8(35), CAB 27/596.

[2] Memorandum by the Chancellor of the Exchequer and the Foreign Secretary on the future of Anglo-Japanese relations. CAB 27/596, CP233(34).

[3] CAB 32/125, PM(35)2.

[4] Ibid.

anxiety; indeed all the more of an anxiety now because of the rise of Nazi Germany. English statesmen took refuge, as Lloyd George had done in 1921,[1] in platitudes whose hopeless inconsistencies were unwittingly expressed by Simon in an address to the Commonwealth prime ministers in 1935, when he said that it was the Far Eastern policy of the United Kingdom 'to maintain their position of friendship' in respect of China, Japan, Russia and the United States.[2]

Yet the potential consequences of this British failure to neutralise Japan were appallingly dangerous, as a memorandum written in the autumn of 1934 by the Chancellor of the Exchequer (Neville Chamberlain) and the Foreign Secretary had pointed out.

> . . . if we had to enter upon such a [European] struggle with a hostile, instead of a friendly, Japan in the East; if we had to contemplate the division of our forces so as to protect our Far Eastern interests while prosecuting a war in Europe; then not only would India, Hong Kong and Australasia be in dire peril, but we ourselves would stand in far greater danger of destruction by a fully armed and organised Germany.[3]

These sombre conclusions were underlined by the 1935 annual review of imperial defence by the Chiefs of Staff. The British armed forces, they wrote, now had to discharge three great tasks; the defence of imperial interests and possessions in the Far East; the fulfilment of European commitments; and the defence of India against Russia:

> So long as the European situation was determined by the results of the Treaty of Versailles, this factor [the strategic situation nearer home] did not seem to be of undue importance . . . since the immense French superiority on land and in the air made [the] chance of war in Europe remote. But we are faced with the position that the re-armament of Germany has not only begun but is, to a large extent, realised, a factor which is increasingly disturbing the existing balance in Europe.
>
> [Moreover] by the signing of the Treaty of Locarno, the United Kingdom undertook definite commitments and to that extent made our participation in a European war more likely without in any way reducing our responsibilities in the Far East.[4]

Here then was a predicament for a partially disarmed country of only

[1] See above p. 266.
[2] CAB 32/125, PM(35)2.
[3] Memorandum to the Cabinet on the Future of Anglo-Japanese Relations, CAB 27/596, CP233(34).
[4] CAB 53/24, COS 372.

forty-five million people, a predicament from which the Chiefs of Staff themselves saw the only possible means of escape as lying in the skill of English foreign policy. As they rather wistfully, and, in the circumstances, naïvely put it: 'That we should be called upon to fight Germany and Japan simultaneously without Allies is a state of affairs to the prevention of which our diplomacy would naturally be directed.'[1]

In the months following the submission of this review in April 1935, however, British diplomacy was directed towards quite a different object. As if the menace of two great powers at opposite ends of the empire was not enough to contend with, British moralising internationalism now proceeded gratuitously to raise up the hostility of a third great power; a power, what was more, whose air and sea striking forces lay athwart the main imperial line of communication between England and the Far East.

Ever since the autumn of 1933 it had been growing more and more apparent that Italy was preparing to conquer Abyssinia, a primitive African state which counted slavery among its institutions. On 5 December 1934 Italian and Abyssinian troops shot each other up at Wal-Wal, on the vague and disputed border between Abyssinia and Italian Somaliland, an occurrence which seemed to bring the expected Italian invasion much nearer. Here was an affair which in former times would have concerned only Italy and the Abyssinians. By 3 January 1935, however, Haile Selassie, the Emperor of Abyssinia, had appealed to the Council of the League of Nations to safeguard peace; i.e. to preserve Abyssinia. By this appeal Haile Selassie launched the biggest crisis in the League's history – subjecting it to a far severer test even than Manchuria. For if the Italians were to attack Abyssinia, it would be a blatant case of international breaking and entering in broad daylight; too blatant to be fudged over by Lytton commissions or like devices.

Nevertheless internationalists in England confidently prepared to meet the challenge. As Lord Allen of Hurtwood (Clifford Allen), the pacifist, explained in a letter to his young daughter Polly:

> . . . Italy is a country of white people, and Italy wants to rule Abyssinia instead of allowing the black people to govern their own country. This, of course, is what used to happen in the old days. Strong countries like England used to allow their Generals and their Admirals like Francis Drake, to go out and capture other peoples' countries. . . .

[1] CAB 53/24, COS 372.

No one could stop us. We just did it because we were the strongest country.

But now that we have got a League of Nations in the world, all the countries have promised not to do that kind of thing any more, and nearly every country, including Abyssinia, whether it consists of white people or black people, has joined the League of Nations. In future if any country feels angry with another country, like Italy does with Abyssinia, it must not go off on its own, like Francis Drake used to, and capture that country. It has to come to the League of Nations and say: 'We are angry with our neighbours.' And then the League of Nations goes into the trouble and tries to make up its mind who is right and who is wrong just like a Judge in our own country.[1]

Internationalists like Allen believed that once the League had successfully asserted its authority over Italy, then other rogues would be deterred from embarking on active roguery. Therefore, in their convictions, the future security of England and France, as well as of all smaller states, lay in absolute fidelity now to the League and its principles in dealing with the question of Italy and Abyssinia. The confidence in the authority of the League demonstrated in Allen's letter to his daughter was general among internationalists. It was a confidence which rested in turn on a trust, curious in the circumstances, in England's own capacity to direct the course of world events from her seat at Geneva. Moralising internationalists indeed made unconscious assumptions about the extent of British power more grandiose than the claims of the most port-complexioned old imperialist; assumptions nobly and sonorously expressed by Dr Hugh Dalton during the Labour Party Conference of 1935:

For better or worse, this country of ours is a Great Power in the world, with correspondingly great responsibilities, not only to our own people but to all mankind. And the question is: Are we going to play the part of a Great Power today, a Great Power for peace, a Great Power for righteousness, a Great Power for justice among the nations?[2]

As the Abyssinian crisis deepened, League-of-Nations men (and women) in Britain bustled about ever more urgently and earnestly, preaching sentiments like Allen's and Dalton's to enthusiastic congregations. As a

[1] Letter written in November 1935, quoted in Martin Gilbert, *Plough My Own Furrow: The Story of Lord Allen of Hurtwood as told through his own writings and correspondence* (London, Longmans 1965), pp. 343–4.
[2] Quoted in Connell, p. 193.

consequence of this evangelism, the British Government came under strong moral pressure to play the part of a great power for righteousness and justice. It was a noble part. Unfortunately those who so passionately urged it on the British Government took no account either of the current world strategic balance or of the factors of comparative national power. For to act over Abyssinia as a great power for righteousness and justice necessarily entailed antagonising Italy; and the more strong-handed and effective the justice, the greater the antagonism. Yet Italy was a traditionally friendly country with whom England had no quarrel of her own – further, a country whose friendship it was of the very highest importance for England and France to retain.

Italy had fought in the Great War at the side of England and France, although she was bound by prior treaty to Germany and Austria, and lost 460,000 men killed. The advent of a Fascist dictatorship under Benito Mussolini in 1922 had not modified the traditionally cordial relations between Italy and England. Despite the brutality with which Fascism dealt with its internal enemies, Mussolini was widely admired in England during the 1920s; Austen Chamberlain and Winston Churchill being among the most eminent of those who saw him as a great patriot and reformer. Italy's foreign policy had remained – on the whole – respectable enough. She was a prominent member of the League of Nations; she signed the Treaty of Locarno as a co-guarantor with England of the Franco-German frontier and of the demilitarised zone of the Rhineland. In 1935 the preservation of the post-war settlement of Europe therefore depended hardly less on Italy than on England and France – particularly in view of Italy's special interest in the independence of Austria, which kept the power of Nazi Germany away from the Brenner Pass. By way of re-affirming their joint interest in the present European *status quo*, the three powers met in conference at Stresa in April 1935; a time when the Abyssinian crisis had already begun to hatch, but which subject the English and French tactfully forbore to mention; an omission Mussolini interpreted as a silent blessing of his purpose.

Since 1931, and the rise of Japanese ambitions in the Far East and Nazi ambitions in Europe, the friendship of Italy had become of immense strategic as well as political value to France and England. In the case of England, the whole rickety and overstrained structure of imperial defence rested on the assumption that, should war break out with Japan, the British battlefleet would be able to pass without hindrance through the Mediterranean on its way to Singapore. If Italy were alienated, this would cease to obtain. Instead there would be a potential enemy astride England's main line of imperial communication at a time when she was already under threat from two existing potential enemies at opposite ends of the line. If – worse – Italy were to fight in a future war as an ally of Germany or Japan, or both, the British would be forced to abandon the Mediterranean for the first time since 1798, thereby vitiating the purpose of the elaborate British involvement in the Middle East and directly endangering Egypt. All these sombre reflections were much to occupy the minds of the Chiefs of Staff during the Abyssinian crisis.

The strategic situation of France too would be greatly weakened if Italy's friendship were cast aside. France would not only lose a political ally – albeit an unreliable one – against German ambitions, but gain a second possible foe on her frontiers at a time when she needed to concentrate all her strategic resources against the existing one.

Thus for England and France to espouse the cause of Abyssinia against Italy would be to inflict far-reaching damage on their own world interests. What was demanded by fidelity to the high principles of the Covenant of the League of Nations ran clean counter to what was demanded by imperative strategic need.

The French solution of this dilemma was simple, and steadily pursued throughout the crisis. For Pierre Laval, the French Foreign Minister, all that really mattered was Nazi Germany. His eyes were on the demilitarised zone of the Rhineland; his thoughts on the Locarno guarantees. To estrange Italy, one of the Locarno powers, over such a question as Abyssinia did not appeal to Laval's Auvergnat peasant mind. In January 1935 he therefore made a private deal with Italy conniving at the absorption of most of Abyssinia into the Italian Empire.

Unfortunately his prudish English colleagues proceeded to try to drag him and France into a chivalrous attempt to save Abyssinia from forceful extinction. Since Laval needed English support against Germany, he could not entirely refuse to co-operate. However, he was deviously careful to limit this co-operation to words as far as he was able; partly in order not to provoke Italy if he could help it, partly in order to try to hold the balloon of English idealism on the ground with a ballast of French realism. Laval has received unfavourable notices in English memoirs[1] on account of his lack of enthusiasm for League action over Abyssinia, his backsliding, his repeated *penchant* for trying to resolve the crisis by private deals with Mussolini at the expense of Abyssinia. Yet in fact his policy, if not his tactics, was remarkably clear and consistent, as well as sane, from start to finish. As he told Eden in June 1935, the policy of France was to

[1] Cf. Avon, Vol. I.

refrain from doing anything which would disturb Italo-French relations.[1] What could be plainer than this? But so simple a motive as unalloyed national self-interest was hard for the British to understand or accept. Nor was Laval himself the kind of Frenchman to appeal to English public-school men. He looked like a dishonest *garagiste* of the Midi; swart, squat, sweaty and inadequately shaven. He wore a white tie during the day. All too clearly he was a bounder.

Unlike the shrewd and cynical Laval, the English themselves were helplessly caught between the fantasy of acting as a great power for righteousness, and the reality that to do so was, in the light of the general world situation, both vastly beyond England's strength and damaging to her own interests. It is the hapless wrigglings of the British Cabinet between fantasy and reality that provide the plot, from a British point of view, of the long drawn-out Abyssinian affair.

On 15 May 1935 the affair first became the subject of a full-dress Cabinet debate; a debate in which the Cabinet deliberately cast away a legitimate, if unsportsmanlike opportunity of allowing England and the League of Nations to slip out of further involvement with Abyssinia. A League Conciliation Commission had been appointed to try to solve the Italo-Abyssinian border disputes, and was now at work. The British Cabinet feared however that the Italians might claim that, since the League's conciliation machinery was thereby in due operation, nothing further need be done at present by the League Council. Unless England took the initiative, therefore, the Cabinet feared that the Abyssinian question would as a consequence be postponed until the next regular meeting of the Council in September. By that time the rainy season in Abyssinia would have ended and the Italian invasion would either have started or be about to start. Moreover, the Italians would be able to claim that their recourse to war was perfectly legal under the Covenant because the specified three months' delay for attempts at conciliation had been exhausted.[2]

Thus the English only had to lie low until the autumn, and the Italian army would wrap up the embarrassing problem of Abyssinia in short order, and in legal fashion. But the Cabinet's opinion, on the contrary, was that 'His Majesty's Government could not acquiesce in procedures at the League which must result in nothing being done before September to stop hostilities and in there not being even an opportunity to do anything.'[3]

So, fatefully, the English committed themselves to an active League-of-

[1] Cf. Avon, Vol. I, p. 233. [2] CAB 23/81, 26(35)9. [3] Ibid.

Nations policy over Abyssinia. At the same time they recognised that a formal quarrel between the League and Italy offered risks better avoided. Therefore they tempered their public spirit by a private attempt to satisfy Mussolini, and thus de-fuse the crisis. But how could anyone satisfy Mussolini, short of handing over most of Abyssinia trussed up in some diplomatic tape and sealing wax, as indeed Laval wished to do? This, however, was not within the orbit of British thinking, for the Foreign Office pronounced against the partition of Abyssinia on the punctilious grounds that Abyssinia was a member of the League of Nations.[1] With an old-fashioned job of carvery by the great powers thus ruled out, any proposal for territorial adjustment would have to be acceptable to both parties. Yet a deal whose terms satisfied Mussolini must *ipso facto* be unacceptable to Haile Selassie, who was looking confidently to the League of Nations to preserve his ancient patrimony. And if there was any question of inducing Haile Selassie to make large concessions, there was also British public opinion to be considered.

The British Government therefore drafted a proposal by which, of all things, *Britain herself* would cede the small port of Zeila in British Somaliland, and a corridor thereto, to Abyssinia, by way of compensating Haile Selassie for minor tracts of territory elsewhere which they hoped he would agree to cede to Italy. In view of the scale of Mussolini's ambitions this proposal was at once pettifogging and misconceived. During the summer and autumn of 1935 however much time and effort was to be expended by the British Government in drafting and re-drafting ingenious schemes of territorial adjustment and economic concession in the impossible hope of eventually pleasing Mussolini and Haile Selassie at the same time; the records suggest that the minds of the Cabinet and the Foreign Office were happier with such petty detail than with broad questions of world strategy.

In their efforts to avert an open rupture between Italy and the League, the British coupled their proposals for a deal with an attempt privately to warn Mussolini off. The means of deterrence took the form of sermons such as that read to Mussolini in Rome on 23 June 1935 by Anthony Eden, the Minister for League-of-Nations Affairs:

> I began by telling Signor Mussolini that His Majesty's Government were gravely concerned at the turn events were taking between Italy and Abyssinia. Our reasons were neither egoist nor African, but European. His Majesty's Government were irrevocably committed to

[1] Cabinet meeting of 19 June, CAB 23/82, 33(35)4.

the League. They could not therefore remain indifferent to events which might profoundly affect the League's future. . . .[1]

Eden attempted to convey to Mussolini how strongly all sections of opinion in Britain believed in the League, and warned him: 'If Italy were to take the law into her own hands in Abyssinia and the consequences were to be fatal to the League, the British people would inevitably and deeply resent it.'[2]

So it was that by midsummer 1935 the British had already reached the point where they were admonishing an old friend and ally, a co-guarantor of the Locarno Treaty and a naval power astride their main imperial artery; and doing so in the tone of Dr Arnold rebuking a boy at Rugby for wickedness and sin.

Eden's visit to Rome, which he acknowledged to be a complete failure,[3] had followed a prolonged meeting of the Cabinet on 19 June; the first on the topic of Abyssinia since Baldwin had become Prime Minister for the third time on 7 June, and MacDonald had stepped down into Baldwin's former post of Lord President of the Council.

In the new Cabinet, some ministers, notably Eden and MacDonald, fully shared the internationalists' faith in the League. Others, like Baldwin, were ambiguous in their outlook, wishing to see the League succeed and its ideals prevail, yet aware of the risks to England herself of a whole-hearted League policy. Others again – especially heads of service departments like Sir Bolton Eyres-Monsell, the First Lord of the Admiralty – took a purely strategic or Palmerstonian line. For them it was, in view of English military and naval weakness and the global threat to the British Empire, highly dangerous nonsense to provoke Italy.

The most passionate advocate of absolute fidelity to the Covenant of the League in dealing with the Abyssinian question was, appropriately enough, the Minister for League-of-Nations Affairs, Anthony Eden. Eden, at thirty-seven, was the young man of the Cabinet, a representative of the new generation of public-school officer present here among ageing Victorians, a veteran of the trenches; idealistic, sensitive; something of a Brooke or a Sassoon. His were the kind of delicately and sensitively handsome features which would have well ornamented the wicket on the night when there was a breathless hush in the close, with ten to make and the last man in. The brave cause of the League could have hardly have found a more appropriate standard-bearer; and, as Vansittart

[1] Eden's record at the time, quoted in Avon, Vol. I, p. 222.
[2] Ibid. [3] Ibid. p. 225.

wrote, Eden's instincts 'harboured few enthusiasms except for the League'.[1]

As Minister for League-of-Nations Affairs during the Abyssinian crisis Eden really acted as a second, and competitive, foreign secretary, urging his own policy in Cabinet, negotiating on England's behalf not only through the League at Geneva, but also directly with foreign governments, as with Mussolini in June. The springs of his policy are to be found in a pure internationalist faith, in a public-schoolboy's sense of honour and doing the right thing. Neither in his actions nor utterances at the time, nor even in retrospect in his memoirs, does he display any interest in, or understanding of, strategy or the world-balance of power, or the likely strategic consequences to England of his League idealism. He was indeed essentially another believer in 'moral authority'. In a memorandum written at Baldwin's request in the latter half of July, he argued that England must support the League, because otherwise 'any opportunity that might still remain of bringing about peace *by the use of the League's moral authority* [author's italics] will be destroyed'.[2]

His rival, the Foreign Secretary *en titre*, Sir Samuel Hoare, had, according to Hoare himself, been chosen for the post in preference to Eden because Eden was adjudged too young and emotional.[3] As Secretary of State for Air from 1922 to 1924, and from 1924 to 1929, Hoare had acquired a reputation for energy and efficiency that was hardly justified by the state of British aviation, and which may have been more a tribute to the sloth and senescence of the Government as a whole. As Secretary of State for India from 1931 to 1935, he had been credited with great skill in reconciling differences, skill which some hoped would now prove useful in the field of foreign affairs.[4] In terms of personal presence, character and force of personality, he was, although different enough from his predecessor, Simon, hardly an improvement as a rider of whirlwinds and a director of storms, being, in Harold Macmillan's phrase, 'a man of modest stature and a certain prim correctness of manner'.[5] It was this primness, accentuated as it was by a mincing speech, which most impressed Hoare's contemporaries. 'He had a very sharp mind,' wrote Sir Basil Liddell Hart later, 'along with a sharpness of facial outline that reflected his primly precise manner – which prompted "FE", Lord Birkenhead, with devastating aptness to describe him as "the last of a long line of maiden aunts".'[6]

Having been brought up, in his own words, 'in a typically Victorian

[1] Vansittart, p. 429. [2] Avon, Vol. I, p. 243.
[3] Viscount Templewood, *Nine Troubled Years* (London, Collins 1954), p. 108.
[4] Ibid. [5] Macmillan, p. 449. [6] Liddell Hart, Vol. I, p. 143.

family, whose traditions had for generations been Quaker, Evangelical . . .', Hoare fully shared the assumptions about the nature of foreign affairs that were current among most of his colleagues and in the country at large.[1] He too entertained hopes that the Great War had been the 'war to end war';[2] that it had been just a 'unique aberration in human affairs'.[3] He too accepted the Covenant of the League of Nations as the guiding principle of English foreign policy.

As Foreign Secretary, however, he was to be exposed to the more powerful mind and will of Sir Robert Vansittart, his Permanent Under-Secretary; and Vansittart ceaselessly urged upon him the need to avert a breach with Mussolini. Hoare, like a maiden aunt caught between the promptings of her upbringing and moral principles and the shrewd advice of some worldly nephew, dithered. Even as summarised by himself in retrospect, his policy was yet another impossible attempt to reconcile the inconsistent, being one 'of negotiation with Italy and respect for our obligations under the Covenant, based on Anglo-French co-operation'.[4] It was he who had to face the fundamental dilemma that, while the British Government was committed to a League-of-Nations policy, it did not wish to incur the inevitable and unpleasant consequences.

At the new Cabinet's first discussion of the Abyssinian question on 19 June, Hoare reported that the problem was now becoming urgent, for Italian forces were proceeding to the Red Sea. France, he went on, who should have supported the League in the event of a clash, was showing every sign of siding with Italy. There was, Hoare argued, every prospect of England being placed 'in a most inconvenient dilemma':[5] 'Either we should have to make a futile protest, which would irritate Mussolini and perhaps drive him out of the League into the arms of Germany, or we should make no protest at all and give the appearance of pusillanimity.'[6] Thus briefly and lucidly did Hoare sum up the predicament into which the British Government had now got themselves.

The Cabinet meeting of 3 July 1935 saw this predicament explored further. It was pointed out that an Italian attack on Abyssinia would be a breach of an agreement of 1906 between Italy, France and Great Britain on the future of Abyssinia, of Article X of the Covenant of the League of Nations and also of the Kellogg Pact. If British obligations under the Covenant were to be ignored or evaded, the Cabinet considered that a heavy blow would be dealt at the whole post-war system of pacts and agreements. So much for principle; the Cabinet now turned to the

[1] Templewood, p. 111.
[2] Ibid.
[3] Ibid.
[4] Ibid. p. 161.
[5] CAB 23/82, 33(35)4.
[6] Ibid.

practical question of what Britain could or should do. Yet even now the Cabinet's internationalist preconceptions remained too strong to permit it to jettison its League policy. Instead it asked the Foreign Office to study the problems arising out of a war between Italy and Abyssinia, and a sub-committee of the CID to report on possible coercive measures against Italy, including the closing of the Suez Canal.[1]

After this meeting and following a private talk with Baldwin, who still favoured action through the League, Sir Warren Fisher, Permanent Secretary to the Treasury and head of the Civil Service, wrote to the Prime Minister and posed those root questions to which the Government had hitherto shirked straight answers: 'If Italy persists in her present policy, is England really prepared not merely to threaten, but also to use force, and is she in a position to do this successfully?'[2]

Britain had not intervened over Manchuria, Fisher went on, nor would she if the Germans seized Memel. He also noted that the greater part of the League's influence derived from British participation; and argued that Britain on her own could not make thee Lague an effective world conscience or policeman.[3]

Although the Cabinet's corporate mind lacked Fisher's ability to pierce through to such fundamentals, the likely consequences of its altruism over Abyssinia nevertheless continued to occur to it piecemeal. On 22 July 1935 it had progressed from pondering upon a war between Italy and Abyssinia to the far more terrifying topic of a war between Italy on the one hand and France and England on the other.[4] Such a war, the Cabinet sagely reflected, would have wider effects in Europe, and hence there was a need to avoid such a contingency.

By midsummer 1935 therefore the British Government had come to enjoy all the comfort and freedom of manœuvre of a man on the rack, wrenched as they were between the fantasy of a League-of-Nations policy and the truth of Britain's weakness and danger. And as Italian preparations mounted apace, and the September campaigning season grew nearer, the distance between fantasy and truth opened wider still.

In Britain at large the cause of Abyssinia and the League was the occasion of an immense bustling about, and a holding of meetings, and an issuing forth of tracts. At the end of June, after Eden's return from Rome, the results of the so-called Peace Ballot were announced.[5] This was an amateurish and unscientific attempt at a poll of the electorate's attitudes to

[1] CAB 23/82, 35(35)2 and 36(35)6.
[2] The Baldwin Papers, quoted in Middlemass and Barnes, p. 840.
[3] Ibid.
[4] CAB 23/82, 39(35)1.
[5] See below pp. 420–4.

various issues connected with peace, war, sanctions and the League of Nations. The nature of its sponsors and organisers, as well as of the volunteers who carried out the leg-work of questioning on the doorstep, guaranteed the partiality of the operation. The questions themselves were so phrased as to angle for the response desired. Nevertheless the results of the Ballot received immense publicity and made an immense impact on public opinion. In particular, the Ballot appeared to demonstrate that an overwhelming majority of the electorate, some 9,000,000 to 600,000, was in favour of economic and non-military action by all nations against an aggressor; and that a smaller, though still decisive, majority of some 6,000,000 to 2,000,000 was even in favour of military action.

What this implied in terms of Abyssinia was plain; here was a general public expectation that England would wield the flaming sword of righteousness. To a government in the middle of an election year, this expectation was a factor impossible to ignore or defy. The influence of internationalist myth over British policy had been decisively strengthened at a time when reality was at last beginning to shed its cold morning light on some of the members of the Cabinet.

Nailed therefore to a League-of-Nations policy by public opinion, the Government sought to dodge at every point the practical consequences that must inevitably flow from it. On 24 July 1935 Hoare explained to his colleagues the subtle line he was taking towards the French in the course of seeking their co-operation in a concerted policy to avert a war between Italy and Abyssinia:

> His aim was to avoid crude questions being put by either side to the other as to whether they were prepared to carry out their obligations under the Covenant. The underlying assumption would be that both Powers realised their obligations and were therefore interested to find a way out of the difficulty.[1]

On 21 August a meeting of ministers discussed at great length the state of the crisis, the autumn campaigning season both at Geneva and in Abyssinia now being only a couple of weeks away.[2]

Eden reported on the failure of the latest talks between Italy, France and England, held in Paris. The Italian representative, Count Aloisi, the ambassador in Paris, had asked for recognition of Italy's special economic and political position in Abyssinia. Eden had replied that this, amounting

[1] CAB 23/82, 40(35)1; see also meeting of 31 July 1935, CAB 23/82, 41(35)4.
[2] Present were Baldwin, MacDonald, Neville Chamberlain (Chancellor of the Exchequer), Simon (now Home Secretary), Hoare and Eden.

as it did to a Class C League mandate, offered no hope of a solution; and he made it clear that Great Britain would not endorse an Italian occupation of Abyssinia. Italy, on the other hand, found the Anglo-French proposals unacceptable, being too favourable towards Abyssinia. The occasion had not proved a meeting of minds. As Eden himself had written home, 'the truth is probably that since Mussolini's own policy is by nature opportunistic and agnostic, he finds it quite impossible to believe in the British faith in a new system of international order'.[1]

Since attempts to settle the business in private had once again come to nought, the ghastly prospect loomed yet nearer that the League (and Britain) would have to live up to the Covenant; have to redeem fine sentiments with strong action. Alternatively the British Government could follow the advice tendered to Eden two days previously by S. M. Bruce, the Australian High Commissioner in London and a former Australian Prime Minister. Bruce argued that if Britain, with her seapower, led the League in stopping Italy by sanctions, this would serve only to establish a precedent for similarly stopping Germany. But Germany was surrounded by weak states which would be hesitant to annoy her by applying sanctions. Bruce then summed up the dilemma as he saw it: if they stopped Italy, they would have to live up to it *vis-à-vis* Germany; if they failed to stop Italy, the League would be undermined. Bruce's solution was radical indeed; it was in essence that henceforth British policy should be based on fact rather than fiction. In his opinion, Britain should announce to the world that owing to the absence of certain major countries from the League, 'the League must admit to the world that it could not carry out the functions embodied in the Covenant at the present time'; and couple this admission with an announcement of an immense British rearmament programme.[2]

However, to acknowledge publicly that the League was a sham called for robuster men than those who dominated Baldwin's Cabinet. For, as Sir Samuel Hoare explained to his colleagues, in referring to his recent conversations with the leaders of the opposition parties, '. . . he had been left with the opinion that there would be a wave of public opinion against the Government if it repudiated its obligations under Article 16. . . . It was abundantly clear that the only safe line for His Majesty's Government was to try out the regular League of Nations procedure.'[3]

This statement provoked a thoughtful discussion among the ministers

[1] Avon, Vol. I, p. 250.
[2] Cecil Edwards, *Bruce of Melbourne; Man of Two Worlds* (London, Heinemann 1966), p. 234.
[3] CAB 23/82, FA(H)7.

present as to what exactly were Britain's obligations to the League, together with various ingenious interpretations which would allow Britain to shirk positive action. It was the topic of sanctions which however best displayed the British dilemma. Chamberlain, the Chancellor of the Exchequer, pointed out that 'even the mildest economic sanction might in the end lead to war', and hence the British armed forces ought now to be put in a state of readiness. Hoare agreed – Mussolini might attack. MacDonald hoped that it would be possible 'to discover a completely pacific method of applying economic sanctions against Italy'.[1]

Next day, 22 August, the full Cabinet met to discuss the British line at the forthcoming critical session of the League Assembly in September. Painful questions occurred to them. What would be the effects of sanctions on Britain's own trade? Would non-League powers like America join in? For if sanctions were to be effective, they must be unanimous. Then again, sanctions might provoke Italy into a sudden attack against British interests. It was remarked that to lay sanctions on Italy would, as the Minutes expressed it, have an effect on future relations between Italy and England.[2]

It had also at last sunk in that England was not really up to the role of a great power for righteousness, for ministers made many anguished references 'to the grave effects on our diplomacy of our present military weakness'.[3]

For the Cabinet had asked the Chiefs of Staff to report on the military implications of applying Article 16 of the League-of-Nations Covenant. Even then, as the Chiefs of Staff pointed out in their report dated 3 August, the Cabinet had not requested them to consider the wider implications in Europe or elsewhere of action against Italy, and that they had therefore not done so. Their paper restricted itself to listing the air, sea and land reinforcements that would be necessary in the Mediterranean and Middle East, and to voicing the need for the armed forces to be given plenty of advance warning of a clash with Italy.[4]

It was only in a memorandum of 9 August 1935 that the Chiefs of Staff put on record their first strategic appreciation of the global effects of embroilment with Italy.[5] It was a document for which the Government would have done well to have asked, and studied, before they originally committed themselves to their League policy over Abyssinia. Coming now, however, it had the dismal ring of a profligate peer's man of business itemising too late the likely consequences of folly already committed. The COS analysed the effect on British seapower, upon which the existence of

[1] CAB 23/82, FA(H)7.
[2] CAB 23/82, 42(35)1.
[3] Ibid.
[4] CAB 53/25, COS 388.
[5] CAB 53/25, COS 392.

the British Empire depended, and concluded: 'There is bound to be a danger, therefore, that the results of a war with Italy would be to leave the British Fleet temporarily weakened to such an extent as to be unable to fulfil its worldwide responsibilities.'[1]

Nor was this all. The despatch of air reinforcements to the Mediterranean would weaken England *vis-à-vis* Germany, and affect our aim of reaching parity with her in the air by April 1937. Moreover, it would not be possible to reinforce the air forces at Singapore.

The Chiefs of Staff concluded their paper by sternly warning the Government against rushing precipitately into sanctions, and asserted that the 'assured military support' of France was 'essential'.[2]

It was a tormenting dilemma that the unfortunate Cabinet faced at this meeting on 22 August 1935. In one ear there was, in these chilling reports by the COS, the voice of reality; in the other, in the emotional rhetoric of the internationalists, the voice of fantasy. The Cabinet had to choose between the grim counts of ships, men and aircraft, the factual analysis of the world strategic situation, and a romantic idealism which could ignore such mundane questions. It was not only that the fantasy and the reality impinged on the Government as external political factors which they must weigh one against the other; the members of the Government, individually and as a whole, were themselves torn asunder between them. As a consequence the Cabinet once again found escape in evasion and inconsistency. While recognising that a war with Italy would be 'a grave calamity', the Cabinet nevertheless decided that the British delegation at Geneva should re-affirm that Great Britain would fulfil her obligations: '. . . they should aim at following closely the procedure laid down in the Covenant, not in any quixotic spirit, and with due regard to the many difficulties'.[3]

More concrete and more ominous was the Cabinet's decision to order the Home Fleet to the Mediterranean, anti-aircraft units to Malta and Alexandria and RAF reinforcements to the Middle East.

Close step, the Cabinet agreed, must be kept with France.

For the nearer the British got to the prospect of really having to take action against Italy on behalf of the League, the more eager were they to ensure themselves the diplomatic and military support of France. The French, for their part, continued to display a lack of enthusiasm which disappointed, wounded and even disgusted the British. Eden regarded Paris as 'a thieves' kitchen'.[4] 'My chief fear', he wrote in August, 'is lest we should be led into taking part in some attempt to make the Abyssinians

[1] Ibid. [2] Ibid. [3] CAB 23/82, 42(35)1. [4] Avon, Vol. I, p. 249.

accept an unjust and unworthy settlement. This would rob us of our good name. . . .'[1] It never seems to have occurred to Eden or other of the League's champions within the British Government that they were calling on the French to take risks in support of a policy which was not France's own, and whose dangers and unprofitability the French Government had repeatedly pointed out;[2] or that this accounted for and justified French deviousness and obstructiveness and French hankering after a bargain with Mussolini. Laval, now the French Foreign Minister, in particular did not budge from his early conviction that to upset Italy at a time of Germany's rapid rearmament was utter folly. He was certain that sanctions must lead to war and therefore wished to be caught up in Britain's Tennysonian chivalry as little as possible. He heaved a shrewdly aimed and sharp-cornered question at Anthony Eden, perhaps the most chivalric minister of all, during a meeting in Paris on 2 September, just before the new session of the League opened. Would Great Britain, he asked, be as firm in upholding the Covenant, even by sanctions, in Europe (i.e. in the case of Germany), as at present over Abyssinia?

Laval here called in question the fundamental validity of League enthusiasts' case over Italy, the League and sanctions – the case not only as passionately argued at the time, but as still to be believed by them in distant retrospect;[3] the case according to which Abyssinia was a crucial test for the League, which, once successfully passed, would have strengthened it against Germany. But faced with Laval's acute enquiry, Eden could return only a lame answer: to stand firm over Abyssinia would, he averred, strengthen the authority of the League, 'and our moral obligation to assist in supporting and enforcing the Covenant correspondingly increased. If, however, the Covenant were now violated with impunity, the authority of the League would be so impaired that its future influence must be negligible in Europe or anywhere else.'

Laval replied, justly enough, that this was the answer he expected, but that it did not meet his question.[4] Eden, writing in retrospect, comments: 'This may have been true, but the British Government's wariness *and the state of our defences* [author's italics] made it impossible for me to promise unconditional support of the Covenant in the future, regardless of the outcome of the present dispute.'[5]

This apologia hardly seems to further his case. Here was an admission, from him of all people, that Britain was really not strong enough to sustain

[1] Avon, Vol. I, p. 249
[2] Cf. Eden in Avon, Vol. I, p. 249.
[3] Cf. Kingsley Martin, p. 171; Avon, Vol. I, *passim*.
[4] Avon, Vol. I, p. 258.
[5] Ibid.

the role he had been urging upon her; that however well the League fared against Italy, this would constitute no precedent for action against Germany. Here too was an admission that, whereas Britain was now counting on France to stand fast, militarily and diplomatically, to the Covenant over Abyssinia, France could not depend in turn on Britain standing fast to the Covenant over Germany.

Since the Cabinet's conclusions on 22 August[1] hardly provided clear guidance as to what Hoare should say and do at Geneva, Hoare asked Baldwin and Chamberlain to dinner on 5 September in order to mull over the British predicament once again. According to Chamberlain, who left the only account of the occasion, he, Chamberlain, recommended that Britain take a firm line, even to the point of sanctions: 'They might force Italy to a halt, which in turn might make Hitler waver.'[2] His companions agreed that England should talk strong at Geneva. Hoare wrote later that he was 'determined to make a revivalist appeal to the Assembly. At best it might start a new chapter of League recovery, at worst it might deter Mussolini by a display of League fervour. If there was any element of bluff in it, it was a moment when bluff was not only legitimate, but inescapable.'[3]

Thus British policy over Abyssinia finally and completely floated away into fantasy. Yet such was the dilemma in which the Government had trussed themselves that, as with the heroes of old-fashioned boys' adventure serials, there was no escape but through the impossible.

On 9 September the COS uttered more warnings against rash action.[4]

On 10 and 11 September Hoare saw Laval in Paris. Hoare had been warned by the British ambassador in Rome, Sir Eric Drummond, that Italy was ready to commit suicide rather than back down. Hoare therefore agreed with Laval that their two countries would only take such measures at Geneva as could not lead to war – no sanctions, no blockades. The reality of the League powers' strategic weakness and danger being thus acknowledged in private, Hoare proceeded to Geneva, and on 12 September delivered himself in public of a speech, drafted in collaboration with Chamberlain and approved by Baldwin, in the very opposite sense:

> . . . on behalf of His Majesty's Government of the United Kingdom, I can say that this Government will be second to none in its intention to fulfil, within the measure of its capacity, the obligations which the Covenant lays upon it . . . the attitude of His Majesty's Government

[1] See above p. 363. [2] Feiling, p. 268. [3] Templewood, p. 166.
[4] CAB 53/25, COS 395.

> has always been one of unswerving fidelity to the League and all that it stands for, and the case now before us is no exception. . . . The recent response of public opinion shows how completely the nation supports the Government in the full acceptance of the obligations of League membership, which is the oft-proclaimed keynote of British policy. . . . In confronting with its precise and explicit obligations, the League stands, and my country stands with it, for collective maintenance of the Covenant in its entirety and in particular for steady and collective resistance to all acts of unprovoked aggression. . . .[1]

It was a speech which brought on a state of extreme euphoric excitement among internationalists – the very speech which they had always hoped to hear from an English foreign minister in such a crisis. They confidently, enthusiastically, looked forward to the Government making good every rash word of it. However, Hoare and his colleagues, having thus committed themselves in the most specific and public manner to a moralising internationalist policy at the most dangerous possible moment for doing so, almost immediately began to feel the chilling onset of doubt. What had they done? The Foreign Secretary, hardly a man bold and brutal enough even at his best to carry great feats of Palmerstonian bluff, was now a sick man, suffering much from arthritis and prone to fainting fits. In the bleak aftermath of his great moment at the rostrum in Geneva, when awareness returned of the gulf between his brave talking and the true state of British world strategic power, Hoare lost his nerve. He assured Mussolini through the British ambassador in Rome that England had not the smallest desire to humiliate Italy, and that she would warmly welcome a settlement.[2] He also informed Mussolini that England had no intention of proceeding to military sanctions or of closing the Suez Canal.

On 18 September a committee of the League mooted a fresh scheme for settling the Italo-Abyssinian dispute under League auspices. Four days later Mussolini rejected it. The long-awaited Italian aggression now seemed inevitable and imminent; inevitable too therefore that the League would have to live up to its pretensions, and England to Hoare's speech.

On 24 September the Cabinet discussed the impending struggle. Hoare opened his report confidently enough. Italy had not a friend in Europe. He was convinced that France had come round to the British point of view, and that she was prepared to join in sanctions. He believed that the United States too would join in. He thought it unlikely that Italy would

[1] Quoted in Middlemass and Barnes, pp. 856–7.
[2] Report to Cabinet on 24 September 1935, CAB 23/82, 43(35)1.

attack Great Britain because of British public opinion and the strengthening of the British fleet in the Mediterranean.

However, when he turned to the question of action by the League against Italy, it was only to point out how unpleasant was the dilemma in which the League was placed:

> If the League confined itself to a moral condemnation of Italy, its futility would be exposed. If sanctions were imposed he thought Italy would probably withdraw, at least temporarily, from the League. He thought that if circumstances required it, collective security ought to be tried out as if it was not effective the sooner we knew it the better.[1]

Nevertheless, in Hoare's opinion, the members of the League were only likely to come to an agreement over sanctions 'on a moderate basis'.[2]

In the ensuing discussion the Government now began to perceive further truths to which its internationalist aspirations had earlier blinded it. There was, the Cabinet noted, little sign at Geneva of other nations taking action in support of our point of view, 'in spite of bold speeches', and England might find herself alone carrying all the economic and strategic consequences of opposing Italy.[3] So much therefore for the internationalist belief that, in Eden's retrospective words, 'Britain had now taken a decision, as one of fifty nations, to try to stop Mussolini.'[4]

Now that it was turning out that the League of Nations was really little more than Britain herself in a world policeman's uniform, the Cabinet was less and less keen on wielding the truncheon alone. As Baldwin said: 'He thought all were agreed that the last thing that must be allowed to happen would be a single-handed war between this country and Italy.'[5]

The First Lord of the Admiralty, Lord Monsell, had sobering facts to put before his colleagues. In order for British seapower to function effectively in the Mediterranean it was essential to have the use of French naval bases, because British bases in that sea lacked adequate docking facilities. Comparison of the British Mediterranean fleet and the Italian fleet led the First Lord to say that 'in event of sanctions the position would not be a pleasant one', although the 'uninformed public' would probably demand that the fleet should be used. The danger of air attack in the narrow waters of the Mediterranean was 'a serious preoccupation',

[1] Ibid. [2] Ibid. [3] Ibid.
[4] Avon, Vol. I, p. 281.
[5] CAB 23/82, 43(35)1.

especially since the fleet's anti-aircraft equipment was not as much as could be wished.

Here then was reality again. Yet the Cabinet was more than ever a prisoner of internationalist fantasy, thanks to the effect of Hoare's speech on public opinion. As the Cabinet minutes record: 'The serious consequences of receding from the previous attitude were emphasised from the point of view of domestic policy no less than from that of foreign policy. It was pointed out that any weakness or vacillation would bring serious consequences.'[1]

And so the Government remained clapped fast in the stocks between fantasy and reality; seeking escape, as always, in an attempt to reconcile both in evasive *formulae*. It decided to fulfil its obligations to the League subject to the French doing likewise. No decision over sanctions would be taken until the attitude of League members and non-League states was known. In answer to the French, who had now officially posed the awkward question first put to Eden by Laval,[2] the Foreign Office was to say that in regard to a resort to force in Europe or elsewhere by other powers 'we reserved our attitude on the form in which Article 16 [of the Covenant] should be applied'. This shifty reply was to be coupled with a request to the French to clear up beyond doubt what *their* attitude would be if Italy attacked Great Britain in the Mediterranean.[3]

On 2 October the Foreign Secretary reported that the French were unlikely to agree to really severe sanctions. Far removed now from the euphoria of his Geneva speech, Hoare reflected Vansittart's urgings, Laval's desires, and his own fears of an Italian attack on British interests, when he expressed the hope that the powers 'would not be too intransigent and would be willing to consider a settlement which, without destroying Abyssinian independence, would give Italy some satisfaction'.[4] Eden, for all his enthusiasm for the League of Nations, had to report that 'the representatives of the other nations at Geneva were most reluctant to speak at all. He would continue his efforts to get them to do so.' He drew attention to the importance of his colleagues in their speeches hammering on the theme that the Italo-Abyssinian dispute was not a British concern 'but a League-of-Nations affair and that the whole future of the League depended on how the question was handled'.[5]

The Cabinet concluded that the severity of sanctions would depend on the attitude of other League and non-League nations; and that in any case military sanctions were 'out of the question'.

[1] CAB 23/82, 43(35)1.
[2] See above p. 364.
[3] CAB 23/82, 43(35)1.
[4] CAB 23/82, 44(35)1.
[5] Ibid.

Next day, 3 October 1935, at 5 a.m., the Italian forces crossed the Abyssinian border and opened the invasion that had been looming nearer for a year. The British Cabinet now faced a new situation altogether: no longer a possible future contingency but a present fact which must be dealt with.

The French reaction to the Italian attack was consistent enough; more urgently than ever Laval wished to conclude a deal with Mussolini at Abyssinia's expense; less than ever was he willing to risk bringing Italy's enmity down upon France by sanctions or military gestures. When the British Cabinet discussed Abyssinia on 16 October for the first time since the Italian attack, Hoare therefore had to report the painful news that Laval 'seemed to be constantly intriguing behind the back of the League of Nations and ourselves with a view to some accommodation with Signor Mussolini'.[1]

The First Lord of the Admiralty, for his part, was 'profoundly disquieted' by the lack of co-operation in the Mediterranean on the part of the French. He pointed out the danger to Malta from Italian attack and referred again to the British fleet's lack of bases.[2]

Thus, now that the British were well and truly committed to riding forth to the rescue of Abyssinia, they looked about them and noticed to their surprise that they were on their own. Indeed there were worse prospects too, for the Prime Minister, remembering Chanak, 'reminded the Cabinet that we must be careful not to be drawn into a quarrel with France as well as Italy as a result of what was happening at Geneva'.[3] In all the circumstances, it was little wonder that the Cabinet concluded that 'great caution must be exercised in the application of sanctions . . .'[4] On 11 October the League Council set up a Committee of Eighteen to recommend what action should be taken under Article 16 of the Covenant. By 19 October, thanks largely to Eden's urging, it had reported in favour of economic sanctions.

Internationalist opinion in Britain, far removed from such matters as French backsliding or a lack of docking facilities and anti-aircraft armament for the fleet, or inadequate reserves of shell or a shortage of sailors, let alone thoughts of possible moves by Japan or Germany, fervently exhorted the Government to lead the League into halting the Italian aggression forthwith by sanctions. The highly wrought-up mood of the internationalists and pacifists and also their immense confusions of thought are vividly conveyed by Kingsley Martin (hardly a hostile witness) in a

[1] CAB 23/82, 47(35)1.
[2] Ibid. [3] Ibid. [4] Ibid.

description of a combined Popular Front meeting in Birmingham Town Hall that autumn:

> The first speaker urged that we must carry out economic sanctions, but in no circumstances must the Labour Party support a war. I followed next and said that, though there was good ground for hoping that economic sanctions would be enough, there was a risk that war would follow, that we should be committed to it if there was war and that we ought to run the risk. The next speaker thanked me for my frankness and said that since sanctions might lead to war, he was altogether opposed to them. The fourth speaker demanded that Britain should at once take drastic steps, including blocking the Suez Canal, but that there must in no circumstances be a war . . . the meeting ended with an eloquent expression of the Christian pacifist case by Canon Stuart Morris, who was later to be chairman of the Peace Pledge Union.[1]

During the final Commons debate of the session on foreign affairs, on 21 and 22 October, Attlee, Leader of the Labour Opposition, wanted to know why economic sanctions had not yet been applied, while averring that the time for re-armament was not yet. Samuel, Leader of the Liberals, also thought it was not time to re-arm but coupled this opinion with a recommendation that military sanctions should be applied and the Suez Canal closed to Italian ships.[2]

And when L. S. Amery (now a backbencher) told the House that sanctions would be no use, that there should be a deal with Italy and a partition of Abyssinia, that the League was only useful for conciliation, and that British policy should rest on the strength of the British armed forces, it was, as he wrote in his Memoirs, 'the only speech I have ever made when I have felt that almost all the House was actually hostile'.[3]

In such a climate of opinion it was not surprising that during the General Election campaign of October 1935 the Government gave due prominence to its internationalist ideals and its loyalty to the League; and when therefore it won the election with a majority of 258 over other parties, it stood more than ever committed to forcing Italy to abandon her invasion of Abyssinia. Yet while the Cabinet itself did not discuss the Abyssinian question from 16 October to 27 November,[4] much was stirring beneath the surface, as Vansittart, Laval and Mussolini wielded

[1] Kingsley Martin, pp. 171–2. [2] Quoted in Middlemass and Barnes, p. 864. [3] Amery, Vol. III, p. 178.
[4] Except to hear from the Foreign Secretary on 23 October that, according to the United States ambassador, the US Government did not wish to invoke the Kellogg Pact over the Italo-Abyssinian dispute. CAB 23/82, 48(35)1.

their spoons. While Mussolini scraped Hoare's nerves with rumours of sudden attack, Vansittart pushed more strongly than ever in the direction of a deal with the Italian dictator. In intimate co-operation with Count Grandi, the Italian ambassador in London, a draft for such a deal was drawn up in the Foreign Office and then amended in Paris in collaboration with the French Foreign Office, all without the British Cabinet's cognisance. On 18 November the League Council in Geneva at last applied mandatory economic sanctions to Italy, even Laval's genius for procrastination having its limits. There was to be an embargo on all imports from Italy, coupled with an embargo on the export to Italy of a whole range of strategic commodities. However, oil, the one commodity of which Italy was desperately short and yet must have in order to carry on her invasion of Abyssinia, was omitted. For, as all the British Cabinet's own discussions on sanctions had foreshadowed, the League powers had found themselves in a hopeless dilemma. The harder sanctions bit into the Italians, the more likely they were to provoke Italy into acts of war by way of reprisal. As a consequence the present sanctions reflected a due sense of prudence, being at once unlikely either to cripple Italy's war effort or invite her reprisals.

It being soon apparent that these gestures were exercising no effect on the progress of Italian forces in Abyssinia, the League's champions began to urge that the sanction on oil should now be applied. Eden submitted a minute to the Cabinet on 2 December in this sense. Oil, he argued, was probably decisive for the success of sanctions. If the League decided on an oil embargo, other nations might join in too; there was a possibility of United States co-operation. On the other hand, if Britain hung back, everybody would be discouraged, especially countries which were already losing trade and money because of the existing sanctions. Here Eden acknowledged what supporters of sanctions often forget: that to apply sanctions against another country is automatically to apply sanctions to oneself. Eden was not impressed by the danger of an Italian attack, although he had to admit it was possible.[1]

In its discussion of oil sanctions on 2 December 1935 the Cabinet was torn yet again, and more deeply than ever, between its fidelity to the League and its awareness of England's world situation. Hoare himself, who was now very much in favour of a deal with Mussolini, offered a gloomy analysis. On the one hand there was the danger of Mussolini being goaded into a 'mad dog' act. On the other, there was at stake the future of sanctions 'and, with them, of the League, and, incidentally, the credit of His

[1] Avon, Vol. I, p. 296.

Majesty's Government'.[1] He referred to alarmist reports from foreign capitals that Mussolini was ready and willing to launch a 'mad dog' attack on British interests. '. . . there was', Hoare went on, 'the question of the serious gaps in our system of Imperial Defence, which were in a weak state as compared with an Italy mobilised for war.'[2]

Hoare expressed his belief that the actual and psychological effects of existing sanctions were already 'great'.[3] However, we could not 'give any appearance of refusing our part in genuine collective action', having fought the election on that line. Oil, he continued, was obviously an effective sanction: 'The more effective it was the more should we be placed in an indefensible position if, having supported what many people thought were ineffective sanctions, we now opposed an effective one.'[4]

But then there were all the concomitant dangers. In Hoare's opinion, Britain needed first to be sure of French, and if possible, American, support before agreeing to oil sanctions. At the same time there was a need to press on with peace negotiations as rapidly as possible in order to bring the conflict to an end.[5]

Sobering though Hoare had been, it was Lord Monsell, the First Lord of the Admiralty, who most effectively pointed out the dangers of pursuing a thorough-going League policy. Monsell pointed out that '. . . although there was no doubt that the Fleet was strong enough to obtain command of the Mediterranean, we might sustain serious losses, since our forces were not in a proper state of readiness for war in a land-locked sea'.[6] There were the repercussions of a war in the Mediterranean on the rest of Imperial Defence: 'The defences of Singapore were still incomplete, and our position in the Far East depended on the British Navy. So long as the fleet was tied up in the Mediterranean the position would be difficult. The air position in the Mediterranean was even worse than that of the Fleet.'[7]

And he summed up Britain's true strategic position, and the political implications thereof: '. . . our defence forces and defences in the Mediterranean were not in a proper condition for war, and from this point of view it was urged that an effort should be made to obtain peace, holding the threat of the oil sanction over Italy.'[8]

The discussion rambled on. The service departments asked that there should be no oil sanction until full French co-operation had been secured. The Cabinet noted that existing sanctions were involving British trade in very serious loss; that United States oil was going into Italy in vast quantities. The Cabinet had even more profound misgivings to ventilate:

[1] CAB 23/82, 50(35)2. [2] Ibid. [3] Ibid. [4] Ibid. [5] Ibid. [6] Ibid. [7] Ibid. [8] Ibid.

> A reverse in the Mediterranean would cost us less than twelve months of sanctions. The real question for decision was whether we were proceeding in the right way. Signor Mussolini as yet had shown no signs of weakness. The gap between our foreign policy and the state of our defence forces and defence was too wide.[1]

Thus, after pursuing its League policy over Abyssinia for eight months and having as a consequence trapped itself in the present appalling dilemma, the Cabinet had at last grasped the simple, obvious truth upon which British policy should have been founded from the start. It therefore decided to join an oil embargo only if all other oil-producing countries did so too; and only then after further efforts at peace talks. The way was at last clear for that policy of realism which Laval in France and Vansittart in England had been urging in vain for so long.

Hoare therefore set off for Paris in order to discuss peace proposals with Laval on his way to Switzerland for a skating holiday. Hoare had been much ground down by the prolonged crisis over Abyssinia; his arthritis was bad and his black-outs worse; he was 'blue and mottled from fatigue and stress'.[2] Unfortunately there was a complete misunderstanding between Hoare and his colleagues as to what he designed to accomplish in Paris. They believed that his purpose was to conduct a general discussion without, at this stage, coming to firm undertakings of any kind. Hoare himself intended, as he himself wrote at the time, 'to go all out for bringing the conflict to an end . . . If as I hope M. Laval and I agree upon a basis for a peace negotiation, Vansittart will stop in Paris for a day or two in order to clinch the details. . . .'[3]

Laval, in opening the talks on 7 December, denounced oil sanctions as a dangerous absurdity. He knew, he said, that an oil embargo would drive Italy to war, and France had no intention of going to war.

> To what end therefore an embargo on oil, which the Americans had no power to enforce . . . and which the Germans would anyhow violate . . . Besides, Italy's consumption of oil was small, because so was the campaign. . . . If we were going to enforce such sanctions, we might as well go to war by less roundabout means; and *he* would not go.[4]

Since Hoare and his colleagues, with the exception of Eden, had come to share these views, the talks proceeded briskly. On the second day Hoare

[1] Ibid.
[2] Sir Horace Wilson, quoted in Middlemass and Barnes, p. 882.
[3] Hoare to Lord Wigram, Private Secretary to the King, 2 December 1935, quoted in Middlemass and Barnes, p. 881.
[4] Ibid. p. 883.

and Laval initialled draft proposals, by which Abyssinia was to cede some 60,000 square miles of territory to Italy in return for a corridor either to the Red Sea or the Indian Ocean, and by which Italy was to be given a monopoly of economic development in the south and south-west of Abyssinia under some kind of League overlordship. These proposals, which owed their substance to earlier exchanges of views between Vansittart and Grandi, differed only in detail from those already negotiated by Sir Maurice Peterson, head of the Abyssinian Department of the Foreign Office and St Quentin, of the French Foreign Office; proposals which were known to the Cabinet at all stages of the negotiation.[1] They did not, however, accord with the proposals of the League Council's Committee of Five.

Hoare and Laval, pleased with their achievement, issued a communiqué in Paris, after which Hoare departed to skate in Switzerland, only to break his nose and retire to bed. According to the communiqué, the two ministers had sought the formulae 'which might serve as a basis for a friendly settlement of the Italo-Ethiopian dispute', and 'were satisfied with the result which we have achieved. The formulae however could not yet be published, the communiqué made clear, because the British Government had still to be informed of them and to agree to them, after which they would have to be put up to the interested parties and to the League.[2]

On Monday, 9 December the Cabinet met to discuss this unpleasantly precipitate development, which, thanks to the communiqué, was now the subject of world speculation. The Minister for League-of-Nations Affairs, Anthony Eden, supported the Foreign Secretary's proposals, although he wanted Abyssinia to receive them at the same time as Italy, and not later, this being in his view 'fairer'.[3]

Such scrupulousness was hardly consistent with the diplomatic strategy underlying the Hoare–Laval proposals, the essence of which was to get Mussolini's agreement and then offer Abyssinia the choice of accepting the joint proposals of the great powers or losing all. In a further discussion of the proposals on 10 December 1935, the Cabinet agreed that the present terms were 'the best, from the Abyssinian point of view, that could be obtained from Italy', or, put another way, 'the lowest terms which the French Government and the Secretary of State for Foreign Affairs thought that Italy might agree to'.[4]

At this time it fell, appropriately and ironically enough, to Eden to convey to his colleagues information that only served to emphasise how

[1] Vansittart, p. 538. [2] Avon, Vol. I, p. 300. [3] CAB 23/82, 52(35).
[4] CAB 23/82, 53(35).

desirable was a bargain over Abyssinia, and how isolated and dangerous was the situation into which Eden's own League idealism had helped to lead Great Britain. Reporting on 11 December as to what support Britain could count on if sanctions led Italy to attack her, he said that he had no news from France, but that Greece and Turkey had promised their full co-operation. The Yugoslavian answer had been less satisfactory.[1] And this was the sum total of what the League and its fifty members were really worth to Britain in a crisis; even a crisis incurred for the sake of the League.

The Cabinet therefore viewed oil sanctions with even greater misgiving. As Baldwin himself summed it up, such sanctions 'ought not to be undertaken unless we were assured that they would be effective', and 'until we knew what America was going to do we should hold our hand'.[2]

Although the Cabinet agreed with Eden over the need to treat Abyssinia and Italy exactly alike during negotiations, the Cabinet had, thus far, on the whole decided to back Hoare's proposals. Such misgivings as it felt were mainly on the score of their timing and circumstances and their likely reception by the League. After all, the alternative to a deal was a continuation of the crisis, with its dreadful prospect of having to make a decision, sooner or later, about oil sanctions.

But this was 1935, not 1835 or 1735. English foreign policy was no longer a matter simply for the foreign secretary or even the Cabinet. When the substance of the Hoare–Laval proposals leaked out to the press on 9–10 December, it detonated an explosion of moral indignation in Britain of a violence and magnitude never before seen. Up till now the internationalist fantasies beloved of articulate public opinion had provided only one factor, if a powerful factor, in the British Government's policy over Abyssinia. Now however public opinion took over the making of policy altogether, dictating to a subservient Cabinet in Downing Street with all the certainty born of strategic ignorance and passionate idealism.

On 10 December British newspapers first pronounced strongly against rewarding the aggressor. The Opposition, in the debate on the Address, pointed out that if the reports were true, the Government had been false to the policy on which it had fought the election; and took the rare course of voting against the Address in order to show their abhorrence of 'this terrible crime that seems likely to be committed'.[3] On 13 December *The Times*, which saw no danger in Nazi Germany and hence no reason to placate Mussolini, denounced the Hoare–Laval proposals in a leading article under the headline 'A Corridor for Camels', in which it said that

[1] CAB 23/82, 54(35). [2] Ibid. [3] Middlemass and Barnes, p. 889.

the proposals were dead from the moment their general tenor was known, because there never had been 'the slightest doubt that British public opinion would recommend them for approval by the League as a fair and reasonable basis of negotiation'.[1] *The Times*, thus striking the keynote of popular feeling by treating the proposals in terms of doctrinaire morality rather than of the strategic interests of England, or the dangers, difficulties and limitations of England's situation, asserted that what Britain could not do was 'to endorse an unjust peace'.[2]

The correspondence columns of *The Times* proceeded to fill up and brim over with lamentation, including a letter, or rather, an epistle, from the Archbishop of Canterbury himself, Cosmo Lang. Several of his bishops also wrote directly to Baldwin, along with many other deeply moved citizens.[3] It was not surprising that the churches and sects were among the loudest voices raised in condemnation of the immorality of England trying to get one of three political enemies off her back by a deal at the expense of the disreputable and obscure state of Abyssinia. Nor was it surprising that the familiar band of internationalist preachers should also have been wringing their hands in public to great effect. But the horror and revulsion at the Hoare–Laval proposals went far beyond these limited circles; it welled up from the depths of the post-evangelical British soul; all parties, all shades of opinion, all social backgrounds.

> During my experience of politics [wrote Duff Cooper], I have never witnessed so devastating a wave of public opinion. Even the easy-going constituents of the St George's division [of Westminster] were profoundly moved. My post-bag was full and the letters I received were not written by ignorant or emotional people but by responsible citizens who had given sober thought to the matter.[4]

To the Conservative rank-and-file the Hoare–Laval proposals were not only a dishonourable act, but a cowardly one. Their feelings were as a consequence hardly less strong than those of the internationalists. Harold Nicolson declared later that he had had sleepless nights wondering whether in all honesty he could retain his seat.[5] Austen Chamberlain, addressing a meeting of the Conservative Foreign Affairs Committee, expressed the general sentiment when he said that 'gentlemen do not behave in such a way'.[6] The Conservative Chief Whip told Baldwin that 'our men won't stand for it'.[7]

[1] *The History of The Times*, Vol. IV, Pt. II, p. 897.
[2] Ibid.
[3] Middlemass and Barnes, p. 890.
[4] Duff Cooper, *Old Men Forget* (London, Rupert Hart-Davis 1954), pp. 192–3.
[5] Macmillan, pp. 411–12.
[6] Ibid. pp. 446–7.
[7] Middlemass and Barnes, p. 890.

While this eruption of British moralism was showering the Government with obloquy, the Chiefs of Staff drafted (on 13 December) a signal to the Commander-in-Chief, Mediterranean (for him to show to his army and air force colleagues), whose contents illustrate just how remote public opinion, in all the heat and turmoil of its feelings, was from real life. The signal warned that no other Mediterranean powers had made preparations for active co-operation in the event of war with Italy, and that they were unlikely to do so before mobilisation. 'It therefore appears that our own forces will have to sustain the war for a not-inconsiderable period.' The situation over French co-operation was 'profoundly unsatisfactory'.[1]

In 1935 however, the apron and gaiters, the dog-collar, carried immensely greater weight than the uniform cap. As a democratic government must, the Government proceeded to defer to public emotion rather than to those strategic realities which it itself now well knew, but which it lacked the political courage to communicate to the nation.

For over the Abyssinian crisis, as over other major questions of strategic policy between the world wars, the Government of the day felt unable to educate democracy in the true facts of the British situation – partly because of fears that the facts would so affront popular prejudice as to bring down displeasure upon the Government itself; partly because publicly to acknowledge the facts would be to announce to other nations the extent to which Britain was living strategically and politically beyond her means, and in this way destroy her precarious credit as a world power.

The Government's horror at the thought of acquainting its mistress, public opinion, with the truth is demonstrated by its attitude to Hoare's forthcoming defence of his policy in the House of Commons. On 17 December Chamberlain reported to the Cabinet Hoare's justification of the Hoare–Laval proposals, after having visited Hoare at home, whence the Foreign Secretary returned from holiday an even sicker man than before, thanks to his accident in Switzerland. There could be, in Hoare's opinion, no further sanctions unless the whole League of Nations was prepared to back them up and face the possible military consequences. 'At the present time there was no indication that any other nation had prepared itself to do that. The result was that the burden of any such consequences would fall on this country alone.'[2]

Chamberlain continued: 'The Foreign Secretary had pointed out that the kind of terms of peace envisaged by those who condemned the Paris proposals was such that could only have been obtained as the result of a League success equivalent to great victories in the field.'[3]

[1] CAB 53/5, COS 159. [2] CAB 23/82, 55(35). [3] Ibid.

Since the world could not dictate terms to Mussolini, then these were the best possible terms. Finally, Chamberlain reported, the Foreign Secretary 'took the view that the League of Nations ought to be faced up to the realities of the situation . . .'[1]

It was the prospect of Hoare defending himself and the Government in the Commons in terms of such uncompromising realism that occasioned growing alarm among his colleagues and a growing feeling that Sam must go. Simon wrote to Eden to express his horror at the idea that Hoare should defend the Government by saying, in effect, that the peace terms were necessary as an alternative to war. 'He did not believe it, and to say so would be to give Mussolini the biggest score of his life.'[2] Halifax agreed that the Hoare–Laval proposals 'were not so frightfully different from those put forward by the Committee of Five. But the latter were of respectable parentage: and the Paris ones were too much like the off-the-stage arrangements of nineteenth-century diplomacy. . . .'[3]

When Hoare faced his colleagues in the Cabinet on 18 December he therefore encountered their general hostility; a general wish that he should make his speech as a back-bencher, not as their Foreign Secretary. It was Halifax who summed up the Cabinet's feeling when he averred that the moral force of the Government was on trial before the world.[4] And so reality bowed to moral force. Hoare resigned, and Eden took his place; a succession not only natural but certain to please the internationalists; and British policy veered back again to romantic chivalry.

Yet after the tempest over the Hoare–Laval proposals there was a lull for some two months in the Cabinet's agonising over Abyssinia, while the Italian forces continued to knock over the ill-armed savages of Haile Selassie's 'army'. The question of oil sanctions next came before the English Cabinet again on 19 February 1936. Eden urged that Mussolini was now in a weaker situation, and was unlikely to go to war if oil sanctions were imposed; that such sanctions might seriously weaken Italian morale. Moreover, if nothing else was done, Italy might win the war over Abyssinia.[5] When on 26 February 1936 Eden argued again that on balance the League ought to impose oil sanctions, all the doubts and objections voiced so often before were again ventilated. There was little likelihood of American co-operation, without which sanctions must be ineffective. Above all there was the risk to the Mediterranean Fleet and hence to England's whole world strategic position. As Lord Monsell, the

[1] CAB 23/82, 55(35). [2] Avon, Vol. I, p. 309. [3] Quoted in Feiling, p. 275.
[4] CAB 23/82, 56(35); also A 16 in Confidential Annexes 1923–37.
[5] CAB 23/83, 8(36)4.

First Lord of the Admiralty, expressed it in strongly opposing oil sanctions: 'We could not afford to overlook Japan.'[1]

It was the Cabinet's belief that the risk of an alliance taking place between Italy and Germany was small. It also thought it unlikely that Italy would forsake the Locarno Pact and the League of Nations as a result of the course of the Abyssinian affair. Yet, as the Foreign Secretary reported on 5 March, this was not the view of Laval's successor as French Foreign Minister, Flandin, who believed that Italy would certainly leave the League if oil sanctions were imposed. Eden nevertheless thought that France, and other nations too, would agree to oil sanctions if conciliation failed.[2] Unfortunately, when Eden met Flandin in Geneva, Flandin refused to support oil sanctions, because of an ultimatum from Mussolini to go to war if the League applied them.

In any case it was still Eden's belief that it was 'the League', with its fifty members, rather than France and England, or really just England, which would be bearing the risks and burdens of oil sanctions. Yet as the Chiefs of Staff had pointed out in a paper of 22 January on the defence of the East Mediterranean and Middle East, other Mediterranean powers had still taken few steps to prepare for military co-operation against Italy, and Great Britain was likely to bear the first brunt of hostilities.[3]

Gradually, in the spring and summer of 1936, reality finally laid its bony fingers on the Cabinet, even on Eden himself. By April it was clear that, thanks to the successes of the Italian armies, Abyssinia was becoming a lost cause. The British service departments continued to point out how England's scarce strategic resources had been sucked into the Mediterranean and the Middle East to the detriment of British strength *vis-à-vis* Germany and Japan. The Admiralty called attention to the strain on the fleet and its manning imposed by months of war-readiness. The Board of Trade reported on the damage done to British economic interests by the sanctions on Italy, particularly to the South Wales coal industry; and the damage was likely to be permanent owing to Britain's place having been taken by competitors such as Germany. Even the Foreign Secretary had noted that Italy was moving diplomatically towards Germany.[4] On 19 May the First Sea Lord, Chatfield, reported that as a result of the Mediterranean crisis and the shortage of manpower in the fleet, four battleships had had to be paid off in order to furnish men for the Mediterranean. When battleships under repair and modernisation were taken into account, 'the Navy was

[1] CAB 23/83, 11(36)5.
[2] CAB 23/83, 15(36)1.
[3] CAB 53/27, COS 426.
[4] See especially the Cabinet of 29 April 1936. CAB 23/84, 31(36)4.

left with seven capital ships only'.[1] Here then, item by item, was the invoice for standing up for the Covenant of the League over Abyssinia.

On 2 May Haile Selassie fled from his country, to arrive in London on 3 June, himself England's only visible gain from her quixotry on his behalf. A deputation of internationalists was there to greet him at Waterloo, including Sylvia Pankhurst, Sir Norman Angell and Lord Allen of Hurtwood. Allen wrote next day to his daughter to describe the occasion: 'He is a very beautiful looking black king with a lovely face. As he got out of the train, lovely flowers were given to him, and then we were introduced to him one by one. Mummy made a lovely curtsey.'[2]

Since there was now no Abyssinian Government left at all, Eden, in his own words, 'grew less confident that any good purpose was being served by continuing sanctions'.[3] Nevertheless he was surprised when, on 10 June, Chamberlain let forth a blast of realism about Abyssinia and sanctions – the first ever uttered in public by a member of the Government. Chamberlain described sanctions – which he had at first supported – as 'the very midsummer of madness'.

> Is it not apparent [he asked] that the policy of sanctions involves, I do not say war, but a risk of war? . . . Is it not also apparent from what has happened that, in the presence of such a risk, nations cannot be relied upon to proceed to the last extremity until their vital interests are threatened?[4]

On 17 June 1936 the Cabinet decided to recommend at Geneva that sanctions should be lifted.[5] The Abyssinian adventure was over. The immediate strategic dangers abated. The strain on the British armed forces and on British trade was relieved. The Chiefs of Staff had already hopefully written on 11 June that 'our interests lie in a peaceful Mediterranean and this can only be achieved by returning to a state of friendly relations with Italy'.[6] Most members of the Government shared this extraordinarily naïve hope. But such a restoration of the traditional friendship and co-operation between Italy and England was out of the question after all that had passed, as Eden himself acknowledged: 'I had to say that I saw no chance of any agreement which would allow us to slow down our defence preparations in the Mediterranean.'[7]

For Mussolini neither could nor would forget or forgive. In 1937 the

[1] The Cabinet Committee on the Position of the Fleet in the Mediterranean, 19 May 1936. CAB 27/606, MF(36)1.
[2] Gilbert, *Plough My Own Furrow*, p. 347.
[3] Avon, Vol. I, p. 384.
[4] Quoted in Avon, Vol. I, p. 385.
[5] CAB 23/84, 43(36)1.
[6] CAB 53/28, COS 477.
[7] Avon, Vol. I, p. 426; see also CAB 23/84, 43(36).

depths of Italy's abiding resentment were brought home to the then First Lord of the Admiralty, Duff Cooper, through the unlikely means of a personal courtesy extended to him by the Italian Government, which provided him and his wife with a special luxury railway coach for a journey from Naples to Calais.

'Unfortunately,' wrote Duff Cooper, 'there was set into the wall of the principal compartment an engraved tablet containing the names of those countries which had applied sanctions against Italy during the Abyssinian war, and an intimation that Italy would never forget. High on the list stood the name of Great Britain.'[1]

In their Annual Review of Imperial Defence for 1937, submitted in February, the Chiefs of Staff glumly recorded that 'we must face the fact that, whether Italy is friendly or the reverse, the days are past when we could count automatically on a friendly and submissive Italy. From hence forward we will have to look to a rival. . . .'[2]

So slow and cumbersome was the machinery by which British strategic policy was shaped and altered, however, that as late as 1 July 1937 Chatfield, the First Sea Lord, was pointing out to the Committee of Imperial Defence that Italy was still officially ruled not to be a probable enemy.[3] On 5 July the CID therefore discussed at length the danger in the Mediterranean now posed by the forfeiture of Italy's friendship, and the effects of this on British global strategy. The CID finally agreed to adopt for the purposes of defence planning the formula that 'Italy cannot be regarded as a reliable friend'.[4] The Cabinet itself approved it on 14 July 1937.

By this formula, so redolent of the governmental language of the period and indeed of the governmental mind, was it finally and formally recognised that England, a weakly armed and middle-sized state, now faced not one, not two, but three potential enemies; enemies inconveniently placed so as to threaten the entire spread of empire from the home country to the Pacific. And the third and most recent potential enemy, in the Mediterranean and Middle East, was the utterly needless creation of the British themselves, as Eden himself admitted to the House of Commons on 5 November 1936, in recalling that 'the deterioration in our relations with Italy was due to the fulfilment of our obligations under the Covenant; there had never been an Anglo-Italian quarrel so far as our country was concerned'.[5]

[1] Cooper, p. 208.
[2] Review dated 22 February 1937, taken note of by the Cabinet on 3 March 1937. COS 560.
[3] CAB 2/6, (2), CID 295.
[4] CAB 2/6, (2), CID 296.
[5] As summarised by Eden in Avon, Vol. I, p. 425.

It was when the British deployment in the Mediterranean during the Abyssinian adventure was at its height, with the navy in home waters reduced to only three ships capable of fighting the new German 'pocket-battleships', the Royal Air Force at home so reduced by reinforcements to Egypt that the Air Minister found it difficult to imagine a worse state, and the army in England equally weakened by drafts to the Middle East,[1] that on 7 March 1936 the German army marched into the demilitarised zone of the Rhineland.

It was a flagrant breach of the Treaty of Versailles, which Germany had signed under the duress of defeat. It was also a flagrant breach of the Locarno Treaty which she had signed of her own free will – double justification for France to order the French army forward to expel the German forces. For England the German violation of the demilitarised zone demanded that she should now make good her signature of the Locarno Treaty, and, as a guarantor of the zone's integrity, herself join in forcing the Germans to withdraw. That contingency had at last arrived which the English negotiator at Locarno, Austen Chamberlain, had never envisaged. What he had signed as a soothing but empty gesture to French fears in 1925 had now become a precise legal and strategic obligation which England, with her vaunted respect for treaties, ought to fulfil to the letter.

The German move had been well timed for a Saturday morning, when many of the British Cabinet was scattered in the country houses of England, breakfasting at leisure. Eden, the Foreign Secretary, was himself in London and it was to him that von Hoesch, the German ambassador, announced the news, coupled with much shrewdly concocted humbug about Hitler's future good intentions.[2] Since there were neither French, nor English, nor joint contingency plans to go automatically into action, there now ensued a period of much agitated communication as to what ought to be done, while the German forces, their leaders amazed that they were not being summarily chucked back over the Rhine, marched on to the cheers of the Rhineland people.

In a broader sense too the Germans had chosen their moment well. English chivalry over Abyssinia had shattered the Stresa front, so-called after the conference of France, England and Italy at Stresa in April 1935.[3] Relations between England and her fellow Locarno guarantor, Italy, were

[1] See reports of the First Sea Lord, and the Air and War Minister to the Cabinet on 16 March 1936. CAB 23/83, 20(36)7.

[2] Avon, Vol. I, pp. 339–40.

[3] See above p. 352, and below p. 405.

at present as hostile as it was possible for them to be, short of outright war. England was now in the absurd situation of having to consult Italy about the German aggression at a time when she was acting as the ringleader at Geneva in the attempts to thwart Italy's ambition in Abyssinia. Some have argued that the so-called 'Stresa front' was an illusion, and that in fact it would have proved ineffective in the present crisis. Whether or not this belief is well-founded can never now be established, but it can hardly be disputed that cordial relations between Italy, England and France would have been preferable to the ridiculous situation that actually prevailed. In any event, the really damaging effect, in regard to the Rhineland crisis, of English chivalry over Abyssinia was upon England herself, and on her own power to fulfil her Locarno obligations. As the Chiefs of Staff reported on 18 March 1936: 'We would at once emphasise . . . that any question of war with Germany while we are as at present heavily committed to the possibility of hostilities in the Mediterranean would be thoroughly dangerous.'[1]

Two months' notice, wrote the Chiefs of Staff, would be needed to bring the air and land forces required against Germany back from the Mediterranean. If there was the smallest danger of war with Germany, then Britain should immediately order the withdrawal of such forces.[2]

On 1 April 1936 the warnings of the Chiefs of Staff against military action under the Locarno Treaty became more urgent. They saw dangers even in lending moral support to the French by the holding of the staff talks.

> If they [the French] think that they are strong enough at the present time to undertake hostilities against Germany, we may find ourselves committed to participation against Germany with forces which are not only inadequate to render effective support, but incapable of assuring our own security, with grave consequences to the people of this country.[3]

On 29 April the British Joint Planners estimated that Britain could only put two divisions into the field, and those without tanks, mortars or anti-tank guns. The strength of the French army, after three weeks' delay for mobilisation, was put at 5 mobile and 48 infantry divisions; the German at 3 panzer and 29 infantry, but these halfway through their training and not yet properly organised and equipped. The French and British air strength was put at 306 bombers and 469 fighters; the German at 405

[1] CAB 53/27, COS 442; see also COS 441, COS 441 (JP).
[2] Ibid.
[3] CAB 53/27, COS 452.

bombers, but able to carry double the French and British bomb load, and 144 fighters. The British joint planners thought that Germany's best hope lay in exploiting the extreme weakness of the British home air defence by unrestricted bombing; they did not however think that such a plan 'would hold out any prospect of complete success . . . in the present stage of German aeronautics'.[1]

The strategic advice of the leaders of the British armed forces might thus well have restrained even a bellicose and impetuous Cabinet from ordering Germany to withdraw her forces forthwith from the Rhineland. As it was, the advice chimed only too harmoniously with the Cabinet's own inclinations – and those of the country. For the country was wholly unprepared to countenance military action alongside the French, partly because of its horror of military action as such, mostly because it could not see that the Germans had done more than, in Lord Lothian's unfortunately effective phrase, walk into their own backyard. Bernard Shaw opined that it was only as if the British had re-occupied Portmouth.[2] On 23 March, Harold Nicolson noted in his diary that 'the feeling in the House is terribly pro-German, which means afraid of war'.[3] The British Government therefore concerned itself not with taking action against Germany, but with discouraging the French from doing so. In a memorandum for the benefit of his colleagues, Eden wrote that 'military action by France against Germany should be discouraged';[4] that we should support any French move to take the matter to the League Council; that we should seek to avoid any such development as French opinion getting so restless and frightened at the slowness of action by the League as to demand armed retaliation.' '. . . as to tactics, I thought we must agree to formal condemnation of Germany's action by the League, but resist any attempt to apply financial and economic sanctions, which would be too slow to be effective in this instance'.[5] The League itself proved instantly useless, as Eden himself admits: 'In general, members of the Council had not been slow to realise that those who were not signatories of Locarno, though they ought to condemn Germany, had no obligation to act against her.'[6]

The French, for their part, were little more willing than the English to march. Because of the defensive strategy and the mass, defensive army adopted in the late 1920s there was no ready strike-force to go forward to meet the Germans. Instead, to take military action meant general mobilisa-

[1] CAB 53/27, COS(JP)460. For COS meetings on the Rhineland crisis, see CAB 53/5, COS 166, 167, 168, 170.

[2] Viscount Maugham, *At the End of the Day* (London, Heinemann 1954), p. 319.

[3] Quoted in James, p. 262.

[4] Avon, Vol. I, p. 345.

[5] Ibid. p. 346.

[6] Ibid. p. 358.

tion – at a time when a General Election was pending, and the climate of French opinion was one of pacifistic demoralisation.[1]

The refusal of the English to fulfil their obligations under the treaties of Versailles and Locarno therefore provided the French with a convenient and welcome excuse for doing nothing themselves; each country gratefully responded to the other's backsliding. After two months of tortuous and vain discussion, including a futile British proposal for an international force in the demilitarised zone and a French complaint to the League, the victors of the Great War allowed Germany to remain in military possession of the Rhineland, contenting themselves with bleats of formal protest and regret.[2]

The German success marked yet another colossal lurch of power in Europe away from France and England towards Germany. The Rhineland could henceforward be used for its traditional purpose of providing the assembly area for great armies intended for the invasion of France and the Low Countries. At the same time fortification of the German side of the French frontier in the future would render it almost impossible for the French to aid their allies in eastern Europe by a relieving offensive in the west. And, finally, German air bases were brought much nearer to the cities and industries in France and England, a circumstance it had been one of the purposes of the English signature of the Locarno Treaty to prevent.[3] The French had now lost almost all the security they and their allies had won in the Great War, and which the Versailles Treaty had originally afforded them; they were back to the situation of before 1914.

For these reasons the unopposed German re-occupation of the Rhineland has been regarded as a turning-point in the history of Europe between the world wars. It has been further argued that this was the last occasion when France and England could have met a German violation of a treaty or an open aggression with superior force; that the Rhineland crisis was therefore the great missed opportunity of stopping Hitler in time. Yet this argument is fallacious, relying only on the fact that the French army, in numbers and fighting power, was still much stronger than the German, but ignoring all those factors of opinion, nerve and determination which made it a foregone conclusion that the superior French power would not be used in the event.

The German march into the Rhineland was in fact merely the culmination, the consummation, of all that had already passed between Germany

[1] For accounts of the French response to the German re-occupation of the Rhineland, see Brogan, pp. 697–701; Alistair Horne, *To Lose a Battle* (London, Macmillan 1969), pp. 34–6; Beaufre, pp. 50–1; John Williams, *The Ides of May: The Defeat of France, May–June 1940* (London, Constable 1968), pp. 70–1.
[2] See Avon, p. 341 and ch. III.
[3] See above p. 332.

on the one hand and France and England on the other in the three years since Hitler had come to power in Germany; three years decisive for the future of England, Europe and the world.

From 30 January 1933 onwards the English had had to deal with a German government whose leader poured public scorn of the utmost brutality on the fundamental beliefs by which the English had come to live. In Nazi Germany and post-evangelical England the utterly incompatible products of two different strains of romanticism now confronted one another – the German, with its mystical and atavistic outlook on race and nationhood, its obsession with power and domination, its neurotic love of violence; and the English, with its faith in the moral law, its vision of the brotherhood of man, its trust in the essential goodness of human nature, its pacific gentleness and compassion. Such a confrontation could only end in a tragedy of misunderstanding.

The English Government did not lack accurate information about the character of the Nazi movement and its leader. All through the autumn of 1932 and into 1933, even before Hitler came to power, Sir Horace Rumbold, the English ambassador in Berlin, had sent back to the Foreign Office constant, detailed and perceptive reports. On 26 April 1933, in a valedictory despatch, he provided a lifelike portrait of the new German Führer and his political convictions. Hitler, he wrote:

> starts with the assumption that man is a fighting animal; therefore the nation is a fighting unit, being a community of fighters. . . . A country or race which ceases to fight is doomed. . . . Pacifism is the deadliest sin. . . . Intelligence is of secondary importance. . . . Will and determination are of the higher worth. Only brute force can ensure the survival of the race.[1]

And hence: 'The new Reich must gather within its fold all the scattered German elements in Europe. . . . What Germany needs is an increase in territory.'[2]

To Hitler, according to Rumbold, 'the idea that there is something reprehensible in chauvinism is entirely mistaken . . . the climax of education is military service' for youths 'educated to the maximum of aggressiveness. . . . It is the duty of the government to implant in the people feelings of manly courage and passionate hatred.'[3]

Rumbold provided samples of Hitler's distinctly non-evangelical views

[1] C 3990/319/18 in CAB 27/599, CP13(36).
[2] Ibid. [3] Ibid.

on life, such as: 'Intellectualism is undesirable. . . . It is objectionable to preach international understanding'; and Rumbold added that Hitler 'has spoken with derision of such delusive documents as peace-pacts and such delusive ideas as the spirit of Locarno'.[1] In Rumbold's conviction, it followed that 'it would be misleading to base any hopes on a return to sanity', for the German Government was encouraging an attitude of mind 'which can only end in one way'.[2] Rumbold concluded this final despatch (he retired because of age in June 1933) by a series of descriptions of Nazi leaders that were as unflattering as cartoons by Gillray, in order to support his final assessment that 'I have the impression that the persons directing the policy of the Hitler government are not normal'.[3]

On 17 May 1933 the Cabinet considered a memorandum by the Foreign Secretary (Simon) based on this last despatch from Rumbold. In the Foreign Secretary's opinion German foreign policy was 'definitely disquieting'. The Government of Germany was 'giving State sanctions and encouragement to an attitude of mind, as well as various forms of military training, which could only end in one way'.[4] In fact, even earlier, on 1 March, within almost a month of Hitler's accession to power, Simon had warned his colleagues that the state of Europe was rapidly worsening, that the situation in Germany was critical and that the Disarmament Conference was likely to break down.[5]

The flow of information about the character and aims of the Nazi dictatorship continued under Sir Eric Phipps, Rumbold's successor. On 31 January 1934 he wrote to Simon:

> [Hitler's] policy is simple and straightforward. If his neighbours allow him, he will become strong by the simplest and most direct methods. The mere fact that he is making himself unpopular abroad will not deter him, for, as he said in a recent speech, it is better to be respected and disliked than to be weak and liked. If he finds that he arouses no real opposition, the *tempo* of his advance will increase. On the other hand, if he is vigorously opposed, he is unlikely at this stage to risk a break. . . .[6]

On 15 October 1934 Phipps sent home a complete account of Nazi education: '. . . the German schoolboy of today is being methodically educated, mentally and physically, to defend his country. . . . But I fear that, if this or a later German Government ever requires it of him, he will

[1] Ibid.
[2] Ibid.
[3] Ibid.
[4] CAB 23/75, 35(33)1.
[5] CAB 23/75, 13(33)1.
[6] In CAB 27/599.

be found to be equally well-fitted and ready to march or die on foreign soil.'[1]

On 1 April 1935 Phipps supplied Simon with a general survey of German power and progress to date, from whose alarming details Phipps drew a moral: '. . . let us hope that our pacifists at home may at length realise that the rapidly-growing monster of German militarism will not be placated by mere cooings, but will only be restrained from recourse to its *ultima ratio* by the knowledge that the Powers who desire peace are also strong enough to enforce it'.[2]

And as early as 26 July 1933 the Cabinet considered a dossier of information from the Foreign Office on German re-armament,[3] and thereafter received copious reports on this topic, albeit inevitably of a more conjectural and conflicting nature than Rumbold's and Phipps's accounts of the character of the Nazi régime.

The British Government therefore received all the information it required upon which to frame in good time a realistic German policy; a policy founded on awareness that England was dealing with a wholly amoral dictatorship which regarded international affairs as an arena of ruthless struggle; a dictatorship which was not only re-arming but glorified arms and war, and which was determined to carve out an empire in Europe, by force if necessary. The claim sometimes made by apologists for the British statesmen of the 1930s that they did not – could not – really know the kind of régime or men they were dealing with until it was too late is without validity. They knew; yet they ignored what they knew. They simply could not bring themselves to believe the evidence placed before them about Nazism, so utterly alien was the Nazi outlook, in all its ramifications, to their own instincts and assumptions.

At the same time they in any case flinched from the kind of policy towards Germany demanded by the evidence – a policy, that was, of headlong re-armament, of close military alliance with France, of a politico-military struggle in Europe between two armed camps. As Sir Samuel Hoare expressed it to his Cabinet colleagues on 19 March 1934: 'What he did object to was going back to the position of 1906 to 1914, that [*sic*] everybody was preparing for a war against Germany. We might eventually be driven to it, but we were not, in his opinion, yet at that point.'[4]

For to this generation of Englishmen the balance of power – of which a realistic policy towards Germany would be the expression – was a con-

[1] In CAB 27/599.
[2] Ibid. C 2839/111/18.
[3] CAB 23/76, 48(33)5.
[4] CAB 23/78, 10(34)3.

ception to be shunned at all costs: had not the balance of power, with its armed camps and armaments races, led to the Great War?

In any event, to re-arm at once and at utmost speed, to conclude an alliance with France, and to inform the German Government, as the great powers had informed the new French revolutionary government in 1830, that any breach of the peace treaty would invite immediate armed intervention, was rendered entirely out of court by British public opinion.

In the first place there was the English proneness to believe well of others, even in the face of the evidence. John Wheeler-Bennett wrote in *International Affairs* after a visit to Berlin in 1933 that Hitler was 'a man of sense . . . who did not want war'.[1] *The Economist* declared on 1 December 1934 that Germany was no threat to Europe.[2] *The Times* (its Editor, Geoffrey Dawson, was a famous and persistent espouser of the German cause) argued on 10 July 1934 that the aggressive speeches made by Nazi leaders were only for home consumption, and on 4 August 1934 that there was no reason to be concerned about the militaristic spirit in Germany. Lord Allen of Hurtwood (Clifford Allen) was quoted by the *Daily Telegraph* on 28 January 1935 as saying after having met Hitler: 'I believe Herr Hitler's position in the country is unassailable. His sincerity is tremendous . . . I am convinced he genuinely desires peace. . . . Germany's aggressive words and warlike phrases do not represent her intentions. . . .'[3]

Secondly, influential British opinion as a whole sympathised with Germany and was hostile to France.[4] This curious reversal partly originated in the contemporary English weakness for trying to see the other man's point of view; an ex-enemy being clearly more the other man than an ex-ally. It was strongly urged that the British people should strive to understand how the Germans felt, how they had suffered, what with being blockaded and defeated in 1914–18, and all their later troubles in the 1920s.[5] A more profound element still, perhaps the decisive element, lay in the deep post-evangelical English sense of guilt. The very existence of Nazi Germany must be our own fault, though even more the fault of the French – the result of all our beastliness to the Germans between 1918 and 1933. If the Nazis *were* in some degree nasty, this too was all our own fault. When Germany left the League of Nations in 1933 Lord Allen of Hurtwood explained why to the House of Lords: '. . . we are compelled

[1] Quoted in James, p. 230.
[2] Ibid.
[3] Gilbert, *Plough My Own Furrow*, pp. 358–9.
[4] See Gannon, pp. 12–14.
[5] Cf. the essay by W. Arnold-Forster in *The Intelligent Man's Guide to Peace*, ed. Leonard Woolf (London, Gollancz 1933), pp. 346–7n.

to admit that we and other nations during the last fifteen years have not handed out to Germany that full measure of wise and fair play which that country merited when it threw out from its own land the régime which made the War'.[1]

Lord Lothian too assiduously set about convincing the British governing class that Nazi Germany was all our own fault. Nazi brutality to its victims at home, Jews, Social Democrats, was, he argued, 'largely the reflex of the external persecution to which Germans have been subjected since the war'.[2]

Of this external persecution to which the Germans had been subjected, people like Allen and Lothian thought that the 'wicked' Treaty of Versailles was the most odious example; in fact the root cause of the present German problem. Even before the treaty had been signed, Lloyd George, Smuts and other members of the British Empire Delegation at the Peace Conference had come to look upon it as too severe, and falling short of the high standards set by the peace given by the British to the Boers.[3] In 1920 regrets and apprehensions about the treaty's alleged severity found expression in a book which was to exercise an immense and far-reaching influence; indeed eventually largely to determine the British governing classes' view of the treaty, and of the treatment of Germany under its provisions. The book, *The Economic Consequences of the Peace*, was written by J. M. Keynes, an economist of genius, but also very much a precious intellectual typical of the period, a contemporary and friend of Lytton Strachey and E. M. Forster at King's, Cambridge, one of the Bloomsbury and Garsington circles, a nonconformist by upbringing, a conscientious objector during the war, a liberal, a man of spinsterish personality.

The core of Keynes's book is an economist's *critique* of reparations, whose essential, and valid, point was that 'Germany cannot pay anything approaching' the sum the Allies demanded, and that in any case the sum itself was grotesquely exaggerated and ill-founded.[4] But it was not this rather technical economic chapter that so appealed to British opinion, but Keynes's bitter attacks on the peace settlement as a whole and on those responsible for it; attacks written with all the moral passion of the true nonconformist. 'It was the task of the Peace Conference', he wrote, 'to honour engagements and to satisfy justice; but not less to re-establish life and heal wounds.' [5] He set out to demonstrate that the conference had

[1] Quoted in Gilbert, *Plough My Own Furrow*, pp. 340–1.
[2] Butler, *Lord Lothian*, p. 206.
[3] See above p. 317.
[4] J. M. Keynes, *The Economic Consequences of the Peace* (London, Macmillan 1920), ch. V.
[5] Ibid. p. 23.

achieved the reverse of these objectives. For Keynes, Clemenceau was the villain of the conference:

> So far as possible therefore, it was the policy of France to set the clock back and to undo what, since 1870, the progress of Germany had accomplished. By loss of territory and other measures her population was to be curtailed, but chiefly the economic system, upon which she depended for her new strength . . . must be destroyed. If France could seize, even in part, what Germany was compelled to drop, the inequality of strength between the two rivals for European hegemony might be remedied for many generations.[1]

Clemenceau, in pursuing these purposes, wrote Keynes, 'sees the issue in terms of France and Germany, not of humanity and of European civilisation struggling forwards to a new order'.[2] The Versailles Treaty was in Keynes's opinion 'a Carthaginian peace' which therefore constituted a breach of a firm contract made between the Allies and Germany during the armistice negotiations that the peace should be in accordance with Wilson's Fourteen Points; hence the justifiable German feelings of betrayal at Versailles.[3]

Keynes therefore demanded that the Peace Treaty should be revised. He returned to this theme in a second book in 1922,[4] in which he recommended that all Allied forces should be withdrawn from German territory in return for a German guarantee of 'the complete demilitarisation of her territory west of the Rhine'.[5] Keynes also hoped that France would reduce her armaments, because:

> That she has anything to fear from Germany in the future which we can foresee, except what she may herself provoke, is a delusion. When Germany has recovered her strength and pride, as in due time she will, many years must pass before she again casts her eyes Westwards. Germany's future now lies to the East, and it is in that direction her hopes and ambitions, when they revive, will certainly turn.[6]

Yet *The Economic Consequences of the Peace* was, except when dealing specifically with economics, simply a moral tract, hot with emotion, which took no account of strategy or the balance of power. Its central argument that the Versailles Treaty was a Carthaginian peace was itself sentimental nonsense, for, in the first place, the treaty was, as the French

[1] Ibid. p. 32. [2] Ibid. p. 33. [3] Ibid. pp. 51–9.
[4] J. M. Keynes, *A Revision of the Treaty* (London, Macmillan 1922).
[5] Ibid. p. 175. [6] Ibid. p. 186.

feared at the time, not Carthaginian enough adequately to reduce German power; secondly, it was extremely lenient in comparison with the peace terms which Germany herself, when she was expecting to win the war, had had in mind to impose on the Allies; and thirdly it was hardly more than a tap on the wrist compared with the peace Germany did in fact impose on Russia at Brest-Litovsk in March 1918, and which the Allies, in their own peace-making, had had before them as an example. By the Treaty of Brest-Litovsk Germany deprived Russia of a third of her population, half her industrial undertakings and nine-tenths of her coal mines, and imposed an indemnity of six thousand million marks.[1]

However it was in the very shortcomings of Keynes's book – its sentimentality, its moral indignation, its sense of guilt, its lack of strategic comprehension – that lay its particular appeal and guaranteed its immense, far-reaching and catastrophic success. Throughout the 1920s and 1930s other influential voices in Britain continued to regurgitate its contents. Thus, as one example among many, Arnold-Forster, a noted pacifist, wrote in 1933:

> It is only right to recognise that the original Treaty was in many respects monstrously unjust and unworkable, that it was imposed in the most woundingly insulting way, that it inflicted many penal injuries now irremediable, and that some of its surviving elements ought to be amended, under favourable conditions, in the interests of justice and reconciliation.[2]

Lord Lothian (Philip Kerr), who at the time the peace treaty was signed could see little fault in it, came in the course of the 1920s to consider Germany as more sinned against than sinning.[3] By the 1930s he had become a passionate advocate of the view that Germany had been denied 'justice'.[4] Allen of Hurtwood shared this conviction; as did Geoffrey Dawson, the Editor of *The Times*, as did all moralising internationalists; as did most leading politicians in both the Government and Opposition parties. For by the early 1930s the Keynesian view of the Versailles Treaty had become to seem the only one an educated, intelligent, liberal-minded man could possibly hold.[5]

It followed that there was no will among the British governing classes whatsoever to defend the provisions of the treaty even from unilateral

[1] See pp. 248–9 and pp. 312–15 above for the terms of the Versailles Treaty.
[2] See Forster's essay in Woolf, p. 349.
[3] Butler, *Lord Lothian*, pp. 77 and 114.
[4] Ibid. p. 206.
[5] See Gannon, p. 11, for a summary of British press attitudes to the Versailles Treaty in the early 1930s. Hostility to its terms ranged from the *Daily Telegraph* to the *Daily Herald*.

German repudiation or violation. On the contrary the prevailing sentiment was that the treaty should be further revised in Germany's favour, not only as a matter of justice, but also because to remedy German grievances was to ensure that the Nazi dictatorship would settle down as a good neighbour. Such was the intellectual foundation of 'appeasement', in the narrow sense of British policy towards Nazi Germany in the 1930s. A return to the balance of power in 1933 by an alignment of England with France against German ambitions was thus out of the question. In any case an alliance with France was abhorrent in itself; France was seen as the villain of post-war Europe, the cause of all the present ills by virtue of her being so beastly to the Germans at Versailles (Keynes's influence again) and in the Ruhr in 1923, and by her refusal to disarm. Lloyd George himself gave vent to this antipathy in his book, *The Truth About Reparations*:

> It may be added that France is the last country that should stand on a punctilio about the Treaty of Versailles [over her then demands for reparations from Germany]. What about armaments; the pledge implicit in the Treaty that German disarmament should be followed and paralleled by her own? Yet France has to-day an army, with reserves, of over five million men, and thousands of heavy guns. No other country in Europe has an armament in any way comparable. . . . The immense land armaments of France are a glaring and arrogant breach of the undertakings of Versailles.[1]

Or, as Allen of Hurtwood wrote to Ellen Wilkinson on 30 April 1934:

> I incline to think it would be a mistake to seem to be on the side of France about the secret re-arming of Germany under the *Versailles Treaty*. To do that means, however carefully we put it, that we appear to re-endorse that wicked Treaty and justify the evil policies of France towards world conciliation during the last ten years.[2]

There was yet another powerful element in British public opinion in 1933 which made a return to the balance of power and the line-up of 1918 wholly out of the question. Despite the failure of the League of Nations over the Japanese aggression in Manchuria, the faith of internationalists in the future of the new world order remained undiminished. That the general situation in the world had so much worsened since the happy days of 1929, with the rise of Nazism in Germany and militarism in Japan,

[1] Lloyd George, *The Truth About Reparations and War Debts*, p. 139.
[2] Gilbert, *Plough My Own Furrow*, pp. 354–5.

only stimulated the internationalists into even greater activity; the more disquieting the facts, the more faith must conquer them. The rather smug optimism evinced by internationalists in the 1920s, when they thought war and aggression had been banished for ever, gave way to a somewhat hysterical eagerness to explain away the inherent impotence and fallaciousness of the League and its Covenant so brutally exposed by the Manchurian affair, and prove how the League nevertheless could and would prevail:[1] '*The League is effective* for organising peace and preventing war,' wrote one believer, '*when* it is used with loyalty and courage. Its Covenant has proved very well-designed for its limited purpose *when* used with a will to breathe life into it. . . .'[2]

And the British people and its Government shared these continued hopes of the internationalists in regard to the League.

Thus it was that the kind of policy towards Nazi Germany demanded by the facts so fully documented by Sir Horace Rumbold and Sir Eric Phipps in their despatches from Berlin ran contrary to all the strongly felt prejudices of national opinion – prejudices common, naturally enough, to the majority of the Cabinet itself.

Between the prejudices and the facts therefore the Cabinet could only follow a tortuous course of evasion. England's German policy became one of inherently futile expedients. Underlying these expedients was the illusion, extraordinary in view of Rumbold's and Phipps's reports, that the Nazi leaders would be accessible to reasoned argument and responsive to proofs of goodwill; a failure, *per contra*, to realise that English policy would carry no weight at all with the Nazis unless backed by English – or French – power and by an evident willingness to use that power. And while more than a decade of internationalist hopes and Treasury economies had left England's own military power in the European theatre sadly below the requirements of foreign policy,[3] the military and naval power of England and France *in combination* was nevertheless still overwhelmingly superior to that of Germany. From 1933 and until the Abyssinian crusade began to drain away British forces to the Middle East in the late summer of 1935, England's German policy was therefore conducted from a position of immense strategic strength – although the style of its conduct belied the fact.

The style was set as early as 17 May 1933, when the Cabinet considered

[1] See e.g. the essays in Woolf.

[2] C. R. Buxton's essay 'Inter-Continental Peace' in Woolf, p. 304.

[3] The Chiefs of Staff in their Annual Review for 1933 (October) particularly noted the gulf between British treaty obligations, such as under Locarno, and the forces available to meet them, especially ground forces. CAB 53/23, COS 310.

the memorandum from Simon on the nature of German foreign policy, based on Rumbold's last despatch. Rather than establish English moral domination at once by high and resolute words in Berlin, the Cabinet decided to instruct Rumbold to tell Hitler that 'we hope Germany will do nothing to make Europe more nervous than it is', and 'work in the framework and spirit of the League of Nations'.[1]

On 26 July the Cabinet pondered a Foreign Office dossier on covert German re-armament, and the likelihood that Germany would violate Article V of the Treaty of Versailles. It decided that the Foreign Office should instruct the British ambassador to express the 'concern of His Majesty's Government at the indications of German re-armament . . . and express their anxiety on the general question'.[2]

The first impressions received of the character of modern English statesmanship by Adolf Hitler from these anxious and old-womanly communications were not such as to earn his apprehensive respect. Yet German re-armament was the key to the future; it was that fundamental violation of the Treaty of Versailles which, if left unresisted, must eventually pave the way for the destruction of all the rest of the post-war settlement, and the enthronement of Germany once more as the super-power of Europe. The British Government however, bemused by its sense of 'fairness' and 'justice', felt that the German demand for equality of status with France could not be resisted, even when, after walking out of the Disarmament Conference in the autumn of 1933, Germany proceeded towards this equality by means of violating the Treaty of Versailles.

At the same time the anxiety of the British over long-term Nazi ambitions caused them to renew that courting of Germany which had been a recurrent feature of England's German policy since D'Abernon's time at the Berlin Embassy. Gradually the British came to pin their continued hopes for European reconciliation on getting Germany back into the League in return for concessions to meet what all believed were rightful German grievances. So it was that in February 1934 a British minister, Anthony Eden, the Lord Privy Seal, set off to visit Paris, Rome and – Berlin. This was in itself an act of deference which could in the circumstances only be a tactical error. In Berlin Eden put forward a British memorandum on the limitation of armaments which the British Cabinet hoped, in the usual way, would somehow satisfy everyone. Hitler put forward counter-proposals well tailored to exploit the British sense of reasonableness and 'justice'.[3] The two men exchanged reminiscences of

[1] CAB 23/76, 35(33)1.
[2] CAB 23/76, 48(33)5.
[3] For details see Avon, Vol. I, pp. 61–71.

the Western Front. Hitler, in this, his first meeting with a minister of the English Crown, did not reveal anything of his true self,[1] being at this time concerned with bamboozling the victors of 1918 with offers and good intentions while the initial stage of Germany's re-armament was got through. At the same time Hitler himself gained through Eden his first personal impression of the character of the present rulers of the British Empire.

Eden returned home sorry that Hitler felt unable to accept the British proposals on arms limitation, sorry too that he displayed no eagerness to return to the League, but pleased with Hitler's counter-proposals on armaments, and convinced that Hitler would, as he promised, be faithful to those treaties like Locarno which Germany had freely negotiated.[2]

On 19 March 1934 the Cabinet considered whether Germany should be taken as the ultimate potential enemy against whom English long-term defence policy should be directed. Simon acknowledged that 'Germany was tearing up the Treaty of Versailles', but consoled his colleagues with the belief that German ambitions lay in eastern Europe – Austria, Danzig and Memel. At the same time Simon noted that 'although it had hitherto been assumed that Germany could not do anything effective against her neighbours, she was rapidly increasing her forces'.[3]

Nevertheless both MacDonald, the Prime Minister, and Neville Chamberlain, the Chancellor of the Exchequer, were, the Minutes record, inclined to look for some alternative to taking Germany as a firm enemy and arming against her.[4]

The Cabinet finally concluded that if the Disarmament Conference did fail, and even if there were an agreement allowing some German re-armament, Germany would soon be a potential danger. In such circumstances the Cabinet must 'without delay' consider whether 'to join in arranging to provide further security against a breach of the peace' or face very heavy further expenditure on re-armament.[5]

So the British Cabinet took refuge in procrastination. Three days later it surveyed the whole question of European security, including such painful topics as Germany's 'illegal re-armament', and the possibility of laying sanctions on her by way of reprisal. While on the one hand no military guarantee to France was possible because of British public opinion, on the other, 'there was a good deal of evidence to show that the German Government meant to get back to the possibility of using force, so that he [*sic*] might obtain his ends, if possible, without fighting, but in the last

[1] For details see Avon, Vol. I, pp. 61, 70.
[2] Ibid. pp. 61–71.
[3] CAB 23/78, 10(34)3.
[4] Ibid.
[5] Ibid.

resort by force'.[1] There were noble efforts to understand and sympathise with the German point of view, taking due note of France's past 'provocations'. Finally the Cabinet decided to ask the Foreign Secretary to draft a memorandum on persuading the French to accept the minimum German terms, but at the same time without involving England in a military alliance with France. Thus the British Cabinet's answer to the blatant German violation of Versailles and the dangers which it posed was doubly to sell the pass, by leaning on the French instead of the Germans and by refusing to join in that most natural and essential of expedients in the circumstances, an Anglo-French alliance.

British policy in 1934 came to rest on two interlinked chimeras: an arms convention between France, Germany and England, which would satisfy German demands for equality of status; and a German agreement to return to the League and generally promise to be a good boy and abide by the school rules. Thus an absurd situation had been reached: Germany, who was violating a key provision of the 1919 peace settlement and thereby offering an immense – and recognised – threat for the future, was being asked by England to be so kind as voluntarily to limit the extent of her violation. At the same time the British were exerting no pressure whatever on the Germans to induce them to carry out this act of self-denial, for there was no suggestion in British diplomacy that if full-scale German re-armament went on, it would invite intervention by the old wartime alliance. So why did the British think that Germany would agree to accept only a fraction of the armaments which there was clearly nothing to stop her having in full?

While during 1934 the British were thus courting a country legally in the wrong and in a currently weak and vulnerable military position, the parade grounds and manœuvre areas of Germany turned out soldiers, and the factories turned out weapons to equip them. On 21 November 1934 the Cabinet's attention was drawn to recent indications 'that German re-armament was proceeding in an alarming manner'.[2] It emerged in the course of discussion that 'all available evidence showed that German re-armament had reached a very formidable stage'.[3] Germany would soon have an army 300,000 strong; within a year the German air force would be as large as the RAF.[4]

The critical state reached by German re-armament now presented the British with an inescapable choice, a choice which, once made, must affect the whole future course of European politics. The Cabinet, in its

[1] CAB 23/78, 12(34).
[2] CAB 23/86, 41(34)1. [3] Ibid. [4] Ibid.

meeting on 21 November 1934, well realised that it stood at such a turning-point. When all information about German re-armament had been collected, the Minutes record, there would then be the 'very important' question for the Cabinet

> . . . whether we ought to abandon our policy of ignoring Germany's action in regard to re-armament. Our information was to the effect that the German authorities were afraid that the Versailles Powers would jointly accuse Germany of violating the Treaty. If such action were taken now, Hitler's prestige might be affected; but with every month that passed, Germany was becoming stronger and therefore better able to disregard such complaints.[1]

It was agreed to appoint a Cabinet Committee to consider a report on the evidence of German re-armament and recommend appropriate action – should we agree to legalise it, or, if not, what?[2]

The lucubrations of this committee turned entirely on the importance of securing agreement with Germany while she was still weak, rather than on taking advantage of this convenient condition by bold and assertive diplomacy. As always in British ministerial discussions, there was constant anxiety as to what Germany might do or think in response to various courses of action that were mooted.[3] The thought that the French might formally denounce Germany under the Treaty of Versailles filled Simon with horror. He said that they must impress on the French the point that 'the choice really lay between uncontrolled and controlled re-armament of Germany';[4] a point which did little credit to his sense of realities. He also said that there could be no question of any concession to Germany over the demilitarised zone of the Rhineland.[5]

In their report to the Cabinet, the committee recommended that the French should be asked to visit London and discuss the problem. Fatalistically they recommended that the German situation should be accepted as it was today, even though they recognised its illegality. There was the importance of getting Germany back into the League, and reaching a general agreement on the limitation of armaments.[6] 'If the French Goverment should raise the point that Germany has, in fact, succeeded by a policy of blackmail, we should not perhaps dissent, but we should ask France what are the alternatives. . . .'[7]

On 26 November 1934 the Cabinet considered this report, especially its recommendation that the evidence as to German re-armament was

[1] CAB 23/86, 41(34)1. [2] Ibid. [3] CAB 27/572. [4] CAB 27/572, GR(34)4.
[5] CAB 27/572, GR(34)5. [6] CAB 27/572, CP295(34). [7] Ibid.

such as could no longer be officially ignored, and that therefore the Government should make an announcement in the House of Commons worded 'in general, *but friendly* terms [author's italics]'.[1] For as an astonishing consequence of the Government's fear of affronting public opinion at home and upsetting delicate Nazi sensibilities in Germany with statements of the truth, the Government had as yet taken no public and official notice of the fact that Germany was re-arming, although the unpleasant topic had been brought up often enough by back-bench politicians like Winston Churchill and military correspondents like Basil Liddell Hart since the middle of 1933.

The Cabinet went on to discuss what could or should be done about German re-armament, coming to the robust decision to take neither firm action nor a hard line towards Germany.[2]

So the Government duly made its parliamentary statements in terms general but friendly to Germany, only to learn to its innocent and pained surprise that the Germans were taking the very mildness of these statements 'as tantamount to a legalisation of their re-armament'.[3] On 12 December the Cabinet again urgently considered what action to take, for its own Committee on German Re-Armament thought that it was 'of the utmost importance that a decision should be taken on this fundamental question of policy'.[4] The Cabinet again dwelt far more on what Germany might do, or want, than on what England might do, or want. There was speculation as to what concessions Germany would demand in return for her agreeing to return to the League. Thus did the British continue to yield up the psychological initiative to a country which was legally in the wrong and strategically still weak and vulnerable. The Cabinet also nursed a happy, though wholly false and totally unjustified, illusion that Germany thought she had much to gain from returning to the League.[5]

A week later the Cabinet finally came to their decision as to what course of action to pursue over German re-armament. The opportunity should be seized to promote Germany's return to Geneva, together with her agreement to some limitation on her re-armament. The 'strongest possible pressure' was to be brought to bear on the French not to obstruct these purposes.[6]

Thus it was that the British answer to the most crucial single question of foreign policy to arise since 1918, the British decision at this point of strategic no-return, was weakly to surrender to the insolence of a past and potential enemy, and toughly to bully a past and potential ally.

[1] CAB 23/80, 43(34)2.
[2] Ibid.
[3] CAB 23/80, 46(34).
[4] Ibid.
[5] Ibid.
[6] CAB 23/80, 47(34).

This perverse British policy now proceeded gradually to unfold. On 9 January 1935 the Cabinet debated on how best to approach the French and get them to agree that a German accession to an eastern European version of Locarno and Germany's return to the League and the Disarmament Conference would give France the security she desired.[1] The whole debate displayed a total unrealism; Chamberlain, for example, expressed his belief that Germany would be reasonable over armaments, once equality of status was conceded.[2] There was no comprehension that in putting her proposals to Germany, Britain had no bargaining leverage at all, since she was not prepared to take any action if Germany turned them down.

Now, however, another aspect of the Versailles Treaty, and this time of the Locarno Treaty as well, came up for the first time for a long period – the demilitarised zone of the Rhineland. This, the Cabinet decided, was not to be a matter of discussion with Germany.[3] On 14 January 1935 the Cabinet returned to this awkward topic. Simon, the Foreign Secretary, foresaw a time when Germany would no longer be willing to put up with the existence of the demilitarised zone[4] – another example of the inverted way the British looked at such questions. Simon therefore thought that there should be no statement to the French about our attitude to the zone. He pointed out however that the zone was part of the Locarno Treaty and that 'in certain circumstances we might be compelled to fight for it . . .'[5] The view of the Cabinet however was that 'the demilitarisation of the Rhineland was not a vital British interest'. It was a view utterly contrary to the Chiefs-of-Staff's opinion at the time when the Locarno Treaty was originally signed;[6] a view reached now without freshly consulting the present Chiefs of Staff. It was also a view in flat contradiction to a speech by Baldwin in the House of Commons on 30 July 1934, when, with the menace of the bomber in mind, he asserted: 'The greatest crime to our own people is to be afraid to tell the truth . . . the old frontiers are gone. When you think of the defence of England you no longer think of the chalk cliffs of Dover; you think of the Rhine. That is where our frontier lies. . . .'[7]

The Cabinet's response to Simon's unwelcome reminder of the obligations entailed by Britain's signature of the Locarno Treaty was to decide to evade any discussion with the French about putting teeth into Locarno, and to avoid making any statement that Great Britain regarded the demilitarised zone as a vital interest.[8]

[1] CAB 23/81, 2(33)1. [2] Ibid. [3] Ibid. [4] CAB 23/81, 3(35)1. [5] Ibid.
[6] See above p. 332. [7] Quoted in Middlemass and Barnes, p. 775. [8] CAB 23/81, 3(35)1.

On 1 February 1935 a French delegation arrived in London by British invitation to discuss what should be done about German re-armament. The British objective at the conference was to sell the idea to the French of attempting to reach an agreement with Germany on the limitation of her armaments and her return to the League.[1] Simon opened the conference in his best legal style by posing three courses of action over German re-armament: drift, which would be the most stupid; combined action by Italy, France and the United Kingdom to stop it by force, which Simon dismissed as 'not practicable'; or an attempt to secure a general agreement. The French delegates, Laval and Flandin, expressed fears of German aims in the East; thought it would do no good to allow Germany to abrogate Article V (on her disarmament) of the Versailles Treaty if there was to be no addition to their security. France also wanted the assurance that rapid British aid would be forthcoming under the Locarno Treaty – indeed they wanted a new 'aerial Locarno' to assure them against German air attack.[2] Simon, for his part, dilated on the need to avoid Anglo-French proposals which might appear to be aimed at Germany – a wholly characteristic wish to deny or dodge the logical implications of the situation.

The French proposal of an 'aerial Locarno' caused much perturbation in a subsequent private meeting of the British delegation. Britain might be drawn into a war simply because of an air raid.[3] In this discussion Sir Maurice Hankey, of all people, joined the ranks of the appeasers. He thought that 'if we tried as hard as we could with Germany, even to the extent of having some temporary difference with France, then our people might be far more ready to accept [the "aerial Locarno"]'.[4] He thought that the position was that Germany was re-arming, and that nothing would stop her at all; but 'we had one weapon, which was to attempt to legalise her re-armament at some level which might be mutually acceptable'.[5] So Hankey too had fallen into the illusion that it was possible to influence German policy without exerting painful leverage on the German arm.

Vansittart, striving for his part to hold an Anglo-French front together, strongly argued against any solely British approach to Berlin. Simon expressed agreement. Yet, after the French had broadly agreed to the British proposals and gone home, it was Simon and Eden without any French colleagues who were to go to Berlin to try them on Hitler.

Before the two of them could set off, however, the German Government, by a brilliant stroke of tactical opportunism, had even more firmly

[1] CAB 29/146, CP23(35).
[2] CAB 29/146, AF(35)1.
[3] CAB 29/146, AF(B)(35)1.
[4] Ibid.
[5] Ibid.

seized the psychological initiative let slip by the British. On 4 March 1935 the British Government issued a White Paper on Defence, itself a novelty, in which, while announcing a cautious programme of re-armament of its own, it made some feebly condemnatory references to German re-armament, to the anxieties it caused Germany's neighbours, and which 'may consequently produce a situation where peace will be in peril'. The references to German policy were innocuous in the extreme compared to the violence of past Nazi denunciations of other nations' policies they disliked. The British programme of re-armament was both modest and legal, following only at long delay a German programme that was neither. Nevertheless, with supreme and successful effrontery, the German Government took vast exception to the White Paper. Hitler became 'indisposed', and unable to receive Simon and Eden. On 6 March 1935 the British Cabinet, instead of denouncing this German hypocrisy, and calling off the visit altogether, agreed to Simon's advice that 'he thought it important to deal with the German Government coolly and calmly; to point out that postponement of the visit was inconvenient in view of other arrangements . . . and without pressing too strongly, to ask Herr Hitler to fix a later date'.[1]

Hitler graciously consented to meet the English ministers on 25–26 March.

On 9 March however Reichsmarschall Göring announced the existence of the Luftwaffe, and on 16 March (a Saturday) the Nazi Government announced the introduction of conscription and the creation of an army of thirty-six divisions; both announcements being outright breaches of the Treaty of Versailles; and justified with characteristic impertinence by reference to the pitiful little British programme of re-armament and a French decision to increase the period of military service from one year to two.

It was a sign of how completely the Germans felt that they now possessed the psychological initiative. It was the moment when England and France, if they wished to regain that initiative, must act boldly and resolutely. They had, after all, far, far better grounds for being bloody-minded than those feeble pretexts by which the Germans themselves had justified their own actions.

On Monday, 18 March, the Cabinet duly pondered the German declarations about conscription, agreeing however that it 'should not be made a reason for abandoning the visit to Berlin, but that the declaration could not be passed over in silence'.[2] Therefore a despatch should be sent to

[1] CAB 23/81, 13(35)1.

[2] CAB 23/81, 15(35)2.

Berlin 'conveying to the German Government a protest against the announcement . . .' and showing how the forthcoming conversations in Berlin would be prejudiced. A final paragraph in the despatch was to 'elicit an assurance that the German Government still desired the visit to take place . . .'[1] – another astounding reversal of what, in the circumstances, ought to have been the natural order of things. The despatch as a whole was to bring out that the purpose of His Majesty's Government had been all along for 'a general settlement freely negotiated between Germany and the other Powers',[2] and 'agreements regarding armaments which in the case of Germany would replace the provisions of Part IV of the Versailles Treaty'.[3]

Thus it was that in dealing with the whole sequence of events from Hitler's well-staged huff over the British White Paper to Germany's open defiance of the key military provisions of the Versailles Treaty, the British Cabinet had done nothing but comply obediently with the initiative more and more masterfully wielded by the German Government. It was little wonder that when Eden met Hitler again on 25 March 1935, a year after his previous visit, he noted that 'Hitler was definitely more authoritative and less anxious to please than a year before'.[4] The calamitous moral defeat the British had just sustained – worse, the surrender they had tamely made – was, after all, the culmination of two years of diplomacy in which England had consistently represented herself to Hitler as a timid, apprehensive and feebly well-meaning old woman. It was an impression unlikely to have been diminished in Hitler's mind by his meetings with Allen of Hurtwood and Lothian, who had visited Hitler privately with the blessings of MacDonald and Baldwin respectively. Meeting Simon could only impress Hitler the more vividly with English feebleness. Here, in Simon, Hitler met for the first time a Foreign Secretary of England, the greatest of all imperial powers, the nation which had thwarted the ambitions of Kaiser Wilhelm II – this sanctimonious and deferential old gentleman of mild and episcopal appearance. In a situation which called for a breezy, brutal arrogance of a Palmerston, the chilling dignity of a Castlereagh, or the blunt, plain-speaking and dominant will of a Wellington, Simon could only make a sorry attempt at ingratiation.

The Cabinet had decided that Simon's objects should be to let Hitler know that the aim of British policy was to secure co-operation between European nations and the creation of regional pacts – instead of the divisions of Europe into two armed camps as at present threatened by Hitler's actions. 'He [the Foreign Secretary] should not hesitate . . . to bring home

[1] Ibid. [2] Ibid. [3] Ibid. [4] Avon, Vol. I, p. 133.

to Herr Hitler, crisply but firmly, the consequences of his recent announcements as affecting the prospects of peace on a co-operative basis.'[1]

The Foreign Secretary's instructions were here derived from another British misapprehension – that the German leader would naturally value, as they did themselves, peace on a co-operative basis.

Simon's opening speech straight away presented Hitler with the dominance of the meetings. He began by assuring the German Chancellor that 'he and Mr Eden were very glad to be in Berlin and that he himself much welcomed Herr Hitler's acquaintance'.[2] He went on to speak of Germany's recent breaches of the Versailles Treaty in terms so elaborately tactful, so anxiously considerate of German feelings, as to deprive his words of all force: referring obliquely to the 'new developments' of the last ten days, and to British hesitations as whether therefore he and Eden should still come to Berlin; and drawing the German leader's attention to the anxiety which British public opinion entertained over the course of German policy. He pointed out how British policy towards Germany in the past – over reparations, the evacuation of the Rhineland, equality of national rights and so on – proved that Britain had always tried to be 'fair and just'.[3] He expressed the British wish to avoid a division of Europe into two camps, and to co-operate with all countries, including Germany, to secure peace.[4] It was a speech indeed whose tone passed beyond the merely tactful into the servile. Hitler, for his part, deployed cunning arguments for evading the British proposals for an 'Eastern Locarno', and for exploiting the weak points of British psychology. Again and again he assured the Englishmen that Germany posed no threat to Austria – Germany was not interested in her. Nevertheless he did not seem to relish Simon's suggestion of a pact over Austria.

Simon and Eden both dilated on the political beauty and utility of the League of Nations, without eliciting any enthusiasm from the man who had poured scorn on it throughout his political career. When Hitler offered an alliance between Germany and England, Simon replied that the British 'did not wish to substitute one friend for another, because they wanted to be loyal friends to all . . .'[5] In answer to a question from Simon, Hitler made the chilling claim that Germany had now reached air parity with Great Britain.

The British mission proved an utter failure: no 'Eastern Locarno'; no promise to return to the League. Simon drew tactful attention to this failure in his closing speech, the tone of which admirably expressed the

[1] Cabinet of 20 March 1935, CAB 23/81, 16(35)1. [2] CAB 23/81, 18(35), CP69(35). [3] Ibid. [4] Ibid. [5] Ibid.

manner of his conduct of the negotiations: '. . . observing the rule of frankness to the end, he must say that the British Ministers did feel somewhat disappointed that it had not been possible in these two days to get a larger measure of agreement'.[1]

Nevertheless: 'Mr Eden and he would report to the British Government, who would continue to use their utmost efforts in a spirit of friendly co-operation. The British Ministers were sincerely thankful for the way in which they had been received in Berlin, and would take away very pleasant memories of the kindness and hospitality shown them.'[2]

Both Simon and Eden recognised their failure.[3] 'All this is pretty hopeless' was how Simon himself summed it up in a note written immediately after his return.[4] Yet the Cabinet's grand strategy remained unaltered: no line-up against Germany; a continued effort to get Germany into a conference and a negotiated arms agreement. On 8 April it decided on the British objectives at the forthcoming Stresa Conference between Italy, England and France. If asked by France and Italy to end conversations with Germany and do nothing more than stand firm with France and Italy, we should not agree with it. 'Our line, therefore, . . . should be that we could not agree to make a complete break with Germany, and to take no action except to threaten her.'[5] Such an act would not be supported in the country. We should admit, however, there that was 'much evidence' to show that Germany could not be brought to agreement, but that 'we were not finally convinced until further exploration'.[6]

England should stand by Locarno, but not join any undertaking to withstand a breach of the peace anywhere – this might mean, for example, Memel. 'Germany', the Cabinet fearfully believed, 'was in a volcanic mood and not inclined to yield to threats.'[7] We ought to let Germany know what was happening at Stresa, as otherwise 'that would undo *the good* [author's italics] of the Berlin visit'.[8] We ought also to let Germany know the effects of her attitude in preventing mutual confidence: 'It was thought that these considerations ought to be put with friendliness to Germany, so that the German people may be impressed morally and spiritually.'[9]

The Cabinet decided that it was important not to be drawn into specific commitments 'in a hypothetical case' over the demilitarised zone. Whatever therefore might have been the substance contributed by France and

[1] Ibid. [2] Ibid.
[3] Viscount Simon, p. 203, and Avon, Vol. I, p. 138.
[4] Viscount Simon, p. 203.
[5] CAB 23/81, 20(35) and 21(35).
[6] Ibid. [7] Ibid. [8] Ibid. [9] Ibid.

Italy to the 'Stresa Front', British policy in itself was enough to wreck it as an effective anti-German combination.

The reference to 'the good' of the Berlin visit is either a tribute to Simon's hypocrisy or to his short memory; or perhaps to his ability to ignore the unpleasant. For he was to tell the Commonwealth prime ministers in May: 'The role of this country in connection with the Versailles Treaty had throughout been that of the conciliator. . . . It would be seen from the Berlin conversations that Herr Hitler had warmly recognised the efforts made by this country as conciliator. . . .'[1]

On 21 May 1935 Hitler further exploited the initiative by a speech aimed with psychological cunning at the yearnings and prejudices of the British public. He gave assurance that German re-armament offered no threat to world peace; that Germany had no intention of breaking any of her foreign obligations. He held out hope that Germany might return to the League of Nations. He promised to abide by the Locarno Treaty. He was willing to accept parity in the air with England, and a fleet only 35 per cent of the British.

The innocent face of British opinion shone with pleasure at this revelation of the German dictator's goodness. *The Economist* thought Hitler's speech gave 'an overwhelming impression of sincerity'. The Archbishop of Canterbury wrote a nice letter about it to *The Times*. The Archbishop of York, Dr Temple, wrote too, saying that 'Hitler had made in the most deliberate manner offers which are a great contribution to the secure establishment of peace'.[2] Tom Jones, Baldwin's private secretary, wrote to Baldwin to tell him: 'All the people I have seen today (Athenaeum, UAB, Geoffrey Dawson, Bishop of Llandaff etc.) are in favour of cordial acceptance of Hitler's advances and determination to exploit them to the uttermost. Good luck!'[3]

On 22 May, in a debate on increases in the defence estimates, Attlee, the Leader of the Opposition, asserted that Hitler's speech offered 'a chance to call a halt in the armaments race'.[4] The parliamentary Labour Party, together with the Trades Union Congress and the Labour Party National Executive, demanded a special international conference to take advantage of Hitler's offer.[5] On 24 May Herbert Morrison told the Fabian Society that the 'Government had either lost the boat or was in danger of losing it, and that Baldwin had missed the opportunity for a big, inspiring and mighty gesture'.[6]

[1] CAB 32/125, PM(35)2.
[2] Quoted in Templewood, p. 133.
[3] Jones Papers, quoted in Middlemass and Barnes, p. 818.
[4] Quoted in Middlemass and Barnes, p. 819.
[5] Templewood, p. 133.
[6] Ibid.

The Cabinet itself felt that Hitler's speech 'should be welcomed and promised careful and sympathetic consideration'.[1] The practical consequence of this sympathetic consideration was an Anglo-German naval conference in London. Far from being willing to *negotiate* an agreement, however, the chief German delegate, von Ribbentrop, told the British in his opening speech that the conversations could not take place unless England first recognised the 35 per cent ratio 'as fixed and unalterable'.[2] When the British haplessly squirmed in an effort to contest this piece of dictation and yet still save the conference, Ribbentrop simply repeated again and again his demand: England was to give 'a clear and formal *recognition* of the *decision* taken by Herr Hitler in laying down a 35 : 100 ratio between the two countries. . . . It was not a matter of agreement between the two countries, but of recognition [of Hitler's decision].'[3] Ribbentrop wanted an answer that day or the following day, otherwise the German delegation would go home. It was a preposterously arrogant demand. Yet Simon, on behalf of England, caved in and formally accepted it.[4] For such were the straits in which the Royal Navy was placed that the Admiralty thought it better to accept the German demand and ratio than have no naval agreement at all.[5]

This abject surrender was the culmination of all the defeats the British had sustained at German hands between March and June 1935. It marked the consummation of a complete German moral ascendancy over the British, already disastrous in its results, but even more fateful for the future. And Hitler had achieved little less of an ascendancy over France. He had taken the measure of France's politicians and French public opinion too. France, forsaken – even betrayed – by England,[6] was herself all too clearly sunk in defensiveness, fear and irresolution, her national will enfeebled. She had, for example, taken no action to prevent the Saar returning to Germany in 1935 after the population had overwhelmingly voted in favour of this in a League-of-Nations plebiscite; thus, in Hitler's judgement, definitely missing 'the opportunity for a preventive war'.[7]

Thus by the middle of 1935, long before Hitler had achieved military ascendancy in Europe, England and France had lost a decisive struggle with Nazi Germany, a struggle in which the English indeed had never even attempted to engage; never even realised was taking place. It had now

[1] CAB 23/81, 30(35)1.
[2] CAB 29/150, NC(G)1.
[3] CAB 29/150, NC(G)2.
[4] CAB 29/150, NC(G)4.
[5] CAB 29/150, NC(G)1, NCM(35)50, NCM(35)50 Annex III, NCM(35)55.
[6] Cf. the Anglo-German Naval Treaty, concluded behind France's back.
[7] Foreign Office, *Documents on German Foreign Policy* (London, HMSO 1959), Vol. III, p. 706; for the political and moral state of France in these years see Brogan, chs. VII and VIII; Williams, pp. 61–70; Beaufre, pp. 53–6, 59–61.

become morally certain that France and England would not make use of their existing joint strategic superiority, whatever the provocation; and this was perfectly apparent to Hitler. Like a commander in battle who divines that he now dominates his opponent's mind and will, Hitler felt able to act boldly, to take great risks, even in the face of superior power.

It was from the beginning of 1936 onwards that the British Government began seriously to consider the possibility that Hitler might make another assault on the crumbling remains of the Versailles Treaty, for the French, who had feared a German re-occupation of the demilitarised zone of the Rhineland throughout the latter part of 1935, now believed that it was imminent. In a memorandum to the Cabinet Committee on Germany,[1] the Foreign Secretary (now Eden) drew attention to the danger that the Germans might march into the zone, and reported that Laval, the French Foreign Minister, was trying to induce England to promise to take action if the Germans should move.[2] Eden had called for reports from the Air Staff and the General Staff as to the grand-strategic importance of the demilitarised zone, the burden of which he summarised for the benefit of his colleagues: '. . . the disappearance of the Demilitarised Zone will not merely change local military values, but is likely to lead to far-reaching political repercussions of a kind which will further weaken France's influence in Eastern and Central Europe, leaving a gap which may be eventually filled either by Germany or by Russia.'[3]

The re-occupation of the Rhineland would lead to these repercussions because fortification of Germany's western frontier would bar the path of a French offensive intended to aid France's eastern allies.[4]

The implications of this strategic assessment, in terms of the British response to a German attempt to re-occupy the zone, were clear. But Eden, on the contrary, wished to avoid discussing 'hypothetical' cases with the French. He thought that it was up to the French and Belgians to take action – it was their security which was involved in the demilitarised zone.[5] Britain, in his view, should not see the alternative as either fighting for or abandoning the zone. Instead there should be negotiations with Germany 'betimes'. Eden's memorandum proved to be just another of those escapist documents to which British diplomacy was so prone, shying away from the fundamental, if unpleasant, issues at stake.

On 5 March, two days before the German army embarked on its first advance in the west since July 1918, the whole Cabinet discussed, amid all its Abyssinian preoccupations, the prospects of such a German forward

[1] One meeting only, 17 February 1936; CAB 27/599. [2] CAB 27/599, G(36)3.
[3] Ibid. [4] Ibid. [5] Ibid. [6] Ibid.

move. Eden reported that Flandin, the new French Foreign Minister, feared that oil sanctions would drive Italy out of the League and also from adherence to the Locarno Treaty: 'This together with the possibility of an Italian *rapprochement* with Germany and of German action in the Demilitarised Zone created a grave situation for France and he wished to be reassured as to the British attitude before taking a decision on the oil embargo.'[1]

Eden added that it was the Foreign Office's opinion that there was no likelihood of such an Italo-German *rapprochement*.

There followed a prolonged and rambling discussion in which it was suggested that 'in the present circumstances that Germany was unlikely to commit a "flagrant" breach of Articles 42 or 43 of the Treaty of Versailles [relating to the demilitarised zone] . . .';[2] but which equally explored at length the exact meaning of these articles and made ingenious attempts to interpret them in ways nugatory of any British obligation to go to the military aid of France.[3] The Prime Minister (Baldwin), the Chancellor of the Exchequer (Chamberlain) and others pointed out that 'the reality of the situation was that neither France nor England was really in a position to take effective military action . . .' and that hence there was a need for a diplomatic approach to Germany in order to avoid being faced with an open breach.[4]

So, as Hitler so well guessed, it was simply a foregone conclusion that England and France would offer no resistance to the German march into the Rhineland when it took place on 7 March 1936.

And now the steel-helmeted sentries of the Wehrmacht stood once more along the frontiers of France and Belgium. As foreseen by the British Air and General Staffs in their reports to Eden, the advent of these sentries marked an immense shift in the European balance – and not least because of the crushing defeat sustained by France herself, with its far-reaching effects not only on her strategic position, but on her national morale and her European prestige.

The re-occupation of the Rhineland was the climax of the strategic and moral successes won by Nazi Germany in the face of opponents who, if only they had been united and resolute of will, were strong enough to crush her. Now, however, that period of French and English superiority was passing away. Soon Germany was to enjoy military as well as moral ascendancy.

At the end of 1936 British planners estimated the ground forces of Germany and Italy combined already to exceed those of England and

[1] CAB 23/83, 15(36)1. [2] Ibid. [3] Ibid. [4] Ibid.

France, while their combined first-line air strength was also believed to be greater, with 'an exceptional advantage where long-range bombers . . . are concerned', giving them a superiority in bomb load of 1,000 tons to France and England's 300 tons.[1] Whereas in 1937 Germany would be herself still weaker on land than France, she would be the stronger by 1939.[2] But in the air Germany would be as far ahead of Great Britain in 1937 as she would ever be, with 800 bombers to Britain's forty-eight.[3] By May 1937 the Italian and German air forces together, it was estimated, would be able to drop 600 tons of bombs a day at a maximum intensity[4] and the Air Raid Precautions Department of the Home Office despondently reported that the limited precautions that could be put into effect 'should be a means of allaying general panic, but no guarantee can be given that the life of the community and the business of governments will not be disorganised'.[5]

Henceforth therefore fear of the German bomber was to be a dominating factor in British policy-making.

For during the three years when England was casting away the opportunity of dealing effectively with Nazi Germany from a position of combined British and French military superiority, she had also allowed herself to suffer another defeat with no less catastrophic consequences; she had lost the re-armament race with Germany, especially in the air.

It was not for want of timely warnings. In 1930 the Chiefs of Staff had warned the Government that other countries' defence expenditure had not shrunk as England's had: that fifty cruisers were insufficient to ensure English command of imperial sea-routes; that the army could not fulfil English obligations under the Locarno Treaty.[6] In March 1931 the Chief of the General Staff referred yet again to the inability of the army to fulfil its European and imperial commitments. He noted that while Germany as yet 'remains comparatively powerless' on land, she had formed the 100,000-man army permitted under the Versailles Treaty into a highly trained cadre; '. . . she intends gradually to resurrect her former military strength . . .'[7] He also drew attention to the enormous war potential of

[1] Report by the Joint Planning Committee comparing British strengths with that of certain other nations as at 1 May, 1937, dated 22 December 1936; CAB 53/29, COS 539 (JP).
[2] Report of the Chiefs of Staff comparing British strengths with that of certain other nations as at 1 May 1937, dated 9 February 1937; CAB 53/30, COS 551.
[3] Ibid.
[4] CAB 53/29, COS 539 (JP).
[5] Report of 31 December 1936, enclosed in CAB 53/29, COS 539 (JP).
[6] CAB 53/21, COS 247. Annual Review for 1930.
[7] Appendix to Memorandum to the Cabinet Committee on Preparations for the Disarmament Conference, 31 March 1931, CAB 27/476, CDC(31)11.

German industry, now reorganised and re-equipped on the most modern lines.[1] In April 1931, the Chief of the Air Staff submitted a memorandum on the state of British air-power relative to other countries: 'I must . . . record my view that, from the strategic as opposed to the political point of view, the existing position is in effect one of unilateral disarmament, which cannot be indefinitely tolerated.'[2]

He also described Germany's evasions of the total prohibition of military aviation laid on her by the Versailles Treaty: members of the German forces flew as 'amateurs'; army and navy officers were being illegally trained, partly in Russia; military aircraft were being built abroad by offshoots of the German aircraft industry; components were being standardised between civil and military types of aircraft.[3]

In November 1931 the Secretary of State for Air, Lord Londonderry, gave his colleagues a fresh warning of British weakness in the air; Britain was now fifth among the powers, spending on aviation (civil and military) a smaller proportion of the national expenditure than Italy, France or the United States.[4]

In 1932, the Chiefs of Staff in their Annual Review analysed at great length all the deficiencies of the British armed forces both in size and in the quality of their equipment that had resulted from cumulative neglect since 1918, placing these deficiencies in the context of the worsening world situation.[5] But the Government took no action except to agree to the abolition of the 'ten-year-rule', and to appoint a committee to survey the whole question of imperial defence.

By midsummer next year, 1933, the English Cabinet had come to know not only the character and ambitions of the new Nazi régime, but also that it had embarked on major programmes of re-armament, including the building of military aircraft. Indeed Germany's re-armament and military expansion were already public knowledge, thanks to articles in great detail by Liddell Hart in the *Daily Telegraph* in May and July 1933.[6] In November 1933 the Chiefs of Staff formally confirmed to the Government that Germany was re-arming and that 'within a few years hence she will again have to be reckoned with as a formidable military power'.[7]

It was only then, November 1933, more than three years after the first warnings by the armed services that the British forces could not fulfil

[1] Ibid.
[2] Memorandum of 27 April 1931 to the Cabinet Committee on Preparations for the Disarmament Conference, CAB 27/476, CDC(31)3.
[3] Ibid. Appendix III.
[4] Memorandum of 26 November 1931, CAB 27/476, CDC(31)22.
[5] See above pp. 342–3.
[6] Liddell Hart, Vol. I, pp. 228–30.
[7] CAB 53/23, COS 310.

Britain's obligations, some two years and eight months after the first warnings of clandestine German re-armament, a year after the Chiefs of Staff's formidable catalogue of British weaknesses, six months after learning that Germany was re-arming on a large scale, that the British Government took action – of a sort. It appointed a committee. This, the Defence Requirements Sub-Committee of the Committee of Imperial Defence, was composed of the Chiefs of Staff and senior civil servants. It was charged with examining and reporting on the subject matter of its title. It rendered its first report on 28 February 1934,[1] recommending a five-year programme to remedy the accumulated deficiencies of the British armed forces. An expeditionary force of five divisions should be prepared; the navy's ships and bases should be modernised; the present strength of the Royal Air Force, far below the peacetime size decided upon as long ago as 1923, should be enlarged by some forty squadrons.

On 29 March 1934, Germany published her new defence estimates, which as a whole were up by a third, while expenditure on aviation was up by 250 per cent.

At the beginning of May the British Cabinet took further action. It referred the Defence Requirements Sub-Committee Report to another, more senior, committee – the Cabinet Committee on Preparations for the Disarmament Conference. On 12 June, while this committee was in the middle of its dignified ponderings, the Chiefs of Staff considered a memorandum by the Chief of the Air Staff, in which he wrote that German airframe and engine production had doubled since 1930; and, given six months' further expansion, could reach 1,000 airframes and 760 engines a month – enough for a first-line strength of 1,000–2,000 aircraft. Germany had 5,000 trained pilots and 10,000 glider pilots. Therefore Germany could rapidly build up an air force of 2,000 aircraft, and, within five years, be able to maintain such a strength in war.[2]

It was only some six weeks later, on 31 July 1934, that the Cabinet Committee on Disarmament at last submitted their report to the Cabinet. This report, based on the now five-months-old recommendations of the Defence Requirements Sub-Committee, was approved by the Cabinet that day. The RAF was to be brought up to the 1923 standard by the creation of forty new squadrons over the next five years. No start, however, was authorised on the remedying of the deficiencies of the other services.[3]

[1] CAB 16/109, DRC 14.

[2] CAB 53/24, COS 341.

[3] See CAB 16/110, Reports and Proceedings of the Cabinet Committee on Disarmament, on Questions Dealing with Defence Requirements, 1934; Interim Report, 16 June 1934, CP193(34); and Report, 31 July 1934, CP205(34).

On 20 November 1934 the Committee of Imperial Defence submitted a memorandum which, by fact and figure, provided the Cabinet with the disquieting news that the belated and modest British measures were being swiftly overtaken by German re-armament, which, as the Cabinet minutes put it, 'had reached a very formidable stage'.[1] The German army would soon reach 300,000 men, with preparations for large-scale training, and there were indications that mechanised divisions were soon to be created. There were 300 munitions factories ready for intensive production. Forty-five new airfields had been constructed in twelve months. The German output of aircraft, put at 100 a month in July, was now put at 140. Within a year Germany would have an air force as big as the Royal Air Force.

On 26 November 1934, therefore, the Cabinet decided to speed up the creation of the new squadrons for home defence and the Fleet Air Arm from four years to two. But still nothing was to be done for the army or the navy. It was now *four years* since the Government had been warned that the army was incapable of fulfilling British obligations under the Locarno Treaty in respect of the Rhineland demilitarised zone.

In March 1935 Germany made her announcements of a peacetime army of thirty-six divisions, conscription, and the existence of the Luftwaffe.

In April the Secretary of State for Air reported to the Cabinet that in air strength Britain would be ahead of Germany for at least three years, but that there was 'grave reason for anxiety for the future', and hence the British programme needed to be increased.[2] The Cabinet therefore authorised a new programme for the RAF, which would provide an extra thirty-nine squadrons for home defence by 1937.[3] In this same month of April 1935, the Chiefs of Staff asked the pertinent question: if the Low Countries were to be defended, 'ought not the state of preparedness of the Field Force be accelerated?'[4] In their Annual Review for 1935 (also submitted in April) the Chiefs of Staff again reminded the Government about British obligations under Locarno, in the context of Britain's worldwide commitments and the menace from both Germany and Japan. Yet the army was, they wrote, reduced to a size barely sufficient for the internal security of the empire and for a field force for service in the East. As for what might be scraped together for Europe, 'to launch so small a force into war on the Continent might well be disastrous'.[5]

On 8 May 1935 the Government learned that Britain was estimated to

[1] CAB 23/80, 41(34)1.
[2] CAB 53/24, CP85(35).
[3] CAB 16/140, DPR 82.
[4] CAB 53/24, COS 374, 29 April.
[5] COS 372.

be already inferior to Germany in the air by 370 aircraft, and that to reach parity again Britain must order 3,800 aircraft for delivery by April 1937 – 1,400 more than the existing programme. It also learned in May that Germany was perfectly capable of outbuilding even this programme.[1] On 21 May 1935 the Cabinet gave its approval for the home defence force of the RAF to be brought up to 1,512 aircraft (of which 840 were to be bombers and 420 fighters).[2]

On 24 July 1935 the Defence Requirements Sub-Committee submitted an interim report, in which was recommended 'a much wider programme of re-armament than hitherto contemplated in Britain', entailing capital expenditure on industrial development – machine tools, jigs and gauges and other resources.[3] Only now, therefore, had general re-armament – expansion of the armed forces, not merely the remedying of deficiencies – made its debut in British thinking. This report was considered by a new Cabinet committee, the Ministerial Sub-Committee on Defence Policy and Requirements; in fact, the old Cabinet Disarmament Committee under a title more appropriate to the times. The new committee authorised the Defence Requirements Committee to work out fresh proposals for re-armament, based on the assumption that by 1939 'each service should have advanced its state of readiness to the widest necessary extent in relation to the military needs of national defence . . .'[4] The DRC was particularly asked to recommend whether special measures were needed to increase factory output.[5]

Thus *five years* after the obsolescence and deficiencies of the army and navy had first been listed to the Government, the stage had only now been reached of *beginning to formulate* detailed proposals for remedying them. And *five years* after it had become known in London that German industry was fully equipped to undertake large-scale munitions production, Britain had only just reached the stage of *investigating* the question of industrial development.

Four months later, on 21 November 1935, the DRC rendered its third report.[6] It recommended a navy large enough and modern enough to provide a deterrent and defensive fleet in the Far East and at the same time meet the German naval threat in home waters; virtually, indeed, the navy for which Beatty and his successors had fought unavailingly in the 1920s. It recommended that the army should be re-equipped over five years, though not enlarged. And it also recommended the creation of a 'shadow'

[1] Middlemass and Barnes, pp. 814–18.
[2] CAB 21/422A.
[3] CAB 16/140, DPR 82.
[4] CAB 16/112, DRC 27.
[5] Ibid.
[6] CAB 16/112, DRC 37.

armaments industry – new factories built with public money and managed by existing industrial firms.

This report was now considered at length by the Defence Policy and Requirements Committee of the Cabinet, which eventually, as the stately saraband of British governmental procedure revolved, submitted *their* report to the Cabinet on 12 February 1936.[1] The Cabinet itself approved their recommendations on 25 February 1936[2] – seven months after the DRC had first put forward broad suggestions for general re-armament and expansion of the armed forces; three months after it had submitted its detailed proposals.

It was thus only in the second month of 1936 that the British Government at last launched a comprehensive scheme of large-scale re-armament, covering industrial development as well as the services. However, it was only *in the course of* 1936 that the programme was gradually set in motion. During the spring and summer, sites were being surveyed and contracts negotiated for the new factories; during the autumn and winter, the factories were being built and the machinery installed.[3] England, therefore, was at least *six years* behind Germany in developing her industrial capacity for war production; and at least *three years* behind in creating a modern air force. England had begun to modernise and expand her sea-power *four years* after the Chiefs of Staff and the Admiralty had first warned that the navy was too weak and run-down adequately to defend the empire. And even now, *six years* after the Chiefs of Staff had pointed out to the Government that the army was incapable of fulfilling England's treaty obligations or protecting her strategic interests in Europe, and *three years* after it had become known that the German army was in the throes of a vast expansion, very little extra was to be spent on the British army.[4]

It was not until 1937, when the new 'shadow' factories came into production by fits and starts, that British re-armament really began to get under way.[5] How much this was too late was brought home to the Government by the Chiefs of Staff in February 1937, when they reported that by May of that year the Luftwaffe would be able to field 800 bombers to the RAF's forty-eight. London and other industrial complexes lay, it was believed, at German mercy.[6]

What were the reasons for these staggering delays and immense inadequacies in British re-armament up to 1936?

In the first place, there was the sheer ponderousness and torpor of the

[1] CAB 16/112, DPR(DR)9.
[2] CAB 16/112, 10(36).
[3] See service department progress reports to the Defence Policy and Requirements Committee in CAB 16/136–137.
[4] CAB 16/123, DPR(DR)4.
[5] CAB 16/137.
[6] See above pp. 409–10.

governmental machine for the framing and deciding of policy – a cumbersome mechanism of over a hundred committees of the Committee of Imperial Defence, to say nothing of various Cabinet committees; a mechanism of which Sir Maurice Hankey in person was the crown wheel. All these committees were leisurely investigating, discussing and reporting on their diverse stocks-in-trade; their recommendations gradually filtering upwards through ever more senior committees until finally the Committee of Imperial Defence or the Cabinet took the major decisions of policy.[1] Thus for example, the Cabinet decided on the first RAF development programme *eight months* after the Defence Requirements Sub-Committee was set up to investigate defence needs; *five months* after the Committee had rendered its first report. The same committee itself took four months to compose its third report in 1935.

The only impetus from the top came from Baldwin, first as the Lord President of the Council and then as Prime Minister, who, as his biographers narrate at length,[2] took special interest in defence and spent much time over it. Yet Baldwin was no dynamic force, no man of immense driving will, such as was needed to set the cumbersome machine rolling and jerk servicemen and civil servants out of the slow rhythms of their existence; he could not be compared to the bluff, brutal and ruthless Göring who was bludgeoning on the headlong – if, as is now known, ramshackle – German effort.

In the second place, the Treasury, under the implacable leadership of the Chancellor of the Exchequer, Neville Chamberlain, resolutely opposed great schemes of re-armament on the grounds that the British economy, hardly yet convalescing from the world slump, could not afford them. In June 1934 Chamberlain himself revised the recommendations of the DRC 'in the light of politics and finance',[3] cutting down the general expenditure from £76 million to £50 million over five years, and deciding that if an air force to defend Britain against German air attack was the prime need, 'we certainly can't afford at the same time to re-build our battle-fleet'.[4] On 2 August 1935 he wrote that Germany was borrowing £1,000 million a year for armaments, and that therefore Britain ought to spend £120 million extra over the next four or five years.[5]

Yet this Treasury 'meanness' was not unreasonable. England was no longer the boundlessly rich country of the Victorian age, or even of 1914.

1 See F. A. Johnson, *Defence by Committee: The British Committee of Imperial Defence 1855–1959* (London, Oxford University Press 1960), especially pp. 221–46.

2 Middlemass and Barnes.

3 Diary for 6 June 1934, quoted in Feiling, p. 258.

4 Ibid.; see also Middlemass and Barnes, pp. 770–1.

5 Feiling, p. 266.

The world slump had only served to make worse a slump peculiar to Britain which had lasted all through the 1920s.[1] Ever since 1931 the British balance of payments had been highly precarious; the chronic problem of the 1950s and 1960s had begun to emerge. Between 1929 and 1932 Britain's foreign dividends fell from £250 million to £150 million per annum, while her other invisible earnings fell from £233 million to £86 million.[2] And re-armament, with its demand for highly advanced technology, would not necessarily help the mass-unemployment in the old and moribund Victorian industries, except in shipbuilding, but only compete with the export trade for the resources of Britain's all too small modern industries: automobiles, chemicals, radio, light engineering. For the question of re-armament brought Chamberlain and the Treasury, if no one else, face to face with the reality that Britain no longer enjoyed the economic strength to support her pretensions as a great power. The financial problem was rendered the more acute by the running down of the British armed forces, for all three now simultaneously needed enormous programmes of re-equipment and enlargement. And whereas for Germany re-armament offered the hope of later carving a way to other nations' riches, for Britain an effort on a similar scale promised nothing but eventual ruin.

Yet a third reason for the belatedness of British re-armament lay in that in 1934–5 the Air Staff was less keen than Baldwin and other members of the Cabinet on embarking on a rapid expansion of the RAF. This was partly because, relying on its own intelligence sources and on information kindly provided by the German air ministry, it believed that the pace of expansion of German air-power was nothing like as fast as the Foreign Office, from its own sources of intelligence, (and outside critics like Churchill) were claiming. Much time was spent inside the Cabinet and its committees in the years 1934–5 disputing various estimates of the current size of the Luftwaffe and its future rate of growth.[3] Whereas the Air Ministry's estimates of the *current* size of the Luftwaffe in these years have been borne out by post-war examination of the German records, it was the Foreign Office whose guesses as to its future rate of growth proved more accurate. Until too late the Air Ministry failed to take sufficient account of the potential growth made possible by German productive resources.[4]

Yet there was another motive behind the Air Ministry's attempts to

[1] E. J. Hobsbawm, *Industry and Empire* (Harmondsworth, Penguin Books 1969), pp. 207–13.
[2] Ibid. p. 211.
[3] See Middlemass and Barnes, pp. 786–9, 812–13; Avon, Vol. I, pp. 183–6.
[4] Avon, Vol. I, p. 186; Middlemass and Barnes, p. 789.

play down the extent of the German menace in the air, and resist the desire of Baldwin and others to embark on a rapid 'shop-window' expansion of the RAF. For in 1934–5 such an expansion could only have lumbered the RAF with obsolescent, indeed obsolete, types of aircraft; slow biplanes of wood and fabric. Despite such well-publicised and gratifying triumphs as winning the Schneider Trophy, the British aircraft industry was now behind those of Germany and America, which had already moved into the era of the all-metal aircraft, both for civil and military purposes.[1] The backwardness of the British aircraft industry at this critical juncture therefore exercised a disastrous long-term effect on British policy.

The British General Staff, like the Air Ministry, also grievously underestimated the speed with which Germany could create her new armed forces. On 20 June 1933 the CIGS expressed the view to his fellow Chiefs of Staff that, while a start should be made now on re-equipping the British army, it would be five or ten years before Germany might be troublesome.[2] A year later on 7 July 1934, the three Chiefs of Staff jointly informed the Government:

> There is, in our opinion, a tendency to exaggerate the immediate danger from Germany, and to treat as imminent a threat which contains many elements of uncertainty. At the same time there appears to us to be an insufficient regard for the difficulties which face Germany . . . and the long period of preparation necessary before she can be in a position to engage in a long war of aggression with good prospects of success.[3]

The British Chiefs of Staff were indeed perfectly correct in judging that it would be a long time before Germany would be strong enough successfully to wage an aggressive war. The professional heads of the German armed forces thought so too; the year 1942 was the target at which they were aiming, given to them by Hitler himself on 28 February 1934.[4] Yet the mistake made by the military men – British and German – was to think exclusively in terms of the date when the German armed forces would be ready successfully *to wage war*. They lacked the political comprehension to perceive that armed forces impressive enough to be brandished effectively in support of an expansionist foreign policy could be created in a far shorter time. And this was in fact the main purpose of

[1] M. M. Postan, D. Hay and J. D. Scott, *The Design and Development of Weapons* (London, HMSO 1964), pp. 3–4; M. M. Postan, *British War Production* (London, HMSO 1952), p. 15.
[2] CAB 53/4, COS 111.
[3] CAB 53/24, COS 343.
[4] See Robert J. O'Neill, *The German Army and the Nazi Party. 1933–9* (London, Cassell 1966), pp. 130–1.

the expansion urged on at such breakneck speed by Hitler and Göring after 1933, much to the German generals' own professional misgivings.

Yet English politicians made the same error as their military advisers, although for different reasons. To them, nineteenth-century liberals in the outlook as they were, armed forces existed in peacetime either to deal with minor military emergencies ('imperial policing') or as a defensive precaution against the contingency of war; but not as an instrument of diplomacy. The presence of the English fleet in the Mediterranean during the Abyssinian crisis was a precaution against an Italian armed attack on English interests, not the means of an English psychological attack on Mussolini's nerve. To commit England to a large-scale re-armament programme therefore seemed to English statesmen tantamount to deciding to take the road to another great war. As Baldwin himself said in a broadcast on 12 October 1933: 'There can be no doubt of one thing, if once re-armament began in Europe, not only would the danger of war become a far more serious menace, but the competition in armaments would impose an intolerable burden of taxation on the people of this and every other country.'[1]

As a consequence, long after Germany had walked out of the Disarmament Conference at the end of 1933, the English Cabinet clung on desperately to the hope of reaching some general agreement on disarmament or arms limitation. As late as November 1935 the Government was still talking arms limitation in its public speeches, and pursuing such an agreement until well into 1936. So long as the Cabinet entertained the faintest hopes in this direction, it was hardly possible for it to throw itself heart and soul into a great re-armament programme. From 1934 onwards indeed the Government was in the ambivalent posture of trying to pursue disarmament and re-armament at the same time.[2]

The truth was that the scale and the pace of Germany's military growth after January 1933 demanded of the British Government that it should reverse course from disarmament to re-armament with an abruptness utterly beyond the agility of its own mind, let alone the mind of the British public. For by tragic coincidence the first two years of the Nazi dictatorship and its military expansion witnessed the rise of pacifistic emotion in Britain to its very climax.

While it was perfectly evident to pacifists and internationalists that the world was becoming more disturbed and violent,[3] their response was only

[1] A. W. Baldwin, *My Father: The True Story* (London, Allen and Unwin 1955).

[2] It is a sign of this that early studies and discussions of British re-armament took place under the auspices of the Cabinet Committee on Preparations for the Disarmament Conference.

[3] Cf. introduction by Leonard Woolf, and essays by C. R. Buxton and W. Arnold-Forster in Woolf.

to advocate the old nostrums of the 1920s, the Covenant of the League, and, above all, disarmament. It was an advocacy in which there was now a high, thin note of panic; a desperate call for faith. Thus one pacifist in 1933, after himself fully describing the shattering defeat of the League at the hands of Japanese military power in 1931–2, the brutal beliefs and practices of the Nazi régime, and the vast Nazi ambitions of conquest, still pleaded:

> The worst of all disservices to disarmament would be to become defeatist . . . To press on, undeterred, with disarmament, in the face of the German situation, is dangerous and difficult; but to call off disarmament, and to try to fall back on the one-sided régime of Versailles – that would be not only dangerous but assuredly disastrous.[1]

Lord Allen of Hurtwood in a letter to the *Manchester Guardian* on 18 May 1933 gave the pacifist and moralising internationalist answer to German re-armament:

> . . . our duty is to call for the disarmament of the old Allies and not to join in the hue and cry against Germany's re-armament. . . . Germany is but little interested either in re-arming or disarming; her one concern is to secure equality. Herr Hitler has declared his willingness for his country to abandon her own armaments if other nations do likewise.[2]

Such convictions as these were preached with ever more frantic ardour in the years 1933–5, as the world situation worsened. All the customary groups were active: the League of Nations, the Churches, the nonconformist sects – and some new ones. In 1934 Canon Dick Sheppard, of St Martin's-in-the-Fields, asked men to send in postcards pledging themselves never again to support war; and this led to the creation of the Peace Pledge Union, with 135,000 members.[3] The various pacifist and internationalist bodies co-operated and coalesced[4] in a great mission in favour of general disarmament and against British re-armament, a mission whose culmination was the so-called Peace Ballot. The moving spirit of the Ballot was Lord Cecil of Chelwood, a founding father of the League of Nations,[5] a man largely responsible for the reduction of the Royal Navy's strength in cruisers to only fifty.[6] From its very inception the Ballot was far from an impartial attempt to sound public opinion, for its first object, according to the Ballot's 'official' historian, was to demonstrate that the

[1] W. Arnold-Forster in Woolf, p. 455.
[2] Gilbert, *Plough My Own Furrow*, p. 351.
[3] Kingsley Martin, pp. 196–8.
[4] Cf. the Federation of Progressive Societies, under the chairmanship of Professor C. E. M. Joad.
[5] See above pp. 244–7.
[6] See above pp. 289–90.

British public supported the League as a cardinal point in British policy.[1] The idea of the Ballot arose in 1934 out of the general atmosphere of gloom by then prevailing over the future of international co-operation after the deadlock in the Disarmament Conference, amid the talk of the possibility of another European war;[2] and throughout that year the faithful enthusiastically organised the Ballot, in co-operation with the League of Nations Union.

The list of the Ballot's public supporters reads like a combined muster roll and pedigree of moralising internationalism: the Labour and Liberal parties; the Archbishops of York and Canterbury and more than fifty bishops; the moderator of the General Assembly of the Church of Scotland; the Roman Catholic Archbishop of Liverpool; the President of the National Council of Evangelical Free Churches; the General Secretary of the Baptist Union; the Moderator of the English Presbyterian Church; the Chief Rabbi and Canon H. R. L. Sheppard. The intelligentsia and the stage were well represented too: Sir Cedric Hardwicke, Sybil Thorndike, Diana Wynyard and St John Ervine; E. M. Delderfield, A. A. Milne, Rose Macaulay, Professor J. B. S. Haldane, Dr A. D. Lindsay (the Master of Balliol), Lady Rhondda, Sir Arthur Salter, Sir Norman Angell and H. A. L. Fisher. Sixty-one leading surgeons and physicians published a manifesto in support of the Ballot.[3]

Half a million disciples carried out the poll of all registered parliamentary electors. The first results were announced in November 1934, and the poll was completed in June 1935. From February 1935 onwards through May (the period of the first British White Paper on Defence and the German announcements of conscription and the Luftwaffe) there was a rapid increase in the numbers of people voting. The total vote was 11,087,660. To the first question of the Ballot: 'Should Great Britain remain a Member of the League of Nations?', 10,642,560 answered yes; 337,964 no. To the second question: 'Are you in favour of all-round reduction of armaments by international agreement?', 10,058,526 voted yes; 815,365 no. To the third question: 'Are you in favour of an all-round abolition of national military and naval aircraft by international agreement?', 9,157,145 answered yes; 1,614,159 no. The Ballot did not, however, offer the voter a direct opportunity of expressing his views on the question of whether Britain herself should re-arm if other countries continued to re-arm.

Summing up the achievement of the Peace Ballot, Lord Cecil expressed

[1] Dame Adelaide Livingstone, *The Peace Ballot: The Official History* (London, Gollancz 1935), p. 6.
[2] Ibid. p. 7.
[3] Ibid. pp. 13–14.

the opinion that it had succeeded in its first object of assuring the British Government that public opinion would be solidly behind it if it took the lead at Geneva, in which case, 'much could still be done to avert the threatened relapse into international anarchy'.[1] With regard to the Ballot's verdict on the question of armaments, Cecil wrote: 'All-round abolition of national naval and military aircraft, which has been supported in eighty-five per cent of those answers, is, I am convinced, the way of true security for the world against the greatest of man-made perils.'[2]

During the great agitation which culminated in the Peace Ballot, it was the Labour and Liberal parties which inside and outside Parliament provided the political spearheads of disarmament.

On 21 December 1933 Attlee declared in the House of Commons: 'For our part, we are unalterably opposed to anything in the nature of re-armament and believe it would be a tragedy if the Disarmament Conference were to result actually in re-armament.'[3]

On 30 July 1934 the Opposition moved a motion of censure regretting the Government's programme to expand the RAF on the grounds that it was unnecessary, would not add to our security, was 'certain to jeopardise' international disarmament and 'encourage a revival of dangerous and wasteful competition in preparations for war'.[4] Attlee asserted in the debate: 'We deny the need for increased air arms. . . . We deny the proposition that an increased British Air Force will make for the peace of the world, and we reject altogether the claim of parity. . . .'[5]

Sir Stafford Cripps, in winding up for Labour, argued: 'It is a fallacy, if one is examining the methods by which security may be obtained, to start upon the assumption that we get security by an increase of air armaments . . .'[6]

Sir Herbert Samuel, the Liberal Leader, for his part, thought that the founders of the League would be shocked by this re-armament.[7]

In March 1935, after the publication of the Government's first White Paper on Defence, timid as it was, and the not-so-timid German announcement of conscription, Attlee declared: 'Let there be no mistake about this White Paper. It marks a complete change of policy. . . . We believe that the policy outlined here is disastrous.'[8]

The Labour MP George Hall (later Lord Hall) told the Commons: 'In our opinion it is madness to assume that more and bigger armaments are required to preserve peace, to give security, and to deter aggression. Let

[1] Livingstone, p. 60.
[2] For other questions and answers in the Ballot, see above p. 360.
[3] Baldwin, p. 193.
[4] Ibid. p. 204.
[5] Viscount Simon, p. 179.
[6] Ibid. p. 180.
[7] Baldwin, p. 205.
[8] Viscount Simon, p. 180.

there be no misunderstanding. We, on these Benches, will vote against the service estimates at every stage.'[1]

In the same debate, Sir Archibald Sinclair, a member of the Liberal front bench, referred to 'the folly, danger and wastefulness of this steady accumulation of armaments . . .'[2]

In May 1935 Cripps was arguing that under collective security there was no need for air parity; parity was just power politics. The only solution was for countries 'to sacrifice their national sovereignty in the interests of international co-operation'. The failure to do this explained 'why we always resist the armament votes of the Government'.[3]

Unfortunately for the Government the course of parliamentary by-elections in 1934–5 offered plain evidence that the electorate shared the profound antipathy to re-armament voiced by the Opposition parties and by the crusaders for pacifism and internationalism. For a candidate to stand for 'peace' was to ensure himself victory. In 1933 Arthur Henderson won Clay Cross on a disarmament ticket. In June 1933, at East Fulham, John Wilmot of the Independent Labour Party also made this the main issue, accusing the Government of having brought the Disarmament Conference to the point of failure and Britain 'nearer to war than we have been since 1918'; and caricaturing his Conservative opponent as a war-monger because he wanted to maintain British defences. George Lansbury, then the Labour Leader, sent a message to the constituency: 'I would close every recruiting station, disband the Army and disarm the Air Force. I would abolish the whole dreadful equipment of war and say to the world "do your worst".'[4]

So much did the East Fulham electorate relish these thoughtful views that a Conservative majority of over 14,000 was turned into a Labour majority of nearly 5,000; a swing of 26·5 per cent.[5] Yet East Fulham was only the first of a series of six by-elections running on into February 1934, all fought on the issue of 'peace', in which the swing against the Government varied between 24·8 per cent and 19·9 per cent.[6] In April and May 1934 three more seats were lost by the Government, with lower swings of 16 per cent to 14 per cent. However, from October 1934 to March 1935, the swing against the Government in by-elections was up again, averaging 23·4 per cent. At Lambeth North, in October 1934, when canvassing for the Peace Ballot was well under way, it was 50 per cent. In November 1934 Edith Summerskill told the electors of Putney that 'war, with all its

[1] Ibid. [2] Ibid. p. 181. Baldwin, p. 231.
[4] Quoted in Middlemass and Barnes, p. 745.
[5] Ibid. [6] Ibid. pp. 745–6.

horrors, may be brought perilously near by the policy of the so-called National Government . . . responsibility for the armaments race in which the nations are now admittedly engaged lies heavily on its shoulders'.[1] The results of the Peace Ballot, coming in from November 1934 to June 1935, only provided further proof that the British had succumbed to a mood of the most profound pacifism.

It was a mood very different from the hopeful, optimistic internationalism of the 1920s; deeper by far than the broad moral and intellectual repugnance to conflict and power bequeathed by nineteenth-century evangelical religion. It welled up from an intense dread of war.

By the early 1930s the British no longer saw the Great War as a victory over perhaps the most formidable foe England has ever had to fight; as a tremendous deliverance; as a time of national regeneration. After all, since the fruits of that victory had already all been cast away, the victory and the sacrifices which had won it had alike been rendered futile. Instead the British now saw the Great War simply as a horror almost beyond imagination: ghastly and yet meaningless in its suffering; hideous and purposeless in its immense squandering of life. More than this even, a national myth had arisen according to which it was the Great War which was responsible for Britain's present decadence and decline. By the early 1930s the Great War had become the great British excuse.

It was believed in the first place that it was the war which had destroyed Britain's Victorian economic supremacy. In the words of Lloyd George:

> Our most serious devastation was invisible – the shattering of our export trade through our being cut off for over four years from our normal overseas markets. . . . Indeed, our export trade has never recovered from the War, as the derelict factories of our industrial districts bear melancholy witness. While world trade had by 1927 risen to 120 per cent of the pre-war level, British export trade was only 83 per cent of its pre-war height.[2]

Yet in objective truth the Great War in no way inflicted crippling economic damage on Britain. No battles or demolitions were carried out on British territory, nor was any part of this territory ever occupied – in contrast to France. Nor did Britain suffer loss of territory or economic resources through the Peace Treaty – in contrast to Germany. The foreign investments sold to pay for the war were, at about £300 million, equal

[1] Middlemass and Barnes, pp. 791–2.
[2] Lloyd George, *The Truth About Reparations and War Debts*, pp. 8–9; cf. also Macmillan, p. 18.

to less than two years' investment at the pre-war rate; hardly more than one-thirteenth of Britain's total foreign investments.[1] Even though the British merchant marine lost 40 per cent of its tonnage to the U-boat, the loss was soon replaced.[2] The collapse of British exports and the stagnation of British industry in the 1920s was not due to the war, but were the final reckoning for the increasing backwardness and uncompetitiveness of the past sixty years.[3]

It is, however, the legend of a crippling *human* loss which is central to the myth that Britain's decline was caused by the war. As Baldwin expressed it in 1935:

> We live under the shadow of the last War and its memories still sicken us. We remember what modern warfare is, with no glory in it but the heroism of man. Have you thought what it has meant to the world to have had that swathe of death cut through the loveliest and best of our contemporaries, how our public life has suffered because those who would have been ready to take over from our tired and disillusioned generation are not there?[4]

Yet this legend too – the legend of 'the Lost Generation' – is unjustified by the facts. The total of United Kingdom dead for all fronts was 702,410.[5] France, from a similar population, lost nearly twice as many – 1,327,000.[6] To make another comparison, had British losses been at the same rate per population as Germany's, her dead would have numbered some 1,200,000 instead of 702,410.[7] Yet it could hardly be said that Germany's national will and energy had been severely and permanently impaired.

But it was the Western Front in particular that loomed so terribly in the British imagination when they thought of the Great War and its supposedly crippling losses. Here United Kingdom dead amounted to 512,564.[8] This is not much more than the losses suffered by Italy in three – not four – years of war on a single front: 460,000.[9] Yet no one seemed to think that Italian life had been drained of its vitality.

Then again, the total United Kingdom dead for all fronts in the Great War was, in proportion to population, less than the total of American

[1] Taylor, *English History 1914–1945*, p. 123.
[2] Ibid. p. 122.
[3] See above pp. 83–112, and below pp. 485–93.
[4] Middlemass and Barnes, pp. 867–8.
[5] *Statistics of the Military Effort of the British Empire during the Great War* (London, HMSO 1922), Table i(a), p. 237.
[6] C. R. M. F. Cruttwell, *A History of the Great War* (Oxford, The Clarendon Press 1934), p. 631.
[7] Germany lost 1,808,545 in killed, out of a population of 66,000,000: ibid.
[8] *Statistics of the Military Effort of the British Empire*, Table (i)(9G), p. 238.
[9] Cruttwell, p. 631.

losses on both sides during the civil war. Yet post-1865 American history is hardly characterised by stagnation and loss of drive.

Even the British losses in officers on all fronts – the true source of the legend of the 'Lost Generation' – was, at 37,452 killed,[1] considerably less than the 55,888 lost by the air crews of Bomber Command during the Second World War,[2] and which led to no comparable legend.

If the Great War casualties are placed in the context of national population statistics, the legend of crippling damage to the national vitality becomes even less well-founded. In 1921 and 1926 the percentage of males between the ages of fifteen and forty-four in the population (roughly the military age-group) was 46, as against 47 per cent in 1911, 48 per cent in 1901 and 45 per cent in 1891 – hardly a significant difference. In terms of loss of population by death, the average annual percentage between 1911 and 1921, the period covering the Great War, was 1·44 per cent – lower than the 1·62 per cent recorded for 1901–11.[3]

The truth was that the Great War crippled the British *psychologically* but in no other way. But how did the British come to believe in the myth that the Great War had bled them of their ancient vigour? How did the legend of the 'Lost Generation' arise?

In the first place, the English governing class was small and intimate, educated in a handful of public schools. Assuming in war its customary right and duty to lead the nation, this narrow governing class supplied the bulk of the subalterns, especially in the early years of the war, and therefore sustained an immensely higher proportionate loss than the nation as a whole; how high the public schools' rolls of honour tragically record. The impact on the governing classes was made the worse because of the number of prominent statesmen who lost relatives or friends. Baldwin's cousin Rudyard Kipling lost a son. Lord Halifax lost four companions out of his undergraduate circle at Christ Church; an example, he wrote, 'typical of the national experience, of the cruel loss suffered by one generation'.[4] Lothian lost a younger brother at La Bassée in October 1914.[5] In Balfour's circle Lord and Lady Wemyss lost two sons, Lord and Lady Desborough two also. Harold Macmillan, himself an officer badly wounded on the Somme, recalled in his memoirs the Eton and Oxford friends killed in action.[6] Herbert Asquith, Prime Minister until 1916, and leader of one

[1] *Statistics of the Military Effort of the British Empire*, Table (i)(G), p. 228.
[2] Sir Charles Webster and Noble Frankland, *The Strategic Air Offensive Against Germany 1939–1945*, 4 Vols. (London, HMSO 1961), Vol. III, pp. 286–7.
[3] A. M. Carr-Saunders and D. Caradog Jones, *A Survey of the Social Structure of England and Wales* (London, Oxford University Press, 1927), Table LXXVII, p. 221.
[4] The Earl of Halifax, *Fullness of Days* (London, Collins 1957), p. 53.
[5] Butler, *Lord Lothian*, p. 61.
[6] Macmillan, pp. 95–6.

wing of the Liberal Party until 1926, lost his son Raymond. Bonar Law, Prime Minister in 1922–3, lost two of his four sons. Lord Crewe's eldest daughter lost her husband in 1914; and Crewe himself lost his brother-in-law. He wrote during the war of the losses among his friends' families: 'The heavy toll goes on, taking so many, as it seems, who have everything to make life delightful, and a brilliant future never to be realised.'[1] Arthur Henderson[2] lost his eldest son on the Somme.[3] Eden's eldest brother was killed early in the war, and his youngest brother at Jutland at the age of sixteen, while his uncle in the RFC was shot down and captured, and his sister's husband badly wounded on the Somme.[4] Neville Chamberlain lost his cousins, Norman, of whom he was deeply fond and whose death much affected him, and Johnnie.[5] Vansittart lost his brother on the Western Front, and in the late 1920s, on a tour of the battlefields with Baldwin, came across his grave.[6] It was little wonder that English statesmen in the 1930s shrank with dread from policies that carried the risk of armed conflict.

Yet it was from these personal losses that the legend of the 'Lost Generation' was woven. So small, even tiny, was this world of the British governing class that it is the same few names that crop up again and again as examples of the brilliant young leaders now lost to Britain – the Desboroughs' sons, Julian and Billy Grenfell, in particular; and Raymond Asquith. And they were exactly the type of men to appeal to the romanticism of the upper-class, public-school mind; perfectly cast as the noble heroes of a tragic legend. Thus Raymond Asquith, according to John Buchan, was a

> scholar of the ripe Elizabethan type, a brilliant wit, an accomplished poet, a sound lawyer – these things were borne lightly, for his greatness was not in his attainments but in himself. He had always borne a curious aloofness towards mere worldly success. He loved the things of the mind for their own sake . . . and the rewards of common ambition seemed too trivial for a man's care. . . .[7]

Buchan, after noting Asquith's 'high fastidiousness', painted a pre-Raphaelite portrait of the young knight at arms: 'Most noble of presence, and with every grace of voice and manner, he moved among men like a being of another race, scornfully detached from the common struggle. . . .'[8]

[1] Pope-Hennessy, p. 147.
[2] Not, of course, a member of the traditional governing class.
[3] Hamilton, p. 112.
[4] Avon, Vol. I, pp. 689.
[5] Feiling, pp. 77–8.
[6] Vansittart, pp. 146, 366.
[7] Quoted with approval in Cooper, p. 55.
[8] Ibid.

Asquith, a legend in himself to his generation, may be taken as representing all that the British governing classes believed had been so fatally taken from England in the war. Yet were these the kind of qualities of which England in the 1920s and 1930s stood most in need? It is hard to see in men like Raymond Asquith – 'aloof towards merely worldly success . . . detached from the common struggle', a man to whom 'the rewards of common ambition' seemed 'too trivial' – the talents required to reorganise and re-vitalise British industry, or carve out new export markets, or solve great social problems, or dominate the course of world affairs. It is therefore by no means certain that in the 'Lost Generation' England lost in quality what she certainly did not lose in quantity.

The British governing classes made the unconsciously arrogant, if understandable, mistakes of thinking that the virtues they admired were necessarily those the future required; and that because their own small circle had been decimated, the vitality of the British nation had been critically impaired.

Yet the peculiar impact of the war on the governing class itself does not explain why British opinion as a whole – especially the broad middle classes – came to accept the myth that Britain had undergone crippling damage in the Great War; why they too came to look back on the war with such shuddering horror, as if Britain had suffered on the French or German scale.

The middle classes' picture of the Great War was the result more than anything else of the tremendous effect produced on their minds by best-selling memoirs and novels about life on the Western Front.

Although there had been a spate of war books immediately after the war, and a steady sale throughout the 1920s,[1] the great bull market for trench memoirs opened in 1927, with fifteen such books, as against six in 1926. In 1928 there were twenty-one; in 1929 twenty-nine. Although the reviewers now began to complain that there was a glut of mud and blood, 1930 proved yet another boom year for trench horror stories, and the market only gradually subsided as the 1930s wore on. Essentially, however, it was these years 1928–31 that made the decisive impression on the public. In 1928 appeared Edmund Blunden's *Undertones of War*, Siegfried Sassoon's *Memoirs of a Fox-Hunting Man*, R. C. Sherriff's play *Journey's End*. In 1929 there was Richard Aldington's *Death of a Hero*, Erich Maria Remarque's *All Quiet on the Western Front*, Robert Graves's *Goodbye to all That*, and Hemingway's *A Farewell to Arms*. In 1930 there followed

[1] Cf. C. E. Montague, *Disenchantment*; R. H. Mottram's *Spanish Farm* trilogy and Ford Madox Ford's quadrilogy.

Frederic Manning's *Her Privates We* and Sassoon's *Memoirs of an Infantry Officer*; and in 1931 Wilfred Owen's *Poems* in an edition by Edmund Blunden.

Despite great contrasts of style and personal response – between, say, the elegance of Blunden and the savagery of Aldington – the outstanding trench reminiscences told much the same story: of idealism turning into sour disillusion, of the futility of the fighting, of the obscenity of death and mutilation on a modern battlefield, of the terrors of battle:

> . . . men, single and in couples, shuffling past them, answering no questions. Tin hats on the back of heads, and no tin hats, tin hats with splinter-ragged sandbag-coverings; men without rifles, haggard, blood-shot eyes, slouching past in loose file, slouching on anyhow, staggering under rifles and equipment, some jaws sagging, puttees coiled mud-balled around the ankles, feet in shapeless mud boots swelled beyond feeling, men slouching on beyond fatigue and hope, on and on and on. GS waggons with loads of sleeping bodies. Stretcher-bearers plodding desperate-faced. Men slavering and rolling their bared-teeth heads, slobbering and blowing, blasting brightness beyond their eye-balls, supported by listless cripples.[1]

Such was the picture of the Great War imprinted on the minds of the British reading public from 1928 onwards; a picture replete with such details as Blunden's description of a lance-corporal killed by a shell: '. . . gobbets of blackening flesh, the earth-wall sotted with blood, with flesh, the eye under the duckboard, the pulpy bone . . .'[2]

The influence of trench reminiscences is to be measured not only from their number, but from the avidity with which they were read. R. C. Sherriff's play *Journey's End*, for example, was reprinted thirteen times between January and October 1929 and had sold to that date 45,000 copies. Blunden's *Undertones of War* was reprinted three times in one month – Manning's *Her Privates We* four times in a month.

Yet in fact the writers of the trench memoirs and novels collectively gave a highly subjective, unbalanced and misleading version both of the experience of the Western Front, and of the British army's reaction to it.[3] For the war writers were not in the least representative of the men of the British army as a whole; they were writers and poets, and with few

[1] Henry Williamson, *Patriot's Progress* (London, Geoffrey Bles 1930), pp. 97–8.

[2] Edmund Blunden, *Undertones of War* (London, Richard Cobden-Sanderson 1928), p. 63.

[3] This is a delicate topic for a historian who has never known a battlefield, for he is sitting in judgement on men who endured ordeals that he fears he himself could not support. The author approaches these writers of the Great War in personal humility, and in wonder at their courage and fortitude.

exceptions they came from sheltered, well-off, upper- or upper-middle-class backgrounds, the products of an upbringing at home and at their public schools which had given them little knowledge or understanding of the real world of their time, but rather a set of unpractical idealistic attitudes. They were indeed flowers of English liberalism and romanticism, all living spiritually at Forster's *Howard's End*, and having delicate emotional responses to the aesthetic stimulus of landscape. It would be hard to guess, for example, from the writings or verse of Sassoon, Blunden or Graves that the English landscape they loved in fact represented British agriculture in distress and decay; or that Britain in 1914 was an overwhelmingly urban and industrial country with profound social problems, where one-third of the population lived in poverty. The social, aesthetic, intellectual and moral world in which the war writers had lived before the war was wholly unreal – as artificial as the pastoral idylls of the French court before 1789. Hence army and trench life – quite apart from the hazards and horrors of war itself – was often their first real introduction to the world of struggle and hardship, as most of mankind knew it. Indeed much of the space in the trench literature is occupied not with battle but with ordinary life in the trenches: 'Washing was a torment. They had three tubs of water between about forty of them a day. Since Winterbourne was a latecomer to the Battalion he had to wait until the others had finished. The water was cold and utterly filthy.'[1]

Dug-outs were a favourite topic: 'Each of the guttering candles had a halo round it. The smoke from them, and tobacco, and acrid fumes from the brazier, could not mask the stale smell of unwashed men, and serges into which had soaked and dried the sweat of months.'[2]

Much attention was devoted by the war writers to rats, and also to the primitive sanitation of the trenches, such as the pole latrines: '. . . while they sat there they hunted and killed the lice on their bodies'.[3]

To the war writers and their middle-class readers it was this squalor of trench life that constituted not the least important and unpleasant aspect of the Great War. Yet nearly *a third* of the British nation lived their entire lives in slums, contemporary descriptions of which remarkably echo those of living conditions in the trenches: 'Two rooms, seven inmates . . . Dirty flock bedding in living-room placed on box and two chairs. Smell of room from dirt and bad air unbearable.'[4] Or: 'Two rooms. In the lower room the brick floor is in holes. Fireplace without grate in bottom. Wooden

[1] R. Aldington, *Death of a Hero* (London, Chatto and Windus 1929), p. 310.
[2] Frederic Manning, *Her Privates We* (London, Peter Davies 1930), p. 418.
[3] Ibid. p. 23.
[4] B. Seebohm Rowntree, *Poverty: A Study of Town Life* (London, Macmillan 1910), p. 156.

floor of upper room has large holes admitting numbers of mice. Roof very defective, the rain falling through on to the bed in wet weather.'[1] Or: 'There is no water supply in the house, the eight families having to share one water-tap . . . with eight other families who are living in other houses. The grating under this water-tap is used for the disposal of human excreta. . . .'[2]

There was little to choose by way of amenity between a slum yard and a trench. Thus Blunden on the trench: 'Under their floors of boards and slats, water swelled and stagnated, and an undesirable nocturnal smell, mortal, greenweedy, ratty, accompanied the tramp of our boots to and fro.'[3]

And the slum yard: 'Large paved yard, full of holes. One ashpit and one closet is used by nine houses . . . the smell from these places is simply horrible in hot and wet weather.'[4]

A no less prominent feature of trench reminiscences is the evocation of the dereliction and desolation of the trench zone: 'The red-brick hollow of a station marked "Cuinchy" [wrote Blunden] told us that we were almost at our journey's end: other ruins of industrial buildings and machinery showed through the throbbing haze; the path became corrupt, and the canal dead and stagnant.'[5]

Sassoon however wrote in almost identical terms and feeling of the surroundings of a camp on the outskirts of Liverpool: '. . . the smoke-drifted munition works, the rubble of industrial suburbs, and the canal that crawled squalidly out into blighted and forbidding farm-lands . . .'[6]

Sassoon himself described the trench zone on returning to it from leave: 'I was entering once again the veritable gloom and disaster of the thing called Armageddon . . . a dreadful place, a place of horror and desolation which no imagination could have invented. Also it was a place where a man of strong spirit might know himself utterly powerless.'[7]

Yet R. H. Sherard, a social investigator, could describe in remarkably similar terms his feelings on return to a great English city in peacetime: 'I never set foot in Manchester without a shrinking at the heart, an instinctive and irrepressible feeling of pale terror. Is it on account of its almost perennial gloom? Is it because I am familiar with the dreadful squalor and surpassing misery of its slums?'[8]

The war writers could thus perhaps as well have found material for

[1] Ibid. [2] Ibid. p. 155.
[3] Blunden, p. 24. [4] Rowntree, p. 189. [5] Blunden, p. 34.
[6] Siegfried Sassoon, *Memoirs of an Infantry Officer* (London, Faber and Faber 1930), p. 103.
[7] Ibid. p. 153.
[8] R. H. Sherard, *The Child Slaves of Britain* (London, Hurst and Blackett 1905), p. 85.

doom-laden descriptions in England as in France; and certainly the British industrial scene would have been just as great a novelty to them as the Western Front.

The war writers also made much of the dangers and hardships of trench life in the quiet times outside the great battles – the patrols, raids, shelling, sniping, digging and carrying. Yet even here much that seemed so novel and unpleasant to them had its parallels in the peacetime life of many of the nation. In a chain works for example: 'I saw women making chain with babies sucking at their breasts . . . I spoke to a married couple who had worked 120 hours in one week . . . I saw heavy-chain strikers who were worn-out old men at thirty-five.'[1]

Or, if it was a question of poison gas, 'the chemical men work amid foul odours and in an intense heat – the temperature being as often as high as 120 degrees. They sweat and toil in an atmosphere charged with biting acids, or deadly gases, or dense with particles of lime.'[2]

It may be wondered what kind of books writers like Siegfried Sassoon would have written after four years of working in such a place. Although it lacked the concentrated, appalling terror of a great battle, it was still far removed from Aunt Evelyn carrying her sweet-peas and roses 'down to the drawing-room while the clock ticked slow, and the parrot whistled and the cook chopped something on the kitchen table'.[3]

Whereas the British industrial population had to cope with squalor and hardship on their own scant and precarious resources, the army in the trenches had the moral and material support of an immense organisation: comradeship, regular food, medical care, canteens, sport, and even entertainment. Many of the rank-and-file were in fact better off in the trenches than at home. The troops themselves therefore were cheerful and stoical rather than outraged and introspective, a fact which deeply puzzled the war writers. Sassoon 'could never understand how they managed to keep as cheery as they did through such drudgery and discomfort, with nothing to look forward to but going over the top or being moved up to Flanders again'.[4] Manning found it a strange thing 'that the greater the hardship they had to endure, for cold and wet bring all kinds of attendant miseries in their train, the less they grumbled. They became a lot quieter, and more reserved in themselves, and yet the estaminets would be swept by roaring storms of song.'[5]

Here, in these comments, is corroborative evidence that the war

[1] Robert Blatchford, *Dismal England* (London, Walter Scott 1901), p. 102.

[2] Description of a Lancashire chemical works in Blatchford, p. 116.

[3] Sassoon, *Memoirs of an Infantry Officer*, pp. 72–3.

[4] Ibid. pp. 32–3.

[5] Manning, p. 335; see also Aldington, *Death of a Hero*, p. 293.

writers were not representative of the army as a whole in their reaction to the experience of the Western Front; that their books gave a distorted impression of the soldier's experiences and state of mind. This is true even of their descriptions of the great Western Front battles, appalling ordeals though these were. For the war writers, being men of acute sensibility, took them far more hard than their more phlegmatic fellows.

It is instructive to compare, for example, Sassoon's – or even Graves's – accounts of the Royal Welch Fusiliers' involvement in the battle of Loos or the Somme with that of Frank Richards, a long-service regular private soldier in the same regiment. Happenings which stirred Sassoon to savage indignation and hysterical horror and outrage, provoked Richards to no more than a laconic comment or a cynical witticism. The casualties, the loss of friends, which is a constant refrain in the books of the war writers, is fatalistically accepted by Richards without much time wasted on introspection.[1] The death or mutilation of comrades could soon be forgotten over a good 'feed' of egg and chips in the canteen.[2] Graves himself records an illustration of the rank-and-file's attitude to death:

> A corpse is lying on the fire-step waiting to be taken down to the graveyard tonight. . . . His arm was stretched out stiff when they carried him and laid him on the fire-step; it stretched right across the trench. His comrades joke as they push it out of the way to get by. 'Out of the light, you old bastard! Do you own this bloody trench?' Or else they shake hands with him familiarly. 'Put it there, Billy Boy.' Of course they're miners and accustomed to death.[3]

Nor did the writers of trench memoirs make much attempt to place their personal experiences in the larger context of the strategy and politics of the war, although they were writing ten years and more after the event. They failed to tackle the hard questions, such as the German occupation of Belgium and northern France and its inescapable effect on Allied policy, and indeed on the nature of a possible compromise peace. Yet it was such insoluble problems which determined the whole course and nature of the war, including the writers' own personal sufferings. Could the war have been stopped? Were the endless offensives really unnecessary? The war writers offered little by way of answer. Blunden wrote virtually nothing on these topics except to say that in early 1917 he 'began

[1] Frank Richards, *Old Soldiers Never Die* (London, Faber and Faber 1964).
[2] Cf. R. H. Haigh and P. W. Turner (eds.), *The Long Carry: The War Diary of Stretcher-Bearer Frank Dunham 1916–1918* (Oxford, Pergamon 1970).
[3] Robert Graves, *Goodbye to All That* (Harmondsworth, Penguin Books 1961), p. 97.

to air his convictions that the war was useless and inhuman'.[1] Aldington's diagnosis of the causes of the war and the factors that determined its continuance was hardly more sophisticated: 'But what were they really against? Who were their real enemies? He saw the answer with a flood of bitterness and clarity. Their enemies – the enemies of German and English alike – were the fools who had sent them to kill each other instead of help each other.'[2]

Graves observed only that by 1917 none of the writers in the army, including himself, 'now believed in the war' – whatever that meant.[3]

Sassoon, rather than offering enlightenment on the gigantic underlying problems of the war, was content to narrate his own pacifist *démarche* of 1917. His reconstruction of his first conversation with Massingham on this topic did his intellect little credit: 'It's only when one gets away from it [the war] that one begins to realise how stupid and wasteful it all is. What I feel is that if it's got to go on, there ought to be a jolly good reason for it and I can't help thinking that our troops are being done in the eye by the people in control.'[4]

Nor was his later formal pacifist declaration about the war, although drafted in collaboration with Bertrand Russell, much more penetrating, although certainly more pompous: 'I believe that this war, upon which I entered as a war of defence and liberation, has now become a war of aggression and conquest . . .' If, he went on, British war aims had been stated '. . . the objects which actuated us would now be attainable by negotiation . . .'[5] Like his fellow writers, Sassoon had nothing to add by way of retrospective understanding of the dilemma which faced the leaders of the belligerent countries.[6]

The war writers therefore shirked the fundamental political and military problems presented by the war; instead they were content to express their emotional revulsion, although with enormous power and cumulative effect.

The middle-class reading public responded to this emotional revulsion with warm sympathy and approval. They seemed only too ready to accept the war writers' accounts, as 'the truth' about the war – as the reviews clearly demonstrate. The *Sunday Times*, for example, wrote of Aldington's *Death of a Hero*: 'The stupidity and humbug of those who "made" the War, and the monstrous futility of the war itself; such is his theme. . . .'[7]

[1] Blunden, p. 199.
[2] Aldington, *Death of a Hero*, p. 296.
[3] Graves, p. 204.
[4] Sassoon, *Memoirs of an Infantry Officer*, pp. 195–6.
[5] Ibid. p. 218.
[6] See also Ford Madox Ford, *No More Parades* (London, Duckworth 1925), pp. 19–20; and Manning, Prefatory Note.
[7] *Sunday Times*, 22 September 1929.

The *Daily Mirror* advised its more numerous readership: '. . . we commend the vituperative novel as a useful reminder and sermon for those who are beginning to forget'.[1] Victoria Sackville-West on the radio was rapturous about Sassoon's *Memoirs of an Infantry Officer:* 'I dare say,' she told her audience, 'that Mr Sassoon's manifesto of protest against the war – which comes at the end of the book – will stir many people to wish that they had had the moral courage to express the same sentiment.' *Time and Tide* wrote of Sassoon's book that it had '. . . a quietness of judgement which does not disguise the deep indignation with which he saw men uselessly slaughtered . . .'[2] The *Sunday Despatch* felt that 'like Mr Aldington, Mr Sassoon leaves us with an abiding sense of the futility of the grim struggle . . . Both books, too, are in their full scope denunciations of the folly of war, more effective than many of the more direct philippics of politicians and orators.'[3] The *Daily Mirror* wrote of Sassoon: '. . . we have his revulsion of feeling against the futility of the nightmare through which he and his fellow soldiers had passed'.[4] And finally, in order to provide a fair spread of opinion, here is the *Tatler* on Williamson's *Patriot's Progress*: 'It leaves one also angry against the people who see in war anything finer than a supreme human disgrace.'[5]

The catastrophically far-reaching effects of the war books on British opinion, and hence on British policy, were compounded by the unlucky coincidence of their historical timing, for they straddled the very turning-point of the inter-war period. The books began to appear in 1928–9, in the era of high internationalist euphoria when the Great War at least seemed to be dead and buried and part of history. Yet long before the boom had spent itself, the world situation had entirely changed; and another war had become for the first time a possibility. Thus whereas the trench reminiscences began to appear in an epoch when they seemed the belated truth about an experience which now belonged completely to the past, they continued to appear in a new epoch where they had an immediate relevance to the present and the future. What began as an epitaph ended as a warning. As a warning, the war books seemed to say that war was so terrible and futile that the British ought to keep out of another one at any cost.

The dread of war which so gripped the British in the 1930s did not however derive only from their image of the Great War; they worked themselves up no less over the novel horrors which, thanks to science, were

[1] *Daily Mirror*, 1 October 1929.
[2] *Time and Tide*, 1 November 1930.
[3] *Sunday Despatch*, 21 September 1930.
[4] *Daily Mirror*, 22 September 1930.
[5] *Tatler and Bystander*, 18 May 1930.

to be expected in the next war. In particular, the British were obsessed by fear of the bomber.

The Royal Air Force, in its campaign to establish its own importance *vis-à-vis* the older services, was the original cause of this obsession, for ever since the end of the Great War its chiefs had been trying to make the politicians' flesh creep by claiming that the air-power could bomb a nation's industry into rubble and reduce its life to anarchy.[1] The claim was taken up and propagated by all forward-thinking writers on strategy.[2] From 1932 onwards in particular the Chief of the Air Staff constantly dwelt in memoranda and in meetings with his colleagues on what the bomber could do to London.[3] By January 1937 the Chief of Air Staff was warning that by 1939, thanks to heavier bomb loads, longer ranges, higher speeds, and better navigational aids, the Germans could drop up to 2,000 tons of bombs on the first day of an air offensive, if they were to concentrate all their aircraft against Great Britain.[4] In 1932, Baldwin told the House of Commons:

> I think it well . . . for the man in the street to realise that there is no power on earth that can protect him from being bombed. Whatever people may tell him, the bomber will always get through. The only defence is offence, which means that you will have to kill women and children more quickly than the enemy if you want to save yourselves. . . .[5]

While this speech was a laudable attempt to tell the people what then seemed to be the truth, it was hardly calculated to stiffen the courage of the nation. It was rather a gift to the pacifists and disarmers, who were to quote it often. No less useful presents to the pacifists were the futuristic predictions of war in the air made by the prophets of air-power. Bertrand Russell in his pacifist tract *Which Way To Peace?*, published in 1936, for example, made brilliant use of quotations both from ministers of the Crown (including Baldwin's 'bomber' speech) and from a whole assortment of experts on air warfare, gas, and air raid precautions. It was Major-General J. F. C. Fuller, who, picturing the results of *one* air raid on London, provided Russell with perhaps the most spine-chilling of all his quotations: '. . . London for several days will be one vast raving Bedlam,

[1] Webster and Frankland, Vol. I, pp. 42–64.
[2] Such as Liddell Hart and J. F. C. Fuller.
[3] Memorandum of 12 June 1934, CAB 53/24, COS 341, discussed by the COS on 27 June 1934, CAB 53/4, COS 130; see also memorandum COS 344; and COS meetings of 20 November 1934, CAB 53/5, COS 135; and 29 October 1935, COS 153.
[4] CAB 53/30, COS 553.
[5] Quoted in Middlemass and Barnes, p. 735.

the hospitals will be stormed, traffic will cease, the homeless will shriek for help, the city will be a pandemonium. What of the Government at Westminster? It will be swept away by an avalanche of terror. Then will the enemy dictate his terms . . .'[1]

Russell himself assured his readers that '. . . undoubtedly the most formidable of the three kinds of bomb will be the one filled with gas. . . . Lewisite is so poisonous that fifty bombers, given perfect conditions, could carry enough of it to poison all London and its suburbs. . . .'[2]

And Winston Churchill himself, in endeavouring to sting the Government and the country into timely re-armament, helped to stir up the nation's terror of another war. In his first major speech on the issue of re-armament, in the House of Commons on 7 February 1934, he provided a characteristically highly-coloured picture of an air attack on Britain, when 'the crash of bombs exploding in London and cataracts of masonry and fire and smoke will apprise us of any inadequacy which has been permitted in our aerial defences'.[3] On 28 November 1934 he informed the House that 'one could hardly expect that less than 30,000 or 40,000 people would be killed or maimed' in a week or ten days of bombing over London, which would also lead to an exodus from the capital of 'at least 3,000,000 or 4,000,000 people'.[4]

All through the first half of the 1930s, therefore, politicians, air marshals, pacifists, disarmers and military commentators constantly vied with each other in portraying the scenes of apocalypse that must inevitably ensue in the capital of the empire immediately war broke out. It was all, however, a science-fiction fantasy founded on a fallacious extrapolation of the statistics of damage done per ton of bombs during the Great War; an error which had originated in the Air Ministry soon after the Great War[5] and which had ever since conveniently served the Air Ministry's undeviating purpose of puffing the importance of the RAF. No less fallacious and exaggerated were the various estimates at different times of the number of bombers which could be deployed over London, and of the operational capabilities, in terms of range and bomb-load, of the aircraft of the epoch. The Air Staff themselves were to admit in a note to the Prime Minister on 13 October 1941 that their pre-war estimates had been largely 'crystal-gazing'.[6]

[1] Quoted in Bertrand Russell, *Which Way to Peace?* (London, Michael Joseph 1936), p. 37.

[2] Ibid. pp. 30–1; see also Kingsley Martin, p. 193, for Russell's letter, written to Martin in August 1935, on the anarchy, starvation and panic which must follow within a few days of the outbreak of war, and which Martin regarded as 'very characteristic of the thought of the period'.

[3] James, p. 231.

[4] Ibid. p. 232.

[5] Cf. speech by Sir Samuel Hoare, then Air Minister, to the Imperial Conference, 1923. CAB 32/9, E-10.

[6] Webster and Frankland, Vol. I, p. 185n.

The 'next war' was therefore visualised by the British nation as a ghastly combination of the Western Front (plus tanks) and the destruction of civilised life at home by air attack. Baldwin only expressed the conviction of all in regarding as a 'truism that the next war will be the end of civilisation in Europe'.[1]

In 1936 the film *Things To Come* (based on a book by H. G. Wells) enacted for the instruction of the mass cinema audience the whole sequence of predicted horrors, from the initial destruction of London to the end of existing civilisation.

The leading circles in British life chose therefore to believe the worst both over the Great War and over the 'next' war too. They dwelt on terrors past and terrors yet to come with a positively morbid relish, terrifying themselves into pacifism. They succeeded, indeed, in breaking their own nerve. And this, as a determining factor in British policy between 1918 and 1939, ranks in importance second only to the post-evangelical British character itself.

In November 1936 Baldwin, in answering an attack by Churchill in the House of Commons on the belatedness of British re-armament, was to say: 'Supposing I had gone to the country [in 1933], and said that Germany was re-arming, and that we must re-arm, does anybody think that this pacific democracy would have rallied to that cry at that moment? I cannot think of anything that would have made the loss of the election from my point of view more certain.'[2]

Churchill in his memoirs, disingenuously choosing to think that Baldwin was referring to the General Election of 1935, bitterly alleged that Baldwin had been afraid of telling the country the truth for fear of losing that election. In fact, although Churchill left this out, Baldwin went on to say, 'we got from the country, with a large majority, a mandate for doing a thing that no one, twelve months earlier, would have believed possible'.[3] Yet, while Churchill's partial quotation and unjust accusation have been misleading enough, Baldwin's own statement was itself disingenuous, for it clearly implied that it was the pacific state of public opinion which had prevented the Government from embarking on a great programme of re-armament in 1933 or 1934. Yet, as the Cabinet records make plain, such was not the case. The Cabinet fully shared the national mood of profound revulsion at the very thought of war and re-armament, although, having the responsibilities of government, it could not indulge in the fantasy of unilateral disarmament enjoyed by the Opposition and by

[1] Quoted in Middlemass and Barnes, p. 937. [2] Quoted in James, p. 268. [3] Ibid.

pacifists and internationalists at large. Baldwin in particular looked on war with a deep and abiding horror as the 'most fearful terror and prostitution of man's knowledge that ever was known'.[1] After the spring of 1932, according to his biographers, a 'preoccupation with air warfare and the constant nightmare of what a rain of incendiary bombs could mean to an open city like London worked remorselessly in Baldwin's mind . . .'[2] Since most of the Cabinet shared Baldwin's own feelings, it was not the outside restraint of a pacific democracy, but their own pacific reluctance which prevented the Cabinet from taking more than the smallest steps towards re-armament which were compatible with increasingly alarming information from Germany. There is no indication that the great crusade against disarmament and in favour of 'peace' mounted by the pacifists and moralising internationalists ever stopped the Government from embarking on a measure of re-armament which it had come to think essential. And as the news from Germany pushed the Government, against its own deepest feelings, into larger and larger measures of re-armament, so the Government proceeded promptly enough to explain and justify to the nation the limited steps it was taking, and the steps it might still be forced to take.[3] There is little discrepancy either in content or timing between the sentiments expressed by the Cabinet in private and in public about re-armament between 1933 and 1936. Only over the first Defence White Paper of 1935 was there some emasculation of the language of the original draft in deference to the susceptibilities of British and foreign opinion.[4]

The truth therefore was that it was neither public opinion which was responsible for the delays in re-armament, as Baldwin made out in 1936, nor that it was all the Government's fault, as Churchill and others have argued. There were no scapegoats: it was the nation as a whole which bore the responsibility for the failure to launch a large-scale programme of re-armament until well into 1936; a failure which henceforth placed the conduct of English foreign policy at an irretrievable disadvantage.

In their Annual Review for 1937,[5] the Chiefs of Staff, those Cassandras in gold braid, despondently surveyed the predicament in which England was now imprisoned:

> . . . we are in a position of having threats at both ends of the Empire from strong military powers, i.e., Germany and Japan, while in the centre we have lost our traditional security in the Mediterranean. . . . So long

[1] Quoted in Middlemass and Barnes, p. 722. [2] Ibid. p. 734.

[3] See the summaries of Baldwin's speeches on re-armament in Baldwin, pp. 188–266; and in Middlemass and Barnes, pp. 864–9. [4] CAB 23/81, 11(35)1, 25 February 1935.

[5] COS 560, 22 February 1937, taken note of by the Cabinet on 3 March 1937.

as that position remains unresolved diplomatically, only very great military and financial strength can give the Empire security.

Although they did not feel it necessary to say so, such military and financial strength did not exist, and never could.

The Chiefs of Staff noted the growth of the German menace since 1935 – her re-armament; the re-occupation of the Rhineland and its weakening effects on France – and concluded that Germany was the primary danger that England had to face, for it was to be doubted, in their view, whether Germany could achieve her aims of expansion by peaceful changes. It was essential to support France and the Low Countries against German aggression. At the same time the Chiefs of Staff pointed out that there was a danger of being drawn into war in Europe at the wrong moment through France's system of alliances in eastern Europe. A war in Europe might open either with an air attack on Great Britain or a land attack on France.

Turning to the Japanese menace, the Chiefs of Staff voiced a hope that because of the distances involved and the need for great superiority of strength, 'it appears unlikely that Japan would embark on major operations against Singapore, although in view of the decisive results at stake the possibility of such action can never be definitely excluded'. However, when the Chiefs of Staff reported on the situation in the Far East in much more detail in May 1937,[1] they struck a less optimistic note, especially in considering what the Japanese might do if England were to become embroiled in a European war. It was possible and in character for the Japanese to prepare a secret expedition before war was declared. The Japanese might aim to establish air forces to operate from shore bases 'and to land army forces in the Malayan Peninsula to advance on Singapore. The Japanese may hope by the combined effect of attrition, air and land attack to force our garrison to surrender before our fleet can arrive to relieve it.'[2]

The Chiefs of Staff remarked that while the east coast of Malaya was difficult country, the west coast enjoyed good communications, although the rubber and coconut plantations afforded poor visibility. They reckoned that the Japanese would need up to two divisions for the invasion of Malaya; and wrote that they could not rule out the possibility of the Japanese landing in Siamese territory at Chumpom and Singora, then moving by road to seize the airfields at Victoria Point and Alor Star. Or the Japanese might land at Penang, giving them an overland advance of some 400 miles to Singapore. Despite the risks of such an invasion 'we

[1] COS Appreciation of the Far East Situation, 28 May 1937, CAB 53/21, COS 590. [2] Ibid.

cannot exclude the possibility that the Japanese may attempt operations of this character . . . If they overcame the difficulties of effecting a landing in Malaya and prevented our reinforcements reaching Singapore, they might consider they had a reasonable chance of capturing the base within two months.'[1]

The COS summarised the form Japanese operations might take: convoys to Malaya, an advance through Malaya, leading to 'close investment of Singapore Island, and command of the naval base by artillery fire'.[2]

The defence of Malaya was weak. No reinforcements could be spared from Singapore except at the cost of weakening the garrison. To defend Malaya successfully, the COS believed, therefore depended on reinforcement from outside: 'If no reinforcements have reached Singapore, the forces at our disposal may be unable to prevent a landing in Malaya . . . these limited forces . . . are unlikely to prevent the Japanese from establishing themselves in Southern Johore within two months of the outbreak of war.'[3]

This COS paper of 1937 constitutes a very remarkable work of accurate prophecy; its existence demolishes the post-1942 legend that the British armed forces had never thought in terms of a Japanese attack on Singapore overland through Malaya.

All turned on the British ability to send the battlefleet to Singapore in good time. Indeed, Sir Samuel Hoare, now First Lord of the Admiralty, told the 1937 Imperial Conference that 'the very existence of the British Commonwealth of Nations as now constituted' rested on this ability. Hoare reassured the delegates that at the present moment England could send a fleet to the East while still covering her European commitments. From spring 1938 to summer 1939, however, we should have to depend on French support in home waters, and even then would only be able to send to Singapore a fleet 'slightly inferior to the full Japanese naval strength'.[4] And Hoare warned that after 1940, when other countries would have completed their building programmes, 'the despatch of a fleet to the Far East would be a most hazardous undertaking unless our battleship strength is increased above the number of fifteen ships [the Washington Treaty limit]'.[5]

No doubt desiring to soothe the painful apprehensions which had by now awakened in dominion minds, Hoare had erred on the side of optimism. Just before the summer recess of 1937 Sir Thomas Inskip, the Minister for the Co-ordination of Defence, admitted to Eden that until

[1] Ibid. [2] Ibid. [3] Ibid.
[4] CAB 32/128, E(PD)(37)5. [5] Ibid.

1940, and owing to refits and reconstruction, England would have only twelve battleships, of which only seven would be fully modernised, to meet all her global requirements.[1]

But twin wars against Germany and Japan were not all that British planners took into account. There was the defence of India against communist Russia; there was the Mediterranean route to India and the Far East. In their Annual Review for 1937, the COS noted that while in Italy 'we will have to look henceforward to a rival', yet: 'If we were at war with Italy, any British convoy passing through the Mediterranean could be attacked by the main Italian Fleet, and would therefore need the escort of equally powerful naval forces, and its passage would thus become a major fleet operation.'[2]

Therefore, the consequence of war with Italy, wrote the COS, must be the diversion of the imperial lifeline to the Cape route – thus, although the COS did not say so, vitiating the whole purpose of the vast and dangerous British involvement in Egypt and the Middle East. However, prestige forbade the voluntary liquidation of this involvement,[3] although, as Lord Chatfield, the First Sea Lord, pointed out to his colleagues on 28 July 1937, 'supposing that the necessity for the defence of Egypt did not exist, the problem of war with Italy would be a comparatively simple one . . .'[4] and although, as the COS wrote in October 1937, any reinforcement of Egypt weakened us in the face of Germany.[5]

The Chiefs of Staff had therefore to consider the prospect of a world war – Great Britain and France *versus* Germany, Italy and Japan. In such a situation they saw the security of the United Kingdom and Singapore as 'the keystones' of British strategy.[6] Weakness in the Mediterranean, in their opinion, would not be nearly so serious as the surrender of our seapower in the Far East.[7]

The order of priority was clear: 'This situation demands recognition of the principle that no anxieties or risks connected with our interests in the Mediterranean can be allowed to interfere with the despatch of a fleet to the Far East.'[8]

Nevertheless it was Germany which offered the greatest danger to British power and independence, as the COS emphasised:

> Strategically, the future of the United Kingdom, and with it the future of the British Empire, is closely linked with that of France and

[1] Avon, Vol. I, p. 490.
[2] COS 560.
[3] Sir Cyril Deverell, COS Meeting, 28 July 1937, CAB 53/8, COS 214.
[4] CAB 53/8, COS 214.
[5] CAB 53/33, 19 October 1937.
[6] Annual Review for 1937, COS 560.
[7] Ibid.
[8] Ibid.

> the Low Countries. If Germany crushed France, she would dominate all Western Europe and would gain power and prestige which would render the situation immensely difficult for the United Kingdom.[1]

But the outcome of a renewed struggle between Germany on the one hand and France and England on the other already appeared much in doubt. On 26 October 1936 the Joint Planning Committee prepared for the Chiefs of Staff an estimate of the balance of strength if there should be a war with Germany in 1939.[2] The German army would enjoy a slight numerical superiority over the French, Belgian and British forces combined, a superiority enhanced because it would be a homogeneous national force. 'Their superiority on land', wrote the Joint Planners, 'might therefore be sufficient to expose the Allied cause on land to considerable danger. The above comparison refers to 1939. In later years Germany's position is likely to be stronger.'[3] In the air too Germany would enjoy superior striking power.

No less alarming than these forecasts was the Joint Planners' judgement that, contrary to popular British prejudices at the time and ever since, Germany was economically better placed to sustain a war than Great Britain. She was reckoned to be 80 per cent self-sufficient in food and animal fodder; 46 per cent in motor fuel. As a result of the thoroughness of German development of their national resources, the Joint Planners believed that 'the capacity of Germany to resist economic pressure has greatly increased since the *last war* . . .',[4] while 'in respect of natural resources Great Britain is more vulnerable than Germany . . .'[5]

England had not had to face so overwhelming a combination of potential enemies with such inadequate resources since the American War of Independence, when, without an ally, she had fought Spain and France as well as the rebellious colonies. It was no comfort to recognise that, as Sir Thomas Inskip rather tactlessly reminded the 1937 Imperial Conference, England had been drawn into 'antagonism' with Italy 'only by virtue of the discharge of its responsibilities as a Member of the League';[6] and that, also in Sir Thomas's words, while England had enjoyed good relations with Japan until 1931, 'the antagonism provoked between ourselves and Japan at the conquest of Manchuria gravely affected the whole military position . . .'[7] The question from 1936 onwards was how to disperse or avoid the perils which, whether inevitable or self-inflicted, beset England ever more closely.

1 Ibid.
2 CAB 53/29, COS 513(JP).
3 Ibid.
4 Ibid.
5 Ibid.
6 CAB 32/128, E(PD)(37)5.
7 Ibid.

There was still the League of Nations; a talisman, however, which had failed to ward off evil. The British armed forces had never believed the League to be other than a sentimental yet dangerous fantasy, and, in their review for 1937, the Chiefs of Staff deferentially reminded their political superiors that:

> The events of the past few years have shown that in the presence of the highly-armed and unscrupulous States with which we have to deal to-day, Members of the League cannot be relied upon to take collective military action against an aggressor State when such action conflicts with their interests, or even where no interest of theirs is vitally affected. We should not therefore rely on other powers' altruism.[1]

Even Anthony Eden had to acknowledge to the new Cabinet Committee on Foreign Policy, at its first meeting on 30 April 1936,[2] that, as he put it, collective security was likely to be less, not more, successful in future. Nevertheless Eden, somewhat inconsistently, still believed that England should follow a League-of-Nations policy.[3] The committee discussed whether there was any chance of abrogating Article XVI of the Covenant,[4] but had to agree that there was not. The Prime Minister (Baldwin) himself said that he accepted that collective security had broken down. So the League of Nations at last ceased to be the vehicle and the inspiration of English policy – twenty years after Lord Robert Cecil's romantic enthusiasms had first begun to prevail over Hankey's all-too-accurately realistic forecasts.[5]

The preservation of English interests had now to be sought in other expedients. The Chiefs of Staff themselves recommended what might be termed strategic appeasement. Since they doubted whether Germany could achieve her aims without war, they wished to concentrate against her the resources at present appallingly over-stretched by the obligation to defend the empire in the Mediterranean and Far East. Their 1937 Annual Review therefore emphasised the importance of reaching an accommodation with Japan, although they recognised that this possibility was now remote; and of achieving good relations with Italy.[6]

Neville Chamberlain, firstly as Chancellor of the Exchequer and after 1937 as Prime Minister, strongly shared these opinions. His was a mind clearer and harder than those of most other senior Cabinet ministers of the era. In 1934 he had seized on the simple fact that it was 'impossible for this country to fight both Germany and Japan';[7] and had never let it

[1] COS 560. [2] CAB 27/622, FP(36)1. [3] Ibid. [4] Providing for economic sanctions.
[5] See above pp. 244–5 [6] COS 560. [7] See above p. 346.

go since, despite the failure of his attempt to promote a reconciliation with Japan in 1934–5.[1] At the very beginning of his premiership he lectured his dominion colleagues on the disastrous consequences of British policy towards Japan at and since the Washington Conference in 1921:

> A threatening situation in Europe was capable of being multiplied in gravity by the difference between our present relations with Japan and those we enjoyed in 1914. There was now the perpetual danger that trouble in Europe might be Japan's opportunity to take some step to our disadvantage in the Far East. At present we should be quite unable to counter such a step.[2]

The ending of the Japanese alliance, Chamberlain went on, had meant 'a great addition to our anxieties'. And he asked: 'Could we not now obtain, not an alliance, but an understanding with Japan?'[3]

In point of fact, this was to prove no more possible in 1937–9 than in 1934–5; partly for the same reason that the British Government was barred by its scruples – and even more by the scruples of public opinion – from paying the purchase price for Japanese friendship; partly because Japan was now allied to Germany by the Anti-Comintern Pact of 1936; and partly because Japan, led by a militarist government, embarked on an invasion of China itself in 1937, and was not in the mood for an understanding with the disapproving but feeble British. Rather, the Japanese were to humiliate British nationals in China and infringe British rights with contemptuous arrogance. In June 1939 the Foreign Secretary (Halifax) had to agree with Sir Robert Craigie, the ambassador in Tokyo, that

> partly owing to the attitude we had adopted, and partly because of the circumstances in which we had been placed, we had got into a position in China *vis-à-vis* Japan very much more difficult than the position of the United States. For years the Government had been pressed to show their sympathy for China in the House of Commons and the League of Nations, and in the circumstances it was perhaps inevitable that we should have become the object of Japan's enmity and irritation.[4]

In view of this enmity and irritation and despite Chamberlain's hopes, Japan was never to cease to figure in the dismal British comparisons between their own strength and that of their worldwide potential enemies.[5] For although in 1936–9 both the Foreign Office and the armed

[1] See above pp. 346–9. [2] CAB 32/128, E(PD)(37)11. [3] Ibid.
[4] CAB 27/625, FP(36)51, 13 June 1939.
[5] Cf. CAB 53/48, COS 886(JP), 20 April 1939; CAB 53/50, COS 931, 16 June 1939.

forces believed and hoped (rightly as it proved) that a Japanese attack on the British Empire in the East was not imminent, the possibility had nevertheless to be provided against, especially in the context of a European war.

Chamberlain – no less than the Chiefs of Staff – also wished to undo the consequences of British opposition to Italy over Abyssinia. If good relations could be restored, it would put an end to the gruesome prospect of having to fight a major war in the Middle East and Mediterranean on top of two other wars elsewhere.

Chamberlain's Italian policy was like his Japanese policy: sound enough in strategic principle, but politically unrealistic. Short of trading away choice portions of the British Empire in Africa, it is hard to see what England could have offered Italy in 1936–9 which, in Mussolini's eyes, would have atoned for her actions as ringleader at Geneva in the efforts to thwart his Abyssinian ambitions. Chamberlain had nothing to offer Mussolini, and nothing to threaten him with. In any case, Mussolini was now gravitating naturally towards his fellow dictator Adolf Hitler; the friendship, or approval, of England was a commodity to be valued less and less. For by 1936 it was all too clear that dictatorship was waxing in power and success; that democracy was dingy and declining. The English in particular, Mussolini perceived, were no longer the swaggering, ruthless pirates who had laid the foundations of England's greatness, and whom he would have respected. As it was, he found Hitler's Germany more *simpatico* than Baldwin's or Chamberlain's or Eden's England.

The Spanish Civil War, which broke out in 1936, not only sharpened this tendency for the powers to array themselves under the banners of their ideologies, but brought England and Italy directly into conflict again.

Communist Russia proceeded to back the Republican Government of Spain with arms, money and men. Germany and Italy, preferring that the civil war should end with a Fascist Government in Madrid, backed General Franco's Falangist insurgents. Although the future of Spain directly bore on the safety of the British imperial lifeline through the Mediterranean and on the preservation of Gibraltar in time of war, England herself backed no party in Spain. Nor did she wholly keep out of the imbroglio either. Instead she pursued a policy of 'Non-Intervention'. England – and France – tried to induce the great powers not to intervene in Spain in any way, directly or indirectly. It was another foredoomed British attempt to run counter to the course of nature. For Russia, Germany and Italy failed to refrain from pursuing their interests. Their intervention in Spain became ever greater and more blatant; they supplied their clients not only with war material but with troops and air-force units. Italian submarines, disavowed by the Italian Government, attacked shipping on its way to Republican ports without enquiring too pedantically whether the vessels were Spanish or otherwise. The Royal Navy therefore replied to the Italian navy's anonymous torpedoes with depth-charges. Such was the public spirit of the British Foreign Secretary that he wished even to employ the Royal Navy to enforce the principle of Non-Intervention, although the Cabinet turned this down. As the Spanish Civil War went on, Italo-British relations grew more and more sour instead of sweeter. In many ways it was Abyssinia all over again.

Nevertheless Chamberlain stubbornly preserved his conviction that Italy could be drawn away from Germany and back to the side of England and France. By the end of 1937 this conviction was bringing him into sharper and sharper conflict with his Foreign Secretary, who, on the contrary, was not only convinced that the wooing of Mussolini would prove a vain undertaking but also found it morally repugnant. Eden did not see foreign affairs in terms of strategy, or strategic appeasement, any more than did the ardent young cavaliers behind him in the Foreign Office.[1] Like a general who demands that every foot of front and every inch of ground must be defended to the last, Eden believed that all dictators must be stood up to, everywhere, all the time, or at least if second-class dictators.[2] With some petulance he resisted Chamberlain's interfering efforts to prod him into a *démarche* with Italy. He refused even to grant the one thing Italy asked of England, *de jure* recognition of her sovereignty over Abyssinia, which would have cost nothing.

It was their differences over Italian policy, coupled with Eden's rising and justified resentment at Chamberlain's contacts with Italian diplomats behind his back, which essentially provoked Eden's resignation in February 1938.[3]

Yet even with Eden out of the way, Chamberlain and his colleagues, although they so strongly desired friendly relations with Italy, could not refrain from moralising to the Italian Government over such matters as the operations of the Italian air force in Spain.[4]

Chamberlain persisted with his fruitless attempts to detach Italy from Germany until 1939. Although he was too stubbornly optimistic to see it,

[1] John Harvey (ed.), *The Diplomatic Diaries of Oliver Harvey* (London, Collins 1970).
[2] Cf. Avon, Vol. I, pp. 434–5.
[3] Avon, Vol. I, chs. VII, XIII and XIV; Harvey, Pt. II; Lord Birkenhead, *Halifax* (London, Hamish Hamilton 1965), pp. 275–80; Feiling, pp. 330–9.
[4] See meetings and memoranda of the Cabinet Committee on Foreign Policy; cf. e.g. CAB 27/626, FP(36)64, June 1938.

there was nothing whatever to induce Mussolini to switch friendships – neither material advantage, nor congeniality of character and outlook. Mussolini preferred the friendship of knaves to that of prigs; the martial boots of Berlin to the prim pin-stripes of London.

And so Chamberlain's – and the Chiefs of Staff's – hopes of lightening England's insupportable strategic burdens came to nothing. In 1939 both Italy and Japan continued to figure in British strategic planning as likely enemies.[1] The consequences of earlier British high-mindedness were not to be repaired by belated, naïve and weightless diplomacy of this kind.

Yet all the while these hopes were being fitfully pursued, it was Nazi Germany which remained the focus of Britain's anxious diplomacy. However much the existence of the empire tended to distract British attention, England's fate was geographically bound to that of Europe. And the fate of Europe was in turn bound up with Nazi Germany. The fundamental question before the British Cabinet, therefore, remained how best to deal with Germany. And the answer depended on the judgement that was made of the nature of the Nazi régime.

In February 1936, even before the re-occupation of the Rhineland had provided a fresh insight into the Nazi conception of international relations, the Foreign Secretary, Anthony Eden, circulated to his colleagues a dossier of reports from the British embassy in Berlin dating from the spring of 1933 until the end of 1935.[2] The dossier fully documented every aspect of Nazism in thought and action. In his covering memorandum Eden himself wrote: 'Hitler's foreign policy may be summed up as the destruction of the peace settlement and the re-establishment of Germany as the dominant power of Europe.'[3]

He believed the German means to these ends were two-fold: '(a) Internally by the militarisation of the whole nation in all its aspects; (b) externally by economic and territorial expansion so as to absorb as far as possible all those of German race who are at present citizens of neighbouring states. . . .'[4]

There was, therefore, little enough room for optimism, as Eden himself recognised: '. . . it will be well to consider whether it is still possible to come to some *modus vivendi* – to put it no higher – with Hitler's Germany which would be both safe and honourable . . .'[5]

After the Germans occupied the Rhineland, Eden's estimate of the

[1] Cf. CAB 23/45, COS 843, COS European Appreciation 1939–40, 20 February 1939. Meeting of Cabinet Foreign Policy Committee, CAB 27/624, FP(36)77, 26 January 1939.
[2] See above pp. 386–8.
[3] CAB 27/599, CP13(36).
[4] Ibid.
[5] Ibid.

Nazi character and of the possibility of a safe and honourable *modus vivendi* became even less encouraging:

> The myth is now exploded that Herr Hitler only repudiates treaties imposed on Germany by force. We must be prepared for him to repudiate any treaty even if freely negotiated (a) when it becomes inconvenient, and (b) when Germany is sufficiently strong and the circumstances are otherwise favourable for doing so. . . .'[1]

All in all, therefore, it was hardly possible by 1936 for the Cabinet to remain under any illusions about Nazi Germany. Nor were they. Ramsay MacDonald saw 'the greatest potential danger of the whole situation in the new Nazi doctrine that the existence of a German population in a foreign country was sufficient to justify an extension of German territorial sovereignty in that direction. If this line were persisted in, negotiations would be impossible.'[2]

Neville Chamberlain, for his part, was troubled at this time by a 'lurking suspicion', which Baldwin shared, that 'there is no real *bona fides* in Germany, and that she is merely playing for time until she feels herself strong enough to make her next spring'.[3]

Baldwin himself had read the unexpurgated edition of *Mein Kampf*. He was therefore well-placed to explain to the dominion premiers in his last days as Prime Minister in 1937 the difference between the democratic and the dictatorial outlook on international affairs:

> In none of these countries [Russia, Italy and Germany] was it possible to make to the people such an appeal as went home to the heart of our people, an appeal based on Christianity or ethics. . . . The whole outlook in the dictator countries was so completely different from ours that for a long time people here could not understand how it was possible for these nations not to respond to the same kind of appeal as that to which our peoples responded. But they were beginning to realise it now. . . . The only argument which appealed to the dictators was that of force.[4]

There was but one conclusion that could logically follow from such assessments as these – that England must at last return to armed diplomacy and the balance of power; that it was time and more than time for England once more to create and lead a great coalition against an overweening European state. Indeed it might have seemed that an anti-German alliance

[1] Avon, Vol. I, p. 345.
[2] Meeting of the Cabinet Committee on Germany, 17 February 1936, CAB 27/599.
[3] Quoted in Middlemass and Barnes, p. 955.
[4] CAB 32/128, E(PD)(37)1.

was not merely the only logical and practical course to take, but in any case, and in the light of historical example, the natural and inevitable consequence, sooner or later, of Germany's power and ambition.

Yet such a policy was never considered by the Cabinet. On the very contrary, the Cabinet – Anthony Eden included – were resolved at all cost to *prevent* a return to the balance of power and the creation of opposing blocs in Europe.[1] The more pressing and urgent the need for a grand anti-German coalition – the more obvious and inevitable an expedient it was to become – the more obstinately did the Cabinet refuse to yield to it. In March 1938, for example, after the Germans had occupied Austria and when Czechoslovakia was plainly the next German objective, Lord Halifax, now Foreign Secretary, was to argue that 'nothing was more likely to aggravate the difficulties of the present situation than any suggestions that our ultimate objective was to unite France, Italy and ourselves against Germany'.[2]

The incongruity between the Cabinet's horror of an anti-German coalition and the facts of the European situation is well, if unwittingly, expressed by Eden in his memoirs: 'Although [in 1937] we might still hope to prevent the divisions of Europe into Fascist and anti-Fascist camps, our real affinities and interests, strategic as well as political, lay with France, a fact which some of my colleagues were most reluctant to realise.'[3]

The Cabinet not only ruled out an anti-German coalition, but also the only strategic alternative, which was to seek to divert German expansion eastwards. Eden informed the 1937 Imperial Conference that Germany could expand either by regaining her colonies, by driving down the Danube, or by establishing a colonial empire in the Ukraine.[4] It would be easy for Britain, Eden went on, to reach an agreement with Germany on the basis of a free hand in the east of Europe.[5] The practical drawback to a bargain of this kind was, as Eden had to point out, that while to divert Germany eastwards might lift the danger from France, England and Belgium for a time, there was always the prospect of a Germany grown immensely stronger on a diet of east European conquest eventually turning back to the west. There was another objection too, though not a strategic one: 'In any case Mr Eden felt that a settlement on these lines would be immoral.'[6]

[1] Cf. CAB 27/622, FP(36)2.
[2] CAB 27/623, FP(36)25, 15 March 1938.
[3] Avon, Vol. 1, pp. 486–7.
[4] CAB 32/128, E(PD)(37)2.
[5] Such a deal was in fact a major aim of German diplomacy, and was repeatedly put forward in Anglo-German conversations.
[6] Ibid.

This was also Vansittart's opinion.[1]

Both the alternative strategic solutions to the problem of Germany alike being repugnant, the Cabinet embraced a third solution. They continued to put their faith in bringing about the 'appeasement' of Europe by negotiation; in other words, in reaching a general settlement of all outstanding European problems with the co-operation and consent of Nazi Germany. The Foreign Secretary concurred with his colleagues in pursuing this policy.[2] The Cabinet thus elected to follow a course of action which stood in flat contradiction to their own expressed convictions about the nature and aims of the Nazi régime, and about the worth of the Nazi signature.

Nothing could be more in the romantic tradition than so to reject what was dictated by knowledge and commonsense, and instead pursue the impossible but ideal. But this was a Cabinet refulgent with high ideals – high Victorian ideals. By the mid-1930s the direction of English policy had fallen even more completely into the hands of clergymen *manqués* than during the 1920s and for the most part clergymen *manqués* now well advanced in middle-age or even into elderliness. In Baldwin's Cabinet in 1936, MacDonald, Runciman, Kingsley Wood, Neville Chamberlain and Simon represented the nonconformist conscience; Halifax and Hoare the High Church; and Inskip the evangelicals. Their approach to world affairs owed no less to Victorian liberalism, for they were deeply imbued with its abhorrence of struggle and its optimistic faith in human reason and goodwill. Indeed four out of twenty-one places in Chamberlain's Cabinet in 1937 were occupied by Liberals in name (National-Liberals), including Simon, a member of the inner Cabinet.

The political and moral equipment of the English cabinet ministers of 1936–7, being thus designed for an historical situation which had long since disappeared, was useless in the present international environment. Indeed it was worse than useless, for it served to bewilder and mislead; it got in the way. English statesmen were like elderly Victorian cavalry generals trying to conduct a great tank battle.

In any case, the balance of power and the creation of alliances lay under a special taboo. English statesmen took it as given truth that these in themselves had brought about the Great War – that, as it were, the game had caused the injury rather than the way it had been played. In view of

[1] Letter to King George V, 7 November 1935, quoted in Harold Nicolson, *King George V* (London, Constable 1952), p. 529.

[2] Cf. meeting of the Cabinet Committee on Germany, 17 February 1936, and his memorandum CP(36), both in CAB 27/599; and Avon, Vol. I, chs. IV and X *passim*.

their terror at the prospect of another war, it was a game which they were resolved never to play again.

And so, even while their intellects acknowledged the truth about Nazi Germany, everything in their characters and upbringing prompted them to flinch from its implications, and urged them instead to seek escape in fantasies. Baldwin could, at one and the same time, state that dictators only understood the language of force, and yet preside over a government long committed to addressing them with the language of goodwill and sweet reason.[1] Eden could follow a penetrating analysis of Nazi policies and intentions by writing a few weeks later: 'On balance, however, I am in favour of making some attempt to come to terms with Hitler.'[2] Ramsay MacDonald could express the blackest doubts as to whether negotiations were possible with Germany, and yet immediately go on to say, if in a warning tone, that 'we must be prepared to pay a heavy price, if we were to buy Germany's return to Geneva . . .'[3] Chamberlain could state his lurking suspicions of German good faith and fears of another German pounce, and then, in the very next sentence, write that 'I am prepared to deal with her on the basis that she means what she says; and, if I could see a prospect of real settlement, I would be prepared to go a long way to get it'.[4]

However, it is possible that it was *because* a general settlement of Europe in collaboration with Germany offered so ideal a solution to the German problem, that the Cabinet were particularly tempted to shut their eyes to its evident impossibility.

For Germany was the key to the English world predicament. If Germany – and Europe – could be appeased, England's strength would then suffice against Italy or Japan. Indeed the appeasement of Germany would make it highly unlikely that those powers would ever attack English interests, for it was believed in London that only if England became first embroiled in a European war would they be tempted into action. And so Baldwin told Eden in May 1936 that he wanted 'better relations with Hitler than with Musso – we must get nearer Germany . . .'[5] Similarly, Chamberlain wrote in his diary after he became Prime Minister: 'If only we could get on terms with the Germans, I would not care a rap for Musso. . . .'[6]

This was not all. Appeasement of Europe would also lift the burden of

[1] See above pp. 394–409.
[2] CAB 27/599, CP13(36). Avon, Vol. I, p. 324; see also above pp. 448–9.
[3] CAB 27/599.
[4] Letter to Lord Lothian in April 1936, quoted in Butler, *Lord Lothian*, p. 215.
[5] Avon, Vol. I, p. 374.
[6] Feiling, p. 329.

re-armament from England's far-from-buoyant economy and far-from-vast financial resources. It was an aspect which particularly appealed to Neville Chamberlain, who was to say to his Cabinet colleagues after the Munich Agreement in 1938:

> Ever since he had been Chancellor of the Exchequer, he had been oppressed with the sense that the burden of armaments might break our backs. This had been one of the factors which had led him to the view that it was necessary to try and resolve the causes which were responsible for the armament race.[1]

The Cabinet, then, were united in clinging to the old policy of wooing Germany. Eden, however, added that 'There must . . . be no concessions merely for the sake of keeping Germany quiet. They should only be offered as part of a final settlement.'[3] There remained only the timing of England's renewed amorous serenade. It was Vansittart's view at the end of 1935 that England should wait until she was re-armed and able to negotiate from strength.[2] It was not the Cabinet's view. Early in 1936 Eden was arguing that it was possible that an economic crisis might force Germany into a foreign adventure, and that hence there was reason for seeking terms quickly.[3] The re-occupation of the Rhineland did not modify his desire for haste, although it was now founded on a wish to anticipate Germany's 'growing material strength and power of mischief in Europe'.[4] The Chancellor of the Exchequer, Neville Chamberlain, also wanted to make haste rather than dally.[5]

There was no less common agreement about the terms England should offer Germany. Vansittart, Eden and Chamberlain all believed that Germany should agree to re-join the League of Nations; conclude an agreement on the limitation of armaments, and an air pact; and offer assurances of her respect for the independence and territories of other European states – in other words, renounce all further territorial claims.[6] Eden and Chamberlain alike wanted Germany to conclude a new European security pact to replace the defunct Locarno Treaty.[7] And Vansittart and Chamberlain alike advocated buying Germany's consent to the British package with colonial concessions in Africa.[8]

[1] CAB 23/94, 47(38), 30 September 1938.
[2] Letter to King George V, 7 November 1935, quoted in Nicolson, p. 529.
[3] CAB 27/599. [4] Avon, Vol. I, p. 345. [5] Cf. CAB 27/626, FP(36)3.
[6] Cf. memorandum by Vansittart, February 1936 in CAB 27/599; memorandum by Chamberlain, April 1937, CAB 27/626, FP(36)23; memorandum by Eden, 25 January 1938, CAB 27/626, FP(36)43. [7] Cf. CAB 27/626, FP(36)43 and FP(36)23.
[8] Ibid.; see also meetings of the Cabinet Committee on Foreign Policy in 1936–8; CAB 27/622, especially 27 July 1936, FP(36)4; 10 March 1937, FP(36)10; and 24 July 1938, CAB 27/623, FP(36)21.

Although in retrospect Eden and Vansittart were to be contrasted favourably with the so-called 'appeasers', not least by themselves in their own memoirs, there were in fact remarkably few differences during 1936–8 between them and Chamberlain over the general lines of England's German policy. There was rather a distinction in tone. When, for example, in spring 1936, Eden proposed that a questionnaire be sent to Hitler as to his real intentions – a document no more likely to receive a satisfactory reply than St Paul's epistle to the Romans – its terms were softened by his colleagues, who found them 'provocative' and 'pinpricks'.[1] Both Chamberlain and Halifax, on the other hand, expressed themselves in favour of using gentle words to Germany over the question of colonies, for fear that otherwise the Germans might become, as they put it, 'sulky and disgruntled', and thus jeopardise the hoped-for conference which was to negotiate a new super-Locarno Treaty.[2] It was this kind of apprehensive timidity which provoked Smuts to write in that same year that 'we are afraid of our shadows. I sometimes long for a ruffian like Palmerston or any man who would be more than a string of platitudes and apologies.'[3]

In 1936 therefore the British Government was resolved to seek escape from England's world predicament by taming Nazi Germany with kindness and concession; and to do so without delay. But, in fact, once the Rhineland crisis died away in midsummer 1936, the British sense of urgency slackened. Germany, her marching done for a time, smiled in encouragingly friendly fashion while she digested her immense successes, and pressed on with the breakneck expansion of her armed forces. It was a time of vague but alluring Nazi offers of pacts and treaties: of Nazi speeches saying all the right things. The 1936 Berlin Olympic Games provided a superb vehicle for a Nazi public-relations campaign to promote Germany's restored might and prosperity. The German team made its entrance into the stadium to the exultant crash and blare of the 'Präsentiermarsch König Friedrich Wilhelm II', and proceeded to conquer Olympic medals as if they were provinces; the British team walked in clad in blazers and trilby hats, all too appropriately the epitome of genteel suburban weekend amateurism, and their performance did no more than bear out their appearance.

The procession of distinguished English visitors to Berlin and Berchtesgaden went on. In the summer Lloyd George, together with Dawson of *The*

[1] Avon, Vol. I, p. 372. For Eden's caution over concessions to Germany, see above p. 453.
[2] Meeting of the Cabinet Committee on Foreign Policy 27 July 1936; CAB 27/622, FP(36)4.
[3] Sir K. Hancock, Vol. II, p. 281.

*Times*, and Baldwin's personal Private Secretary, Dr Tom Jones, a nonconformist Liberal and a man of a simplicity and naïveté remarkable in politics even for that age, all visited Hitler, and came away completely taken in. The dinner tables of London, the parterre at Blickling and the lawns of the country retreats of the intelligentsia were busier than ever with talk of how Germany would settle down as a good neighbour in Europe, once Britain had appeased all her entirely legitimate grievances. There was much looking forward to super-Locarno conferences and the appending of Herr Hitler's valuable signature to all kinds of pacts, agreements and guarantees.

There were other reasons for the relaxation in the British sense of urgency. Baldwin, now in his third term as Prime Minister, was old, very tired and in poor health, and much preoccupied with the personally delicate and constitutionally critical business of Edward VIII's wish to marry an inappropriate American woman. Eden – and the Cabinet as a whole – became much engrossed with the Spanish Civil War, which broke out in July 1936.[1] Spain came to seem the great arena where democracy and dictatorship confronted one another; an arena which provided Eden, that picador of good causes, with the opportunity of lodging some shrewd banderillas in the hide of his old adversary Mussolini.[2] Spain equally provided a wonderful new trigger for left-wing romantic emotion. There was clamorous support in Britain for the Spanish Republican Government, which idealists failed to perceive had decayed into the front for a communist apparatus. The Labour Party, which denounced arms for England as a shockingly immoral policy, loudly called for arms for Spain.[3] And so from midsummer 1936 onwards into 1937 the menace presented in the heart of Europe by Nazi Germany receded in the British mind.

Yet by the end of 1937 the Cabinet was once again, as in 1935–6, clutched by a feeling of approaching peril; its diplomacy was again animated by a sense of working against time in order to anticipate and prevent a general catastrophe. Two factors conjoined to inspire this mood: firstly, signs that the onward march of German ambition was about to be resumed, and secondly, the advent of a new Prime Minister in England, energetic, brisk, businesslike, and determined to settle the affairs of Europe once and for all.

* * *

[1] See CAB 27/622.

[2] See above pp. 446–7; Avon, Vol. I, chs. V, VI, VIII.

[3] Cf. Hugh Dalton's tart comments on this piece of illogic in a letter to Kingsley Martin on 26 July 1937, quoted in Martin, p. 190.

Chamberlain succeeded Baldwin in May 1937, during the Imperial Conference and just after the Coronation of George VI, at a time of ceremonial affirmation of the unity of the empire under the Crown, and, behind the scenes, of feeble and unavailing British effort to impart some strategic meaning to this unity in the face of unprecedented and potentially overwhelming dangers.[1] The new Prime Minister made the sharpest contrast with his two half-Celtic predecessors in office, the dreamy and emotional MacDonald and the genial, gentle, easy-going and emollient Baldwin. Chamberlain was a man of sinewy strength of will; energetic, masterfully self-confident, cocksure even. He ran his Cabinet like a managing director. 'His personal influence', wrote Sir Samuel Hoare, one of his senior colleagues, 'was due to his mastery of facts, his clear head and his inherited gift of incisive speech.'[2] His was the forbidding personality of a Victorian headmaster, aloof, authoritative; the very embodiment of rectitude.

> Spare, even ascetic, in figure, dark-haired and dark-eyed; with a profile rather corvine than aquiline [wrote Sir Arthur Salter (later Lord Salter) in 1939], he carries his seventy years well and looks and seems less than his age. His voice has a quality of harshness, and with an occasional rasp, and is without music or seductive charm. . . . In debate and exposition his speech is lucid, competent, cogent, never rising to oratory, unadorned with fancy and rarely touched with emotion. But it gives a sense of mastery of what it attempts, well reflects the orderly mind behind. . . .[3]

Chamberlain was devoid of charm and outward warmth; he had none of the graces of humour and gentleness, the gestures of personal interest and concern, which so endeared Baldwin even to his political opponents. He was devoid of insight into other men's feelings or motives. The unfortunately sardonic line of the mouth under the moustache and beaky nose heightened the impression of a man ready to sneer and snub those who had the temerity to disagree with him. Chamberlain chilled members of his own party and the opposition alike.[4]

Yet his appearance and manner belied him. His reserve, his quickness to strike down criticism, sprang from shyness and sensitivity,[5] a shyness that had been evident to his masters during his school days.[6] Only close

[1] See above pp. 220–7.
[2] Templewood, p. 375.
[3] Arthur Salter, *Security; Can We Retrieve It?* (London, Macmillan 1939), pp. 284–5.
[4] Cf. H. Morrison, *An Autobiography* (London, Odhams Press 1960), p. 175; Macmillan, pp. 172–3.
[5] Halifax, pp. 227–9.
[6] Feiling, pp. 10, 12.

friends and colleagues realised that behind that austere, dark exterior there was both tenderness and responsive warmth of heart:

> It was not universally known with how many sides of life Chamberlain moved on terms of close and intimate relationship. Few men had a more real enjoyment of all things of beauty and art, whether in the world of nature or of men, which make life colourful and rich, and few had his knowledge and deep appreciation of all that is greatest in music. No one was a truer lover of the countryside. . . .[1]

Yet in one essential particular Chamberlain's outward self did not belie the inner truth. He not only looked but *was* the embodiment of Victorian rectitude. One biographer wrote that Chamberlain was 'nearer his father's generation than his own in that he was predominantly a moralist, and an intellectual'.[2] and that in him 'morality owed more than in most men to heredity, or at least to a family piety of religious force'.[3]

Chamberlain was born on 18 March 1869, and so was already past early manhood before the Victorian age was over, and in middle-age by the time the Great War broke out. His father, Joseph Chamberlain, was a successful businessman who first became, as Lord Mayor of Birmingham, a great municipal reformer, and then an outstanding statesman. Both his father and his mother were devout Unitarians. Chamberlain spent his childhood amid solid Forsytian comfort and security and under the spiritual influence of strict nonconformist moral teaching.[4] His school-days at Rugby preparatory school and then at Rugby in the 1880s were however far from happy, for he disliked cricket and games (except for rugger) and was badly bullied. It was perhaps little wonder in the circumstances that his masters noted him to be 'rather quiet and shy'.[5] Later he went to a technical college, by way of balancing the academicism of the public school, and studied science, metallurgy and engineering. Though he became much interested in the writings of Darwin and Huxley at this time, his religious faith was not thereby affected, for he became a Sunday-school teacher at the Church of the Messiah in Broad Street, Birmingham.

In 1897 he was appointed a director of a Birmingham copper works. Like the Baldwin family ironworks, this firm was typical of all that was by then inadequate in British technology; small in size, with poky work-shops unchanged since the heyday of British world industrial supremacy in the 1830s.[6]

Chamberlain, now a Liberal-Unionist in political allegiance, was no

[1] Halifax, p. 231; see also Feiling, p. 124.
[2] Feiling, p. 121.
[3] Ibid. p. 120.
[4] Ibid. ch. 1.
[5] Ibid. p. 10.
[6] Ibid. p. 38.

moralising internationalist at this period of his life, no 'appeaser'; far from it indeed. In 1908, at the time of the Bosnian crisis, he asserted in a speech that the crisis 'has opened the eyes of some of our cranks and shown them that treaties are not to be depended on for keeping the peace, and that we have got to make ourselves too strong to be attacked'.[1]

Next year he joined in the popular demand for eight new battleships to counter the German building programme, instead of the four proposed by the Liberal Government; and in 1910 he was speaking for the National Service League in favour of conscription. But all this was before the Great War; before his cousins had been killed on the Western Front. Thereafter he was inspired instead by a profound detestation of force as a means of solving disputes between nations: 'War wins nothing, cures nothing, ends nothing. When I think of the seven million young men who were cut off in their prime, the thirteen million who were maimed and mutilated, and the misery and the sufferings of the mothers or the fathers – in war there are no winners, but all are losers.'[2]

Chamberlain entered the House of Commons in 1922, as a Conservative, in his fifty-third year; hardly the age when a man might look forward to a distinguished political career culminating in the premiership. As Lord Mayor of Birmingham in 1911–16 he had already shown himself a superbly efficient administrative reformer; and in 1923 he was appointed Minister of Health. For five years he was busy with all the administrative detail of social insurance, housing and local government; tirelessly he carried through immense schemes of reform, vast and complicated legislation, tidying up a labyrinth of muddle with brisk and punctual efficiency. He was indeed the last of the great Victorian social reformers. In 1932 he took his restless energy and efficient mind to the Treasury. It was now that he began to form clear and strong views on England's strategy and foreign policy[3] and to urge them on the Cabinet.

Yet there was another theme in Chamberlain's life which ran in counterpoint to this efficient progress to the top; the theme of failure and personal eclipse, beginning with his unhappiness and unsuccess at school.

In 1891 Chamberlain had gone to the Bahamas to attempt to grow sisal. After six years of the most stubborn and tenacious effort in conditions of great loneliness and hardship, he was forced to give up. Failure came upon him again during the Great War when Lloyd George first appointed him Director of National Service, and then sacked him; a failure which was by no means his own fault. There are signs that this failure in particular, and the circumstances and manner of his dismissal by

[1] Feiling, p. 48. [2] Quoted in Feiling, p. 320. [3] See above pp. 346–9, 380.

Lloyd George, stung him deeply into a determination to prove himself before the world. When in 1940 he sacked Hore-Belisha from the War Office, and Hore-Belisha hesitated about accepting his offer of the Board of Trade, Chamberlain, in Hore-Belisha's words, 'reiterated that I was an ambitious man and that if I stayed in the Government I might have a great career. He had been thrown out by Lloyd George – "and look where I am now", he said.' [1]

Chamberlain had always before him the examples of the brilliant careers of his father and step-brother. At the age when he first entered the Commons as a virtually unknown provincial, his father had been a commanding figure of English politics; his step-brother Austen had been both a cabinet minister and a leader of a party. And even when Chamberlain was making a complete success of his vast work of social and local government reform in the 1920s, Austen, as Foreign Secretary and a highly respected international statesman, still eclipsed him. Anthony Eden has an anecdote which casts a pencil-beam of light on the relationship of the two brothers. Early in 1937 Austen and Eden dined with Neville Chamberlain at No. 11 Downing Street, and Austen expounded his views on the situation in Austria and Czechoslovakia, which he had just visited. When however Neville then ventured some views of his own, his brother told him: 'Neville, you must remember you don't know anything about foreign affairs.' It was as wounding as it was patronising. Neville, according to Eden, only smiled wryly and remarked that 'this was rather hard on a man at his own dinner table'.[2]

It is difficult not to feel therefore that there was in Chamberlain's masterful manner as Prime Minister some element of glee and pride in self at having wiped out the failures of the past, and at having risen higher than either his father or his brother. It is hard not to think that he must have felt a certain determination to prove now that he *did* know something about foreign affairs; hard not to wonder whether perhaps he cherished an ambition to bring off an even greater *coup* in the service of European peace than Austen's Locarno Treaty.

Certainly such a personal motive would chime harmoniously enough with the high and noble object which he set himself; an object determined alike by his detestation of war and by his entire upbringing. It was no less than 'the appeasement of the whole world'.[3]

He brought to this task a stubborn and undeviating purpose. He also

[1] Hore-Belisha's Diary, 4 January 1940, quoted in R. J. Minney (ed.) *The Private Papers of Hore-Belisha* (London, Collins 1960), p. 270.

[2] Avon, Vol. I, p. 445.

[3] Speech in July 1938, quoted in Feiling, p. 335.

brought to it all the virtues of a 'sensitive and high-minded product of the Victorian peace';[1] and in particular the 'simplicity which must belong to integrity'.[2] Unfortunately Adolf Hitler, the principal object of Chamberlain's hopes and endeavour, was not himself in any way a sensitive and high-minded product of the Victorian peace. In the circumstances, Chamberlain's virtues could serve only to betray him. In particular, the simplicity that belongs to integrity could too easily become the credulity that belongs to the dupe.

And yet although trust in the reasonableness and good faith of dictators was necessarily the very foundation of his whole policy, Chamberlain was repeatedly troubled by doubts on this score, both before and after he became Prime Minister. In 1934, when Mussolini moved troops to the Brenner Pass at the time of the murder of the Austrian President Dolfuss, Chamberlain wrote in his diary: 'It's the only thing Germans understand . . . What does not satisfy me is that we do not shape our foreign policy accordingly.'[3] In April 1936 he was again expressing suspicion of the Nazi character.[4] In March 1937 he wrote that '. . . the main source of this fear of war in Europe is to be found in Germany', and that the only thing which would make Germany give up aggressive designs 'would be the conviction that her efforts to secure superiority of force were doomed to failure by reason of the superior force which would meet her if she attempts aggression'.[5] Chamberlain in fact, like most of his colleagues, *willed* himself to believe the best despite the evidence before him. In 1937, after reading *The House That Hitler Built*, a comprehensive and fair account of the Nazi political and social system, he wrote: 'If I accepted the author's conclusions, I should despair, but I don't and won't.'[6]

It was a misfortune that Chamberlain found ready to hand, in Sir Horace Wilson and Sir Nevile Henderson, instruments all too apt for his purpose. Wilson, although technically only the Government's chief industrial adviser, became his principal counsel and the go-between in foreign affairs. A man with the appearance of 'an ageing and unsuccessful clerk whose firm expects to be bankrupted next week',[7] Wilson was a drab, highly efficient, conscientious bureaucrat whose whole career had been spent in industrial relations. Chamberlain and Wilson shared the illusion that the same arts of round-table negotiation which served with English employers and trade unionists would also serve with Adolf Hitler. As Vansittart (whose functions Wilson usurped) put it, Wilson

[1] Feiling, p. 358. [2] Ibid. pp. 121–2. [3] Ibid. p. 253. [4] See above p. 449.
[5] Letter to Morgenthau, the US Secretary of the Treasury, quoted in James, pp. 325–6.
[6] Quoted in Feiling, p. 328. [7] *Daily Herald*, quoted in Connell, p. 255.

had 'enormous talents, a pure personality and a *sancta simplicitas* in foreign affairs'.[1]

Nevile Henderson, the English ambassador in Berlin from April 1937 onwards, although a professional diplomat, was blessed with no less of a *sancta simplicitas*. Formerly ambassador to the Argentine, he was appointed to Berlin by Eden on the advice of Vansittart. As Eden wrote later, 'No one foresaw the opinions he was to hold.'[2] Henderson took his appointment to mean that 'I had been specially selected by Providence for the definite mission of, as I trusted, helping to preserve the peace of the world'.[3] He was a man of artless sincerity of purpose, as he was proud to claim in his memoirs:

> What I wish to stress, however, is the honesty of the intentions which inspired me when I went to Berlin in 1937. . . . I may have erred in optimism, but not in cynicism, in hoping as long as possible for the best and in refusing to be convinced, until the worst proved me wrong, that the intentions of others were as evil as they seemed.[4]

Although Henderson had read the unexpurgated version of *Mein Kampf* on the voyage home from Buenos Aires, he still trusted that once the grievances arising out of the Versailles Treaty had been rectified, 'Hitler and the reasons for his existence and the methods of his régime would disappear'.[5] Henderson was in truth a living caricature of what the nineteenth-century religious revival had finally done to the English governing classes.

Chamberlain's convictions and Henderson's coincided all too exactly, for before he went to Berlin, as Henderson recounted later, Chamberlain, then still Chancellor of the Exchequer '. . . outlined his views on general policy towards Germany, and I think I may honestly say that to the last and bitter end I faithfully followed the general line which he set me, all the more easily and faithfully since it corresponded so closely with my private conception . . .'[6]

Believing therefore that the peace and stability in Europe depended on conciliating Germany and on the achievement of understanding between Germany and England, Henderson, in his own words, 'was consequently determined, firstly to do all in my power to associate with the Nazi leaders, and if possible to win their confidence, and even sympathy and secondly, to study the German case as objectively as possible and,

[1] Vansittart, p. 442.
[2] Avon, Vol. I, p. 504.
[3] Sir Nevile Henderson, p. 13.
[4] Ibid. p. 19.
[5] Ibid. pp. 35–6.
[6] Ibid. p. 17.

where I regarded it as justified, to present it as fairly as I could to my own Government'.[1]

This came to mean in practice that Henderson represented German interests in London far more eloquently and determinedly than he ever represented English interests in Berlin. A more ill-starred coincidence could hardly be imagined therefore than that which brought together an ambassador like Henderson, a go-between like Horace Wilson, and a Prime Minister like Chamberlain.

In April 1937, Chamberlain expounded his ideas on foreign policy in a memorandum to the Cabinet Committee on Foreign Policy, while he was still Chancellor of the Exchequer. First and fundamental was his contention that England should open up general discussions with Germany rather than adhere to a policy of drift possibly leading to war.[2] In such discussions, 'our objective should be to set out the political guarantees which we want from Germany as part of a general settlement . . .'[3] These guarantees, in Chamberlain's view, should consist of a new European security pact to replace Locarno; the return of Germany to the League of Nations; an agreement on the limitation of armaments; and, the crucial provisos, treaties to assure Germany's intention to respect the integrity of European states, including a non-aggression and non-interference pact with Czechoslovakia. Chamberlain suggested that by way of inducement to Germany, we could offer our financial help in restoring her economic system[4] – a suggestion which, in the relative circumstances of the two countries and coming from a prudent Chancellor, is not a little amazing.

The specific reference to Czechoslovakia revealed that particular new anxiety which, together with his own temperamental impatience and energy, impelled Chamberlain towards action rather than dalliance. For by the spring of 1937 signs were accumulating that Germany intended to resume her march of expansion, and that her direction would be to the East; and during the rest of the year, the signs were to grow yet more ominous.

It had been in the autumn of 1936 that the Foreign Office had first felt disquiet on this score, when Czechoslovakia's Sudeten-German minority began to voice grievances against their alleged unfair treatment by the Czech authorities.[5] By the early months of 1937 the Foreign Office began to entertain renewed, if still distant, fears for the independence of Austria. By May Eden was informing the Imperial Conference that the main

[1] Sir Nevile Henderson, p. 18. [2] CAB 27/626, FP(36)23. [3] Ibid.
[4] Ibid.
[5] Avon, Vol. I, p. 503.

danger of war lay in central Europe in connection with such countries as Czechoslovakia and Austria.[1] At the end of July the Foreign Office's secret German sources were warning that Germany might take violent action against Austria under cover of a staged Nazi uprising.[2] During the summer and autumn the Sudeten-Germans grew still more vociferous about their alleged wrongs.

In the course of 1937 therefore the English Cabinet was brought to face the disagreeable prospect that the German forward moves predicted by Eden in February 1936[3] might shortly be put into execution. It was a prospect which, with a chill wind of dismay, awoke English statesmanship from another of the illusions which had so comforted it since the Great War; in this case, the illusion that the affairs of eastern and central Europe in no way bore on English interests and were therefore no concern of England.

The illusion owed its origins to an English dislike of the 1919 peace settlement as it affected Germany's frontiers to the east; a dislike particularly strong in the case of the new German–Polish frontiers, with the creation of the so-called 'Polish Corridor' to the Baltic between East and West Prussia and the incorporation of a large German-speaking minority into Poland. The British delegation at the peace conference had tried without success to have these frontiers amended in Germany's favour, for they were convinced that they were not only politically and racially unjust to Germany, but could never be maintained. In British opinion at that time, the new German–Polish frontiers would serve only to offer a resurgent Germany a standing provocation; worse, an irresistible temptation. For Poland, however much she was blown out into the semblance of an important power by the peace treaties, would no more be able to make head against her great neighbours in the twentieth century than in the eighteenth.

The British delegation in 1919 had felt similar qualms about Czechoslovakia, another weak new creation whose frontiers were so drawn as to include a large German-speaking population of former Austrian nationality; and also about the German-speaking rump of the old Austria, whose apparently natural and inevitable destiny as part of a union with Germany was forbidden by the peace treaties at French insistence. The peace settlement of eastern and central Europe, taken as a whole, therefore seemed to the English to offer about as much hope of long-term peace and

[1] CAB 32/128, E(PD)1.
[2] CAB 27/626, FP(36)36, 29 July 1937.
[3] See above p. 408.

stability as penning up together three small hens and a large fox harbouring a grievance. As Lloyd George said during the peace conference:

> I cannot conceive any greater cause of future war than that the German people should be surrounded by a number of small states, many of them consisting of people who have never previously set up a stable government for themselves, but each of them containing large numbers of Germans clamouring for reunion with their native land.[1]

As a consequence the English in the early 1920s came quietly to abdicate their responsibility for the eastern European aspects of the peace treaties. They accepted with equanimity that sooner or later, when Germany revived her power, she would expand to the east; they were in fact well aware that this was in the mind of every German Government, however 'respectable'.[2] They believed however that this process would in no way harm English interests; rather, by turning German policy in the opposite direction from France, the Low Countries and the North Sea, the contrary.[3] English diplomacy therefore simply took good care to disengage itself from the process in advance. Germany's eastern frontiers were deliberately excluded from guarantee by England under the Locarno Treaty.[4]

There was yet another reason why the English had wanted to convince themselves that developments in eastern Europe were no concern of theirs: it was geographically impossible for them either to intervene directly there or to exert pressure directly.

The English therefore came to regard their vital interests in Europe as limited to the preservation of France and the Low Countries.[5]

Yet now that, in 1937, German expansion eastwards was no longer an intellectual question relating to a misty future, but a practical and more and more immediate issue, it did not seem quite so right and easy just to sit back and let it happen. For one thing, England, as the self-proclaimed upholder of international law and order, could hardly stand by silent while frontiers were violated and states were conquered or subverted.[6] Sermons at least would be called for, and, some would no doubt say, as in the case of Abyssinia, gestures too. For another thing, and in coarse terms of

[1] Quoted in Martin Gilbert, *The Roots of Appeasement* (London, Weidenfeld and Nicolson 1966), p. 48.
[2] Cf. D'Abernon, *passim.*
[3] See e.g. Keynes, *The Economic Consequences of the Peace*, p. 186.
[4] See above pp. 331–3.
[5] See COS Annual Reviews from 1926 onwards, and especially that for 1937, COS 560: and Eden's statement to the 1937 Imperial Conference, CAB 32/128 E(PD)(37)1.
[6] Cf. Eden's and Vansittart's views, above pp. 450–1.

strategy and power, the creation of a greater Germany through expansion in central and eastern Europe did not seem quite so acceptable after all. Supposing this greater Germany eventually turned westwards again?[1]

There was yet another reason, and the most compelling of all, why English statesmen found that they could not wash their hands of eastern Europe. Because of her relationship with France, England could be dragged into war by a German quarrel with Poland or Czechoslovakia just as easily and inescapably as she had been in 1914 by an Austrian quarrel with Serbia. A remote local crisis over the Polish Corridor or the Sudetenland could bring down on London the dreaded cataract of fire from the air. For Poland or Czechoslovakia were key members of that system of alliances which France had laboriously created since 1919 in order to counter-balance Germany's preponderant national power. If Germany moved against either country, it must be expected that France would go to war, both in honour of her treaties of alliance and out of self-preservation. Since the independence of France was, as in 1914, a cardinal English interest, England would have little choice but to fight too.

The truth was that, in believing that England could disengage herself from the fate of Poland, Austria and Czechoslovakia, English statesmen had only repeated the self-deception practised by Sir Edward Grey before the Great War with regard to the Balkans. Europe in fact presented a single, indivisible grand-strategic problem, of which German power was the heart. Now, in 1937, it therefore dawned that England must have an active eastern European policy of her own, if she was not simply to be dragged helplessly behind French policy, and perhaps into war itself. But what policy? And how to make it effective?

On behalf of the Cabinet, Eden explored the possibilities for the benefit of the Imperial Conference. In the first place:

> We might disinterest ourselves altogether in Central Europe and confine ourselves strictly to our vital interests in the Low Countries and Northern France.
>
> [However] such a policy would be most unwise and would most certainly invite aggression.
>
> [Alternatively therefore] we might declare our readiness to fight for Czecho-Slovakia or Austria if they became victims of aggression.
>
> [But] that would be going far beyond our obligations under the Covenant and far beyond where the people of this country were prepared to go. There could be no greater danger than for the Government

[1] Cf. Eden's memorandum of February 1936, above p. 450.

to declare themselves in favour of a policy which did not command the general support of public opinion at home. This would only make things infinitely worse.[1]

With one of the practical alternatives being unacceptable in its consequences and the other being found politically impossible although strategically right, here was a dilemma of a familiar enough kind. The Cabinet sought escape by the no less familiar device of compromise:

> There remained [said Eden] the third possibility, namely, that without undertaking any military commitment we should make it clear that we were interested in events in Central Europe. . . . This, then, was our policy in regard to that part of Europe which gave rise to the greatest anxiety.[2]

As a policy, this was less compromise than compromised. To be 'interested' in central Europe – whatever that might mean – meant perilously to combine involvement and impotence. It served only to put off the inevitable moment of decision, for sooner or later the English 'interest' in events in central Europe must either be exposed as bluff, mere wind and paper, or it must be made good. And that could only be done, in the geographical circumstances, by a proclaimed willingness to go to war.

In fact, the policy enunciated by Eden on behalf of the Cabinet only made sense in the context of the larger hopes, shared equally by Eden and Chamberlain, of a freely negotiated settlement of all European problems with Germany. In terms of eastern Europe, as of everywhere else, this dream offered the English the escape-hatch they so desperately sought from the reality of the power struggle. The more likely, therefore, a German pounce on Austria or Czechoslovakia appeared to be, the more urgent became Chamberlain's desire to get into discussion with the Nazi leaders.

In November 1937 the Nazis provided him with the opportunity by inviting Lord Halifax, a noted rider to hounds, to the International Hunting Exhibition in Berlin, organised under the auspices of Reichsmarschall Göring. The German Government suggested that Halifax might care to go on to Berchtesgaden to see Hitler afterwards. The German Government however insisted that, although the initiative for the visit came from them, the British Government should itself formally request the meeting with Hitler. Eden spotted the German manœuvre; but Chamberlain, in

[1] CAB 32/128, E(PD)(37)1.

[2] Ibid.

his eagerness to establish personal contact with the German Führer, was not thinking of tactical positioning. For all the world knew, Halifax went to Berchtesgaden as another obedient English suitor.

The encounter with Hitler nearly opened with the tall, gaunt English nobleman unwittingly but effectively humiliating the little German upstart. For Halifax, on getting out of his car, mistook Hitler's legs, dark-trousered and ending in black patent-leather shoes, for those of a footman. The German Foreign Minister, Neurath, muttered 'Der Führer! Der Führer!' just in time.[1] Thereafter Halifax, with his gentle and stately courtesy, made no attempt to use his rank and background to exploit the inferiority complex from which he believed Hitler to suffer, and thus to throw the German dictator off balance. The tactical successes were all Hitler's, for, as was his cunning gambit in negotiation, he waited in his prepared positions until the other man advanced across the open. Although it was Hitler who had designs on central and eastern Europe, it was Halifax who brought the subject up:

> I said that there were no doubt other questions arising out of the Versailles settlement which seemed to us capable of causing trouble if they were unwisely handled, e.g., Danzig, Austria, Czechoslovakia. On all these matters we were not necessarily concerned to stand up for the *status quo* as to-day, but we were concerned to avoid such treatment of them as would be likely to cause trouble. If reasonable settlements could be reached with the free assent and goodwill of those primarily concerned, we certainly had no desire to block.[2]

Far from keeping Hitler guessing, as Eden had instructed, Halifax had guilelessly told him exactly what he wanted to know. It was not Hitler, but Chamberlain, via Halifax, who had kicked off the central European cup game. Nevile Henderson, however, was delighted with Halifax's visit, and allowed himself 'to cherish the dream' that it was 'the beginning of better things'.[3] As he wrote in his memoirs: 'Hitler cannot but have been – and in fact, so I heard, was – impressed by the obvious sincerity, high principles and straightforward honesty of a man like Lord Halifax.'[4]

Chamberlain too congratulated himself on Halifax's visit, confiding to his diary: 'From my point of view, great success, because it achieved its object, that of creating an atmosphere in which it is possible to discuss

[1] Halifax, p. 185.
[2] Account of the visit of the Lord President of the Council to Germany, 26 November 1937, CAB 27/626, FP(36)39.
[3] Sir Nevile Henderson, p. 100.
[4] Ibid. p. 98.

with Germany the practical questions involved in a European settlement. . . .'[1]

Yet the encounter between Halifax and Hitler ought on the contrary to have opened the eyes of Chamberlain and his Cabinet to the unreality of their hopes, for, as Halifax wrote in his diary:

> One had the feeling all the time that we had a totally different set of values and were speaking in a different language. It was not only the difference between a totalitarian and democratic state. He gave me the impression that, whilst he had attained to power only after a hard struggle with present-day realities, the British Government was still living comfortably in a world of its own making, a fairy-land of strange, if respectable illusions. It clung to shibboleths – 'collective security', 'general settlement', 'disarmament', 'non-aggression pacts' – which offered no practical prospect of a solution of Europe's difficulties.[2]

Despite all this, Hitler struck Halifax, as he told his colleagues, as 'very sincere'.[3]

On 29 and 30 November the French Prime Minister, Camille Chautemps, and his Foreign Minister, Delbos, visited London so that Halifax could report on his German visit, and both governments discuss future policy over Austria and Czechoslovakia. The discussions revealed a fundamental divergence, especially in regard to the latter country. The English saw the issue in their favourite 'objective' manner in terms of a 'fair' and peaceful settlement between Germany and Czechoslovakia which would remedy what they believed to be the just grievances of the Sudeten-Germans. This was Eden's view as much as Chamberlain's.[4] They saw Right as being rather with Germany than with Czechoslovakia over the Sudeten question. Chamberlain told the French ministers: 'It seemed to His Majesty's Government that Germany wanted two things . . . These were: first, colonies; secondly, *assurances about Central and Eastern Europe* [author's italics]. . . .'[5]

It followed therefore, in the English view, that if France and England used their influence to bring about Czech concessions to the Sudeten-Germans, it would both avert the immediate danger of war, and, in the long-term, make a valuable contribution towards the general appeasement of Europe. As Chamberlain argued: 'Germany did not seem to be

[1] Quoted in Feiling, pp. 332–3.
[2] Diary, quoted in Halifax, p. 189.
[3] CAB 27/626, FP(36)39.
[4] Record of Anglo-French Conversations at Downing Street, 29 and 30 November 1937, CAB 27/626, FP(36)40.
[5] Ibid.

contemplating the use of force at present, as she recognised that this would plunge us all into chaos. So long as Germany was prepared to use peaceful methods, we could perhaps do something to see that the steps she took were as little objectionable as possible. . . .'[1]

What, after all, was the alternative? Chamberlain asked Delbos whether he 'saw any way of preventing German expansion in Central Europe short of using force?'[2] Here indeed was the crux of the whole matter. But the English Government had long made up their minds[3] against resorting to so unthinkable an expedient as force, or in the first and perhaps last instance, the threat of force. Chamberlain therefore informed the French ministers that he 'thought it right to say that he did not think it would be possible to mobilise opinion in England in support of forcible intervention against Germany on behalf of Czechoslovakia'.[4]

So it was that, by the end of 1937, the English policy of 'interest' without commitment in eastern Europe had come to mean in practice that England was content to acquiesce in Germany's expansion to the east so long as the process was decently garbed in due legal form. By this means would be avoided such acts of open aggression as would be publicly embarrassing to the English conscience and might drag England into a war. It made a perfect solution to the English dilemma, but for the fact that it wholly ignored the equilibrium of power in Europe.

It was otherwise with the French ministers, who saw the Czechoslovak question in terms of the relative balance of strength between the dictatorships and the democracies. The French failed to share the comforting English conviction that Germany's aims in regard to Czechoslovakia did not even extend as far as autonomy for the Sudeten-Germans inside the Czechoslovak state.[5] On the contrary Delbos expressed an uncharitable suspicion that Germany really wanted to absorb Czechoslovakia rather than simply to secure better civic treatment for the Sudetens. The absorption of Czechoslovakia and Austria, he pointed out, could not be without consequence to the structure of Europe. It would mean German hegemony and a new appetite for conquest.[6]

Though the French ministers were realists, they were also funks. French politics and society were now in a state of progressive demoralisation, in which dread of another war was not the least element.[7] France now wore the role of a great power like a decrepit old man shrunken

[1] Ibid.
[2] Ibid.
[3] Cf. Eden's statement to the Imperial Conference in the spring.
[4] CAB 27/626, FP(36)40.
[5] Ibid.
[6] Ibid.
[7] For accounts of France in *her* decadence at this time, see Brogan, ch. IX; Beaufre, pp. 55–61; Horne, pp. 47–59, 73–7.

inside the uniform he had worn so bravely long ago. Since Chamberlain's policy offered a respectable escape from their obligation to fight for Czechoslovakia if Germany used force, and since they dare not forfeit England's friendship, they began to trail along behind the masterful, self-certain English Prime Minister. They used their special relationship in Prague only to press the Czechs to make concessions to their Sudeten-German citizens.

As 1938 opened, therefore, Chamberlain and his colleagues could feel that the grand design for the appeasement of Europe was making encouraging progress, what with Halifax's *tête-à-tête* with Hitler, and France's acquiescence in England's grasping of diplomatic leadership. Anthony Eden was no less eager than Chamberlain to press on with the courting of Germany while Halifax's kiss was still damp on Hitler's cheek; no more aware than Chamberlain that to chase after Germany in this way was to continue to yield her the tactical advantage. On New Year's Day 1938 Eden submitted his recommendations for 'The Next Steps Towards a General Settlement with Germany'.

> The conversations between Lord Halifax and Herr Hitler showed that, if we wish for a general settlement with Germany, it will be for us, and not for the German Government, to take the next step by putting forward some concrete proposals. . . . The next step, therefore, lies with us. It is important, if we are really anxious to prevent the hopes created by the recent conversations from evaporating, that we should keep moving, that there should be no long delay. We must keep moving . . .[1]

Since the Germans had spoken much in the previous year of their lost colonies and of their need for access to colonial raw materials, Eden and Chamberlain alike still saw colonial concessions as the most hopeful way of bribing Germany to accept English proposals for a European settlement.[2] On 24 January 1938 Chamberlain unveiled to the Cabinet Committee on Foreign Policy, not without some evident self-satisfaction, a cut-and-dried plan for re-partitioning Africa rather as he might have once re-drawn untidy local government boundaries. A large zone in central Africa, mostly and conveniently consisting of Belgian and Portuguese territory, was to be yielded to Germany under new, common rules of colonial administration.[3] Hoare, the Home Secretary, dampeningly expressed the thought that German reactions would not be as favourable as the Prime Minister hoped. Chamberlain argued that he was 'anxious

[1] CAB 27/626, FP(36)41. [2] Ibid. [3] CAB 27/623, FP(36)21.

to get the Germans interested in a general settlement', and that colonies were a good bait.[1] The Cabinet was not enthusiastic about the Prime Minister's plans for Africa. On 25 January and 10 February 1938 Eden submitted further memoranda on 'the German Contribution towards General Appeasement'.[2] As well as looking forward as usual to new Locarno treaties and disarmament agreements, he also suggested that Germany be asked to renew her 1936 recognition of Austria's full sovereignty, and that the Czech question should be settled too, on the lines of Czech concessions to the Sudeten-Germans in return for a German guarantee of Czechoslovakia's integrity. In his memorandum of 10 February, Eden, in terms that closely echoed what Halifax had told Hitler in November, continued:

> It would not be our intention, in discussing this question with Germany, to imply that we regard the present territorial disposition in Central and Eastern Europe as rigid and unchangeable for all time. But we should make it clear that we could not condone any change in the international status of a country achieved by force against the will of its inhabitants, or any forcible interference in its internal affairs.[3]

In the years that followed Eden's resignation from Chamberlain's Government on 20 February 1938, it came to be widely believed that Eden had disagreed with Chamberlain over the 'appeasement' of Germany. The documents make it clear, however, that to the very end of his tenure of the Foreign Office Eden shared Chamberlain's reliance on the worth of the hope of negotiating a genuine and general settlement with Germany; that Eden shared Chamberlain's belief that it was for England urgently to go and court Germany; that he shared his aversion to giving Hitler a blunt warning that England would go to war if Germany forcibly interfered with the *status quo* in central and eastern Europe; and that Eden agreed broadly with Chamberlain on the terms which should be offered Hitler, including Czech concessions to the Sudeten-Germans. It was not over the appeasement of Hitler but the appeasement of Mussolini that Eden and Chamberlain fell out.[4] There was also Chamberlain's high-handed interference in the Foreign Secretary's own sphere of responsibility, culminating in the famous snub, while Eden was abroad on holiday, to President Roosevelt's suggestion of an international conference of lesser powers, though under United States leadership, to work out proposals for

[1] Ibid.
[2] CAB 27/626, FP(36)43; CAB 27/627, FP(36)51.
[3] CAB 27/627, FP(36)51.
[4] See above p. 447.

a world peace settlement. Chamberlain, who had disliked and distrusted Americans ever since their sharp practice over naval questions in the 1920s, believed – rightly as it turned out – that Roosevelt's suggestion was just more fine American words; and that no solid American commitment to the maintenance of peace would ever be forthcoming.[1]

The new Foreign Secretary, Lord Halifax, was completely Chamberlain's man. Halifax accepted his new post less with enthusiasm than a sense of duty, for he had never been greatly interested in European affairs and knew little about them.[2] Having few clear ideas or convictions of his own, he was content loyally to acquiesce in his Prime Minister's conduct of foreign policy. As a Victorian Christian and gentleman like his chief, moreover, Halifax found Chamberlain's aims and aspirations entirely congenial.

> Although Edward was very clever the world was an innocent world to him. To live in it during Hitler's epoch with the ideas his father had planted in him was extremely difficult. He was so bound by tradition that he never wavered in the principles he was taught when he was young. No new view of the world or violent change dented his orthodoxy.[3]

Sir Samuel Hoare noted that Halifax enjoyed many of the characteristics of his reforming Whig ancestor, Lord Grey, and his Liberal kinsman Sir Edward Grey. 'In India [as viceroy] he had shown his wisdom in reconciling bitter differences. . . . Might he not have the same success in Europe that he had won [*sic*] in Asia?'[4]

So with Halifax at the Foreign Office, Henderson in Berlin, and Chamberlain in Downing Street with Horace Wilson at his ear, English foreign policy more than ever took on the character of an evangelical mission to convert the heathen.

On 12 March 1938 the invasion of Austria by the German army and the triumphal entry of Hitler into Vienna strongly suggested, however, that the heathen were not entirely hungry for the Word. Nevertheless the invasion was not, as some darkly suspected at the time, long premeditated. Hitler had intended to destroy Austrian independence gradually from within, by means of the indigenous Nazi Party; a process which Halifax's incautious remarks during his visit to Berchtesgaden had made clear would arouse no English wrath. The orders to march were given in the utmost

[1] See Avon, Vol. I, chs. XII and XIII.
[2] Birkenhead, pp. 418, 419.
[3] Lord Brand, quoted in Birkenhead, p. 422; see also above p. 156.
[4] Templewood, p. 280.

haste to prevent the Austrian president, Schuschnigg, from carrying out his plan of holding a plebiscite to ascertain whether or not the Austrian people were in favour of union with Germany. Since France and England contented themselves once again with whinnies of protest and disapproval, Hitler had now discovered that, apparently, he could get away even with open invasion of a neighbouring state and the destruction of its independence.

The wiping-out of Austria did not shake Chamberlain's faith in his policy. He admitted to his colleagues in the Cabinet Committee on Foreign Policy on 15 March 1938 that 'Hitler's violent actions had . . . greatly strengthened the hands of those persons in this country who urged that we should cease to have any dealings of any kind with Dictators'.[1] Nevertheless he 'did not think anything that had happened should cause the Government to alter their present policy; on the contrary, recent events had confirmed him in his opinion that that policy was the right one and he only regretted that it had not been adopted earlier'.[2]

It was plain enough to the Cabinet that Czechoslovakia was next on the list, and plain too that Germany could no longer be counted upon to refrain from the use of force against her. The time was past for enunciating evasive academic formulae such as that of England's 'interest' without commitment in eastern Europe, or for holding broad discussions as how best to open up negotiations with the Nazi leaders, and as to the terms on which Europe should be finally settled. English statesmen had now to face the urgent, practical question of how to deal with the great European crisis that was about to explode. On 18 March 1938 the Cabinet Committee on Foreign Policy held its first full-scale discussion of the problem of German designs on Czechoslovakia.[3]

The President of the Board of Trade, Oliver Stanley, roundly suggested that England should issue a declaration that she would stand by France if Germany attacked her because she had fulfilled her obligations to Czechoslovakia. The suggestion sank without a ripple. Halifax himself resolutely refused to see the problem in strategic terms. He said he did not agree with the argument for a 'deterrent commitment' on the 'assumption that when Germany secured the hegemony over Central Europe she would then pick a quarrel with France and ourselves . . .' He believed rather that 'the more closely we associate ourselves with France and Russia the more we produced on German minds the impression that we were plotting to encircle Germany and the more difficult would it be to make any real settlement with Germany'.[4]

[1] CAB 27/623, FP(36)25. [2] Ibid. [3] CAB 27/623, FP(36)26. [4] Ibid.

Then again, he 'distinguished in his own mind between Germany's racial efforts, which no one could question, and a lust for conquest on a Napoleonic scale which he himself did not credit'.[1]

Chamberlain himself reassured his colleagues with the belief that 'the seizure of the whole of Czechoslovakia would not be in accordance with Herr Hitler's policy which was to include all Germans in the Reich but not to include other nationalities . . .'[2]

It was his view therefore that some arrangement with Hitler on the lines of Sudeten autonomy 'might be worth exploring'.[3]

The Cabinet Committee finally decided to undertake no further commitment to France in regard to Czechoslovakia; and to try instead to persuade the Czechs and the French that an amicable settlement was necessary, and to persuade the Germans that there should be 'an orderly settlement of the Sudeten problem'.[4]

And thus did the Cabinet Foreign Policy Committee lay down the broad lines of English policy for the approaching Czechoslovakian crisis. It was a policy which, far from being founded on the realities of power and the principles of strategy, flatly denied them, like a house designed in defiance of the structural properties of its materials and of the laws of physics and mathematics.

On 21 March 1938 the Chiefs of Staff reported on 'The Military Implications of German Aggression against Czechoslovakia'[5] – a document which it may be thought the Foreign Policy Committee ought to have studied *before* deciding on its Czechoslovakian policy. In any case, however, the burden of the COS report was exactly what Chamberlain and his friends needed to justify their own views and bludgeon down their critics when the full Cabinet met on 22 March formally to decide policy over Czechoslovakia. It was, as Halifax said, 'an extremely melancholy document'.[6]

It was melancholy not merely in its broad assessment of the balance of military strength in Europe, but particularly so in its survey of the state of the British armed forces.[7]

Of the three armed services, the Royal Navy was in the best case, strong enough to ensure sea superiority except in the Baltic. However, the essential base of Rosyth was still at a year's notice; the defence of

1 CAB 27/623, FP(36)26. 2 Ibid. 3 Ibid. 4 Ibid.

5 CAB 27/627, FP(36)57, COS 698. 6 CAB 23/93, 15(38)1.

7 Colonial and Indian forces were not included, because none was available or earmarked for employment in Europe; dominion forces were not included because dominion participation in a war could not be automatically assumed; and, in the case of South Africa and Canada, was much in doubt. See above pp. 229–30.

merchant shipping against air attack was incomplete; and the anti-aircraft defence of naval bases and fuel storage was 'quite inadequate'.[1]

The army, however, was in hardly better shape than at the end of the 1920s. In support of France, England could field only one corps of two divisions 'seriously deficient of modern equipment'.[2]

Yet it was in the Royal Air Force and the Air Defence of Great Britain that the most crippling shortcomings were found, although these had been the first and paramount concerns of the British re-armament programme.

The present programme of expansion of the air force was still a year short of the scheduled date of completion. Of the 30 squadrons (420 aircraft) of fighters, only 27 could be mobilised. Of them 20 squadrons were of obsolete types slower than the majority of German bombers. There were only one and a half weeks' reserves of aircraft.

The first-line strength of the air striking force (bombers) on 1 April 1938 would be 67 squadrons (804 aircraft), but of these only 35 squadrons (420 aircraft) would be mobilisable. Twenty-five out of the 35 squadrons were capable of attacking Germany from Great Britain, but most could not penetrate deeply except from French bases. No staff arrangements had been reached, however, with the French for basing British bombers in France. Ten out of the 35 squadrons were light bombers and were useless against modern fighters.

The COS, having enumerated all kinds of further deficiencies in the RAF, wrote: 'The net result of these deficiencies . . . is that the air force cannot at the present time be said to be in any way fit to undertake operations on a major war scale.'[3]

The state of the air defence of Great Britain was worse still. Of the present approved scale of 640 3·7-inch and 4·5-inch anti-aircraft guns, not one was yet available. Instead there were 252 obsolete guns of 3-inch calibre. Of the planned 3,027 searchlights, there were only 969. Anti-aircraft defences would therefore have to be concentrated on London. Barrage balloons were 'of no practical value as yet'.[4] Radar defence, on which so much depended, consisted so far of only four stations, and was only of value to detect attacks approaching London from the east and south, and for tracking aircraft flying north or south down the Channel. There were almost no air-raid shelters. There was no centralised control of civil defence (or Air Raid Precautions, in the civil-service language of the time). As a result, '. . . we cannot ignore the fact that our Air Raid Precautions Organisation has not yet reached a stage when air attacks could be faced with any confidence . . .'[5]

[1] CAB 27/627, FP(36)57, COS 698. [2] Ibid. [3] Ibid. [4] Ibid. [5] Ibid.

Such then was the pitiable state of the British armed forces and the defence of the Realm two full years after the Government had launched its comprehensive programme of re-armament, and four years after it had first begun to remedy the weakness and obsolescence of the Royal Air Force. It was a state which owed itself not to the dilatoriness of peace-loving politicians but to the inadequacies of British technology and of the British industrial machine.

The navy's programme of modernisation and new construction had been particularly hampered by the running-down and even disappearance of the specialised industrial resources and skilled manpower necessary to make naval guns, gun-mountings and armour-plate – just as Beatty and the naval staff had vainly predicted in 1921–2 at the time of the Washington Conference.[1] Such plant as the Admiralty had been able to keep in being during the disarmament of the 1920s and early 1930s by carefully doling out the limited amount of work available were not always blessed with the most modern methods, organisation or equipment. In October 1937 Beardmores, a major supplier of guns and gun-mountings both for the navy and for anti-aircraft defence at home, presented, according to Lord Weir, the 'problem of raising what might be termed a scrap-heap to an efficient unit'.[2] Beardmores were then in fact six months behind in their production.[3] British trade unionism had made its own contribution to this delay, with all its implications for the air defence of Great Britain, by an unofficial strike which was calculated to have put back production by up to three months.[4]

The crippling inadequacy of British plant for making armour-plate (also largely owing to the naval standstill from 1922 to 1935), provided another major brake on the modernisation of ships and on new construction, and forced the Admiralty to buy armour from abroad; from the United States, from Krupps even. The new aircraft carriers *Indomitable* and *Implacable*, which were to see famous service during the Second World War, and the Fiji class cruisers were clad in Czechoslovakian armour.[5]

The specialist British armament firms, and Woolwich Arsenal too for that matter, were not only backward in their equipment and methods of production, but also in their design departments. In the spring of 1937 the

[1] Hornby, pp. 15–17, 20–2; Postan, pp. 3–4; see above pp. 270–2.
[2] Meeting of the Defence Policy and Requirements Committee, 21 October 1937, CAB 16/137, DPR/44.
[3] CAB 16/137, DPR/43, 30 September 1937.
[4] See 14th Progress Report of the Admiralty and the War Office to the DPRC, July 1937, CAB 16/142, DPR 206 and 207.
[5] 19th, 20th, 22nd and 25th Admiralty Reports to the DPRC, January, February, May and December 1938, CAB 16/142, DPR 244 and 249; CAB 16/143, DPR 271 and 293.

decision had to be taken to buy 40-mm 2-pounder anti-aircraft guns from the Swedish firm of Bofors, because the Vickers light anti-aircraft gun had proved useless and no other British design existed. Buying Bofors equipment would save a year. It was not even possible to manufacture the Bofors guns in Britain under licence; in April 1937 Lord Weir, the industrialist and a member of the Defence Policy and Requirements Committee, expressed himself 'very perturbed' at the 'limited and inexperienced' capacity in Great Britain for manufacturing automatic guns and their mountings.[1] Orders for the Bofors had therefore to be eventually placed not only in Sweden, but also in Belgium, Poland and Hungary.[2] The British army's new standard light machine-gun, the Bren (named after its place of origin), was Czech; the RAF's new monoplane fighters were to be armed with the American Browning,[3] of which 2,000 were ordered from the United States to bridge the gap until they could be manufactured in Britain.[4]

Yet it was not the small size and partial decrepitude of Britain's specialised armaments industry that were mainly responsible for throttling back British re-armament. For specialised armaments firms constitute only a small part of the production of modern war equipment, which is a matter of general industrial resources and technology, especially in all kinds of advanced engineering. It was such general, and varied, resources that Germany had been able swiftly to convert to producing munitions after 1933. But it was such resources that Great Britain terribly lacked, just as in 1914–15. As the Defence Policy and Requirements Committee had warned in submitting its recommendations for large-scale re-armament in February 1936: 'The most serious factor in the completion of the proposed programme is the limited output of our existing industrial resources. The key to the successful completion of the Service programmes lies in the solution of the industrial problem. . . .'[5]

The first and fundamental lack, which exercised a crippling and ubiquitous influence, was of enough highly skilled, highly trained personnel: production managers to plan and run new factories; draughtsmen and designers; tool and pattern makers; fitters. Not only the various re-armament programmes but also the expanding armed services themselves competed in fishing the small pool of skilled manpower.[6]

[1] Meetings of the DPRC 18 March, 22 and 29 April 1937, CAB 16/137, DPR/36, DPR/38, DPR/39.
[2] 25th Report by the War Office to the DPRC, 15 December 1938, CAB 16/143, DPR 290.
[3] In preference to the French 20-mm Hispano-Suiza cannon.
[4] DPRC meeting 22 April 1937, CAB 16/137, DPR/38.
[5] CAB 16/112, DPR(DR)9, 12 February 1936.
[6] See meeting of the DPRC, 7 May 1936, CAB 16/136, DPR/20.

For although there were over a million unemployed, they were mostly men from the wreckage of Victorian industry, coal, cotton, shipbuilding; men often either unskilled or skilled in some redundant and outdated craft. Neither British industry nor the British State possessed enough training schools to re-train those suitable on the scale required.

The very first progress reports of the service departments and the Ministry of Labour on re-armament to the Defence Policy and Requirements Committee uttered what were to be continued groans about the shortage of highly trained industrial personnel. The Air Ministry admitted that the scale of difficulties that would be caused by this shortage was 'not sufficiently foreseen'.[1] The Ministry of Labour noted that the shortages existed among the most highly skilled and therefore most highly needed trades – tool makers, precision fitters and highly skilled machinists.[2]

Because of this lack both of skilled manpower and of manufacturing resources of the right kind, Lord Weir told the DPRC in January 1936, that he was 'bound to state that the programme recommended could not be carried out in the period envisaged, unless a definite turn-over to a semi-war organisation was undertaken'.[3]

This of course was politically impossible in a liberal democracy in peacetime, especially in the climate of national opinion prevailing in 1936. Equally, as Weir himself believed, Britain could not afford to cut drastically the normal commercial production of her all-too-small modern exporting industries, the very ones most needed for re-armament, and already fully occupied. There was no slack.

Weir reiterated that the real bottleneck was skilled labour.

The fundamental problem which Britain therefore faced in embarking on large-scale re-armament was, therefore, as crisply summed up by Lord Weir: 'We were short of fundamental facilities for making certain articles.'[4]

The truth of this bleak assessment and the dimension of the shortage were to become more and more clear as the re-armament programme got under way.

The British aircraft industry on the eve of re-armament was, when compared with its American and German competitors, a cottage industry. All that remained by the early 1930s of that great industry which had been built up during the Great War were small, sleepy firms with factories

[1] CAB 16/140, DPR 82, 30 April 1936.
[2] CAB 16/140, DPR 83; see also meetings of the DPRC and progress reports submitted to it, 1936–8 *passim* in CAB 16/123–143.
[3] Meeting of the DPRC, 13 January 1936, CAB 16/123, DPR(DR)1.
[4] CAB 16/123, DPR(DR)1.

little more than experimental aircraft shops employing hand-work methods, and built round small design departments.[1] Whereas 30,000 aircraft had been produced in 1918, the figure for 1924 was only 503 and even in 1930 only 1,456.[2] This sad failure of the British to retain their wartime lead in a major new branch of technology was partly owing to the aircraft industry's own lack of commercial ambition and acumen, but also owing to the parallel British failure to develop civil aviation on the German or American scale.[3] While the German and American aircraft industries thrived in the 1920s on designing and selling civil air transports, the British aircraft firms were only kept alive by a trickle of Air Ministry orders for military aircraft.[4] By the early 1930s, when the Germans and Americans had successfully pioneered all-metal aircraft, mostly fast monoplanes, the British aircraft industry was still in the era of the slow wood and fabric biplane, whether fighters or airliners.[5]

The leaders of the British aircraft industry themselves were self-made, 'practical' men of the kind traditional in British industry since the great days of the early nineteenth-century Industrial Revolution: men who were often designers of genius, happy at the drawing-board or in the workshops, but qualified neither by training nor by experience to direct large industrial corporations. Beneath them, there was an almost total lack of production engineers and managers of the kind now common in American and German industry, and able to organise and manage assembly-line production. Except for its stock-in-trade therefore, the British aircraft industry in the early 1930s presented the classic picture of British industry a hundred years earlier.[6]

When after 1934 the industry was flooded, and later deluged, with Air Ministry orders, it coped well enough therefore with the *design* of new aircraft, profiting from the earlier foreign developments. Production, however, was another matter. Headlong large-scale expansion presented the industry with problems of scale and of complexity of organisation utterly new to it and, for several years, beyond it. From senior and middle management to design-staff and skilled labour, there was a critical shortage of appropriate training and experience.[7] All this applied equally to the industry's sub-contractors.

As a consequence the progress reports of the Air Ministry to the Defence Policy and Requirements Committee in 1936–8 were a gloomy catalogue of the industry's shortcomings, and of muddles, delays, disappointments

[1] Postan, Hay and Scott, pp. 36–7.
[2] Hornby, p. 18.
[3] See above pp. 213–15.
[4] Hornby, p. 19.
[5] Postan, Hay and Scott, pp. 33–4.
[6] Ibid. pp. 29–36.
[7] Ibid. pp. 36–8.

and missed delivery dates which resulted therefrom. As early as May 1936 the Air Ministry was referring to delays because of the difficulties in getting new, and, for the British aircraft industry, revolutionary types of aircraft into production.[1] In October and in December 1936 the DPRC again was told of delays in production owing to the changeover to new types, and their size and complication.[2] On 19 February 1937 the DPRC discussed the state of Vickers aviation, which rendered production of their aircraft 'extremely unsatisfactory'.[3] In April the DPRC took note that deliveries of airframes were well below the contractors' forecasts.[4]

In May 1937 the Air Ministry reported that the Blenheim, Whitley and Harrow bombers were now being delivered, but without defensive armament because of troubles with the turrets, whose production was not expected to be adequate until October.[5] In June, Lord Swinton gave the DPRC the reason for the delays in turrets. The head of the company responsible, he said, was 'a brilliant designer, but his firm was not good at production'.[6] Fairey's production was also behindhand and only three Battles had so far been produced. The firm was reported to be weak in production management.[7] Handley-Page however was noted as being well organised.[8]

In July 1937 the Air Ministry had much bad news to report. Of bomber contracts supposed to be completed by June, only 14 out of 80 Whitleys, 26 out of 150 Blenheims and 34 out of 100 Harrows had been delivered. Of 96 Wellesley bombers due by April only 22 had been delivered. The delivery date of the Spitfire fighter had been put back from November to December 1938; no production was expected in the current year. In September Lord Swinton, the Air Minister, was telling the DPRC with some emphasis that Fairey's management was 'totally unsatisfactory', which accounted for the delays with the Battle. There was a threat of cancelling the contract.[9] In this same month the Air Ministry was able to report that 130 out of 177 Gladiators, an already obsolescent fighter, had been delivered.[10] In October however there was less joy: only 24 of the new Hurricane fighters were expected in 1937 as against an earlier forecast of 52 for the period November 1937–January 1938; and, while

[1] Meeting of the DPRC, 7 May 1936, CAB 16/136, DPR/30.
[2] Meeting of 1 October 1936, CAB 16/136, DPR/26; 7th Report by the Air Ministry, December 1936, CAB 16/141, DPR 148.
[3] CAB 16/137, DPR/35.
[4] CAB 16/137, DPR/38.
[5] CAB 16/141, DPR 193.
[6] Meeting of 24 June 1937, CAB 16/137, DPR/40.
[7] Ibid.
[8] Ibid.
[9] Meeting of 30 September 1937, CAB 16/138, DPR/43.
[10] 15th Progress Report of the Air Ministry, September 1937, CAB 16/142, DPR 213.

4 Spitfires had after all been hoped for in December, there would now be none.[1]

In November there was more gloomy news: from 26 September to 31 October, only 213 airframes had been delivered as against the manufacturers' forecasts of 269, and only 383 engines as against 435. Because of difficulties with sub-contractors, there were going to be further delays with the Spitfire.[2] And the Air Ministry's report for December 1937[3] rounded off the year seasonally with a final gift package of delays and broken manufacturers' promises. Of the Blenheims and Whitleys due for delivery in June 1937, only 34 out of 80 and 117 out of 140 had even now been received. Of 155 Battles contracted for June 1937, only 84 had arrived by December. While the contract for the Harrow had now been completed, production of its spares was badly behindhand. The Air Ministry had now ceased to give a delivery date for the Spitfire at all in its progress charts because the 'firm state they are unable to forecast deliveries at present'.[4] However there would at least be 5 Hurricanes in the current month, and 7 were hoped for in January 1938 – as against earlier estimates of 52 for November–January.[5] In fact 20 had been delivered by the end of January. Spitfire deliveries could still not be forecast.[6]

The delays in British aircraft production which led to the weakness of the RAF described by the Chiefs of Staff in their March 1938 report to the Cabinet appear the more appalling when compared with the performance of the German aircraft industry.

The specification which the Spitfire and Hurricane were designed to meet was issued by the Air Ministry in December 1934;[7] the same year as the German specification which led to the Messerschmitt ME 109. The prototype of the ME 109 flew at the end of October 1935; of the Hurricane in November 1935; of the Spitfire not until May 1936.[8] But whereas the first version of the ME 109 (then known as the BF 109) was in squadron service with the German contingent in Spain by March 1937, there were only 20 Hurricanes with the RAF by the end of *January 1938*; and no Spitfires until the late summer of 1938. Thus the weakness and obsolescence of the RAF at the beginning of the Czechoslovakian crisis, with all its immense and far-reaching political and strategic consequences, was not

[1] 16th Progress Report of the Air Ministry, CAB 16/142, DPR 222.
[2] 17th Report by the Air Ministry, CAB 16/142, DPR 228.
[3] 19th Progress Report by the Air Ministry, CAB 16/142, DPR 241.
[4] Ibid. [5] Ibid.
[6] 21st Report by the Air Ministry, CAB 16/143, DPR 255.
[7] Postan, Hay and Scott, Appendix V and VI. [8] Ibid. Appendix II.

because of politicians, but because the British were not only trying to build aircraft in 1934–8, but an aircraft industry as well.

This immense task of development was tackled partly by expanding the plant of the aircraft firms themselves; partly by building 'shadow' engine and airframe factories to be operated by the motor-vehicle industry – firms like Rover, Austin and Morris. The whole operation was financed by government capital. The problem of manufacturing equipment for the other armed forces was solved in like fashion by expansion of existing private plant or Royal Ordnance Factories, and by the erection, with government aid, of new factories of the most modern kind and on the largest scale – plant for chemicals, propellants and explosives; for shell-production; small arms; fuses; instrumentation and equipment of all kinds. Most of these installations were really large general-purpose light-engineering factories of the kind unfortunately still rare in Britain but long commonplace in the United States and Germany, who owed their export successes in all kinds of modern industrial and consumer goods to them. It had taken therefore the urgent need to re-arm, together with government leadership and public money, to push British industry into emulating the scale and type of their commercial rivals' operations.

However, the vast new factories required machine tools in a quantity and of a sophistication of design wholly beyond Britain's own machine-tool industry.[1] Lord Weir warned the DPRC as early as January 1936, when large-scale re-armament was still under discussion, that the 'worst bottle-necks existed in the production of machine-tools, gauges, all precision work and, above all, skilled labour'.[2] For despite the sharp lessons of the Great War the British machine-tool industry had largely relapsed in peacetime – and had been allowed by the Government to relapse – into its old conservatism of design and its small-scale handicraft methods of production. It particularly neglected the kind of machines, often automatic, needed for mass-production of such articles as typewriters, components for radios and vacuum cleaners and other electrical apparatus, cycles, motor-vehicles and engines, and aero-engines, all of which industries in Britain were equipped with foreign machinery. In 1933–7, when Germany enjoyed 48·3 per cent of the world's trade in machine tools, and the United States 35·3 per cent, the United Kingdom's share was only 7·1 per cent.[3]

And so in the late 1930s, just as in 1914–15, the modernisation and expansion of British industry after a long and profound slumber depended

[1] Cf. Swinton's comments in DPRC meeting on 22 October 1936, CAP 16/136, DPR/28.
[2] Meeting of the DPRC, 13 January 1936, CAB/123, DPR (DR)1.
[3] Hornby, pp. 324–5.

critically on foreign technology, whose products had to be bought with precious and steadily dwindling reserves of foreign exchange. United Kingdom imports of machine tools leaped from 7,765 tons in 1935 to 20,058 tons in 1936, and 31,591 in 1937.[1] By contrast, as Vice-Admiral Sir Harold Brown, Director of Munitions Production at the War Office, pointed out to the DPRC on 22 October 1936, the Germans had not only provided themselves with their own machine tools, but had a surplus for export.[2]

The dependence on foreign supplies related not only to quantity, but also to key equipment of highly advanced performance.

In October 1936 the War Office reported to the DPRC that there was a bottleneck in shell-forging because the existing equipment was old-fashioned and useless for modern production methods. As a consequence, there would have to be recourse to German or Hungarian types of press, for which British firms had the manufacturing rights. The War Office also thought that the purchase of German machine tools should be considered, because similar types could not be obtained in Britain.[3] Next month the War Office reported that German shell-machinery plant had been bought.[4] Again, the new petrol-tin factory was to be entirely equipped with American machines.[5]

The British machine-tool industry was also amazingly tardy and slack about delivery dates. In July 1937, for example, the DPRC discussed the lateness of new factories in getting into production owing to slow deliveries of machine tools. Some ordered six months ago were two months late, and as a result Swiss machines had been bought instead. On the other hand, the same meeting took note that production of bombs had been speeded up owing to a new German lathe, which could absorb seven times the horsepower of any other lathe in the world.[6]

Yet British dependence on foreign technology went far beyond the equipment for the new factories. So small and inadequate were existing British resources in regard to the technology of the age of electricity, flight and motor transport that finished products had to be bought abroad in order to avoid even more protracted delays in re-armament. For example, there being almost no capacity in Britain for making clockwork fuses for anti-aircraft shells, orders had to be placed with a Swiss firm, to

[1] Ibid. p. 326; see also pp. 321–31 for a general discussion of the weaknesses of the British machine-tool industry.
[2] CAB 16/136, DPR/28.
[3] 5th Progress Report by the War Office, 15 October 1936, CAB 16/141, DPR 126.
[4] 6th Report by the War Office, November 1936, CAB 16/141, DPR 138.
[5] 9th Progress Report by the War Office, 15 February 1937, CAB 16/141, DPR 169.
[6] Meeting of 21 January 1937, CAB 16/136, DPR/33.

bridge the gap until the same Swiss firm should have built a factory in Britain, and supplied Swiss skilled labour for a period of several years to enable it to start to function.[1] Eventually it was decided instead simply to buy fuses from Switzerland until a British type could be manufactured at home.[2] As well as being dependent on Swiss fuses to detonate its shells, anti-aircraft defence had to fall back on American predictors and French height-finders.[3] The RAF likewise had to turn to foreign sources for the highly sophisticated equipment it needed for its new bombers and fighters. In July 1937 the Air Ministry reported to the DPRC that owing to difficulties in getting from British industry the desired quantities and types of 'rate-of-climb' indicators, 700 American indicators were to be bought, in order to see the RAF through to October, when the American type would begin to be manufactured in Great Britain.[4] Large contracts had to be placed in the United States for aircraft instrument panels. Four thousand American instruments were also ordered, to tide over until a new British instrument factory was finished in March 1939.[5] The RAF had to depend on American altimeters, too, until these could be made under licence in Britain.[6]

The Royal Navy had similar difficulties over fire-control gear, another field demanding highly advanced design and manufacture; it was in fact the major brake on new construction. The Admiralty reported: 'The country has been scoured to find firms willing to undertake the work, but without success.'[7] As a consequence ships would be delivered without their second or third High Angle Control Systems.[8]

And common to all three services were the effects of a shortage of optical instrument capacity in Britain, which again made it necessary to buy abroad.[9]

Even the production and installation of radar, a British invention later to take its place in the national folk-myth as a proof of British technological leadership, was delayed because of a bottleneck in production of valves, which Britain was forced to consider buying instead from America. The bottleneck in valve manufacture was attributed to British manufacturers lagging behind in research.[10]

[1] CAB 16/137, DPR/32 and DPR/33, DPRC meetings of 17 December 1936 and 21 January 1937.
[2] DPRC meeting of 24 June 1937, CAB 16/137, DPR/40.
[3] 9th War Office Report to the DPRC, 15 February 1937, CAB 16/141, DPR 169.
[4] 14th Progress Report of the Air Ministry to the DPRC, July 1937, CAB 16/142, DPR 205.
[5] 2nd Progress Report of the Air Ministry to the DPRC, May 1936, CAB 16/140, DPR 93.
[6] 3rd Progress Report of the Air Ministry to the DPRC, June 1936, CAB 16/140, DPR 93.
[7] 16th Report of the Admiralty to the DPRC, October 1937, CAB 16/142, DPR 224.
[8] Ibid.
[9] DPRC meeting of 23 July 1936 in CAB 16/136, DPR/25.
[10] Meeting of the Joint Defence Committee, 20 May 1938, CAB 36/4, 54.

Re-armament therefore put British industry to the proof, and found it wanting. It harshly demonstrated to the British governing classes the diminished vigour with which was beating the very heart of British world power, the United Kingdom industrial machine. Yet it was twenty years since the desperate munitions crisis of 1914–15 had served its fearsome warning of Britain's advancing industrial senility. It was twenty years since the subsequent wartime industrial revolution had begun the task of rejuvenation; since Lloyd George had expressed the resolve of government and people that this task would be carried through to completion after the war: 'Old principles have vanished, new ideas are abroad: employers and workers, the public and the State, are favourable to new methods. This opportunity must not be let slip.'[1]

It was twenty years since the exhaustive wartime reports of the Committee on Commercial and Industrial Policy had recommended what needed to be done:

> It is in our opinion a matter of vital importance that, alike in the old-established industries and in the new branches of manufacture which have arisen during the war, both employer and employed should make every effort to attain the largest possible volume of production, by the increased efficiency of industrial organisation and processes. . . . It is only by the attainment of this maximum production and efficiency that we can hope to secure a speedy recovery of the industrial and financial position of the United Kingdom and assure its economic stability and progress.[2]

How then had these twenty years come instead to witness only continued relative decline?

It might have appeared beyond a doubt in 1918 that the economic and social doctrines of liberalism had been utterly and finally discredited by the experiences of the war; doubly discredited, in the first place by the appalling deficiencies in British national power revealed in 1914–15, and secondly by the spectacular success in remedying these deficiencies which was achieved by collective national purpose and organisation. It might have seemed indeed that since England had only escaped catastrophe by hastily reverting to the Elizabethan or Cromwellian conception of the nation-state as a single great strategic and commercial enterprise, this conception would henceforth inspire her national policy. Yet such was not at all the case.

When the guns ceased to fire on 11 November 1918 it was for Britain

[1] See above p. 116.

[2] Cd. 9032, p. 23; see above p. 117.

what the stroke of midnight was for Cinderella. The brilliant coach of national reorganisation and development changed back to the now dried-up pumpkin of *laissez-faire* individualism. For what had been done in wartime was looked upon as an extraordinary response to an extraordinary situation, having no relevance to peacetime. Indeed, by a paradox, the war rendered British businessmen more self-satisfied rather than less, because, forgetting that foreign machines had alone made the colossal output of munitions possible, they took victory as being a proof that British industry was superior to German.

All that came of the wartime reports and good intentions was the 1921 Act of Parliament to safeguard certain strategically vital industries – optical glass, scientific glassware, scientific instruments, wireless valves, magnetoes and so on – from extinction by renewed foreign, in truth German, competition; an act without which British dependence on foreign technology in 1936–8 would have been even heavier.

Once the Great War was over, therefore, and with one accord, government, industry and trade unions hastened to carry on where they had left off in 1914 – and with the same results. In 1927, when the volume of world exports as a whole had risen to an index figure of 118 (taking 1913 as 100), British exports had sunk to 73.[1] It was an index figure which stood not only for the collapse of those Victorian staple industries which had been growing more and more out of date for so long – iron and steel, coal, cotton – but also for the want of vigorous growth in Britain's new industries.[2]

All those factors of tradition and prejudice, of psychological attitude, which had underlain the British decline from 1860 to 1914 remained in full operation. Businessmen clung to the familiar, hallowed methods and the beloved machinery they were used to; and sought to preserve the independence of the cosy little firms which, however inefficient, gave them perks, precedence and an income. They continued to lack the inner restlessness of American and German businessmen and the pleasure of these nations in efficiency and growth *per se*; to lack their contempt for incompetence and failure. They seemed more interested in getting their golf handicaps down than their profitability up. As for exports, overseas markets were a long way off; there seemed no compelling reason to go to all that bother when there were the tame British and empire markets at hand. If the foreigners wanted the best, they knew where to come.

Unpushing and gentlemanlike behaviour, as inculcated by the public schools, was an attribute of the boards and managements of large concerns

[1] W. K. Hancock, Vol. II, p. 206.

[2] Hobsbawm, p. 221.

as well as of the little firms. A diplomat in the American Department of the Foreign Office (whose functions now included those of intermediary between British firms and foreign governments) found in the 1930s that

> . . . even if one had an important report affecting a matter in which hundreds of thousands of pounds were involved, it was impossible to talk to any responsible person in the firm concerned except on Tuesdays, Wednesdays and Thursdays – and perhaps Friday mornings; from Friday to Monday business seemed to be at a standstill.[1]

The mentality of British trade unionism was no less conservative and nostalgic; in fact, it presented in some respects an even greater obstacle to change and growth. Now that the war was over, the trade unions' consent to work modern factories in a modern way, so as to achieve the utmost efficiency and productivity, was revoked. Their main purpose in life, stubbornly pursued, became once again to preserve the ancient skills and prescriptive rights of their members, often by opposing the introduction of new machines and methods, but alternatively by demanding that men rendered superfluous by new equipment should nevertheless be retained on the payroll. Theirs was the behaviour of cavalry regiments which, if finally forced to accept tanks, nevertheless insisted on keeping their horses, and employing cavalry drill. The trade unions used their control of apprenticeship – in any case a medieval system of industrial education – not to increase the amount of skilled labour, but to restrict it.[2] Traditional right rather than modern function also determined those convoluted borderlines between one union and another which divided up work in a British factory like a map of Germany in the eighteenth century. The British trade union's aim was maximum manning rather than maximum efficiency and profitability and hence maximum wages. As a consequence the more go-ahead a firm or industry was, the more it was bound to run into dour, pig-headed trade-union obstruction. Trade unionism was therefore particularly to blame for the fact that even new industries in Britain grew far more slowly than their foreign rivals.

Despite the growth of State education since the Education Act of 1902, it was, though the very fountainhead of national efficiency, still far from adequate. In the 1920s and even 1930s the British remained largely an ignorant and untrained nation. In 1921 only 19 per cent of the population between the ages of fourteen and seventeen were in full-time education, and only another 3 per cent in part-time education.[3] In the three years

[1] Kelly, p. 207. [2] Cf. evidence to the Emmott Committee on Technical Education, p. 16.
[3] Carr-Saunders and Caradog Jones, p. 125.

1922–5 only 12·3 per cent of elementary-school children went on to secondary, technical or other full-time education.[1] Only about a quarter of the boys leaving elementary schools every year could hope for some form of training which would make them more or less skilled.[2] Whereas the consultative committee of the Board of Education reported as early as 1909 in favour of compulsory day-continuation schools, nothing had been done in this direction even by the 1930s.[3] The public schools for their part, although their scientific departments were slowly growing, were still turning out district commissioners rather than production engineers; it was still the best form to go into public service, the 'liberal' professions or even the City rather than into industry, unless, of course, it was into the family firm.

Despite the furore during the debates on the 1902 Bill about the urgent need for better technical and higher education, fewer than twenty first-class technical schools were built between 1902 and 1918.[4] In 1927 an investigating committee, made up of representatives of different industries and professions and of the teachers' associations,[5] noted the fragmentary nature of British technical education. For example, fourteen institutions of university rank offered courses in mining engineering to 200 students, whereas in Germany there were three times as many students in just four mining colleges. In any case British technological colleges remained dismally penny-pinched institutions compared with their lavishly equipped foreign counterparts. In one college:

> The equipment for the practical study of electrical engineering is meagre, and the room in which the electrical machines are housed is a very small and dingy store on the basement. . . . The lecture room is so badly lighted that it is impossible to see anything on the blackboard, and in the laboratory the lighting is so poor that volumetric or colorimetric work is impossible. . . .'[6]

And in the universities, except for admittedly brilliant original research, science and technology made slow progress: whereas in 1922 there were 9,852 students in these fields, in 1939 the number had crept up to only 10,278.[7]

[1] Carr-Saunders and Caradog Jones, p. 125.

[2] Ibid. p. 136.

[3] G. A. N. Lowndes, *The Silent Social Revolution* (London, Oxford University Press 1937), pp. 192–3.

[4] Ibid.

[5] The Emmott Committee Report of an enquiry into the relationship of technical education to other forms of education and to industry and commerce (1927).

[6] Board of Education: *Survey of Technical and Further Education in England and Wales* (London, HMSO 1926).

[7] Michael Argles, *South Kensington to Robbins: An Account of English Technical Education since 1851* (London, Longmans 1964), p. 77.

Here then, in the continuing deficiencies of the British system of education, was the root cause of that scarcity of highly trained personnel and skilled labour which was to throttle back British re-armament in the late 1930s. Yet the truth was that, with the exception of the all-too-few progressive firms, British industry did not *want* the products of technical and higher education. It remained sentimentally loyal to the 'practical man' self-taught on the job, whether the job was that of fitter or managing director. As the Balfour Committee on Industry and Trade reported in 1929:

> The available information makes it clear that the present response of the leaders of industrial and commercial enterprises to the educational efforts made to train candidates for entry into the higher grades of these organizations is much less certain and widespread than in certain foreign countries, e.g., Germany or the United States.[1]

The Report quoted one progressive managing director as saying that

> . . . the old-fashioned type of more or less self-made man, who had grown up as a practical man inside a factory, and reached a position of works manager, is now definitely out of date. His continuance in this position is, in my opinion, largely responsible for the parlous condition of many of our industries, particularly engineering and textiles. . . .[2]

The Balfour Committee equally noted the way in which the results of state-aided scientific research were wasted and neglected by industry, and admonished:

> Before British industries, taken as a whole, can hope to reap from scientific research the full advantage which it appears to yield to some of their most formidable trade rivals, nothing less than a revolution is needed in their general outlook on science; and in the case of some industries at least, this change of attitude is bound to be slow and difficult, in view of our old and deeply rooted industrial traditions.[3]

The Balfour Report was the latest of those periodic and monumental reports on British industrial failings which had served since the 1860s not as the prelude to action, but as its substitute. It provides a picture of the British industrial machine as it was between the return to liberal economics after the Great War and the beginning of re-armament; it portrayed the truth behind the myth of individual 'enterprise' and 'free competition',

[1] Cmd. 3282, p. 213.
[2] Ibid.
[3] Ibid. p. 218.

which still commanded the belief of British industry and of the Conservative and Liberal parties.

There was, in the first place, the failure of competition to act according to theory; it did not swiftly eliminate the inefficient as it was supposed to do: 'The tenacity of life shown by businesses working at a loss is sometimes extraordinary . . . the results of the prolonged competition of inefficient undertakings react on the more efficient and tend to depress the whole industry. . . .'[1]

Then, instead of the entrepreneurial enterprise and flexibility expected by classic economic theory, there was what the Balfour Report called 'the human factor':

> . . . the conservative habits of mind which prevent many British employers from pursuing so energetic and (as it appears to them) so ruthless a policy of 'scrapping' old plant and replacing it by new as their competitors (say) in America or Germany, and the corresponding qualities of mind which lead many workmen and some of their Trade Unions to cling tenaciously to obsolete trade customs and lines of demarcation and thus prevent them from co-operating to the full in getting the best value out of machinery at the lowest cost.[2]

The Balfour Committee returned to this question of entrenched trade union privilege in the final conclusions to their report:

> We are aware of no other country that suffers nearly so much as Great Britain from artificial and hard and fast lines of demarcation between different skilled crafts, or between workers of different grades of skill, and this disability is more acutely felt than ever in a period of rapid economic change, when old lines of distinction are necessarily becoming less and less consistent with the realities of productive economy.[3]

Earlier in its report the committee had pointed out by way of instructive contrast how different was the American attitude to wages and productivity: 'The characteristic feature of the economy of the great industrial establishments of the United States is not merely the high wages which prevail, but the combination of high wages and low labour costs per unit of output, and this combination depends on the power of making the freest use of mechanical aids to productivity. . . .'[4]

In their summary of the recent history of the iron and steel industry the

[1] Cmd. 3282, p. 179. [2] Ibid. pp. 80–1. [3] Ibid. p. 361.
[4] Ibid. p. 151.

Balfour Committee provided a convenient epitome of their entire voluminous report; the more so because steel was the very framework that supported national power:

> . . . British practice in the manufacture of iron and steel tended over a period of years before the war to fall behind continental practice . . . the war-time extension and improvements in the industry did not completely modernise it, and, *owing to the extensive re-construction effected in the iron and steel plants of Germany and other continental countries* [author's italics], the average British practice probably remained behind the average continental practice . . . the need for modernising British iron and steel plants has become more pressing.[1]

Yet the Balfour Committee were not free themselves from the 'conservative habits of mind'. In their case the conservative habit of mind was that of Victorian individualism; the obsolete equipment they could not bring themselves to scrap was the nineteenth-century liberal economic dogma of *laissez-faire* and the nineteenth-century liberal idea of the role of the State. For the general assumption of their report was that private enterprise could be left to put itself in order without compulsory reconstruction; an assumption from which five out of fifteen members of the committee nevertheless dissented.

It was an assumption hardly warranted by the course of the past sixty years of British industrial history, or by the supine picture painted by the committee itself. Yet it was shared not only by Conservative and Liberal politicians, but also by the Treasury, which was haunted by Gladstone, and the Board of Trade, wherein still dwelt the spirit of Cobden. Baldwin himself, Prime Minister in 1923 and again from 1924 to 1929, was, having sat on the wartime committee on commercial and industrial policy, deeply aware of the dire condition of British industry, and adverted to it in speech after speech.[2] But beyond admonition and encouragement he would not go. As he told his audience in a speech in Birmingham Town Hall in March 1925: 'What this Government will not do is attempt to control the industries of this country. . . . It is little that the Government can do [about re-organising industry into large-scale groups of capital and labour]; these reforms, these resolutions, must come from the people themselves.'[3]

For believers in *laissez-faire* economic orthodoxy, the plight of British

[1] Ibid. p. 185.
[2] Cf. speech at Birmingham 5 March 1925, quoted in Middlemass and Barnes, pp. 295, 391; see also pp. 304, 311–16, 379–84, 423, 463–78.
[3] Middlemass and Barnes, pp. 380–1.

industry presented indeed a baffling conundrum. What did you do when private enterprise simply refused to display enterprise? The classic liberal economists had never envisaged a situation where entrepreneurs responded neither to the carrot of maximum profit nor the stick of competition, but simply lay down in the shafts and snoozed.

Yet the only alternative to the nation remaining the passive spectator of the decay of its industrial strength was compulsory reconstruction by the State, as in the war. Only the Labour Party favoured it, and their solution of 'nationalisation' was an emotive symbol, a slogan, rather than a thoroughly worked-out practical scheme based on a grasp of the technology and organisation of modern industrial processes. 'Nationalisation' indeed, as the Labour Party understood it in its pseudo-religious fashion in the 1920s and 1930s, was a secularised Wesleyan conversion. Upon industry, in its sinful state of exploitation and decrepitude, the act of nationalisation would, like baptism, confer a state of grace, and instantly the convert would enter upon a new life.

The two political cries of 'nationalisation' and 'private enterprise' between the world wars therefore served only to transform into emotional questions of ideology what ought to have been pragmatic questions of the functional organisation of industry; it was not the least contribution of party politics to British decline.

Yet wartime experience had shown that there was, in objective fact, no reason why the State should not successfully compel that modernisation and reconstruction which industry lacked the will to carry out for itself. Baldwin's government was inhibited solely by taboo – just as in the 1930s his government and that of his successor were also to be inhibited by taboo from returning to the balance of power in foreign affairs; the taboo in both cases being a legacy of Victorian liberalism. What might have been achieved was demonstrated by the one isolated example of major government intervention in industry for which Baldwin was responsible during the 1920s.

At Baldwin's request Lord Weir headed a small committee to 'review the national problem of electrical energy'. Weir's committee reported on 14 May 1925. Since the existing electricity-supply industry comprehended 438 separate generating stations all with their own frequencies and voltages, Weir recommended instead that a Central Electricity Board should be set up; a State monopoly half financed by Government-guaranteed stock, half by local undertakings. Although the government was somewhat taken aback by so unorthodox and thorough-going a scheme, Baldwin was keen and pushed it through. It became law at the end of 1926. By 1929 output of electricity was up four-fold, while generating costs had fallen; and there were nine million consumers as against only three-quarters of a million in 1926.[1] Nevertheless, despite the outstanding success of this experiment, and although it offered a prototype for directly tackling the problems of inefficiency in other industries, it was not repeated. Like Jehovah's Witnesses at the death bed of a loved one, the Government shunned surgery. As Baldwin's biographers write: 'Baldwin's political philosophy did not permit the application of such a solution to a staple industry like coal, not even in the form of a national holding company, first suggested by Sir Arthur Duckham in 1919, and revived as a suggestion in 1926.'[2]

So the decline went on, passively watched by government and nation, while at the same period the German State was co-operating with its industrialists in colossal reorganisations and re-equipment of German industry, and in research and development. By 1931 the British Chief of the General Staff was pointing out to his Government that 'the enthusiasm for modernisation and rationalisation has caused the capacity of German industry in general to outstrip that of any other continental nation . . .'[3]

It was only the coming of another great emergency, the world slump, which finally broke the taboo of liberal economic doctrine in Britain. Free Trade itself was abandoned in 1931. It was nearly a hundred years since it had opened the way to British dependence on overseas markets and supplies for very existence; a dependence whose lethal dangers were revealed by the Great War, and which represented, to paraphrase Adam Smith, the triumph of opulence over defence. The restoration of Free Trade after the war had once again laid the British home market itself open to foreign conquest. Now, in 1931, that market was to be preserved for British industry by protective tariffs. It was not however the protection the nursery afforded to lusty infants, like German and American tariffs in the nineteenth century, but that of the geriatric ward.

And while the British Government at last began in the 1930s to take a part in industry, the purpose of this co-operation was not to renew and develop national strength, like the earlier co-operation of State and industry in Germany, but to *reduce* capacity, to limit output to the quantity that the present slumped market could absorb. A twilight of liberalism still lingered on, for the Government intervened in industry timidly, piecemeal, as little as it could, hoping that the forces of 'natural recovery' would do the job for them. There was no great programme of

[1] See Middlemass and Barnes, pp. 393–4.
[2] Ibid. p. 394.
[3] See above p. 334.

modernisation; no immense capital investment. That had to wait, together with thorough-going government intervention, for re-armament; and by then it was all too late. On 11 February 1938, a month before Germany marched into Austria and the danger to Czechoslovakia became immediate, the Chiefs of Staff wrote in a report on the state of British military preparations: 'What we desire to do in this paper is to call the attention of the Committee of Imperial Defence to the fact that our approved re-armament programme is falling behind and that in our opinion it will fail to give us security in time.'[1]

There were however particular reasons why in March 1938, at the opening of the Czechoslovakian crisis, England had only two ill-equipped divisions to place in the scales of European power. From the very beginnings of re-armament the British army had been placed a bad third, an extremely bad third, in priority behind the Royal Air Force and the Royal Navy.

For re-armament in Britain was dominated throughout its course by an obsession with air power. It was the comparative progress of the Luftwaffe and the RAF which fascinated the attention of most governmental discussions on re-armament, and which no less formed the subject matter of public debate, thanks to the ferocious criticisms of government tardiness voiced by Winston Churchill. To the British therefore re-armament came to seem almost a question of air power alone. Cabinet discussion tacitly assumed that the next war, if it came, would take the form of a direct, almost a private, duel between the British and German air forces; the implications of another decisive land battle in the west, of which the French would bear the brunt, were largely ignored.

This obsession with aerial warfare was in the first place owing to the success since 1918 of Air Ministry propaganda, helped along by the futuristic military commentators, in convincing 'informed' public opinion that the next war would be decided by the bomber before the floundering armies got to grips, thus rendering land forces obsolete and largely redundant. The advent of re-armament in 1934 inspired the Air Ministry to a fresh effort to convince the other armed services, and even more so the politicians, that Germany's strategy in the next war would be to ignore the French army and strike on the instant against Britain in the air. The Air Staff, relying on what their successors of 1941 were to admit was no better than 'crystal-gazing',[2] provided figures, revised upwards from time to time, of the enormous tonnages of gas and explosive which they

[1] Memorandum on Military Preparations in Relation to Imperial Defence, 11 February 1938, CAB 53/36, COS 683.

[2] See above p. 437.

believed could be dropped day after day for weeks by the German aircraft of the epoch.[1] As the Chief of the Air Staff, Sir Edward Ellington, wrote, in a memorandum of 12 June 1934 which was to exert an immense and long-lasting influence: '... we must be prepared for an attack far more severe in weight and continuity, than anything experienced in this country during the last war; and the organisation necessary to ensure the continuance of the war effort of this country will require the most careful consideration ...'[2]

The Chief of the Air Staff redoubled the impact of this forecast by writing a little later of the likelihood that the war would open with a 'knock-out' blow against London, a specially vulnerable target.[3]

None the less, his fellow Chiefs of Staff disputed his figures and his estimate of the possible scale of a German air offensive. The Chief of Naval Staff (Sir Earle Chatfield) thought Ellington was quite wrong in thinking that Germany could still concentrate all her air forces on Great Britain even if France were Britain's ally. The CIGS (Sir Archibald Montgomery-Massingberd) agreed that Ellington had left France out of his calculations.[4] The argument dragged on. In November 1934 the CIGS, in a discussion on the draft annual defence review, said he thought it over-emphasised German air re-armament, whereas in fact it was the expansion of the German army which was more important.[5] A year later the Chiefs of Staff (the same three officers) were still disputing, army and navy versus air force, as to whether the opening major German effort would be by air or land; or, if in the air, would be concentrated against England. Both Chatfield and Montgomery-Massingberd believed that a land offensive through Belgium was the most likely German course, and an air attack against England the least likely.[6]

It was the Air Ministry's view which none the less prevailed upon the Cabinet and in particular upon Neville Chamberlain, then Chancellor of the Exchequer. It chimed exactly with their own feelings and prejudices, not to say their sense of political convenience. In the first place the Cabinet, like the rest of public opinion, had long ago accepted that the next war would indeed open with cataclysmic scenes of destruction and panic beneath the bomber fleets.[7] Leaving aside cold strategic calculation, their dread was itself enough to prompt them to make it their principal care in

[1] See above p. 436.
[2] Memorandum by the Chief of the Air Staff (Sir Edward Ellington), 12 June 1934, CAB 53/24 COS 341.
[3] CAB 53/24, COS 344.
[4] COS meeting of 27 June 1934, CAB 53/4, COS 130.
[5] COS meeting of 20 November 1934, CAB 53/5, COS 135.
[6] COS meeting of 29 October 1935, CAB 53/5, COS 153.
[7] See above pp. 438–9.

re-armament to prevent or mitigate such scenes by re-equipping and expanding the Royal Air Force, even if at the expense of the other armed forces. In the second place, the air force benefited as much from the politicians' memory of the last war as from their apprehensions about the next. For the Government recoiled in horror from the mere thought of large-scale British participation in another Western Front; and they were only too well aware that public opinion at large recoiled as well.[1] This was why the Government was to devote so little attention to the possibility and implications of a great German land offensive in the west.

Yet at the same time politicians and service leaders alike recognised that France and the Low Countries were vital British interests. Even the Chief of the Air Staff had written that it was of 'vital importance to prevent Germany from establishing air bases in the Low Countries . . .'[2] Until the mid-1930s it had always been assumed that these vital interests would be defended, as in 1914, by an expeditionary force. Unfortunately, as the Great War had shown, once England became entangled at all with a land war in Europe, it was not easy to limit liability to a small regular-army field force. It came to seem to some politicians in the 1930s, and most of all to Chamberlain, that to find a major place within the re-armament programme for a modern field force was to incur the grave risk of being drawn into another Western Front. By the same token it would be, unlike spending on the RAF, in the highest degree politically unpopular.

Here then was a dilemma. The apostles of air power however provided a neat solution to it – England should offer France the aid of an air-striking force instead of an army. In this enticing suggestion lay the second major reason why British re-armament concentrated on the RAF, to the neglect both of the army and the Fleet Air Arm.

For it appeared that air power, necessary in any event to defend London against the virtually certain German opening onslaught, also offered a convenient and relatively painless alternative to another Western Front. And it offered a cut-price alternative at that. For all these reasons Chamberlain, first as Chancellor of the Exchequer and later as Prime Minister, resolutely opposed expediture on the army's field forces, in favour of the RAF. As he argued to the Cabinet Committee on Disarmament in the summer of 1934, he was against an expeditionary force for Belgium, on the grounds that if the French and Belgian defences were impregnable, there was no need for it, and if they were not, then the BEF could not stop the Germans from overrunning Belgium. This might seem strongly to argue in favour of the creation of a much bigger British field army, but

[1] See above pp. 424–35. [2] CAB 53/24, COS 341.

such was far from Chamberlain's thinking. He referred instead to the trench stalemate of 1914–18 and what he took to be the lessons of the Great War, and said that it 'seemed to him that our experience in the last war indicated that we ought to put our major resources into our Navy and our Air Force'.[1] He considered that the best and cheapest deterrent would be a strong United Kingdom air force; expenditure on the army over the next five years could therefore be reduced from the £40 million proposed by the DRC to £19·1 million.[2] The Cabinet settled on £20 million over four years – a clear-cut victory for Chamberlain.

Yet although the army had been allotted so minor a share in the re-armament budget, the question still remained undecided whether British interests in western Europe could be defended adequately by air power. In 1935–6 the Air Ministry – and Chamberlain – received the influential backing of B. H. Liddell Hart, who had by now achieved a reputation as a strategic thinker of genius, and whose views, proffered either in numerous books and articles or over discreet but important dinner tables, were devoured by politicians with somewhat uncritical appetite; possibly because he so often gave intellectual shape and respectability to their own instinctive fears and wishes. Chamberlain in particular was much influenced by Liddell Hart, whose ideas he found extremely sympathetic.[3]

In the course of three major articles in *The Times* in November 1935 Liddell Hart suggested that 'the offensive role of an expeditionary force might be entrusted to the air force . . . it would avoid many of the complications involved, and evolving, when we land an army on the Continent . . .'[4]

In a leading article in the same newspaper on 10 February 1936 he further argued: 'Unless our field force could arrive on the scene during this opening phase – it is difficult to see how it could, since it is to cross the sea – our assistance might be more profitably given in the form of a proportionately larger contribution in air strength.'[5]

And in November 1936 Liddell Hart returned to this theme in another *Times* leader: there were, he wrote, greater risks than in 1914 in committing the BEF to the Continent, especially of its being stranded in the depths of France; and it would be wiser therefore to give up the idea of intervening on the Continent with a land force, and make clear to the French that they might get more value from air assistance.[6]

When at the beginning of 1936 the Defence Policy and Requirements

[1] CAB 16/110, DCM(32)41.
[2] Ibid.
[3] Liddell Hart, Vol. I, p. 384, et seq.; also Vol. II, p. 39; Minney, p. 54.
[4] Quoted in Liddell Hart, Vol. I, pp. 296–7.
[5] Ibid. p. 298.
[6] Ibid. pp. 380–1.

Committee began to discuss proposals for large-scale re-armament,[1] Chamberlain argued along the same lines as Liddell Hart in the previous November, suggesting that a strong offensive air force would be a more effective deterrent to a German attack in the west than a field army, and especially a more effective deterrent if Germany attacked elsewhere instead. He recommended that RAF expansion should aim at an 'offensive' rather than a 'defensive' force – in itself an excellent idea.[2] However Chamberlain's views meant that the future of the British army as more than a colonial gendarmerie was much in question – so much so that on 15 January 1936, before the DPRC met, Sir Maurice Hankey wrote a memorandum to Baldwin, the Prime Minister, to plead the necessity of a field army for Europe in terms almost of desperation:

> War can only be averted or won by a combination which includes at least France and Belgium. These states as well as other Continental States are not satisfied that aircraft can defend them against invasion and still look on armies and fortifications as their mainstay. If we have no efficient army they will feel that we do not mean business. Without some aid from us France will collapse; London will be exposed to the worst horrors of aerial bombardment. . . .
>
> In a word, an efficient army, if only a small one, is essential to re-assure our potential allies. . . . Aircraft, in spite of their vast potentialities, have never yet proved a decisive factor even against second-rate forces. . . .[3]

The CIGS himself argued in the DPRC meeting later that day: 'It is vital to our security that France and Belgium should not be defeated on land and a war lost in the first round. For this reason we cannot afford to neglect the provision of a Field Army, attractive as the proposition [of doing without one] may seem from many points of view.'[4]

Such had in fact always been the collective opinion of the Chiefs of Staff Committee. In May 1934 in answer to the specific question of whether a land force was essential for Europe, or whether, as Chamberlain was arguing, air forces would be sufficient, they had replied: 'Refusal on our part to provide direct assistance will inevitably be interpreted by our Allies as equivalent to abandoning them to their fate. . . .'[5]

They had gone on to note how European powers – friendly and otherwise – thought in terms of armies; and therefore it followed that unless

[1] See above p. 415.
[2] CAB 16/123, DPR(DR)2.
[3] Memorandum of 15 January 1936, CAB 21/422.
[4] CAB 16/123, DPR(DR)6.
[5] CAB 16/123, DCM(M)(32)109, Enclosure No. 1 to Annex, 8 May 1934.

England had land forces ready for intervention, European states would consider our power to 'influence a decision by arms inadequate. The influence which this may have on international policy and the cause of peace may be far-reaching in the extreme.'[1]

The struggle in the DPRC in early 1936 over the future of the army ended, thanks to Baldwin's balancing diplomacy, in a compromise or stalemate. The army, despite Chamberlain, would retain its field force role, but not specifically for intervention in Europe. The Defence White Paper of 3 March 1936 laid down the tasks of the army in order of importance as imperial defence, home defence and lastly the provision of a field force for use 'overseas'.

It was a compromise which, being as imprecise as it was, satisfied neither side; it left the army still a poor third in its share of re-armament funds. Chamberlain continued implacably to oppose any suggestion that the army ought to be made ready to fight in a European campaign; and his arguments were to be inspired throughout, directly or indirectly, by the writings of Liddell Hart. In December 1936, when the War Minister, Duff Cooper, argued in a memorandum that in order to supplement the proposed field force of five regular divisions (to be ready in 1939), a reserve of twelve Territorial divisions should be equipped for the field,[2] it drew forth a complete and blistering statement of Chamberlain's strategic views. He claimed that the War Secretary was asking for something completely new – a force of seventeen divisions ready to take the field immediately. It was impossible, he wrote, to create such a force out of our resources because of the competing demands of the navy and the RAF. The RAF and anti-aircraft defences were the first essentials, so as to defend Great Britain against air attacks and counter-attack Germany. Already the strain was showing on British industry; the re-equipment of five regular divisions was as much as it would stand. '. . . to add to that programme any substantial degree of re-equipment of the Territorial Force would only result in the breakdown of the whole scheme.'[3]

And even if resources were not limited, would seventeen divisions be the best investment? The air force, thought Chamberlain, 'might well exercise a preponderating influence' and a small (*sic*) military force not. As to the political aspects: 'No doubt the existence of a substantial British Army strong enough for immediate and effective intervention in Continental disputes . . . would in some respects strengthen our influence on the

[1] Ibid.

[2] Appendix B to Memorandum by the Secretary of State for War, 4 December 1936, CAB 53/29 COS 537.

[3] Appendix C to COS 537, CAB 53/29.

Continent. . . .'[1] But there was a limit to our resources, and in allotting them between the services,

> we should not lose sight of the fact that the political temper of people in this country is strongly opposed to Continental adventures . . . they will be strongly suspicious of any preparation made in peacetime with a view to large-scale military operations on the Continent, and they will regard such preparations as likely to result in our being entangled in disputes which do not concern us.[2]

On 14 December Duff Cooper retorted with another memorandum which argued that the Cabinet *had* sanctioned a field force of seventeen divisions, and forthrightly attacked the Chamberlain–Liddell Hart strategy.

> I would say that the simplest and the gravest emergency which can be envisaged is an attack by Germany on France and Belgium. . . .
>
> If the view is now taken that we should in no circumstances send a land force to take part in a Continental war and that such a possibility no longer existed, the whole of our military policy would, of course, require immediate and fundamental re-adjustment.[3]

Duff Cooper pointed out that he was not even asking for an increase in what he called 'the extraordinary low demands made on the manpower of the nation', which were lower than in the case of any other European nation.[4]

This exchange of memoranda was considered by the Cabinet on 16 December 1936,[5] which decided to ask the Chiefs of Staff for *their* recommendations as to the role of the army.

The discussions in the Chiefs of Staff Committee opened up the fundamental question of the correct balance between army and air force. When the CIGS (Sir Cyril Deverell) argued that it was necessary to have twelve fully equipped Territorial divisions behind the BEF, the Chief of Air Staff (Ellington) replied that there was a danger that concentration on the army would weaken the air force, and repeated the old assertion that the main peril was in the air: 'the effect of an air attack on industrial production would be certainly very serious in a future war'.[6] Ellington continued throughout the discussions to paint a terrifying picture of shattered morale, industrial dislocation and absenteeism. Deverell pointed out that the

[1] Appendix C to COS 537, CAB 53/29.
[2] Ibid.
[3] Appendix D, COS 37, CAB 53/9.
[4] Ibid.
[5] CAB 53/00, 75(36)6.
[6] COS meeting of 12 January 1937, COS 192, CAB 53/6.

present number of divisions contemplated was less than a quarter of the Great War figure. He believed they would never have time to build such huge forces as in that war, 'because he felt that no war in the future would last four years'.[1] Therefore what were needed were ready forces able to defeat a dictator's attempt at a quick decision. Ellington, on the other hand, thought that it was not wise, in the light of the prophecies current in 1914, to count on a short war. The Chief of Naval Staff (Chatfield) expressed awareness that the Chancellor of the Exchequer (Chamberlain) was apprehensive about the creation of a huge continental army again.

In the next COS meeting, on 19 January 1937, Inskip, the Minister for the Co-ordination of Defence, virtually laid down the role of the army on behalf of Chamberlain, saying that the Chancellor was not happy about the economic implications of equipping an army of seventeen divisions. Deverell tried to point out that this was not proposed; but rather the five Regular divisions first, and the Territorial divisions in batches after the outbreak of war. Ellington gave tongue to the underlying but usually unspoken assumption of the Chamberlain–Liddell Hart school of thought by complacently suggesting that 'we might rely on the French army to stop the German army . . .'[2] Deverell reminded the committee that there was still no Treasury sanction for the re-equipment of the regular army. He was, however, against giving a precise mandate to employ the army on the Continent: 'This would result in our becoming tied to the heels of France.'[3] In a later meeting on 22 January he drew attention to the delay in re-equipping the army caused by the failure to decide its role.[4]

The COS reported to the Government on 28 January 1937. To some extent Ellington had been overborne, for the report criticised the opinion that all land forces should be supplied by England's allies, while England restricted herself to sea and airpower, and criticised it especially because of the effect on our allies of such a decision.[5] Thereafter however the COS report only havered: '. . . though it is undesirable that we should accept such a commitment [of a land force for France] in advance . . . We cannot . . . discount the possibility that we may be compelled to despatch land forces to the Continent at some stage in a war. . . .'[6]

As a consequence the field force ready for employment in imperial defence should be equally available for Europe. On the other hand: '. . . we think it right to say that we should greatly deprecate the develop-

[1] Ibid. [2] COS 193, CAB 53/6. [3] Ibid.
[4] COS 194, CAB 53/6.
[5] COS 550, 28 January 1937, in CAB 53/30. [6] Ibid.

ment of such a land campaign, so far as this country is concerned, on the scale experienced in 1914–18 with large national armies'.[1]

Since the circumstances in which war might break out in Europe could not be predicted, 'the decision as to the role of our army may well remain in doubt until the last moment . . .'[2]

Except that no Cabinet sanction was given for the equipment of twelve Territorial Army field divisions, the form of British intervention in support of France and Belgium still lay all in vagueness. When however Chamberlain became Prime Minister in May 1937 he was able to push his strategic ideas even more effectively than as Chancellor. Liddell Hart now became the decisive intellectual influence on British grand strategy. In May 1937 he prepared schemes for the reorganisation of the British army for Sir Thomas Inskip, the Minister for the Co-ordination of Defence, 'with a view primarily to the role of Imperial Defence'.[3] In June he was introduced by Duff Cooper to his successor at the War Office, Leslie Hore-Belisha. It was the commencement of extremely close, though unofficial, collaboration which was to last until July 1938. Liddell Hart played a strategic Jeeves to Hore-Belisha's political Bertie Wooster, laying out the elegant suits of ideas and schemes which Hore-Belisha was to wear later in Cabinet or Committee.[4] Liddell Hart thus not only enjoyed an intellectual influence over Chamberlain himself, but directly participated in the policies of his War Minister. On 29 October 1937 Chamberlain wrote to Hore-Belisha, 'I have been reading in *Europe in Arms* by Liddell Hart. If you have not already done so you might find it interesting to glance at this, especially the chapter on the "Role of the British Army".'[5] Hore-Belisha replied two days later: 'I immediately read the "Role of the British Army" in Liddell Hart's book. I am impressed by his general theories.'[6]

With Liddell Hart drafting schemes for the future employment and appropriate reorganisation of the British army for Hore-Belisha to put up to a Cabinet dominated by Chamberlain, the strategic emphasis swung further and further away from British participation in a decisive land battle in Europe. At the beginning of November 1937, when Chamberlain had himself made it clear that imperial and home defence came first and that no great increase of spending on a field force for Europe was

[1] COS 550, 28 January 1937, in CAB 53/30.
[2] Ibid.
[3] Liddell Hart, Vol. II, p. 3.
[4] See ibid. chs. 1–3; Minney, p. 54 et seq.
[5] Minney, p. 54.
[6] Ibid. In view of his decisive influence over British grand strategy in the Chamberlain era, the reputation that Liddell Hart later acquired of being the man who was not listened to in Britain before the Second World War was not entirely justified.

possible, Hore-Belisha and Liddell Hart drafted a paper on 'The Role of the Army' which pointed out that 'home defence (i.e. anti-aircraft) and empire defence were the primary responsibilities, and that the defence of other people's territory was, in comparison at least, secondary'.[1] On 15 November Hore-Belisha informed Liddell Hart that 'the Cabinet was moving towards the discontinuance of an Expeditionary Force for the Continent'.[2] Next day he told his mentor that the Prime Minister was delighted at the general line taken by his paper on the role of the army; Liddell Hart was now asked for a further contribution on 'The Re-orientation of the Regular Army for Imperial Defence'.[3]

All this was a fulfilment of Liddell Hart's long-argued conviction, which Chamberlain fully shared, that the commitment of a great army to the Continent in the Great War had been a terrible mistake and that historically 'the British way in warfare' was to leave European land battles to allies, and, by means of seapower, employ the British army to fight isolated enemy forces away from the principal front.[4] Yet this was not Liddell Hart's – or Chamberlain's – only contribution to the unpreparedness of the British army in 1938 for operations in Europe. Both men remained obsessed with the aerial danger to the United Kingdom. In Chamberlain's case, the obsession had already led to higher priority within the army's restricted re-armament budget being given to new equipment for the anti-aircraft defence of the United Kingdom than to new equipment for the field force. It was the subject of anti-aircraft guns, not new field and medium artillery, which filled the reports of the War Office to the Defence Policy and Requirements Committee in 1936–7.[5] In 1937 however Liddell Hart strongly advocated that even more resources should be devoted to anti-aircraft defence.[6] His opinion, naturally a congenial one to Chamberlain, prevailed. On 8 November 1937, at a meeting in the Prime Minister's room at the House of Commons, it was decided 'that the Secretary of State for War should be authorised to instruct the War Office that the *provision of anti-aircraft defences is to have absolute priority over all other forms of war material*'.[7]

[1] Liddell Hart's notes at the time, quoted in Liddell Hart, Vol. II, p. 50; for summary of the paper, see pp. 53–4.
[2] Ibid. p. 55.
[3] Ibid. pp. 56–7.
[4] For a historical critique of this strategic conception, see Correlli Barnett, *Britain and Her Army 1509–1970* (London, Allen Lane The Penguin Press 1970), *passim*.
[5] Cf. also Chamberlain's memorandum of December 1936, CAB 53/29, Appendix C to COS 537; see above pp. 499–500.
[6] Cf. Liddell Hart, Vol. II, pp. 6–7, 37, 39, 41, 48, 50.
[7] Also present were the Chancellor of the Exchequer, Sir John Simon; the Foreign Secretary, Anthony Eden; the War Secretary, Leslie Hore-Belisha, and the Minister for the Co-ordination of Defence, Sir Thomas Inskip, CAB 3/7, 271–A.

As a consequence, whereas in March 1937 it had been proposed to spend, over five years, £37 million on anti-aircraft defence and £80 million on the field force, by January 1938 the proportion had been altered to £98 million and £80 million.[1] So it proved that the British obsession with aerial warfare *doubly* enfeebled the British ability to intervene by land in Continental affairs – by cutting the army's overall share of re-armament expenditure to no more than a fifth, on average, over the period 1934–7 inclusive,[2] and then again by drastically cutting the field force's share of even that.

It was in December 1937, at a time when apprehensions about German designs on Austria or Czechoslovakia were fast rising, that the Minister for the Co-ordination of Defence submitted a crucial report on Defence Expenditure in Future Years which carried Chamberlain's and Liddell Hart's strategy of 'limited liability' or isolation from Europe to its ultimate.[3] Having reiterated that the air defence of the United Kingdom was the first priority of British strategy and re-armament, Inskip went on: 'On the basis of the policy now proposed, the Continental hypothesis ranks fourth in order of priority and the primary role of the Regular Army becomes the defence of Imperial commitments, including the anti-aircraft defence of the United Kingdom.'

While he gave as one of the main reasons for this decision the competing demands on industrial manpower and resources, he also believed that

> a number of recent events have occurred which go far to justify this change of policy. Thus it has, I understand, been suggested that France no longer looks to us in the event of war to supply an expeditionary force on the scale hitherto proposed in addition to our all-important co-operation on the sea and in the air.
>
> [Secondly] Germany has guaranteed the inviolability and integrity of Belgian neutrality and there seems good reason for thinking that it would be in Germany's interests to honour this commitment.
>
> [And thirdly there was the empire] . . . external events have conspired to increase the probable demands on our forces in respect of our Imperial commitments overseas, and to render it probable that in a major war they would go far to absorb our military resources.[4]

Here was plain acknowledgement that the empire served not to enhance British power, but to drain her strength away, leaving her virtually impotent in that part of the world whose destiny and her own were in-

[1] Postan, p. 31.
[2] Ibid. p. 28n.
[3] CAB 24/316, CP276(37).
[4] Ibid.

escapably entangled because of geography. Inskip himself recognised that to give priority to the defence of the Empire over that of western Europe was a decision of the most fateful character:

> I must, however, warn my colleagues of the possible consequences of this proposal in order that they may share my responsibility for the decision to be taken with their eyes open. . . . If France were again to be in danger of being overrun by land armies, as in the last war, a situation may arise when, as in the last war, we had to improvise an army to assist her. Should this happen, the Government of the day would most certainly be criticised for having neglected to provide against so obvious a contingency.[1]

Nevertheless, for the reasons he had given, Inskip saw no alternative but to adopt the more limited role for the army recommended in his report. Nor did the Cabinet, which on 16 February approved the reorganisation of the army for its new role, as laid down in a memorandum by the War Secretary.[2] The Cabinet merely altered a reference to the field force being 'equipped for an eastern theatre', which was thought politically undesirable, to being 'equipped for general purposes'. It was decided at the same Cabinet meeting that the French should be informed that henceforward they could not expect more than a total of two divisions.[3]

Thus whereas since 1934 England had pursued a foreign policy of ever more active intervention in the affairs of Europe, her grand strategy – her re-armament and defence policies – had taken the very opposite direction, that of disengagement and defensive isolationism. These contrary policies had both been pursued with far greater vigour since Chamberlain had become Prime Minister. As it happened, the British Government finally washed its hands strategically of Europe on the very eve of the crisis over Czechoslovakia, in which crisis it confidently proposed to play a leading diplomatic role.

The Chiefs of Staff's Report on 'The Military Implications of German Aggression against Czechoslovakia', of 21 March 1938, was by no means limited to a survey of the fighting strength of the British armed forces only.[4] The COS had been asked by the Prime Minister to give general advice on the basis of two alternative courses of action; firstly that Great Britain should concert with France, Czechoslovakia, Yugoslavia,

[1] Ibid.
[2] CAB 23/92, 5(38)11.
[3] CAB 23/92, 5(38)12.
[4] See also pp. 474–5.

Romania, Hungary, Turkey or Greece, or any of them, to resist by force any German aggression against Czechoslovakia; or secondly, that Britain should give assurance to the French that, if France went to war over Czechoslovakia, Britain would support her. The COS were instructed to assume that Italy would be hostile or neutral; that there was a risk of Japan being hostile; and that Russia, Poland and the United States of America were to be taken as neutral.

The COS's account of the present state of the French forces showed how far France's military power had declined since 1936. The French, they estimated, could mobilise fifty-three divisions, though only at the cost of industry and agriculture; 'she could not hope to keep this number of divisions in the field',[1] but only thirty. At present however the French armaments industry was seriously disorganised, and the COS doubted whether the output of shells was adequate, while there were reports of deficiencies in the reserve stocks. The French field artillery was 'greatly outranged' by the German. On the other hand, there were enough anti-aircraft guns and searchlights for the defence of important areas, and 'the French frontier fortifications would prove of great value in defence'.[2] The French metropolitan air force consisted of 297 fighters and 456 bombers, half of which were short-range, together with some 248 army-co-operation and general-purpose aircraft which could be used in a general counter-offensive. With an output of fewer than 100 aircraft a month, the state of the French aircraft industry was 'deplorable'. The reserves were obsolescent and the factories vulnerable to air attack because of their location. There were indications that the fighting value of the French air force was 'not of a high standard'.[3] And the French navy, although it would enhance the British superiority at sea, would not provide a remedy to the deficiencies in the Royal Navy.

The Czechoslovakian army, according to the COS, was of a peacetime strength of seventeen infantry and four cavalry divisions 'with adequate reserves well-equipped'. The front-line strength of the Czech air force was approximately 400 aircraft – 64 bombers, 156 fighters and 180 reconnaissance aircraft, all trained to work with the army. However, by occupying Austria, the Germans had turned the Czech field defences, for there were no fortifications along the Czech–Austrian frontier except for a fortified bridgehead at Bratislava. And since 75 per cent of Czech trade by weight passed over German territory, the occupation of Austria would enable Germany to strangle Czechoslovakia economically.

When the COS turned to Germany their tone changed noticeably, for

[1] CAB 27/627, FP(36)57, COS 698. [2] Ibid. [3] Ibid.

whereas they had been at pains to bring out the weaknesses of England, France and Czechoslovakia, they were equally at pains to look for, and emphasise, the strengths of Germany's position. While the German navy was only large enough to secure command of the Baltic, the three 'Deutschlands' (the fast 10,000-ton, 11-inch-gun 'pocket battleships') represented a serious potential danger to our trade routes. By the end of March, the German air force would enjoy a front-line strength of 2,860 aircraft – 1,570 bombers and dive-bombers, 540 fighters, 270 army-co-operation aircraft, 210 aircraft for coastal defence, and 270 for reconnaissance. Behind the first line were 100 per cent reserves, and an aircraft industry with great future powers of producing airframes and engines; an industry which could make good a 50 per cent wastage per month by the second month of war.

The COS attributed a superiority to Germany on land as well. They put the total strength of the German Reich army (*sic* – i.e. now including the former Austrian army) at 90 divisions, of which 57 were fit for the field: 30 active infantry divisions (6 of them motorised), 3 active armoured divisions, 18 reserve divisions, 24 *Landwehr* and 4 Austrian divisions. After three months of war, German industry would be capable of maintaining 70 divisions in the field.

According to the COS estimates, therefore, England, France and Czechoslovakia would oppose 2,209 aircraft (but many of them obsolete) to 2,860 German. In bombers, with only 940 to 1,570, they were particularly inferior. Only in fighters, a purely defensive weapon, did they enjoy a combined superiority of 831 to 540. On land they could mobilise 76 divisions to the German 90, although it should be noted that the COS only gave the Czech army's peacetime strength.

The Chiefs of Staff's examination of possible courses of action open to the 'allies' and Germany was no more cheering than their comparison of forces. They assumed that Germany would take advantage of engineered internal risings in Czechoslovakia to invade her, in which case, because of the shape of the country and the German occupation of Austria, the Czech defences could be turned from the south. While the COS had to acknowledge that the Czech–Austrian frontier was 'close and hilly' except for an open area just east of Vienna, they took it that Germany would be able to occupy Bohemia and the sites of the Czech armaments industry before allied action could take any effect. What then could the allies do?

Naval action was little use, because unless Germany 'considered that the intervention of Great Britain would necessarily involve her in a long war she might be inclined to disregard the threat of economic pressure' through seapower.[1] As for action by land, it was geographically impossible directly to aid Czechoslovakia. An offensive in the west would run into strong German defences. Since French military doctrine was defensive, a French attack into open country was unlikely. The British field force was useless for offensive operations. Even in the air it would be impossible to aid the Czechs directly because of the distance. An air attack on German targets was open to the objection that the allies would not care to bomb the kind of target not yet bombed by Germany. In any case British air attacks would be carried out less to help the Czechs than to try to reduce the scale of German attacks on Great Britain. Since the Germans' anti-aircraft defences were better and their bomb-lift an estimated 1,825 tons compared with the Allies' 575 tons, the COS concluded that 'at the best we cannot anticipate that the Franco-British air force would have a great deterrent effect'.[2]

While the COS were of the opinion that there was virtually nothing militarily effective, direct or indirect, that the allies could do to help Czechoslovakia, they saw Germany as being able to take not only direct but highly effective action against England if England should go to war in aid of the Czechs. They considered that the strength of the French army and of the Maginot line might deter a direct German offensive against the French, in favour of an attack on the British, as in March 1918, except that in the present case the offensive would come in the form of – the COS repeated the favourite phrase – a 'knock-out blow' from the air. In such circumstances, England could look forward to receiving regular deliveries of 400 tons of bombs a day. The COS went on:

> The crux of the situation, in our view, is whether this would be a knock-out blow. The Germans in their present state could not keep it up indefinitely, and it seems unlikely that they would take on a ruthless attack on London or other centres of population . . . unless they were satisfied that they had a reasonable chance of success.
>
> The outcome of an unrestricted air attack on this country by Germany is impossible to forecast with any accuracy. All we can say is that we are not in a position to prevent them dropping bombs in this country on the scale suggested above, which we think they might be able to sustain for not less than two months.[3]

There was also Italy to think about, and the effects of possible Italian hostility on the strategic situation in the Mediterranean and Middle East; Japan too: 'The advent of Japan on the side of our enemies, Germany and

[1] CAB 27/627, FP(36)57, COS 698. [2] Ibid. [3] Ibid.

Italy, would produce a situation which neither the present nor projected strength of our defence forces is designed to meet.'[1]

The British fleet, with three out of fifteen capital ships under reconstruction, would have to be divided between home waters and the Far East, leading to the abandonment of the Eastern Mediterreanean, a circumstance which would render critical the British position in Egypt, Palestine and the rest of the Middle East. It was hardly surprising that the COS were led to remark: 'It is not possible to envisage, without the deepest misgivings, the military implications of a situation arising in which the British Empire became engaged in war with Germany, Italy and Japan, and with France as our only major ally.'[2]

The Chiefs of Staff saw the only hope therefore in deterring Germany rather than fighting. A concerted undertaking by France, Great Britain and central European powers to resist by force any German aggression against Czechoslovakia 'might have a psychological effect on Germany'.[3]

> A pronouncement by Great Britain that she would fight for the maintenance of Czechoslovakian integrity would change the issue for Germany from a *coup* executed with overwhelming force to the possibility of a long war, in which they might reckon that the staying power of the British Empire might eventually prevail. This consideration would be bound to have a deterrent effect on Germany's decision. . . .
>
> [That was, unless she considered that] public opinion in Great Britain was not unanimously behind the Government and that she had, in the present inadequate state of our defences, of which she must be fully aware, a good chance of dealing a knock-out blow on Great Britain, in which case our undertaking would lose almost all its deterrent value.[4]

The Chiefs of Staff felt it necessary to repeat in their final summing-up: 'The deterrent effect of Great Britain and France opposing German aspirations in Central Europe would depend on the degree of Germany's expectations that she could obtain a knock-out blow against this country by the ruthless use of the German air-striking force.'[5]

And their coda brought to a climax the general theme of the work; the theme of 'we are not yet ready for war'.[6]

It was a lugubrious report, providing apparently incontrovertible expert backing for the policy the inner Cabinet had already decided to pursue; providing also a future reference work with which to confound any Cabinet member who might have the hardihood to question the Prime Minister's wisdom. It therefore merits critical examination.

[1] Ibid. [2] Ibid. [3] Ibid. [4] Ibid. [5] Ibid. [6] Ibid.

In the first place, the Chiefs of Staff were not asked by Chamberlain – whether deliberately or whether because he did not think of it – the one fundamental strategic question which needed to be answered, and that was: what would be the effect on the whole strategic balance in Europe of the successful achievement of German domination over Czechoslovakia? Not being asked the question, the Chiefs of Staff nowhere in their long report answered it. Chamberlain's omission was the more regrettable since by 18 March 1938 his Foreign Secretary, Halifax, had placed his initials on a Foreign Office memorandum which indeed foresaw that present events marked the beginnings of German hegemony over central Europe.[1]

Secondly, there was the harping in the COS report on the possibility of the 'knock-out blow' against British cities, which so effectively probed a sensitive area of the Cabinet's collective imagination. This harping was a manifestation of that constant British tendency to emphasise air power to the neglect of the likelihood and implications of a great conventional land battle, and to think of war as a kind of lone duel between Britain and Germany, to which the French and other possible allies were largely irrelevant. Since Germany was a land-power surrounded by other land-powers, and since expansion of the German army was the centrepiece of German re-armament, this emphasis was less than objective. In any event, the COS seemed in considerable doubt as to whether the German air force was at present really capable of inflicting a 'knock-out blow'; doubt which the politicians chose to ignore. And the COS themselves contradicted their prophecy that the entire German air-striking force might attack Britain, by writing in another part of their report that 'Germany might in the first instance employ her own bombing force in support of her operations against Czechoslovakia'[2] – which was indeed much more likely.

At the same time the balance-sheet drawn by the Chiefs of Staff of the relative strengths on land of the 'allies' and Germany was also unbalanced, savouring allied weaknesses and German strengths, and playing up both. Whereas they believed the German field fortifications in the west to be 'strong', it was the opinion of General Gamelin, the French Commander-in-Chief, that they were weak and unfinished – an estimate now known to have been correct.[3] Whereas they put the German army's strength on mobilisation as 57 field divisions, the Czech army (in peacetime) at 17, and the French (on mobilisation) at 53, General Gamelin was to tell Chamberlain in September 1938 that there were 34 Czech divisions facing an equal

[1] CAB 27/622, Appendix I to FP(36)26. [2] Ibid. [3] CAB 23/95, 45(38).

number of German, while in the west France was then opposing 23 divisions to 8 German.[1] Indeed the estimates the COS themselves were to give of comparative army strengths in September 1938 were markedly at variance with their March figures. In September they put the Czech army at a peacetime strength of 21 divisions and double that on mobilisation, and the German forces, then on the Czech frontier, at 27 divisions, with 2 more moving up and 7 in reserve. A map attached to this September report shows an estimated German strength in the west of only 14 divisions.[2]

Taken as a whole therefore the March 1938 COS Report was excessively pessimistic; and particularly unbalanced in its emphasis on air-power and the imagined danger to the United Kingdom, and in its corresponding neglect of Germany's lack of superiority on land. Curiously enough, the Commander-in-Chief of the German army, General Beck, was to submit two memoranda to the Chief of the Armed Forces General Staff in May 1938 in the exactly opposite sense, dwelling on Germany's military weaknesses and her unreadiness for war over Czechoslovakia, and describing the superior potential strength of the allies, which must spell Germany's ultimate defeat.[3] But whereas Hitler, if he ever saw Beck's memoranda, ignored his gloomy analysis, and gambled that even if the German armed forces were not yet fit to wage a great war, they were at least powerful enough to break his opponents' nerve, Chamberlain and his friends drank in the British Chiefs of Staff's pessimism; their fears, thus confirmed, ruling out any thought on their part of trying to bend Hitler's nerve, as the COS had suggested as the only possible course of action at all likely to be effective.

How decisive was the support to Chamberlain and his closest colleagues afforded by the 21 March 1938 COS report was to be demonstrated immediately.

On the very day the report was submitted, the Cabinet Foreign Policy Committee again discussed whether or not to offer France a further guarantee of support over Czechoslovakia, a course once more advocated by Oliver Stanley, the President of the Board of Trade, because he thought such a guarantee might restrain German adventurousness. But Halifax replied that it seemed to him that

> the President of the Board of Trade did not attach sufficient weight to the very grave considerations contained in the Report of the Chiefs of

[1] As reported by the Prime Minister to the Cabinet on 26 September 1938, CAB 23/95, 45(38).

[2] COS Report on situation if there was a war with Germany, 14 September 1938, CAB 53/41, COS 765.

[3] Quoted in O'Neill, pp. 152–7.

> Staff. That Report showed conclusively that it was hopeless to prevent Germany overwhelming Czecho-Slovakia [sic] by violence if she chose to do so, and it accordingly behoved us to take every step that we could and use every argument that we could think of to dissuade France from going to the aid of Czecho-Slovakia.[1]

In the full Cabinet on the following day, when it met to consider the COS Report and reach a final and formal decision as to the line to be taken over Czechoslovakia, Halifax outlined two possible policies. The first was to guarantee Czechoslovakia, and guarantee support to France if she carried out her treaty obligations to that country. But in view of the COS report ('an extremely melancholy document'), he felt 'he was not in a position to recommend a policy involving the risk of war'.[2] Turning therefore to his second, and preferred, alternative, Halifax recommended that 'we should endeavour to induce the Government of Czecho-Slovakia to apply themselves to producing a direct settlement with the Sudeten-Deutsch'.[3] We should persuade the French to use their influence in Prague. Halifax explained, however, that the settlement he contemplated was one between the Czechs and the Sudeten-Deutsch, not Germany.

Chamberlain too, in a long speech, dwelt on the implications of military weakness and the consequent need to make a deal, since it was impossible to prevent the Czechs from being overrun.

Nevertheless, some members of the Cabinet[4] argued that the proposed policy was too weak. More than this, they brought up that fundamental question of grand strategy neither touched on by Chamberlain, nor discussed by the COS in their report, by arguing that it would be better to fight now than later, when Germany had conquered all Europe. They indeed pointed out that the COS had not dealt with the possible situation in a year or two's time.

Gradually however the Cabinet came to accept the line taken by the Prime Minister and Foreign Secretary that the Czechs could not be helped. It was argued that once Czechoslovakia had fallen, France would be stuck behind the Maginot Line, while it would be two months before England could send effective help. There was also the habitual over-emphasis on aerial warfare: 'The Germans, owing to the strength of their Air Force, could damage us more than we could damage them ... Meanwhile the people of this country would have been in a position of being subjected to constant bombing, a responsibility no Government ought to take.'[5]

[1] CAB 27/623, FP(36)27.
[2] CAB 23/93, 15(38)1, 22 March 1938.
[3] Ibid.
[4] Not identified in the record.
[5] Ibid.

Then again: 'In regard to the position two years hence, the Cabinet were reminded that the Royal Air Force at any rate would be armed with up-to-date aeroplanes and the anti-aircraft defences with modern weapons.'[1] And so: 'In all the above circumstances it was generally felt that any policy of bluff would be dangerous. . . .'[2]

The Cabinet therefore agreed that, as Chamberlain and Halifax recommended, Britain should attempt to de-fuse the Czechoslovakian question before it could explode into an international crisis, by pressing the Czechs into remedying the Sudeten-Germans' grievances in good time.

Unless this policy was nothing but the dismal expedient of apparent weakness and consequently of funk (for which the discussions in Cabinet and the Cabinet Foreign Policy Committee indeed provide strong evidence), it necessarily assumed that what was at issue were Sudeten-German grievances against the Czechoslovak state, not German designs against Czechoslovakia's independence or territorial integrity. It necessarily assumed therefore that, once the Sudeten-Germans were accorded full civic rights, they would happily settle down as Czechoslovak citizens; whereupon the present tension in central Europe would relax. Furthermore, it necessarily assumed that Hitler himself would be satisfied with such a solution; that there really was a limit both to his ambitions and to his willingness to promote them by threats or force.

What is by no means clear however is whether the British inner Cabinet really made any of these assumptions. Halifax certainly expressed himself confident that, in his own words, Hitler did not entertain a lust for conquest on a Napoleonic scale.[3] Chamberlain too told the Cabinet Foreign Policy Committee at the same time that he thought the seizure of the whole of Czechoslovakia would not be in accordance with Hitler's policy; and that a settlement along the lines of Sudeten autonomy was worth exploring.[4] He had also said at earlier meetings that the German occupation of Austria, far from causing the Government to alter its line of policy, only confirmed, in his opinion, that it was the right one.[5] Yet two days before this Chamberlain had written in his private diary: '. . . it is perfectly evident, surely, now that force is the only argument Germany understands, and that collective security cannot offer any prospect of preventing such events, until it can show a visible force of overwhelming strength backed by determination to use it . . .'[6] But then again, he also wrote further down in the same entry in his diary: 'If we can avoid

[1] Ibid.
[2] Ibid.
[3] Meeting of the Cabinet Committee on Foreign Policy, 18 March 1938, CAB 27/623, FP(36)26; see above p. 474.
[4] Ibid.
[5] Meeting of 15 March, CAB 27/623, FP(36)25.
[6] Quoted in Feiling, p. 342.

another violent *coup* against Czechoslovakia, which ought to be feasible, it may be possible for Europe to settle down again, and some day for us to start peace talks again with the Germans.'[1]

The truth was that Chamberlain's diagnosis of Nazi Germany and its intentions was not constant and consistent; that behind his policy lay not a single, simple motive, but several interwoven motives, partly idealistic, partly expedient, partly inspired by hope and partly by fear; and sometimes one element and sometimes another came to the fore.

None the less, in the spring of 1938 Chamberlain and his Cabinet embarked on the same kind of futile Utopian quest for a 'just' solution as had been pursued over Manchuria and Abyssinia, to say nothing of over Germany herself in the past. They again adopted the posture of the honest broker who was interested only to see fair play done and the disputants reconciled. From the evidence, it does not seem ever to have occurred to them that the Sudeten grievances were simply a pretext: tactical ground or a tactical gambit in a struggle for Europe. Lacking the advantage of such cynical mistrust, Chamberlain and his closest colleagues utterly mistook the nature of the business into which they were venturing.

Yet the belief that the Czechoslovakian problem was a moral rather than a strategic one was not peculiar to the Cabinet: ambassadors (Henderson in Berlin, Sir Eric Newton in Prague) shared it; so did *The Times*, the *Observer*, the *News Chronicle* and the *New Statesman*.[2] The liberal-minded intelligentsia, spurred by their fear of war, were quick to see and sympathise with the Sudeten-Germans' point of view, and, adopting like the Government, a posture of high-minded concern for 'fairness', were at pains to persuade the nation of the justice of the Sudeten-German case, believing this to be of relevance to the issue.[3]

The French Government, for their part, took the same view as their predecessors the previous November.[4] When the French Prime Minister, Daladier, visited London on 28 April and 29 April with Bonnet, his Foreign Minister, he advanced that simple and obvious truth about German intentions to which Chamberlain and Halifax were so blind: 'I am myself convinced that Herr Henlein [the Sudeten-German leader] is not in fact seeking any concessions, and that his real object is the destruction of the present Czechoslovak state. We are confronted by German policy designed to tear up treaties and destroy the equilibrium of Europe.'[5]

However – again as in November 1937 – clear perception of the truth

[1] Quoted in Feiling, p. 342.
[2] See *The History of The Times*, Pt. III, pp. 913–50.
[3] See Gannon, pp. 16–19 and Pt. 4.
[4] See above pp. 468–70.
[5] *Documents on British Foreign Policy* (London, HMSO 1949), Third Series, Vol. 1, No. 217.

failed to lead the French to an appropriately resolute policy. They were too conscious of their political weakness, of the loss of the overwhelming military superiority France had enjoyed even as late as 1936, of the bitter disunity of French society and of the strength of pacifistic feeling among the French people.

When the British refused their request for an agreement to stand by Czechoslovakia if Hitler moved against her, the French ministers tamely yielded up the diplomatic leadership to Chamberlain, just like their predecessors in 1937, hoping that somehow or other they might thereby escape having to fulfil their treaty obligations to the Czechs. Chamberlain was now free to play a diplomatic role of such pre-eminence as his brother had never enjoyed – as indeed even Palmerston or Castlereagh had never enjoyed. For the destiny of Europe lay between him and one other man.

The British and the French began to apply their persuasion in Prague. It was timely, because in the Sudetenland riots and processions and clamorous utterings of alleged wrongs and consequent demands had been under way since the end of March, the tempo being gradually worked up by Henlein, leader of the Sudeten Party. He had been given his general instructions by Hitler on 28 March, which were, in Henlein's words: 'We must always demand so much that we can never be satisfied.'[1] On 24 April Henlein, at a party congress at Carlsbad, made a fresh demand – self-government for the Sudetenland, which meant virtual independence from the central Czechoslovakian Government. Since Czechoslovakia comprised other national minorities as well – Slovaks, Poles and Hungarians – Henlein's demand, if granted, would lead inevitably to the break-up of the Czechoslovak state.

Germany herself screwed up the general tension by anti-Czech propaganda of mounting violence and by veiled threats to use force if the Czechs failed to be 'reasonable'. In May rumours of German military concentrations thickened the atmosphere of menace, and lent a sharper urgency to British efforts to persuade Czechoslovakia to make radical concessions to the Sudetens. Already British policy was subtly changing its character, from a search for a just and peaceful solution into a yielding under psychological pressure. On 20 May the Czechs, fearing an early German stroke, wrongly as it turned out, mobilised their forces and moved them towards their frontiers.

On 25 May the British Cabinet agreed to authorise staff talks with the French, though only between relatively junior officers. The British

[1] A. J. P. Taylor, *The Origins of the Second World War* (Harmondsworth, Penguin Books 1963), p. 192.

representatives were instructed not to agree to any French suggestion of contacts between seniors. There was to be no commitment in advance to send troops to France.[1] On 31 May the Chiefs of Staff reviewed plans for an emergency.[2]

The French were terrified that their ally, Czechoslovakia, might drag them into war at any time by some ill-considered and provocative action. Chamberlain, according to his diary, believed that Germany had intended to march, but had been deterred by the risks. He wrote that 'the incident shows how utterly untrustworthy and dishonest the German Government is . . .'[3] Both France and Britain redoubled their pressure on Prague to give way to the Sudetens. As June and July passed, Hitler screwed the tension tighter and tighter still, exercising the initiative in his customary fashion, so that his opponents obligingly ran about to do his business for him. On 25 July, at a gymnastic festival in Berlin, Henlein, the Sudeten leader, made a fresh claim, which held disturbing implications: 'We are and remain German national citizens serving voluntarily under the laws of the German nation. We have become one people, a community of all Germans throughout the world.'[4]

On 31 July 40,000 Sudetens in Germany marched past Hitler. With a charmingly spontaneous gesture, women and children broke ranks to lay flowers at Hitler's feet and scream: 'Führer, help us! Take us home to the Reich!'[5]

Along the German side of the Franco-German frontier work was pushed on day and night on a zone of field fortifications; only one of the ominous signs of military bustle apparent inside Germany. The British and French governments grew yet more fearful. Yet Chamberlain, despite the reference in his diary in May to the utter untrustworthiness of the German Government, still acted as if the crisis were a matter of a genuine dispute between the Czechs and the Sudetens. At the end of July he pressed on the Czech Government the services of an impartial British arbitrator, who would investigate Sudeten grievances and make recommendations for a settlement. For this fantasy role he chose Lord Runciman. Runciman was an elderly North-Country millionaire ship-owner, a teetotaller, a non-conformist, 'a gentle fellow',[6] and one of those members of the Liberal Party who had opposed going to war in 1914. Like Chamberlain and Halifax, like Simon, like Inskip, he was an exemplar of Victorian virtues

[1] CAB 53/39, COS 790, quoting Cabinet decision 26(38)4.
[2] CAB 53/39, COS 733.
[3] Feiling, p. 354.
[4] Keith Eubank, *Munich* (Oklahoma, University of Oklahoma Press 1963), p. 77.
[5] Ibid. p. 78.
[6] Hore-Belisha's diary, 25 February 1939, quoted in Minney, p. 138.

to the tips of his wing-collars, a man selected for this mission because of, in Chamberlain's own words, his 'fearlessness, freedom from prejudice, integrity and impartiality'.

Runciman went to Czechoslovakia at the beginning of August, and was instantly subjected to ceaseless Sudeten-German propaganda – 'spontaneous' demonstrations, faked statistics, carefully planned tours of the Sudetenland, agreeable hospitality. Runciman responded to this elaborate and unscrupulous public-relations operation with credulous trust, his sympathy being quickly enlisted for the 'plight' of the Sudetens. But before he could complete his mission and make his report, the British Cabinet had at last had to acknowledge that the Czechoslovakian question was more than a matter of righting Sudeten wrongs; more than just a domestic dispute between the Sudetens and the Czech Government; that it was in fact a question of the territorial integrity of Czechoslovakia. They had come to fear that Hitler might soon send the German army into the Sudetenland, and thereby provoke a general European war.

On 30 August 1938, during the summer recess, there was a meeting of ministers at Downing Street to discuss what to do. Halifax offered two interpretations of the situation. One was that Hitler, against the advice of the German army, was determined to intervene by force; there was plenty of evidence for this. The second was that Hitler had not made up his mind, although he was determined to have everything ready; that he was relying on a 'mixture of bluff and reliance on force'.[1] If the first interpretation were true, then, in Halifax's opinion, the only effective deterrent 'would be an announcement that if Germany invaded Czechoslovakia we should declare war upon her. He thought that this might well prove an effective deterrent.'[2] But the results of such a declaration might be to split British public opinion. And if the deterrent failed, Czechoslovakia could not be saved. Even after a general war it was unlikely that Czechoslovakia could be reconstituted as now. 'It might, therefore, be said that there was not much use in fighting a war for an object which we could not secure.'[3]

However, Czechoslovakia was not all; we were in effect, Halifax went on, 'concerned with an attempt of the dictator countries to attain their ends by force. But he asked himself whether it was justifiable to fight a certain war now in order to forestall a possible war later.'[4]

This indeed was one of the fundamental questions; but having stated it, Halifax shied away from investigating it more deeply. He thought that an invasion of France by Germany would be a different matter. Then again, if Germany were to absorb part of Czechoslovakia it would bring

[1] CAB 23/94. [2] Ibid. [3] Ibid. [4] Ibid.

world opinion against her – the United States, for example. Therefore it was Halifax's opinion that, on the assumption that Hitler had not made up his mind, 'we should try to keep Herr Hitler guessing'.[1] Halifax referred to the many moderate Germans who were pressing us to go further, because they believed it would stop the attempt to coerce the Czechs, at which 'the Hitler régime would crack'. He said that he received these messages 'with some reserve'.

This muffled speech, clogged with caution and qualification, warmed the meeting up for Chamberlain, who stated that a decision must be reached at the present meeting as to how far we were prepared to go. He acknowledged that 'many people in this country and in Germany took the view that if we made it clear now that, if Germany used force, we should come in on the side of Czechoslovakia, there would be no war. . . .'[2]

They also took the view, according to Chamberlain, that a revolution to topple Hitler would then follow; and he quoted a letter from Robert Boothby MP on the opinions communicated to him by German industrialists. None the less, the Prime Minister still agreed with Halifax: 'No State, certainly no democratic state, ought to make a threat of war unless it was both ready to carry it out and prepared to do so.'[3]

If Hitler took the view, Chamberlain went on, that the British statement was a bluff, 'we should then have to choose between being shown up as bluffers and going to war'.[4]

He thought that the strategic situation was even worse than in May. There was also the question of public opinion in Britain. And what line would be taken by South Africa? 'The policy of an immediate declaration or threat might well result in disunity in this country, and in the Empire.'[5]

The other gentlemen who made up the inner circle of the Cabinet hastened to support the Prime Minister and the Foreign Secretary. Simon, the Chancellor of the Exchequer, pronounced himself in favour of continued appeasement. Hoare, the Home Secretary, drew attention to the dangers of the empire breaking up because of differences over Czechoslovakia. He thought we should hesitate before accepting that, if France were at war with Germany, we were inevitably bound to go to her assistance. He was against making a declaration that we would fight if the Czechs were attacked. Inskip, Minister for the Co-ordination of Defence, agreed with the Foreign Secretary, said that Britain was not ready for war, and drew the meeting's attention to an interesting circumstance which had apparently just dawned on him; to wit, that for four years British foreign policy and grand strategy had been moving apart in opposite directions:

[1] CAB 23/94. [2] Ibid. [3] Ibid. [4] Ibid. [5] Ibid.

'There was a further point, that we had based our re-armament programme on what was necessary for our own defences. We had concentrated on the navy and the air. We could not put an army into the field large enough to have any decisive effect for many months. . . .'

The rest of the Cabinet now had their say. Since Malcolm MacDonald, the Colonial Secretary, had supported a policy which avoided a showdown with Mackenzie King, it is not surprising to find him now supporting his seniors in the avoidance of a showdown with Adolf Hitler. He thought the Foreign Secretary's statement exactly expressed the opinion of the great majority in the country. Though Australia and New Zealand would follow England into war, it was rather doubtful if the other dominions would in the present case. In any event, he did not believe that a British threat would effectively prevent Hitler going to war.

Duff Cooper, the First Lord of the Admiralty, tried to back oars against this tide of pusillanimity. He thought that a successful *coup* in Czechoslovakia would enormously strengthen Germany. He believed that the Czechs would fight well. He advocated that the Fleet should go to the North Sea for manœuvres not in fourteen days as now planned, but four or five days earlier, and that the crews should be brought to war strength. The resolute effort of all this was somewhat marred when he added that 'he put these measures forward somewhat tentatively . . .'[1]

The Secretary of State for Air, Sir Kingsley Wood, disagreed with the belligerent ideas of the First Lord, and prodded the Cabinet's tender spot: 'Any attempts to bomb Germany would bring down a terrible retaliation on this country and he would look with great misapprehension at the prospect of war at the present time.'[2]

In his view, a declaration that we should declare war if Germany marched into Czechoslovakia 'would divide the people of this country and in a few weeks' time there would be a majority against such a policy'. He therefore favoured trying to reach a settlement.

Hore-Belisha, the War Secretary, like Chamberlain and others, sought refuge in the sanctions of public opinion, ignoring, again like them, the fact that the Government had an overall majority in the House of Commons of 281, and need not go to the country until 1940. He thought that 'a threat of war could only be made if there was an overwhelming public demand first. Such a demand did not exist.' There was no way of preventing the Sudetens joining their compatriots.

Lord De La Warr, the Lord President of the Council, was also against making a declaration on Czechoslovakia's behalf, on similar grounds that

[1] Ibid. [2] Ibid.

the country would not be behind it. However, unlike senior ministers, he did emphasise the importance of Czechoslovakia in the general European situation, and the effects of her 'crumpling up'. Somewhat ambiguously, he pronounced in favour of a policy of moderate action, combined with a show of resolute strength.

Apart from Duff Cooper, only the President of the Board of Trade, Oliver Stanley, showed a grasp of the strategic realities. It was he who alone had argued in March in favour of guaranteeing both France and Czechoslovakia. Now he said that if Germany attacked Czechoslovakia, and France became involved, then England should fight. He referred to the known doubts of the German generals about Germany's readiness for war,[1] and said: 'In a year or so Germany would be in an immeasurably stronger position for fighting a long war than at the present time.'

Therefore, while we should try for a peaceful settlement, we should not try to stop France going to war if there was aggression by Germany. Earl Winterton, the Chancellor of the Duchy of Lancaster, for his part, supported the immediate proposals of the Foreign Secretary, while finding himself in general agreement with Oliver Stanley's views.

The Prime Minister summed up: 'The Cabinet was unanimous in the view that we should not utter a threat to Herr Hitler, that if he went into Czechoslovakia we should declare war on him. It was of the utmost importance that the decision be kept secret.'

No decision, Chamberlain continued, would be taken now as to what should be done if Germany should attack Czechoslovakia. There should be no 'pin-pricks' to Germany in regard to our naval manœuvres, because he 'thought it very important not to exacerbate feeling in Berlin against us'.

So this crucially important meeting, having dwelt with satisfaction on all the risks and drawbacks attendant upon being resolute, and having neglected almost entirely the less congenial topic of the possible weaknesses in Germany's own position, finally decided on doing nothing more positive than 'trying to keep Hitler guessing'.

However, whereas the British Government were being so careful not to exacerbate feelings in Berlin, they had no such tenderness about feelings in Prague. Since April they had become more and more Palmerstonian in their bullying of the unfortunate Czechs, aided and abetted by the French

[1] See Cabinet meeting of 1 June 1938, which considered the report of Mr Strang of the Foreign Office on his tour of Prague, Berlin and Paris. Halifax summarised Strang's impressions in Berlin as follows: 'The German Army had advised on the side of prudence, for the reason that they were not yet ready for a European war. Mr Strang said that the Germans were not so conscious of our weaknesses as we ourselves, and they were more concerned with their own weaknesses.' CAB 23/93, 27(38)2.

Government in their own rising fear of war. There were threats of abandoning Czechoslovakia to her fate unless she was 'reasonable'. On 4 September President Benes at last gave way to months of pressure. He met the Sudeten leaders, asked them to write down their full demands, then signed beneath to signify his complete acceptance. It was an astute manœuvre, because, unless the crisis now instantly evaporated, the Sudeten demands must be exposed as mere pretexts to cover the intended destruction of Czechoslovakia. At the same time, by making all the concessions demanded of him by Britain and France, he placed these countries under a moral obligation to defend Czechoslovakia against further encroachment. Three days later however an outbreak of violence between Czechs and Sudetens in the Sudeten town of Mayrisch-Ostrau gave the Sudeten leaders a heaven-sent opportunity to break off negotiations in a huff and so escape from the predicament in which Benes had placed them. A march by the German army into the Sudetenland now seemed very near. Chamberlain wrote to his sister: 'Is it not horrible to think that the fate of hundreds of millions depends on one man, and he is half mad? I keep wracking my brains to try to devise some means of averting the catastrophe.'[1]

On 9 September the French cancelled army-leave and called up reservists; the British called up reserve crews for minesweepers and mine-layers. On 11 September violent rioting boiled throughout the Sudetenland. On 12 September the British Foreign Secretary expressed to the Cabinet sentiments similar to those confided by Chamberlain to his sister: 'Herr Hitler', said Halifax, 'was possibly or even probably mad.' For this reason Halifax was still against issuing any ultimatum to Germany, because of the danger of 'driving Hitler over the edge'.[2] Chamberlain passed on the information that Anthony Eden concurred in this view that a declaration was more likely to drive Hitler into action than otherwise. Lord Maugham, the Lord Chancellor, and later to be a notable apologist for the policies of Chamberlain's Government,[3] wondered whether there was a possibility of France agreeing to Britain remaining neutral at the beginning; a suggestion remarkable even for a member of that Cabinet.

This was a fateful Cabinet meeting, for it marked the last time serious consideration was given to preserving Czechoslovakia's present territorial integrity by threatening Germany with a general war if she marched. Yet the evidence suggests it was at least possible that Hitler would have been deterred in the event by a blunt and resolute English ultimatum.

Hitler himself, although he had ordered the German armed forces to

[1] Feiling. p. 357.    [2] CAB 23/95, 37(38).    [3] See Maugham, *passim.*

be ready to advance on 1 October, had not irrevocably committed himself to attacking Czechoslovakia, either in his directives or his public speeches. Good tactician that he was, he used the initiative, the moral domination which he had long since won, to pluck his opponents' nerves with undefined threats of violence while preserving his own freedom of political manœuvre.

The leaders of the German army – as the English Government well knew at the time[1] – were utterly opposed to risking a general war over Czechoslovakia, recognising as they did that Germany's present strength offered her no hope of victory.[2] In July Brauchitsch, the Chief of the Armed Forces General Staff, had convened a conference of senior generals to consider the dangers of a general conflict. The conference agreed that the mood of the German people and the troops was against war. They were also of one mind that while the standard of training and equipment of the army would probably suffice to defeat Czechoslovakia, it would not suffice for a struggle with the powers of Europe.[3]

Brauchitsch conveyed the opinion of this conference to Hitler, who, on 15 August, met his mutinous generals and assured them that as long as Chamberlain and Daladier were still in power, there would be no European war over Czechoslovakia.[4] The generals' misgivings were not stilled. On 27 August Beck, having failed to convince Hitler, resigned. In late August and early September other generals turned to plotting to overthrow Hitler if he should give the order to attack Czechoslovakia.[5] Brauchitsch and Halder, who had succeeded Beck as Chief of the Army General Staff, continued to urge caution on the Führer.

While it is much in doubt whether the plotters could have succeeded in toppling Hitler in that 'revolution' which the English Government was promised by its German sources, the fact remains that Hitler knew that his generals believed that to march against Czechoslovakia must bring down a general war on Germany's head, a war which could only end in catastrophe. An English ultimatum would have provided just the kind of lever the German generals needed in their controversy with Hitler. The combined moral pressure of his own generals' opposition and of an English declaration to stand by Czechoslovakia might therefore have dissuaded Hitler, when it came to the point, from issuing the order to march. But the summer had passed and no English ultimatum had come, and now never would. English policy had played on Hitler's side against

[1] See above p. 520 and footnote.
[2] Cf. Beck's memoranda of May 1938, and his further memorandum of 3 June, in O'Neill, pp. 152–7.
[3] O'Neill, pp. 158–9. [4] Ibid. p. 160. [5] Ibid. pp. 163–5.

his generals. The English Cabinet finally therefore threw away in the Cabinet meeting of 12 September their one chance, uncertain though it must seem even in retrospect, both of preserving Czechoslovakia within her present frontiers and also avoiding a war. Instead the destiny of Europe took another course.

At the Nazi Party rally in Nuremberg that evening, as the massed banners stirred in the wind, and the silent ranks of uniformed men listened under the stars, there was none of the old-womanly anxiety and apprehension manifested by the rulers of England earlier amid the inappropriate Georgian masculinity of the Cabinet room at Downing Street. Hitler was in his best, most malignant, form:

> I am a National-Socialist, and as such I am accustomed on every attack to hit back immediately. I know too, quite well that through forbearance one will never reconcile so irreconcilable an enemy as are the Czechs; they will only be provoked to further presumption. . . .
>
> Herr Benes plays his tactical game: he makes speeches, he wishes to negotiate . . . and to make little appeasement presents. But in the long run that is not good enough! . . . The Germans in Czechoslovakia are neither defenceless nor are they deserted, and people should take notice of that fact.[1]

Next day there was an armed rising in the Sudetenland, easily crushed by the Czechs. Henlein and other Sudeten leaders broke off all contacts with the Czech Government, and fled to Germany. Henlein issued a proclamation which showed how far Sudeten civil rights or Sudeten autonomy had now been left behind, dumped once that they had exhausted their purpose: 'We wish to live as free Germans. We want peace and work again in our homeland. We want to return to the Reich.'[2]

To the British and French governments it now seemed inevitable that the Germany army would very soon enter the Sudetenland. This would force the French to honour their alliance with Czechoslovakia. Once France was at war with Germany, England could hardly leave her to her fate. The Soviet Union too was bound by a treaty with Czechoslovakia to go to her aid if she was attacked, providing France had first honoured her own obligations. A general European war therefore seemed desperately near, a prospect under which the French nerve, never robust, now broke.

Daladier sent a message to London that the entry of German troops into

[1] Quoted in Alan Bullock, *Hitler: A Study in Tyranny* (London, Odhams Press 1952), p. 414.
[2] Ibid.

Czechoslovakia must be prevented at all costs. This gave Chamberlain *carte blanche* to make the move he had been mulling over for some days – a move of a kind unprecedented in history. On 13 September he sent a personal message to Hitler: 'In view of increasingly critical situation, I propose to come over at once to see you, with a view to finding a peaceful solution. I propose to come across by air, and am ready to start tomorrow.'[1]

It was a dramatic, not to say melodramatic, gesture, and much out of keeping with Chamberlain's outwardly cold and matter-of-fact personality. What he had to say to the Cabinet on 14 September about his great plan suggests indeed an unwonted mood of excitement.[2] He reported Sir Eric Phipps (the English ambassador in Paris) as saying that Bonnet, the French Foreign Minister, was in a state of collapse, believing that English and French cities were certain to be laid in ruins if there was a war. Colonel Lindbergh,[3] who had just visited Berlin, had informed Bonnet that Germany had 8,000 aircraft and could produce 1,500 a month. Chamberlain went on that he had put what he rather sensationally called his 'plan Z' into operation without consulting the full Cabinet, only the inner circle. He hoped the idea 'would appeal to the Hitlerian mentality'. He thought 'it might be agreeable to his vanity that the British Prime Minister should take so unprecedented a step'. He then outlined his tactics. In his own words, he should open by appealing to Hitler on his chance of obtaining fame for himself by making peace in Europe. He would point out that if Germany were to have Britiain's goodwill, it was essential that the Czechoslovakian dispute should not be settled by force.

Now Chamberlain came to the terms he proposed to put to Hitler. He was, he said, in favour of a plebiscite to decide the political future of the Sudetenland. But if part of Czechoslovakia should be then ceded to Germany, what would happen to the rest of the country? 'It might be said that there would be a helpless little strip of territory liable at any moment to be gobbled up by Germany.'

Therefore the Czechs might rather prefer to die fighting. Chamberlain's solution to this problem was one 'which he was most unwilling to contemplate' – namely, a British guarantee of the integrity of what was left of the Czech state. This, he acknowledged, could only be a deterrent, since we could not save Czechoslovakia if Germany did decide to overrun it.

Chamberlain made it clear that he was not only hoping to avert the

[1] Feiling, p. 363.
[2] CAB 23/95, 38(38).
[3] The American transatlantic flyer and in 1938 an admirer of the Nazis.

immediate danger of war, but was still looking ahead to the fulfilment of his long-cherished dreams, for he argued that the proposed personal negotiations with Hitler offered the chance of securing better relations between Germany and England.

Chamberlain had unveiled both a course of action and a scheme for a settlement which demonstrate that even now he failed to see, or refused to see, the European situation in terms of conflict, strategy and the equilibrium of power. In the first place, by himself going to visit Hitler at his own suggestion he was only bringing to its climax that process of chasing after Germany which for so long had made that country a gift of the diplomatic upper-hand. Not only the location of the coming negotiations, but the very circumstances in which they had been arranged must place Hitler in a tactically commanding position – all of which Chamberlain, in his simple enthusiasm, appeared totally unaware. Secondly, Chamberlain clearly accepted that, even if under the decent democratic covering of a plebiscite, the Sudetenland would have to be ceded by Czechoslovakia to Germany.

Yet it was here in the mountainous terrain of the Sudetenland that were situated the formidable Czech frontier defences; a crucial military fact which Chamberlain either forbore to mention or of which he was ignorant; or, more likely still, which he simply did not consider relevant. However, he had himself admitted that what remained of Czechoslovakia would be 'helpless' in the face of renewed German aggression. None the less, to this helpless rump he was prepared to give the British guarantee he refused to give to the present Czechoslovakia, with its fine army of some forty divisions and a powerful zone of fortifications covering all its frontier with Germany except along the old Austrian border. He had made it clear to the Cabinet that this guarantee would in any case be 'deterrent' only, and, by implication, valueless if Germany chose to ignore it.

In other words, in order to win a present respite, Chamberlain was now quite prepared to countenance the disappearance of a well-armed and well-organised Czechoslovakia from the European scene; to see forty divisions, and powerful defences, struck from the balance-sheet of 'allied' strength, and their first-class equipment added instead to Germany's. He was prepared for these things to happen because, as the record makes clear, they held little importance for him. They were outside his system of political thought.

The Cabinet nevertheless generally welcomed Chamberlain's plan of action with approval not a little tinged with adulation and sycophancy.

Kingsley Wood, the Secretary of State for Air, who was good at both, said 'the plan was an adventurous one which would appeal to the imagination of the whole world'. Maugham, the Lord Chancellor, not to be outdone, regarded it as a 'magnificent proposal, which would have a great influence over the whole world'.

It was Duff Cooper again, the First Lord of the Admiralty, together with Walter Elliot, the Minister of Health, who took some of the bubbles out of the occasion. Duff Cooper said that in his view 'the choice was not between war and a plebiscite, but between war now and war later. He had never been optimistic about our catching up Germany in our re-armament programme. . . .'

And Elliot thought that 'we were being led by pressure to do something which we should not have done of our own free will'.

On the same day the Chiefs of Staff submitted a fresh report on the military situation if there should be a war with Germany.[1] It largely went over ground similar to that of the COS report of 21 March, although with some changes in the estimated size of forces.[2] The COS now noted however that the British army's first commitment after the United Kingdom was Egypt, while also writing that it was essential to send a field force to France. They again went into the question of a German 'knock-out blow' on England from the air, and again their final conclusion was by no means clear-cut: 'We are still in considerable doubt as to the range and capacity of the bombers with which the German squadrons are now equipped. . . .' They thought that there was 'some reason to believe that the German air-striking force, *if concentrated against this country alone*', might be able to drop 500–600 tons a day for the first two months.[3]

The general conclusion of the Chiefs of Staff's new report was not such as to stiffen quaking political knees:

> It is our opinion that no pressure that Great Britain and France can bring to bear, either by sea, on land, or in the air, could prevent Germany from overrunning Bohemia and from inflicting a decisive defeat on Czechoslovakia. The restoration of Czechoslovakia's lost integrity could only be achieved by the defeat of Germany and as the outcome of a prolonged struggle, which from the outset must assume the character of an unlimited war. . . .[4]

However the new COS Report failed to cast any strategic light at all

[1] CAB 53/41, COS 765. It is not clear whether the Cabinet had seen this document before it met.
[2] See above pp. 474–5 and pp. 505–9.
[3] CAB 53/41, COS 765. [4] Ibid.

on the proposals Chamberlain intended to put to Hitler for the solution of the Czechoslovakian crisis. This was not surprising. For the COS had never been asked for their counsel on the fundamental grand-strategical questions at issue in the crisis – neither about the consequences of the Czechs having to abandon their frontier defences if they ceded the Sudetenland, nor about the effects on the general European strategic balance of the disappearance of Czechoslovakia as a military power, nor as to whether it would be better for France and Britain to fight Germany now or later. On these vital issues Chamberlain and his colleagues made up their own minds, unencumbered with professional strategic advice.

At 12.30 p.m. next day, 15 September, Chamberlain stepped out of his aircraft at Munich Airport after his first long journey by air, during which he was, according to one of his fellow passengers, 'as always, aloof, reserved, imperturbable, unshakeably self-reliant'.[1] Now at last he was seeing Nazi Germany at first hand, this dictatorship which for more than a year had been the focus of all his hopes of a peaceful and lasting settlement in Europe. Amid the brazen pomp of military bands, the raucous orders, the stamp of shining jackboots, the flash of ceremonial small swords, he walked to his car, a gaunt, intensely civilian figure in his ministerial black and pin-stripes: the Prime Minister of one of the victorious nations of the Great War, the representative of a world empire, on his way to plead with the leader of a nation which twenty years ago had been defeated in the field, and which only four years ago had still been weak and helpless.

At the Berghof, Hitler's residence high in the Bavarian Alps, the two men met on the stone steps: the upper-class Englishman born to wealth and family distinction and reared in public school and Unitarian chapel, and the lower-middle-class German whose education had been the street and the doss-house; Chamberlain who thought that the noblest ambition for an English statesman was to make gentle the life of the world, Hitler who believed that 'the idea of struggle is as old as life itself. In this struggle, the stronger, the more able win, while the less able, the weak lose. Struggle is the father of all things. . . .'[2] Evangelical England was face to face with Nazi Germany.

Now, in the course of their three-hour conversation, Chamberlain had the opportunity of weighing up the man on whose good faith his European policy rested. The Prime Minister gave his reading of Hitler's character to his Cabinet on his return. 'On a first view, Herr Hitler was

[1] Lord Strang, *At Home and Abroad* (London, André Deutsch 1956), p. 137.
[2] Bullock, p. 31.

unimpressive. There was nothing out of the common in his features.'[1] Later in the meeting his impression had become more favourable, however; there were

> no signs of insanity but many of excitement. Occasionally Herr Hitler would lose the thread of what he was saying and would go off into a tirade. It was impossible not to be impressed with the power of the man. He was extremely determined; he had thought out what he wanted and he meant to get it. . . . Further, and this was a point of considerable importance, the Prime Minister had formed the opinion that Herr Hitler's objectives were strictly limited.[2]

Chamberlain's view of Hitler's assurances, he told the Cabinet, was that he 'meant what he said'. Chamberlain believed 'that Herr Hitler was telling the truth'.[3]

The simple Chamberlain had been gulled – so much for *Mein Kampf*; so much for all the Foreign Office reports on Nazi Germany since 1933; so much for the whole course of Nazi policy since that date; so much even for Chamberlain's own recurrent mistrust of the Nazi leadership, confided to his diary as recently as May. Yet Chamberlain had, after all, an immense vested interest in believing well of Hitler: his present extraordinary mission depended on the premise that Hitler was honest and reliable, even if a shade rough; as no less did his grander vision of a Europe settled by peaceful negotiation, a vision which he had been following since the spring of 1937 with the true evangelist's steadfast and undeviating purpose and blindness to worldly doubts. As one of his closest colleagues, Sir Samuel Hoare, wrote later: 'This belief in his mission underlay the whole of his talks to me in the spring and summer of 1938. When he told me of any new project for furthering his objects, it was not so much to ask for my comments, although he was a good listener . . . as to explain why this or that step was necessary. . . .'[4]

The meeting at the Berghof provided Hitler with yet another tactical victory. Since 1933 he had had the pleasure of seeing a Lord Privy Seal, a Lord President of the Council and a Foreign Secretary come to visit him with their suits; now he had landed the Prime Minister of England himself – and all of them without even having to cast a line. While he sat on the bank and waited, they had leaped eagerly out of the water and into his creel. Hitler consolidated his moral initiative over Chamberlain by some initial storming and raging, making much of the unendurable

[1] Cabinet meeting of 17 September 1938, CAB 23/95, 39(38).
[2] Ibid. [3] Ibid. [4] Templewood, pp. 297–8.

sufferings of the Sudeten-Germans, which made a quick solution necessary, otherwise Germany would have no alternative but to march to their rescue. He demanded the cession of the Sudetenland. To this idea of 'self-determination', as Chamberlain was later to express it in 1919 Wilsonian jargon, Chamberlain agreed, saying that he would put it to his own Cabinet and to the French and Czechs. In return he asked Hitler not to take precipitate military action. Since the preparations of the German armed forces were in any case not due to be completed until 1 October, Hitler graciously consented to give Chamberlain this assurance.

Next day, on his return to England, Chamberlain reported to the Czechoslovakian Crisis Committee of the Cabinet.[1] As he told it, it made a dramatic story, which he repeated in very similar terms and with no less sense of excitement and occasion to his breathless Cabinet on the following day.[2] The Prime Minister said he believed that the situation when he went to Germany was 'of desperate urgency. If he had not gone he thought that hostilities would have started by now. The atmosphere had been electric. . . .'[3]

He quoted Hitler's thoughtful statement that the German military machine was 'a terrific instrument', ready to act at any moment. He also expressed to the Cabinet his belief that he, Chamberlain, had favourably impressed Hitler as a man. And he went on to give an account of what had passed between them both at Berchtesgaden.[4]

Yet outside the tight little circle of Chamberlain's senior colleagues, and the wider circle of his loyal sycophants, his report was greeted by uneasy doubts and criticism. Oliver Stanley, Walter Elliot and Duff Cooper all spoke of the dangers inherent in a plebiscite. Duff Cooper expressed his fear that 'we might be led into a complete surrender', and said that he did not believe in Hitler's word. He referred to the traditional wisdom of the balance of power, and attacked the Chamberlain–Halifax line that we were militarily too weak to do other than seek to avoid war: 'As regards the condition that we should not intervene unless we had overruling force, we had not got it now and were unlikely to attain it.' He thought that even if the present crisis were solved, it would not be an end to their troubles; there was no chance of peace in Europe while there was a Nazi régime in Germany.

Lord De La Warr, the Lord Privy Seal, said it was impossible to make the concessions asked for, which were 'unfair to the Czechs and

[1] CAB 27/646, CS(38)5, 16 September 1938. Present were Simon, Hoare and Halifax, with Vansittart, Cadogan and Horace Wilson in attendance.
[2] CAB 23/95, 39(38). [3] Ibid. [4] Ibid.

dishonourable to ourselves'. It was wrong to assume that the only alternatives were war or complete surrender. He went on: 'No one was particularly anxious to embark on war on behalf of Czechoslovakia; but he for his part was prepared to face war in order to free the world from the continual threat of ultimatums.'

By contrast, the Lord President of the Council, Lord Hailsham, was quite blatantly defeatist: 'It was in our interests to prevent a single power dominating Europe; but that had come to pass, and he thought we had no alternative but to submit to what the Lord Privy Seal regarded as humiliation.'

This limp acquiescence provoked a crisp rebuke from Lord Winterton, the Chancellor of the Duchy of Lancaster, who was 'profoundly disturbed' at Hailsham's remarks: 'In his opinion the issue now before the Cabinet raised the same issue as had been raised in 1914, when Belgium had been invaded. There was hard fibre in the British people which did not like to be told that, unless they acquiesced in certain things, it was all up with them.'

If Germany kept mobilised, he continued, then our action (over concessions to Hitler's demands) was a surrender. It was essential for Germany to make a concession.

The Foreign Secretary now proceeded to defend the proposals Chamberlain had brought back from Germany. Yet he himself was forced to agree that 'the present affair contained an element of German blackmail'; but he went on, 'this should not blind us to other considerations'. In the first place, there was the necessity in any case for revisions of the 1919 peace treaties, even if belated. Swiftly abandoning these statesmanlike considerations, however, Halifax came to the heart of the matter as he saw it. If the alternative to the Prime Minister's proposal was war, 'then he asked himself what was the ultimate justification of war? In his view, he would fight for the great moralities which knew no geographical boundaries. But there was no greater urge to fight for Czechoslovakia than to fight for Japan because of the bombing of civilians in Canton.'

Therefore we should arrange the transfer of the Sudeten population, but get Hitler publicly to promise that he would then be satisfied. We should give a guarantee to the remainder of Czechoslovakia, although he disliked the idea. As regards procedure, 'it was very important that we should avoid allowing the French to say that they came to London and found that we had decided to give the show away'.

Halifax, then, showed himself motivated by an uneasy blend of high moralism and sheer expediency; but what was still absent from his thinking was any consideration of grand strategy – the effect on the European balance of the destruction of Czechoslovakia as an efficient, if only second-class, military power; the effect of opening Germany's way to further expansion eastwards and south-eastwards. These, the fundamentally important issues which Chamberlain and Halifax consistently failed to face and discuss, were ventilated by Oliver Stanley, the President of the Board of Trade:

> Like the First Lord of the Admiralty, he regarded this question as almost as direct an attack upon us as, say, an attack on the Isle of Wight. The present Nazi régime could not exist without coups. If the choice for the Government in the next few days was between surrender or fighting, we ought to fight. His view was that the present was a better rather than a worse time to fight.[1]

Germany, he went on, would be better off in six months' or a year's time, when the same points could arise over the Polish Corridor, Memel or the ex-German colonies.

Walter Elliot, the Minister of Health, agreed: it was better to fight than surrender; we should resist intolerable demands. Duff Cooper too re-affirmed a like belief.

But, in winding up the discussion, Chamberlain argued: 'The alternatives to-day were not between abject surrender and war. Acceptance of the principle of self-determination was not an abject surrender.'

No, no, on the contrary: '. . . it had never entered his head that he should go to Germany and say to Herr Hitler that he could have self-determination on any terms he wanted. He would not assent to any such agreement.'

By way of supporting this contention Chamberlain said that it was only the fact that our re-armament programme had progressed and we were now 'a formidable Power' that enabled us to speak with any influence. It was an argument which in all the circumstances was perfectly breath-taking.

Chamberlain's had been a shifty performance for an honourable man. Nevertheless his opponents failed to achieve anything more valuable than the relief of their own feelings. Chamberlain informed his colleagues that he did not want to have his negotiating hands tied by pre-conditions, and nor were they. He also said that there ought to be no more military measures, such as naval mobilisation, for the time being; and nor were there.

[1] CAB 23/95, 39(38).

On 18 September Daladier and Bonnet flew to London to hear Chamberlain's now well-rehearsed story of how he bearded Hitler in his lair, and to consult about the next move. In a sense Daladier's and Bonnet's personal tragedy was greater than that of Chamberlain and his colleagues, for while the Frenchmen's desire was to avert war was as overpowering – perhaps even more overpowering – they had not, like the Englishmen, the comfort of illusion to hide from themselves what they were doing and what the consequences of it must be. As Daladier said, 'Germany's real aim was the disintegration of Czechoslovakia and the realisation of Pan-German ideals through a march to the East. Within one year we might expect her to turn back against France and Great Britain, who would then have to meet her in much more difficult circumstances than those existing today.'[1]

Chamberlain ignored these arguments, just as he ignored them when advanced by members of his own Cabinet. Instead he went straight for the Frenchmen's nerves: '. . . he was convinced that it would not be the slightest use to suggest any alternative proposals. . . . Negotiations could not be resumed except on the basis of considering ways and means to put the principle of self-determination [for the Sudetens] into effect. It we would not accept this basis it meant war. Let there be no mistake about that.'[2]

Threatened by their ally with the alternative of war or surrender, the French gave way again. Next day in Paris the French Cabinet approved the agreement reached in London that Czechoslovakia should be induced to cede the Sudetenland with or without the ceremony of a plebiscite. In return however, the English agreed – as foreshadowed in Cabinet discussions – to a French demand that England should guarantee the integrity of the future rump of Czechoslovakia. England and France therefore passed on Hitler's demands to Czechoslovakia in the guise of Anglo-French proposals for a settlement. These proposals failing to elicit a favourable answer from Prague, the British and French ambassadors delivered President Benes an ultimatum at 2 a.m. on 21 September the harshness and brutal clarity of language of which would have been admirable if addressed to the aggressor rather than to the victim:

> One. That which has been proposed by England and France is the only hope of averting war and the invasion of Czechoslovakia.
>
> Two. Should the Czechoslovak Republic reply in the negative, she would bear the responsibility for war.

[1] *Docs. on Brit. Foreign Policy*, Vol. II, p. 384.

[2] Ibid. p. 386.

Three. This would destroy Franco-English solidarity, since England would not march.

Four. If under these circumstances the war starts, France will not take part; i.e. she will not fulfil her treaty obligations.[1]

At midday the Czechs unconditionally accepted the German proposals as passed on by England and France. Next day, 22 September 1938, Chamberlain flew to Germany again, to meet Hitler at Bad Godesberg and tell him of his wonderful success in securing the Czechs' agreement to his demands. But, to his vast surprise and pain, Hitler failed to evince gratitude and delight:

> He was sorry but these proposals were no longer enough. . . . Representatives of Poland and Hungary had recently visited him and said that they would not in any circumstances agree to their nationals remaining under Czech rule. . . .
>
> A settlement must be reached within a few days. There were, as the whole world knew, military preparations on both sides, but this situation could not be held for very long and a solution must be found one way or another, either by agreement or by force. He desired to say, categorically, that the problem must be settled definitely and completely by 1 October at the latest.[2]

To this outrageous speech, Chamberlain replied in hurt reproach rather than with the anger which it merited.

> He was both disappointed and puzzled at the Führer's statement. . . . He [Chamberlain] had induced his colleagues, the French and the Czechs to agree to the principles of self-determination, in fact he had got exactly what the Führer had wanted and without the expenditure of a drop of German blood. In doing so he had been obliged to take his political life in his hands.[3]

A crestfallen and bewildered old gentleman, Chamberlain returned to his hotel, there at least to write a letter to Hitler warning him that if the German army should take precipitate action, it would mean war. Chamberlain reported to the Cabinet:

> Herr Hitler takes the line that the only way of preserving order and preventing situation degenerating is for Germany to occupy Sudeten territory by German military forces. Boundary he proposes is based on

[1] Gilbert, *The Roots of Appeasement*, p. 154.
[2] *Docs. on Brit. Foreign Policy*, Vol. II, p. 466.
[3] Ibid. p. 467.

> a language map and he has drawn it as to give the most favourable results to Germany. He is willing that a plebiscite should be held within two or three months.
>
> Failing acceptance of his proposals he intimates he will be obliged to seek a military solution.[1]

On the morrow the two men met again. Hitler produced new proposals for Chamberlain to pass on to the Czechs. Though entitled a memorandum, the document was, as Chamberlain pointed out, couched like an ultimatum.

Even now Chamberlain still saw the negotiations as genuine and sincere; it still apparently did not dawn on him that he was caught up in a rigged game of political poker. He took Hitler's threats completely at face value; he appealed to Hitler's humanity and love of peace: 'He could not believe that Herr Hitler would deliberately gamble away all chances of working together, the prospect of peace and a happy future for Europe merely for the sake of avoiding a delay of a few days . . . to rush things like this was to take fearful chances.'[2]

While they were arguing, news came that the Czechs had mobilised. 'In that event,' said Hitler, 'things are settled.'[3] Chamberlain returned to England with pockets empty. Yet *even now* he failed to realise that he was being mercilessly and cynically played for a dupe. Worse, and in a peculiarly terrible way, he seemed to have fallen more deeply under Hitler's influence – partly because of his own rather pathetic vanity; partly because the more harsh and pressing reality became, the more desperately he clung to his vision of a Europe at peace, all its problems solved by negotiation. It was a vision with which a villainous Hitler was quite incompatible.

When on 24 September Chamberlain gave the Cabinet Czechoslovakian Crisis Committee his account of the Bad Godesberg meetings, he told them that he 'thought he had established some degree of personal influence over Herr Hitler. The latter had said to him, "You are the first man for many years who has got any concessions from me." '[4]

Later the same day, in rendering much the same account of the meetings to the full Cabinet, he was at pains to act as Hitler's apologist, attributing his behaviour to his lack of trust in Czech good faith.[5] He even sought to excuse the peremptory nature of Hitler's ultimatum: 'The tone

[1] *Docs. on Brit. Foreign Policy*, Vol. II, p. 478. [2] Ibid. p. 501. [3] Ibid.
[4] CAB 27/646, CS(38)13, 24 September 1938.
[5] CAB 23/95, 42(38).

was not as courteous or considerate as one would wish, but it was worth remembering that Germans were apt to express themselves curtly.'[1]

He went on to say that, although he had felt indignant when Herr Hitler first pressed new demands, he had now modified his views. He proceeded to give his latest assessment of Hitler's character, having now had the advantage of being cheated and browbeaten by him:

> In his view Herr Hitler had certain standards . . . Herr Hitler had a narrow mind and was violently prejudiced on certain subjects but he would not deliberately deceive a man whom he respected and with whom he had been in negotiation, and he was sure that Herr Hitler now felt some respect for him. When Herr Hitler announced that he meant to do something it was certain that he would do it.[2]

This Lear-like self-delusion not only marked the tragic decline of Chamberlain's own character, but also the climax of the whole tragedy of the England whose virtues Chamberlain so well represented, virtues which he was now misapplying to the conduct of foreign affairs more catastrophically than any English statesman before him. The tragedy was all the more poignant because, while Chamberlain still embodied the virtues of liberal England, he no longer reflected its present state of mind. Chamberlain was himself clinging to illusions and hopes from which British opinion, right and left, was fast awakening under the sting of Hitler's gangster diplomacy at Berchtesgaden and Bad Godesberg.

*The Times* – even *The Times* – wrote on 27 September that 'the Godesberg Note reverts to the worst form of Prussianism in using the language of a bully, fixing a time limit of a few days'; and went so far as to question Germany's ultimate intentions *vis-à-vis* Czechoslovakia.[3] On the previous day the *Daily Telegraph*'s diplomatic correspondent had argued that if Hitler's demands at Godesberg were met, Czechoslovakia 'would be militarily indefensible, economically broken and politically subjugated completely to German domination'.[4] *The Manchester Guardian*, once a gas cylinder of internationalist optimism, consistently advocated throughout the Czech crisis that Czechoslovakia should be preserved within her existing boundaries, and that Hitler should be resisted by a coalition of Britain, France and Russia.[5] The *News Chronicle*, although it had hoped earlier in the year for a 'just' settlement by compromise, now demanded that England should stand firm on the Covenant of the League of Nations, in defence of Czech democracy; she should combine

1 Ibid.
2 Ibid.
3 Gannon, p. 187.
4 Ibid. p. 195.
5 Ibid. pp. 198–203.

with Russia and France to resist any German aggression.[1] The *Daily Herald*, although also once hopeful of a negotiated settlement, wrote on 26 September that Hitler's ambition was to dominate Europe, and that the Czech dispute was only a ploy in the game.[2] And the *Herald* was later to urge Chamberlain at the Munich Conference to 'Stand Firm'.[3] *The Observer*, which, under J. L. Garvin as editor, had for so long expressed liberal trust in human reasonableness and goodness, even of dictators, wrote on 25 September, after Godesberg, that two visits to Hitler had produced two ultimata and no concessions. Britons, the paper said, must steel their hearts.[4] Of the 'quality' papers, only the *Sunday Times* remained wholeheartedly in favour of appeasement.[5]

The Labour Party, having decisively contributed to England's present military weakness by its advocacy of disarmament in the 1920s and by its fanatical opposition to re-armament in the crucial years 1933–6, had long been demanding – without any sense of inconsistency – steadfast resistance to the ambitions of dictators. It had been urging the Government to create a grand anti-Fascist European coalition. So strongly was the Labour Party moved by the new ideological cause of anti-Fascism that in 1937 it went so far as to cease voting against the defence estimates. During the Czech crisis therefore, the Labour Party, while it remained in favour of a just, negotiated settlement if that were possible, was nevertheless wholeheartedly against yielding to German pressure and blackmail. On 8 September the National Council of Labour published a manifesto – accepted by the TUC at its annual conference – which proclaimed:

> BRITAIN SHOULD LEAD AGAINST AGGRESSION. The time has come for a positive and unmistakable lead for collective security. . . . The British Government must leave no doubt in the mind of the German Government that they will unite with the French and Soviet Governments to resist an attack on Czechoslovakia. . . . Whatever the risks involved, Great Britain must take its stand against aggression. . . .[6]

On 19 September, the Labour Party organised a mass protest meeting in Trafalgar Square against the Anglo-French proposals, which Labour leaders in deputations to Chamberlain and Halifax described as an 'absolute surrender' and 'one of the biggest disasters in British history'.[7] On

[1] Gannon, pp. 206–11. [2] Ibid. p. 218. [3] Ibid. [4] Ibid. p. 224.

[5] Ibid. p. 22. For an able survey of the shifting attitudes of the British press towards Germany in 1936–8, and the conflicts of opinion within the editorial staffs of individual newspapers, see Gannon, especially Pts. 3 and 4.

[6] Carl F. Brand, *The British Labour Party; A Short History* (Stanford, California, Stanford University Press 1965), p. 205.

[7] Ibid. p. 206.

the eve of Chamberlain's flight to Godesberg the three Labour executives protested that 'this dishonour will not bring us peace. Hitler's ambitions do not stop at Czechoslovakia.'[1] Thus it was that by September 1938 the idealism and ideological zeal which had led the Labour movement to a Quaker-like quietism and pacifism between 1920 and 1935 now inspired it with a Cromwellian resolve to smite unrighteous tyrants.

The Liberals too had been moved by ideology to abandon their old trust in reason and goodwill, and instead prepare to resist Fascist expansion by countervailing power. In 1935, after the German announcements of the existence of the Luftwaffe and introduction of conscription, the Liberal Party had decided to vote for instead of against the defence estimates. On 10 September 1938 Lord Samuel, the Liberal leader in the Lords, warned Germany in a speech that Great Britain would support France and Russia in defending Czechoslovakia in the event of a German attack. 'I know', he said, 'of no important section of the nation which would oppose such a policy.'[2] After Chamberlain's return from Godesberg, Sir Archibald Sinclair denounced Chamberlain's policy as 'a humiliating rout'.[3]

In the Conservative Party itself, the majority of MPs were – as the vote of 7 May 1940 was to demonstrate – uncritically and limitlessly loyal to Chamberlain, no matter what his policies, while a dissenting minority was urging that appeasement be ended, and that Czechoslovakia's present integrity should be preserved even at the cost of war.

It was among some of the intellectuals – Lord Lothian, Allen of Hurtwood, C. E. M. Joad – that old illusions still lingered on. Kingsley Martin, for example, convinced as he admits by letters from Maynard Keynes, wrote in the *New Statesman* at the beginning of September (antedating the famous *Times* leader on a similar theme on 7 September) that a solution to the crisis might have to be found in a revision of Czechoslovakia's frontiers. 'The strategical value of the Bohemian frontier', wrote the *New Statesman*, 'should not be made the occasion of a world war. We should not guarantee the *status quo*.'[4]

Given therefore Chamberlain's absolute mastery of his Cabinet and party, given the state of opinion in the opposition parties and the national press, there is no substance in the claim made by Chamberlain and some of his colleagues in the Cabinet meetings[5] during the Czech crisis and by his apologists later that to threaten Germany with war if she moved against Czechoslovakia would be so unpopular as to be politically impossible;

[1] Ibid.
[2] John Bowle, *Viscount Samuel* (London, Victor Gollancz 1957), p. 312.
[3] Ibid. p. 315.
[4] Gannon, p. 178; Kingsley Martin, pp. 254–7.
[5] See above pp. 517–20.

or in the parallel claim that to go to war over Czechoslovakia would split the nation. On the contrary, the conversion of the Labour and Liberal parties from pacifistic appeasement to militant anti-Fascism since 1935 had offered Chamberlain the opportunity, had he wished to take it, of organising an anti-German coalition under the guise of 'collective security'; and of pursuing a balance-of-power foreign policy in the chic costume of a crusade against dictatorship – exactly as Palmerston in his time had dressed up his opportunist pursuit of English interests as the promotion of liberal ideals. It was, however, as the records make clear, the particular aim of Chamberlain and Halifax to *avoid* such a division of Europe into opposing coalitions, no matter whether founded on considerations of power or ideology. By the time of his return from Godesberg, therefore, Chamberlain was, except for his docile senior colleagues and obedient backbenchers, very much a lone man, blindly pursuing his vision against the general tide of national feeling.

The Prime Minister, therefore, did not feel Bad Godesberg to have been a final and humiliating defeat; on the contrary, as he remarked to the Cabinet, in view of how Hitler valued British friendship, there was a possibility of a turning-point in Anglo-German relations. 'He thought that he had now established an influence over Herr Hitler, and that the latter trusted him and was willing to work with him. If this was so, it was a wonderful opportunity to put an end to the horrible nightmare of the present armament race. That seemed to him to be the big thing in the present issue.'[1]

Insidiously he asked the Cabinet to consider whether the difference between the previous and the present proposals justified us going to war. Then, to help them make up their mind, he played on all their deep Victorian peaceableness and love of peace, their horror of conflict and violence, and their humanitarian concern:

> That morning he had flown up the river over London. He had imagined a German bomber flying the same course. He had asked himself what degree of protection we could afford to the thousands of homes which he had seen stretched out before him, and he had felt that we were in no position to justify waging a war to-day in order to prevent a war hereafter.[2]

He repeated much the same argument later, in touching almost for the first time in the entire course of the crisis, and then only in passing, on the crucial question of whether it would be better to fight now or later. He

[1] CAB 23/95, 42(38). [2] Ibid.

argued that if we went to war, it would not be for Czechoslovakia in its present form 'but because we thought that we could check Herr Hitler's ambitions more effectively by war now than by war hereafter'. Chamberlain however thought that it was possible that protection against German bombers would be more effective in the future.[1]

Only a short debate followed the Prime Minister's statement. Duff Cooper repeated that he did not believe in Hitler's promises; nor did he believe Hitler would respect the new Czech frontiers. He thought the Czechs would choose to fight rather than accept Hitler's terms, and that the Cabinet should order general mobilisation forthwith. Hore-Belisha too, referring to a report on this topic by the Chiefs of Staff,[2] urged the importance of early mobilisation; he suggested it might deter Hitler. Walter Elliot the Minister of Health, agreed. But Chamberlain wanted to put off mobilisation, and again had his way.

That weekend Europe prepared itself for war. In London the unemployed dug hasty trenches in the parks to shelter civilians from the expected bomber fleets. Air-raid sirens under test squeezed the stomach. Thirty-eight million gas masks were distributed to regional centres.

On Sunday, 25 September 1938, the British Cabinet met again, and this time searched its collective soul.[3] Even Halifax was now deeply troubled, a circumstance for which Sir Alexander Cadogan, the Permanent Under-Secretary at the Foreign Office, was largely responsible.[4] Halifax admitted he was now far less certain in his views. Much turned on Hitler's future intentions and on Anglo-German *rapprochement*. 'Nevertheless, he could not rid his mind of the fact that Herr Hitler had given us nothing and that he was dictating terms, just as though he had won a war but without having to fight.'[5]

Halifax went on to say that he did not altogether share the First Lord's views on a 'March to the East', but he nevertheless wished to see the destruction of Nazism because 'so long as Nazism lasted peace would be uncertain'.

Therefore: 'His reflections during the night led him to think we should put no pressure on the Czechs to accept. If they reject, France would join in and we should join with them. If Hitler was driven to war the result might bring down the Nazi régime.' But he also argued that the present proposals did not involve a difference of principle. Halifax concluded by

[1] Ibid.
[2] CAB 53/41, COS 770, 23 September 1938: if immediate hostilities were assured, 'we are most strongly of opinion that immediate general mobilisation is a first, and vitally essential measure.'
[3] CAB 23/95, 43(38).
[4] Birkenhead, p. 400.
[5] CAB 23/95, 43(38).

saying that 'he had worked most closely with the Prime Minister throughout the long crisis. He was not quite sure that their minds were still altogether at one.'

The Lord President of the Council, Hailsham, an earlier supporter of the Prime Minister, now averred that they could not trust Hitler, and provided examples of his past duplicity to prove it. The Lord Chancellor, Maugham, and the President of the Board of Education, Earl Stanhope, were both in favour of pressing the Czechs to accept. The Chancellor of the Duchy of Lancaster, Lord Winterton, believed that the Cabinet should not support acceptance of Hitler's latest proposals on moral grounds: '. . . the Memorandum was an ultimatum and was couched in almost offensive terms'.

Inskip, the Minister for the Co-ordination of Defence, with a subtlety worthy of the lawyer he was, thought that England should put the facts to the Czechs, but not apply pressure. He went on to argue that victory in a war might well result in the virtual destruction of both sides. The remedy was worse than the disease, and therefore he thought it was not in our interest to go to war. Inskip did however provide a titbit of military information welcome to those who were wishing to be encouraged rather than discouraged; apparently the Germans only had a thin *couverture* on their western frontier.

Kingsley Wood, the Air Minister, gratefully noted the weakness of the French and Russian air forces, and recommended acceptance of Hitler's proposals.

Duff Cooper, the First Lord of the Admiralty, discounted Lindbergh's alarmist information about the German air force, since he was an admirer of the Nazi régime; and told the Cabinet what he believed it ought to do: 'we should now tell the Czech Government that we regarded the terms as intolerable, and that, if they refused the ultimatum presented to them, we should stand by them and that we hoped France would do the same. He thought that the future of Europe, this country and of democracy was at stake.'

He was again supported by Oliver Stanley, the President of the Board of Trade, who likewise was against accepting Hitler's terms, believing that his price would only rise again. And he continued: 'No doubt war was horrible but it would be equally horrible in six months' time. Further, Germany was not now prepared for a long war. . . .' If we waited, Stanley said, Germany would be stronger owing to her expansion to the south-east of Europe.

The Secretary of State for the colonies, Malcolm MacDonald, reported on the attitudes of the dominions. Te Water, Dulanty and Massey – High Commissioners respectively of South Africa, the Irish Free State and Canada – were definitely of the view that we had 'accepted the principle of transfer [of the Sudetenland to Germany] a week ago and that we ought now to accept proposals which merely concerned the method of the transfer'. Bruce, the Australian High Commissioner, 'inclined' to the same view, providing there was a guarantee of the new Czechoslovakia, and that we made it clear that we would fight if Germany went any further. MacDonald himself was in favour of accepting Hitler's demands, because only the method of the transfer was at issue, and it was not worth going to war about that. However he thought there should be no pressure on the Czechs and no further concessions.

The Lord Privy Seal, Lord De La Warr, said that Hitler's demands 'became daily more preposterous. He thought that a vital question of principle was at stake. Herr Hitler's proposals in effect amounted to an ultimatum.' He pointed out that the Germans would get behind the Czechs' fortified line, and added that it was impossible to have any confidence in Hitler. He was 'afraid that we were being drawn along and slowly abandoning the moral basis of our own case'. There was a risk of losing the sympathy of the world and our own moral conviction. Therefore we should not ask the Czechs to accept the terms. 'Further, we should not shelter behind the French, nor the French behind us.' We should say to the French that if they fulfilled their obligations, we should march.

The Secretary of State for India, the Marquess of Zetland, made haste to disperse the effects of such stout speaking. Hitler, he said, was not bluffing, but quite ready to plunge the world into war. Zetland drew the Cabinet's attention to our 'Achilles Heel' in the Middle East; to Palestine (where a large British garrison was engaged in fighting Arab rebels). Then there was the attitude of the Moslems of India. Zetland went on to evoke another gloomy prospect – after a world war, might the new German régime be more dangerous to us than the Nazis? He was therefore in favour of all possible steps to avoid war.

Sir John Simon, the Chancellor of the Exchequer, agreed with Zetland – hardly surprisingly, in view of his earlier record as Foreign Secretary. But he did say that there was 'no dispute about the fact that Herr Hitler's proposals were a shocking document'.

The Minister of Transport, Leslie Burgin, asked whether this was the best time to attack (*sic*) Germany? Our forces, he rather tactlessly reminded the Cabinet, were mostly for defence.

Hore-Belisha, the War Secretary, had now stiffened his attitude. The issue, he thought, was now a moral one. Czechoslovakia was a democracy. 'If we forced Czechoslovakia to yield, we should not be able to escape strong condemnation.'

Hoare, the Home Secretary, was also 'much shocked' by the style of the document containing the German proposals, with its character of an ultimatum. As a consequence he believed that we should apply no pressure to the Czechs. We should indeed offer to send a division of troops to Czechoslovakia.

W. S. Morrison, the Minister of Agriculture and Fisheries, came back to the fundamental issue: 'There was a feeling in this country that war with Germany was quite inevitable, and that if the bastion of Czechoslovakia was surrendered, the position would really be worsened.'

Yet he still thought that we must make every effort to secure peace. We should present the facts to the Czechs without applying pressure. He believed it was important for Britain to get back to the position of 'honest broker'.

The Minister of Labour, Ernest Brown, could not accept the inevitability of war. We should still try for a settlement.

It was a deeply and evenly divided Cabinet. Of the inner circle of Chamberlain's closest colleagues, Hoare and Halifax had pronounced themselves against acceptance of Hitler's Godesberg demands.

It was characteristic however that it should have been considerations not of strategy but of morality, which had caused Chamberlain's former supporters in the Cabinet to waver. Whereas up to the beginning of September 'morality' had seemed to be on the German side, in the demand for civic rights or even self-government for the Sudetens, it had now turned its coat and was fighting for the Czechs. For at long last Hitler had torn off his disguise as the rectifier of German 'wrongs' under the 1919 peace settlement, and stood revealed to all but Chamberlain and those who remained loyal to him as a scoundrel bent on seizing what he wanted from a small democratic country by threats or actual force.

Chamberlain now sought to get his Cabinet back into orderly ranks behind him. He emphasised the importance of the Cabinet maintaining a united front. He said it was wrong to talk of *us* (author's italics) accepting or rejecting the German terms, or feeling humiliation, because, he went on, 'the proposals were not addressed to us, and we were only acting as an intermediary'.[1] The responsibility for accepting or rejecting the terms rested with the Czechs.

It was, to say the least, a disingenuous argument. No less disingenuous

[1] CAB 23/95, 43(38).

were Chamberlain's efforts to blur the distinction between putting pressure on the Czechs and simply putting the facts of the situation before them.

The First Lord's suggestion of telling the Czechs to reject the terms, and that we would come in on their side was, Chamberlain said, impossible, because the Cabinet was divided. He thought the attitude of France was the key. It would be impossible to carry public opinion and the empire if we were to go to war; hence the need to strive for peace up to the last. In talking to the French, we should avoid either undertaking to go to war if Hitler's proposals were rejected, *or* saying that in no circumstances would we go to war.

In the end, all the agonised debate came to nothing more than agreement to postpone a final decision as to English policy until after the forthcoming meeting with Daladier and Bonnet in London in the evening.

But that afternoon the Czechs in any case rejected Hitler's Godesberg proposals. The British and French ministers had therefore simply to consider what their countries should do if, as now seemed certain, Germany invaded Czechoslovakia. Daladier brought to London a shaky and precarious determination to honour France's treaty obligations with the Czechs. Chamberlain, supported by Simon, set out to destroy this determination.

Chamberlain asked Daladier:

> What would we then do if we found ourselves faced, as we well might in two or three days, with a German invasion of Czechoslovakia? It might take place very rapidly . . . they must know what attitude the French Government intended to take . . . M. Daladier had indicated that the French plan was to undertake offensive operations against the Siegfried Line . . . and also to bomb German factories and military centres. He wished to speak quite frankly and say the British Government had received disturbing reports of the condition of the French Air Force . . . he therefore felt he must ask what would happen if war had been declared and a rain of bombs descended upon Paris, upon French industrial districts . . .? Could France defend herself, and was she in a position to make an effective reply?[1]

The course of the meeting was in fact a model of how British ministers ought to have handled Hitler from the time of Simon and Eden's first visit in 1935 onwards – the relentless assertion of moral domination, the

[1] *Docs. on Brit. Foreign Policy*, Vol. II, pp. 531–2.

ruthless exploitation of every weak spot in the other man's position or argument; the bluntness, even the cruelty, of the language. Yet it was all employed not to prevent a dangerous rival from re-building his power and from seeking again to dominate Europe, but to prevent a friendly country from honouring its obligations to a small state in danger of attack; employed not to block the aggressor's path, but to open the way for him.

The meeting, like the British Cabinet meeting earlier, came to no decision, except to agree to Chamberlain's idea of sending a last personal appeal to Hitler by letter via Horace Wilson, suggesting a four-power conference to solve the crisis; an idea later that day approved by the Cabinet.[1]

On Monday, 26 September, General Gamelin, the French Commander-in-Chief, came to London. He informed Chamberlain that France *would* attack in the west; that the Czechs had thirty-four divisions opposing an equal number of German divisions; and that the Czech air force numbered 500 aircraft, plus another 280 recently received from Russia. Gamelin believed that the Czechs would fight well, aiming to hold open the bottleneck between Silesia and Austria so that the main body of their army could, if forced to retire, escape and fight on in the east of the country. France had twenty-three divisions in the west; the Germans only eight. The Siegfried Line was 'far from complete'; in fact 'in many respects it was improvised', and therefore the French believed they could make an attack which would at least draw off German troops from Czechoslovakia.[2]

On 26 September Hitler, in the Sportpalast in Berlin, delivered one of the most violent speeches of his life, in which he told his baying followers that either Benes accepted his offer and gave the Sudetens their freedom, or 'we will go and fetch this freedom for ourselves'.

On 27 September the Prime Minister reported to the Cabinet that Nevile Henderson had said that unless we advised Czechoslovakia 'to make the best terms she could with Berlin, we should be exposing her to the fate of Abyssinia'.[3] He also reported that the British military attaché in Berlin, after visiting Czechoslovakia, was of the opinion that the morale of the country was very poor, and that he had 'formed the impression that they would offer a feeble resistance'.[4] Chamberlain further bolstered his

[1] CAB 23/95, 44(38).
[2] As reported to the Cabinet on 26 September 1938 by the Prime Minister, CAB 23/95, 45(38).
[3] CAB 23/95, 46(38).
[4] See also Chamberlain's account of the attaché's opinion to the Czechoslovakian Crisis Committee on the same day, CAB 27/646, CS(38)15.

Cabinet's fighting spirit by saying that all the dominions felt that Hitler's proposals were better than war.

Horace Wilson gave the Cabinet an account of his unhappy interviews with Hitler in the course of delivering the Prime Minister's letter proposing a four-power conference. Hitler, he said, saw only two alternatives: one, acceptance of his memorandum, or, two, that German troops would overrun Czechoslovakia.[1]

The Cabinet reached agreement that the Prime Minister in his coming speech in the House of Commons on 28 September should say that if France were at war in fulfilment of her obligations to Czechoslovakia, 'we should feel obliged to support them'. At last England was to give the guarantee urged by Oliver Stanley and Duff Cooper in March – too late to be of the faintest diplomatic use. Chamberlain also announced that he had authorised the First Lord to mobilise the navy, but that there would be no general mobilisation of the RAF.[2]

With the English Cabinet almost evenly divided between standing fast and surrender, with the French reduced again to irresolution, Chamberlain, the one man on the 'allied' side absolutely certain that he was right, took charge of Anglo-French policy again. Without consulting the full Cabinet, but with the firm backing of Halifax,[3] he wrote that night to Hitler personally to suggest a four-power conference, to include Mussolini.

> I feel certain you can get all essentials without war, and without delay. I feel convinced that we could reach agreement within a week. However much you doubt the Prague Government's intentions, you cannot doubt the power of the British and French governments to see that the promises are carried out fairly and fully and forthwith.[4]

The purpose of the proposed conference was therefore to avert war at all costs – and to do so by means which Chamberlain had been advocating since Godesberg, but to which half his Cabinet were now opposed: to wit, hand over the swag to the criminal in return for a due receipt, in order to save him the trouble of having to rob his victim.

At the same time Chamberlain wrote to Mussolini requesting him to urge Hitler to agree to a conference. Mussolini, impressed by the mobilisation of the Royal Navy and himself not at all ready for war, did as he was asked.

In the forenoon of 28 September, with the German ultimatum to

[1] CAB 23/95, 46(38).
[2] Ibid.
[3] Birkenhead, p. 405.
[4] Quoted in Feiling, p. 372.

Czechoslovakia due to expire at 2 p.m., Chamberlain spoke in the House of Commons. In the middle of his speech a message was passed to him that Hitler had agreed to stay his troops for twenty-four hours in order to give time for a conference. When Chamberlain announced this to the Commons there were hysterical cheers of relief from all parts of the House.

Next morning Chamberlain was seen off by members of his Cabinet and by Geoffrey Dawson, the Editor of *The Times*, at Heston Airport on his third flight to Germany. From the depths of failure Chamberlain found himself raised again to the role of possible saviour of Europe. The newsreel film shows him that morning as a man full of himself, his manner masterful and confident, even cocksure. His dark eyes were agleam with impending triumph while he was telling the assembled journalists: 'When I was a little boy, I used to repeat, "If at first you don't succeed, try, try, try again!" This is what I am doing. When I come back I hope I may be able to say, as Hotspur says in *Henry IV*, "out of this nettle danger, we pluck this flower, safety".'

If it was a singular impertinence to associate himself with Harry Hotspur, that gallant heart, that high-mettled warrior, it was also a great pity that he chose not to quote also the letter read by Hotspur which immediately follows his quotation: 'This purpose you undertake is dangerous; the friends you have named uncertain; the time itself unsorted; and your whole plot too light for the counterpoise of so great an opposition. . . .'[1]

The conference in the Führer House in Munich took its shameful, farcical course. Russia was not invited; the Czechoslovakian representatives were kept under German police guard in their hotel while their country was being butchered. Mussolini produced a draft agreement in the guise of a proposal from a 'neutral'; it had in fact been drafted by the German Foreign Office. There followed thirteen hours of haggling. Characteristically enough, Chamberlain, who was conniving quite happily at the upset of the entire European strategic balance, proved stubborn over such details as compensation for the loss of private property rights in the transferred areas. The final agreement gave Hitler all he had demanded at Godesberg, but under the respectable trappings of international consent. The only essential difference was that the German occupation would take place in five stages up to 10 October, instead of in one bound on 1 October. The Czechs were given thirteen hours in which to make up their minds to accept. Deserted by those they thought were their friends, and whose own interest they had believed lay in supporting them, they

[1] *Henry IV*, *Part One*, Act II, Scene III.

accepted. Chamberlain returned home in a state of triumphant exaltation, to a welcome such as traditionally followed a famous victory. Indeed *The Times* actually opened its leading article on the Munich settlement with the words: 'No conqueror returning from a victory on the battlefield had come adorned with nobler laurels.'[1]

He had done it; he had given Europe peace; he had placed himself in the ranks of England's very greatest statesmen. When he spoke to joyful crowds from the balcony of No. 10 Downing Street, he was ill-advised enough to say, with reference to Disraeli's return from the Congress of Berlin in 1878: 'This is the second time in our history that there has come back from Germany to Downing Street peace with honour. I believe it is peace in our time.'

Next day, 30 September 1938, Chamberlain basked in the adulation of his Cabinet. The Chancellor of the Exchequer, Lord Simon, opened the feast by saying that

> he thought the present occasion justified a departure from the normal procedure at Cabinet meetings, and that, before the Prime Minister spoke, he should express, on behalf of the whole Cabinet, their profound admiration for the unparalleled efforts the Prime Minister had made and for the success that he had achieved. He would also like to say how proud they were to be associated with the Prime Minister as his colleagues at this time.[2]

Then Chamberlain gave his report of the Munich Conference. He explained that at the outset of the conference he had suggested that a Czech representative be sent for, 'but it had been represented that the matter was too urgent to permit of the delay that this course would involve'. But he said he had done his best for the Czechs in the absence of their own representatives. He then explained the differences between the Godesberg Memorandum and the Munich Agreement: the one was an ultimatum, the other an international agreement; German occupation would take place in five stages over ten days instead of at once; the line of occupation would be fixed by an International Commission, instead of being laid down by Hitler. 'He thought it could be fairly said that the Munich Agreement was a vast improvement. . . . He thought it was a triumph for diplomacy that representatives of the Four Powers concerned should have met and reached a peaceful settlement of the matter.'[3]

Of the earlier 'rebels' in the Cabinet, only Duff Cooper now felt it necessary to resign – when it was now in any case a useless gesture. For

[1] *The Times*, 1 October 1938. [2] CAB 23/95, 47(38). [3] Ibid.

before Munich the Cabinet had never once had the opportunity of approving or not approving the decisive initiatives and policies of the Prime Minister. All the Cabinet meetings in which the agonised soul-searching had taken place had ended with the postponement of the crucial decisions, so that the 'rebels' never found themselves with an issue and an occasion for resigning. Chamberlain's fateful decisions – to fly to Germany in the first place, to offer Hitler all he wanted if he would agree to a conference – were taken behind the Cabinet's back. By a curious inversion, Chamberlain was, at home, the cunning and ruthless tactician he so utterly failed to be in Germany.

Except for Duff Cooper, the 'rebels' were content to share in the Prime Minister's glory. Chamberlain received a fan mail of praise and gratitude from correspondents ranging from King George VI to humble people grateful that they were not after all going to be bombed.[1] Perhaps Alan Herbert, the Independent MP, best expressed their mood when he wrote long afterwards:

> My soul revolted at the thought of another, and, I was convinced by many expert opinions, a much worse war. . . . But, 'wishful thinker', 'anxious hoper', 'old soldier', or 'Christian believer' – what you will – I wanted Mr Chamberlain to be right, and keep the peace successfully . . . I voted sadly for Munich: and the whole thing made me feel ill.[2]

At least two prominent veterans of moralising internationalism nevertheless approved of the Munich Agreement enthusiastically rather than sadly. Lord Lothian, who was in Australia at the time, was profoundly relieved, and thought that Chamberlain had done 'a marvellous job', being 'the only man who steadfastly refused to accept the view that Hitler and the Nazis were incorrigible and would understand nothing but the big stick'.[3] And Clifford Allen (Lord Allen of Hurtwood) wrote so gushing a personal letter to Chamberlain that it drew from the Prime Minister the warm reply that 'I feel I must . . . send you a few words of thanks for having written to me in such generous terms and for letting me see the the notes which you are sending to your correspondents. If I may say so, they present a masterly statement of the case.'[4]

Allen also wrote to *The Manchester Guardian* to rebuke those who were ungrateful enough to criticise the Munich Agreement: 'We must force ourselves to remember that if we had had to buy peace today by what

[1] See Feiling, pp. 378–80 for a summary.
[2] Quoted in James, p. 339.
[3] Butler, *Lord Lothian*, p. 226.
[4] Quoted in Gilbert, *Plough My Own Furrow*, p. 416.

some would call dishonour, it was because twenty years ago we imposed peace by dishonour.'[1]

The critics of Chamberlain's policies however now included Lord Cecil of Chelwood, a founding father of the League of Nations, a man described by Allen in his letter to *The Guardian* as 'that noblest of international thinkers', but whose idealism, fervent though it had been from the middle of the Great War right through the 1920s and early 1930s, had finally succumbed to fact. In May 1938 he had noted in a letter that German diplomacy had never in history been founded on honest dealing. 'The Germans', he wrote, 'really conceive of their country as always under war conditions in this respect. No one expects a belligerent to tell the truth and, to the German mind, they are always belligerent. The Germans take the view that war is only intensified peace. . . .'[2]

Now after Munich, Cecil wrote to *The Guardian* to ask:

> But supposing there is a German guarantee, of what is its value? It is unnecessary to accuse Germany of perfidy. Not only the Nazi Government but all previous German Governments from the time of Frederick the Great downwards have made their position perfectly clear. To them an international assurance is no more than a statement of present intention. It has no absolute validity for the future.[3]

It was such sentiments coming from Cecil, of all people, which provoked Clifford Allen to write his own post-Munich letter to the same newspaper, a letter of pained reproach: 'I cannot but feel with great respect that this is an appalling view to take of any nation. . . . If Lord Cecil's statement was accepted as true it could only mean that we have been playing a hideous farce in trying to build up the League of Nations. . . .'[4]

In the House of Commons debate on Munich, the Labour and Liberal parties were ranged solidly against the Government; not on strategic grounds, but on the score of morality and ideology. A robber power – and, what was worse, a Fascist power – had been positively helped by the British Government to enlarge itself at the expense of a small country, and, what was worse, a democratic country. Attlee, the Leader of the opposition, called it 'a victory for brute force';[5] Sinclair, the Liberal

[1] Letter published 20 October, quoted in ibid. pp. 416–20.
[2] Letter to Lord Londonderry, quoted in the Marquess of Londonderry, *Wings of Destiny* (London, Macmillan 1943), p. 211.
[3] Quoted in Gilbert, *Plough My Own Furrow*, pp. 416–20.
[4] Ibid.
[5] Hansard, *Parliamentary Debates* (House of Commons), Fifth Series, Vol. 339, col. 51.

Leader, 'a travesty of self-determination'.[1] But it was Churchill, that ignored, scorned figure on the Conservative back benches, who almost alone perceived what was really important about the Munich Agreement:

> ... We have suffered a total and unmitigated defeat, and ... France has suffered even more than we have ... you will find that in a period of time which may be measured by years, but may be measured by months, Czechoslovakia will be engulfed in the Nazi régime. We are in the presence of a disaster of the first magnitude. ... Do not let us blind ourselves to that. ...
>
> The system of alliances upon which France depended for her safety has been swept away. We have passed an awful milestone in our history, when the whole equilibrium of Europe has been deranged, and ... the terrible words have for the time being been pronounced against the Western democracies: 'Thou art weighed in the balance and found wanting.'[2]

Yet perhaps the most dangerous of all consequences of the Munich crisis was the total contempt in which Hitler now held Chamberlain. An English diplomat in the Berlin embassy was informed by reliable sources in Hitler's entourage that 'Hitler regarded the Prime Minister as an impertinent busybody who spoke the ridiculous jargon of an outmoded democracy. The umbrella, which to the ordinary German was a symbol of peace, was in Hitler's view only a subject of derision.'[3] According to the same sources, Hitler had been heard to observe: 'If ever that silly old man comes interfering here again with his umbrella, I'll kick him downstairs and jump on his stomach in front of the photographers.'[4]

On 14 November a meeting of the Cabinet Foreign Policy Committee discussed a number of confidential reports from hitherto reliable sources in Germany to the effect that Hitler was no longer worried by British re-armament; and that he no longer believed the British would go to war, and that he was therefore ready to embark on a vast programme of national expansion. This information led Halifax to argue: 'As regards Germany the immediate objective should be the correction of the false impression that we were decadent, spineless and could with little impunity be kicked about.'[5]

Chamberlain however discounted these reports as to the state of Hitler's opinion.[6] For he, for his part, emerged from the Munich crisis

[1] Hansard, *Parliamentary Debates* (House of Commons), Fifth Series, Vol. 339, col. 51.
[2] Ibid. cols. 359–73. [3] Kirkpatrick, p. 122. [4] Ibid. p. 135.
[5] CAB 27/624, FP(36). [6] Ibid.

with the happy conviction that both the Munich Agreement itself and the high respect which he believed Hitler now entertained for him as a man meant that his dream of settling the affairs of Europe was beginning to come true. As he wrote to the Archbishop of Canterbury on 2 October 1938: 'I sincerely believe that we have at last opened the way to that general appeasement which alone can save the world from chaos.'[1]

The very next day he expressed the same conviction to the Cabinet, though in more cautious language: 'He thought that we were now in a more hopeful position, and the contacts which had been established with the Dictator Powers opened up the possibility that we might be able to reach some agreement with them which would stop the armament race.'[2]

None the less he added that it would be 'madness' to stop re-arming until we were convinced that others would act likewise: 'For the time being, therefore, we should relax no particle of effort until our deficiencies had been made good. That, however, was not the same thing as to say that as a thank-offering for the present *détente*, we should at once embark on a great increase in our armaments programme.'[3]

So strongly did Chamberlain wish to nurture the tender plant of mutual respect and amity which he believed to have germinated at Munich that he even wanted to discourage the Lord Mayor of London from opening a fund for Czechoslovakian refugees for fear that it 'might have a bad effect on public opinion in Germany'.[4]

The Munich crisis was nevertheless followed by a lull prolonged throughout the winter of 1938–9, as if the English needed time to draw breath before the next round of concession no less than the Germans before the next bout of coercion. It was the unsleeping quiet of a night before a battle, uneasy with rumour, busy with stealthy preparation.

On 26 October the Cabinet appointed a committee to investigate and report on 'Defence Programmes and their Acceleration'.[5] All three services demanded large increases in their budgets; all reported continuing hold-ups in production owing to the shortage of skilled manpower and of appropriate British industries; all wished therefore to buy more foreign equipment.[6] The Chancellor of the Exchequer, Simon, had to point out, however, that British economic resources could not sustain these programmes, especially since revenue was 'sagging with the declining activity of the country as a whole'.[7] 'The Air Ministry's programme is . . .

[1] Feiling, p. 375. [2] CAB 23/95, 48(38). [3] Ibid.

[4] Ibid. The apologia sometimes made on Chamberlain's behalf that his motive during the Munich Crisis was to win time so that Britain might the better be prepared for an inevitable war is, therefore, on the documentary evidence, without foundation.

[5] CAB 27/648. [6] CAB 27/648, CP247(38). [7] Appendix to CP247(38).

so costly as to raise serious doubt whether it can be financed beyond 1939–40 without the gravest danger to the country's stability.'[1]

He noted, moreover, that the re-armament programme was leading to increasing imports and reduced exports: 'Our balance of payments – already a serious problem – will become more and more serious.'[2] Our monetary resources were already being heavily depleted, and 'might be still more rapidly exhausted and we should have lost the means of carrying on a long struggle altogether'.[3]

He therefore wished the Cabinet to concentrate on getting the full number of fighters for 1940 (1,850) but only enough bombers to keep the factories going – a policy which was not adopted.

On 1 December 1938 Inskip rendered to the Committee of Imperial Defence a general survey of British industrial war-potential in relation to the needs of the armed forces. He reported, in particular, that the War Office had pointed out that owing to the priority given to anti-aircraft defence, the field force, if war occurred within the next two years, 'would be compelled to take the field with obsolete medium artillery, which would be totally outranged by modern German artillery'.[4] The War Office therefore wanted the priority given to anti-aircraft defence to be reconsidered.

The very next day the CIGS himself (Lord Gort) reminded the Government, in a report on the state of readiness of the army,[5] that although a year ago the Cabinet had put the assistance of Britain's allies fourth in order of importance, the danger still remained of a German advance through the Low Countries against France. Germany was stronger because of the fall of Czechoslovakia; she would now have to fight on one front only. Yet owing to the Cabinet's decision in 1937 to create a 'general purpose' army, we could only send to France, and for a defensive role, two Regular infantry and one mobile division by the twenty-first day after mobilisation; two more Regular divisions equipped on a half-scale by forty days after mobilisation, and then nothing more for ten months. The CIGS went on to write that, despite our military weakness for a role against a first-class power, 'we may be called upon to implement it [this role], with all our available resources, as a matter of great emergency, to stave off a disaster'.[6]

Gort in fact wished to undo the effects of Liddell Hart's earlier advice to Hore-Belisha, Inskip and Chamberlain, and put Europe and the field force first, before imperial defence and the anti-aircraft defence of the

[1] Appendix to CP247(38).
[2] Ibid.
[3] Ibid.
[4] CAB 16/143, DPR 295.
[5] CAB 53/43, COS 811.
[6] Ibid.

United Kingdom. It was an only too timely recommendation, because at the turn of the year the Foreign Office reported that the French were now saying that they could not defend themselves alone, and needed British assistance.[1] Gort's proposals began to pass through the slowly grinding wheels of the Government decision-mill. However, in reopening the question of the proper role of the army, Gort provoked a fresh debate about the aims of British grand strategy and the assumptions on which it was based. On 21 December he sought to persuade his fellow Chiefs of Staff that we needed to help the French to go to the aid of Holland and Belgium; in order to fulfil this purpose he asked for complete equipment for four Regular army infantry divisions and two mobile (armoured) divisions; as regards the Territorial army, he wanted training equipment first, and then war-equipment for four divisions.[2]

The First Sea Lord (Sir Roger Backhouse) agreed that the French would want help on land or otherwise they might back out. But he conjured up an old spectre: he said that there was a danger that our land commitment could not be limited. Gort, in a reply which in a single sentence demolished the escapist British strategy of the past twenty years, recalled that 'Lord Kitchener had clearly pointed out that no great country can wage a "little" war'.

The Chief of Air Staff (Sir Cyril Newall) nevertheless himself dilated on the danger that a small BEF in France would open the way to an unlimited land war; a line he took up with even greater vigour at the COS meeting on 18 January 1939,[3] when he pronounced himself strongly against a policy 'which bound us to a land Continental commitment. Once we were launched on land in support of the French in France it might well be impossible to turn off the tap.' He wanted to know whether in fact England *was* committed to sending an army to France. Backhouse answered him by saying: 'We were morally committed, even though probably the Prime Minister's remarks to M. Daladier did not constitute an actual promise.'[4]

Gort then launched a ferocious attack on the whole theory of strategic mobility by means of seapower, which he characterised as a fallacy. In modern war, land transport was faster and more economical than sea transport. Tonnage was the Achilles Heel. The Alexandretta project favoured by Lloyd George in 1917 would have needed one million tons of shipping. '. . . experience proved that [maritime side-shows] invariably

[1] CAB 53/43, COS 825, December 1938–January 1939.
[2] CAB 53/10, COS 265.
[3] CAB 53/10, COS 268.
[4] Ibid.

led to vast commitments out of all proportion to the value of the object attained'.[1]

He warned that the Maginot Line, despite its strength, would sooner or later be broken, if there were only passive defence. He reminded his colleagues that the army (including the anti-aircraft defence of the United Kingdom) was only receiving £277 million out of some £2,000 million allotted for defence purposes.[2]

So it was that at the beginning of 1939 Britain's service leaders were still disputing the fundamental nature of British grand strategy, of which the rôle of the army was the touchstone. The impulse to turn the back on Europe, the facile lure of sea- and air-power, the distraction of imperial defence, were as strong as ever – except in the army – and this despite the inescapable preoccupation of all, service leaders and politicians alike, with Germany's military power and her plans for using it; a preoccupation constantly fed by rumour and report.

On 19 January 1939 the Foreign Office circulated to the Cabinet Foreign Policy Committee a memorandum on recent visits to Germany by two British 'Germanophiles', one of whom acknowledged that he had been an earlier apologist for the Nazis. These reports quoted various German sources and contacts to demonstrate the contempt which Germans from Hitler downwards now felt for Britain because of our 'feebleness' and 'gentleness'.[3] Vansittart believed that there was now an even chance that Germany would attack in the west before the east.[4]

In the same month the War Office reported to the Defence Policy and Requirements Committee that the immense delays in the delivery of armoured fighting vehicles under contracts originally due for completion by 31 March 1939 'may be attributed to several factors, but principally to the very real difficulty which has been experienced in specifying the characteristics (thickness of armour, speed, armament etc.) of the types to be put into production'.[5] Although the report did not say so, part of the difficulty in specifying the characteristics lay in the havering over the army's role which had gone on from 1934 to 1937, a role which was again a matter of dispute.

This bad news about the army's lack of tanks could hardly have been less fortunately timed, because on 23 January the Cabinet Foreign Policy Committee discussed whether or not England should give the Dutch a public guarantee against German aggression.[6] The committee was not

[1] CAB 53/10, COS 268. [2] Ibid. [3] CAB 27/627, FP(36)74.
[4] Ibid.
[5] CAB 27/627, DPR 297, Annex B to the 25th Progress Report by the War Office.
[6] CAB 27/624, FP(36)35.

eager, but debated the question again three days later[1] when it had the benefit of a COS Report on the subject.[2] The Chiefs of Staff were of the opinion that 'we have, as we see it, no choice but to regard a German invasion of Holland as a direct challenge to our security'.[3] When they looked at the broader implications of a war in Europe, however, the Chiefs of Staff proved no more sanguine about British prospects than in earlier years: 'If we were compelled to enter such a war in the near future we should be confronted with a position more serious than the Empire has ever faced before. The ultimate outcome of the conflict might well depend upon the intervention of other Powers, in particular the United States of America.'[4]

There was little, in the opinion of the COS, that we could do directly to save Holland. None the less they concluded that 'failure on our part to intervene would undermine our position in the world and would only mean that at some later stage we should have to face the same struggle with Germany with fewer friends and in far worse circumstances'.[5]

Both Chamberlain and Halifax expressed agreement with this point of view[6] – although throughout 1938 they had brushed the same arguments aside when put forward in regard to Czechoslovakia by Daladier, Duff Cooper and Oliver Stanley. It was a sign that Chamberlain and Halifax had undergone a notable reversal of opinion.

The Foreign Policy Committee agreed that forthcoming staff talks with the French should assume that Italy as well as Germany would be an enemy.[7]

On 1 March a new Cabinet Committee, the Strategical Appreciation Committee (set up on 24 February primarily to consider the Chiefs of Staff European Appreciation 1939–40), surveyed the entire strategic situation and noted glumly that with Germany, Italy and Japan as possible enemies and only France, in her present poor condition, as an ally, the British Empire was not very well placed. Hore-Belisha provided the information that it would take six months from the date of mobilisation to produce four Territorial divisions for France, and then only if war did not break out until a year's time.[8] But at least it had come to be accepted again that England would have to send a field force to Europe, although it was not until April that it was formally confirmed that in terms of land-forces France took priority over all other theatres.[9]

On 13 March, the new committee returned to these depressing topics.

[1] CAB 27/624, FP(36)36.
[2] CAB 27/627, FP(36)77.
[3] Ibid.
[4] Ibid.
[5] Ibid.
[6] CAB 27/624, FP(36)36.
[7] Ibid.
[8] CAB 16/209, SAC.
[9] CAB 16/209, SAC 13, CID Paper No. DP(P)45.

Hore-Belisha reported that by the end of the year we should be able to send two Regular divisions to France by mobilisation plus twenty-one days, and two more after four months. The first Regular armoured division would not be ready until the middle of 1940; the second not until later. The Committee turned to the problems that might arise in the Far East if England became fully involved in Europe; and in particular to the burden presented by Australia and New Zealand; 'this heavy commitment', as Chatfield (now Minister for the Co-ordination of Defence) put it.[1] At the same time there was the defence of the Low Countries, in which connection Hore-Belisha quoted a paragraph from the Chiefs of Staffs' 1939–40 Appreciation: 'It is, however, difficult to say how the security of the United Kingdom could be maintained if France was forced to capitulate. . . .'[2]

Europe or the Empire? – after nearly twenty years of speculation the British still found themselves unable to choose. They were still racked apart by opposite and irreconcilable strategic demands; still striving to find a solution to the insoluble. But on 15 March 1939, as the committees on this and the committees on that were treading their stately and slow-paced saraband of memoranda and meetings, there came an unseemly interruption. The German armed forces lunged forward in a sudden stroke and extinguished what remained of Czechoslovakian independence.

Chamberlain's surrender at Munich was thus finally consummated in the way that Churchill had foretold in October. The Czech army of forty divisions finally disappeared from the European balance, to provide equipment instead for forty new German divisions. It was a turnover of eighty divisions in Germany's favour; equivalent, as General Beaufre points out, to the army of France.[3] The great Czech armaments industry went to swell Germany's already enormous technological superiority. With German troops along the old Czech–Polish frontier in the Carpathians, Poland was even more deeply outflanked than hitherto. And German troops now also stood on the border of Romania, a country rich in the oil resources necessary for the waging of modern war. Chamberlain in his well-meaning blindness had brought about the greatest of all the catastrophes which had befallen France and England since Hitler came to power.

Nevertheless he and his colleagues felt themselves absolved from fulfilling their guarantee of Czech integrity, since the German occupation of Prague had followed the break-away of Slovakia from the Czech state

[1] CAB 16/209, SAC 2. [2] Ibid. [3] Beaufre, p. 84.

and an agreement signed in Berlin, if under duress, by Hacha, the Czech President, that Bohemia and Moravia should become a German protectorate. As Sir John Simon explained, it was impossible to fulfil a guarantee to a state which had ceased to exist.[1] Both sides, in their own way, had thus liquidated their pledges at the time of Munich.

The German occupation of Czechoslovakia finally shook English opinion awake from its beautiful twenty-year-old dream that the world was governed by morality and goodwill, and not by power and ambition. Even those most stubborn in self-delusion – Lothian, Smuts, *The Times* – at last perceived, like flat-earthers converted to Copernican astronomy, that moralising internationalism did not accord with the observable facts.[2] The most notable convert of all was the Prime Minister himself. He announced his conversion to his Cabinet on 18 March: '... up to a week ago we had proceeded on the assumption that we should be able to continue with our policy of getting on to better terms with the Dictator Powers, and that although those powers had aims, those aims were limited'.[3]

At the back of their minds, however, Chamberlain continued, there had been a reservation that this might not be the case, although it was right to try out the possibilities. 'He had now come definitely to the conclusion that Herr Hitler's attitude made it impossible to negotiate on the old basis with the Nazi régime.'[4]

The Prime Minister said that he regarded his own Birmingham speech on 17 March – 'any attempt to dominate the world by force was one which the Democracies must resist' – as 'a challenge to Germany on the issue whether or not Germany intended to dominate Europe by force. It followed that, if Germany took another step in the direction of dominating Europe, she would be accepting the challenge'.[5]

And in going on to discuss the new fear planted on 16 March by the Premier of Romania, who believed his country was next on Germany's list, Chamberlain argued: 'A German attempt to dominate Romania was, therefore, more than a question whether Germany would thereby improve her strategical position; it raised the whole question whether Germany intended to obtain domination over the whole of south-eastern Europe.'[6] It was a demonstration how utterly his way of looking at things

[1] Taylor, *Origins of the Second World War*, p. 251.

[2] Butler, *Lord Lothian*, p. 227; Sir K. Hancock, Vol. II, pp. 308–9; *History of the Times*, Vol. 4, Pt. II, pp. 960–1; Gannon, pp. 233–8; for the reaction of the rest of the British press to the occupation of Prague, see Gannon, pp. 239–62.

[3] CAB 23/98, 12(39)1.

[4] Ibid. [5] Ibid. [6] Ibid.

had changed since the previous March, when it had been Austria and Czechoslovakia which were in danger.

The Prime Minister therefore proceeded to put forward a new foreign policy – viz., to see if Russia, Poland, Yugoslavia, Turkey and Greece would join with France and England in resisting any act of German aggression aimed at south-eastern Europe.[1]

And so, in the third week of March 1939, England at last returned to the balance of power as the guiding principle of her diplomacy. Now, at the worst possible time, when the European equilibrium was already steeply tilted in Germany's favour, and tilting more and more every day as the German army grew, England set out to create the grand alliance which she had so bigotedly refused to contemplate since 1933, since the early 1920s indeed. But while she strove during the spring and summer to halt Germany's further expansion, she had also simultaneously to contend with all the other elements that were making for the collapse of British power – the consequences of past folly and neglect, the competing and irreconcilable demands on England's inadequate strength, the burden and distraction of empire.

In London, the month of March, following the occupation of Prague, was a time of panic activity. On 18 March the Cabinet appointed a new committee on 'Defence Programmes and their Acceleration', which sat until 12 July. In fact, British industrial capacity could not support larger or faster programmes of re-armament without damage to exports and hence to the fragile balance of payments. Hore-Belisha reported that deliveries of machine tools were now quoted from fifty to sixty weeks. There was only one possible way, therefore, in which to increase munitions production, a way put forward by Chatfield (now Minister for the Co-ordination of Defence): 'Would it not be possible to put industry on a war production basis immediately, not necessarily at the expense of our export trade, but by curtailing internal consumption?'[2]

But Stanley, the President of the Board of Trade, showed a proper Cobdenite horror at such authoritarian interference in time of peace: 'Such a step would be almost revolutionary, and must be proved absolutely essential before introduction.'[3]

On 23 March German troops occupied Memel on the Baltic and thereby raised another gust of March windiness in London lest Germany might strike again soon at Poland; a gust which filled the sails of Chamberlain's project of a grand alliance with the countries of eastern Europe. But

[1] CAB 23/98, 12(39)1. [2] CAB 27/657, DP(39)1, 20 March 1939. [3] Ibid.

already he had come up against another dilemma; whether to try for Poland or Russia as the principal ally in Eastern Europe. Poland enjoyed the dubious advantage of being contiguous with Germany, while Russian troops could only intervene against Germany by arrangement with Poland and the Baltic states. Russia was Communist; did France and England wish to arrange a march of the Red Army far to the westwards into central Europe? Chamberlain himself was of opinion that Poland was more important than Russia.[1] On 27 March the Cabinet Foreign Policy Committee discussed the problem. Chamberlain said that the evidence was that attempts to build up a front against German aggression were likely to be frustrated if Russia was to be associated with it. He himself believed Romania would be Germany's next victim, and he pointed out the necessity 'for urgent and immediate action'.[2]

Halifax quoted a despatch of 10 March from the British ambassador in Moscow to the effect that the Russian army had been greatly weakened by the political purges of its officer corps in 1937–8, and that its offensive value was small; and thought that 'if we had to make a choice between Poland and Soviet Russia, it seemed clear that Poland could give the greater value'.[3] Inskip, now Dominions Secretary, said that Poland was probably the best of possible eastern allies militarily, but that he thought Russia would be a greater deterrent to Germany. Halifax remarked that the Polish army of fifty divisions would make a 'useful contribution'. Inskip asked a highly pertinent question: could Poland and Romania draw off enough German troops to enable the French to breach the Siegfried Line? This aspect had, he said, not yet been examined from a military point of view. Stanley quoted the Chiefs of Staff's opinion that Romanian independence was vital to us and said that 'her subjection by Germany was an issue on which we must fight'.

But it was Halifax who reminded the Cabinet of the long-standing and fundamental British predicament in regard to eastern Europe – one to which Austen Chamberlain had tried to find an answer in 1926, Eden in 1937,[4] and Chamberlain in 1938. Geography made it impossible for England to lend military weight to her diplomacy in that region. There was, Halifax said, no way in which we could save Poland or Romania. 'We were faced with the dilemma of doing nothing, or entering into a devastating war.' If we did nothing, the result would be a great accession of German strength, and a weakening of our own position and support. 'In these circumstances,' said Halifax, 'if we had to choose between two great evils, he favoured going to war.' Inskip agreed with him: 'In a

[1] CAB 23/95, 15(39). [2] CAB 27/624, FP(36)38. [3] Ibid. [4] See above pp. 465–6.

sentence, we were in a weak military position to meet a political situation we could not avoid.'

The committee gave its consideration to the usefulness of assuring Poland and Romania that, if they should resist aggression, we should go to their aid – a proposition hardly compatible with the views just voiced that it was not within our power to bring them aid.

Sir Samuel Hoare alone was of the firm opinion that Russia ought to be included in an Eastern Pact, because in his own words, 'all experience showed that Russia was undefeatable'.

On 30 March came another panic. The Foreign Secretary called a Cabinet at short notice because of information that an imminent German *coup de main* against Poland was likely. The Cabinet decided that, as the record expresses it, the Germans could not be allowed to take us by surprise – that Poland could not be allowed to let slip [*sic*], and that the Foreign Secretary, in answering a forthcoming arranged question in the House of Commons should answer that 'if . . . any action was taken which clearly threatened the independence of Poland so that Poland felt bound to resist with her national forces, His Majesty's Government would at once lend them all the support in their power'.[1]

That afternoon Beck, the Polish Foreign Minister, accepted this British assurance between, as he put it, 'two flicks of the ash off his cigarette'.

In such panicky haste therefore did the British finally and totally reverse their traditional eastern European policy by giving to Poland the guarantee they had refused to give to Czechoslovakia in 1937–8, and thereby accept at last that Europe posed a single, indivisible strategic problem. Yet it was an incautious guarantee. It was unconditional; it was up to the Poles, not the British, to decide when and whether the time had come to fight. It was one-sided; for Poland was not asked to give a reciprocal assurance.[2]

The circumstances in which so fateful a guarantee was given, together with the rashness and looseness of its wording, serve to show that, although Chamberlain and his colleagues had at last recognised what kind of game they were playing, it did not follow that they could play it very well. In Chamberlain's attempts to create an anti-German front there was – hardly surprisingly – the same direct simplicity, or naïveté, of approach, the same lack of wariness and tactical sense which he had displayed when his foreign policy had been inspired by moral idealism.

[1] CAB 23/95, 16(39).

[2] See also Foreign Policy Committee meeting on the same day and on 31 March, CAB 27/624, FP(36)39; FP(36)40.

Contrary to what is sometimes supposed, however, the Cabinet had enjoyed the benefit of the advice of the Chiefs of Staff[1] before offering their guarantee to Poland. The Chiefs of Staff had recommended that the British announcement should make clear that Britain would not intervene unless there had been a definite act of aggression against Polish territory; unless the Poles resisted and asked us for aid; and unless the French were fully committed with us. In fact Chamberlain issued the guarantee in France's name without consulting the French Government, thus giving the French little choice but to consent. Chamberlain however ignored the Chiefs of Staff's further opinion that it was important that the Poles should make a simultaneous declaration that they would aid Great Britain or France if those countries were attacked.[2]

April blossomed profusely with trouble: old predicaments put forth fresh life; new dilemmas sprang out of the ground. On 3 April the COS reported fully on the military implications of the terms of Anglo-French guarantee to Poland – and of a possible extension of the guarantee to Romania.[3] The report only served to emphasise the allied dilemma: 'Neither Great Britain nor France could render direct assistance to Poland or Romania by sea, land or air; nor could they supply them with armaments.'[4]

There was little doubt, in the COS's opinion, that Germany was capable of occupying Romania, Polish Silesia and the Polish Corridor, and that it would only be a matter of time before all Poland was eliminated. No rapid or spectacular success, on the other hand, was possible in the west against the Siegfried Line. However, a two-front war would serve to increase the strain on the German forces.[5]

On 10 April, one of the British Empire's other potential enemies, Italy, carried out a fresh aggression of her own, invading and swiftly conquering Albania. The Cabinet Foreign Policy Committee therefore not only discussed at its meeting that day what to do if Germany attacked Romania and what form and scope a British guarantee to that country would take, but also how best to implement the general principle adopted by the Cabinet earlier in the morning of 'reinforcing Greece and Turkey against possible Italian expansion and aggression'.[6] The Foreign Secretary defined the latest predicament: 'We had to find a middle road between provoking Italy on the one hand, and on the other not doing enough to give Italy clear warning that we should join in resisting aggression.'[7]

[1] CAB 53/11, COS 288, 30 March 1939.
[2] Ibid.
[3] CAB 53/47, COS 872.
[4] Ibid.
[5] Ibid.
[6] CAB 27/624, FP(36)41.
[7] Ibid.

Next day the committee got back to the problems of creating an anti-German coalition; there was now a suggestion of creating a Balkan bloc, including Turkey, Yugoslavia and Bulgaria. It was thought Greece would serve our purposes better as a neutral.[1] No one seemed to note that, since France and Britain had virtually nothing to offer these countries by way of aid or protection, all projected coalitions were fantasies. Yet on 19 April there was more talk about an approach to Turkey, which was seen as the key to a Balkan bloc.[2]

Russia too was still regarded as a possible runner, and the Foreign Policy Committee, in the meeting of 11 April, regretted the lack of recent and good information on her armed forces. It was decided to refer this question to the Chiefs of Staff. Chatfield however observed that it was clear that the political arguments against Russia being an ally outweighted any military advantages; and that therefore the COS should not be asked to give a military appreciation for or against a Russian alliance, but confine themselves to Russia's military capability.[3]

On this same busy day, 11 April, was rendered the Stage 1 Report on the Anglo-French Staff conversations about joint plans and strategy in the event of war.[4] These exchanges, between senior military, naval and air representatives, were not the hasty result of the German march on Prague, but the slowly matured fruit of a French suggestion after Munich.

The Strategic Memorandum which was put before the conference by the British delegation[5] was a no less melancholy document than the COS report a year earlier on the military implications of war over Czechoslovakia. At sea the combined strength of England and France as at 1 April 1939 was only slightly greater than that of the Axis Powers (Germany, Italy *and* Japan), with 19 capital ships to 14; 7 aircraft carriers to 6; and 72 cruisers to 67. In destroyers and submarines they were outnumbered 135 to 194, and 134 to 224.[6] On land, as at 1 April, France and Britain were now overwhelmingly outnumbered. Britain herself could put no divisions at all into the field in Europe by the eighteenth day after mobilisation, but 3 in Egypt. France would initially field 54 divisions (including one armoured and five mobile) to Germany's 96 (including five armoured); and later 76 to 106. Italy could field a total of 76 divisions; Japan 28 in China and another 16 in Japan itself, Manchuria and Formosa. The 13 British Territorial divisions had no equipment and would not be ready for the field for another year. India could only furnish 3 brigade-groups

[1] CAB 27/624, FP(36)42. [2] CAB 27/624, FP(36)43. [3] CAB 27/624, FP(36)420.
[4] CAB 16/209, AFC 7 (Revise); see CAB 29/159 for the proceedings and memoranda of the conversations.
[5] 20 March 1939, AFC 1, CAB 29/159. [6] Ibid.

for service outside India. 'It will be seen that at no time in the initial phases will the combined British and French army formations available in Europe be equal to that of Germany.'[1]

In the air too the lapse of a year had done little to remedy the crushing Allied inferiority. In the European theatre, England and France opposed 1,290 and 1,450 aircraft to Germany's estimated 3,700, and Italy's 1,393. In the Middle East they opposed 328 and 246 to Italy's 414, although much of Italy's metropolitan strength would also be available for a war in the Mediterranean. In India there were 96 British aircraft; in the Far East 38. The Japanese air force was estimated to number 1,343 aircraft. 'It must be admitted that the Allied Air Forces are very greatly inferior to those of Germany and Italy in air-striking power, judged on the basis of firstline strength, and that in April 1939 the position regarding allied reserves will be most unsatisfactory.'[2]

The memorandum summarised the possible plight that England and France now had to face:

> We are considering a situation in which we, allied to France, would be engaged in war with Germany and Italy simultaneously and when Japan would also be a potential enemy. . . . The British Empire and France would thus be threatened at home, in the Mediterranean and in the Far East at the same time, and it would be hard to choose a worse geographical combination of enemies.[3]

In 1939, the memorandum continued, 'our state of readiness for war will not compare, on the whole, with that of the nations we have assumed as hostile . . .'[4]

And the memorandum's final conclusion was: 'It is clear, therefore, that in facing Germany and Italy in 1939, France and Great Britain would be undertaking a considerable commitment. . . .'[5]

This then was the sombre strategic reality behind Chamberlain's hasty guarantee to come to the aid of Poland – behind his efforts to create a great anti-German coalition. Chamberlain in his eagerness to proffer British 'guarantees' was like a bankrupt passing dud cheques.

The facts and figures contained in the British Strategic Memorandum seemed to offer little enough promise of eventual victory if war should come. Nevertheless, the same memorandum hopefully put forward a strategy[6] which was adopted with little alteration by the two delegations:

> . . . we must be prepared to face a major offensive directed against either England or France. To defeat such an offensive we should have

[1] Ibid. [2] Ibid. [3] Ibid. [4] Ibid. [5] Ibid. [6] Ibid.

> to concentrate all our initial efforts, and during this time our major strategy would be defensive.
>
> Our subsequent policy should be directed to holding Germany and to dealing decisively with Italy, while at the same time building up our military strength to a point at which we shall be in a position to undertake the offensive against Germany.[1]

This strategy of protracted war, however, absolutely depended on an assumption that the financial and economic resources of France and England were such as could support a long conflict; an assumption also shared by the Chiefs of Staff's 1939–40 Appreciation. Unfortunately this assumption was – at least so far as England was concerned – utterly and completely mistaken. Indeed, the truth was quite the contrary, as was pointed out to the Strategical Appreciation Committee on 6 April by Sir Alan Barlow, Under-Secretary at the Treasury: 'The position had radically changed for the worse compared with 1914. First of all our internal stability was not so great, and secondly we had not the same resources for purchasing supplies from abroad. ... We were already experiencing anxiety as to payment for stores from abroad for which dollars are required. ...'[2]

Borrowing abroad offered little hope: 'Everyone knew how shaky our position was and world opinion was so susceptible that no one could tell when the slide might not begin.'[3] Sir Alan drew the conclusion that 'if we were under the impression that we were as well able as in 1914 to conduct a long war we were burying our heads in the sand'.[4]

Whereas, therefore, the British could only hope to win a long war, they could only afford a short one. It was one of the most interesting of all the dilemmas of 1939.

While the Anglo-French staff delegations were busy evolving their economically nonsensical grand strategy, and the British Government were continuing to play at European coalitions, the potential danger in the Far East was the subject of attention by the Foreign Office and the COS Joint Planning Staff. On 20 April the Joint Planners examined the possibility of Japanese attacks on Singapore by means of landing in Johore and on North Borneo; in each case they considered that the Japanese might set up bases in Siam as a preliminary. Since the garrison at Singapore was not a war establishment, reinforcements would have to be sent without delay if the Japanese attacked. At the same time, the British fleet would have to be despatched promptly to the Far East,

[1] CAB 29/159, AFC 7. [2] CAB 16/209, SAC 4. [3] Ibid. [4] Ibid.

because Singapore held only three months' reserve supplies. This would mean the abandonment of the eastern Mediterranean; a decision 'not lightly to be undertaken' because, under Anglo-French war strategy, there was hope of launching early attacks on the Italians.[1]

Unfortunately the Foreign Office had to report at the same time that while Japan was a potential enemy, the United States was not a potential ally: '. . . it would appear as matters now stand that His Majesty's Government should expect no more from the United States Government in wartime than the maximum degree of assistance compatible with the preservation of United States' neutrality'.[2]

On 24 April it was the turn of the Chiefs of Staff to render their report on the Military Effectiveness of Russia.[3] They rated it low. Although they believed Russia possessed 9,000 good but lightly armoured tanks, and could mobilise thirty cavalry divisions and a hundred infantry divisions after three months of war, poor road and rail communications between Poland and Russia meant that 'any substantial military support to Poland is out of the question'. The Russian aircraft industry was not much good. The state of Russian industry as a whole was so bad, so disorganised, that when taken together with poor rail communications, '. . . we consider it doubtful whether the national economy of the Soviet could deliver war stores at a greater rate than would suffice to keep in the field [on the Western Frontier] thirty divisions'.[4]

After two or three weeks, military mobilisation would have to be abandoned to prevent a complete breakdown in industry and the national life.[5]

On 25 April Chatfield summed up this report for the benefit of the Cabinet Committee on Foreign Policy: 'Russia, although a great Power for other purposes, was only a Power of medium rank for military purposes. . . . Her assistance would be of considerable, though not of great, military value. . . .'[6]

There were therefore apparently good military as well as political reasons for not prizing a Russian alliance very highly or making very strenuous efforts to secure one. Indeed on 5 May Halifax was giving vent to a positive fear that we might get drawn into a formal alliance with Russia.[7]

Yet in point of fact the Chiefs of Staff were themselves strongly *in favour* of a Russian alliance, although the terms of reference given to them

[1] CAB 53/48, COS 886 (JP).
[2] Quoted in COS 881 (JP) of 19 April 1939, CAB 53/48.
[3] CAB 53/48, COS 887; also CAB 27/627, FP(36)82.
[4] CAB 53/48, COS 887.
[5] Ibid.
[6] CAB 27/624, FP(36)44.
[7] CAB 27/624, FP(36)45.

in preparing their report had denied them the opportunity of saying so. They were not only in favour of it for its own sake, but because they were afraid that otherwise there was a danger that Russia might become allied to Germany.[1] Chatfield passed on their point of view to the Cabinet Foreign Policy Committee on 16 May.[2] He also expressed their conviction that England should aim at a full reciprocal alliance with Russia, because otherwise she was unlikely to get any agreement with her.

Chamberlain himself thought that the military and strategic considerations pointed one way, the political another.[3] Halifax believed the political reasons against a Russian alliance were the stronger. Chatfield, as always a voice of clear-headed strategic realism in a Cabinet hardly distinguished for this quality, argued however: '... if for fear of making an alliance with Russia we drove that country into the German camp we should have made a mistake of vital and far-reaching importance'.[4]

But Chamberlain had another idea, or rather another fantasy, to propound: 'Rather than consent to a Triple Alliance to include Russia he, the Prime Minister, would prefer to extend our guarantee against aggression to the Baltic States, though this was a proposition on which he would like to have time to reflect.'[5]

Hoare, the Home Secretary, again expressed himself in favour of a Russian alliance.

But although France desperately wanted a Russian alliance – which had saved her in 1914 – and although Churchill and Lloyd George too passionately advocated it, Chamberlain, stubborn as ever, confident in his own judgement as ever, was not convinced. On 19 May he argued that 'there were still important moderate elements in Germany which it was desirable to foster and encourage. He greatly feared that an alliance with Russia would drive those moderate elements into Hitler's camp.'[6]

On 22 May came news of another alliance: Italy and Germany had signed the 'Pact of Steel', by which they committed themselves to waging war in common. It was a conclusive end to Chamberlain's long-standing hope of winning Mussolini back from Hitler's side; payment of the penultimate instalment of the price for British high-mindedness over Abyssinia.

As May gave way to June, all the flurry and urgent bustle stirred up by the German march on Prague gradually subsided; instead there was a mutter of protracted but indecisive diplomatic exchanges: England and

[1] Cf. Aide-Mémoire by the COS, Appendix II to CAB 27/625, FP(36)47.
[2] CAB 27/625, FP(36)47.
[3] Ibid.
[4] Ibid.
[5] Ibid.
[6] CAB 27/625, FP(36)48.

Germany; France and Poland; France and England and Russia. On 13 June a discussion in the Cabinet Foreign Policy Committee on the problem of defending Denmark provided Chamberlain with an opportunity of making a fresh statement of his current foreign policy:

> ... our general policy towards Germany was directed not to protecting individual States which might be threatened by Germany but to preventing German domination of the Continent resulting in Germany becoming so powerful as to be able to menace our security.
>
> German domination of Poland or Romania would increase her military strength and it was for this reason that we had given guarantees to those countries.[1]

It would have been an admirable policy, but for the fact that it was six, ten, twenty years late; too late.

Germany, however, was not the only item on the agenda of this meeting; there was a new crisis in the Far East to consider. The British concession area at Tientsin in China had been violated by Japanese troops and British subjects put to brutal indignities. This caught England, as the Foreign Policy Committee sadly remarked, when she was trying to build up a Balkan front, and needed her naval strength in the Mediterranean. On 16 June the Chiefs of Staff reported that the absolute but undesirable minimum strength for a fleet for the defence of Singapore was seven capital ships. However, to denude the eastern Mediterranean completely would only yield five, and therefore two more would have to be detached from the Home Fleet.[2] Two days later the COS advised that if England sent an adequate fleet to the Far East, then her position in Europe would be endangered.[3] A joint committee of representatives of the Foreign Office, Colonial Office and Board of Trade reported on 16 June on possible reprisals against Japan in language no less despondent:

> Japan, counting – as she evidently might – upon action by the totalitarian powers in Europe if we became involved in the East ... might well answer reprisals with counter-reprisals and even with warlike measures against exposed British interests in the Far East. If we could not effectively fight back, our prestige in those regions would be far more seriously damaged.[4]

Halifax himself wrote that the Japanese aim was to get us and other foreign interests out of China, and gain control of China, Manchuria and

[1] CAB 27/625, FP(36)51.
[2] CAB 53/50, COS 931, 16 June 1939.
[3] CAB 27/627, COS 928.
[4] CAB 27/627, FP(36)94.

East Asia as a base for a later southwards move against the British Empire. There was a need to do something to deter them, but what? And he went on to delineate the predicament in which England had been finally landed by her Far Eastern and Pacific policy since 1921. Compromise or co-operation with the Japanese, he wrote, 'appears to be ruled out, since it would lead to the downfall of China, it would put Japan in a better position to undermine the British Empire in the Far East, and it would alienate America, whose goodwill is essential to us in the West as well as in the East'.[1] But to do nothing, Halifax went on, would only encourage Japan and other totalitarian states.[2]

In the end the Cabinet Foreign Policy Committee could only decide that because of British weakness there was no other course but to seek a peaceful settlement of the Tientsin affair.[3]

Meanwhile half-hearted negotiations were still dragging on with Russia. While the French desired a straightforward pact of mutual assistance with Russia, the English feared that this might commit them to go to the aid of Russia if she were attacked by Germany with Polish or Romanian acquiescence or connivance. The Russians, on their side, demanded the right to move forward into the Baltic states (Latvia, Estonia and Lithuania) whenever they judged those states threatened by aggression; a condition the British could not swallow, it being against their principles 'to traffic', as Nevile Henderson put it later, 'in the honour of neutral Baltic States',[4] even in order to buy a valuable ally. Here was yet another dilemma; how could Russia in fact intervene unless Poland and the Baltic states, or Romania, agreed in advance to let the Red Army in? The British Government was reluctant so to persuade them, for reasons as much political as moral.[5]

As the summer progressed, the question of German designs on Poland still remained: a continual source of latent tension; thunder grumbling beneath the European horizon. On 4 July, in the Cabinet Foreign Policy Committee, Halifax canvassed the idea that Danzig as a Free City inside the Reich might satisfy Hitler without war.[6]

Next day the Chancellor of the Exchequer lectured the Cabinet on the problem that underlay all the others: Britain's economic weakness. Our balance of trade, said Simon, was not as favourable as in 1914; our sterling balances and gold reserves were falling [as a result of overseas purchases for the re-armament programme]: 'We should realise that we were

[1] CAB 27/627, FP(36)95. [2] Ibid. [3] CAB 27/625, FP(36)53.
[4] Nevile Henderson, p. 239.
[5] See the May–August files of the Cabinet Foreign Policy Committee CAB 27/625.
[6] CAB 27/625, FP(36)55.

steadily reducing our war chest. It was impossible to say when war might break out. If it should break out some years hence, it was important that those who were responsible for policy should realise that our financial strength was then likely to be much weaker than it was to-day.'[1]

And Sir Richard Hopkins, the Second Secretary to the Treasury, observed that Germany was in fact better off than England in terms of a long war. According to a 'Note on the Financial Position' provided by the Treasury for the Cabinet's enlightenment, British gold reserves would barely last three years at the present rate, let alone at a war rate, and therefore: '. . . unless, when the time comes, the United States are prepared either to lend us or to give us money as required, the prospects for a long war are becoming exceedingly grim'.[2]

On 19 July the Chiefs of Staff decided that there were no grounds for assuming that Italy could be knocked out of a war in its early stages.[3]

On 23 July the Russian Foreign Minister, Molotov, sought to overcome British hesitations about a full political alliance by suggesting that instead there should be purely military talks. The French were enthusiastic; the English fell in reluctantly. On 1 August, at long last, a joint French and English mission set off for Russia – a mission headed not by foreign ministers with full powers, but only by staff officers, even if of high rank.

The mission proceeded to Russia by sea, taking nine days on the voyage. Rail travel via Berlin was ruled out for obvious reasons. The reasons why the mission did not fly to Moscow were less obvious, but much in character. The only available airliners, two old short-range 'Hannibal' biplanes, would have to fly overland, necessitating a refuelling stop in Berlin, a place the mission wished to avoid. The alternative was to fly by the oversea route to Russia via Denmark, which would require eight 'Sunderland' flying boats. Unfortunately these eight aircraft were the only modern flying boats available to the British fleet, and could not therefore be spared.[4]

Thus while Europe began its final lurch towards war, the British and French military missions were sailing leisurely through the North Sea and the Baltic in the SS *City of Exeter*, whose solid comforts, Indian crew, and superb curries breathed the last enchantments of the Edwardian Empire.

In August 1939, the League-of-Nations Free City of Danzig, an enclave between East Prussia and Poland with a predominantly German-speaking population and a Nazi-controlled Senate, served the place of the Sudeten-

[1] CAB 23/100, 36(39).
[2] CAB 23/100, CP149(39).
[3] CAB 53/11, COS 309.
[4] CAB 27/625, FP(36)60, 1 August 1939.

land a year before: anti-Polish demonstrations, demands to be allowed to join the Reich. Hitler, having stated his demands on Poland in the spring, followed his usual strategy of vague menace – military preparations, the uttering of blood-curdling threats of forcible intervention to visiting statesmen – a strategy well designed to give him both the initiative and freedom of manœuvre. But in 1939 the strategy did not work as it had in 1938; the Poles, unlike the Czechs, simply refused to budge. Since Britain was now unconditionally committed to go to war for Poland if the Polish Government thought its independence threatened, the British Government had locked themselves into yet another fearsome predicament, and this time the most dangerous of all.

For Chamberlain and Halifax, aware as they were of England's military, and even more her economic, weakness, still wished above all things to *avoid*, not fight, a European war. The purpose of the Polish and Romanian guarantees, and of the military convention with Russia (if it ever came off), was deterrent; to have to fulfil them could only lead to a catastrophe for England. All through the spring and summer the British Government sought to bring about a peaceful solution of the German–Polish dispute by pressure in Warsaw and by trying to demonstrate to Hitler how much more profitable it would be for him if he refrained from force. This was a new and different kind of appeasement, no longer motivated by idealism, but expediency; appeasement wholly justified by the state of British world power.

Unfortunately its chances were ruined by Polish pride, obstinacy and *folie de grandeur*. Unfortunately too Chamberlain's attempt to propel Hitler along the right course by threatening him with war if he were violent and offering him rich rewards if he were not, suffered from Hitler's total disbelief since Munich that this sanctimonious old gentleman with the umbrella would ever really go to war. It was a year too late for a show of British resolution to exert any deterrent power; perhaps four or five years too late. As Hitler told Ciano, the Italian Foreign Minister, on 12 August, he proposed to attack Poland by the end of the month unless he got complete satisfaction beforehand: 'he was absolutely certain that the Western democracies . . . would shrink from a general war'.[1]

On 14 August Marshal Voroshilov, the chief Russian representative in the Anglo-French-Russian Staff talks, cut through the evasions and inconsistencies of the proposals put forward by the English and French delegations by asking: '. . . will Poland accept the entry of Soviet troops in the Vilna corridor in order to make contact with the enemy; likewise will

[1] Quoted in Taylor, *Origins of the Second World War*, p. 309.

Poland give our troops access to Galicia; likewise allow them passage to get to Romania?'[1]

But Admiral Sir Reginald Plunkett Ernle-Erle-Drax, the chief English representative, and General Doumenc, the chief French representative, could only return Voroshilov a shuffling answer, for he had asked the key questions which their governments had never been able to bring themselves to face and answer. Twice Voroshilov bluntly pressed his questions home, saying: 'I consider that a reply to these questions is of cardinal importance. Without a precise answer, any continuation of these discussions is useless.'[2]

The Anglo-French delegations reported to their governments, requesting that Polish agreement be sought to the Russian requests; agreement that was in the highest degree unlikely to be forthcoming. While it was being sought, the talks in Moscow carried on, an empty and tedious ritual. On 17 August Voroshilov said that there was no point in meeting again until his question about Polish permission for the entry of Russian troops was answered. On 21 August the French Government, tired of British hesitations and scruples and Polish obstruction, instructed the French delegation to negotiate and sign any agreement that would secure Russia as a military counterpoise to Germany. On 23 August the Poles at last agreed to a formula according to which common action between Poland and the USSR against German aggression 'is not excluded'.[3]

It was all too late. On 23 August Ribbentrop, the German Foreign Minister, and Molotov, the Russian Foreign Minister, signed a pact of friendship in Moscow. Publicly it was a non-aggression pact; secretly Germany gave Russia all she wanted, all that France and England had dithered so long over giving – recognition of the Baltic states and Eastern Poland as a sphere of Russian expansion. It was only nine days since Germany had first put forward suggestions of a Nazi–Soviet agreement; three days since Ribbentrop himself had arrived in Moscow. Germany, not France and England, had won Russia, and won her by swift decision, prompt action, and a realistic willingness to pay the full purchase price.

Chamberlain himself not only shared the general shock in England and France that these two ferocious old ideological enemies should sign a pact of friendship, but was also surprised and pained for another reason, for, as

[1] Beaufre, pp. 109–10. General Beaufre was a member of the French delegation, and provides in ch. 6 of his book a vivid picture of the confused minds and contradictory hopes in London and Paris which the unfortunate English and French delegations represented; and the consequent ineffectiveness of their attempts at negotiating.

[2] Ibid. p. 111.

[3] Taylor, *Origins of the Second World War*, p. 317.

he confided to his Cabinet on 24 August: 'It appeared to be contrary to good faith that, while we were conducting negotiations with the Russians in all confidence, they should have been negotiating with Germany behind our backs.'[1]

What the British Chiefs of Staff had warned against in May had thus come to pass: Chamberlain and his colleagues in their squeamishness about making an alliance with Russia had indeed driven her into the German camp; had indeed, in Chatfield's words back in May, committed a mistake of 'vital and far-reaching importance'.[2] Once again a British Government had been unable to bring itself to make clear-cut choices: in this case between Poland and Russia, and between a Russian alliance and the sovereign rights of Poland and the Baltic states.

Poland now stood alone in the east, beyond hope of direct aid. Chamberlain's clumsy and naïve attempts to create an anti-German coalition had been brought to nothing. Russia and Germany alike therefore took it that England and France would have the sense to abandon a lost cause, and compel the Poles to yield, like Czechoslovakia in 1938. Chamberlain however still clung to his double policy of appeasement and deterrence. On 22 August, the day after it became known that Ribbentrop had been invited to Moscow, the Cabinet agreed to Chamberlain's suggestion that the Government should make it clear that they stood firm by their obligations to Poland, while at the same time appealing to Hitler, by means of a personal letter from the Prime Minister,[3] to seek a peaceful solution.[4] The Government's announcement in Parliament later the same day that England would honour her guarantee was received with much enthusiasm; an enthusiasm into which cold calculations of British interest did not enter. It was concern for moral principle which now impelled the British to resist Germany, just as in earlier years it was moral principle which had impelled them to make concessions to her.

On 1 September 1939, despite a last flurry of personal correspondence between Chamberlain and Hitler, and frenzied official and unofficial diplomatic activity in London, Berlin and Warsaw, the German armed forces invaded Poland. Thus ended in ruin Chamberlain's 1939-model foreign policy, of deterrence combined with appeasement. In particular, the British guarantee to Poland had entirely failed of its deterrent purpose. Was it therefore still in England's interest to fulfil it? Poland herself could not be saved, but only restored after a great war – an argument which, when applied to Czechoslovakia in 1938, had seemed to the Cabinet

[1] CAB 23/100, 42(39).
[2] See above p. 566.
[3] The idea was Nevile Henderson's.
[4] CAB 23/100, 41(39)5.

decisive in favour of abandoning that country to its fate. If on the other hand – as the Cabinet rebels had rightly argued in 1938 – it was a larger question of German ambition, was it now too late successfully to halt Germany by force? Had the strategic balance been allowed to tilt too far in Germany's favour?

Financially and economically, as the Treasury analyses made clear, England was less well able to support a long conflict in 1939 than in the previous year. Militarily the balance had swung further against the Allies in the last twelve months, for whereas the British field force available for Europe was still no larger, the superiority of the German army over the French army on mobilisation had risen from 57 field divisions to the French 53 in March 1938,[1] to 96 to 54 in March 1939.[2] The German strength in panzer divisions had risen from 3 to 5 in the same period, while France had only one such division. The Siegfried Line, unfinished in 1938, had now been completed. Nor had the Allied inferiority in the air been remedied since the Czech crisis, except in terms of the air defence of Great Britain, which was irrelevant to the issue of a European campaign. On the contrary, the German superiority was believed to have increased. In March 1938 the Luftwaffe had been estimated to oppose 2,860 first-line aircraft to France and England's combined metropolitan strengths of 2,209.[3] In March 1939 it was estimated to oppose 3,700 aircraft to 2,740.[4] And, as the Chiefs of Staff had pointed out in March 1939, the Allies were 'very greatly inferior' to Germany in bombers.[5] The broad conclusion of the Chiefs of Staff in March had been: 'It is clear, therefore, that, in facing Germany and Italy in 1939, France and Great Britain would be undertaking a considerable commitment. . . .'[6]

Yet in point of fact no general discussion even took place in the Cabinet as to whether it would be expedient to fulfil the British guarantee to Poland. There were no prolonged and anguished debates such as had taken place during the Czechoslovakian crisis. Nor were the Chiefs of Staff asked for an assessment of the military implications of going to war over Poland. For throughout the Polish crisis there had been no doubt whatsoever in Chamberlain's mind, or in the mind of his Cabinet, or in the mind of Parliament and public, that there was only one course of action England could follow if Germany should attack Poland: the course of action dictated by moral obligation. On 1 September, as news came in of the bombing of Polish towns and the killing and maiming of women and children, Chamberlain told his colleagues: '. . . the Cabinet met under

[1] COS estimate CAB 27/627, FP(36)57, COS 698. [2] COS estimate, CAB 29/159, AFC 1.
[3] CAB 27/627, FP(36)57, COS 698. [4] COS estimate CAB 29/159, AFC I. [5] Ibid. [6] Ibid.

the gravest possible conditions. The event against which they had fought for so long and so earnestly had come upon us. But our consciences were clear, and there should be no possible question now where our duty lay.'[1]

Yet even now Chamberlain hoped that Hitler might consent to a conference, and thereby save England from a war which must, whatever its course, inevitably ruin her. The French Government too, having seen France's military superiority stripped from her since 1929 epaulette by epaulette and medal by medal, not least owing to the well-meant offices of England, was even less keen to fight for Poland than for Czechoslovakia. While the very last possibilities of a conference were being pursued. England and France therefore delayed their declaration of war.

At 7.30 p.m. on 2 September, as the Luftwaffe smashed a passage for the panzer divisions, and Poland began to realise that she was not, after all, a great power, Chamberlain made a statement in the House of Commons in the course of which, while he talked hopefully of a conference, he said nothing of British ultimatums. The Commons saw in this disappointing omission a sign of continued weakness and appeasement. Chamberlain sat down to a silent House, to listen to other speakers giving vent to stirring demands that an ultimatum should be despatched to Germany forthwith, on the grounds of honour and obligation – calls which much appealed to the emotional and chivalric mood of MPs of all parties that evening. After the debate, the pressure on Chamberlain to send an ultimatum without further delay continued to mount. There was a mutiny among his own Cabinet colleagues, the spokesman for which was – of all people – Sir John Simon. At 11.30 p.m. the Cabinet met – and agreed to instruct Sir Nevile Henderson to seek an interview with Ribbentrop next morning at 9 a.m. and inform the German Government that

> unless they were prepared to inform His Majesty's Government by 11 a.m. that they would . . . give satisfactory assurances that they had suspended all aggressive action against Poland, and were prepared promptly to withdraw their forces from Polish territory, a state of war would exist between Great Britain and Germany as from that hour.[2]

When the British ultimatum was delivered by Henderson next morning, it flabbergasted Hitler, as well it might, in view of all that had gone before since 1933. Who could have imagined that the British should have chosen such a moment and such a pretext for opposing German ambitions by force, when they had neglected so many better opportunities in the past? But just as the British had utterly failed to comprehend the outlook of

[1] CAB 23/100, 47(39)1.

[2] CAB 23/100, 49(39)1.

Nazi Germany until too late, so Hitler on his side completely misjudged the British. As Nevile Henderson justly observed in his memoirs, Hitler's 'great mistake was his failure to understand the inherent British sense of morality, humanity, and freedom'.[1]

It was this sense which at 11 a.m. on 3 September impelled the British into a war which, according to the Treasury, they could only afford to wage if short, but, according to the Chiefs of Staff, could only hope to win if long.

The crisis of British power had begun. Yet the war at first took an unexpectedly auspicious course, despite the extinction of Polish resistance in only three weeks. In the first place, the long-predicted instant 'knock-out blow' from the air on London and other British cities, dread of which had exerted so fatal an influence over pre-war British policy, failed to take place. The Luftwaffe, being a tactical and not a strategic air force, was fully occupied in supporting the German army's operations in Poland. Secondly Italy, unready for war, remained neutral, although the threat she represented compelled the French to allot twenty divisions to watch the Franco-Italian frontier and the frontier between Tunisia and Libya, and the English to keep naval forces in the Mediterranean which, as the Chiefs of Staff wrote on 21 April 1940, could 'ill be spared'.[2] And thirdly Japan forbore to descend on the British Empire in the East, although she, like Italy, remained a constant menace that could not be ignored. Instead therefore of the three enemies spaced out across the world which had been the nightmare of the British armed forces since 1935, France and England had only to contend with Germany.

And in 1939 Germany not only refrained from attacking England by air, she also refrained from that other course of action predicted by the Chiefs of Staff before the war, an attempt to bring about the collapse of France by a great offensive on land.

The Allies were thus accorded a reprieve in which to arrange themselves for the fray. On 12 September 1939 Chamberlain and Daladier, at a meeting of the Supreme War Council, confirmed the strategy of the protracted war which had been agreed by the English and French Staff delegations in April. Since, as the Allied leaders agreed, time was on their side, they decided to plan for a three-year war. There were to be no large-scale Allied operations until the Allies' full strength had been developed.[3]

Chamberlain for his part still could not bring himself to believe that the war would go on for long, or ever come to great battles. He still

[1] Nevile Henderson, p. 266. [2] CAB 66/7, WP(40)134. [3] CAB 66/1, WP(39)38.

hoped rather for a miraculous deliverance from the mortal predicament in which England found herself, for, with a present realism little shared by his countrymen, he privately 'very much doubted the feasibility' of military victory.[1] Instead he looked to early peace talks, brought about by the 'widespread desire for peace', a desire 'so deeply rooted'.[2] In the Supreme War Council he expressed a hope that before the time for the great Allied offensive had come Germany might have collapsed because of internal tension.[3]

Yet even during the 'Phoney War' of the winter of 1939–40 the ultimate collapse of British power was drawing steadily nearer. For the fundamental dilemma remained: the better the British equipped themselves to prosecute the war, the quicker they brought on their economic ruin.

On 22 September 1939 the War Cabinet discussed a proposal to create a British and Imperial army of fifty-five divisions – a proposal which marked the total demise of Liddell Hart's and Chamberlain's pre-war strategy of 'limited liability', or the avoidance of a large military commitment in Europe.[4] It had finally dawned that, just as in 1914–18, France would need the help of a great British army; that if France went, the British plight would be parlous indeed. However a memorandum by the Chancellor of the Exchequer, which was considered by the Cabinet at the same meeting, pointed out that the proposed fifty-five-division programme would depend on dollar machine tools and raw materials. Together with the current air programme for an eventual output of 2,500 aircraft a month and the naval building programme, it meant that we would be in 'very serious difficulties' over dollar exchange by the end of the second year of war.[5] This was a further prediction which made utter nonsense of the agreed Allied strategy of a three-year war.

The hapless Cabinet nevertheless authorised the erection and equipment of factories to equip an army of fifty-five divisions.[6]

In February 1940 Lord Stamp's 'Survey of the National Resources in relation to the War Effort', a document which the Chancellor of the Exchequer told his colleagues was of outstanding importance, again reminded the War Cabinet that their grand strategy had only the bog of national bankruptcy for a foundation.[7] According to Stamp's calculations – with which the Treasury agreed – Britain would have a balance-of-payments deficit of £250 million in the first year, even when all saleable

[1] Diary for 10 September 1939, quoted in Feiling, p. 418.
[2] Ibid.
[3] CAB 66/1, WP(39)38.
[4] CAB 65/1, 23(39)1; Second Report of the Land Forces Committee, War Cabinet Paper WP(39)37.
[5] CAB 65/1, WP(39)42.
[6] CAB 65/1, 23(39)1.
[7] See above p. 13.

British overseas assets had been realised at their market value, and even if the slender gold and dollar reserves were drawn upon to the extent of £150 million.[1]

The Cabinet discussed all manner of expedients for closing this vast gap, but without success.[2] Even during the inactivity of the 'Phoney War', therefore, England was quietly bleeding to death.

On 7 April 1940 Germany put an end to the delusive tranquillity by occupying Denmark and invading Norway in brilliantly improvised operations which exploited surprise and boldness to the uttermost. England and France responded by going to the aid of Norway with forces originally earmarked for defending Finland against Russia, a lunatic expression of altruism prevented, fortunately for the Allies, by a timely Finnish defeat. Nevertheless these were forces that could be ill-spared from the Western Front. Their operations, although also improvised like the German operations, were not similarly brilliant, being muddled and mishandled in every possible way. On 2 May the Allied forces ignominiously evacuated the central part of Norway. On 7 and 8 May there was a debate in the House of Commons on the handling of the Norwegian campaign, in which the critics attacked not the man most responsible, Winston Churchill, the First Lord of the Admiralty, but the unfortunate Chamberlain. The debate turned into a great inquest on Chamberlain's policies and leadership, in which many of those who had cheered him in relief and gratitude at the time of Munich expiated their own shame by putting the boot in now. Chamberlain in fact became the scapegoat not only for the nation's pre-war illusions and mistakes but also for its present frustrations. In the vote on the Opposition of censure, the Government's majority of about 240 sank to only 81; 41 Government supporters voted with Labour, and some 60 more abstained. On 10 May Chamberlain resigned, on the day the long-awaited German offensive in the west opened, a coincidence of events which fittingly closed the era of covenants without swords.

[1] See above p. 13.
[2] CAB 65/5, 40(40)1, 13 February 1940.

# VI

# VI: VICTORY AT ALL COSTS

Now came the reckoning for the escapist British refusal in the 1930s to accept the obvious lesson of the Great War that the security of France and the Low Countries depended on there being a powerful British army on the Western Front. The decision early in 1939 to reverse Liddell Hart's and Chamberlain's strategy of military isolation from Europe came too late; and far, far too late the decision in September 1939 to create an army of fifty-five divisions. The British contribution to the battle for Europe which opened on 10 May 1940 was only ten field divisions, plus four more in training in the Maginot Line, and a small air component ill-equipped and ill-trained for intervention in ground operations. The only British armoured division was in Egypt, a long way away from the Meuse; the second was forming in England. In April 1940, after eight months of war there were only 366,000 British troops in France, as against 936,000 still being trained and equipped in the United Kingdom, 19,000 in Norway, 76,500 in garrisons and defended ports throughout the empire (52,000 of them in the Middle East), plus 39,000 in India and Burma.[1]

Apart from the ten British divisions the French could only look to the Belgian army of twenty-two divisions, mostly fortress troops, and the Dutch army of eight divisions – allies to be rescued rather than significant sources of added strength. The brunt of the battle fell on the French army – 94 divisions against 134 German, ten of them panzer, of which number the Germans had been able to create four thanks to the Czech tanks which fell into their hands in March 1939.

And the French army, standing now at the end of a long process of moral and professional decline,[2] its equipment, doctrine and methods of command out of date, its commanders the ageing survivors of the great days of Foch and Joffre, was no match for the new German army. On 15 May, the day the Dutch surrendered, Paul Reynaud, now French

[1] War Office Progress Report for April 1940, 15 May 1940, CAB 68/6, WP(R)(40)145.

[2] See General A. Beaufre, *1940 The Fall of France* (London, Cassell 1967); John Williams, *The Ides of May: The Defeat of France May–June 1940* (London, Constable 1968), Pt. I; Guy Chapman, *Why France Collapsed* (London, Cassell 1968), Pts. I and II; Alistair Horne, *To Lose a Battle* (London, Macmillan 1969), Pt. I; Colonel H. Goutard, *The Battle of France 1940* (London, Frederick Muller 1958), Pts. I and II.

Premier, informed the new British Prime Minister, Winston Churchill, that the road to Paris lay open. Churchill had nothing to offer but rhetoric. On 20 May the panzer spearheads stood on the Channel coast. The BEF fell back on Dunkirk, its retreat made possible by the last stand of the French First Army round Lille. On 3 June the destruction of the Allied northern army group was completed when the last of some 330,000 survivors were evacuated from Dunkirk to England. General Maxime Weygand, called home from Syria to replace Gamelin and to attempt to save an already lost battle, prepared to defend the line of the Somme and the Aisne with 49 weak French divisions and one British against 104 German.

On 5 June the Germans renewed their offensive. On 11 June Italy declared war. On 14 June, despite a defence on the Aisne as stout as the French army had ever fought in its history, Paris fell. The exhausted and overwhelmingly outnumbered French began finally to break up. In Bordeaux, where the French Government had finally taken refuge, Churchill urged the French to fight on, though offering them nothing of greater substance in that undertaking than more rhetoric and an offer of common English and French citizenship. It was easier for the British, able to fly back after a conference to the sanctuary of England, to urge a fight to the last, than for the French to implement the advice, knowing as they did that between them and the fast-advancing panzer divisions lay not the English Channel, but handfuls of soldiers in the last extremities of exhaustion.

On 16 June Reynaud resigned; on 17 June his successor, Marshal Pétain, sued for an armistice. On 22 June the armistice was signed. On 25 June the French forces ceased to fight. France had come down like a rotten elm, and England was left without shelter from the gale.

The British complained at the time, and were long to complain afterwards, that the French had let them down; that the French army had not fought well enough; that France, by capitulating, had left them to carry on the war alone against overwhelming odds. These were complaints which the British, who had been hardly more than spectators of the battle, were singularly ill-qualified to make. For it was, after all, only the logical, if not the inevitable, consequence of the entire course of British policy towards France in the previous twenty years, and of the whole pattern of British grand strategy and re-armament in the 1930s, that France should virtually alone have to fight the decisive land battle against Germany, a nation twice her size; and that she should therefore lose that battle.

Now the British were face to face with the doom which, step by step, illusion by illusion, they had brought down on themselves – a war without an ally against two great powers, possibly three; their own island in danger; an ill-defended and immensely vulnerable empire; and an inadequate industrial machine; and insufficient and fast-dwindling national wealth.

It was the grimmest legacy ever inherited by an English Prime Minister; a situation probably beyond remedy even by statesmanship of the most far-sighted and cool-headed genius. The first and urgent question, the question which filled the minds of War Cabinet and nation alike, was whether the United Kingdom itself could for long survive in the face of the immensely powerful forces, elated with victory, which were gathering just across the narrow seas; or whether the swastika would fly above the Houses of Parliament and on the church towers of the English countryside, and the boots of a foreign conquerer stand on the soil of England for the first time since the Middle Ages.

It was a time for former moralising internationalists either to repent, or skulk behind the armed forces they had sought so devotedly to dismantle. For this was the hour, an hour too long delayed, when England returned to herself; when English policy once again spoke in broadsides instead of sermons. To the world's astonishment, the nation which had allowed itself to be represented by – which had even seen itself mirrored in – men like Baldwin, MacDonald, Henderson, Simon, Chamberlain, reverted of a sudden to its eighteenth-century character, hard as a cannon.

But could the island survive? 'The crux of the matter', wrote the Chiefs of Staff on 26 May in answer to a direct question from the Prime Minister, 'is air superiority.'[1] As the summer months passed, the thoughts of the English themselves and of the waiting world beyond were fixed on the ferocious battle of attrition in the English sky between Fighter Command and the Luftwaffe. The long-dreaded German attempt at the 'knock-out blow' had come at last, and, thanks to the fall of France, the German bombers enjoyed the immense advantage of being able to run a shuttle-service from French bases instead of having to fly all the way to England and back from Germany. None the less, despite this unlooked-for German advantage, and owing to the overriding priority given to the air defence of Great Britain by Baldwin's and Chamberlain's governments in their re-armament programmes, the Battle of Britain was won, if only by a narrow margin. Yet the battle only took place at all because of their

[1] See above p. 8.

concomitant failure to ensure that the allies won the Battle of France. For the German aim in the Battle of Britain was not to defeat England by air attack alone, as British opinion had believed before the war would be the case, but to pave the way for invasion by the German army; an operation which Germany was only able to contemplate at all because the Allies had lost the land battle in Europe. That England, alone, should have to fight a defensive battle for her life in her own skies was as much the logical consequence of pre-war British grand strategy as that France should first have had to fight the decisive ground campaign virtually alone also.

Nevertheless, Fighter Command gained the victory in the first decisive battle of its kind in history: and the two aircraft on which the battle had turned, the Hurricane and the Spitfire, took their place in national folklore as triumphant vindications of British technology – although, unfortunately for legend, their guns and much of their instrumentation were foreign, while their engines and airframes had been largely fabricated on foreign machine tools.

Without air superiority the Germans would not risk what could only prove a particularly disagreeable Channel crossing. By the autumn of 1940, therefore, the immediate, urgent question of the survival of the United Kingdom itself had been answered. Yet the long-term questions remained – questions of which the British public was happily unaware at the time, and which even in retrospect have been obscured by the obvious and dramatic dangers of the year. Even if outright defeat had so far been averted, even if it could be averted in the future, what were the prospects of ultimate victory?

Although the empire had been awakened once again by the kiss of war to a common purpose and a common action, it still remained on balance an immense strategic burden and source of weakness and danger to England.[1] Moreover, it was never to cease being so, even when its military resources had been fully developed. For the lucky circumstances of 1914–1918, when only England and not the empire was directly threatened by an enemy, had not been repeated. This time Japan was not to be an ally, but after 7 December 1941, an adversary, against whom Australia and New Zealand were incapable of defending themselves. War in the Far East coinciding with war in Europe – it was the situation of which Billy Hughes, the Australian Prime Minister, had so vividly expressed his fears in the 1921 Imperial Conference.[2] England, instead of being able to concentrate all her strength, especially at sea, on her own struggle with Germany, was obliged to wage a fresh war against Japan on behalf of

[1] See above pp. 8–11.

[2] See above p. 252.

Australia and New Zealand, and in defence of India. Yet the only directly British interests in the Far East were the rubber and tin of Malaya and the oil of Borneo, and the meat, dairy produce and wool of Australia and New Zealand, resources which, though valuable, were far from being vital enough to British existence to warrant in themselves fighting Japan.[1]

The sinking of the *Prince of Wales* and *Repulse* – the one a new battleship conscientiously built within the Washington Treaty limit of 35,000 tons and therefore more easily sinkable than, say, the 45,000 ton *Bismarck*, and the other an unmodernised Great War battlecruiser; all that could be spared to serve as the 'main fleet' for which the Singapore base had been constructed – marked the tragic, terrible consummation of English naval policy between the world wars. The ensuing Japanese conquest of the British Empire in the East no less marked the dénouement of English policy towards Japan and the United States since 1921; it was General Percival, the luckless fortress commander of Singapore, and his soldiers who paid the final instalment on the Washington Treaty. Yet the imperial catastrophe in the Far East also owed itself to English chivalry over Abyssinia. For by the time Japan attacked on 7 December 1941, England had become deeply embroiled in the war with Italy in the Mediterranean and the Middle East; a war to which Churchill had given naval, air and military priority over the Far East, thus reversing pre-war English strategy and compounding the ill-consequences of Italy's hostility.

Yet the war with Italy too had to be fought in defence of *imperial* rather than *English* interests; a drain on English resources that was to be by no means made good by the military and naval forces contributed to it by Australia, New Zealand, India and South Africa. The only *direct* English interest in the Middle East lay in the oilfields of the Persian Gulf, whose defence – even against long-range bombers – would not in itself have required keeping a large fleet in the Mediterranean at a time when the Atlantic trade routes were under heavy German attack. Nor would defence of the Persian Gulf oilfields have demanded the creation of so vast a base in the Middle East, a miniature war economy, as was in fact built up in 1940–2; a base stocked and supplied by sea round the Cape; and thus an immense additional strain on limited British resources of merchant shipping. Nor would the defence of the Persian Gulf oilfields have necessitated the locking-up, by 1942, of over half a million men in a struggle against two and a half German divisions. For the truth was that this enormous British effort in the Middle East from 1940 onwards sprang

[1] See J. Hurstfield, *The Control of Raw Materials* (London, HMSO 1953), pp. 165–9.

not from a clear sight of England's own essential interests, but grew willy-nilly out of the traditional defence of the route to India and the Far East and Churchill's impatient desire to strike at the enemy on the then only available front. Yet as the Chiefs of Staff had predicted before the war, it took major and costly fleet actions in 1940–1 to pass convoys through the Mediterranean in the face of Italian belligerence, and therefore, as they had also predicted, the Mediterranean route to India could not in any case be used. The Mediterranean and Middle East campaign was completely to bear out Gort's warning, as CIGS, in January 1939 that side-shows maintained by long sea communications 'invariably led to vast commitments out of all proportion to the value of the object attained'.[1]

And the presence of a Canadian corps in southern England, though morally heartening to the natives, went no way towards replacing the British land forces sent overseas because of imperial entanglements in the Middle East and Far East. Indeed, the highly publicised despatch of dominion and Indian forces overseas to 'help' the Mother Country was, taken as a whole, only a kind of strategic general post, after which England was still left with far smaller forces by land and sea available for her own war with Germany than she could have deployed if there had been no British Empire. For all their loyalty and for all the skill and courage of their forces, the nations of the empire were true 'daughters' of the Mother Country in that at no time during the war did their contributions defray the cost of their own strategic keep. To the last, the existence of the empire forced on England a world role she had not the resources to sustain.

And it was shortage of resources – economic and financial – which posed by far the gravest question of all for the British Government after the fall of France in 1940. For whether or not England escaped defeat at the hands of the enemy, the mere continuance of the war would itself inevitably, inexorably, bring independent British power to an end through national bankruptcy and economic ruin. It was a situation which no British Government had had to face since England first emerged as a great power in the wars against Louis XIV.

This inevitability of economic collapse, coupled with the bleak long-term strategic prospects, might have seemed to point to one answer: to accept that Germany now dominated Europe, and make the best possible peace with her. This solution was unthinkable as long as England itself remained unconquered. The English people, slow but formidable in their anger, aware of their military weakness and unreadiness but still believing themselves to be a rich and technologically advanced nation, could think

[1] See above pp. 553–4.

of nothing now but crushing Hitler and the Nazi tyranny, come what may, cost what it might. Churchill himself, a statesman of powerful emotions and grand dramatic attitudes, shared and expressed this national temper. Peace with Hitler, peace with such a man and such a régime, was out of the question.

The alternative was to postpone the collapse of the economic foundations of British power as long as possible by waging war on a scale commensurate with Britain's reserves of gold and dollars; and by holding a judicious balance between the industrial resources devoted to war and those devoted to paying for it (and for the national livelihood) by exports. While war on so limited a scale could offer no possible hope of defeating Germany and Italy, the English might nevertheless have hoped that if they simply kept the war alive, other and greater powers might eventually be drawn in.

It was a choice that no more occurred to Churchill and his colleagues than that of making peace with Hitler. Instead they opted to wage war on a scale far, far beyond British economic resources. They opted to mobilise the entire nation and the entire economy for purposes of war. It was a decision exactly similar to that which Hindenburg and Ludendorff took in Germany in 1916–17, and for which those leaders have been condemned, on the grounds that they achieved a vast short-term increase in Germany's military strength at the cost of making her ultimate collapse inevitable. But in 1940 the British choice followed naturally, and without discussion, from the principal aim of Churchill's policy, as he explained it to the House of Commons on first taking office:

> You ask, What is our policy? I will say: it is to wage war, by sea, land and air, with all our might and with all the strength that God can give us; to wage war against a monstrous tyranny, never surpassed in the dark, lamentable catalogue of human crime. That is our policy. You ask, What is our aim? I can answer in one word: Victory – victory at all costs, victory in spite of all terror; victory, however long and hard the road may be; for without victory there is no survival. . . .[1]

Yet 'victory', or the defeat of Nazi Germany, was not, as Churchill and his colleagues and the British people themselves believed at the time, and were still to believe in retrospect, synonymous with the preservation of British power. The defeat of Germany was only one factor, if a highly important factor, in such a preservation. For Germany might be defeated and yet British power still be brought to an end. What counted was not

[1] Quoted in J. R. M. Butler, *Grand Strategy* (London, HMSO 1957), Vol. II, p. 181.

so much 'victory' in itself, but the circumstances of the victory, and in particular the circumstances in which England found herself in that happy hour. Churchill failed to understand this until too late; even by his own later account his consuming obsession was not the preservation and extension of British power, but simply 'victory'. Stalin made no such mistake. Cold realist that he was, he recognised that the defeat of Germany was not an end, but a means. As early as December 1941, when the German army was fighting just outside the suburbs of Moscow, Stalin was already looking ahead to the post-war settlement of Europe, and to Russia's dominating role within it.[1] Churchill, for his part, in his total absorption in the waging of war, did not begin seriously to look beyond 'victory' until late 1943 or even 1944.[2] Even in retrospect, in the British memoirs and histories of the Second World War, there is the same emphasis on 'victory' alone, the same exclusive preoccupation with the defeat of Germany, the same neglect of the whole question of the preservation and if possible the furtherance of British interests in the course of the war.

In the summer of 1940, therefore, Churchill and his government quite deliberately, if in their view inevitably, chose to sacrifice England's existence as an independent power, a power living and waging war on her resources, for the sake of 'victory'. It was the most romantically noble gesture of them all; the climax of British altruism in foreign policy.

The decision redounded immediately to the benefit of the United States, where the British Government, far from husbanding gold and dollars, now proceeded to pour out its last reserves on American munitions, raw materials and industrial equipment.[3] England's plight and profligacy was America's prosperity. By late August 1940, while the Luftwaffe was still rumbling over southern England, glinting silver crosses in the sky, the Chancellor of the Exchequer reckoned that the English gold and dollar reserves would run out by December.[4] By June 1941 the adverse balance with the United States would have grown to some £800 million. The Chancellor added somewhat nervously that his note had been written on the assumption that the Cabinet's 'confident expectation of abundant American help would not be falsified; otherwise we should have to fall back on our own resources, and therefore it was important to husband what was left just in case. . . .'[5]

Yet in point of fact the British had little reason at this time for their

[1] The Earl of Avon, *The Eden Memoirs* (London, Cassell 1965), Vol. III, pp. 289–97.
[2] Ibid. pp. 428–9; but especially pp. 441–2.
[3] See above pp. 13–14.
[4] CAB 66/11, WP(40) 324, 21 August 1940.
[5] Ibid.

'confident expectation' that America would pension them once they had gone broke, for no reassuring promises had been forthcoming from Washington. So far as the British Government knew in August 1940, as they poured out their gold and dollars, the beginning of 1941 would present them with the unimaginable catastrophe of being unable to keep the nation in food and work, let alone wage war even in the most limited fashion.

The readiness with which Churchill entrusted England's future to American charity was prompted not only by his resolve to wage war beyond the national means in pursuit of victory, but also by a belief that America was not just another rival nation-state, but a friend. For Churchill, half-American in blood himself, was a life-long believer in the romantic British myth of Anglo-American cousinhood and of the common destiny of the English-speaking peoples; that myth which had already exercised so calamitous an effect on British policy in the past.[1] There was to be little less appeasement under Churchill than under Chamberlain; the difference lay in that Washington instead of Berlin was now its focus, in that the American President instead of the German Führer was now the recipient of concessions and ingratiating missives.

The Second World War therefore saw the disastrous culmination of the long-standing but unreciprocated British belief in the existence of a 'special relationship' between England and America. For the Americans – like the Russians, like the Germans, like the English themselves in the eighteenth century – were motivated by a desire to promote their own interests rather than by sentiment, which was a commodity they reserved for Pilgrim's Dinners, where it could do no harm. Churchill's policy therefore provided the Americans with the opportunity firstly, of prospering on British orders, and secondly, of humbling British world power, a long-cherished American ambition. From 1940 to the end of the Second World War and after, it was America, not Russia, which was to constitute that lurking menace to British interests which Churchill, in his passionate obsession with defeating Germany, failed to perceive.

The opportunity for the most ruthless of American attempts at hard bargaining during the summer of 1940 was provided by the desperate English shortage of destroyers, of which they possessed only ninety-four, the result of the refusal of the disarming governments of the 1920s and the early 1930s to hearken to the warnings of the Admiralty that imperial defence and the protection of trade routes demanded all the 433 destroyers which had been at sea in 1918.[2] The English asked for fifty 'moth-balled'

[1] See above pp. 255–73, 286–91, 346–8. [2] See above p. 297.

American four-stack destroyers dating from the Great War. The United States Secretary of State, Cordell Hull, proposed that these fifty ancient vessels should constitute the full purchase price for the naval and air bases which England had offered the United States in Newfoundland, Bermuda, the Bahamas, Jamaica, Santa Lucia, Trinidad and British Guiana; not only that, but, as the British War Cabinet minutes put it: 'The draft letters proposed by Mr Cordell Hull also included a definite statement that if the waters surrounding the British Isles became untenable to British ships of war, these would be sent to other parts of the empire for the continued defence of the Empire.'[1]

In other words the British were to agree not to use their fleet as a bargaining counter in peace negotiations with Germany, should a German invasion prove successful.

The War Cabinet discussed this heart-warming example of American cousinliness on 21 August 1940:

> The view of the War Cabinet was that a formal bargain on the lines proposed was out of the question.
>
> It was pointed out that no monetary relationship could be established between the benefits conferred by either side. From our point of view, the facilities we were offering were worth far more than the fifty old destroyers and other war material which we were to receive and whose chief value lay in our urgent need for this type of vessel. If a formal bargain was concluded, it could be asked why we were not obtaining more valuable consideration; e.g. cancellation of the American debt [incurred by England during the Great War].[2]

Yet, in the manner so familiar in previous British governments, the Cabinet could not avert surrender, except over the question of the future of the fleet, but only seek to disguise it with sophistry. The Prime Minister and Cabinet therefore agreed that the British line would be that we were spontaneously offering the base facilities without asking for a consideration. If the USA liked to link the two transactions it was up to them. We should make it plain that we were offering *facilities*, not *bases*; there would be no transfer of sovereignty.[3]

On 29 August, when the Battle of Britain was rising to its ferocious climax, the War Cabinet considered a telegram from the British ambassador in Washington (Lord Lothian) which stated that the US Government wished Britain to offer the facilities in Newfoundland and Bermuda

[1] CAB 65/8, 231(40); 21 August 1940.
[2] Ibid.
[3] Ibid.

as a 'free gift', while they wanted ninety-nine year leases on the Caribbean and British Guiana facilities.[1] Lord Beaverbrook, the Minister of Aircraft Production, argued that if the United States insisted on a bargain, it ought not to be 'an unfair bargain, such as was now proposed'.[2] Nevertheless, in its extremity of need, the War Cabinet could only authorise Lord Lothian to accept.[3]

The last months of England's existence as a fully independent great power, able out of her own resources both to maintain her national existence and to wage war, passed away. By the third quarter of 1940 the volume of British exports (*including* munitions for the empire) was down by 37 per cent on 1935.[4] By the turn of the year 1940–1, the dark mid-winter of the Blitz, England's stock of gold and dollars was near exhaustion.[5] Yet she had committed herself to vast purchasing programmes in the United States which still had to be paid for.[6] The United States Government had therefore to consider whether, now that nothing more was to be got out of the British, it would really be in America's interest to cut off supplies and see England collapse or make peace, or whether it would be more in her interest to prop England up between herself and a European continent under German control. On 10 January 1941 a bill was put before Congress whose title accurately enough proclaimed it to be an 'Act to promote the defense of the United States';[7] it was enacted on 11 March 1941; it was the beginning of what became known misleadingly as 'Lend-Lease'. By this time British resources were utterly at an end; all fresh purchasing had had to be stopped, and payments currently due had only been met thanks to a loan of gold from the Belgian Government in exile.[8] In April 1941, the month in which Germany invaded Greece and Yugoslavia and threw British imperial forces out of their last foothold in Europe, the British reserves of gold and dollars sank to their lowest point ever, of $12 million.

For obvious reasons the advent of 'Lend-Lease' was represented as an act of unparalleled generosity. In fact it was clearly to America's advantage that American weapons should be carried into battle by the fighting men of England and the empire rather than by the sons of American mothers. Even after the United States entered the war in December 1941 – and not then by her own volition – it was still clearly to her advantage that England should be enabled to wage war on a far greater scale than would have been possible on English resources alone.

[1] CAB 65/8, 236(40)6, 29 August 1940. [2] Ibid. [3] Ibid.
[4] W. K. Hancock and M. M. Gowing, *British War Economy* (London, HMSO 1953), p. 243.
[5] Ibid. p. 232. [6] Ibid. [7] Ibid. p. 235.
[8] H. Duncan Hall, *North American Supply* (London, HMSO 1955), pp. 208, 215–16, 247–78.

Lend-Lease gradually consummated the process Churchill had begun of transforming England into an American satellite warrior-state dependent for its existence on the flow of supplies across the Atlantic. Indeed the very terms under which Lend-Lease was operated both encouraged England to become the more dependent on America and emphasised the fact of her dependence. England had to agree not to sell any articles abroad which contained Lend-Lease material, nor any goods, *even if British-made*, similar to goods received under Lend-Lease. An organisation of American officials in England policed observance of these requirements,[1] whose essential purpose was to ensure that British industry was switched wholly from exports to war production. By June 1944, while 13 million out of a total British labour force (over fourteen years of age) of 23·5 million were either in the armed forces or civilian war employment, the American figure was 24·9 million out of 62·2 million;[2] or only 40 per cent as against the British 55 per cent; an unequal sacrifice.[3]

Not only did the British export trade in the products of advanced technology collapse as the result of Lend-Lease[4] but, when the war was drawing to an end, it was to prove difficult or impossible for Britain to revive such exports because of Lend-Lease regulations and American supervision of them.[5] It was an illuminating aspect of the 'special relationship' that this American control was only extended to the English, and not to the less compliant Russians, who took all they could by way of aid without surrendering a jot of their independence.[6] By 1944 British exports were down to 31 per cent of the 1938 figure,[7] a figure which testified to the destruction of the essential basis of England's existence as an independent and self-sufficient power; testified likewise to the degree to which, like a patient on a heart-lung machine, she was now dependent for life itself on the United States.

Thus the British and imperial armies which marched and conquered in the latter half of the war, in North Africa, in Italy, in Burma, in Normandy and north-west Europe; the great bomber forces which smashed and burnt German cities; the navy which defeated the U-boat; these were not manifestations of British imperial power at a new zenith, as the British believed at the time and long afterwards, but only the illusion of it. They were instead manifestations of *American* power – and of the decline of England into a warrior satellite of the United States. Thus the 'victory' of 1945 itself was, so far as the British were concerned, partly illusion too;

[1] Hall, p. 245.
[2] Hancock and Gowing, p. 366.
[3] Ibid. p. 370.
[4] Ibid. p. 245.
[5] Ibid. pp. 244–5.
[6] Ibid. p. 245, note 2.
[7] Ibid. p. 354.

for although Germany had been defeated, England was not, of her own right and resources, a victor. She emerged into the post-war era with the foundations of her former independent national power as completely destroyed as those of France or Germany, but with the extra, and calamitous drawback that, as a 'victor', she failed to realise it.

For, unlike the collapse of French power in 1940 and German power in 1945, the collapse of British power had not been made evident by defeat in the field; its historical moment was not fixed by the entry of conquering troops into the capital, or by well-filmed and photographed ceremonies of surrender. Instead, British power had quietly vanished amid the stupendous events of the Second World War, like a ship-of-the-line going down unperceived in the smoke and confusion of battle.

# *BIBLIOGRAPHY*

# *BIBLIOGRAPHY*

PUBLISHED SOURCES

For ease of reference the Command and Parliamentary Papers and other official documents are listed separately on pp. 611–14. All other published sources are divided into parts corresponding with the parts in the text. Because of this, a title which is cited in more than one part is only listed under the part of its first citation.

*Part I – between pages 1 and 15*

BUTLER, J. R. M. *Grand Strategy*. London, HMSO 1957. **II**.
CHURCHILL, WINSTON. *The Second World War*. London, Cassell 1964.
HALL, H. DUNCAN. *North American Supply*. London, HMSO 1955.
HANCOCK, W. K. and GOWING, M. M. *British War Economy*. London, HMSO 1953.
HORNBY, WILLIAM. *Factories and Plant*. London, HMSO 1958.
HURSTFIELD, J. *The Control of Raw Materials*. London, HMSO 1953.
KIRBY, S. WOODBURN. *The War Against Japan*. London, HMSO 1957. **I** *The Loss of Singapore*.
*Marlburian, The*. **XXII**, 360 (12 November 1887).
POSTAN, M. M. *British War Production*. London, HMSO 1952.
ROSKILL, S. W. *The War At Sea*. London, HMSO 1961. **I**.
*Statesmen's Year Book 1940*. ed. M. Epstein. London, Macmillan 1936–41.
*War Illustrated*. **III**, 32 (12 April 1940).
*War, The*. 26 (19 April 1940).

*Part II – between pages 17 and 68*
*(sources not previously cited)*

ABBOTT, EVELYN and CAMPBELL, LEWIS. *The Life and Letters of Benjamin Jowett M.A.* London, John Murray 1897. 2 Vols.

AMERY, L. S. *My Political Life*. London, Hutchinson 1953. 3 Vols.
ANGELL, NORMAN. *The Great Illusion*. London, Heinemann 1910.
ARCHER, R. L. *Secondary Education in the Nineteenth Century*. London, Frank Cass 1966. First edition 1921.
BAINTON, R. *Christian Attitudes to War and Peace*. London, Hodder and Stoughton 1961.
BAMFORD, T. W. *Rise of the Public Schools*. London, Thomas Nelson 1967.
— *Thomas Arnold*. London, The Cresset Press 1960.
BARKER, ERNEST. *National Character and the Factors in Its Formation*. London, Methuen 1928.
BEALES, A. C. F. *The History of Peace*. London, George Bell 1931.
BEER, M. *A History of British Socialism*. London, George Bell 1919 and 1920. 2 Vols.
BELL, QUENTIN. *Bloomsbury*. London, Weidenfeld and Nicolson 1968.
BOUTMY, E. G. *The English People: A Study of their Political Philosophy*. tr. E. English. London, T. Fisher Unwin 1904.
BOWEN, W. E. *Edward Bowen: A Memoir*. London, Longmans 1902.
BROCKWAY, F. *Inside the Left*. London, Allen and Unwin 1942.
BUTLER, J. R. M. *Lord Lothian (Philip Kerr) 1882–1940*. London, Macmillan 1960.
BUTTERFIELD, H. *Christianity, Diplomacy and War*. London, The Epworth Press 1951.
— *Christianity in European History*. London, Oxford University Press 1951.
— *Christianity and History*. London, George Bell 1950.
CECIL OF CHELWOOD, VISCOUNT. *A Great Experiment*. London, Jonathan Cape 1941.
— *All the Way*. London, Hodder and Stoughton 1949.
CONNOLLY, CYRIL. *Enemies of Promise*. Harmondsworth, Penguin Books 1961. First edition 1938.
COULTON, G. C. *Pacifist Illusions: A Criticism of the Union of Democratic Control*. Cambridge, Bowes and Bowes 1915.
CROSBY, G. D. *Disarmament and Peace in British Politics 1914–1919*. Cambridge, Massachusetts, Harvard University Press 1957.
DALE, H. E. *The Higher Civil Service of Great Britain*. London, Oxford University Press 1941.
DARWIN, BERNARD. *The English Public School*. London, Longmans 1929.
EDWARDS, MALDWYN. *Methodism and England*. London, The Epworth Press 1957.
ENSOR, R. C. K. *England 1870–1914*. Oxford, The Clarendon Press 1966. First edition 1946.

FEILING, KEITH. *A Life of Neville Chamberlain*. London, Macmillan 1970.

FINER, HERMAN. *The British Civil Service*. London, Fabian Society 1927.

FITCH, JOSHUA. *Thomas and Matthew Arnold and Their Influence on English Education*. London, Heinemann 1897.

GAUS, J. M. *Great Britain: A Study in Civic Loyalty*. Chicago, Chicago University Press 1929.

GRAVES, ROBERT. *Goodbye to All That*. Harmondsworth, Penguin Books 1961. First edition 1929.

GUTTSMAN, W. L. *The British Political Elite*. London, MacGibbon and Kee 1963.

HALPÉRIN, VLADIMIR. *Lord Milner and the British Empire*. London, Odhams Press 1952.

HAMILTON, MARY AGNES. *Arthur Henderson*. London, Heinemann 1938.

HEUSSLER, ROBERT. *Yesterday's Rulers: The Making of the British Colonial Service*. New York, Syracuse University Press 1963.

HIRTZEL, SIR ARTHUR. *Church, the Empire and the World*. London, SPCK 1919.

HOBSBAWM, E. J. *Labouring Men: Studies in the History of Labour*. London, Weidenfeld and Nicolson 1964.

— *Industry and Empire*. Harmondsworth, Penguin Books 1969.

HOBSON, J. A. *Imperialism: A Study*. London, Allen and Unwin 1902.

HOLLIS, CHRISTOPHER. *Eton: A History*. London, Hollis and Carter 1960.

HOLROYD, MICHAEL. *Lytton Strachey: A Critical Biography*. London, Heinemann 1967 and 1968. 2 Vols: **I** *The Unknown Years*; **II** *The Years of Achievement*.

HYAMS, EDWARD. *The New Statesman: The History of the First Fifty Years 1913–1963*. London, Longmans 1963.

JOHNSTONE, J. K. *The Bloomsbury Group*. London, Secker and Warburg 1954.

JONES, R. TUDOR. *Congregationalism in England 1662–1962*. London, Independent Press 1962.

JONES, THOMAS H. *A Diary with Letters 1931–1950*. London, Geoffrey Cumberlege, Oxford University Press 1954.

LAMBERT, SIR HENRY. *The Nature of History*. London, Humphrey Milford, Oxford University Press 1941.

LEATHES, SIR STANLEY. *The People of England*. London, Heinemann 1920–2. 3 Vols.

— *What is Education?* London, George Bell 1913.

LOWNDES, G. A. N. *Public School Life: Boys, Parents, Masters*. London, Collins 1922.

— *The Silent Social Revolution*. London, Oxford University Press 1937.

LYMAN, RICHARD W. *The First Labour Government 1924*. London, Chapman and Hall 1957.

MCCALLUM, R. B. *Public Opinion and the Last Peace*. London, Oxford University Press 1944.

MCINTOSH, P. C. *Physical Education in England Since 1800*. London, George Bell 1968.

MACK, EDWARD C. *Public Schools and British Opinion Since 1860*. New York, Columbia University Press 1941.

MACMILLAN, HAROLD. *Winds of Change*. London, Macmillan 1966.

MARTIN, DAVID A. *Pacifism: An Historical and Sociological Study*. London, Routledge and Kegan Paul 1965.

MARWICK, ARTHUR. *The Deluge: British Society and the First World War*. London, The Bodley Head 1965.

MASSEY, VINCENT. *What's Past Is Prologue*. London, Macmillan 1963.

MAUGHAM, VISCOUNT. *At the End of the Day*. London, Heinemann 1954.

MEEHAN, E. G. *The British Left Wing and Foreign Policy*. New Brunswick, Rutgers University Press 1960.

MIDDLEMASS, KEITH and BARNES, JOHN. *Baldwin: A Biography*. London, Weidenfeld and Nicolson 1969.

MILLER, KENNETH E. *Socialism and Foreign Policy: Theory and Practice in Britain to 1931*. The Hague, Martinus Nijhoff 1967.

MURRAY, GILBERT. *The Ordeal of this Generation: the War, the League and the Future, being the Halley Stewart Lectures for 1928*. London, Allen and Unwin 1929.

MURRAY, G. W. and HUNTER, T. A. A. *Physical Education and Health*. London, Heinemann Educational Books 1966.

NEWMAN, J. H. *The Idea of a University*. New York, Longmans Green 1947.

NEWSOME, DAVID. *Godliness and Good Learning*. London, John Murray 1961.

NORWOOD, CYRIL. *The English Tradition in Education*. London, John Murray 1929.

NUTTALL, G. *Christian Pacifism*. Oxford, Basil Blackwell 1958.

PLUMB, J. H. *England in the Eighteenth Century*. Harmondsworth, Penguin Books 1959.

RANULF, S. *Moral Indignation and Middle-Class Psychology*. Copenhagen, Levin and Munksgaard 1938.

RENIER, C. J. *The English: Are They Human?* London, Williams and Norgate 1931.

RIDLEY, JASPER. *Lord Palmerston.* London, Constable 1970.

ROBSON, W. A. (ed.) *The British Civil Servant.* London, Allen and Unwin 1937.

*Sanderson of Oundle* (various authors). London, Chatto and Windus 1926.

SEELEY, J. R. *The Expansion of England.* London, Macmillan 1883.

SIMON, BRIAN. *Education and the Labour Movement 1870–1920.* London, Lawrence and Wishart 1965.

SIMON, VISCOUNT. *Retrospect: Memoirs of the Rt. Hon. the Viscount Simon.* London, Hutchinson 1952.

SPENCER, HERBERT. *Education: Intellectual, Moral and Physical.* London, Williams and Norgate 1861.

STANLEY, A. R. *The Life and Correspondence of Thomas Arnold D.D.* London, Ward Lock 1890.

STEDMAN, A. M. M. *Oxford: Its Life and Schools.* London, George Bell 1887.

STRATTMAN, F. *The Church and War.* London, Sheed and Ward 1929.

SWANWICK, H. M. *The Roots of Peace.* London, Jonathan Cape 1938.

THRING, EDWARD. *Theory and Practice of Teaching.* Cambridge, Cambridge University Press 1910.

TREVELYAN, G. M. *English Social History.* London, Longmans Green 1942.

VANSITTART, LORD. *The Mist Procession.* London, Hutchinson 1958.

WARD, W. R. *Victorian Oxford.* London, Frank Cass 1965.

WAUGH, ALEXANDER. *The Loom of Youth.* London, Grant Richards 1917.

WEARMOUTH, R. F. *Methodism and the Struggle of the Working Classes 1850–1900.* Leicester, Edgar Backus 1954.

— *The Social and Political Influence of Methodism in the Twentieth Century.* London, The Epworth Press 1957.

WELLESLEY, SIR VICTOR. *Diplomacy in Fetters.* London, Hutchinson 1944.

WILKINSON, RUPERT. *The Prefects. British Leadership and the Public School Tradition.* London, Oxford University Press 1964.

WILLIAMS, RAYMOND. *The Long Revolution.* London, Chatto and Windus 1961.

WILLIS, IRENE COOPER. *How We Came Out of the War.* London, International Bookshops 1921.

— *How We Got On With the War.* Manchester, National Labour Press 1920.

— *How We Went Into the War.* Manchester, National Labour Press 1918.

WILSON, TREVOR. *The Downfall of the Liberal Party 1914–1935*. London, Collins 1966.

WINSTANLEY, D. A. *Later Victorian Cambridge*. Cambridge, Cambridge University Press 1947.

WORSLEY, T. C. *Barbarians and Philistines*. London, Robert Hale 1940.

WRENCH, JOHN EVELYN. *Alfred Lord Milner*. London, Eyre and Spottiswoode 1958.

YOUNG, KENNETH. *Arthur James Balfour*. London, George Bell 1963.

*Part III – between pages 69 and 120*
*(sources not previously cited)*

ARNOLD, MATTHEW. *Culture and Anarchy*. New York, Macmillan 1894. First edition 1869.

BORDEN, SIR ROBERT LAIRD. *His Memoirs*. Toronto, Macmillan 1938. 2 Vols.

CLAPHAM, J. H. *Economic Development of France and Germany 1815–1914*. Cambridge, Cambridge University Press 1923.

CLOUGH, S. B. and COLE, C. W. *Economic History of Europe*. Boston, D. C. Heath 1952.

COLE, D. H. *Imperial Military Geography*. London, Sifton Praed 1936.

CORBETT, SIR JULIAN. *History of the Great War; Naval Operations*. London, Longmans Green 1920. I.

GORDON, DONALD C. *The Dominion Partnership in Imperial Defence 1870–1914*. Baltimore, Johns Hopkins Press 1965.

HANCOCK, W. K. *Survey of British Commonwealth Affairs*. London, Oxford University Press 1942. II *Problems of Economic Policy 1918–1939*.

HEINDEL, R. H. *The American Impact on Great Britain 1898–1914*. New York, Octagon Books 1968.

LLOYD GEORGE, DAVID. *War Memoirs*. London, Odhams Press 1938. 2 Vols.

MANSERGH, NICHOLAS. *The Commonwealth Experience*. London, Weidenfeld and Nicolson 1969.

O'DWYER, SIR MICHAEL. *India As I Knew It 1885–1925*. London, Constable 1925.

PLAYFAIR, LYON. *Industrial Instruction on the Continent*. London, Royal School of Mines 1852.

PRESTON, R. A. *Canada and Imperial Defense*. Durham, North Carolina, Duke University Press 1967.

ROSKILL, S. W. *Naval Policy Between the Wars*. London, Collins 1968. **I** *The Period of Anglo-American Antagonism.*

ROYAL INSTITUTE OF INTERNATIONAL AFFAIRS, STUDY GROUP OF THE. *The Colonial Problem.* London, Oxford University Press 1937.

— *Political and Strategic Interests of the United Kingdom.* London, Oxford University Press 1939.

SEMMEL, B. *Imperialism and Social Reform: English Social-Imperial Thought 1895–1914.* London, Allen and Unwin 1960.

SMITH, ADAM. *The Wealth of Nations.* London, Dent 1929. First edition 1776.

WINSTEDT, SIR RICHARD O. *Malaya and Its History.* London, Hutchinson's University Library 1948.

*Part IV – between pages 121 and 233*
*(sources not previously cited)*

Australian Defence Policy. *The Round Table.* **XXVI** (December 1935).

BEAVERBROOK, LORD. *The Decline and Fall of Lloyd George.* London, Collins 1963.

BIRKENHEAD, LORD. *Halifax.* London, Hamish Hamilton 1965.

BUTLER, IRIS. *The Viceroy's Wife: Letters of Alice Countess of Reading from India 1921–5.* London, Hodder and Stoughton 1969.

'CANUCK'. Canada and Imperial Defence. *Army Quarterly.* **XXVI,** 2 (July 1933).

CAREY, JOYCE. *Britain and West Africa.* London, Longmans Green 1946.

CHATFIELD, ADMIRAL OF THE FLEET LORD. *It Might Happen Again.* London, Heinemann 1947. **II** *The Navy and Defence.*

COUPLAND, R. *The Indian Problem 1833–1935.* London, Oxford University Press 1942.

COWIE, DONALD. *An Empire Prepared.* London, Allen and Unwin 1939.

CROCKER, W. R. *On Governing Colonies.* London, Allen and Unwin 1947.

CROSS, J. A. *Whitehall and the Commonwealth.* London, Routledge and Kegan Paul 1967.

CURTIS, LIONEL. *The Round Table.* **XI,** 43 (June 1921).

DAVIDSON, MAJOR-GENERAL SIR J. H. Defence of the British Empire. *Army Quarterly.* **I,** 2 (January 1921).

DAWSON, R. MACGREGOR. *William Lyon Mackenzie King: A Political Biography, 1874–1923.* London, Methuen 1958. **I.**

EAYRS, JAMES. *In Defense of Canada: From the Great War to the Great Depression.* Toronto, University of Toronto Press 1964.

EDWARDES, MICHAEL. *High Noon of Empire*. London, Eyre and Spottiswoode 1965.
— *The Last Years of British India*. London, Cassell 1963.
EDWARDS, CECIL. *Bruce of Melbourne, Man of Two Worlds*. London, Heinemann 1966.
ELLIOTT, W. Y. and HALL, H. DUNCAN (eds.). *The Commonwealth at War*. New York, Alfred Knopf 1943.
FIDDES, SIR GEORGE. *The Dominions and the Colonial Offices*. London, Putnam 1926.
GANN, L. H. and DUIGNAN, PETER (eds.). *Colonialism and Africa 1870–1960*. Cambridge, Cambridge University Press 1969. **II.**
GIBBS, N. H. *The Origins of Imperial Defence*. London, Oxford University Press 1955.
GREENBERGER, ALLEN J. *The British Image of India*. London, Oxford University Press 1969.
HANCOCK, SIR K. *Smuts: Biography*. Cambridge, Cambridge University Press 1962 and 1968. 2 Vols: **I** *The Sanguine Years*; **II** *The Fields of Force 1819–1950*.
HANCOCK, W. K. *Survey of British Commonwealth Affairs*. London, Oxford University Press 1937. **I** *Problems of Nationality 1918–1936*.
HASLUCK, PAUL. *The Government and the People 1929–41*. Canberra, Australian War Memorial 1952.
HEEVER, C. M. VAN DEN. *General J. B. M. Herzog*. Johannesberg, APB Bookstore 1946.
HOARE, SAMUEL (VISCOUNT TEMPLEWOOD). *Empire of the Air*. London, Collins 1957.
HYDE, H. MONTGOMERY. *Lord Reading*. London, Heinemann 1967.
KEITH, A. BERRIEDALE. *Speeches and Documents on the British Dominions 1918–1931*. London, Humphrey Milford, Oxford University Press 1938.
KNAPLUND, PAUL. *Britain, Commonwealth and Empire*. London, Hamish Hamilton 1956.
LAVARACK, COLONEL J. D. The Defence of the British Empire with special reference to the Far East and Australia. *Army Quarterly*. **XXV**, 2 (January 1933).
MANSERGH, NICHOLAS. *Survey of British Commonwealth Affairs*. London, Oxford University Press 1952. **III** *Problems of External Policy 1931–9*
MAYO, KATHARINE. *Mother India*. London, Jonathan Cape 1927.
MILLER, J. D. B. *Britain and the Old Dominions*. London, Chatto and Windus 1966.

NEATBY, H. BLAIR. *William Lyon Mackenzie King*. London, Methuen 1963. **II** *The Lonely Heights 1924–1932*.

ORR, COLONEL G. M. The Military Forces in India. *Army Quarterly*. **XVIII,** 2 (July 1929).

PARKINSON, SIR COSMO. *The Colonial Office from Within, 1909–1945*. London, Faber and Faber 1947.

POSTAN, M. M., HAY, D. and SCOTT, J. D. *Design and Development of Weapons*. London, HMSO 1964.

PURCELL, VICTOR. *The Chinese in Malaya*. London, Oxford University Press 1948.

RICHMOND, ADMIRAL SIR HERBERT. An Outline of Imperial Defence. *Army Quarterly*. **XXVI,** 2 (July 1932).

ROBERTSON, MAJOR H. C. H. (Australian Army). The Empire and Modern War. *Army Quarterly*. **XXVI,** 2 (July 1933).

RUSSELL, SIR THOMAS (Pasha). *Egyptian Service 1902–46*. London, John Murray 1949.

SMITH, VINCENT A. and OTHERS. *The Oxford History of India*. Oxford, The Clarendon Press 1958.

THOMPSON, E. *The Reconstruction of India*. London, Faber and Faber 1933.

— *A Letter from India*. London, Faber and Faber 1932.

THORNTON, A. P. *The Imperial Idea and Its Enemies*. London, Macmillan 1959.

TOYNBEE, ARNOLD J. *The Conduct of British Empire Foreign Relations Since the Peace Settlement*. London, Oxford University Press 1928.

TUCKER, G. N. *The Naval Service of Canada*. Ottawa, King's Printer 1952. **I** *Origins and Early Years*.

WALEY, SIR DAVID. *Edwin Montagu*. London, Asia Publishing House 1964.

WERTHEIMER, EGON. *Portrait of the Labour Party*. London, Putnam 1929.

WHYTE, WILLIAM FARMER. *William Morris Hughes. His Life and Times*. Sydney, Angus and Robertson 1957.

WINSTEDT, SIR RICHARD. *Britain and Malaya*. London, Longmans Green 1964.

WOOD, F. L. *The New Zealand People at War: Political and External Affairs*. Wellington, War History Branch, Dept. of External Affairs 1958.

WOODRUFF (MASON), PHILIP. *The Men Who Ruled India*. London, Jonathan Cape 1953 and 1954. 2 Vols: **I** *The Founders*; **II** *The Guardians*.

WYNTER, BREVET LT-COL. H. D. (Australian Army). The Command and Administration of the Military Forces of the Empire in War. *Army Quarterly*. **IX,** 2 (January 1925).

ZINKIN, MAURICE and TAYA. *Britain and India*. London, Chatto and Windus 1964.

*Part V – between pages 235 and 577*
*(sources not previously cited)*

ALDINGTON, R. *Death of a Hero*. London, Chatto and Windus 1929.
— *Collected Poems 1915–1923*. London, Allen and Unwin 1929.
ALLEN, H. C. *The Anglo-American Relationship Since 1783*. London, Adam and Charles Black 1959.
ARGLES, MICHAEL. *South Kensington to Robbins: An Account of English Technical Education since 1851*. London, Longmans 1964.
AVON, THE EARL OF (ANTHONY EDEN). *The Eden Memoirs*. London, Cassell 1962. 3 Vols: **I** *Facing the Dictators*.
BALDWIN, A. W. *My Father: The True Story*. London, Allen and Unwin 1955.
BALFOUR, MICHAEL. *West Germany*. London, Ernest Benn 1968.
BARNETT, CORRELLI. *Britain and her Army 1509–1970*. London, Allen Lane, The Penguin Press.
— The New Military Balance. *The History of the Twentieth Century*. 24 (1968).
— *The Swordbearers*. London, Eyre and Spottiswoode 1963.
BEAUFRE, GENERAL ANDRÉ. *1940 The Fall of France*. London, Cassell 1967.
BERGONZI, BERNARD. *Heroes' Twilight: A Study of the Literature of the Great War*. London, Constable 1965.
BLATCHFORD, ROBERT. *Dismal England*. London, Walter Scott 1901.
BLUNDEN, EDMUND. *Undertones of War*. London, Richard Cobden-Sanderson 1928.
BOWLE, JOHN. *Viscount Samuel*. London, Victor Gollancz 1957.
BRAND, CARL F. *The British Labour Party; A Short History*. Stanford, California, Stanford University Press 1965.
BRITTAIN, VERA. *Testament of Youth*. London, Victor Gollancz 1933.
BROGAN, SIR DENIS. *The Development of Modern France*. London, Hamish Hamilton 1967.
BROOKE, RUPERT. *Complete Poems*. London, Sidgwick and Jackson 1932.
BRYCE, JAMES. *The American Commonwealth*. New York, Macmillan 1911. 2 Vols.
BUCK, PHILIP W. *Amateurs and Professionals in British Politics 1918–59*. Chicago, University of Chicago Press 1959.
BULLOCK, ALAN. *Hitler: A Study in Tyranny*. London, Odhams Press 1952.

CAMPBELL, A. E. *Great Britain and the United States 1895–1903*. London, Longmans 1960.

CAMPBELL, CHARLES S. *Anglo-American Understanding 1898–1903*. Baltimore, Johns Hopkins Press 1957.

CARLTON, DAVID. *MacDonald Versus Henderson*. London, Macmillan 1970.

CARR-SAUNDERS, A. M. and JONES, D. CARADOG. *A Survey of the Social Structure of England and Wales*. London, Oxford University Press 1927.

CHURCHILL, SIR WINSTON. *The Second World War*. London, Cassell 1948. I *The Gathering Storm*.

CONNELL, JOHN. *The Office; a Study of British Foreign Policy and Its Makers 1919–1951*. London, Allan Wingate 1958.

COOPER, DUFF (VISCOUNT NORWICH). *Old Men Forget*. London, Rupert Hart-Davis 1954.

CRAIG, GORDON A. and GILBERT, FELIX (eds.). *The Diplomats 1919–39*. Princeton, NJ, Princeton University Press 1953.

CRAIGIE, SIR ROBERT. *Behind the Japanese Mask*. London, Hutchinson 1946.

CRUTTWELL, C. R. M. F. *A History of the Great War*. Oxford, The Clarendon Press 1934.

D'ABERNON, VISCOUNT. *Ambassador of Peace*. London, Hodder and Stoughton 1929–30. 3 Vols.

DUGDALE, BLANCHE E. *Arthur James Balfour*. London, Hutchinson 1936.

EDMONDS, CHARLES (CARRINGTON). *A Subaltern's War; being a memoir of the Great War from the point of view of a romantic young man*. London, Peter Davies 1929.

EUBANK, KEITH. *Munich*. Oklahoma, University of Oklahoma Press 1963.

FALLS, CYRIL. *War Books: A Critical Guide*. London, Peter Davies 1930.

FORD, FORD MADOX. *Some Do Not*. London, Duckworth 1924.

— *No More Parades*. London, Duckworth 1925.

— *A Man Could Stand Up*. London, Duckworth 1926.

— *Last Post*. London, Duckworth 1928.

GANNON, FRANKLIN REID. *The British Press and Germany 1936–1939*. Oxford, The Clarendon Press 1971.

GELBER, L. M. *The Rise of Anglo-American Friendship 1898–1906*. Hampden, Connecticut, Archon Books 1966.

GILBERT, MARTIN. *Plough My Own Furrow: The Story of Lord Allen of Hurtwood as told through his own writings and correspondence*. London, Longmans 1965.

GILBERT, MARTIN. *The Roots of Appeasement*. London, Weidenfeld and Nicolson 1966.

GILBERT, MARTIN and GOTT, R. *The Appeasers*. London, Weidenfeld and Nicolson 1963.

GREGORY, J. D. *On the Edge of Diplomacy*. London, Hutchinson 1928.

HAIGH, R. H. and TURNER, P. W. (eds.). *The Long Carry: The War Diary of Stretcher-Bearer Frank Dunham*. Oxford, Pergamon Press 1970.

HALIFAX, EARL OF. *Fullness of Days*. London, Collins 1957.

HARDINGE OF PENSHURST, LORD. *The Old Diplomacy*. London, John Murray 1947.

HART, SIR BASIL LIDDELL. *Memoirs*. London, Cassell 1965. 2 Vols.

HARVEY, JOHN (ed.). *The Diplomatic Diaries of Oliver Harvey*. London, Collins 1970.

HENDERSON, SIR NEVILE. *Failure of a Mission*. London, Hodder and Stoughton 1940.

*History of The Times: Part II 1921–1948, The*. London, The Times 1952.

HORNE, ALISTAIR. *To Lose a Battle*. London, Macmillan 1969.

HUSSEY, MAURICE (ed.). *Poetry of the First World War*. London, Longmans 1967.

IONS, EDMUND. *James Bryce and American Democracy. 1870–1939*. London, Macmillan 1968.

JAMES, ROBERT RHODES. *Churchill: A Study in Failure 1900–1939*. London, Weidenfeld and Nicolson 1970.

JOAD, C. E. M. *Why War?* Harmondsworth, Penguin Books 1939.

JOHNSON, F. A. *Defence by Committee: The British Committee of Imperial Defence 1880–1959*. London, Oxford University Press 1960.

JOHNSTON, JOHN H. *English Poetry of the First World War*. Princeton NJ, Princeton University Press 1964.

JONES, DAVID. *In Parenthesis*. London, Faber and Faber 1937.

KELLY, SIR DAVID. *The Ruling Few*. London, Hollis and Carter 1952.

KEYNES, J. M. *The Economic Consequences of the Peace*. London, Macmillan 1920.

— *A Revision of the Treaty*. London, Macmillan 1922.

KIRKBRIDE, SIR ALEC. *A Crackle of Thorns*. London, John Murray 1947.

KIRKPATRICK, SIR IVONE. *The Inner Circle*. London, Macmillan 1959.

KNATCHBULL-HUGESSEN, SIR HUGHE. *Diplomat in Peace and War*. London, John Murray 1949.

LIVINGSTONE, DAME ADELAIDE. *The Peace Ballot: The Official History*. London, Victor Gollancz 1935.

LLOYD GEORGE, DAVID. *The Truth About Reparations and War Debts.* London, Heinemann 1932.

LONDONDERRY, MARQUESS OF. *Wings of Destiny*. London, Macmillan 1943.

MANNING, FREDERIC (Private 19022). *Her Privates We.* An abridged version of *The Middle Parts of Fortune*. London, Peter Davies 1930.

MARTIN, KINGSLEY. *Editor: A Second Volume of Autobiography 1931–45.* London, Hutchinson 1968.

MILNE, A. A. *Peace with Honour.* London, Methuen 1934.

MINNEY, R. J. (ed.). *The Private Papers of Hore-Belisha.* London, Collins 1960.

MONTAGUE, C. E. *Disenchantment.* London, Chatto and Windus 1922.

MORRISON, H. (LORD MORRISON OF LAMBETH). *An Autobiography.* London, Odhams Press 1960.

MOTTRAM, R. H. *The Spanish Farm Trilogy 1914–1918.* London, Chatto and Windus 1927.

MURRAY, ARTHUR C. (LORD MURRAY OF ELIBANK). *Reflections on Some Aspects of British Foreign Policy Between the World Wars.* Edinburgh, Oliver and Boyd 1946.

NICHOLS, BEVERLEY. *Cry Havoc!* London, Jonathan Cape 1934.

NICOLSON, HAROLD. *King George V. His Life and Reign.* London, Constable 1952.

OLIPHANT, SIR LANCELOT. *Ambassador in Bonds.* London, Putnam 1946.

O'NEILL, ROBERT J. *The German Army and the Nazi Party 1933–9.* London, Cassell 1966.

OWEN, WILFRED. *Poems.* ed. Siegfried Sassoon. London, Chatto and Windus 1921.

— *Poems.* ed. Edmund Blunden. London, Chatto and Windus 1931.

PELLING, HENRY. *America and the British Left: From Bright to Bevan.* New York, New York University Press 1957.

PETRIE, SIR CHARLES. *The Life and Letters of Sir Austen Chamberlain.* London, Cassell 1939–40. 2 Vols.

POPE-HENNESSY, JAMES. *Lord Crewe 1858–1945: The Making of a Liberal.* London, Constable 1955.

READ, HERBERT. *In Retreat.* London, L. and V. Woolf 1925.

REMARQUE, E. M. *All Quiet on the Western Front.* London, Putnam 1929.

RICHARDS, FRANK. *Old Soldiers Never Die.* London, Faber and Faber 1964. First edition 1933.

ROSENBERG, ISAAC. *Poems.* ed. Gordon Bottomley. London, Chatto and Windus 1922.

ROWNTREE, B. SEEBOHM. *Poverty: A Study of Town Life*. London, Macmillan 1910.

RUSSELL, BERTRAND. *Which Way to Peace?* London, Michael Joseph 1936.

SALTER, ARTHUR. *Security; Can We Retrieve It?* London, Macmillan 1939.

SASSOON, SIEGFRIED. *Counter-Attack and Other Poems*. London, Heinemann 1918.

— *Memoirs of a Fox-Hunting Man*. London, Faber and Faber 1929.

— *Memoirs of an Infantry Officer*. London, Faber and Faber 1930.

SHERARD, R. H. *The Child Slaves of Britain*. London, Hurst and Blackett 1905.

SHERRIFF, R. C. *Journey's End*. London, Victor Gollancz 1929.

SHIGEMITSU, MAMORU. *Japan and her Destiny*. London, Hutchinson 1958.

SORLEY, CHARLES H. *Marlborough and Other Poems*. Cambridge, Cambridge University Press 1919.

*Statesman's Yearbook 1926*. ed. M. Epstein. London, Macmillan 1926–30.

STORRY, RICHARD. *A History of Modern Japan*. Harmondsworth, Penguin Books 1960.

STRANG, LORD. *The Foreign Office*. London, Allen and Unwin 1955.

— *At Home and Abroad*. London, André Deutsch 1956.

TAYLOR, A. J. P. *English History 1914–1945*. Oxford, The Clarendon Press 1965.

— *The Origins of the Second World War*. Harmondsworth, Penguin Books 1964. First edition 1961.

TEMPLEWOOD, VISCOUNT (SAMUEL HOARE). *Nine Troubled Years*. London, Collins 1954.

TILLEY, SIR JOHN. *London to Tokyo*. London, Hutchinson 1942.

TILLEY, SIR JOHN and GASELEE, STEPHEN. *The Foreign Office*. London, Putnam 1933.

TROUGHTON, E. R. *It's Happening Again*. London, John Gifford 1944.

WALTERS, F. P. *A History of the League of Nations*. London, Oxford University Press 1952. 2 Vols.

WATT, D. C. *Personalities and Policies*. London, Longmans 1965.

WEBSTER, SIR CHARLES and FRANKLAND, NOBLE. *The Strategic Air Offensive Against Germany 1939–45*. London, HMSO 1961.

WEIR, L. MACNEILL. *The Tragedy of Ramsay MacDonald*. London, Secker and Warburg 1938.

WILLIAMS, JOHN. *The Ides of May: The Defeat of France May–June 1940*. London, Constable 1968.

WILLIAMSON, HENRY. *Patriot's Progress*. London, Geoffrey Bles 1930.

WINTERTON, THE RT HON EARL OF. *Orders of the Day*. London, Cassell 1953.

WOOLF, LEONARD (ed.). *The Intelligent Man's Guide to Peace*. London, Victor Gollancz 1933.

WRENCH, SIR EVELYN. *Geoffrey Dawson and Our Times*. London, Hutchinson 1955.

ZETLAND, MARQUIS OF. *Essayez: The Memoirs of Lawrence, Second Marquis of Zetland*. London, John Murray 1956.

ZILLIACUS, K. *Mirror of the Past*. London, Victor Gollancz 1944.

*Part VI – between pages 579 and 593*
*(sources not previously cited)*

AVON, THE EARL OF (ANTHONY EDEN). *The Eden Memoirs*. London, Cassell 1965. 3 Vols: **III** The Reckoning.

CHAPMAN, GUY. *Why France Collapsed*. London, Cassell 1968.

GOUTARD, COLONEL H. *The Battle of France 1940*. London, Frederick Muller 1958.

*Command Papers*

| | |
|---|---|
| 3288 | *(Public Schools) Report of H.M. Commissioners on Revenues and Management of certain Colleges and Schools, studies pursued and instruction given. Vol. I. Report.* (1864) **xx**, I. |
| 3966 | *Endowed Schools (Schools Inquiry) Commission, Report of the. Vol. I.* (1867–8) **xxxviii**, Pt. I, I. |
| 4139 | *Report of the Committee of Council of Education.* (1868–9) **xx**, |
| C. 3981 | *Second Report of the Royal Commissioners on Technical Instruction. Vol. I. Report.* (1884) **xxix**. |
| C. 7862 | *Royal Commission on Secondary Education. Vol. I. Report.* (1895) **xliii**. |
| Cd. 4757 | *Report of the Consultative Committee on Attendance, Compulsory or Otherwise at Continuation Schools. Vol. I.* (1909) **xvii**, I. |
| Cd. 5130 | *Report of the Board of Education 1908–9.* (1910) **xx**. |
| Cd. 5246 | *Reports from those Universities and University Colleges in Great Britain which participated in the Parliamentary Grant for the University Colleges in the year 1908–9.* (1910) **xxiv**. |
| Cd. 5745 | *Imperial Conference 1911. Minutes of Proceedings.* (1911) **liv**, 103. |

Cd. 7338 *Fourth Report of the Royal Commission on the Civil Service.* (1914) **xiv,** 1. *Appendix* (1914) Cd. 7339. **xvi,** 165.

Cd. 7339 See *Appendix* to Cd. 7338.

Cd. 8181 *Report of a Sub-Committee of the Commercial Intelligence Committee on Measures for securing the position after the War of certain branches of British Industry.* (1916) **xv,** 591. *Evidence* (1916) Cd. 8275. **xv,** 611.

Cd. 8275 See *Evidence* to Cd. 8181.

Cd. 8462 *Final Report of the Dominions Royal Commission.* (1917) **x,** 1.

Cd. 8566 *Imperial War Conference 1917. Extracts from Proceedings and Papers laid before the Conference.* (1917–18) **xxiii,** 319.

Cd. 8657 *Report of the Committee appointed by Lords Commissioners of His Majesty's Treasury to consider and report upon the scheme of Examination for Class I of the Civil Service.* (1917–18) **viii,** 119.

Cd. 9032 *Interim Report on certain essential Industries of the Committee on Commercial and Industrial Policy.* (1918) **xiii,** 205.

Cd. 9035 *Final Report of the Committee on Commercial and Industrial Policy.* (1918) **xiii,** 239.

Cd. 9109 *Report on Indian Constitutional Reforms (Montagu–Chelmsford Report).* (1918) **viii,** 113.

Cd. 9177 *Imperial War Conference. Extracts from Proceedings and Papers laid before the Conference.* (1918) **xvii,** 691.

Cmd. 153 *Treaty of (Versailles) Peace between the Allied and Associated Powers and Germany.* (1919) **liii,** 127.

Cmd. 1474 *Imperial Conference of Prime Ministers and Representatives of the United Kingdom, the Dominions and India, held in June, July and August 1921. Summary of Proceedings and Documents.* (1921) **xiv,** 1.

Cmd. 1922 *Memorandum relating to Indians in Kenya.* (1923) **xviii,** 141.

Cmd. 1987 *Imperial Conference 1923. Summary of Proceedings.* (1923) **xii,** Pt. I, 25. *Appendices* (1923) Cmd. 1988. **xii,** Pt. I, 25.

Cmd. 1988 See *Appendices* to Cmd. 1987.

Cmd. 2009 *Imperial Economic Conference of Representatives of Great Britain, the Dominions, India and the Colonies and Protectorates held in October and November 1923. Record of Proceedings and Documents.* (1927) **x,** 313.

Cmd. 2029 *Report of the Sub-Committee of the Committee of Imperial Defence on National and Imperial Defence (with a report on the relations between the Navy and the Air Force).* (1924) **x,** 277.

Cmd. 2083 *The Singapore Naval Base: Correspondence with the self-governing Dominions and India regarding the development of the Singapore Naval Base.* (1924) **xv**, 841.

Cmd. 2084 *Imperial Economic Conference 1923. Resolutions relating to Imperial Preference passed at the Imperial War Conference, 1917, and the Imperial Economic Conference 1923; with detailed Statements of the proposals laid before the Conference of 1923, and of the Preference in force from 1919 to 1924.* (1924) **xviii**, 45.

Cmd. 2301 *Correspondence with the Dominion Governments with respect to consultation on matters of Foreign Policy and general Imperial interest.* (1924–5) **xxi**, 1.

Cmd. 2768 *Imperial Conference 1926. Summary of Proceedings,* (1926) **xi**, 545. *Appendices to the Summary* (1926) Cmd. 2769. **xi**, 607.

Cmd. 2769 See *Appendices* to Cmd. 2768.

Cmd. 2883 *Colonial Office Conference 1927. Summary of Proceedings.* (1927) **vii**, 751. *Appendices* (1927) Cmd. 2884. **vii**, 825.

Cmd. 2884 See *Appendices* to Cmd. 2883.

Cmd. 3282 *Final Report of the Committee on Industry and Trade.* (1928–9) **vii**, 413.

Cmd. 3554 *Report on the system of appointment in the Colonial Office and the Colonial Service (Warren Fisher Report).* (1929–30) **viii**.

Cmd. 3568 *Report of the Indian Statutory Commission. Vol. I. Survey.* (1929–30) **xi**, 1. *Vol. II, Recommendations* (1929–30) Cmd. 3569. **xi**, 443.

Cmd. 3569 See *Vol. II* of Cmd. 3568.

Cmd. 3628 *Colonial Office Conference 1930. Summary of Proceedings.* (1929–30) **ix**, 1.

Cmd. 3717 *Imperial Conference 1930. Summary of Proceedings.* (1930–1) **xiv**, 569.

Cmd. 3778 *Indian Round Table Conference 1930–1. Proceedings of the Conference.* (1930–1) **xii**, 91.

Cmd. 4268 *Proposals for Indian Constitutional Reform.* (1932–3) **xx**, 997.

Cmd. 5482 *Imperial Conference 1937. Summary of Proceedings.* (1936–7) **xii**, 1.


*Parliamentary Papers and other Official Documents*


Air Ministry Directorate of Civil Aviation. *Report on the Progress of Civil Aviation 1930*, London, HMSO 1931.

Air Ministry Directorate of Civil Aviation. *Report on the Progress of Civil Aviation, 1931* London, HMSO 1932.

*Army, General Return of the* (by command of the Army Council) 1939.

Central Office of Information. *Consultation and Co-operation in the Commonwealth.* London, HMSO 1957.

*Civil Service Commission Open Competition Reports and Examination Papers for August.* London, HMSO 1900, 1905 and 1910.

*Civil Service Commission Regulations, Examination Papers and Table of Marks for Class One Clerkships.* London, HMSO 1885 and 1891.

*Civil Service Commission Reports.* London, HMSO 1895, 1896 and 1900.

Education, Board of. *Survey of Technical and Further Education in England and Wales.* London, HMSO 1926.

Foreign Office. *Documents on British Foreign Policy 1919–39.* London, HMSO 1949. Third Series **I** 1938; **II** 1939.

Foreign Office. *Documents on German Foreign Policy 1918–45.* (From the archives of the German Foreign Ministry.) London, HMSO 1959. Series C. **III** *The Third Reich: First Phase.*

Hansard, *Government of India Bill.* House of Commons, 1935. Fifth Series, **296–304.**

Hansard. *Parliamentary Debates.* House of Commons, 10 July 1833. Third Series, **19.**

Hansard. *Parliamentary Debates.* House of Commons, 18 March 1924. Fifth Series, **171.**

Hansard. *Parliamentary Debates.* House of Commons, 18 November 1925. Fifth Series, **188.**

Hansard. *Parliamentary Debates.* House of Commons, 10 December 1934. Fifth Series, **296.**

Hansard. *Parliamentary Debates.* House of Commons, 11 February 1935. Fifth Series, **297.**

Hansard. *Parliamentary Debates.* House of Commons, 5 June 1935. Fifth Series, **302.**

Hansard. *Parliamentary Debates.* House of Commons, 3 and 5 October 1938. Fifth Series, **339.**

*Indian Constitutional Reform, Joint Committee on.* (Session 1932–3.) London, HMSO 1933. **I** Report.

*Ministry of Munitions, History of.* London, HMSO 1922. 12 Vols.

*Scientific Instruction, Report from the Select Committee on; with the Proceedings of the Committee, Minutes of Evidence and Appendix.* House of Commons 1867–8. **xv.**

*Sedition Committee Report* (*Rowlatt Report*). Calcutta, Superintendent Government Printing 1918. **viii, 423.**

*Statistics of the Military Effort of the British Empire during the Great War.* London, HMSO 1922.

UNPUBLISHED SOURCES

L. S. Amery Papers.
Curriculum and set books at Uppingham School. 1870–1900.
Emott Committee. Report of an enquiry into the relationship of technical education to other forms of education and to industry and commerce. 1927.
Marlborough College House Reports. 1879–85.
Syllabuses and set books at Winchester. 1888.
Syllabuses at Marlborough College for 1851, 1863, 1873 and 1893.

*Cabinet Papers (Public Record Office)*

| | |
|---|---|
| CAB 2/3–9 | Minutes of the Committee of Imperial Defence Meetings 1912–39. |
| CAB 16/109–12 | Report, Proceedings and Memoranda of the Defence Requirements Sub-Committee of the Committee of Imperial Defence 1933–5. |
| CAB 16/123 | Defence Policy and Requirements Committee of the Cabinet 1936. |
| CAB 16/136 | Minutes of Meetings of the Defence Policy and Requirements Committee of the Cabinet 1936–9. |
| CAB 16/209 | Strategic Appreciation Committee of the Committee of Imperial Defence 1939. |
| CAB 21/188 | Cabinet: Registered Files. Naval Defence scheme for the Empire 1921. |
| CAB 21/336 | Cabinet: Registered Files. Imperial Conference 1930 – Foreign Policy and Defence. |
| CAB 21/386 | Cabinet: Registered Files. Defences of Australia – Visit by Sir M. Hankey, November 1934. |
| CAB 21/397 | Cabinet: Registered Files. Defence of Australia 1935. |
| CAB 21/406 | Ministerial Committee on Defence Requirements. |
| CAB 21/422A | Cabinet: Registered Files. Defence Policy and Requirements – CID Committee 1936. |
| CAB 23/2–6 | Minutes of the War Cabinet Meetings 1917–18. |
| CAB 23/15 | 'A' Minutes of the War Cabinet Meetings 1919. |
| CAB 23/25–31 | Conclusions of the Cabinet Meetings 1921–2. |
| CAB 23/46 | Conclusions of the Cabinet Meetings 1923–4. |
| CAB 23/52–100 | Conclusions of the Cabinet Meetings 1926–39. |

| | |
|---|---|
| CAB 27/361–3 | Minutes and Memoranda of the Reductions and Limitations of Armaments Policy Committee 1927–1929. |
| CAB 27/407 | Fighting Services Committee 1929–30. |
| CAB 27/476, 512, 514 | Minutes and Memoranda of the Committee on Preparations for the League of Nations Disarmament Conference 1931–2. |
| CAB 27/482 | Far East Committee 1932. |
| CAB 27/504–11 | Ministerial Committee on League of Nations Disarmament Conference 1932–5. |
| CAB 27/572 | German Re-armament Committee 1934. |
| CAB 27/596 | Japan – Political and Economic Relations Committee 1935–6. |
| CAB 27/599 | Cabinet Committee on Germany 1936. |
| CAB 27/603 | Germany and the Locarno Treaty Cabinet Committee 1936. |
| CAB 27/606 | Mediterranean Fleet Cabinet Committee 1936. |
| CAB 27/622–7 | Minutes and Memoranda of the Cabinet Committee on Foreign Policy 1936–9. |
| CAB 27/646 | Czechoslovakian Crisis Cabinet Committee 1938. |
| CAB 27/648 | Defence Programmes and their Acceleration Cabinet Committee 1938. |
| CAB 27/653 | Defence of India Cabinet Committee 1938–9. |
| CAB 27/657 | Defence Programmes and their Acceleration Cabinet Committee 1939. |
| CAB 27/662 | Defence Preparedness Cabinet Committee 1939. |
| CAB 29/117, 128 | Naval Conference, London 1930. |
| CAB 29/146 | Anglo-French Ministerial Conversations, London 1935. |
| CAB 29/147, 150, 157, 158 | Naval Conference, London 1935–6. |
| CAB 29/159 | Anglo-French Staff Conversations, London 1939. |
| CAB 30/1A | Cabinet: Washington (Disarmament Conference) – Minutes of the British Empire Delegation Conference 1921–2. |
| CAB 30/1B | Cabinet: Washington (Disarmament Conference) – Memoranda of the British Empire Delegation Conferences 1921–2. |
| CAB 30/9–10 | Cabinet: Washington (Disarmament Conference) – |

| | |
|---|---|
| | Committee on the Limitations of Armament 1921–1922. |
| CAB 30/11–13, 26 | Cabinet: Washington (Disarmament Conference) – Meetings of the Heads of the Delegations 1921–2. |
| CAB 30/15–16 | Cabinet: Washington (Disarmament Conference) – Committee on the Pacific and Far Eastern Question 1922. |
| CAB 30/31 | Cabinet: Washington (Disarmament Conference) – Sir Maurice Hankey's correspondence 1921–2. |
| CAB 32/1/1 | Imperial War Conference 1917. Minutes of Proceedings and Papers laid before the Conference. |
| CAB 32/1/2 | Imperial War Conference 1918. Minutes of Proceedings and Papers laid before the Conference. |
| CAB 32/2–3 | Stenographic Notes of the Meetings of the Imperial Conference 1921. |
| CAB 32/9 | Stenographic Notes of the Meetings of the Imperial Conference 1923. |
| CAB 32/44 | Imperial Conference, London 1926 – CID Committee on Foreign Policy and Defence. |
| CAB 32/46 | Documents and Stenographic Notes of the Imperial Conference, London 1926. |
| CAB 32/47 | Memoranda on general subjects of the Imperial Conference, London 1926. |
| CAB 32/49 | Documents of the Imperial Conference, London 1926 – British Representatives' Memoranda. |
| CAB 32/56 | Imperial Conference, London 1926 – Conference Committee on Certain Aspects of Inter-Imperial Relations. |
| CAB 32/76 | Memoranda on general subjects of the Imperial Conference, London 1930. |
| CAB 32/77 | Imperial Conference, London 1930 – CID Committee on Foreign Policy and Defence. |
| CAB 32/87 | Imperial Conference, London 1930 – Fighting Services Committee. |
| CAB 32/88 | Imperial Conference, London 1930 – Committee on Certain Aspects of Inter-Imperial Relations. |
| CAB 32/91 | Imperial Conference, London 1930 – Singapore Base Committee. |
| CAB 32/100 | Imperial Conference, London 1930 – Sub-Committees of the Committee on Certain Aspects of Inter-Imperial Relations. |

| | |
|---|---|
| CAB 32/125 | Commonwealth Prime Ministers' Meetings, London 1935. |
| CAB 32/127 | Imperial Conference, London 1937 – Cabinet Committee 1936–7. |
| CAB 32/128 | Imperial Conference, London 1937 – Documents of Plenary Sessions. |
| CAB 32/129 | Imperial Conference, London 1937 – Memoranda. |
| CAB 32/130 | Imperial Conference 1937 – Meetings of the Principal Delegates on Special Subjects. |
| CAB 36/1–13 | Minutes and Memoranda of the Joint Oversea and Home Defence Committee 1920–39. |
| CAB 53/1–11 | Committee of Imperial Defence: Meetings of the Chiefs of Staff Committee 1929–39. |
| CAB 53/12–54 | Committee of Imperial Defence: Memoranda of the Chiefs of Staff Committee 1923–39. |
| CAB 65/1–2 | Conclusions of the War Cabinet Meetings 1939. |
| CAB 65/3–4 | Confidential Annexes to the War Cabinet Meetings 1939. |
| CAB 65/5–10 | Conclusions of the War Cabinet Meetings 1940. |
| CAB 66/1–11 | Memoranda of the War Cabinet 1939–40. |
| CAB 68/6 | Memoranda of the War Cabinet 1940. |
| CAB 75 series | Chiefs of Staff Meetings 1939–40. |
| CAB 80 series | Chiefs of Staff Memoranda 1939–40. |

# INDEX

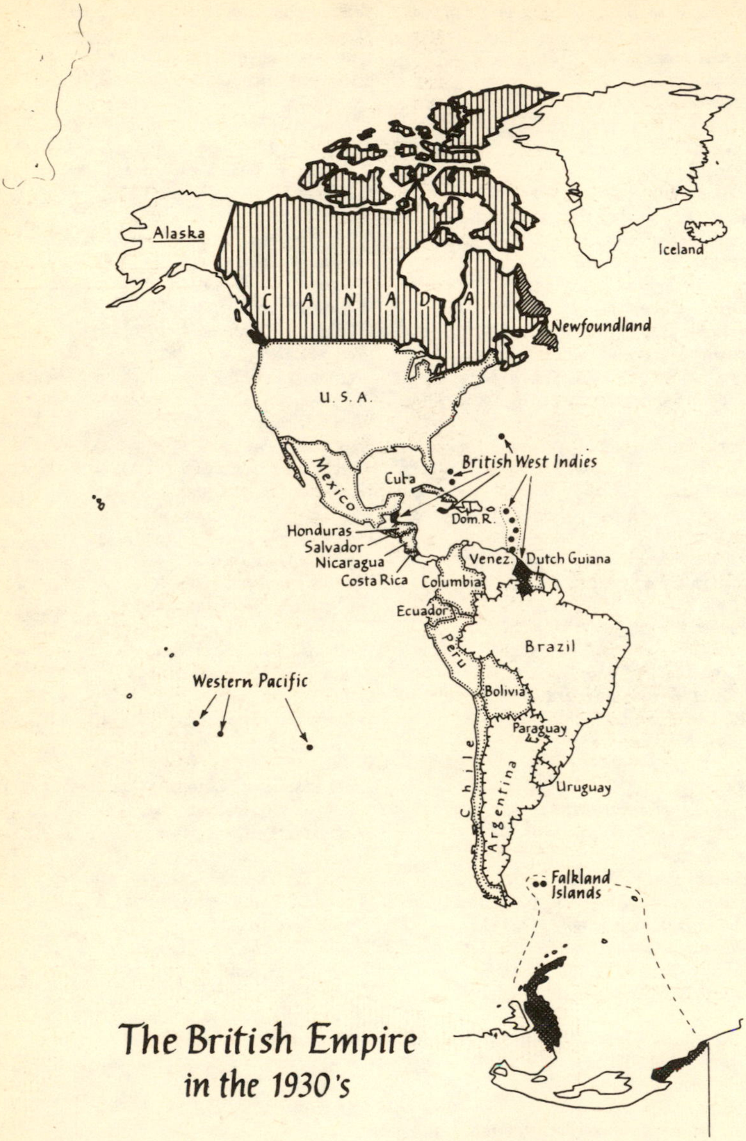


The British Empire in the 1930's

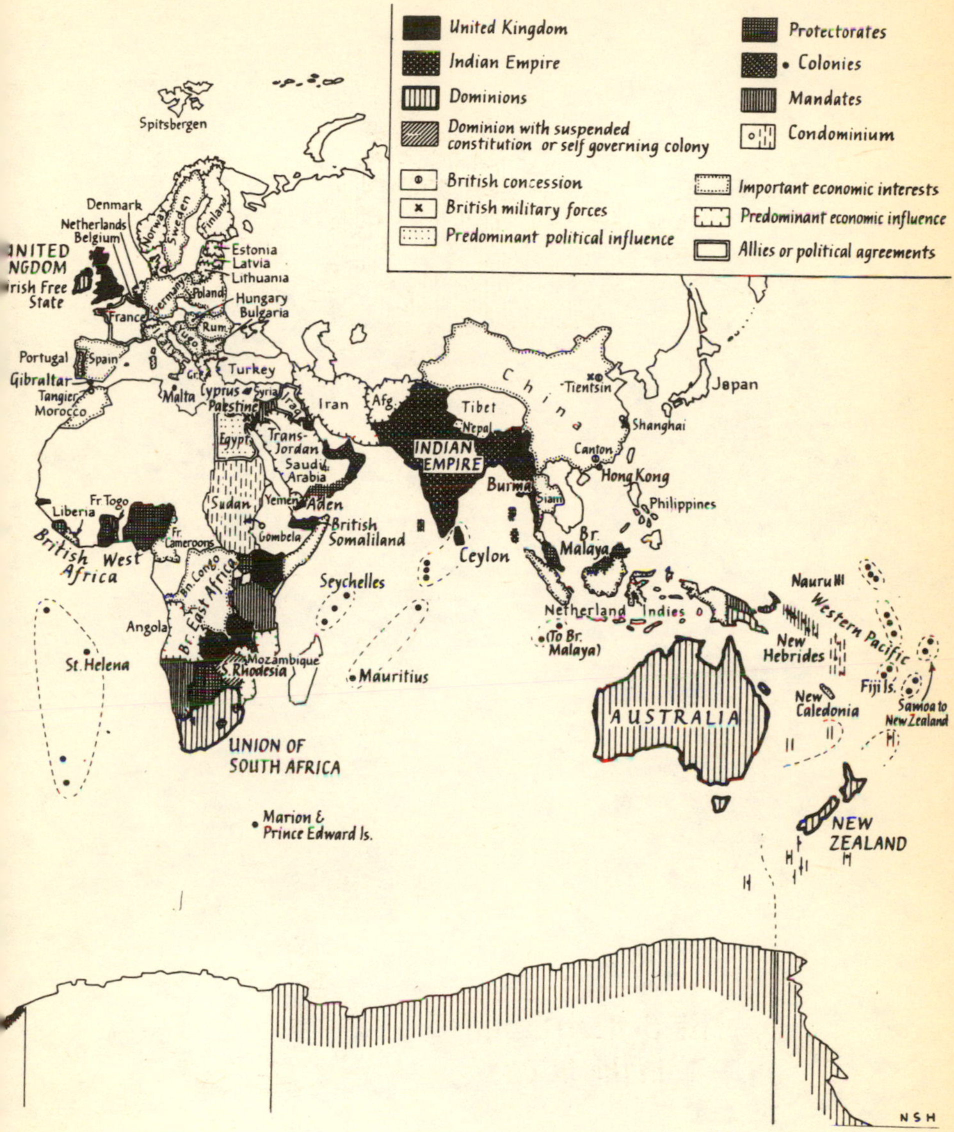

United Kingdom
Indian Empire
Dominions
Dominion with suspended constitution or self governing colony
Protectorates
Colonies
Mandates
Condominium
British concession
British military forces
Predominant political influence
Important economic interests
Predominant economic influence
Allies or political agreements
Spitsbergen
Denmark
Netherlands
Belgium
Norway
Sweden
Finland
Estonia
Latvia
Lithuania
Poland
Germany
Hungary
Bulgaria
Rum.
France
Portugal
Spain
Gibraltar
Tangier
Morocco
Malta
Turkey
Cyprus
Syria
Palestine
Iraq
Iran
Afg.
Tibet
Nepal
China
Tientsin
Shanghai
Canton
Hong Kong
Japan
Philippines
INDIAN EMPIRE
Burma
Siam
Br. Malaya
Ceylon
Egypt
Trans-Jordan
Saudi Arabia
Yemen
Aden
Sudan
British Somaliland
Gombela
Liberia
Fr Togo
Fr. Cameroons
British West Africa
Bn. Congo
Br. East Africa
Angola
Mozambique
S. Rhodesia
St. Helena
Seychelles
Mauritius
UNION OF SOUTH AFRICA
Marion & Prince Edward Is.
Netherland Indies
(To Br. Malaya)
AUSTRALIA
Nauru
Western Pacific
New Hebrides
New Caledonia
Fiji Is.
Samoa to New Zealand
NEW ZEALAND
NSH